D1329596

A HISTORY OF
AMERICAN PHILOSOPHY

Number 18 of the
Columbia Studies in American Culture

A HISTORY OF
AMERICAN
PHILOSOPHY

HERBERT W. SCHNEIDER

COLUMBIA UNIVERSITY PRESS
NEW YORK

Columbia Studies
in American Culture

EDITED AT COLUMBIA UNIVERSITY

A series bringing together scholarly treatments
of those aspects of American culture
that are usually neglected in political histories and in
histories of American literature and education

THE ARTS AND SCIENCES

PHILOSOPHY AND RELIGION

FOLKWAYS

INDUSTRY AND AGRICULTURE

in short, whatever has contributed significantly
to the patterns of American life and to its heritage

First printing 1946
Second printing January, 1947
Third printing July, 1947

PREFACE AND ACKNOWLEDGMENTS

PART IX of this work is entitled "New Realism and New Naturalism," but I shall not live to write it. I could, if there were need for it, expound the chief contemporary systems current in America, but their history cannot yet be written. Of their origins this work gives an account, for the reader will find here how and when realistic and naturalistic ideas emerged from evolutionism, idealism, and empiricism. But the careers of these ideas are still too young to merit biography, and their significance is still veiled in the future. The historian must therefore be content to end his story where his own reflections begin. It may be permitted, however, that in this preface the historian turn prophet and attempt to discern the perspectives from which a later generation may view the thought of his own time. It seems highly probable, though it cannot yet be regarded as historical truth, that something genuinely new is brewing. One should not be misled by all the talk and hope about new realisms, new naturalisms, new logics, new republics, and new deals, for such preoccupation with novelties is itself an old story. There may be nothing new under our patient sun except new names for old ways of thinking and new ways of arriving at old discoveries. But even this much novelty is worth noting. There are good reasons, however, for suspecting that we stand at the beginning as well as at the ending of a cultural epoch. The times have been too eventful not to be creative of new ideas, especially among men who for at least a generation have focussed their attentions on events. We ought to be prepared intellectually for understanding changes even though it is most difficult to understand historically the changes with which we are most familiar.

The fact which above all others should make us aware of a new epoch is the impact of recent importations on American ideas. The reader of the story that follows will note that American philosophy has continually been given new life and new directions by waves of immigration. In America, at least, it is useless to seek a "native" tradition, for even our most genteel traditions are saturated with foreign inspirations. Spanish Franciscans, French Jesuits, English Puritans, Dutch

Pietists, Scottish Calvinists, cosmopolitan *philosophes*, German Transcendentalists, Russian revolutionaries, and Oriental theosophists have all shared in giving to so-called American philosophy its continuities as well as its shocks. The extent to which American intellectual life has been dependent on non-American scholars is incommensurate with the extent to which American philosophers have enjoyed influence abroad. Emerson himself, with all his independence, was certainly not made in America alone; he absorbed from Europe and Asia much more than he gave them. America was intellectually colonial long after it gained political independence and has been intellectually provincial long after it ceased being intellectually colonial. We still live intellectually on the fringe of European culture.

No more striking illustration of this fact is afforded than the tremendous impact made on our own minds by ideas generated and nourished elsewhere. More conspicuous in the history of today and tomorrow than the ideas contained in this volume are the recent intellectual imports from Cambridge, Paris, and Vienna. I mention these three as outstanding sources of contemporary American thought, though there are many others that might well be named in order to remind ourselves that we have an unfavorable balance of foreign trade in ideas. The type of philosophical analysis that grew up in Cambridge under the leadership of Whitehead, Russell, and G. E. Moore, the sophisticated, modernized versions of Catholic scholasticism that have come to us from Paris, and the schools of value theory, existentialism, phenomenology, logical positivism, psychoanalysis, and socialism that have come to us either directly or indirectly from Vienna —these are now pervasive forces in American culture. I venture to predict that all the types of philosophic thought described in this volume are being so radically revised, reviewed, and reconstructed because of these new importations that a decidedly new chapter in American philosophy is being written, the outlines of which we can still not see, though the labor of it is evident on all sides. But the imported goods are not being swallowed raw; they must be blended with those homegrown ideas, for which an established taste and preference exists.

How shall we measure the vitality and momentum of American traditions in the face of this revolutionary situation? Have they a central content, a dominant note, or a moral lesson? I think not. The reader of this story will probably be at least as bewildered as I am in trying to tell what American history teaches us or what American philosophy "stands for." From a European distance and on the basis of learned ignorance such generalizations can be ventured without fear of contradiction. But for us at home who must live with the facts, it is prudent to let others draw the portraits of our ancestral soul and outline the basic dialectic in our national existence. Our past is fully as confused as our present. Its vitality, therefore, must be sought, not in any definable quality or direction of movement, but in that vague yet tangible energy which it exerts when it is faced with new ideas. When a new idea comes to us we project it, semi-consciously, against one historical perspective after another to discover what meanings or significances it may acquire when placed in various contexts. After a series of experiments in interpretation, we discover how and where the new idea can best be used and assimilated. The variety of contexts at our disposal gives us many handles by which to take hold of novelties. But we do take hold of them as much as they get a hold on us. The many ways in which we resist, distort, adapt, revise new importations is the best evidence that an American tradition lives. Occasionally even the dead past is revived through the stimulus of a sudden turn in affairs or in thought, and we discover new uses for American antiques. The renewed interest in Jonathan Edwards, Thomas Jefferson, Tom Paine, Andrew Jackson, Walt Whitman, to take conspicuous examples, is the product of fresh challenges to ideas which had repeatedly been laid to rest in peace, but which have risen unexpectedly, not as ghosts, but as "living thoughts of great Americans." Much that is carried along as sheer gentility or academic exercise may, without much notice, crowd out our up-to-date notions, when the latter are compelled to meet a new tomorrow. It is for this reason that no enduring evaluation of what is living and what is dead in our tradition is possible. Nevertheless, I confess to a hope that some of the episodes which I have laboriously exhumed for the purposes of this narrative may never suffer further revivification, for I have included them more out of academic scruple and professional etiquette than because I believe that someday it will profit someone to have remembered them.

I must add a few words about the relation of the history told in this volume to other attempts at giving a general pattern to the development of American thought. Whether or not it be true that the history of the past must everlastingly be rewritten, it is certainly true that the writing of American intellectual history is in a highly experimental stage; and I have no illusion that my outline will endure when my successors get to work. I have departed widely from the outlines suggested by my predecessors; in fact, no two historians of American thought have told similar stories. I have, of course, profited by the works (see Index) of I. W. Riley, Morris R. Cohen, H. G. Townsend, Perry Miller, R. B. Perry, V. L. Parrington, Charles Beard, Merle Curti, and others, even when I have not followed them. I regret that two recent works of major critical importance came too late to give me the extensive help which I should have derived from them had they come sooner: Arthur M. Schlesinger's *The Age of Jackson* and Joseph Dorfman's *The Economic Mind in American Civilization*— two works which seem to me in general to confirm and enrich the story here told and at a few points to amend it. Dorfman's work, particularly, should be regarded as an essential part of an adequate history of American philosophy. It is already clear that political, economic, theological, and metaphysical principles have been more closely associated in American thought than we have hitherto been led to believe and that a truly comprehensive history of American philosophy still remains to be written.

My volume is, of course, not my work in any strict sense. Besides the works of the historians whom I have mentioned and other contributors to American history, it embodies some of the labors and discoveries of students at Columbia University with whom I have been privileged to work and the cream of whose dissertations I have skimmed for the benefit of those who cannot take the milk of the Word whole. The published works of these students are referred to here and there in this volume; I wish to express my indebtedness to their researches, particularly to those of Marguerite B. Block, J. Edward Dirks, James E. Dombrowski, W. J. B. Edgar, Frances B. Harmon, Joseph Haroutunian, Eugene C. Holmes, Marc E. Jones, Morris Judd, Estelle Kaplan, Adrienne Koch, G. Adolf Koch, Edward McNair, Eugene T. Mudge, Martha Pingel, Herbert E. Richards, Niels H. Sonne, Ronald V. Wells, Morton G. White, and Daniel D. Williams. Their works shall now live after them, and they will know their proper places in the objective reason of history, which until now had eluded us. They will forgive me, I trust, for fixing them "definitively" as contributors.

My greatest debt is to my collaborator Dr. Joseph L. Blau, who has prepared the anthology of *American Philosophic Addresses*, which is intended to be used with this volume, has compiled the bibliographical references, has dug scores of dusty volumes out of many libraries, has compelled me to study them, has criticized my manuscript, and has in general done so much important research in this field that he is co-inventor of this history, whoever may be its author.

The help I have received in special ways from friends and colleagues ever since Professor Coss first urged me to undertake this work twenty years ago is too varied and detailed to be recalled here. I should mention, however, that my colleagues Joseph Dorfman, Raymond M. Weaver, Charles W. Everett, Henry W. Wells, Arthur E. Christy, Edwin N. Garlan, and Quentin Anderson have given me generously of their expert knowledge. I am likewise indebted for information to Charles M. Bakewell, Philip P. Wiener, Bert J. Loewenberg, Sidney Ratner, Kurt F. Leidecker, and Miss Edith Harris. The task of transforming the chaos of my manuscript into something fit to print fell to Jean Allen Wilson, Shirley Carson O'Connell, Eleanor W. Blau, and Ida M. Lynn; I am deeply grateful to them.

For permission to quote copyrighted material we are indebted to Henry James, who kindly consented to the extensive use of the letters published in his and Ralph Barton Perry's volumes; to the Harvard University Press for the use of many excerpts from Peirce's *Collected Papers*; to Longmans, Green and Company for quotations from James, *A Pluralistic Universe*; to Charles Scribners's Sons for quotations from Santayana, *The Genteel Tradition at Bay*; to Houghton Mifflin Company, publishers of the writings of Henry Adams, for permission to quote generously from them; to The Macmillan Company for a quotation from *E. A. Robinson*, by H. Hagedorn; to the Chicago University Press for selections from the works of Mead; to the Open Court Publishing Company for a quotation from Dewey's *Experience and Nature*; to Minton, Balch and Company for a quotation from Dewey's *Art as Experience*. I have here reproduced in part and with revisions several articles previously published in *The Journal of the History of Ideas, Church History, Studies in the History of Ideas,* and the co-operative volume, *The Constitution Reconsidered,* edited by Conyers Read.

The "Guides to the Literature" of the various parts of the story told here are not meant as exhaustive bibliographies. They are, rather, attempts to provide a selective list of both primary and secondary materials for the reader who may wish to continue his studies in American philosophy.

H.W.S.

Columbia University
July, 1946

CONTENTS

CONTENTS

— I —

PLATONISM AND EMPIRICISM IN COLONIAL AMERICA

THE PLATONIC HERITAGE
OF THE NEW ENGLAND PURITANS

CONGREGATIONALISM was at one time more than a sect; it was a social reform movement with a complete ideology. Though this branch of Puritan philosophy was imported ready made into New England and was soon corrupted, it is well to begin the study of American philosophy with it, partly because it deserves a place among well-constructed and technically erudite systems and partly because it continued to pervade the institutions of New England and haunt its imagination long after it ceased to be believed literally and practically.

In France, the Netherlands, and England a small but enterprising and educated group made a determined attack not only on the Roman Catholic ecclesiastical and sacramental system but also on the scholasticism in which this system found philosophic expression and justification. To attack so well-grounded and deep-seated a tradition required a very elaborate mechanism. To challenge the synthesis of Catholicism and Aristotelianism, the reformers were obliged to construct a no less scholastic synthesis of Protestantism and Platonism. No Protestant groups worked at this task so painstakingly as did the disciples of Peter Ramus, especially the "covenant," or Congregationalist, theologians.[1]

The path of the European Congregationalists was exceptionally tortuous and treacherous, because this small minority was a middle-of-the-way group, not only struggling with other Protestants against Catholicism, but struggling among Protestants for a tenuous *via media* which met with vigorous opposition from both extremes of the Reformation. These covenanting dissenters had to contend, in the New World as well as in the Old, against the Presbyterian wing of Protestantism on the Right, and on the Left against the Separatists, Ana-

---

[1] Strictly speaking, the Covenant Theology was not confined to the Congregational churches, nor were all Congregationalists familiar with this theory. The Dutch Collegiate Church, too, was inspired by these theologians. This Covenant Theology or Federal (*foedus*, covenant) Theology is, of course, not to be confused with the Scottish Covenanters who had a quite different origin.

baptists, Independents, and Antinomians. In addition to meeting all these opposing forces within the Church, they confronted the rising power of secular law and secularized "covenant" theory as popularized by Hobbes.

Against the Catholics and the Anglicans, all dissenters repudiated the mediatorial office of the priesthood, the sacraments and the doctrine of the Apostolic succession of authority. Against the Presbyterians and the orthodox Calvinists, these Congregational dissenters refused to admit that God's decrees are arbitrary and sovereign, asserting that election is based on a "covenant" of grace in the most literal sense and that the elect therefore have a *right* to justification through grace; they also opposed the special powers of elders and synods, regarding them as a compromise with episcopal or aristocratic government. Against the Separatists, they recognized the union of church and state, and against the Antinomians, they admitted that the elect are under the obligation of obedience to the commandments of God, even though they are not liable to the punishments merited by the divine law. Finally, against the Hobbesians, they repudiated purely secular law and temporal peace as a basis for the commonwealth and insisted that a true society must be a theocracy whose aim and duty it is to govern not only "in matters of righteousness and honesty, but also in matters of godliness, yea of all godliness."

The covenant theory of the church was really the ecclesiastical aspect of "social-contract" theory, and its basic aim was to transform the "status" of the elect of Calvinistic theory into a "contract" relationship of voluntary obligation. The theory was welcomed chiefly in middle-class and mercantile circles and was part of the general movement away from feudal and toward commercial conceptions of authority and government.[2] The theory was democratic in the sense that it provided for the regular election of magistrates and church officers by all members, and in that sense it championed equality and representative government; but in another sense it was not democratic, since it denied that the elected officers are responsible to the will of the people and asserted that law and authority come from God.

[2] For example, an early version in England of the Ramist logic, written by Abraham Fraunce in 1588, was entitled *The Lawiers Logike*. See John Milton, *Works*, Columbia University Press edition, Vol. XI.

The sources of Congregational Puritanism take us back to Renaissance Platonism, specifically to Peter Ramus (1515–86). He was a French humanist and Platonist who launched a vigorous attack on the logic and rhetoric of Aristotelian scholasticism, especially on the categories and predicables which seemed to him useless. In 1561 he was converted to Calvinism and at the Synod of Nîmes (1572) attained some notoriety for defending a pure congregational theory of the church against the Presbyterians, who denounced his theory as too "democratic" and hence "completely absurd and pernicious." He was murdered during the Massacre of St. Bartholomew. Both his life and his death thus contributed to making him a Protestant saint and martyr. His chief philosophical contribution was to revive and systematize a Platonic dialectic or dichotomy as basic to and more useful than the scholastic and Aristotelian logic of demonstration. He conceived logic as an art, rather than as a science of proof—an art for disciplining man's natural intelligence (*sagesse*). By dialectic or systematic dichotomy he taught the art of making distinctions or discriminations. This art of logical analysis he called invention. The other branch of logic he called judgment, or disposition, which is the art of joining properly what dialectic has disjoined. Ramus defended his system primarily for its pedagogical value, but some of his disciples, notably one of Melanchthon's German students, named J. H. Alsted, developed the dialectic method into an encyclopedia of arts and sciences. Alsted's *Encyclopaedia* (1630) became a popular text for Puritan philosophy. It distinguished three basic disciplines in addition to the educational discipline, *didactia: hexilogia,* the knowledge of the habits and constitution of the mind; *technologia,* the system of arts arranged dialectically to show the essential relations and unity of knowledge; and *archelogia,* the system of archetypes, ends, or principles of both knowledge and being, equivalent roughly to a system of Platonic ideas. The general aim of learning or encyclopedic philosophy was to transform man's natural ("inartificial") *sagesse* into disciplined ("artificial") argument until the human mind became an *imago Dei.*

The Ramist system was introduced into Cambridge University by Sir William Temple, in 1580, and contributed to the growth of Cambridge Platonism. It became the basis of Congregational apologetics. The Cambridge Puritans were represented by Alexander Richardson,

George Downame, Anthony Wotton, and especially by William Ames, whose writings became the favorite philosophy texts of early New England. In 1672, the same year in which Ames's edition of Ramus's *Dialectics with Commentary* appeared, Milton published his *Institutions of the Art of Logic Based on the Method of Peter Ramus*. Other Puritan divines who popularized the Ramist philosophy and Covenant Theology were William Perkins, John Preston, and Thomas Hooker.

Hooker later emigrated and became one of the early leaders in New England. He had studied Ramist philosophy under Richardson at Cambridge before he emigrated to New England, where he became the best-informed expositor of the system and, together with an adequately educated group of New England ministers, continued the philosophical defense of Congregationalism for several generations. This philosophical Puritanism in New England created a distinctive, intellectual tradition, whose chief themes were the theory of theocratic towns, and the academic development of *technologia*.

In Europe the primary aim of the Ramist philosophy and Covenant Theology was to give laymen the intellectual tools for breaking down the privileges of the priesthood, the necessity for sacraments, and the power of establishments. In England the Congregationalists could hope at most that parishes might be permitted to organize on covenant principles as recognized and established parts of the Church of England. Though they continued to preach the Calvinistic gospel that all kingdoms should become holy commonwealths, they could not carry out their program in practice. In New England, on the contrary, it was practical to organize by covenants or social contracts small independent communities, towns, or congregations, small kingdoms of Christ, or theocracies, in which popularly elected magistrates and ministers were jointly responsible for enforcing the law of God. Jonathan Mitchell explained in 1662 that "The Latter Erecting of Christs Kingdom in whole Societies . . . was our Design, and our Interest in this Country: tho' with Respect to the Inward and Invisible Kingdom, as the Scope thereof." [3] And Professor Perry Miller comments very aptly: "That which made New Englanders unique in all seventeenth-century Christendom, which cut them off from all reformed churches and constituted them in truth a peculiar people,

[3] Quoted in Perry Miller, *The New England Mind* (New York, 1939), p. 433.

was their axiom: 'The Covenant of Grace is cloathed with Church-Covenant in a Politicall visible Church-way.' " [4] Though the New England divines formed the habit of promulgating divine decrees from their pulpits and took on the airs and powers of a privileged order, the laymen were able in the long run to assert their covenant rights, and they gradually undermined the clerical theocracies in favor of democracies. The clergy, of course, raised an outcry against the growth of ungodliness, but the younger generation, even of the clergy, paid little attention to such lamentation. In other words, what was in Europe primarily a revolt of the middle classes against ecclesiastical privilege became in America a positive basis for the founding of independent political communities in which the clergy gradually lost their power and kept their prestige only to the extent that they themselves adopted the "lay" point of view. The New England towns were neither mere investments for merchant adventurers nor holy commonwealths; they pretended to be both, but gradually there was evolved a distinct type of independence which embodied a mixture of Platonic idealism and Yankee mercantile prosperity. The "election" and the "providence" of God became the sanction or ideology of independent commonwealths.

The theory of nature and the philosophy of history were unified for the New England Puritans by their Christian Platonism. They defined nature as the art (*technē*) of God. A typical text, that of Samuel Johnson, of Yale College, begins as follows:

TECHNOLOGY OR TECHNOMETRY

1. Art is the idea representing and directing *eupraxia* [well-doing].
2. An idea is the matter of art.
3. An idea is the pattern of a thing.
4. An idea is representing and by means of the representation directing *eupraxia* in action.
5. On which the form of art is based.
6. The object and end of an idea is *eupraxia*.
7. A thing is an object in so far as it is engaged in being represented;
8. An end, in so far as it directs by means of representing.
9. *Eupraxia* is the orderly procedure or action of an agent in acting.

[4] *Ibid.*, p. 447.

10. We have to consider the effective agent, object, effect and parts of *eupraxia*.

11. An action is an effective agent when it produces an effect consequent on an idea.

12. An object is the material about which an effective agent and its *eupraxia* are concerned in practice—and is also the material out of which it proceeds.

13. The effect which is produced by the agent and his *eupraxia* according to an idea is a *euprassomenon*—which is on the other hand the deed done.

14. The parts or factors of *eupraxia* are two—generation and analysis.

15. Generation is a regular advance from simples to the composites which they compose.

16. Analysis is an orderly regress from the composites to the simples into which they can be resolved.

17. Where generation ends analysis begins, and this holds good for all *generalia*.

Thus we see that there are four things necessary for any *euprassomenon*: (1) An art or idea, namely something representing and directing it. (2) An action which is done consequent upon an idea. (3) A good deed represented and directed. (4) Something about which this deed is concerned and which may be the material out of which the action produces the effect consequent on the idea.[5]

God Himself is interpreted as "art," and the discipline of the human mind is the attempt at ordered understanding of the divine wisdom. There is no secular science; the so-called "secondary causes" are intelligible, not as merely secondary, but as intrinsic instrumentalities of God's "economy of redemption." "Technology" is thus sanctified. The New England educators emphasized Ramus's scorn for Aristotelian metaphysics and ethics as secular inquiries and extended it to all the sciences. All means are God's means, and all agency is divine art. Samuel Johnson prefaced his book on physics with the following question and answer:

Q. Why do not the Peripatetics follow this [Ramist] method?
A. The Peripatetics do not follow this method because they do not follow Moses but Aristotle; and learn their philosophy not from the sacred

[5] Samuel Johnson, *The Career and Writings of Samuel Johnson*, ed. by H. W. and C. Schneider (New York, 1929), II, 63–65.

pages, but from the heathen Aristotle, and because they do not run through the whole course of the nature of things, but deal only with certain parts of it. For they restrict the object of physics and exclude many things from physics as for example, the highest heaven and the angels, whose nature is nowhere considered.[6]

And President Charles Chauncy told his students at Harvard that physics, politics, rhetoric and astronomy "in the true sense and right meaning thereof are Theological & Scripture learning, and are not to be accounted as humane learning." [7]

Though the dialectics or dichotomies of the Ramist texts became, in the course of a generation or two, little more than academic exercises, there persisted the Platonic habit of regarding the divine government not merely as an object of worship but also as a method of inquiry. "Tho' God's Will be His Rule, yet God hath in Himself an Idea of that which He will manage the Creatures by, and it is wise and just." [8] The *eupraxia*, or skill, exhibited in the works (*euprassomena*) of God or man was the basic category of philosophic analysis and enabled the Puritans to interpret their arts and crafts, including the most mercantile and menial, in the perspective of God's will. They took seriously and literally Peter Ramus's maxim "The exercise and practice make the artisan. . . . To know only the universal rules, without knowing the particular usage, is not to know absolutely and actually." [9] In short, Puritan philosophy was a system of practice, intended to be practical as well as scientific.

The transition from this Puritan Platonism to deism and natural religion was easy, gradual, and largely unconscious. For the Puritans were obviously not so dependent on the Biblical revelation of law and covenant as they pretended to be. Their system was from the start more genuinely philosophical than Biblical.

When the first attempts were made in New England to assert "natural" rights against the magistrates and the clergy in the interests of more democratic government, Governor Winthrop made a very effective reply, condemning in terms of the Puritan philosophy any appeal to "natural liberties" as being also an appeal to "corrupt liberties."

[6] *Ibid.*, p. 27.   [7] Quoted in Miller, *The New England Mind*, p. 105.
[8] Samuel Willard, quoted in *ibid.*, p. 167.   [9] Quoted in *ibid.*, p. 142.

There is a twofold liberty, natural (I mean as our nature is now corrupt) and civil or federal. The first is common to man with beasts and other creatures. By this, man, as he stands in relation to man simply, hath liberty to do what he lists; it is a liberty to evil as well as to good. This liberty is incompatible and inconsistent with authority, and cannot endure the least restraint of the most just authority. The exercise and maintaining of this liberty makes men grow more evil, and in time to be worse than brute beasts: *omnes sumus licentia deteriores*. This is that great enemy of truth and peace, that wild beast, which all the ordinances of God are bent against, to restrain and subdue it. The other kind of liberty I call civil or federal, it may also be termed moral, in reference to the covenant between God and man, in the moral law, and the politic covenants and constitutions, amongst men themselves. This liberty is the proper end and object of authority, and cannot subsist without it; and it is a liberty to that only which is good, just, and honest. This liberty you are to stand for, with the hazard (not only of your goods, but) of your lives, if need be. . . . This liberty is maintained and exercised in a way of subjection to authority; it is of the same kind of liberty wherewith Christ hath made us free.[10]

Hobbes would have made the same reply! Nevertheless, these civil or covenant liberties came increasingly to the fore. John Wise gave the Puritan case away when he showed that the covenant theology of "Christian liberty" could be paralleled by secular social contract theory as interpreted by Pufendorf, provided the "consideration of man's moral turpitude be waived." With the gradual decline in the consciousness of corruption and with the growing irritation in the colonies against British mercantilism, Locke's *Treatises* were welcomed increasingly in New England and were finally used to justify rebellion.

What was true of social theory was also true of natural philosophy. Cambridge Platonism was closely associated with the rise of Newtonian science, and when, about 1700, Bacon, Newton, and Locke became available in New England, they quickly supplanted the antiquated physics and astronomy of the Ramist texts.

The condition of learning (as well as everything else) was very low in these times, indeed much lower than in the earlier time while those yet lived who had had their education in England and first settled the country. These were now gone off the stage and their sons fell greatly short of their ac-

---

[10] John Winthrop, *The History of New England*, ed. by J. K. Hosmer (New York [c. 1908]), II, 238–39, "Original Narratives of American History."

quirements as through the necessity of the times they could give but little
attention to the business of education. . . . It was nothing but the scholastic cobwebs of a few little English and Dutch systems that would hardly
now be taken up in the street, some of Ramus and Alsted's Works was considered as the highest attainments. They heard indeed in 1714, when he
[Johnson] took his Bachelor's Degree of a new philosophy that of late was
all in vogue and of such names as Descartes, Boyle, Locke, and Newton,
but they were cautioned against thinking anything of them because the
new philosophy, it was said, would soon bring in a new divinity and corrupt
the pure religion of the country, and they were not allowed to vary an ace
in their thoughts from Dr. Ames' *Medulla Theologiae* and *Cases of Conscience* and Wollebius, which were the only systems of divinity that were
thumbed in those days and considered with equal if not greater veneration
than the Bible itself for the contrivance of those and the like scholastical
authors to make curious systems in a scientific way out of their own heads,
and under each head to pick up a few texts of Scripture which seemed to
sound favorably and accommodate them to their preconceived schemes.
Indeed there was no such thing as any book of learning to be had in those
times under a 100 or 150 years old, such as the first settlers of the country
brought with them 70 or 80 years before and some few used to make
synopses or abridgements of these old scholastic systems.[11]

This *rapprochement* between Puritanism and Newtonian science is
most clearly exhibited in the case of Jonathan Edwards.

— 2 —

THE PIETIST THEORY OF LOVE

THAT Puritanism drifted easily into the principles of the Enlightenment and away from strict Calvinism is plausible on two
grounds:

1) Puritanism made God intelligible in terms of art and contract,
both principles of general order or reason, whereas Calvin had insisted that the decrees of God are in exercise of His absolute sovereignty, that they are inscrutable and arbitrary. For strict Calvinism
any attempt to reduce grace to either art or justice was impious as well

[11] Quoted from Johnson, *Autobiography*, in *Works*, ed. by Schneider, I, 5–6.

as futile. It was no accident that the system of Ramus made headway
first among the Arminians and then among the Dutch Congregationalists, for it was in the Netherlands and later in Scotland that Calvinism
was transformed from an absolutistic theocratic system into something
approaching constitutionalism and republicanism. In Dutch and British
Puritanism philosophical Platonism and political reform were intimately associated. In America this association was developed into an
integrated system.

2) By emphasizing the Church-Social Covenant, Puritanism confused and subordinated the "covenant of grace" or individual election.
Individualism was persistently sacrificed to "church order." Ramist
Platonism emphasized God's *general* providence and respect for covenants. In this sense God's justice was clearly embodied and exhibited
both in the social order and in natural law. As the New England church
covenants gradually became secularized and were increasingly in-
distinguishable from the town ordinances, the "standing order" (as
the New England theocracy was called) was put on the defensive and
resisted the growth of both political and religious individualism. Thus,
the Puritans were well prepared to interpret natural law as divine
order and social obligations as divine law.

Precisely these two traits of Puritan thinking increasingly segregated
them from their near neighbors on the Protestant Left. The Quakers,
Anabaptists, and Antinomians in general were pietists or "enthusiasts,"
who subordinated law to revelation and general order to personal
inspirations. The more these groups (especially in America) made
trouble for the Puritans, the more the latter became "sober," emphasizing an "enlightened mind" rather than "raised affections" (in the
words of Charles Chauncy) and repudiating mysticism, private revelations, and religious individualism in general.

This basic conflict between individualism and ecclesiasticism flared
up in the Great Awakening, when European pietism and evangelicalism migrated to America and swept large portions of the populace off
its balance. Of all the Puritans, the one who felt this conflict most
keenly and dealt with it most radically was Jonathan Edwards. He
learned his Ramist and Cambridge Platonism at Yale (probably under
Samuel Johnson, who was his tutor for a short time), but during his
college years the Dummer Library came over from Europe, contain-

ing the chief works of the "new learning," and both he and Johnson grasped at them eagerly. He was especially impressed by two philosophical works, Locke's *Essay* and Hutcheson's *An Inquiry into the Original of Our Ideas of Beauty and Virtue;* the former in 1717 while he was still in college, the latter about 1730, while he was a young minister at Northampton. His personal religious struggle was most intense during the years 1722–25, and in 1734 the "Revival" or "Awakening" broke out in his congregation. During these years he read and reread, in addition to the "new" philosophers, a work which was familiar to the Puritan divines, but gained new significance for Edwards—Petro van Mastricht's *Theoretico-practica theologia,* which was also available in a popularized, English version. Van Mastricht, though closely related to the Dutch Covenant theologians, was one of the founders of Dutch pietism. Through this Continental pietism Edwards was prepared theologically for the British and the American pietism of the Great Awakening. Edwards soon became the intellectual leader among the "New Lights," as those Puritans were called who inclined toward religious individualism and participated in revivalism; he constructed a philosophy which is impressive for its personal intensity as well as for its masterly dealing with the intellectual currents of his day. In our next chapter we shall consider how he dealt with Locke and Newton as scientists; our concern here is with his reworking of the Puritan tradition under the stimulus of pietism.

Taking his clue from Locke's emphasis on simple ideas of sense as the ultimate source of reflection, and from Hutcheson's doctrine of the moral sense, Edwards argued that God must be experienced by a kind of sense experience, instead of being understood by "justification of His ways to man," as the Puritan and other rationalistic theologians had tried to understand Him. He remembered how as a youth he had resented the doctrine of the absolute sovereignty of God until there suddenly came over him an "inward, sweet delight in God." His own eloquent account is worth quoting:

From my childhood up, my mind had been full of objections against the doctrine of God's sovereignty, in choosing whom he would to eternal life, and rejecting whom he pleased; leaving them eternally to perish, and be everlastingly tormented in hell. It used to appear like a horrible doctrine to me. But I remember the time very well, when I seemed to be convinced, and fully satisfied, as to this sovereignty of God, and his justice in thus eternally disposing of men, according to his sovereign pleasure. But never could give an account, how, or by what means, I was thus convinced, not in the least imagining at the time, nor a long time after, that there was any extraordinary influence of God's Spirit in it; but only that now I saw further, and my reason apprehended the justice and reasonableness of it. However, my mind rested in it; and it put an end to all those cavils and objections. And there has been a wonderful alteration in my mind, with respect to the doctrine of God's sovereignty, from that day to this; so that I scarce ever have found so much as the rising of an objection against it, in the most absolute sense, in God shewing mercy to whom he will shew mercy, and hardening whom he will. God's absolute sovereignty and justice, with respect to salvation and damnation is what my mind seems to rest assured of, as much as of any thing that I see with my eyes; at least it is so at times. But I have often since that first conviction, had quite another sense of God's sovereignty than I had then. I have often since had not only a conviction, but a *delightful* conviction. The doctrine has very often appeared exceedingly pleasant, bright, and sweet. Absolute sovereignty is what I love to ascribe to God. But my first conviction was not so.

The first instance, that I remember, of that sort of inward, sweet delight in God and divine things, that I have lived much in since, was on reading those words, I Tim. i. 17. *Now unto the King eternal, immortal, invisible, the only wise God, be honour and glory for ever and ever. Amen.* As I read the words, there came into my soul, and was as it were diffused through it, a sense of glory of the Divine Being; a new sense, quite different from any thing I ever experienced before. Never any words of Scripture seemed to me as these words did. I thought with myself, how excellent a Being that was, and how happy I should be, if I might enjoy that God, and be rapt up to him in heaven, and be as it were swallowed up in him for ever! . . .

After this my sense of divine things gradually increased, and became more and more lively, and had more of that inward sweetness. The appearance of everything was altered; there seemed to be, as it were, a calm, sweet, cast, or appearance of divine glory, in almost everything.[1]

The "almost everything" is significant, for he relates how the cultivation of this new sense led him into solitude, into communion with nature, and how his academic tasks and social relations reduced him to "a low, sunk estate and condition, miserably senseless . . . about

---

[1] Jonathan Edwards, *Representative Selections*, ed. by C. H. Faust and T. Johnson (Cincinnati, 1935), pp. 58–60.

spiritual things" and made him realize that he had "abundant reason to be convinced of the troublesomeness and vexation of the world, and that it will never be another kind of a world." He was troubled by the "proud and self-righteous spirit" which he sensed in himself and saw in his fellows, and he wrote, apparently without humor:

I have greatly longed of late, for a broken heart, and to lie low before God; and, when I ask for humility, I cannot bear the thought of being no more humble than other christians. It seems to me, that though their degrees of humility may be suitable for them, yet it would be a vile self-exaltation in me, not to be the lowest in humility of all mankind.[2]

Thus, in Edwards's mind there grew a master passion, a single concern that the sovereignty of God become literally an all-pervasive and all-inclusive motive, transforming passion into subjection and moral benevolence into "holy love."

Partly on the basis of this interpretation of his own experience, partly through his observations of "the religious affections" during the Awakening, and partly under the influence of pietist theology, he came to believe in a "divine and supernatural light" through which God reveals himself inwardly. He was careful to explain that "those convictions that natural men may have of their sin and misery, is not this spiritual and divine light,"[3] that "this spiritual and divine light does not consist in any impression made upon the imagination,"[4] that "this spiritual light . . . is quite a different thing from inspiration: it reveals no new doctrine, it suggests no new proposition to the mind, it teaches no new thing of God, or Christ, or another world,"[5] and that "not every affecting view that men have of the things of religion is this spiritual and divine light."[6] It is "a real sense of the excellency of God."[7]

There is a difference between having an opinion, that God is holy and gracious, and having a sense of the loveliness and beauty of that holiness and grace. There is a difference between having a rational judgment that honey is sweet, and having a sense of its sweetness. . . . There is a wide difference between mere speculative rational judging any thing to be excellent, and having a sense of its sweetness and beauty. The former rests only in the head, speculation only is concerned in it; but the heart is concerned in the

---

[2] *Ibid.*, pp. 70–71.   [3] *Ibid.*, p. 102, from "A Divine and Supernatural Light."
[4] *Ibid.*, p. 104.   [5] *Ibid.*, p. 105.   [6] *Ibid.*   [7] *Ibid.*, p. 106.

latter. When the heart is sensible of the beauty and amiableness of a thing, it necessarily feels pleasure in the apprehension.[8]

Edwards was convinced that he had abundant empirical evidence, such as Locke might demand, that men find pleasure in God. But he is careful to point out that love toward God and the pleasure found "in the things of religion" are not natural affections, because the means used are not natural. Following Locke, Edwards believed that in natural "willing" the will is determined by "the last dictate of the understanding"; in the case of this supernatural sense, on the contrary, the sense or appreciation of God's excellency creates the understanding of it. Edwards thus worked out very carefully an empiricist argument for supernatural or holy love.

Not content, however, with the empirical approach, he cast the same idea into Platonic form. He argued not only, as the pietists did, that God must be approached through the "heart" not the "head," but that this "holy" or supernatural love is the love of the universal. He called it "benevolence to Being in general" or "being's consent to Being." All natural or moral virtue is but a reflection and derivative of this "true virtue," which is based, not on a "moral sense" in the humanitarian form of disinterestedness, but on the excellence of Being itself, an excellence of harmony or proportion among the parts of Being. "Wherefore all the Primary and Original beauty or excellence, that is among Minds, is Love; and into this may all be resolved that is found among them." [9]

Edwards made an ingenious synthesis of his two approaches to God —the Lockean and the Platonic—in his sketch on the Trinity. God the Father is Love. In order to have an object of love, the Father must have an Idea of Himself. This Idea is the Son. Their unity in action is the Holy Spirit or Divine Will.

The F. is the Deity subsisting in the Prime, unoriginated & most absolute manner, or the deity in its direct existence. The Son is the deity generated by Gods understanding, or having an Idea of himself & subsisting in that Idea. The Holy Gh. is the Deity subsisting in act, or the divine essence flowing out and Breathed forth in Gods Infinite love to & delight in himself. & I believe the whole divine Essence does Truly & distinctly subsist both in

[8] *Ibid.*, p. 107
[9] *Ibid.*, p. 35, from "Notes on the Mind."

the divine Idea & divine Love, and that each of them are Properly distinct Persons.[10]

Edwards projected a "Body of Divinity," which he did not live to write. He indicated, however, that he wanted to entitle it "Lovely Christianity," and referred in explanation to van Mastricht and the pietists. His chief ambition, in other words, was to reconcile the doctrine of God as Platonic Archetype of Excellence with the Lockean system of "ideas," and the Puritan theory of grace with the pietist conception of love.

He reconstructed the Ramist Platonism, based on the idea of the Divine Art, into a pietist version of Platonic love. He made it quite clear that this "holy love" or benevolence is nothing sentimental or merely emotional. It is empirical and empiricist "sense." And it is certainly not to be confused with either the inspiration of the Quakers or the ecstatic "affections" of the religious revivals. Edwards's *Treatise on the Religious Affections* is severely critical, and his conception of "Christian practice" or practical holiness is neither mysticism nor enthusiasm. It is Puritan sobriety suffused with a Platonic sense and sensitivity for beauty.

But for the New England Puritans it had a disquieting meaning and effect. When young Edwards of Northampton preached to the Boston aristocracy on the theme "God Glorified in Man's Dependence," the effect was sensational. To have the Calvinistic orthodoxy—the doctrine of absolute and arbitrary decrees, the doctrine of original corruption, the doctrine of determinism, damnation, and redemption—revived, not as a covenant for a holy commonwealth, but as an "inward" or "sensible" revelation of the love of God was both refreshing and disconcerting. As the divergence between "New Lights" and "Old Lights" became more apparent, Edwards's attempt to reconcile Puritanism and Pietism proved increasingly impractical. When he and, even less tactfully, his followers Bellamy, Emmons, and Hopkins attempted to repudiate the popular "Half-way Covenant," to revive in the New England congregations the practice of strict communion and public confession of godliness or regeneration, they became an unpopular minority and ended by becoming a small sect of philosophically erudite but socially unfashionable Calvinists. In self-defense and also

[10] *Ibid.*, p. 379, from "An Essay on the Trinity."

in the interest of "holy love," the Edwardean New Lights were forced to affiliate with the Presbyterians, who corrupted their philosophy, welcomed their pietism, and substituted for their individualism the Presbyterian brand of Protestant Jesuitism (to use Jefferson's apt term), the attempt to organize a centralized "Christian party in politics." [11] Not only in New England but throughout the country philosophy and piety became estranged, and the cause for which Edwards labored was hopelessly lost.

— 3 —

IMMATERIALISM

PURITAN scholasticism conceived God in terms of art, not of substance. But those Cambridge Platonists who were not of the school of Ramus were less concerned to combat scholastic concepts of substance and more worried by Descartes's innovations in ontology. Henry More, in particular, dwelt on the theological difficulties arising from the Cartesian distinction between extended substance and thinking substance. *Where,* then, is God? More's answer, which Newton repeated, was that God is extended and that material things literally and spatially exist *in* the divine mind. This led Newton to deify absolute space, and Jonathan Edwards did not hesitate to follow him.

Deprive the world of light and motion and the Case would stand thus with the world, there would [be] neither white nor black neither blew nor brown, bright nor shaded pellucid nor opake, no noise or sound neither heat nor Cold, neither fluid nor Wet nor Drie hard nor soft nor solidity nor Extension, nor figure, nor magnitude nor Proportion nor body nor spirit, what then [is] to become of the Universe Certainly it exists no where but in the Divine mind.[1]

It is self-evident I believe to every man, that Space is necessary, eternal,

---

[11] See the pamphlet by Ezra Stiles Ely, *The Duty of Christian Freemen to Elect Christian Rulers* (1827), reprinted in Joseph Blau, ed., *American Philosophic Addresses, 1700–1900* (New York, 1946), pp. 551–62, and Joseph Blau, "The 'Christian Party in Politics,' " *Review of Religion*, XI, no. 1, Sept. 1946.

[1] Edwards, *Representative Selections*, ed. by C. H. Faust and F. Johnson, pp. 22–23; from "Of Being."

infinite, and omnipresent. But I had as good speak plain: I have already said as much as, that Space is God.[2]

When we say that the World, i.e. the material Universe, exists no where but in the mind, we have got to such a degree of strictness and abstraction, that we must be exceedingly careful, that we do not confound and lose ourselves by misapprehension. That is impossible, that it should be meant, that all the world is contained in the narrow compass of a few inches of space, in little ideas in the place of the brain; for that would be a contradiction; for we are to remember that the human body, and the brain itself, exist only mentally, in the same sense that the other things do; and so that, which we call place, is an idea too. Therefore things are truly in those places; for what we mean, when we say so, is only, that this mode of our idea of place appertains to such an idea. We would not therefore be understood to deny, that things are where they seem to be. For the principles we.lay down, if they are narrowly looked into, do not infer that. Nor will it be found, that they at all make void Natural Philosophy, or the science of the Causes or Reasons of corporeal changes; For to find out the reasons of things, in Natural Philosophy, is only to find out the proportion of God's acting.[3]

In his early "Notes" Edwards represented this Cambridge Platonism, which is the background of Newton as well as of Puritanism, as making no pragmatic difference for scientific knowledge. "It is just all one," he said, whether "ideas" exist in the divine mind or whether things exist "in the same manner as is vulgarly thought." Whether the order of cause and effect is interpreted as proportion in the divine excellence or as natural law makes no difference to science; there is only the difference to religion and the imagination, for idealism leads men to look upon material things as the "shadows of beings" and to see the beauty or art of God, "when one part has such consonant proportion with the rest, as represents a general agreeing and consenting together," "that they seem to have respect one to another, as if they loved one another." But, as Edwards read Locke and saw the general drift of natural religion toward the faith in *necessary* connections, he revised his estimate of idealism somewhat and emphasized an idealistic theory of causation. In his *The Great Christian Doctrine of Original Sin Defended*, which was not published until 1758, he argued against

[2] Edwards, *Works*; with a memoir of his life by Sereno E. Dwight, I, 706; from "Notes on the Mind."

[3] *Ibid.*, I, 669; from "Notes on the Mind."

the idea of necessary connection, much as Hume was doing at about the same time. Edwards apparently arrived at his critique independently of Hume, and certainly had quite different objectives in view. He argued against all "secondary causes" and attributed all causation directly to God's "arbitrary constitution." God is the *only* "agent" in the world; material things are used by him as means, but, strictly speaking, material things do not act as "efficient causes."

Prior existence can no more be the proper cause of the new existence, in the next moment, or next part of space, than if it had been in an age before, or at a thousand miles distance, without any existence to fill up the intermediate time or space. Therefore the existence of created substances, in each successive moment, must be the effect of the *immediate* agency, will, and power of GOD. . . .

It will certainly follow from these things, that God's *preserving* of created things in being, is perfectly equivalent to a *continued creation*, or to his creating those things out of nothing at *each moment* of their existence.[4]

The whole *course of nature*, with all that belongs to it, all its laws and methods, constancy and regularity, continuance, and proceeding, is an *arbitrary constitution*. In this sense, the continuance of the very being of the world and all its parts, as well as the manner of continued being depends entirely on an *arbitrary constitution*. For it does not at all *necessarily* follow, that because there was sound, or light, or colour, or resistance, or gravity, or thought, or consciousness, or any other dependent thing the last moment, that therefore there shall be the like at the next. All dependent existence whatsoever is in a constant flux, ever passing and returning; renewed every moment, as the colours of bodies are every moment renewed by the light that shines upon them; and all is constantly proceeding from God, as light from the sun. *In him we live, and move, and have our being.*[5]

Edwards's doctrine of God's omnificence represented not merely a return to orthodox Calvinism but also a positive argument for pantheism based on Newton and Locke. It did not deny the existence of matter; it asserted that matter exists and operates in God. It denied the existence of substance or substances, for God is more than substance; he is Being, continually creative. And it denied mechanical causation

[4] Edwards, *Representative Selections*, ed. by Faust and Johnson, pp. 333–34; from *The Great Christian Doctrine of Original Sin Defended.*
[5] *Ibid.*, pp. 336–37.

or necessary relations. It is important to note that for Edwards human wills, too, exist in the Divine Will and act only *in* God. The immediate antithesis to Edwards's idealism was not materialism, but Arminianism. Edwards's idealism was opposed to Berkeley's. Samuel Johnson's, on the other hand, was intended to be faithful to Berkeley's; but the Puritan heritage was so strong in Johnson that his immaterialism combined superficially his old Platonism with his new Anglicanism.

When Samuel Johnson was converted to Anglicanism, he was converted on grounds of "church order" or episcopal, as contrasted with democratic authority.[6] Having made his decision, he was practically obliged to become converted also to Arminian theology and turned to Bishop Berkeley for help in this problem. It is clear from their correspondence that neither Johnson nor Berkeley appreciated each other's difficulties. Johnson had just turned from his Ramist system, with great relief, to the study and appreciation of Bacon, Locke, and Newton. The latitudinarian Anglican divines, especially Clarke, who had induced him to return to the "devout, grand, and venerable administration" of the Church of England, had also led him along the fashionable road toward "the reasonableness of Christianity." Wollaston's natural religion was his new bible. Consequently, when he found Berkeley attacking Newton, he was disconcerted. He called Berkeley's attention to Newton's conception of space as God's boundless sensorium and added, "nor can I think you have a different notion of these attributes from that great philosopher, tho' you may differ in your ways of expression or explaining yourselves." He even was so bold as to suggest that "I can't see how external space and duration are any more abstract ideas than spirits." But Berkeley was firm and told Johnson he had no use for absolute space or for the deification

[6] "Considering first that this country is in such a miserable state, as to Church government (let whatever hypothesis will, be right) that it needs reformation and alteration in that affair. . . .

"That peace without one of Christ's institutions is a false peace and it is best erring on the surest side.

"There may be offence taken where there is none given; if others are damnified by my doing my duty, I cannot help that, however I endeavor the contrary.

"There may be more souls damnified for want of Episcopal government in the country and that by far at length than by my making this appearance."

(*Samuel Johnson, President of King's College; His Career and Writings*, Herbert and Carol Schneider, eds. New York, 1929, I, 63–64.)

of space, and he gradually led Johnson to understand why he was so intent on attacking abstract ideas. Johnson had carried over into his idealism the Puritan distinction between archetypes and ectypes and had preached this doctrine to Berkeley, who had considerable difficulty in persuading Johnson that this distinction was subject to the same criticism that he was making of the materialists who held "that an ideal existence in the divine mind is one thing, and the real existence of material things another." In fact, Johnson's *Noetica*, which embodied his interpretation of Berkeley's idealism, is an uncritical mixture of Puritan Platonism and Berkeleyan immaterialism. The following passage plainly illustrates this mixture, the first part being Berkeleyan, the rest Puritan.

There are archetypes of these sensible ideas existing, external to our minds; but then they must exist in some other mind, and be ideas also as well as ours; because an idea can resemble nothing but an idea; and an idea ever implies in the very nature of it, relation to a mind perceiving it, or in which it exists. But then those archetypes or originals, and the manner of their existence in that eternal mind, must be entirely different from that of their existence in our minds; as different, as the manner of His existence is from that of ours: in him they must exist, as in original intellect; in us, only by way of sense and imagination; and in Him, as originals; in us only as faint copies; such as he thinks fit to communicate to us, according to such laws and limitations as he hath established, and such as are sufficient to all the purposes relating to our well-being, in which only we are concerned. Our ideas, therefore, cannot otherwise be said to be images or copies of the archetypes in the eternal mind, than as our souls are said to be images of Him.[7]

In his subsequent polemics with Calvinists, Johnson took a more vigorously Arminian stand. There it was made quite clear that human "spirits" are not primarily mere perceivers or merely images of the divine, original and absolute Being, but genuine "agents." The argument for moral responsibility was here his chief reliance, and he used it effectively against his Calvinist opponents, who had neither the dialectical skill nor the theological boldness of Jonathan Edwards. What helped Johnson's *Ethics*, however, was not its relation to Berkeley's idealism or to his own *Noetica*, for it had little, but its open assertion of human independence and free will, which was becoming an increasingly popular doctrine in the American colonies.

[7] *Ibid.*, II, 376–77; from Johnson's *Elementa Philosophica*.

The metaphysics of "agency" took a new turn with Cadwallader Colden, of New York. He was something of a naturalist, but his ambitions as a scientist overreached themselves when he tried to "explain" the law of gravitation on Newton's mechanical principles, thus bringing to theoretical completion the great Newtonian physics. He was disappointed in this, for the Newtonian scientists found too many "hypotheses" in Colden's system to make it of any scientific (that is, experimental) use. But philosophically Colden's analysis of "the first causes of action in matter" is of considerable interest, though he, himself, may have been too much an amateur to have known what he was doing. However, he formulated his basic contribution admirably in a letter to an Edinburgh friend, to whom he sent his "papers" in the hope that at Edinburgh at least their value might be recognized.

National Prejudices, as well as personal often prevail in many points of philosophy. Perhaps the Principles which I have adopted may be more favourably received in Scotland than in England. You'll pardon the fondness which a man naturally has for his own productions when I desire of you, in case you do not think these papers proper to appear in public, please to deposit them in the library of the University of Edinburgh where I had my Education in the Rudiments of Science, for I am persuaded they will sometime or other be found to contain the true principles of physical knowledge, and to be of real use.

We have no knowledge of substances or of things themselves, as little knowledge of material substance as of the Intelligent or of Spirit. All our knowledge consists in this that from the effects of phenomena we discover something which we call substances have the power of producing certain effects. How they produce these effects we in no manner conceive. Yet all the objections to my principles which I have seen arise from an expectation that I should explain in what manner the primary powers produce their effect.[8]

Colden had a clever, pragmatic (I would almost venture to say, behavioristic) method of cutting short the metaphysical problems of what mind can do and what matter can do. He had evidently understood the point of Locke's *Essay* and assumed as a scientific maxim the following principle:

Our knowledge of the powers in nature can only be attained by an accurate

[8] Letter to Robert Whyte, professor of medicine at the University of Edinburgh, dated February 25, 1762, in *The Colden Letter Books*, Vol. I.

observation of the phenomena or effects produced by them and from thence collecting the general rules or laws which these powers observe in producing their effects in different circumstances. We thereby have obtained all the knowledge of nature which can be obtained by our faculties.[9]

From this principle he concluded that the science of matter reduced itself to a description of types of action. "Everything that we know is an agent," but all we know of an agent is "its action and the effects of that action."

I hope to shew, that we may have as clear and distinct an idea or conception of spirit, as we can have of matter: and that all the difficulties or absurdities, which many have fallen into, arise from an error in the conception of the power, force, energy, or manner of acting, and which are commonly called the properties or qualities of things; or from the confusion which arises by the using of different terms, or words to express things, which in themselves are not different. The property, or quality of any thing, is nothing else but the action of that thing: and the different qualities or properties of any thing or substance are no other than the different actions or manner of acting of that thing.[10]

He then proceeded to distinguish the different "essences," "powers," or "forces" in things or substances according to the differences observable in their "manner of acting." Accordingly, he discovered three types of material agents: resisting (having the *vis inertiæ*), moving (having the power to continue in a straight line at a given velocity), and elastic (having the power to communicate resistance or motion in any direction, i.e., the power of a medium or *aether*). Momentum is a combination of the first two; friction a conflict between the first two; radiation is a product of the first and third.

When Colden had elaborated his system to this extent, he sent it to Samuel Johnson for criticism (and, of course, admiration!). Johnson replied that he had always been taught that matter is by nature, if not by definition, inactive, passive, inert, and that it must be moved by an immaterial agent. Furthermore, he could not understand how "action" and "intelligence" could be separated, since unconscious action (that is, agency) seemed to him a contradiction in terms.

[9] P. R. Anderson and M. H. Fisch, eds., *Philosophy in America* (New York, 1939), p. 98, from *The Letters and Papers of Cadwallader Colden*, Vol. VI.
[10] *Ibid.*, p. 103, from *The Principles of Action in Matter*.

To this Colden replied promptly and confidently that "they who perceived the necessity of this connection [between action and intelligence] must show it." "I observe, I think, every day multitudes of actions, without that the idea of intelligence is necessarily connected with those actions." However, Colden revised his *First Causes of Action in Matter*, and under the title *First Principles of Action in Matter* he added a section on a fourth type of action, viz., "perception, intelligence and will." He labeled this type of agent "intelligent being," and then made the following significant observations.

We have no idea of substances; we have as little knowledge of the substance of material beings as of intelligent ones. . . .

Therefore in all actions of intelligent beings, which are likewise called *moral actions*, the intention, purpose, or will, is principally to be considered. This is the guiding principle in morality, policy, and religion. . . .

The intelligent agent never acts in opposition or contradiction to the material agents; for if it did, nothing but confusion, contradiction and absurdity could ensue: and there could be no need or use of machinery, or of a certain order and disposition of the parts of matter in the several systems, which compose the universe. But the intelligent either so disposes of the parts of the system, that their complicated actions shall serve the purpose, which the intelligent being has in forming of the systems: or where the action of the material agent is not determined, by any thing external to it, and its action is indifferent to any direction, in such case the intelligent being gives the action such direction, as best suits its own purpose.[11]

Insofar as there is a single system of design or purposive action we must assume a single intelligent being which Colden calls *Archeus* or Nature.

Samuel Johnson was, of course, not completely satisfied with this mere addition of a fourth agent, even when Colden was willing to call it *immaterial*, but the discussion at least revealed that as far as "morality, policy, and religion" are concerned, the naturalists and the immaterialists could join hands, provided they confined themselves to "action."

The larger significance of the introduction of the philosophies of immaterialism into American philosophy at this time is that the chief issues out of which these philosophies arose were subordinated to new

[11] *Ibid.*, pp. 119–120, from "Of the Intelligent Being."

ones. Idealism itself made practically no headway in America until a century later, and immaterialistic idealism least of all. For Johnson and Edwards the problem of idealism arose out of two ancient concepts—substance and free will. In the course of the development of both the Arminian and the Puritan types of idealism, the ideas of substance and free will proved increasingly irrelevant and were practically discarded in favor of the newer ideas of material causation and action. "Matter" not only took the place of "substance" as the context of "agency," but in turn was crowded out of the argument by the more empirical study of cause and effect relations. Arguing on this empirical basis, Edwards defended a type of supernatural (but observable) sense, *in addition to* the natural senses, and a type of immaterial "constitution" in which the natural succession of events can be included. In other words, Edwards and Colden might have come to terms with each other on the interpretation of nature, whereas Colden and Johnson could come to terms on matters of morals. The two immaterialists, Johnson and Edwards, could probably not have agreed on even the meaning of immaterialism. But it is clear that underlying the strictly philosophical arguments among these men, were deep-seated divergences of interest. Edwards was anxious to revive faith in the supernatural in the interests of piety; Johnson, increasingly fearful of the growth of "free thinking," fled to what might be called a "fundamentalist" interest in biblical science; and Colden turned toward the natural sciences. None of them was prepared for the moral issues that were becoming increasingly urgent and that clustered around the cry of "liberty."

GUIDE TO THE LITERATURE FOR PART I

CHAPTER I

For the more general background of English Puritanism William Haller, *The Rise of Puritanism* (New York, 1938), is authoritative and makes good use of the polemic pamphlets. For the still more general background, the basic, if not indispensable, work is John Calvin, *Institutes of the Christian Religion* (1st American ed., Philadelphia, 1816).

By far the most adequate exposition of the philosophy of the New England Puritans is Perry Miller, *The New England Mind; the Seventeenth Century* (New York, 1939). Chapters IV–IX and Appendix A are particularly valuable, since they contain the only comprehensive treatment of the Ramist branch of Puritan philosophy. Chapters XIV and XV give a good account of the social theory of the covenant theology. For criticism of this book see the review by H. W. Schneider in *Journal of the History of Ideas,* I (1940), 119–22. Until Professor Miller's projected sequel, giving a similar account of eighteenth-century thought in New England, appears, the reader might profitably consult Perry Miller and Thomas H. Johnson, *The Puritans* (New York, 1938), which covers a wider range than *The New England Mind.* Ralph Barton Perry, *Puritanism and Democracy* (New York, 1944) gives an excellent account of Puritan social philosophy. Joseph Dorfman, *The Economic Mind in American Civilization* (New York, 1946), I, 42 ff., 111 ff. has a good discussion of Puritan economic ethics and of the secular aspects of Puritan "corporations"; see also Dorfman's discussions of Davenport, p. 39, Winthrop, pp. 60–65, Williams, pp. 66–74, and Morgan, p. 120. George F. Willison, *Saints and Strangers* (New York, 1945), gives a good account of the Plymouth Separatists.

Samuel Eliot Morison, *Harvard College in the Seventeenth Century* (Cambridge, Mass., 1936), is the chief collection of relevant materials for the early period of American Puritanism, but it is still useful to refer to an older classic, Henry Martyn Dexter, *The Congregationalism of the Last Three Hundred Years as Seen in Its Literature* (New York, 1880), since it contains much detailed information on Connecticut Puritans. Another useful reference work is Williston Walker, *The Creeds and Platforms of Congregationalism* (New York, 1893).

In S. E. Morison, *Builders of the Bay Colony* (New York, 1930), there are good sketches of John Winthrop, Thomas Shepard, Nathaniel Ward, and John Eliot. In S. E. Morison, *The Puritan Pronaos; Studies in the Intellectual Life of New England in the Seventeenth Century* (London, 1936), there are references to the chief sources and expressions of New England thought. Clifford K. Shipton, *Roger Conant; a Founder of Massachusetts* (Cambridge, 1944) and "The Autobiographical Memoranda of John Brock 1636–1659," *Proc. American Antiquarian Society,* LIII, part i, add to our knowledge of early Puritan leaders. Kenneth B. Murdock, *Increase Mather; the Foremost American Puritan* (Cambridge, Mass., 1925), and his "The Puritan Tradition," in *The Reinterpretation of American Literature,* ed. by Norman Foerster (New York, 1928), are sympathetic presentations of Puritanism, intended to counteract the unsympathetic accounts of the preceding generation of historians as represented in Brooks Adams, *The Emancipation of Massachusetts* (1st ed., Boston, 1887; rev. and enl. ed., Boston, 1919), George E. Ellis, *The Puritan Age and Rule in the Colony of Massachusetts Bay, 1629–1685* (Boston, 1888), Sanford H. Cobb, *The Rise of Religious Liberty in America* (New York, 1902), and I. Woodbridge Riley, "Philosophers and Divines, 1720–1789," in *The Cambridge History of American Literature*, I, 72–89. See, too, Parrington, *Main Currents in American Thought*, I, 98–106, for a valuable criticism of Murdock's work; note also Parrington's treatment of Hooker and Roger Williams.

Chapters I–III of Herbert W. Schneider, *The Puritan Mind* (New York, 1930), give a running commentary on the general ideas of New England Puritanism, but are inadequate for the technical philosophical orientation, which is given by Professor Miller. In Chapter V, on Samuel Johnson, pp. 158–64, however, brief mention is made of the Ramist philosophy as taught at Yale, and Herbert and Carol Schneider, *Samuel Johnson, President of King's College; His Career and Writings* (New York, 1929), II, 57–186, reproduce, and in part translate, Samuel Johnson's typical Ramist texts.

Of the selections in Anderson and Fisch, the following are relevant to this chapter: "A Model of Church and Civil Power," and the selections from John Winthrop, Urian Oakes, and John Wise.

It is difficult to select from the voluminous writings of the New England Puritans. For general orientation, two classics supplement each other admirably—John Winthrop, *The History of New England from 1630–1649* (various editions), and Cotton Mather, *Magnalia Christi Americana; or, The Ecclesiastical History of New England, from Its First Planting in the Year 1620, unto the Year of Our Lord, 1698* (London, 1702). There is an excellent full bibliography of Puritan writings in Miller and Johnson, *The Puritans* (New York, 1938). Below are listed the chief American Puritan philosophical writings in chronological order.

1634   John Cotton and others (?), A Model of Church and Civil Power (London, 1634).

1640   Thomas Shepard, The Sincere Convert (London, 1640).

1644   John Cotton, The Keys of the Kingdom of Heaven, and Power Thereof, according to the Word of God (London, 1644).

1645   John Cotton, The Covenant of Gods Free Grace (London, 1645). —— The Way of the Congregational Churches Cleared (London, 1645).

Thomas Shepard, The Sound Beleever (Boston, 1645; London, 1653).

1647   Nathaniel Ward, The Simple Cobler of Aggavvam in America (London, 1647).

1648   Thomas Hooker, A Survey of the Summe of Church-Discipline (London, 1648).

1651   Peter Bulkeley, The Gospel-Covenant. 2d ed. (London, 1651).

1659   John Eliot, The Christian Commonwealth: or, The Civil Policy of the Rising Kingdom of Jesus Christ (London, 1659).

1668   William Stoughton, New-Englands True Interest; Not to Lie 2d ed. (Cambridge, Mass., 1670).

1672   John Davenport, The Power of Congregational Churches (London, 1672).

1682   Urian Oakes, The Soveraign Efficacy of Divine Providence (Boston, 1682).

1700   Increase Mather, The Order of the Gospel, Professed and Practised by the Churches of Christ in New England (Boston, 1700).

1702   Cotton Mather, Magnalia Christi Americana (London, 1702).

1717   John Wise, A Vindication of the Government of New-England Churches (Boston, 1717).

1721   Cotton Mather, The Christian Philosopher (London, 1721).

1726   Samuel Willard, A Compleat Body of Divinity in Two Hundred and Fifty Expository Lectures on the Assembly's Shorter Catechism (Boston, 1726).

CHAPTER 2

The best biography of Edwards is by Ola Elizabeth Winslow, New York, 1940. The best exposition of his philosophy is by Clarence H. Faust, pp. xiv–xcviii in Jonathan Edwards, *Representative Selections*, with Introduction, Bibliography, and notes by Clarence H. Faust and Thomas H. Johnson (Cincinnati, 1935). The selections in this volume are admirable; on pp. cxix–cxlii there is an extensive bibliography with brief analytic comments on much of the material listed. A. C. McGiffert, Jr., *Jonathan Edwards* (New York, 1932), is an excellent study of Edwards's psychology of religion. Chapter IV of H. W. Schneider, *The Puritan Mind*, gives a critical account of Edwards's relations to Puritanism, but fails to do justice to his doctrine of supernatural sense and to his pietism. W. J. B. Edgar has made important researches on Edwards's pietism, but they have not been published.

To the bibliographies in these works it is necessary to add only a few recent publications. Theodore Hornberger, "Edwards and the New Science," *American Literature*, IX (1937–38), 196–207, presents Edwards as an antagonist of materialism on the grounds of natural science itself, while H. G. Townsend, "Jonathan Edwards' Later Observation of Nature," *New England Quarterly*, XIII (1940), 510–18, and James H. Tufts, "Edwards and Newton," *The Philosophical Review*, XLIX (1940), 609–22, present evidence connecting Edwards with the "new" science. Conrad Wright, "Edwards and the Arminians on the Freedom of the Will," *Harvard Theological Review*, XXXV (1942), 241–61, finds Edwards's position on the freedom of the will close to that of the Arminians in some respects. Perry Miller, "Jonathan Edwards to Emerson," *New England Quarterly*, XIII (1940), 589–617, considers Edwards typical of the same sort of revolt out of which Emerson arose.

The works of Edwards have been published in many editions. *The Works of President Edwards;* with a memoir of his life by Sereno E. Dwight (New York, 1829), is of particular value because of the "memoir." Thomas Herbert Johnson, *The Printed Writings of Jonathan Edwards, 1703–1758: a Bibliography* (Princeton, 1940), is a useful study of the various printed editions of Edwards's individual works.

I. Woodbridge Riley, *American Philosophy; the Early Schools* (New York, 1907), is valuable because it contains the "Notes on the Mind" and "Of Being." Substantial excerpts from the first of these important youthful works are given in Muelder and Sears, *The Development of American Philosophy* (Boston, 1940), together with selections from "God Glorified in Man's Dependence," "A Divine and Supernatural Light," and "The Freedom of the Will," and a chapter, "The Insufficiency of Reason as a Substitute for Revelation," from *Miscellaneous Observations on Important Theological Subjects*. P. R. Anderson and M. H. Fisch, eds. *Philosophy in America* (New York, 1939), contains the sections on "Excellency" from the "Notes on the Mind" and a very good selection entitled "Personal Identity," from *The Great Christian Doctrine of Original Sin Defended*.

In addition to these philosophical essays by Edwards, the reader's attention is called to the following important philosophical sermons and essays. Those marked with an asterisk are contained in part in the volume of selections edited by Faust and Johnson. "God Glorified in Man's Dependence * " (reprinted in full in Joseph Blau, ed., *American Philosophic Addresses, 1700–1900,* pp. 521–36); "A Divine and Supernatural Light * "; "The Justice of God in the Damnation of Sinners * "; "Christian Love"; "Decrees and Elections"; "Efficacious Grace"; "Treatise on Grace"; "Observations on the Trinity * "; "Treatise Concerning Religious Affections * "; "Freedom of the Will.* "

CHAPTER 3

The long search for the sources of Edwards's idealism (see C. H. Faust and T. H. Johnson, *Jonathan Edwards*, p. xxvii, and H. W. Schneider, *The Puritan Mind*, p. 137) now seems superfluous, since recent researches on Puritan philosophy have proved the prevalence of Cambridge Platonism in New England. The attempt to decide which of the numerous Platonist works were most influential on Edwards is a comparatively trivial question. . Consult the literature on Edwards referred to in the section for Chapter 2. The "Notes on the Mind," which are pervaded by the Lockean approach, should be supplemented by the fragment "Of Being," where the approach is more dialectical.

The published writings of Samuel Johnson are scarce. His *Elementa Philosophica* was published by Benjamin Franklin (Philadelphia, 1752); it is composed of two parts: "Noetica" (in which Berkeley's influence is conspicuous) and "Ethica," which had been published separately in 1746 as *A System of Morality*. Of the four volumes ed. by H. W. and C. Schneider, *Samuel Johnson, President of King's College. His Career and Writings* (New York, 1929), Volume II contains the important philosophical works, including Johnson's correspondence with Berkeley and Cadwallader Colden. The introductory essay by H. W. Schneider in this volume is practically identical with Chapter V of *The Puritan Mind*. Volume I contains Samuel Johnson's highly instructive and readable "Memoirs," or autobiography, together with selections from his personal correspondence. Volume III contains his ecclesiastical correspondence and reprints his chief polemics with dissenters; of these, his pamphlets against Jonathan Dickinson and Hezekiah Gold are particularly important philosophically. Volume IV concerns Johnson's labors in connection with the founding of King's College, New York, and reprints some of the anti-Anglican polemics. At the end of this volume is a calendar of the Johnson Papers, most of which are in the Columbia University Library.

E. E. Beardsley, *Life and Correspondence of Samuel Johnson, D.D.* (New York, 1873), is the most complete biography of Samuel Johnson and contains the correspondence with Berkeley and Colden. P. R. Anderson and M. H. Fisch, *Philosophy in America* (New York, 1939), gives part of the Berkeley correspondence and a selection from Johnson's *Noetica*. W. G. Muelder and L. Sears, *The Development of American Philosophy* (Boston, 1940), give selections from Johnson's *Noetica* and *Ethica*. In connection with Johnson's *Ethica*, the reader should refer to William

Wollaston, *The Religion of Nature Delineated* (Glasgow, 1746),* [1] the significance of which as a source for Johnson's work escaped the editors of his writings. For general bibliographies on Samuel Johnson see H. W. Schneider, *The Puritan Mind*, p. 287, and P. R. Anderson and M. H. Fisch, *Philosophy in America*, p. 54. Theodore Hornberger "Samuel Johnson of Yale and King's College. A note on the relation of science and religion in Provincial America," *New England Quarterly*, VIII (1935), 378–97, discusses the relation of Johnson to Bacon, Locke, Newton, and Berkeley.

In addition to Cadwallader Colden's correspondence with Samuel Johnson, referred to above, the published philosophical works of Colden are: *An Explication of the First Causes of Action in Matter, and of the Cause of Gravitation* (New York, 1745); *The Principles of Action in Matter, the Gravitation of Bodies, and the Motion of the Planets, Explained from Those Principles* (London, 1751). *The Letters and Papers of Cadwallader Colden*, from the Collections of the New York Historical Society, 9 vols. (New York, 1917–23; 1934–35), especially Volume III and the list of unpublished Colden manuscripts in VII, 359–76, some of which are of philosophic interest. One of these, "An Introduction to the Study of Phylosophy," is included in Joseph Blau, ed., *American Philosophic Addresses, 1700–1900* (New York, 1946), pp. 289–311.

[1] See below, pp. 37–38.

— II —

THE AMERICAN ENLIGHTENMENT

THE Enlightenment is indefinable philosophically, especially in America, where it was least literary and most active. There was no systematic formulation of human reason in this country—no *Encyclopédie*, no *philosophes*, no *esprit de système*; yet there was no period in our history when the public interests of the people were so intimately linked to philosophic issues. To recapture the intellectual life of the revolutionary generation in America we must turn, not to academic texts or to systems of theology and ethics or to the products of reflective solitude, but to the center of public affairs—to state documents and to political platforms, presses, and pulpits. Never in America were philosophical thinking and social action more closely joined. Though much of the philosophizing was *ad hoc*, finding universal solutions for particular problems, it will not do to dismiss the thought of the Enlightenment as mere rationalization. For the conspicuous fact about American life then was that not only were the eyes and hopes of the world centered on America but also American men of affairs themselves were genuinely concerned with the wider, if not the universal, implications of their interests and deeds. They had, indeed, "a decent respect to the opinions of mankind." It is amazing to see how far into the past and the future they looked in order to understand their present. Never was history made more consciously and conscientiously, and seldom since the days of classic Greece has philosophy enjoyed greater opportunity to exercise public responsibility.

It is impossible to read and write dispassionately of the American Enlightenment, for it contains the heart of our heritage as a people and our deepest tie to the rest of humanity. America was then the cosmopolitan frontier in a double sense: it gathered into action the reflections and passions of several generations of European thinkers, and it also led the way toward the bold political, religious, and moral experiments in which the whole world has ever since participated. It is somewhat embarrassing to the historian of philosophy to point to John Adams, Benjamin Franklin, Thomas Jefferson, and James Madison as cosmopolitan and distinguished expressions of the philosophy of the Enlightenment and then be compelled to admit that their writings are full of commonplaces and their minds full of confusions.

They had no systems of thought, and they consciously borrowed most of the scattered ideas which they put into action. They are poor material for the classroom, but they are, nevertheless, still living forces as well as classic symbols in American philosophy. Under these circumstances any failure to make the American Enlightenment appear as a "glorious revolution" in thought as well as in fact must certainly be a failure on the part of the historian, not of the Enlightenment itself.

Yet, in a sense the Enlightenment did fail miserably. Its ideas were soon repudiated or corrupted, its plans for the future were buried, and there followed on its heels a thorough and passionate reaction against its ideals and assumptions. It was a dramatic episode. Its great themes —natural rights, religious liberty, liberal religion, free thought, universal progress and enlightenment—how soon they had a hollow sound! How pervasive the disillusionment! A Virginia planter, about 1850, wrote that he considered democratic doctrines to have "caused more evil than the avowed opposers of popular rights could have effected if their power had equalled their wishes. . . . A government based on universal suffrage will be a government of and by the *worst* of the people." [1] A German liberal in Cincinnati, celebrating Jefferson in 1855, bewailed the utter collapse of freedom in American culture.[2] And in 1859 Lincoln wrote:

The principles of Jefferson are the definitions and axioms of free society and yet they are denied and evaded, with no small show of success. One dashingly calls them "glittering generalities." Another bluntly calls them "self-evident lies" and others insidiously argue that they apply to "superior races." These expressions . . . are the vanguard, the miners and sappers of returning despotism.[3]

But this reaction fails to prove that the Enlightenment was not really enlightened. On the contrary, there is an increasing and nostalgic return among American philosophers to the memory of those great days, and no American thinker who is more than a professor can refrain from occasional thoughtful wishing for the utility and freedom which philosophy then enjoyed.

[1] Avery O. Craven, *Edmund Ruffin: Southerner* (New York, 1923), p. 44; similarly George Fitzhugh, in his *Sociology for the South* (Richmond, 1854) especially ch. xix.
[2] J. B. Stallo, *Reden, Abhandlungen und Briefe* (Cincinnati, 1893), p. 19.
[3] Thomas Jefferson, *The Writings*, ed. by A. L. Bergh (Washington, D.C., 1903), I, xvi–xvii. [Memorial edition.]

BENEVOLENCE

THE Enlightenment began in complacency and ended in fear. During its early stages the faith in universal benevolence arose out of theological optimism. In America this trait became conspicuous with Cotton Mather, a pompous old theocrat, who conceived his professional duty to be "doing good." He not only wrote *Essays to Do Good,* but went about from house to house "doing good" wherever he suspected the presence of vice. He became a conscientious busy-body. In Edwards's conception of benevolence and "Christian love" the object is God and the beneficiary is one's own soul. But more puritanical Puritans conceived benevolence in terms of doing good to others, imagining that God himself is interested not so much in his own glory as in the happiness of his creatures. Mather's *Christian Philosopher* is one of the earliest American exhibitions of this conceit, based on the argument from fitness and design in nature. Butler's *Analogy of Religion* and Paley's *Natural Theology* became fashionable expositions of the argument from design. The belief in universal providence was increasingly acceptable to the prosperous "elect" of New England. Even Wollaston's *Natural Religion* was widely read and recommended. Samuel Johnson made it the basis of his *Ethica.* With Wollaston as his model, he explained that God treats everything for what it really is, "according to truth," and that He therefore treats man as a being created for happiness (eternal, of course).

We must . . . take into the account, the whole of our nature and duration, as being sensitive and rational, social and immortal creatures. It must therefore be the good and happiness of the whole human nature, and the whole moral system, in time, and to all eternity. Hence the good of the animal body, or the pleasure of sense, is but imaginary, and ceaseth to be good, and hath even the nature of evil, so far forth as it is inconsistent with the good and happiness of the soul: which is also the case of private good, so far forth as it is inconsistent with the good of the public; and temporal good, so far forth as it is inconsistent with that which is eternal. . . . And this our good and happiness in the whole, does necessarily coincide with, and even result from, the truth and nature of things, or things, affections and actions, considered as being what they really are; for thus to consider them, is the same thing with considering them as being fit and tending, in the nature of them, to render our rational, social and immortal nature, in the whole ultimately happy.[1]

Benjamin Franklin, who not only read Wollaston's book but also set type for it during his brief sojourn in London, was inclined to ridicule such complacency, and his *Dissertation on Liberty and Necessity, Pleasure and Pain* succeeded admirably in this. For example:

The late learned Author of The Religion of Nature . . . has given us a Rule or Scheme, whereby to discover which of our Actions ought to be esteem'd and denominated *good*, and which *evil*: It is in short, this, "Every Action which is done according to *Truth*, is good; and every Action contrary to Truth, is evil: To act according to Truth is to use and esteem every Thing as what it is, &c. Thus if A steals a Horse from B, and rides away upon him, he uses him not as what he is in Truth, *viz.* the Property of another, but as his own, which is contrary to Truth, and therefore *evil*." But, as this Gentleman himself says, (Sect. I. Prop. VI.) "In order to judge rightly what any Thing is, it must be consider'd, not only what it is in one Respect, but also what it may be in any other Respect; and the whole Description of the Thing ought to be taken in": So in this Case it ought to be consider'd, that A is naturally a *covetou*s Being, feeling an Uneasiness in the want of B's Horse, which produces an Inclination for stealing him, stronger than his Fear of Punishment for so doing. This is Truth likewise, and A acts according to it when he steals the Horse. Besides, if it is prov'd to be a *Truth*, that A has not Power over his own Actions, it will be indisputable that he acts according to Truth, and impossible he should do otherwise. . . . 'Tis as just and necessary, and as much according to Truth, for B to dislike and punish the Theft of his Horse, as it is for A to steal him. . . .

How necessary a Thing in the Order and Design of the Universe . . . Pain or Uneasiness is, and how beautiful in its Place! Let us but suppose it just now banish'd from the World entirely, and consider the Consequence of it: All the Animal Creation would immediately stand stock still, exactly in the Posture they were in the Moment Uneasiness departed; not a Limb, not a Finger would henceforth move; we should all be reduc'd to the Condition of Statues, dull and unactive. . . .

As the *Desire* of being freed from Uneasiness is equal to the *Uneasiness*, and the *Pleasure* of satisfying that Desire equal to the Desire, the Pleasure thereby produc'd must necessarily be equal to the *Uneasiness* or *Pain* which produces it. . . .

[1] Johnson, *Works*, ed. by Schneider, II, 448.

From these Propositions it is observ'd,

1. *That every Creature hath as much Pleasure as Pain.*
2. *That Life is not preferable to Insensibility; for Pleasure and Pain destroy one another: That Being which has ten Degrees of Pain subtracted from ten of Pleasure, has nothing remaining, and is upon an equality with that Being which is insensible of both.*
3. *As the first Part proves that all Things must be equally us'd by the Creator because equally esteem'd; so this second part demonstrates that they are equally esteem'd because equally us'd.*
4. *Since every Action is the Effect of Self-Uneasiness, the Distinction of Virtue and Vice is excluded; and* Prop. VIII. *in* Sect. I *again demonstrated.*
5. *No State of Life can be happier than the present, because Pleasure and Pain are inseparable.*

Thus both Parts of this Argument agree with and confirm one another, and the Demonstration is reciprocal.

I am sensible that the Doctrine here advanc'd, if it were to be publish'd, would meet with but an indifferent Reception. Mankind naturally and generally love to be flatter'd: Whatever sooths our Pride, and tends to exalt our Species above the rest of the Creation, we are pleas'd with and easily believe, when ungrateful Truths shall be with the utmost Indignation rejected. "What! bring ourselves down to an Equality with the Beasts of the Field! with the *meanest* part of the Creation! 'Tis insufferable!" But, (to use a Piece of *Common* Sense) our *Geese* are but *Geese* tho' we may think 'em *Swans;* and Truth will be Truth tho' it sometimes prove mortifying and distasteful.[2]

Benjamin Franklin, when a youth, also ridiculed Cotton Mather. Under the pen name Mrs. Silence Dogood he began to attack the Harvard students, their wealthy parents, their pretentious professors, the fashionable clergy, and Mather personally, all in the name of "essays to do good." After his arrival in Philadelphia, Franklin continued his ridicule by the publication of a series of "Busybody Papers." Years later he wrote to Cotton Mather's son, Samuel, that his father's *Essays to Do Good* "gave me such a turn of thinking, as to have an influence on my conduct through life; for I have always set a greater value on the character of a doer of good, than on any other reputation and if I have been, as you seem to think, a useful citizen, the public

[2] Anderson and Fisch, eds., *Philosophy in America*, pp. 133–43.

owes the advantage of it to that book." [3] It is possible that Samuel Mather, like more recent readers, failed to see the joke in this letter.

These personal incidents illustrate a general trend: theological complacency, which generated "natural religion" in England and New England, soon had to face a more critical and often a satirical "natural religion," which could not readily be reconciled with Christianity. The theory of benevolence became increasingly secularized, until natural religion meant simply humanitarian ethics. The characters in Hume's *Dialogues on Natural Religion* could all have been found in America, and young Franklin was a good Philo, the skeptic. Franklin was a homespun and picturesque, but impressive, embodiment of secularized humanitarianism, a man who devoted himself wholeheartedly and effectively to public service and to useful projects. His "art of virtue" and *Poor Richard*, which are usually interpreted as the cult of thrift and capitalist ethics, were to his mind "essays to do good." What makes Franklin a truly revolutionary figure in America is the thoroughgoing secularization of his mind and morals. He retained much of the Yankee complacency and acquired some of the Quaker variety in addition. He was complacent about the economic value of Puritan virtues. But he removed the veneer of holiness from them completely and put them on a plain utilitarian footing. The reader of *Poor Richard's Almanac* would never suspect that the common sense and proverbial wisdom embodied in it was an achievement of intellectual struggle and laborious liberation. It all seems so commonplace and naïve. But the reader of his *Autobiography* and, even better, of his early pieces on deism can see how much enlightenment, sophistication, and critical honesty went into his discovery of common sense amid so much theological pomp and circumstance.

We sometimes disputed, and very fond we were of argument . . . which disputatious turn is apt to become a very bad habit . . . besides souring and spoiling conversation, it is productive of disgusts, and perhaps enmities, with those who may have occasion of friendship. I had caught this by reading my father's books of dispute on religion. Persons of good sense, I have since observed, seldom fall into it, except lawyers, university men, and generally men of all sort, who have been bred at Edinburgh.

I grew convinced that truth, sincerity, and integrity . . . were of the utmost importance to the felicity of life. [4]

[3] Anderson and Fisch, eds., *Philosophy in America*, p. 125.
[4] Benjamin Franklin, *Autobiography*.

Thus, Franklin made explicit and complete a philosophical change that was gradually coming over the Puritans; more or less consciously they began to understand that the so-called "Puritan ethic" had a utilitarian basis as well as a theological expression. The New Englanders were forced to be Puritans because of their desire to build a New England, not, as is commonly supposed, because of their Calvinism. The direct and principal cause of the "agonized conscience" or sense of sin, supposedly consequent on the Calvinistic doctrine of depravity and of predestination, is to be found in the exacting demands of pioneer life. The clergy were careful that God should command whatever needed doing and prohibit whatever proved an obstacle.

Benjamin Franklin made the attempt to maintain the Puritan virtues in all their rigor, but to abandon entirely their theological sanctions. He placed the frontier morality on a utilitarian footing and gave it empirical sanctions. In this he was eminently successful. Franklin put the whole matter in a few words: "Revelation had indeed no weight with me, as such; but I entertained an opinion, that, though certain actions might not be bad, *because* they were forbidden by it, or good, *because* it commanded them; yet probably these actions might be forbidden *because* they were bad for us, or commanded *because* they were beneficial to us, in their own natures, all the circumstances of things considered." [5] All that remained to be said was simply what Franklin did say over again: If you want to achieve anything, these are the necessary means: Temperance, silence, order, resolution, frugality, industry, sincerity, justice, etc. And if one were to ask for proof, Franklin could point to his own experience and to the colonies themselves as evidence.

Philosophers are offended by the simplicity, almost simpleness, of this philosophy. In his preoccupation with instrumental values, Franklin is typical of what Europeans call "Americanism." Final values, being taken for granted, seldom become consciously defined and discussed, for in America (and elsewhere too for that matter) ends are adopted early and easily, much as religions are adopted by children; they are taken for granted as part of the intellectual environment, and there seldom arises an occasion for criticizing them seriously. Franklin was not interested in establishing his puritanic discipline as an end in itself. He assumed that people have ends, that they want to be "free

[5] *Ibid.*

and easy," and that they understand wealth as merely the necessary means for enjoying the real ends of leisure society. "Early to bed and early to rise, makes a man healthy, wealthy and wise." Health, wealth, and wisdom—this combination is not a bad summary of the natural goods of human life. But none of them occurs in Franklin's table of virtues, which is concerned exclusively with the "early to bed and early to rise" side of life.

In other words, Puritan virtues, inasmuch as they are not a philosophy of human ideals, were neither a substitute for the Aristotelian ethics nor a glorification of bourgeois commercialism. If Puritan morality substitutes for anything it is for the traditional "Christian" virtues, for they, too, constitute a philosophy of the discipline of life. The Christian life is traditionally portrayed as one of humility, charity, penitence, poverty, self-denial, and a forgiving spirit. The Puritan virtues, in spite of the fact that they were sanctioned by a Christian theology, were not traditionally Christian. This divorce from the Christian moral tradition, which Franklin made explicit in his philosophy, is at the heart of the contrast between the Yankee and the Christian. It is also at the heart of the American Enlightenment in general. Had the American Enlightenment followed Franklin into the pursuit of practical benevolence and secular humanitarianism it would have created what Europe expected of it. But it followed the more conventional pattern, engaging in the sentimental cult of benevolence and creating a "liberal religion." [6] Meanwhile Franklin's "virtues," divorced from his benevolence, which led him to conceive them as means toward a "free and easy" life, hardened into the stuff of unbridled competition and sordid business.

— 5 —

THE THEORY OF FREEDOM

THE secular triumph of the English Whigs in 1688 was the continuation and culmination of the Puritan rebellion, and the political philosophy of John Locke embodied in secularized form most of the practical aims of the dissenters—constitutional rights,

[6] See below, pp. 59–67.

toleration, and security. There was a similar development in New England, a secularization of Puritanism into the theory of freedom. But the clergy failed to take the lead in this transition, for the Puritan theocrats were afraid of secular trends, and a few of them revived the old Calvinist doctrine of resistance to tyrants. One of the most striking and amusing illustrations of this is the famous "rebellion" sermon by President John Witherspoon to the Princeton students, May 17, 1776, in which he argued that the sovereign will of God was arousing the "disorderly passions" of the colonists against their oppressors. "The wrath of man in its most tempestuous rage, fulfills his will, and finally promotes the good of his chosen." [1] But even Witherspoon, after he has expounded his orthodox theory of God's use of the passions of men, devotes the last half of his sermon to a plain, secular appeal to the youth to fight bravely in defense of their rights and in "the cause of justice, of liberty, and of human nature." He attempts to unite the two doctrines by arguing on the basis of history that the loss of civil liberty always entails the loss of religious liberty, and that "if we yield up our temporal property, we at the same time deliver the conscience into bondage." [2]

There was precedent for such adaptations of Puritan theology to rebellion in the case of John Wise, who in vindicating the liberties of local congregations (1717) had turned from the ecclesiastical arguments and principles of Puritanism to the "law and light of nature" (specifically to Pufendorf) for a theory of "the immunities of man," and who had specified as "capital immunities belonging to man's nature" the liberty to follow one's own rational judgment, personal liberty and equality, and the opportunity to join with one's fellows in the exercise of popular sovereignty and social contract. John Wise had concluded quite pointedly that of all governments "possibly the fairest in the World is that which has a Regular Monarch, (in Distinction to what is Despotick) settled upon a Noble Democracy as its Basis." [3] Some of the New England clergy now were emboldened to follow

---

[1] Sermon on *The Dominion of Providence over the Passions of Men*, p. 16. In the same paragraph Witherspoon comments with his customary theological wit: "There is often a discernible mixture of sovereignty and righteousness in providential dispensations."

[2] *Ibid., p.* 28.

[3] Anderson and Fisch, eds., *Philosophy in America*, p. 39n.

the example of Jonathan Mayhew, who in his *Sermons to Young Men* (1763) declared that the love of liberty and country and the hatred of all tyranny and oppression are the very essence of true religion. But Mayhew and his fellow rebels made little attempt to derive this doctrine from Puritanism. In fact, he was not a minister in "good standing" and was described by Samuel Johnson, a Tory, as one of those "loose thinkers who can scarcely be accounted better Christians than the Turks."

It was simpler for prosperous and rebellious Yankees to discard their Puritan pretense of believing in entire dependence on God and in dutiful obedience to "magistrates" and to become out and out Whigs, if not republicans, in preparation for their amazingly secular declaration of independence. And so there spread rapidly throughout the colonies a secular conception of history and progress. One of the most popular and powerful expressions of this new point of view was Adam Ferguson's *An Essay on the History of Civil Society* (Edinburgh, 1767). Imagine the effect of the following sentences on a young mind steeped in Edwardean theology.

If the question be put, What the mind of man could perform, when left to itself, and without the aid of any foreign direction? We are to look for our answer in the history of mankind. . . . We speak of art as distinguished from nature; but art itself is natural to man. He is in some measure the artificer of his own frame, as well as of his fortune, and is destined, from the first age of his being, to invent and contrive. . . . If we are asked therefore, where the state of nature is to be found? We may answer, it is here . . . all situations are equally natural. . . . "Man is born in society," says Montesquieu, "and there he remains." [4]

Can you imagine the wrench this must have given the Puritan reader? In place of the Fall, the primitive animal. In place of regeneration, progress by degrees. In place of the divine plan of redemption in history, history is "the mind of man left to itself without the aid of any foreign direction." In place of the congregational covenant with God, man is naturally born into society and simply stays

[4] Adam Ferguson, *An Essay*, pp. 5, 10, 12, 28. Ferguson was professor of pneumatics and moral philosophy at Edinburgh from 1765 to 1785. He was inspired directly and chiefly by Montesquieu. The seventh edition of his *Essay* was published in Boston, 1809; the eighth in Philadelphia, 1819. This is an index to its extreme popularity.

there. Society is here conceived of as both a human art and a state of nature. Ferguson's reader is being prepared to understand Plato, Aristotle, Cicero, Machiavelli, Hobbes, Harrington, Sidney, Locke, Montesquieu, and in general the classics of political theory, without benefit of clergy.

In spite of the popularity of Tom Paine's and Benjamin Franklin's appeals to prudence and "common sense," the American leaders took the trouble to reassert the classic principles, not merely of the modern classics, but of the ancient as well. The invasion of America by Roman law and Greek political philosophy, to which the Puritans had paid only lip service, was in itself a major event in the history of American thought and a major contribution of the Enlightenment. Without tracing them back to their classical origins, we can at least mention the chief philosophical ideas and issues that emerged in the attempts to justify the rebellion and in the long deliberation and debate over the Constitution:

a) *Social contract and the commonwealth.*—It was a simple matter to secularize the Puritan theory of the church covenant. This had been achieved in large measure by Locke and the British Whigs; all that was needed to adapt Locke's version of the social contract to American needs was to republicanize it with bits of the Roman classical theories of social contract, the public weal, and the law of nature. For a time it looked to colonial lawyers such as John Adams and Thomas Jefferson that the theoretical, as well as the practical, problems could be solved within the framework of the British Empire, much as the non-separatist Congregationalists had hoped to remain within the Church of England. Let the colonies be regarded as so many "realms" each with its own legislature, each with its own voluntary contract of allegiance to the common Crown, to the common law of the Empire, and to the statute laws its own legislature, then they, together with their "fellow free states," Great Britain, the Isle of Man, etc., would form an imperial federation of free states, analogous to the Congregationalist theory of free parishes federated into the Anglican Church under Christ the only and supreme head. To regard the colonies thus was possible because their charters were obviously contractual. Such states, though federated, would be free, since each enjoyed its own representative government and each, within the limits of the common law, could vote on the nature and extent of its contribution to the common weal. The only agency needed to insure unity, in addition to the common bond of loyalty to the Crown, would be an independent, imperial supreme court, whose sole function it would be to judge the constitutionality of the acts of each legislature. This conception of a federal commonwealth of free (i.e., contractual) societies was being urged in the 1760's on both sides of the Atlantic by conciliatory statesmen who hoped that the economic strife between motherland and colonies could be subordinated to a scheme of constitutional reform,[5] but, as the world knows, what proved to be an impractical scheme for an imperial commonwealth quickly became a working basis for colonial co-operation and then for a federal union of states. Everyone expected the federal legislature to be the chief center of trouble and factionalism, for the same reason that the British Parliament was the storm center of colonial policy. It was essential to liberty that this should be so. But a single executive and a supreme court might nevertheless keep the peace, on which the safety of all depended. This basic pattern of American political thought from about 1760 to about 1820 was not merely a practical expedient to win a war and establish a peace, it was the practical embodiment of a social philosophy. The "federal scheme," of which its founders were very proud indeed, was a double application of social contract theory—or, as Jefferson explained, it was a great republic built out of little ones. Each New England town, each ward, or "hundred," each state, was, like the great federation, regarded as a complete contractual society. Thomas Jefferson, especially, was concerned that these "little republics" be maintained in vigor, for, he argued, on the republican virtues and vigilance of these local societies depends the health of the great one.

I dare say that in time all these as well as their central government, like the planets revolving round their common sun, acting and acted upon according to their respective weights and distances, will produce that beautiful equilibrium on which our Constitution is founded, and which I believe it will exhibit to the world in a degree of perfection, unexampled but in the planetary system itself. The enlightened statesman, therefore, will endeavor to

[5] In the colonies Benjamin Franklin and Samuel Johnson were early advocates of a federation before the question of independence arose, and Johnson, curiously enough, regarded even his plea for American bishops as an ecclesiastical version of this idea.

preserve the weight and influence of every part, as too much given to any member of it would destroy the general equilibrium.[6]

A republic, *res publica,* or commonwealth according to this contractual theory is a voluntary, legal union of citizens who promise each other to protect each other's natural rights and *to this end* appoint an "agent," "trustee," or government to establish civil rights or justice. It is not a mutual compact of subjection to a sovereign (Hobbes) or a recognition of the will of the majority as sovereign (Locke). It is a people exercising its freedom or sovereignty (if that concept *must* be retained) by asserting, respecting, enforcing the rights of each, not by surrendering those rights to a government. Thomas Paine, a virulent republican, proclaimed baldly the "sovereignty of the people"; whereas James Wilson worked out conscientiously the legal implications of such a theory of sovereignty. The Americans had not heard of Rousseau's doctrine of the sovereignty of the General Will when this theory was being formulated; they would have been suspicious of it if they had. For their doctrine was based rather on a subordination of both particular and general wills to respect for natural and civil rights, i.e., to the *res publica.* The *res publica* is related to the *res privata,* they maintained, as means to end; civil liberties, laws, powers, etc. are the instruments of securing the properties and promoting the happiness of the several citizens.

We hold these truths to be self evident: that all men are created equal; that they are endowed by their creator with [*inherent and*] inalienable rights; that among these are life, liberty, and the pursuit of happiness; that to secure these rights, governments are instituted among men, deriving their just powers from the consent of the governed; that whenever any form of government becomes destructive of these ends, it is the right of the people to alter or to abolish it, and to institute new government, laying its foundation on such principles, and organizing its powers in such form, as to them shall seem most likely to effect their safety and happiness.

These "self-evident truths" were believed to belong to a larger body of self-evident truth. It was one of the basic aims of the Enlightenment, formulated in Locke's *Essay,* to put the moral and political

[6] Letter to Peregrine Fitzhugh, Feb. 23, 1798; Thomas Jefferson, *The Living Thoughts of Thomas Jefferson,* ed. by John Dewey (New York, 1940), pp. 51–52.

sciences on the foundation of demonstrative knowledge. Mathematics was the ideal pattern, and axioms of right were the obvious starting point for such a system. This general attempt to construct deductive systems in the sciences of mind and morals was a thoroughly rationalistic ideal; it often went by the French label of "ideology." There was no enthusiasm as yet for the Hutcheson-Hume theory of moral sense, and any attempt to regard these "principles of natural law" as merely principles of human nature was repudiated along with the belief in innate ideas. Though there was a constant appeal by pamphleteers like Samuel Adams and Thomas Paine to "common sense," and though Jefferson explained that when he referred to "self-evident truths" in the Declaration of Independence he meant nothing more than "the common sense of the subject," this faith in common sense was not yet a philosophical principle or a psychological discovery. Common sense, in this connection, meant common reason, and the science of any subject was based on the common sense or self-evident principles *of that subject*. To build on such "ideas" or first principles was to achieve certainty without metaphysics and to be empirical without being either utilitarian or sensationalist.[7]

b) Natural rights and constitutional right.—By the pamphleteers and lawyers "the rights of man" were used as a convenient shibboleth. To them it mattered little whether they be "rights of Englishmen," "birth rights," "inherent rights," or "rights endowed by our Creator." Nor was it prudent to distinguish too clearly between natural rights

---

[7] Jefferson generalized these doctrines of method more than his co-laborers in "the science of government" did, with the possible exception of John Taylor of Caroline; John Adams, James Wilson, and James Madison developed systems of government, but they failed to make explicit their more general philosophical ideas; and Alexander Hamilton, who philosophized liberally, was inclined to pick up his principles from the classics when he happened to need them. Jefferson explained that in a formal or academic scheme of studies "in the Philosophical department, I should distinguish: (1) Ideology; (2) Ethics; (3) the Law of Nature and Nations; (4) Government; (5) Political Economy." Here "ideology" represents the general theory of ideas, and the other philosophical "sciences" represent particular bodies of truth. In ideology Jefferson recommended first of all De Tracy; in ethics, Lord Kames; in "the law of nature and nations" next to the ancient Stoics, Grotius or Vattel (secondarily Pufendorf and Burlamaqui); in government De Tracy's *Commentary* and Review of Montesquieu; and in political economy De Tracy's revision of the physiocrats (especially Smith and Say). See Adrienne Koch, *The Philosophy of Thomas Jefferson* (New York, 1943), pp. 60 ff. and 144 ff.

and civil rights. They were inclined to do what Pufendorf did, whom the French in 1789 followed—cut the Gordian knot by speaking grandiloquently of "the rights of man and citizen." A vague, popular conception of natural rights, liberty, and popular sovereignty was current in the discussions centering about the colonial legislatures and state constitutions. Samuel Adams and James Otis in New England and George Mason, Patrick Henry, and George Wythe in Virginia were typical early popularizers of republican ideas, who set the problems for the next generation of more critical theorists.

But among the philosophically inclined statesmen the great debate in America was really a continuation of the great debate begun (for Englishmen, at least) in Cromwell's army between the Presbyterians and the Independents. Locke had used the concept of natural rights loosely, since he could grind his axe better on distinctions none too sharp. Similarly, in America the basic theoretical issues were subordinated until after the War of Independence had been won, but then they came increasingly to the fore; it was impossible to evade them in making the Constitution and in dealing with revolutionary France. The basic philosophical issue that emerged out of this conflict may be stated as follows: Can right, or law, be defined as an institutional moral structure so that the general and permanent framework or constitution of a state may be said to be either just or unjust, rational or arbitrary? Or must the right be defined in terms of particular acts, which by their individual nature are just or arbitrary? In the case of England, this issue amounted in practice to the question of whether the sovereignty of parliament, that is, of the people's legislators, is *ipso facto* right, or whether even the law of the land may be arbitrary and hence require the people to "reserve" particular rights or liberties against its own representatives and laws. John Adams, following James Harrington, conceived an institutional, structural, self-regulating order. His idea was so to construct the constitution that private interest and public interest would be identical, an idea that hypnotized social philosophy for more than a century. He would depersonalize law by distributing property or power in such a way that no particular interest could dominate. In other words, in a perfect republic the various classes and interests check and balance each other and thereby create a natural equilibrium that automatically does justice to each. By increasing the number of proprietors, by rotation of office and secret ballot, by separation of the deliberative and "prerogative" bodies, and by other such constitutional devices his "equal" or equilibrating commonwealth would enable each citizen in seeking his own interest to promote that of the whole. Had we adopted his "scientific" frame of government, the depravity of human nature would have been so nicely checked and balanced by the institutions of government that we would have nothing to fear from the "insatiable and unlimited" "passions and desires of the majority of the representatives." Could he be here now, he might be much gratified by the magnificent spectacle of checking and balancing which even our imperfect Constitution affords.

At the other extreme was Thomas Jefferson, who because he feared the "tyranny of the legislatures" fought for the Bill of Rights as a "legal check" in the hands of the judiciary, which body, "if rendered independent and kept strictly to their own department merits great confidence for their learning and integrity." [8]

That these extremes were juxtaposed without being reconciled is evident from the argument of Alexander Hamilton, who in his eagerness to defend the Constitution appealed to both philosophies. He argued that bills of rights "have no application to constitutions professedly founded upon the power of the people, and executed by their immediate representatives and servants. Here, in strictness, the people surrender nothing." [9] But on the following page he writes: "The Constitution is itself, in every rational sense, and to every useful purpose, a bill of rights." [10]

The rights outlined in the Bill of Rights appended under Jeffersonian pressure to our Constitutional "right" are clearly civil, not natural rights, and they resemble more closely those formulated in England in 1689 than the natural rights mentioned in the Declaration of Independence. However, the "law of the land" is still a combination of the two ideas of freedom, new "rights" being embodied from time to time in new amendments to the constitutional framework, and new

[8] Letter to James Madison, March 15, 1789.

[9] *The Federalist*, No. LXXXIV.

[10] See the article by James Truslow Adams, "Rights without Duties," in *The Yale Review*, XXIV, 237–50; also Charles W. Hendel, Jr., "The Meaning of Obligation," in *Contemporary Idealism in America*, ed. by Clifford Barrett (New York, 1932), pp. 237–95.

"freedoms" being added to legal freedom. In practice the issue turned largely on who ultimately is the guardian of the people's liberties. The Federalists, under the leadership of John Marshall, erected the Supreme Court, which James Wilson had likened to an international tribunal for the advancement of natural law, into the ultimate voice of "the sovereignty of the people" and the guarantor of the reign of law. Tom Paine had given a popular expression to this ideal in *Common Sense,* which when it appeared in 1776 was decidedly more sensational than it was in the days of John Marshall.

But where, say some, is the king of America? I'll tell you, friend, he reigns above, and doth not make havoc of mankind like the Royal Brute of Great Britain. Yet that we may not appear to be defective even in earthly honors, let a day be solemnly set apart for proclaiming the charter; let it be brought forth placed on the divine law, the Word of God; let a crown be placed thereon, by which the world may know, that so far as we approve of monarchy, that in America THE LAW IS KING.[11]

Jefferson, on the other hand, relied primarily on the civic virtues of the people and on periodic opportunities (theoretically, once in every generation) to revise their government as radically as they choose.

In government, as well as in every other business of life, it is by division and subdivision of duties alone, that all matters, great and small, can be managed to perfection. And the whole is cemented by giving to every citizen, personally, a part in the administration of the public affairs. . . .

Private fortunes are destroyed by public as well as by private extravagance. And this is the tendency of all human governments. A departure from principle in one instance becomes a precedent for a second; that second for a third; and so on, till the bulk of the society is reduced to be mere automatons of misery, to have no sensibilities left but for sinning and suffering. Then begins, indeed, the *bellum omnium in omnia,* which some philosophers observing to be so general in this world, have mistaken it for the natural, instead of the abusive state of man. And the fore horse of this frightful team is public debt. Taxation follows that, and in its train wretchedness and oppression.[12]

c) *Class society.*—Republican theory was both by tradition and on

---

[11] Thomas Paine, *Representative Selections,* ed. by Harry Hayden Clark (Cincinnati, 1944), pp. 32–33.

[12] Thomas Jefferson, *The Living Thoughts of Thomas Jefferson,* ed. by John Dewey, pp. 59–60. "Letter to Samuel Kercheval, July 12, 1816."

principle the antithesis of feudal theory. Feudalism, with its class privileges, was not to be permitted to arise in America; that was the first and foremost meaning of the dictum that all men are created equal. On the other hand, there was general agreement also that all societies are class societies. How reconcile political equality with economic inequality? That was the crux of the problem. That there had already arisen a colonial landed aristocracy, especially in the middle and southern colonies, was readily admitted; that a financial and industrial aristocracy was in the making was generally seen. That "every man ought to be supposed a knave and to have no other end, in all his actions, but private interest" [13] was one of those self-evident truths on which rest the sciences of government and political economy. John Adams proclaimed it more formally when he wrote: "Harrington has shown that power always follows property. This I believe to be as infallible a maxim in politics, as that action and reaction are equal, is in mechanics." [14] There will inevitably be factions, and the problem is to devise a mechanism whereby factions will govern each other without injury to "the rights of other citizens, or to the permanent and aggregate interests of the community." [15] Looking back, we can readily see here a clear formulation of the problem of party government. But our Constitution and its fathers made no provision either in theory or in practice for parties; they debated everlastingly the relative merits of other systems of checks and balances and hoped to devise a form of government which by its very form might withstand those tendencies toward corruption which have been described and explained in all the classics. The chief theoretical argument against party government was: "Representation, limited to the alternative of enlisting under one of these parties, ceases to be an instrument of national self-government, and dwindles into an instrument of oppression." [16] The chief practical reason why an enduring government could not be based on a party system, according to their theories, was that the factions and the class-interests which they expressed, though ever-present, would be ever-

[13] Alexander Hamilton, *Works* (New York, 1904), II, 51.
[14] Parrington, *The Colonial Mind, 1620–1800*, p. 318.
[15] *Federalist Papers*, No. X (Madison).
[16] John Taylor, *An Inquiry into the Principles and Policy of the Government of the United States* (Fredericksburg, Va., 1814), p. 196; quoted in E. Mudge, *The Social Philosophy of John Taylor of Caroline* (New York, 1939), p. 148.

shifting. To speculate on the enduring classes in American society seemed at that time the least profitable form of speculation.

It was easy enough to predict that there would always be rich and poor, propertied and propertyless classes, but it was also easy enough to see that the kinds of property were apt to change radically and that it was idle to build on a landed aristocracy. For even within the ranks of the landed aristocracy pro- and anti-slavery factions were rising, sectional interests were cutting across class interests, and property in land was as unstable and as inflationary as any property could be. It is true that agricultural theorists like Jefferson and Taylor defended agrarian interests as in a peculiar sense "the national interest," but this old semi-feudal argument became quite specious, and Jefferson finally abandoned it, for the landholders did not have the "fixed" interests in America which the theory required to make it plausible. Even Taylor wrote to Jefferson in 1799, "it would be happy indeed for us if agriculture and farming still continued to be interesting." Nevertheless, Taylor tried doggedly to maintain it:

Next in importance to arms for defending our country, should be instruments for cultivating it; and the latter enhance the value of the former, in the degrees that they render the country more worthy of being defended. . . . [The duties of agriculture], like the duties of moral rectitude, spread from the narrow circle of providing sustenance for one man or one family, into a wide expanse, created by the obligations arising from society, and the interests interwoven with national prosperity. In the United States, the responsibility of agriculture does not stop at food for all eaters. It extends to the support of government, to the encouragement of commerce, to the sustenance of the learned professions, to the introduction of the fine arts, and to the support of the more useful mechanical employments. . . . Being the sources from which all classes, and particularly the numerous family of the "*nati consumere fruges,*" must derive their subsistence and prosperity; all classes have a deep interest in rendering it more copious, because the success of each must expand with its growth, and contract with its decline. . . . Every stab given to agriculture reaches their own [the politicians'] vitals. . . . Where then, can be found a difference of interests between agriculture and the other useful occupations of society, when their prosperity must result from hers, and she can only reap the blessings of a well organized social state, by providing for them? . . . A common interest ought to suggest the national policy in regard to agriculture. . . . To what object more glorious, can the powers of the mind and of the purse be directed, than to one which with oracular certainty, deals out happiness or misery in extremes, and in all the intermediate gradations? . . . As agriculture is a national property [no group must harm it]. As our country is one great farm, and its inhabitants one great family, in which those who work the least receive the greatest share of the profit, those who are not farmers have a deeper interest for increasing the profit of agriculture, than the farmer himself; because his subsistence must precede theirs, and theirs can only be supplied from his surplus.[17]

Both the rich in land and the rich in banknotes took for granted, it seems, that they would be a minority of the citizens and foresaw the day when, with the rapid decline in property qualifications for voters, they would be a minority of the voters. The problem of class government was, therefore, to them primarily one of protecting the minority rights of the propertied classes. John Adams did not hesitate to put the matter offensively.

It must be remembered, that the rich are *people* as well as the poor; that they have rights as well as others; that they have as clear and as sacred a right to their large property as others have to theirs which is smaller; that oppression to them is as possible and as wicked as to others.[18]

If you give more than a share in the sovereignty to the democrats, that is, if you give them the command or preponderance in the sovereignty, that is, the legislature, they will vote all property out of the hands of you aristocrats, and if they let you escape with your lives, it will be more humanity, consideration, and generosity than any triumphant democracy ever displayed since the creation. And what will follow? The aristocracy among the democrats will take your places, and treat their fellows as severely and sternly as you have treated them.[19]

Thomas Paine, in opposing the single executive, reverted to the classic, republican doctrine that it is laws, not men, that should be obeyed:

[17] *American Farmer*, II (Sept. 15, 1820), 194–95; quoted in E. Mudge, *op. cit.*, pp. 155–56.

[18] "A Defence of the Constitution, etc.," in *Works*, VI, 65; quoted in Parrington, *The Colonial Mind, 1620–1800*, p. 317.

[19] "Letter to John Taylor," in *Works*, VI, 516; quoted in Parrington, *op. cit.*, pp. 315–16.

I have always been opposed to the mode of refining government up to an individual, or what is called a single executive. Such a man will always be the chief of a party. A plurality is far better; it combines the mass of a nation better together. And besides this, it is necessary to the manly mind of a republic that it loses the debasing idea of obeying an individual.[20]

From this point of view the will of the majority, too, or, for that matter the will of the people as a whole might constitute a faction, a danger to the *res publica*. Jefferson was almost alone among his contemporaries in giving a democratic turn to his republican theory, and even he came to it late in life, when executive experience had made him dubious of some of the "self-evident truths."

At the birth of our republic, I committed that opinion to the world, in the draught of a constitution annexed to the "Notes on Virginia," in which a provision was inserted for a representation permanently equal. The infancy of the subject at that moment, and our inexperience of self-government, occasioned gross departures in that draught from genuine republican canons. In truth, the abuses of monarchy had so much filled all the space of political contemplation, that we imagined everything republican which was not monarchy. We had not yet penetrated to the mother principle, that "governments are republican only in proportion as they embody the will of their people, and execute it." Hence, our first constitutions had really no leading principles in them. But experience and reflection have but more and more confirmed me in the particular importance of the equal representation then proposed. Where then is our republicanism to be found? Not in our constitution certainly, but merely in the spirit of our people. . . . The true foundation of republican government is the equal right of every citizen, in his person and property, and in their management. Try by this, as a tally, every provision of our constitution, and see if it hangs directly on the will of the people.[21]

Though Jefferson here shifts the emphasis in the theory of freedom from government by impersonal reason to government by popular will, he still retains the faith that the people can be trusted precisely because it can judge reasonably its own interests in the face of factional interests.

[20] Thomas Paine, *Representative Selections*, ed. by H. H. Clark, p. 388*n*.
[21] Thomas Jefferson, *The Living Thoughts of Thomas Jefferson*, ed. by John Dewey, pp. 58–59.

RELIGIOUS LIBERTY

WHEN, in 1644, Roger Williams argued that "civility and Christianity may both flourish in a state or kingdom notwithstanding the permission of divers and contrary consciences, either of Jew or Gentile" there were few who thought his contention plausible. The separation of "civility" and religion was, as a matter of fact, not tenable for most of the consciences of his day. Both politics and religion had to undergo basic changes before such a separation could become conscientious; these changes came with the Enlightenment. Williams used an argument which foreshadowed them:

The Church or company of worshippers (whether true or false) is like unto a Body or Colledge of Physitians in a Citie; like unto a Corporation, Society, or Company of East-Indie or Turkie-Merchants, or any other Societie or Company in London: which Companies may hold their Courts, keep their Records, hold disputations; and in matters concerning their Societie, may dissent, divide, breake into Schismes and Factions, sue and implead each other at the Law, yea wholly breake up and dissolve into pieces and nothing, and yet the peace of the Citie not be in the least measure impaired or disturbed; because the essence or being of the Citie, and so the well-being and peace thereof is essentially distinct from those particular Societies.[1]

This "essential distinctness" of "city" and church has been only gradually and indirectly realized. No Puritan could afford to admit that temporal and eternal peace could be separated in idea, nor could he conceive of a church as a private corporation which was not essential to the welfare of the commonwealth. Two factors made the separation possible: (1) the growth of political morality and secular bases for conscience; (2) the growth of religious individualism through pietism, and of evangelical sects, such as the Baptists, whose concerns were nonpolitical. The principles of civil peace became during the eighteenth century independent of the "economy of redemption," and conversely the pietistic pursuit of salvation was *in practice* distinct from the pursuit

---

[1] *The Bloudy Tenent of Persecution*, p. 73. Quoted in Anderson and Fisch, eds., *Philosophy in America*, p. 25.

of happiness on earth. The contents of popular politics and of popular religion were so distinct by the end of the eighteenth century that James Madison's *Memorial and Remonstrance on the Religious Rights of Man* (1785) and Jefferson's famous Act Establishing Religious Freedom in Virginia (1786) were less debatable than they would have been in the time of Roger Williams.

The religion of every man, must be left to the conviction and conscience of every man; and it is the right of every man to exercise it as these may dictate. This right is, in its nature, an unalienable right. It is unalienable, because the opinions of men, depending only on the evidence contemplated in their own minds, cannot follow the dictates of other men; it is unalienable, also, because what is here a right towards men, is a duty towards the creator. It is the duty of every man to render the creator such homage, and *such only*, as he believes to be acceptable to him; this duty is precedent, both in order of time and degree of obligation, to the claims of civil society. Before any man can be considered as a member of civil society, he must be considered as a subject of the governor of the universe; and if a member of civil society, who enters into any subordinate association, must always do it with a reservation of his duty to the general authority, much more must every man who becomes a member of any particular civil society do it *with the saving his allegiance to the universal sovereign.*[2]

Our civil rights have no dependence on our religious opinions, more than our opinions in physics or geometry. . . . It is time enough for the rightful purposes of civil government, for its officers to interfere when principles break out into overt acts against peace and good order; and finally, that truth is great and will prevail if left to herself, that she is the proper and sufficient antagonist to error, and has nothing to fear from the conflict, unless by human interposition disarmed of her natural weapons, free argument and debate, errors ceasing to be dangerous when it is permitted freely to contradict them.[3]

Jefferson and Madison here confess a triple faith: that civil rights are secular; that religion thrives best in freedom; and that truth will prevail. They were religiously and intelligently devoted to freeing religious as well as political institutions from "the deliria of crazy imaginations" and arbitrary authorities. To a Unitarian clergyman

[2] Bernard Smith, ed., *The Democratic Spirit* (New York, 1941), p. 104.
[3] Anderson and Fisch, eds., *Philosophy in America*, pp. 197–98.

who knew that he held the Unitarian faith, Jefferson wrote substantially in the same vein.

You ask my opinion of the items of doctrine in your catechism. I have never permitted myself to meditate a specified creed. These formulas have been the bane and ruin of the Christian church, its own fatal invention, which, through so many ages, made of Christendom a slaughterhouse, and at this day divides it into castes of inextinguishable hatred to one another. Witness the present internecine rage of all other sects against the Unitarian. The religions of antiquity had no particular formulas or creeds. Those of the modern world none, except those of the religionists calling themselves Christians, and even among these the Quakers have none. And hence, alone, the harmony, the quiet, the brotherly affections, the exemplary and unschismatizing Society of the Friends, and I hope the Unitarians will follow their happy example.[4]

For the reasons which led him to refrain from expressing himself on religious subjects he expected the clergy to keep politics out of their pulpits.

There is not an instance of a single congregation which has employed their preacher for the mixed purposes of lecturing them *from the pulpit* in Chemistry, in Medicine, in Law, in the science and principles of Government, or in anything but Religion exclusively. Whenever, therefore, preachers, instead of a lesson in religion, put them off with a discourse on the Copernican system, on chemical affinities, on the construction of government, or the characters or conduct of those administering it, it is a breach of contract, depriving their audience of the kind of service for which they are salaried, and giving them, instead of it, what they did not want, or, if wanted, would rather seek from better sources in that particular art or science. In choosing our pastor we look to his religious qualifications, without inquiring into his physical or political dogmas, with which we mean to have nothing to do. I am aware that arguments may be found, which may twist a thread of politics into the cord of religious duties. . . . I agree, that on all other occasions, the preacher has the right, equally with every other citizen, to express his sentiments, in speaking or writing, on the subjects of Medicine, Law, Politics, etc., his leisure time being his own, and his congregation not obliged to listen to his conversation or to read his writings.[5]

[4] Thomas Jefferson, *The Writings*, ed. by A. L. Bergh (Washington, D.C., 1903), Memorial edition, XV, 373–74; letter to Rev. Thomas Whittemore, June 5, 1822.

[5] *Ibid.*, XIII, 281–82; letter to P. H. Wendover, March 13, 1815, indorsed "Not Sent."

Jefferson's religious conviction that religious beliefs should remain private is explained in large part by the circumstances which I have narrated, but it is traceable also to the two literary sources which, according to him, influenced his religious opinions most: that is, to Joseph Priestley and to Conyers Middleton. These were both anticlerical Anglicans. They looked upon the growth of clerical power and of theological conflict as corruptions of Christianity and took a personal religious interest in the "pure and simple" teachings of Christ. They were exceptionally broad churchmen, who were persecuted and became personally embittered against "cannibal priests." And yet they were sincerely religious.

The power and eloquence of Jefferson's writing on religious freedom is due largely to his evident religious devotion. Unlike the typical *philosophe* of the Enlightenment, he had little relish for satire. Benjamin Franklin, who cultivated skeptical satire as a youth, abandoned it completely for the pursuit of his secular "art of virtue." Jefferson's enlightenment was no less than Franklin's a serious concern for morals, but his ethics were distinctly religious. He agreed with the Scottish intuitionists, loosely identifying the intuitions of what they called the moral sense with reason and common sense, but his favorite identification was with the Gospel of Christ. His reverence for "the peculiar superiority of the system of Jesus over all others" was fundamental for both his philosophy of religion and his character.

— 7 —

LIBERAL RELIGION

MEANWHILE, the Enlightenment was bringing with it a type of religion more "worldly" than either Jeffersonian piety or the pietism of the popular churches, a philosophical, public faith which took puritanism's place as the guardian of the commonwealth. Though the roots of religious liberalism reached far back into the history of New England and reflected its increasing prosperity during colonial times, the first outspoken departures from puritanism on the part of the clergy came with the Revolution. Jonathan Mayhew, of

West Church, Boston, was inclined toward deism and Arianism. King's Chapel, Boston, after 1782, when it openly called itself Unitarian and made James Freeman of Harvard its minister, was a seedbed of Arminianism. Charles Chauncy, of the First Church, Boston, preached an optimistic gospel to the effect that the "infinitely benevolent Creator" was concerned for the happiness of each of his creatures and that discontent with his "government" originates, not in good judgment, but in "a bad temper of mind." Gradually, and until 1784 secretly, he came to believe that God would ultimately save all sinners from damnation. In that year he took courage and published his sensational *The Salvation of All Men: the Grand Thing Aimed at in the Scheme of God*, which marks the beginning of professed universalism in New England. Hosea Ballou, who inspired both Universalists and Unitarians, finally came to the conviction that there would be no punishment whatsoever in the future world.

Harvard was notoriously a fountain of latitudinarianism. But the most picturesque of all the early liberals was the Reverend William Bentley (1759–1819), of East Church, Salem. His congregation was full of maritime traders and owners of clipper ships, who brought back marvelous reports from the Orient. Bentley was a newspaper editor as well as a clergyman, and a Jeffersonian Republican. A paraphrase of his sermons would run about as follows.

"For what good ends Christians have shaken the foundations of their own religion by depreciating natural religion may not be easy to determine. . . . Natural religion is still the most excellent religion." "How much more pure the charity of a savage than the pulpit-anathemas of a priest against churches which differ from his own." God befriended Israel that he might use them to promote universal religion, and although Mohammedans and Jews may err in detail, their devotion, zeal and obedience are certainly acceptable to the Universal Father of all. Religion leads us to consider ourselves "not of small societies only . . . but as belonging to the household of the faithful who dwell in every nation and in every clime with one God and Father who hateth nothing that he has made, but loveth and cherisheth it." By natural religion the will of God is made known to us and Christianity only assists us in the further knowledge and practice of it. Revelation acts merely in an auxiliary capacity until "a variety of causes, wisely fitted to act, may render this assistance unnecessary. . . . The Son himself shall then be put under, and God by perfecting human nature, be all in all." "Heaven and happiness were not designed by God as the exclusive rights of learned priests or ingenious doctors; they are the end which God had proposed for all mankind, and are therefore by the same means, attainable by all men." "Happiness is not only the reward of virtue, but it is the end for which we have been created. Often earthly circumstances seem not to correspond to a design of immediate good, but through knowledge, the evil consequence of the decrees of Heaven which cannot be changed, can at least be avoided. It is therefore education that promotes the greatest usefulness and happiness. Through the development of the social principle in him, man will discover other means of overcoming evil, even the evils of society, itself." [1]

The culmination of the native, genteel liberalism in and around Boston came with William Ellery Channing, who was an American Schleiermacher, standing at the turning point from the Enlightenment to transcendentalism. In the Revolutionary generation three distinct systems of thought, three historically separate faiths, were flourishing; for want of better terms I shall call them rationalism, pietism, and republicanism. Channing inherited each of these faiths, understood the issues at stake, felt the struggle intimately, and attempted to formulate a synthesis of all three. His humanitarianism may therefore fittingly be studied as the meeting point of the ideals of the American Enlightenment, the heritage of puritanism, and the emotional enthusiasm of the religious revival. He was, on the whole, not willingly a prophet of transcendentalism, and when he saw dimly where it was leading, he was repelled by much of it and looked back almost wistfully to revealed Christianity. It is nonetheless a just fate that overtook him, for by principle and by habit Channing was forward-looking. He did not attempt a literal synthesis of pietism, natural religion, and republicanism; though his mind was molded by all three, it gave to all three a new stimulating expression that transformed them from a mere heritage of the eighteenth century into the guiding principles of the nineteenth. He had sufficiently mastered the heritage of the Enlightenment to be willing to take it for granted and to turn toward the practical problems it suggested. "God designs us for activity, pursuit of ends, efficiency. Action originating in God, and attended with

[1] William Bentley, *Sermon Preached at Stone Chapel* (Boston, 1790); this selection was made by G. A. Koch and published in his *Republican Religion*, pp. 214–17.

the consciousness of his favor, is the highest source of enjoyment." [2]
He gave to purely practical religion an adequate theoretical basis.

Channing's early life and thought were dominated by a pietistic
environment. The legend has grown up, started by Channing himself, that his love of religious liberty came to him naturally in his
birthplace, Newport, Rhode Island, that he inherited it, so to speak,
directly from Roger Williams. The Newport of his boyhood, however, was dominated theologically by Samuel Hopkins, the champion
of "consistent Calvinism," whose followers even at that time were
being called Hopkinsians and whose faith that his own system was
the only true gospel was so strong that it bore the fruits of sectarian
fanaticism and intolerance. Channing writes: "I was attached to Dr.
Hopkins chiefly by his theory of disinterestedness. I had studied with
great delight during my college life the philosophy of Hutcheson,
and the Stoical morality, and these had prepared me for the noble,
self-sacrificing doctrines of Dr. Hopkins." [3] He turned to Hopkins,
not in the darkness of depression, but because he realized that, though
the old theologian was harsh and polemical, his system was the most
"noble" and enlightened philosophy in New England. Channing
pointed out the boldness of Hopkins in reconciling Calvinism to Platonic moral philosophy and natural religion. The pietistic doctrine of
the distinctive quality of holiness and the pietistic cultivation of the
sense or feeling for the divine remained the dominant theme of Channing's thought to the end. It made doctrinaire Unitarianism distasteful to him. Though he defended the Unitarian cause when its rights
and liberties were threatened, he preferred not to call himself a Unitarian or to engage in polemics concerning historical Christian doctrines. This was due not only to his dislike of sectarianism but even
more to his New Light evangelicalism. Channing's Platonic idealism
thus came to him through Calvinistic pietism, and he had already

[2] William Henry Channing, *Memoir of William Ellery Channing;* with extracts
from his correspondence and manuscripts (Boston, 1848), I, 189.

[3] *Ibid.,* I, 137. Cf. the remark of the Hon. D. A. White of Salem, who was in the
class above Channing at college and knew him well. "About the time he commenced
preaching, he spoke of Dr. Hopkins with warm esteem, both as a friend and a theologian, dwelling with particular emphasis on the strong feature of benevolence which
marked both his character and his divinity, and observing very pointedly, that 'those
who were called Hopkinsians . . . appeared to know little of him or of his true
theological views.' " (*Ibid.,* I, 161.)

reacted against Locke's empiricism and rationalism before he learned of Coleridge, Kant, and the growth of transcendentalism in general.

A second general strain in Channing's thought was his liberalism, or republicanism. By the latter term I mean to suggest his civic, or social, conception of virtue. At Harvard he discovered the Edinburgh Enlightenment. Professor David Tappan, of Harvard, under whose influence Channing came, was himself decidedly influenced by Hutcheson and by moral liberalism in general. He preached as follows: "Christian patriotism is nothing else than general benevolence embracing, with peculiar sensibility and active energy, that portion of mankind, to which our capacity of usefulness eminently reaches." [4] Through Professor Tappan and Harvard in general Channing discovered Hutcheson and then the other Scottish liberals. As Hutcheson revealed to Channing that holiness might be a natural capacity of man, so Ferguson [5] suggested to him that regeneration is a gradual and a social process. More congenial to Channing than Ferguson's radical secularism was a combination of Hutcheson and Ferguson, which he found in the *Dissertations* of Richard Price, the English liberal and dissenter, whose defense of American independence won him many friends in this country. He wrote:

Price saved me from Locke's philosophy. He gave me the Platonic doctrine of ideas, and like him I always write the words Right, Love, Idea, etc., with a capital letter. His book, probably, moulded my philosophy into the form it has always retained, and opened my mind into the *transcendental depth*. And I have always found in the accounts I have read of German philosophy in Madame de Staël, and in these later times, that it was cognate to my own. I cannot say that I have ever received a new idea from it; and the cause is obvious, if Price was alike the father of *it* and of *mine*. [6]

Had Channing's philosophy of social progress proceeded no further, he might have turned out a typical New England idealist, but immediately after his graduation circumstances pushed him into the heart of the Jeffersonian aristocracy in Richmond, Virginia. For almost two years, 1798–1800, two crucial years, he lived in a family of

[4] David Tappan, *Sermon on the Annual Fast in Massachusetts, April 5, 1798* (Boston, 1798), p. 13.

[5] On Ferguson see above, pp. 44–45.

[6] Elizabeth Palmer Peabody, *Reminiscences* (Boston, 1880), p. 368.

Randolphs as private tutor. With his characteristic enthusiasm he explains what he is learning to his college friends at home.

My political opinions have varied a little since I saw you; but it would be unfair to charge them to the Jacobinic atmosphere of Virginia. . . . I view the world as a wide field of action, designed by its Framer to perfect the human character. Political institutions are valuable only as they improve and morally elevate human nature. Wealth and power are subordinate considerations, and are far from constituting the real greatness of a state. I blush for mankind, when I see interest the only tie which binds them to their country, when I see the social compact improved for no purpose but the accumulation of riches, and the prosperity of a nation decided by the successful avarice of its members. I wish to see *patriotism* exalted into a moral *principle*, not a branch of avarice.[7]

I have of late, my friend, launched boldly into speculations on the possible condition of mankind in the progress of their improvement. I find *avarice* the great bar to all my schemes, and I do not hesitate to assert that the human race will never be happier than at present till the establishment of a community of property.[8]

I am convinced that virtue and benevolence are *natural* to man. I believe that selfishness and avarice have arisen from two ideas universally inculcated on the young and practised upon by the old,—(1.) that *every individual has a distinct interest to pursue from the interest of the community;* and (2.) that *the body requires more care than the mind.*

I believe these ideas to be false; and I believe that you can never banish them, till you persuade mankind to cease to act upon them; that is, till you can persuade them (1.) to destroy all distinctions of property (which you are sensible must perpetuate this supposed distinction of interest), and to throw the produce of their labor into one common stock, instead of hoarding it up in their own garners; and (2.) to become really conscious of the powers and the dignity of the mind.[9]

All my sentiments and affections have lately changed. I once considered mere moral attainments as the only object I had to pursue. I have now solemnly given myself up to God. I consider supreme love to him as the first of all duties, and morality seems but a branch from the vigorous root of religion. I love mankind because they are the children of God.[10]

Channing was apparently on the verge of "joining himself as minis-

[7] *Memoir*, I, 86–87.   [8] *Ibid.*, p. 111.
[9] *Ibid.*, pp. 113–14.   [10] *Ibid.*, pp. 126–27.

ter to a settlement of Scotch emigrants, whose fundamental principle was common property," [11] when his relatives called him back to New England. Intellectually, too, the young communist returned home. He had been converted by his political enthusiasm to a religious faith, and his fanatic mortification of the flesh made of him a physical wreck and gave him that "spiritual" pallor of countenance for which he became famous. Henceforth he was neither a secular republican, devoting himself out of a patriotic sense of duty to the public good, nor a pietist, looking down upon mere secular morality. He saw piety and duty reconciled in the religion of humanity.

He projected a philosophic treatise, which he never wrote. Its title is significant, "The Principles of Moral, Religious, and Political Science." The aim was to show the union of morality, religion, and politics —that is, the inter-relatedness of piety, virtue, and republican patriotism. In the Preface intended for his work he wrote as follows:

> The true perfection of man is the great idea of the moral sciences. His nature is therefore to be examined so as to determine its central law, and the end for which all religious and political institutions should be established. . . . Just views of human nature are, then, all-important. In comprehending men . . . we have the key to the Divine administration of the world.[12]

Throughout the Enlightenment this emphasis on human nature was a familiar theme, but note the significant shift in aim. Locke's aim was to find the origin of human understanding in order to reveal its natural limitations; Channing's aim was to find the perfection of human nature in order to realize its possibilities. These possibilities he pronounced boldly in his famous sermon, "Likeness to God," which was one of the first American formulations of transcendentalism.

Pursuing this aim, Channing made significant modifications in the concepts he had inherited from the Enlightenment. The idea of "disinterested benevolence" he transformed into the idea of "diffusive charity." According to him, the characteristic of true benevolence is its social diffusion, not, as according to Edwards, its distinct object, i.e., general being. This social and humanitarian concept of love combined the concepts of holy love in pietism, of disinterestedness among the

---

[11] *Ibid.*, p. 116.   [12] *Ibid.*, II, 403–4.

moralists, and of public virtue among republicans.[13] Thus, God's justice is really only a form of his mercy. He assists man to become perfect gradually. This regeneration of man or moral progress also implies "social regeneration," which also must be gradual and is thus identical with reform or progress. However, the fact that Channing continued to use the terminology of regeneration is not a merely verbal matter; it is a tribute to his abiding pietism. Only it is now a socialized pietism.[14] Channing turned from the churches as particular "societies" to society in general as a channel of regenerating grace. The "perpetual regeneration" of its members is the duty of society as such. At times Channing talked much like a Jeffersonian republican, in terms of political reform, but on the whole he seems disillusioned on that score. The moral elevation cannot come through politics. He was especially outspoken on this point after his return from Europe in 1823.

I return with views of society which make me rejoice as I never did before in the promise held out by revealed religion of *a moral renovation* of the world. I expect less and less from revolutions, political changes, violent struggles,—from public men or measures,—in a word, from any outward modification of society. Corrupt institutions will be succeeded by others equally, if not more, corrupt, whilst the root principle lives in the heart of individuals and nations; and the only remedy is to be found in a moral change, to which Christianity and the Divine power that accompanies it, are alone adequate.[15]

We all see that civil liberty has not produced that sudden melioration and exaltation of human nature which was confidently hoped; nor has religious

[13] He wrote: "I fear it has been the influence of many speculations of ingenious men on the Divine character to divest God of that paternal tenderness which is of all views most suited to touch the heart. I fear we have learnt insensibly to view him as possessing only a *general* benevolence" (*ibid.*, I, 253). "I felt, I saw, that God is most willing to impart his 'Holy Spirit,' his strength and light, to every man who labors in earnest to overcome evil, to press forward to that perfection which is the only heaven" (*ibid.*, p. 345).

[14] "It seems to me that the signs of the times point to a *great approaching modification of society*, which will be founded on and will express the essential truth, that the chief end of the social state is the elevation of all its members as intelligent and moral beings, and under which every man will be expected to contribute to this object according to his ability. The present selfish, dissocial system must give way to Christianity, and I earnestly wish that we may bear our full part in effecting this best of all revolutions" (*ibid.*, III, 38).

[15] *Ibid.*, II, 249.

liberty borne all the fruits we hoped. Still a good work is going on. Slavery and bigotry and worldliness will not reign forever.[16]

Slavery, bigotry, and worldliness are the three enemies, respectively, of republicanism, rationalism, and pietism; and it was to the struggle against these enemies that Channing's humanitarianism was wholeheartedly devoted. This glorification of morality and human nature thus turned out to be the culmination of Channing's thought, as it was also of the Enlightenment in general. The transition from the Enlightenment to transcendentalism is here so smooth that it is difficult to detect.

— 8 —

FREE THOUGHT

THE extreme left wing of the Enlightenment was militant rationalism as expounded by laymen, usually lawyers or physicians, in the interests of anticlericalism and antiecclesiasticism. The writings of Blount and Collins, and later of Voltaire, Volney, and Paine, were models for American deism of this militant type, and there is nothing very distinctive or original in the American output. The first and most picturesque figure of the type was Ethan Allen, of Vermont. As a youth he came under the influence of a free-thinking physician, and as a captive of the British he heard and read the opinions of "infidels." His *Reason the Only Oracle of Man* appeared in 1784. In it he attacked clerical impostures, revelation, miracles, appeals to authority, and everything that was specifically Christian. He not only believed in God and immortality, but attempted rational justification for his beliefs in typical deist fashion. Philosophically more interesting than his *Oracle* is his little-known *Essay on the Universal Plenitude of Being and on the Nature and Immortality of the Human Soul and Its Agency;* from which the following is worth quoting here.

Perhaps we are the most selfish, oddest, and cunningest medley of beings, of our size, in the universe. However to compleat the schale of being, it seems to have been requisite, that the link of being called man, must have

---

[16] *Ibid.,* III, 308.

been, and since under the Divine government, we have a positive existence, we can not ultimately fail, of being better than not to have been.[1]

In this essay Allen expounds a radical deism. God is "infinite intelligent substance," omnipresent in particular spiritual substances or souls, which are likewise spatial and "not immaterial."

A more substantial though smaller work than Allen's is Elihu Palmer's *Principles of Nature* (1801), which is an expression of free thought as an organized movement. Palmer was one of a number of itinerant preachers of rationalism. In several cities he helped to organize "temples of reason" or "theistic societies" (among them Tammany in New York). The *Theophilanthropist* and *The Temple of Reason* were typical periodical publications of the movement, and Palmer was one of the ablest editors. He lectured up and down the Atlantic coast; his *Principles of Nature* is a compendium of his lectures.

By "principles of nature" Palmer meant that in formulating the laws of motion modern scientists had also liberated the energies in matter and the "moral energies in human nature" to such an extent that the natural "power of intellect" must soon destroy the artificial and oppressive faiths. Men would naturally embrace the following principles:

1. That the universe proclaims the existence of one supreme Deity, worthy of the adoration of intelligent beings.

2. That man is possessed of moral and intellectual faculties sufficient for the improvement of his nature, and the acquisition of happiness.

3. That the religion of nature is the only universal religion; that it grows out of the moral relations of intelligent beings, and that it stands connected with the progressive improvement and common welfare of the human race.

4. That it is essential to the true interest of man, that he love truth and practise virtue.

5. That vice is every where ruinous and destructive to the happiness of the individual and of society.

6. That a benevolent disposition, and beneficent actions, are fundamental duties of rational beings.

7. That a religion mingled with persecution and malice cannot be of divine origin.

8. That education and science are essential to the happiness of man.

[1] Anderson and Fisch, eds., *Philosophy in America*, p. 165.

9. That civil and religious liberty is equally essential to his true interests.

10. That there can be no human authority to which man ought to be amenable for his religious opinions.

11. That science and truth, virtue and happiness, are the great objects to which the activity and energy of the human faculties ought to be directed.

Every member admitted into this association shall deem it his duty, by every suitable method in his power, to promote the cause of nature and moral truth, in opposition to all schemes of superstition and fanaticism, claiming divine origin.[2]

On the basis of this faith in natural religion Palmer prophesied the renovation of "civil science" through the American Revolution.

It is not to be presumed, that men will long remain ignorant of their moral condition in nature, after being instructed in the principles of civil science. The moral condition of man will be as essentially renovated by the American revolution as his civil condition; and certainly it is equally necessary, and equally important that this should be done. The science of morality is of all sciences the most necessary to the happiness of man. . . . Awakened by the energy of thought, inspired by the American revolution, man will find it consistent with his inclination and his interest to examine all the moral relations of his nature, to calculate with accuracy the effects of his own moral energies.[3]

A similar faith in the rapid growth of a universal moral order of peace and happiness was voiced in Joel Barlow's epic of the American Enlightenment, the *Columbiad*.

> Sun of the moral world! effulgent source
> Of man's best wisdom and his steadiest force,
> Soul-searching Freedom! here assume thy stand
> And radiate hence to every distant land;
> Point out and prove how all the scenes of strife,
> The shock of states, the impassion'd broils of life,
> Spring from unequal sway; and how they fly
> Before the splendor of thy peaceful eye;
> Unfold at last the genuine social plan,
> The mind's full scope, the dignity of man,

[2] Elihu Palmer, *Posthumous Pieces; Principles of the Deistical Society of the State of New York*, pp. 10–11; quoted in G. Adolf Koch, *Republican Religion*, p. 79.

[3] Elihu Palmer, *An Inquiry relative to the Moral and Political Improvement of the Human Species* (New York, 1797), pp. 26–27.

Bold nature bursting thro her long disguise
And nations daring to be just and wise.

      . . .

Mold a fair model for the realms of earth,
Call moral nature to a second birth,
Reach, renovate the world's great social plan
And here commence the sober sense of man.

      . . .

Each land shall imitate, each nation join
The well based brotherhood, the league divine,
Extend its empire with the circling sun,
And band the peopled globe within its federal zone.[4]

The conception these freethinkers had of reason and "sober sense" was as romantic as their theory of progress, and eventually it bore fruit in romantic education. They took for granted that the truths and spirit of science, especially of moral science, were as simple and elementary as their "principles of nature," and they expected this sunlight of reason, since it was a natural energy, to take possession of all men easily. Barlow's conception of the future of public education is worth taking seriously as an expression of the faith prevalent among merchants, lawyers, and liberal laymen.

Instruction clear a speedier course shall find,
And open earlier on the infant mind.
No foreign terms shall crowd with barbarous rules
The dull unmeaning pageantry of schools;
Nor dark authorities nor names unknown
Fill the learn'd head with ignorance not its own;
But wisdom's eye with beams unclouded shine,
And simplest rules her native charms define;
One living language, one unborrow'd dress
Her boldest flights with fullest force express;
Triumphant virtue, in the garb of truth,
Win a pure passage to the heart of youth,
Pervade all climes where suns or oceans roll
And warm the world with one great moral soul . . .[5]

[4] Joel Barlow, *The Columbiad*, Bk. IV, ll. 487–98; Bk. VIII, ll. 151–54; Bk. IX, ll. 699–702.
[5] *Ibid.*, Bk. X, ll. 451–64.

The poets Barlow and Freneau were active participants in deistic societies, not only as political propagandists for Jefferson but also as expounders of the faith. As Henry Wells has pointed out, this faith in progressive change, in human rights, and in independence of mind was consciously related by the Revolutionary poets to a classic philosophical tradition. Freneau was especially explicit in linking it to Lucretius and in picturing the realm of matter as intensely active. According to him, the nature of the soul is "activity, that knows no rest"; the soul is thus energetic because it is vitally related to matter. Hence, the faith in the *natural* power of freedom in the face of tyranny and, for that matter, of law in general.

> All human sense, all craft must fail
> And all its strength will nought avail,
> When it attempts with efforts blind
> To sway the independent mind,
> Its spring to break, its pride to awe,
> And give to private judgment, law.[6]

It is worth noting that these "intellectuals" of the democratic movement, even the left-wing leaders, such as Tom Paine, were neither atheists nor labor leaders. They were very bourgeois, and freedom to them meant a combination of individualistic religion and individualistic freedom of trade. There were not a few politically conservative anticlericals who failed to participate in the public activities of Democratic clubs, but read the writings of their members, together with those of Volney, Godwin, and the European anticlericals. Typical of these were Chancellor James Kent, of New York, William Dunlap, the New York dramatist, George Washington, an Anglican infidel, Stephen Hopkins, governor of Rhode Island, and others. When they attacked Christianity they explained that they meant to attack primarily religious establishments and other clerical privileges. Barlow even sang the praises of free churches in his *Columbiad;* he expected the evangelical and popular churches to follow the lead of the Unitarians in becoming deistical. The politics and economics even of the Jefferson republicans were more antifeudal and antimonarchic than radically democratic. When during the Jacksonian era labor leaders

[6] Philip Freneau, *On the Abuse of Human Power as Exercised over Opinion;* quoted in Henry Wells, *The American Way of Poetry*, p. 15.

tried to capture the free-thought press and clubs, they failed to attract more than a small group of leaders, for the members of these societies were far from being of the rank and file of labor, and few of them took an active part in radical reforms such as the antislavery crusade, to say nothing of socialism.

— 9 —

NATURAL PHILOSOPHY

THE freethinkers, with their cult of reason, were really the prophets of the growth of natural philosophy; their religious enthusiasm was matched by the secular, constructive energy of the Enlightenment, which found its culmination and justification in the progress of the natural sciences. The transition from natural philosophy to natural science is almost imperceptible and represents what might be called the disintegration or differentiation of the sciences. During the Enlightenment the encyclopedic ideal of knowledge, which found American expression in Puritan scholasticism and was given its classic impetus toward natural science by the great French *Encyclopédie*, maintained itself. It lost much of its ambition for the formal unity of science, but it encouraged a co-operative spirit and communicative habits among scientists. When Cadwallader Colden wished to introduce his son to philosophy, he warned him as follows:

I told you before that the school learning is really a misapplication of time, in learning of things which exist nowhere but in the imaginations of idle, monkish, useless men, and serves no good purpose in life. It is otherwise in acquiring knowledge of the powers and force of those things on which our well-being depends. Our life and health, our pleasures and pain all depend on the powers of those beings, which constitute the human system, and on the powers of other things, which are continually acting upon it. Not only the speculative sciences, the explaining of all the phenomena which strike our senses, depend on the knowledge of these powers; but likewise all the practical arts depend on them. This knowledge is useful to us in every circumstance of life, whether as individuals and private persons, or as members of society: as will very evidently appear to you, when you shall apply your thoughts to any particular art or science. . . .

The gentleman, who proposes to be generally useful in society, ought not to fix his thoughts singly on any one branch of science, but to have a competent knowledge of the principles of every branch, which he may obtain without fatiguing his imagination, by too continued an application. While he reads and thinks by turns, he should, in the intervals, cultivate his intellectual faculties by general conversation, where he may obtain more useful knowledge, than can be learned from books. The mere Scholar, the mere Physician, the mere Lawyer, Musician, or Painter, take them out of their own way, and they are often more insipid than the mere plowman.[1]

The chief visible embodiment in America of this spirit was the American Philosophical Society, founded in 1742 through the cooperation of Cadwallader Colden, Benjamin Franklin, David Rittenhouse, and several other scientists. In 1769 Franklin persuaded the members of the Philosophical Society, whom he called "*virtuosi*, or ingenious men," to unite with his Junto "for promoting useful knowledge." He recommended that in addition to "a physician, a botanist, a mathematician, a chemist, a mechanician, and a geographer" (i.e., the *virtuosi*), the society always include a "general natural philosopher," and that these men meet and correspond to exchange discoveries and to examine practical means for solving technical problems in medicine, agriculture, engineering, and the other arts. A similar society (the Library Society) was founded in Charleston, South Carolina, in 1748.

Jefferson's *Notes on the State of Virginia* (1787) is the first important American work in natural history. The great encouragement given to both pure and applied science by men of affairs such as Franklin, Jefferson, and Colden was evidence not merely of the union of natural and political interests in the same persons but also of the dominant philosophical interest in discovering "principles of nature" in all fields. Medical men took the lead in the cultivation of such natural philosophy, but the clergy, too, were infected with scientific curiosity (illustrated by the researches in natural history and biology of Jonathan Edwards, Timothy Dwight, Jeremy Belknap, L. D. von Schweinitz, Henry Muhlenberg, and F. E. Melsheimer) as well as with the more philosophical itch for natural religion.

[1] Cadwallader Colden, *An Introduction to the Study of Phylosophy* (MS, New York Historical Society), reprinted in Blau, ed., *American Philosophic Addresses, 1700–1900*, pp. 301–2, 311.

Three men besides those already mentioned deserve special consideration as "general natural philosophers." David Rittenhouse (1732–96), of Philadelphia, was an excellent astronomer and mathematician. Though he enjoyed distinction in his profession, his extraordinary influence on his fellow citizens is due more to the fact that he was a living symbol of devotion to natural science. He was not a philosopher of nature, except for the fact that he preached the value of experimental verification of theories, but he was able to impress on the general public the beauty of mathematical method and precision in understanding natural motion. His famous "orrery," or model of the solar system, and his ability to explain and predict astronomical events made him the kind of hero in the popular imagination that Albert Einstein is today.

Another important man of science was Benjamin Rush (1745–1813), likewise of Philadelphia, a physician and teacher of medicine, whose experimental successes in medicine and extraordinary lectures on "the influence of physical causes upon the moral faculty" gave an enduring stimulus to biological psychology. He was the embodiment of the Edinburgh school of natural philosophy and worldly wisdom.[2] He therefore exhibited to his Philadelphia students a strange combination of experimental science, piety, and enthusiasm for humanitarian reforms. He applied his inquiries into the power of passions not merely to individual cases in pathology but also to social problems. He tried, for example, in a very disconcerting way, to defend religion on the ground of its "salutary operation" in making man happy in this life.

The different religions of the world, by the activity they excite in the mind, have a sensible influence upon human life. Atheism is the worst of sedatives to the understanding, and passions. It is the abstraction of thought from the most sublime, and of love, from the most perfect of all possible objects. Man is as naturally a religious, as he is a social, and domestic animal; and the same violence is done to his mental faculties, by robbing him of a belief in God, that is done, by dooming him to live in a cell, deprived of the objects and pleasures of social and domestic life. The necessary and immutable connection between the texture of the human mind, and the worship of an object of some kind, has lately been demonstrated by the atheists of Europe,

[2] He was personally responsible for inducing Witherspoon to come to Princeton.

who after rejecting the true God, have instituted the worship of nature, of fortune, and of human reason; and in some instances, with ceremonies of the most expensive and splendid kind. Religions are friendly to animal life, in proportion as they elevate the understanding, and act upon the passions of hope and love. It will readily occur to you, that Christianity when believed, and obeyed, according to its original consistency with itself, and with the divine attributes, is more calculated to produce those effects, than any other religion in the world.—Such is the salutary operation of its doctrines, and precepts upon health and life, that if its divine authority rested upon no other argument, this alone would be sufficient to recommend it to our belief. How long mankind may continue to prefer substituted pursuits and pleasures, to this invigorating stimulus, is uncertain; but the time we are assured will come, when the understanding shall be elevated from its present inferior objects, and the luxated passions be reduced to their original order.—This change in the mind of man, I believe, will be effected only by the influence of. the Christian religion, after all the efforts of human reason to produce it, by means of civilization, philosophy, liberty, and government, have been exhausted to no purpose.[3]

He likewise tried to prove in a genial way that the American environment was full of salutary "stimuli."

In no part of the human species, is animal life in a more perfect state than in the inhabitants of Great Britain, and the United States of America. With all the natural stimuli that have been mentioned, they are constantly under the invigorating influence of liberty. There is an indissoluble union between moral, political and physical happiness; and if it be true, that elective and representative governments are most favourable to individual, as well as national prosperity, it follows of course, that they are most favourable to animal life. But this opinion does not rest upon an induction derived from the relation, which truths upon all subjects bear to each other. Many facts prove, animal life to exist in a larger quantity and for a longer time, in the enlightened and happy state of Connecticut, in which republican liberty has existed above one hundred and fifty years, than in any other country upon the surface of the globe.[4]

Rush's philosophical importance lies chiefly in the fact that he made an impressive scientific attempt to demonstrate the underlying unity of man's "excitability" and consequently of man's knowledge; he sug-

[3] Benjamin Rush, *Three Lectures upon Animal Life*, pp. 67–68.
[4] *Ibid.*, p. 62.

gested, though he did not preach, that there was no radical separation possible between body and soul, medicine and morals, natural and social philosophy.

The most picturesque among the scientists, and the least scientific, was Thomas Cooper (1759–1839), a student of chemistry under Priestley in England and, like his teacher, a refugee from religious and political persecution. He came closer to being a thoroughgoing materialist than any of his friends (including his closest friend, Jefferson), who were often accused of materialism and atheism. Cooper was the most outspoken anticlerical among the scientists, as he was also the most ready to apply his materialistic psychology to the more general problems of morals and religion. He came to America in 1794 and threw himself wholeheartedly into the Jeffersonian campaign, became a judge in Pennsylvania, was forced out of office under charges of corruption in 1811, taught chemistry and mineralogy at several schools in Pennsylvania until 1819, was scheduled by Jefferson to be first president of the University of Virginia, but instead became professor of chemistry and, later, president of the University of South Carolina, where he had an influential career. He became a leader in preaching nullification and states' rights, and wrote a treatise on political economy.

Thus, in various ways various scientists made natural philosophy an exciting field of exploration and a symbol of the direction which moral philosophy should take in order to make similar progress. In stimulating the public imagination they were for a brief generation more effective than the clergy, and they were most effective when they most neglected theology. For their achievements in exhibiting the unity and utility of secular reason were themselves the most eloquent proof of the "vanity of dogmatizing." Natural philosophy's ability to make progress did more toward establishing the "principles of nature" in American morals and education than all the naturalistic philosophy preached by the freethinkers ever could do. In the natural sciences the Enlightenment still lives, but the so-called mental and moral sciences were fated to endure another century of philosophical polemics.

Ralph Barton Perry, *Puritanism and Democracy* (New York, 1944), not only is the most recent exposition of American social ideas, but also emphasizes (possibly overemphasizes) the continuity between the Puritan doctrines of the church and salvation and the democratic features of the Enlightenment. Vernon L. Parrington, *Main Currents in American Thought; Volume I: The Colonial Mind, 1620–1800* (New York, 1927), is at his best in giving portraits of the intellectual leaders and in exposing the prevalence of antidemocratic theories. Parrington is a good antidote to Perry, but the reader should be cautioned that during this period what is usually meant when democracy is referred to, is not representative government, but government through the immediate voice of the people. Carl Becker, *The Heavenly City of the Eighteenth Century Philosophers* (New Haven, 1932), gives a description of the utopian ideals of the Enlightenment which is illuminating because it reverses the usual method, describing its theories not as a secularization, but as a new form of religious mythology. Evarts B. Greene, *The Revolutionary Generation, 1763–1790* (New York, 1943), and John A. Krout and Dixon Ryan Fox, *The Completion of Independence, 1790–1830* (New York, 1944), Vols. IV–V, in *A History of American Life*, ed. by Schlesinger and Fox, contain sketches and excellent bibliographies of the nonpolitical aspects of the period. They are especially worth consulting on science and on the arts. Charles A. Beard and Mary R. Beard, *The Rise of American Civilization; Vol. I: The Agricultural Era* (New York, 1924), Chapters VI–VIII, should be read as background for the intellectual currents of the times. J. Mark Jacobson, *The Development of American Political Thought; a Documentary History* (New York, 1932), contains in Chapter III excellent selections from the documents of the period and a critical essay by the editor, who follows Beard closely. Joseph Dorfman, *The Economic Mind in American Civilization*, Vol. I (New York, 1946), presents relevant materials in Chapters X and XI of Book I, "Colonial America," and in Book II "From Independence to Jackson;" note, in particular, Dorfman's discussions of Franklin, pp. 178–95, Woolman, pp. 196–204, Huntington, p. 241, Barton, p. 252, Blodgett, p. 336, John Adams, pp. 417–33, Jefferson, pp. 433–47, Paine, pp. 417–59; and Barlow, pp. 459–71.

CHAPTER 4

For the transition from Puritanism to the Enlightenment in addition to Perry's *Puritanism and Democracy* see I. Woodbridge Riley, *American Philosophy; the Early Schools* (New York, 1907), where Deistic elements in Cotton Mather and other Puritan theologians are exaggerated. H. W. Schneider, *The Puritan Mind* (New York, 1930), Chapters III, "The Loss of the Sense of Sin," and VI, "The Declaration of Independence," picture the Enlightenment as an undermining of Puritanism and therefore underestimate the Puritan contribution to the Enlightenment. F. A. Christie, "The Beginnings of Arminianism in New England," in *Papers of the American Society of Church History*, 2d series, Vol. III, is an excellent account of the early attacks on Calvinism among the New England clergy. Alice M. Baldwin, *The New England Clergy in the American Revolution* (Durham, N.C., 1928), and Edward F. Humphry, *Nationalism and Religion in America, 1774–1789* (Boston, 1924), throw light on the contributions of the New England clergy to liberalism. Bernard Faÿ, *The Revolutionary Spirit in France and America; a Study of the Moral and Intellectual Relations between France and the United States at the End of the Eighteenth Century* (New York, 1927), gives a somewhat exaggerated account of secular tendencies in the period.

The following list gives the most important literature relating to the chief figures in the growth of secular philosophy.

Bentley, William, A Sermon Preached at the Stone Chapel in Boston, September 12, 1790 (Boston, 1790).

—— The Diary of William Bentley, D.D., Pastor of the East Church, Salem, Massachusetts, 1784–1810. 3 vols. (Salem, Mass., 1905–11). Vol. I contains a biographical sketch of Bentley by J. G. Waters.

—— Oration in Commemoration of the Birthday of Washington, Delivered at Salem, Massachusetts, Feb. 22d, 1793 (Morrisania, N.Y., 1870).

Chauncy, Charles, Divine Glory Brought to View in the Final Salvation of All Men; a Letter to the Friend of Truth; by one who wishes well to all mankind (Boston, 1783).

—— The Benevolence of the Deity, Fairly and Impartially Considered; in three parts (Boston, 1784).

Franklin, Benjamin, Autobiography, ed. by John Bigelow (Philadelphia, 1868).

—— A Dissertation on Liberty and Necessity, Pleasure and Pain (New York, 1930).

FRANKLIN, BENJAMIN

Frank L. Mott and Chester E. Jorgenson, ed. Benjamin Franklin; Representative Selections, with Introduction, Bibliography and Notes. New York, 1936. American Writers Series. An excellent selection; the bibliography is good, the introduction most useful.

Carl Van Doren, Benjamin Franklin (New York, 1938).

Phillips Russell, Benjamin Franklin, the First Civilized American (New York, 1926).

Bernard Faÿ, Franklin, the Apostle of Modern Times (Boston, 1929).

Eduard Baumgarten, Benjamin Franklin, in *Die geistigen Grundlagen des amerikanischen Gemeinwesens* (Frankfurt am Main, 1937), Vol. I. Makes an elaborate analysis of Franklin's Puritan ethics on the basis of Max Weber's theories.

Herbert W. Schneider, "The Significance of Benjamin Franklin's Moral Philosophy," Studies in the History of Ideas (New York, 1925), II, 293–312. An abbreviated version of this is contained in Schneider, "The Puritan Mind," pp. 237–56.

Gay, Ebenezer, Natural Religion as Distinguished from Revealed; a Sermon Preached at the Annual Dudleian Lecture at Harvard-College in Cambridge, May 9, 1759 (Boston, 1759).

Johnson, Samuel, "Ethica," in Elementa Philosophica. See H. W. Schneider, and C. Schneider, eds., Samuel Johnson, President of King's College: His Career and Writings (New York, 1929), 4 vols. especially Vol. II, containing the philosophical writings, including the "Ethica," which was a pious redaction of Wollaston's principles.

Mather, Cotton, Reasonable Religion; or, The Truths of the Christian Religion Demonstrated (London, 1713).

—— The Christian Philosopher (London, 1721).

—— Essays to Do Good; Addressed to All Christians, Whether in Public or Private Capacities (Boston, 1710).

MATHER, COTTON

R. P. Boas and Louise Boas, Cotton Mather, Keeper of the Puritan Conscience (New York, 1928).

Mayhew, Jonathan, Seven Sermons upon the Following Subjects: viz., The Difference between Truth and Falsehood, Right and Wrong; The Natural Ability of Man for Discerning These Differences; The Right and Duty of Private Judgment; The Love of God; The Love of Our Neighbour, etc. (Boston, 1749).

—— A Discourse, concerning Unlimited Submission and Nonresistance to the Higher Powers; with some reflections on the resistance made

to King Charles I . . . in which the mysterious doctrine of that
Prince's saintship and martyrdom is unriddled (Boston, 1750).
—— Two Sermons on the Nature, Extent and Perfection of the Divine
Goodness, Delivered December 9, 1762, being the Annual Thanks-
giving of the Province (Boston, 1763).
—— Sermons to Young Men, 1763 (London, 1767).

CHAPTER 5

For discussion of the more technical details in the political theories of the
American Enlightenment, V. L. Parrington, *Main Currents in American
Thought. Vol. I. The Colonial Mind, 1620–1800* (New York, 1927) and
Charles E. Merriam, *A History of American Political Theories* (New
York, 1903) are the most informative. Randolph G. Adams, *Political Ideas
of the American Revolution* (Durham, N.C., 1922) emphasizes the theories of imperial federation, and especially John Adams. Carl Becker, *The
Declaration of Independence: A Study in the History of Political Ideas*
(New York, 1922) is an interesting though not always accurate account
of the sources and fortunes of the political ideas of the American Revolution;
chapter II, "The Natural Rights Philosophy," shows the continuity between Puritan political theory and that of Locke. This theme is more elab-
orately discussed in Herbert D. Foster, "International Calvinism through
John Locke and the Revolution of 1688," *American Historical Review*,
XXXII (1926–27), 475–99. Otto Vossler, *Die Amerikanischen Revolu-
tionsideale in ihrem Verhältnis zu den Europäischen untersucht an Thomas
Jefferson* (München und Berlin, 1929) gives a valuable account from a
European point of view. Conyers Read, ed., *The Constitution Reconsidered*
(New York, 1938), especially Part I, "The Background of Political, Economic, and Social Ideas behind the Constitution," is a collection of critical
essays, of which those by Charles H. McIlwain, William Haller, and Herbert Schneider are especially relevant. Bernard Smith's anthology, *The
Democratic Spirit* (New York, 1941), contains good selections for this
period.

The following list gives the most important literature of the Revolutionary political philosophy.

Adams, John, Works; ed. by C. F. Adams, with a life of the author (Bos-
ton, 1850–56).
ADAMS, JOHN
    C. M. Walsh, The Political Science of John Adams. New York, 1915.
Gilbert Chinard, Honest John Adams. Boston, 1933.

Adams, Samuel, Writings; ed. by H. A. Cushing (New York, 1904–8).

Hamilton, Alexander, Works; ed. by H. C. Lodge. New York, 1904.

—— Alexander Hamilton and Thomas Jefferson; representative selections, with introduction, bibliography, and notes, by Frederick C. Prescott. New York, 1934. American Writers Series.

Hamilton, Alexander, John Jay, and James Madison. The Federalist; sesquicentennial ed. Washington, D.C., 1937.

Jefferson, Thomas, Writings; ed. by A. L. Bergh. Washington, 1903.

—— The Life and Selected Writings of Thomas Jefferson; ed. by Adrienne Koch and William Peden. New York, 1944.

—— The Living Thoughts of Thomas Jefferson; ed. by John Dewey. New York, 1940.

—— The Commonplace Book of Thomas Jefferson; ed. by Gilbert Chinard. Baltimore and Paris, 1926.

—— The Literary Bible of Thomas Jefferson; ed. by Gilbert Chinard. Baltimore and Paris, 1928.

JEFFERSON, THOMAS

Adrienne Koch, The Philosophy of Thomas Jefferson. New York, 1943.

Gilbert Chinard, Jefferson et les idéologues. Baltimore and Paris, 1925.

Claude G. Bowers, The Young Jefferson (Boston, 1945).

—— Jefferson in Power (Boston, 1936).

—— Jefferson and Hamilton (Boston, 1925).

Clement Eaton, "The Jeffersonian Tradition of Liberalism in America," *South Atlantic Quarterly*, XLIII (1944), 1–10.

Charles M. Wiltse, The Jeffersonian Tradition in American Democracy (Chapel Hill, N.C., 1935).

Ethics, Vol. LIII, No. 4 (July, 1943), contains a symposium on Thomas Jefferson with papers by Claude G. Bowers, Herbert W. Schneider, Gilbert Chinard, and Horace M. Kallen, and supplementary papers by T. V. Smith, and by Charles E. Merriam and Frank P. Bourgin.

Madison, James, Writings; ed. by Gaillard Hunt (New York, 1900).

MADISON, JAMES

Gaillard Hunt, The Life of James Madison (New York, 1902).

Edward M. Burns, James Madison, Philosopher of the Constitution (New Brunswick, N.J., 1938).

Paine, Thomas, The Complete Works; ed. by Philip S. Foner (New York, 1945). Especially "Common Sense," "Agrarian Justice," and the "Letter to George Washington."

—— Thomas Paine; Representative Selections, with Introduction, Bibliography, and Notes, by Harry H. Clark (New York, 1944). American Writers Series. Professor Clark's introduction is particularly valuable.

PAINE, THOMAS

W. E. Woodward, Thomas Paine, America's Godfather (New York, 1945). The most recent popular biographical justification of Paine.

Taylor, John, of Caroline, Arator; Being a Series of Agricultural Essays, Practical and Political (Columbia, S.C., 1813).

TAYLOR, JOHN

Eugene T. Mudge, The Social Philosophy of John Taylor of Caroline (New York, 1939).

Wilson, James, Works; ed. by James D. Andrews (Chicago, 1896).

—— Selected Political Essays of James Wilson, ed. by Randolph G. Adams (New York, 1930). Especially "Of the General Principles of Law and Obligation," pp. 215–57.

Witherspoon, John, Works (Edinburgh, 1815).

—— Lectures on Moral Philosophy; ed. by Varnum L. Collins (Princeton, N.J., 1912).

WITHERSPOON, JOHN

Varnum L. Collins, President Witherspoon; a Biography (Princeton, N.J., 1925).

CHAPTER 6

Evarts B. Greene, *Religion and the State* (New York, 1941), is a good survey and analysis of the relations between church and state. W. W. Sweet, *Religion in Colonial America* (New York, 1942), and "Natural Religion and Religious Liberty in America," *Journal of Religion* XXV (1945), 45–55 and Conrad H. Moehlman, *School and Church—The American Way* (New York, 1944), add suggestive materials and interpretation. Sanford H. Cobb, *The Rise of Religious Liberty in America* (New York, 1902), is still useful. Brooks Adams, *The Emancipation of Massachusetts* (Boston, 1919), is an account of the overthrow of the theocracy written by an enthusiastic anticlerical. Hamilton J. Eckenrode, *Separation of Church and State in Virginia; a Study in the Development of the Revolution* (Richmond, Va., 1910), and William T. Thom, *The Struggles for Religious Freedom in Virginia; the Baptists* (Baltimore, 1900), give good accounts of this theme in the Old Dominion.

CHAPTER 7

The origins of New England liberalism are best described in F. A. Christie's account of "The Beginnings of Arminianism in New England." There is a brief survey in G. A. Koch, *Republican Religion; the American Revolution and the Cult of Reason* (New York, 1933), "Introduction—Political Freedom and Free Thought." John Wingate Thornton, *The Pulpit of the American Revolution; or, The Political Sermons of the Period of 1776* (Boston, 1860), contains sermons by Mayhew, Chauncy, West, Stiles, and others.

The contributions of the Universalists have been inadequately treated, but see Abel C. Thomas, *A Century of Universalism in Philadelphia and New York* (Philadelphia, 1872), and Richard Eddy, *Universalism in America* (Boston, 1884). Charles Chauncy, *Mystery Hid from Ages and Generations, Made Manifest by the Gospel-Revelation; or, The Salvation of All Men; the Grand Thing Aimed at in the Scheme of God* (Boston, 1784), is the first outspoken American expression of Universalism. The *Works* of Hosea Ballou should be read as the classical expression of Universalism in America, while the early writings of Orestes A. Brownson present the views of the left wing of the movement.

William Ellery Channing's *Works* have appeared in many editions. W. H. Channing, *Memoir of William Ellery Channing; with Extracts from His Correspondence and Manuscripts* (Boston, 1848), and Elizabeth Palmer Peabody, *Reminiscences of Rev. Wm. Ellery Channing, D.D.* (Boston, 1880), are useful. Herbert W. Schneider, "The Intellectual Background of William Ellery Channing," *Church History*, VII (1938–39), 3–23, emphasizes Channing's position as the summation of the Enlightenment rather than as the forerunner of transcendentalism. Neal F. Doubleday, "Channing on the Nature of Man," *The Journal of Religion*, XXIII (1943), 245–57, shows how much closer Channing's theology was to transcendentalism than to natural religion.

CHAPTER 8

G. Adolf Koch, *Republican Religion; the American Revolution and the Cult of Reason* (New York, 1933), discusses this theme with emphasis on the contributions of individuals such as Allen and Palmer to the development of free thought. Herbert M. Morais, *Deism in Eighteenth Century America* (New York, 1934), is more concerned with "infidelity" as a movement. Albert Post, *Popular Freethought in America, 1825–1850* (New York, 1943), Chapter I, "Early American Freethought," is a good historical survey. Freethinking among the Anglicans of the South is treated in Virginius Dabney, *Liberalism in the South* (Chapel Hill, N.C., 1932), and Clement Eaton, *Freedom of Thought in the Old South* (Durham, N.C., 1940). I. Woodbridge Riley, *American Philosophy; the Early*

Schools (New York, 1907), and *American Thought from Puritanism to Pragmatism and Beyond* (New York, 1923). Chapters III, "Deism," and IV, "Materialism," while somewhat naïve and presenting an oversimplified account, are worth consulting.

The following list gives the most important literature of early freethought in America.

Allen, Ethan, Reason the Only Oracle of Man; or, A Compenduous System of Natural Religion, alternately adorned with confutations of a variety of doctrines incompatible to it, deduced from the most exalted ideas which we are able to form of the divine and human characters, and from the universe in general (Bennington, Vt., 1784).

—— "An Essay on the Universal Plenitude of Being and on the Nature and Immortality of the Human Soul and Its Agency," *The Historical Magazine, and Notes and Queries concerning the Antiquities, History and Biography of America*, 3d series, I (1872–73), 193–96, 274–82, 330–33; II (1873), 29–32, 76–82. This supplement of Allen's Oracles of Reason was written about 1787 and is philosophically more interesting.

ALLEN, ETHAN

John Pell, Ethan Allen (Boston, 1929).

Alexander Kadison, "An Unfamiliar Figure in American Rationalism," in *The Rationalist Press Association Annual for the Year 1926* (London, 1926), pp. 76–80.

B. T. Schantz, "Ethan Allen's Religious Ideas," *Journal of Religion*, XVIII (1938), 183–217.

Barlow, Joel, The Columbiad. Philadelphia, 1807.

—— Political Writings. New York, 1796.

BARLOW, JOEL

Charles Burr Todd, Life and Letters of Joel Barlow (New York, 1886).

Joseph Dorfman, "Joel Barlow: Trafficker in Trade and Letters," *Political Science Quarterly*, LIX (1944–45), 83–100.

John Dos Passos, The Ground We Stand On (New York, 1941). Includes a vivid sketch of Barlow as the summation of libertarian tendencies.

Freneau, Philip, Poems; ed. by Harry H. Clark (New York, 1929). Contains a good introduction.

FRENEAU, PHILIP

Henry W. Wells, The American Way of Poetry (New York, 1943). "New Destinations" treats of Freneau.

Paine, Thomas, The Age of Reason (1794, 1796), in The Complete
Writings of Thomas Paine, ed. by Philip Foner (New York, 1945).
Palmer, Elihu, An Enquiry Relative to the Moral and Political Improve-
ment of the Human Species (New York, 1797).
—— The Principles of Nature (London, 1823).

CHAPTER 9

William M. and Mabel S. C. Smallwood, *Natural History and the
American Mind* (New York, 1941), is of some value, but is little concerned with the philosophical approach to nature. Some information may
be found in various monographs on the development of the specific sciences
in the United States, listed in Smallwood's bibliography. The best sources
are biographies and biographical sketches of the natural philosophers. Harry
H. Clark, "The Influence of Science on American Ideas from 1775 to
1809," *Transactions of the Wisconsin Academy of Sciences, Arts, and Letters, XXXV* (1944), 305–49, and F. E. Brasch, "The Royal Society of
London and Its Influence upon Scientific Thought in the American Colonies," *Scientific Monthly,* XXXIII (1931), 336–55, 448–69, and "The
Newtonian Epoch in the American Colonies (1680–1783)," *Proceedings
of the American Antiquarian Society,* October, 1939, pp. 3–21, contain
useful material.

Benjamin Rush, *The Influence of Physical Causes on the Moral Faculty*
(1786), is reprinted in Blau, ed., *American Philosophic Addresses, 1700–
1900,* pp. 315–43. Nathan G. Goodman, *Benjamin Rush; Physician and
Citizen* (Philadelphia, 1934), is an excellent biography. Thomas Cooper's
Scripture Doctrine of Materialism and *A View of the Metaphysical and
Physiological Arguments in Favor of Materialism* were published together
(Philadelphia, 1823). Dumas Malone, *The Public Life of Thomas Cooper*
(New Haven, 1926), presents carefully the various activities of its subject.

— III —

NATIONALISM AND DEMOCRACY

WHIG NATIONALISM

THERE were two schools of Federalist philosophy current during the American Enlightenment, and eventually they faced each other bitterly in civil war. In their early days, however, they were partners. The "constitutionalist" school flourished in New England, found its fullest exposition in the writings of John Adams, and was particularly congenial to Calvinists, both to Puritan traders and to Dutch patroons. It served to give a common front to the vested interests of landed and commercial aristocrats, first against British mercantilism, then against Southern agrarianism, and finally against the urban propertyless classes, whose interests were thought by the wealthy to be contemptible because they were not "fixed." The "public" interest was usually identified in the minds of those Federalists with the security of capital in land and ships. The phrase "common defense and general welfare" enshrined in the preamble to the Constitution was interpreted by them in such a "strict" way that "general welfare" meant little more than "common defense." In fact, the term "commonwealth" was used technically by these theorists to mean no more than a union of "justice and equality," law and order. We might call this school, following Adams's own terminology, the "Novanglian" federalism.

The other school, the "bill of rights" school, found its chief exponents in Thomas Jefferson and the Virginia Republicans. By the Novanglians these men were usually called Jacobins, and, in truth, during the days of the French Revolution and Napoleon the two schools diverged rapidly, because the one was pro-British and the other pro-French, on general principles as well as in foreign policies. The Republicans of the South were no less aristocratic than the Federalists of the North, but they looked down on different classes—they took for granted (with a few notable exceptions, among them Jefferson himself) that there are creatures who are *naturally* slaves, by nature intended as the recipients of the benevolent despotisms of "plantation" government, but these Southern aristocrats made friends with the "common" men in the northern colonies, whom they greeted as fellow citizens and equals in their "Jacobin clubs" or "democratic societies." The legend grew and still lives that in the South "there are no common men"! Be that as it may, the Virginia Republicans, who were as deeply concerned as the New Englanders in an enduring federation, soon found themselves, to their dismay, to be a faction or a party, representing sectional and class interests. They were, therefore, forced to put increasing emphasis on state sovereignty rather than on federal government.

Alexander Hamilton, meanwhile, was radically antifederal in his philosophy. He was not a child of the Enlightenment, but the founder of a new nationalism, an American Burke, as Jefferson correctly called him. He suffered an ironical fate, being compelled to write many of the *Federalist Papers* and to play New England Federalist politics; his thinking, however, had entirely different foundations and aims. He called himself a "continentalist" and, like later New Yorkers, conceived his type of provincialism as a truly American program. Historians, to say nothing of politicians, are still debating whether Hamilton's economic nationalism was in practice more influential than federal-republican politics in establishing the United States, but it certainly established American capitalism.

Hamilton was exceptional in his time not only in being an ardent nationalist but also in basing his theory on political economy rather than on "the science of government." Intellectually Hamilton was farther removed from his Federalist allies than the Federalists were from the Republicans: witness John Adams's growing distrust of Hamilton's policies. As a young man he had learned the philosophies of the Enlightenment, and his first essays in political controversy, published just before the Revolutionary War, reflect the stock in trade of "natural rights," "liberty," and the rest. His ultra-Tory schooling at King's College made him an enlightened rebel. Before graduating he organized a militia company. Most of his life he spent in close association with "General" Washington, and he seems to have regarded himself as primarily a soldier. He was pleased when his followers were dubbed "the military party." It was in this military atmosphere that he acquired the dominant themes of his social philosophy.

He had studied the classics and would, on occasion, quote Hobbes, Hume,[1] and Montesquieu, but his ideas were for the most part hammered out of military experience. He had acquired from Montesquieu one pregnant belief, "that a government must be fitted to a nation as much as a coat to the individual." [2] He set to work fitting a government to America. His most genuine arguments in the *Federalist Papers*, when he is not catering obviously to the prejudices of "the People of the State of New York," are attempts to prove the fitness of federalism for American circumstances; and they stand in marked contrast to Madison's learned applications of the classics. Madison later criticized Hamilton for seeking to "administer the government into what *he* thought it ought to be," failing completely to understand that the emphasis placed on "administration" by Hamilton and his "executive party" (as the Republicans sarcastically called it) was not incipient monarchism, but a conscientious program of "fitting" the government continually to the nation's changing needs. As early as the Constitutional Convention Hamilton became convinced that only a republican government was fitted for the American "genius," though he personally had little faith in it.[3] He later described American party government as "a vibration of power."

More significant than Hamilton's view of federalism was his analysis of politics in terms of power and of power in terms of money. During the dark days of the war, when he shared Washington's concern for the demoralized remnants of the army, he became convinced that the military power could be revived only on the basis of financial power, and it was as early as 1780 that he went to Robert Morris with his proposal to found a "continental bank." Political power is ultimately, according to Hamilton, based on credit. It was no jest when he insisted that a public debt is a public asset or when he defended an

---

[1] Of Hume's works he knew best the *History of England* and the *Essay on the Jealousy of Commerce*.

[2] To Lafayette, January 6, 1799.

[3] "It appeared to me to be in some sort understood that, with a view to free investigation, experimental propositions might be made, which were to be received merely as suggestions for consideration. Accordingly, it is a fact that my final opinion was against an Executive during good behavior. . . . In the actual situation of the country, it was in itself right and proper that the republican theory should have a fair and full trial."—To Timothy Pickering, September 18, 1803.

expensive government on the ground that since it needed more taxes it would get more power. He thought of government less in terms of legislation than of taxation. Madison complained that Hamilton had no objection to using the "general welfare" clause of the Constitution for whatever concerns the "general interests of learning, of agriculture, of manufactures, and of commerce . . . as far as regards an application of money." [4] Thus, to conceive of government as the active promotion of "general interests," instead of limiting it to "justice and equality," was indeed revolutionary in American political theory. But it was the very essence of Hamilton's program, and he at once gave "to that government a tone and energy far beyond what was contemplated by the founders." [5]

From the point of view of money power Hamilton envisaged the nation, bound in "strict and indissoluble Union," as primarily a union of credit and of commerce. To fund the public debt, "consolidate" and expand credit in the hands of the Federal Government, seemed to him an elementary business necessity, and the objection that this would enrich speculators was no real objection to his mind. Fluid capital for industrial expansion was his prime concern, and if this power were concentrated in the hands of bankers and other investors, so much the better. Not the distribution of wealth, but the direction of speculation was what mattered in the end. Hamilton's great idea was to encourage manufacturing. He conceived the manufacturing interest, which was in his time particularly strong in the middle states and the hinterland of New England, as in a peculiar sense the national interest, because it mediated (economically and geographically) between the more "factional" interests of the New England maritime traders and the planters of the South.[6] The benefits of manufactures,

---

[4] William C. Rives, *History of the Life and Times of James Madison* (Boston, 1868), III, 233.

[5] *Ibid.*, p. 173.

[6] The same point was made by Henry Clay in his famous *Speech in Defence of the American System* (1832): "Gentlemen are greatly deceived as to the hold which this system has in the affections of the people of the United States. They represent that it is the policy of New England, and that she is most benefitted by it. If there be any part of this Union which has been most steady, most unanimous, and most determined in its support, it is Pennsylvania. Why is not that powerful State attacked? Why pass her over, and aim the blow at New England? New England came reluctantly into the policy. In 1824 a majority of her delegation was opposed to it. From the largest

he argued, would be nationwide. In his famous *Report on Manufactures* (1791) he consciously applied Adam Smith's arguments for the division of labor on a national scale. Let the labor of America be diversified, let the government give encouragement to those forms of labor that most need it, let there be free trade within the Union,[7] and let America thus become an independent world power.

In Hamilton's mind public and private credits and debts, public and private societies for promoting industry were all lumped together as sources of "national wealth." An illustration of how he himself put his theories into practice is the fact that while he was preparing his famous *Report* he (and two fellow-promoters) were organizing the New Jersey Society for Useful Manufactures.

The charter for this concern was secured from the New Jersey Legislature in spite of objectors who said that it was dangerous to the landed and the artisan interests. Another use was now found by Hamilton for the public debt. It was to be the only means of securing stock in the society and in turn this subscribed public debt could be invested in National Bank stock. This multiple use, said Hamilton, would increase the market value of the public stocks, and so both the venture and the public stood to gain from what the prospectus described as a patriotic enterprise for the promotion of domestic industry.[8]

State of New England there was but a solitary vote in favor of the bill. That enterprising people can readily accommodate their industry to any policy, provided it be *settled.* They supposed this was fixed, and they submitted to the decrees of government. And the progress of public opinion has kept pace with the developments of the benefits of the system. Now, all New England, at least in this house (with the exception of one small still voice) is in favor of the system. In 1824 all Maryland was against it; now the majority is for it. Then, Louisiana, with one exception, was opposed to it; now, without any exception, she is in favor of it. The march of public sentiment is to the South. . . . And finally, its doctrines will pervade the whole Union, and the wonder will be, that they ever should have been opposed."—*The Life and Speeches of Henry Clay* (New York, 1844), II, 60–61.

[7] Hamilton's idea of an American "customs union" was the direct inspiration of Friedrich List's *Outlines of American Political Economy* (1827); List was the chief economist of the German Zollverein and one of the fathers of European nationalist economics. See William S. Culbertson, *Alexander Hamilton* (New Haven, 1916), pp. 140–41, and Johns Hopkins University, *Studies in Historical and Political Science*, XV, 46–63, 581–82.

[8] Rexford Guy Tugwell and Joseph Dorfman, "Alexander Hamilton: Nation Maker," *Columbia University Quarterly*, XXX (March, 1938), 63n.

That Hamilton was thinking in terms of power politics and that he worked out a substantial political economy for his "one great American system" is clear not only from his private speculation, from his *Report on Manufactures* and from his *Reports on Public Credit,* but even from his *Federalist Papers.* He would not have dared to be so outspoken, had he not been addressing the people of the State of New York (i.e., the influential people), and even as it was, his bold use of the terms "national," his references to "the streams of national power" and "the fabric of American Empire," required much clever explaining by his fellow author, Madison. Putting together a few of these scattered passages, we can expose the boldness as well as the modernity of Hamilton's philosophy.

Have republics in practice been less addicted to war than monarchies? Are not the former administered by *men* as well as the latter? . . . Has commerce hitherto done anything more than change the objects of war? Is not the love of wealth as domineering and enterprising a passion as that of power or glory? Have there not been as many wars founded upon commercial motives since that has become the prevailing system of nations, as were before occasioned by the cupidity of territory or dominion? Has not the spirit of commerce, in many instances, administered new incentives to the appetite, both for the one and for the other? Let experience, the least fallible guide of human opinions, be appealed to for an answer to these inquiries.

Is it not time to awake from the deceitful dream of a golden age, and to adopt as a practical maxim for the direction of our political conduct that we, as well as the other inhabitants of the globe, are yet remote from the happy empire of perfect wisdom and perfect virtue?

Our position is . . . a most commanding one. . . . By a steady adherence to the Union, we may hope, erelong, to become the arbiter of Europe in America, and to be able to incline the balance of European competitions in this part of the world as our interest may dictate.

Under a vigorous national government, the natural strength and resources of the country, directed to a common interest, would baffle all the combinations of European jealousy to restrain our growth. This situation would even take away the motive to such combinations, by inducing an impracticability of success. An active commerce, an extensive navigation, and a flourishing marine would then be the offspring of moral and physical necessity. We might defy the little arts of the little politicians to control or vary the irresistible and unchangeable course of nature.

An unrestrained intercourse between the States themselves will advance the trade of each by an interchange of their respective productions, not only for the supply of reciprocal wants at home, but for exportation to foreign markets. The veins of commerce in every part will be replenished, and will acquire additional motion and vigor from a free circulation of the commodities of every part. Commercial enterprise will have much greater scope, from the diversity in the productions of different States.

The speculative trader will at once perceive the force of these observations, and will acknowledge that the aggregate balance of the commerce of the United States would bid fair to be much more favorable than that of the thirteen States without union or with partial unions.

A unity of commercial, as well as political, interests, can only result from a unity of government.

Let Americans disdain to be the instruments of European greatness! Let the thirteen States, bound together in a strict and indissoluble Union, concur in erecting one great American system, superior to the control of all transatlantic force or influence, and able to dictate the terms of the connection between the old and the new world!

Upon the same principle that a man is more attached to his family than to his neighborhood, to his neighborhood than to the community at large, the people of each State would be apt to feel a stronger bias towards their local governments than towards the government of the Union; unless the force of that principle should be destroyed by a much better administration of the latter.

There is one transcendent advantage belonging to the province of the State governments, which alone suffices to place the matter in a clear and satisfactory light,—I mean the ordinary administration of criminal and civil justice. This, of all others, is the most powerful, most universal, and most attractive source of popular obedience and attachment. It is that which, being the immediate and visible guardian of life and property, having its benefits and its terrors in constant activity before the public eye, regulating all those personal interests and familiar concerns to which the sensibility of individuals is more immediately awake, contributes, more than any other circumstance, to impressing upon the minds of the people, affection, esteem, and reverence towards the government. This great cement of society, which

will diffuse itself almost wholly through the channels of the particular governments, independent of all other causes of influence, would insure them
so decided an empire over their respective citizens as to render them at all
times a complete counterpoise, and, not unfrequently, dangerous rivals to
the power of the Union.

The operations of the national government, on the other hand, falling less
immediately under the observation of the mass of the citizens, the benefits
derived from it will chiefly be perceived and attended to by speculative men.
Relating to more general interests, they will be less apt to come home to the
feelings of the people; and, in proportion, less likely to inspire an habitual
sense of obligation, and an active sentiment of attachment.

The great and radical vice in the construction of the existing Confederation
is in the principle of legislation for states or governments, in their corporate
or collective capacities, and as contradistinguished from the individuals of
which they consist.

It has not a little contributed to the infirmities of the existing federal
system, that it never had a ratification by the people. Resting on no better
foundation than the consent of the several legislatures, it has been exposed
to frequent and intricate questions concerning the validity of its powers, and
has, in some instances, given birth to the enormous doctrine of a right of
legislative repeal. . . . The fabric of American empire ought to rest on
the solid basis of the consent of the people. The streams of national power
ought to flow immediately from that pure, original fountain of all legitimate
authority.

In disquisitions of every kind, there are certain primary truths, or first principles, upon which all subsequent reasonings must depend. These contain
an internal evidence which, antecedent to all reflection or combination,
commands the assent of the mind. Where it produces not this effect, it must
proceed either from some defect or disorder in the organs of perception, or
from the influence of some strong interest, or passion, or prejudice. Of this
nature are the maxims in geometry, that "the whole is greater than its parts;
things equal to the same are equal to one another; two straight lines cannot
enclose a space; and all right angles are equal to each other." Of the same
nature are these other maxims in ethics and politics, that there cannot be an
effect without a cause; that the means ought to be proportioned to the end;
that every power ought to be commensurate with its object; that there
ought to be no limitation of a power destined to effect a purpose which is
itself incapable of limitation.

A government ought to contain in itself every power requisite to the full accomplishment of the objects committed to its care, and to the complete execution of the trusts for which it is responsible, free from every other control but a regard to the public good and to the sense of the people.

As the duties of superintending the national defence and of securing the public peace against foreign or domestic violence involve a provision for casualties and dangers to which no possible limits can be assigned, the power of making that provision ought to know no other bounds than the exigencies of the nation and the resources of the community.

As revenue is the essential engine by which the means of answering the national exigencies must be procured, the power of procuring that article in its full extent must necessarily be comprehended in that of providing for those exigencies.

Money is, with propriety, considered as the vital principle of the body politic; as that which sustains its life and motion, and enables it to perform its most essential functions. A complete power, therefore, to procure a regular and adequate supply of it, as far as the resources of the community will permit, may be regarded as an indispensable ingredient in every constitution.

Nations in general, even under governments of the more popular kind, usually commit the administration of their finances to single men or to boards composed of a few individuals, who digest and prepare, in the first instance, the plans of taxation, which are afterwards passed into laws by the authority of the sovereign or legislature.

Inquisitive and enlightened statesmen are deemed everywhere best qualified to make a judicious selection of the objects proper for revenue; which is a clear indication, as far as the sense of mankind can have weight in the question, of the species of knowledge of local circumstances requisite to the purposes of taxation.

There is an idea, which is not without its advocates, that a vigorous Executive is inconsistent with the genius of republican government. The enlightened well-wishers to this species of government must at least hope that the supposition is destitute of foundation; since they can never admit its truth, without at the same time admitting the condemnation of their own principles. Energy in the Executive is a leading character in the definition of good government.

There are some who would be inclined to regard the servile pliancy of the Executive to a prevailing current, either in the community or in the legislature, as its best recommendation. But such men entertain very crude notions, as well of the purposes for which government was instituted, as of the true means by which the public happiness may be promoted. The republican principle demands that the deliberate sense of the community should govern the conduct of those to whom they intrust the management of their affairs; but it does not require an unqualified complaisance to every sudden breeze of passion, or to every transient impulse which the people may receive from the arts of men, who flatter their prejudices to betray their interests. It is a just observation, that the people commonly *intend* the public good. This often applies to their very errors. But their good sense would despise the adulator who should pretend that they always *reason right* about the *means* of promoting it. They know from experience that they sometimes err; and the wonder is that they so seldom err as they do, beset, as they continually are, by the wiles of parasites and sycophants, by the snares of the ambitious, the avaricious, the desperate, by the artifices of men who possess their confidence more than they deserve it, and of those who seek to possess rather than to deserve it. When occasions present themselves, in which the interests of the people are at variance with their inclinations, it is the duty of the persons whom they have appointed to be the guardians of those interests, to withstand the temporary delusion, in order to give them time and opportunity for more cool and sedate reflection. Instances might be cited in which a conduct of this kind has saved the people from very fatal consequences of their own mistakes, and has procured lasting monuments of their gratitude to the men who had courage and magnanimity enough to serve them at the peril of their displeasure.[9]

The practical upshot of this theory of national administration is that problems of justice may be entrusted to local governments, whereas the prime concern of the national government should be to promote the "general interests" of the people, interests which the common people themselves fail to understand and which must, therefore, be entrusted to men of affairs. Those will govern best who most enhance the wealth of the nation by energetically applying the principles of political economy. Hamilton's program for developing the diversification and eventual self-sufficiency of American economy was not patterned on the principles of traditional mercantilism, nor did it rely primarily on protectionism. Hamilton specifically pointed out

[9] Alexander Hamilton, John Jay, and James Madison, *The Federalist* (Washington, D.C., 1937), Sesquicentennial ed., ed. by Sherman F. Mittell, pp. 30, 33, 65–66, 68, 69, 102–3, 103–4, 89, 140–41, 188, 190, 182–83, 218, 454, 464–65.

that government could "liberate" industry best by removing barriers to interstate commerce and by giving subsidies rather than by imposing tariffs. He relied chiefly, however, on the theory of balanced production; the various sectional interests and classes can, by proper "administration," be made to supply each other's needs. And the nation's needs, Hamilton asserted on the basis of experience rather than of principle, may be presumed to be ever equal to the nation's resources.

Hamilton's open disdain for popular opinion and demagogic methods bore its natural fruit; he was turned out by the politicians at Washington when his policies became extremely unpopular and spent the remainder (1795–1804) of his short life in retirement from office, a "disappointed politician" and an increasingly cynical philosopher. One of his last letters contained the bitter words: "Dismemberment of our empire will be a clear sacrifice of great positive advantages without any counterbalancing good, administering no relief to our real disease, which is *democracy*, the poison of which, by a subdivision, will only be the more concentrated . . . and the more virulent." [10] But even more bitter and cynical was his scheme for beating Jacobin societies at their own game, consciously "corrupting public opinion" by appealing to passion and prejudice. He proposed to make Federalist capital out of the growing power of popular religion:

Nothing is more fallacious than to expect to produce any valuable or permanent results in political projects by relying merely on the reason of men. . . . Our adversaries . . . at the very moment they are eulogizing the reason of men, and professing to appeal only to that faculty, are courting the strongest and most active passion of the human heart, *vanity!* . . . In the competition for the passions of the people . . . we must renounce our principles and our objects, and unite in corrupting public opinion till it becomes fit for nothing but mischief. . . . I do not mean to countenance the imitation of things intrinsically unworthy, but only of such as may be denominated irregular. . . . Let an association be formed to be denominated "The Christian Constitutional Society." Its objects to be: First the support of the Christian religion. Second the support of the Constitution of the U. S. . . . The populous cities ought particularly to be attended to; perhaps it would be well to institute in such places—first, societies for the relief of

[10] To Theodore Sedgwick, July 10, 1804.

emigrants; second, academies, each with one professor, for instructing the different classes of mechanics in the principles of mechanics and the elements of chemistry." [11]

He was evidently attempting to imitate (or, possibly, to satirize) the demagogic methods of Aaron Burr, the Presbyterian hypocrite.

During the French Revolution American conservatives such as Hamilton had lost their faith in Europe in general and had learned from troublesome experience that it was difficult to do business with "European caprice." The embargo had made it practically compulsory to turn inward and westward toward America's own resources. After 1815 the disillusionment with Europe was shared by all parties, and there spread throughout America a romantic nationalism. Even Americans came to believe in the romantic portraits of their country which had long been current in Europe. A century earlier Bishop Berkeley had written in his *Verses on the Prospect of Planting Arts and Learning in America:*

> In happy climes, the seat of innocence,
>   Where nature guides and virtue rules
>
>   . . .
>
> There shall be sung another age,
>
>   . . .
>
> Not such as Europe breeds in her decay;
>
>   . . .
>
> Westward the course of empire takes its way;
>   The four first Acts already past,
> A fifth shall close the Drama with the day;
>   Time's noblest offspring is the last.

Joel Barlow drew essentially the same picture in his *Fourth of July Oration* (1787), repeated it in his sensational *Advice to the Privileged Orders in Europe* (1792), and in his address "to his fellow citizens of the U.S." (Paris, 1799), referring to his country as "the fairest fabric of human policy that the world has hitherto seen." In America, he claimed, moral force was supplanting physical force, and American

---

[11] To James A. Bayard, April, 1802.

"efforts might point out to Europe the great desideratum of good men, the means of establishing perpetual peace" and "prove beyond contradiction that an unarmed neutrality is better than an armed one." The most widely circulated version of this sentiment, copied and recited for generations as an oracle of Whiggism, was Noah Webster's Preface to his Speller.

Europe is grown old in folly, corruption, and tyranny. In that country laws are perverted, manners are licentious, literature is declining, and human nature is debased. . . . American glory begins at dawn at a favorable period, and under flattering circumstances. We have the experience of the whole world before our eyes; but to receive indiscriminately the maxims of government, the manners and literary taste of Europe, and make them the ground on which to build our systems in America, must soon convince us that a durable and stately edifice can never be erected upon the mouldering pillars of antiquity. •

President Monroe's famous Message (1823) to Congress and to the world was based on the premise that "our system" is antithetical to Europe's and that, therefore, any attempt on the part of "old world powers" to extend "their system" to this hemisphere would be "dangerous to our peace and safety." Thus, "the American system" became the symbol of a new world. Since political developments favored the inclusion of South America in the field of American expansion, the "continental" view of Hamilton was enlarged by the Whig orators into a grand hemispheric design. Both the isolationist position toward Europe and the positive concept of the "moral state" were expanded by Edward Everett, whose oratorical powers were heightened by his enthusiasm for "a well-constituted, powerful commonwealth," which he brought back with him from Germany.

The true principle of American policy, to which the whole spirit of our system, not less than the geographical features of our country invites us, is *separation from Europe*. Next to *union at home*, which ought to be called not so much the essential condition of our national existence as our existence itself, separation from all other countries is the great principle by which we are to prosper. . . . This is the voice of our history, which traces everything excellent in our character and prosperous in our fortunes to dissent, non-conformity, departure, resistance, and independence.

The greatest engine of moral power known to human affairs is an organized, prosperous state. All that man in his individual capacity can do . . . is as nothing, compared with the collective, perpetuated influence on human affairs and human happiness, of a well-constituted, powerful commonwealth. . . . Man is in his nature neither a savage, a hermit, nor a slave, but a member of a well-ordered family, a good neighbor, a free citizen, a well-informed, good man, acting with others like him. This is the lesson which is taught in the charter of our independence; this is the lesson which our example ought to teach the world.[12]

This was the lesson which was *not* taught in the Declaration of Independence, but it mattered little whether it was taught to Everett in Germany, to Monroe in Washington, to John Quincy Adams in Boston, or to Charles Jared Ingersoll in Philadelphia, for it was the lesson which they all joined in teaching to the world.

The expansionist program, which began as a speculative venture, became in 1815 a grim necessity. President Madison was finally compelled to admit the disastrous effects on American economy of his foreign policy and of the Napoleonic blockades, and in his message of 1815 he gave the Whigs the signal to go ahead by urging the creation of a national currency, the protection of manufactures, and the construction of roads and canals. Though an arch-Republican, Madison was somewhat prepared theoretically for this emergency and shift of policy. It had long been his doctrine that though public opinion is the true sovereign, it was part of the duty of the government to attempt "a modification of the sovereignty," i.e., to mold or "enlighten" public opinion. Madison and Monroe now went to work on their Republican "sovereign" and began "refining and enlarging the public views" until "the will of society," even in the South, was sufficiently "enlightened" to understand the need for a program of public works and protective tariff. Calhoun and the Southern "War Hawks" now took the lead in a program of nationalism, giving the Whig Party, or National Republicans, a truly national scope and burying the soured remnants of the old New England Federalism, such as Squire Fisher Ames and Colonel Timothy Pickering.

The best theoretical expositor of the new Whig nationalism was John Quincy Adams. He consciously departed from the faith of his

---

[12] *Orations and Speeches*, pp. 53, 129–30. The first paragraph is 1824; the second, 1826.

father, who had conceived government as an affair of checks and balances, not only among the powers of government but also among various group interests, and conceived the public interest as an overall concern based on the unity of the people, whereas government he conceived to be a "co-operation of the departments" in the service of the public interest.

The very object and formation of the *National* deliberative assemblies was for the compromise and conciliation of the interests of all—of the whole nation. . . . It is not through the medium of personal sensibility, nor of party bias, nor of professional occupation, nor of geographical position, that *the Whole Truth* can be discerned, of questions involving the rights and interests of this extensive Union. . . . [Representatives] should cast all their feelings and interests as Citizens of a single State into the common Stock of the National concern.[13]

What made Adams's theory more than lip service to "the national concern" was the positive, concrete content which he included in this term. His first message to Congress (1825) closed with the following outline of his theory of public "improvement":

The great object of the institution of civil government is the improvement of the condition of those who are parties to the social compact, and no government, in whatever form constituted, can accomplish the lawful ends of its institution but in proportion as it improves the condition of those over whom it is established. Roads and canals, by multiplying and facilitating the communications and intercourse between distant regions and multitudes of men, are among the most important means of improvement. But moral, political, intellectual improvement are duties assigned by the Author of Our Existence to social no less than to individual man. For the fulfillment of those duties governments are invested with power, and to the attainment of the end—the progressive improvement of the condition of the governed— the exercise of delegated powers is a duty as sacred and indispensable as the usurpation of powers not granted is criminal and odious. . . .

. . . if these powers and others enumerated in the Constitution may be effectually brought into action by laws promoting the improvement of agriculture, commerce, and manufactures, the cultivation and encouragement of the mechanic and of the elegant arts, the advancement of litera-

[13] John Quincy Adams, *A Letter to the Hon. Harrison Gray Otis on the Present State of Our National Affairs* (Boston, 1808), p. 5.

ture, and the progress of the sciences, ornamental and profound, to refrain from exercising them for the benefit of the people themselves would be to hide in the earth the talent committed to our charge—would be treachery to the most sacred of trusts.

The spirit of improvement is abroad upon the earth.[14]

Brooks Adams wrote that his grandfather believed that "by the gift of Providence" "an unlimited store of wealth" would raise the American people

above the pressure of any competition which would be likely to engender war. The only serious problem for them to solve, therefore, was how to develop this gift on a collective, and not on a competitive and selfish basis. . . . This task might be done by an honest executive . . . were he supported by an intelligent and educated civil service . . . capable of conducting a complex organism on scientific principles.[15]

The Whigs undoubtedly used this concept of the "American system" and the "public interest" to camouflage their investments in land speculation and industry and their private profits from protective tariffs, national banking, and commercial development in the West and in South America. In the hands of Henry Clay the party and the doctrine became conspicuously sectional. Calhoun, too, repented of his nationalism after 1828 and challenged the Whigs, declaring that "no such political body as the American people collectively, either now or ever, did exist." Calhoun's later and elaborate doctrine of "the concurrent majority" was clearly based on a reversion to Jeffersonian principles and scarcely deserves the recognition it has received as an original contribution to political philosophy. It was, to be sure, a clever defense of minority rights without the customary defense of natural rights and of the social contract theory, and it modernized the theory of checks and balances by applying it to Democratic Party politics as well as to the separation of powers in constitutional government, but apart from these technical innovations his aims and ideas were Jeffersonian.[16] He is most clearly Jeffersonian in repudiating

[14] Willard Thorp, Merle Curti, and Carlos Baker, ed., *American Issues* (Philadelphia, 1941), I ("The Social Record"), 157, 159–60.

[15] Cited in Charles A. Beard, *The American Spirit* (New York, 1942), pp. 158–59.

[16] "He regarded himself as a democrat but he never really accepted the principles of democracy and never learned to cope successfully with the vast unpredictable force represented by the common man."

the nationalism of his youth and reasserting the rights of local interests. Calhoun's case is the most dramatic illustration of the general tendency among Whig politicians to sacrifice their nationalist principles to partisan exigencies. The case of Daniel Webster should, perhaps, be mentioned here, though he was not a philosopher; his nationalistic rhetoric was from the start in the service of New England commerce. By the time he began to proclaim that liberty and union are inseparable he was clearly evading the real philosophical issue, sharpened by Calhoun, namely: How are liberty and union compossible? Politically the solution to this question seemed as hopeless as it did philosophically. The faith in liberty and the faith in national unity both grew, but the conflict between them grew likewise.

While "the American system" was thus degenerating into factionalism among the politicians, it received a more adequate intellectual development among political economists. It was natural and in the spirit of Hamilton that Whiggism should find its best embodiment in economics rather than in politics. It was also natural that the headquarters for this type of nationalism should be located in and around Pennsylvania. One of the first and most eloquent blasts of American economic nationalism came from a Philadelphia lawyer and Congressman, Charles Jared Ingersoll, who in 1808, when American commerce was at its lowest, published a vigorous attack on British interference under the text, "Saul, Saul, why persecutest thou me?" He first pointed out the futility of relying on international law.

We Americans, who make our first appearance in the ranks of independent nations while the battle is raging, with a modest determination to do what is right, according to the best of our judgment, are alternately denounced by the combatants for not abiding by their irreconcilable interpretations, and can for ourselves discover nothing but the din and dissonance of that comity

---

"A single selfish interest had gained control of the machinery of government and was indirectly but none the less thoroughly looting a third of the nation. The democratic process had run its full cycle before his eyes, and he saw the problem at last as Randolph and John Taylor had seen it long ago. He realized now that men were moved primarily by love of gain, and that it was asking more than human nature could give to ask for personal disinterestedness in the majority of any body of men on earth. . . .—Charles M. Wiltse, *John C. Calhoun, Nationalist, 1782–1828* (Indianapolis, 1944), pp. 271, 396.

of nations, which each party asseverates, according to his construction, is so harmonious and interesting. . . .

It may, therefore, without a paradox, be declared, that the law of nations, as an uncertain compilation, by unauthorized and discordant editors, of international usages and relations has been entitled, is in fact law with no nation.

It is the baseless fabric of this vision the United States of America have placed for a corner stone of their jurisprudence, the law of nations being considered part of the common law, said to have been transmitted hither an inestimable inheritance from the mother country, and a rule of supreme force in all decisions of the courts of the United States, and of most of the individual states.[17]

Ingersoll then argued that since neither legal nor military measures are practical remedies, a tariff war was necessary to make America "really independent." [18] Meanwhile, an ardent Irish refugee named Mathew Carey was editing in Philadelphia *The American Museum*, a periodical devoted chiefly to the discussion of economic problems and the denunciation of England. He and his son, Henry, reading proof for the articles in this magazine as well as for the books which issued from his publishing house, became homemade economists. In 1814 Mathew Carey published *The Olive Branch*, in which he tried to suggest a practical basis of co-operation for all the factions generated by the War of 1812. He became the leading promoter of anti-British protectionism, but he also preached a constructive economic gospel of "harmony of interests" as an ideology for the Whig program of public works and economic expansion.[19] Carey became host to the German exile Friedrich List, who published (1827) his *Outlines of American*

[17] Charles Jared Ingersoll, *A View of the Rights and Wrongs, Power and Policy, of the United States of America* (Philadelphia, 1808), pp. 34, 39.

[18] Ingersoll later amplified his views to include cultural nationalism. See his address, "The Influence of America on the Mind" (1823), reprinted in Blau, ed., *American Philosophic Addresses, 1700–1900*, pp. 20–59.

[19] "Carey saw the limitations of the agricultural communities of the United States. He wished America to advance from simplicity to complexity. He hoped to multiply many times the number of callings open to the young men of America. Only in such a mature and complex society could the democratic ideal of the free individual be realized. . . . The nation must become independent in an economic as well as in a political sense. Until such independence had become a reality, Americans could not call themselves free men."—Ralph Henry Gabriel, *The Course of American Democratic Thought* (New York, 1940), p. 83.

Political Economy, under the inspiration of the American nationalists and in refutation of Thomas Cooper's *Lectures on Political Economy* (1826). Cooper had been a personal friend of Jefferson, and in his earlier Pennsylvania days (1813) had lectured in favor of the encouragement of domestic manufactures. He had interpreted the classical economy as an argument against foreign trade. However, in the revision of his *Lectures*, after his removal to South Carolina, his views became more agrarian, and he relied largely on the physiocratic doctrines of Jean Baptiste Say. List's attack thus made evident the persistence of the basic issues between the Jeffersonians and the Hamiltonians.

Philosophically the most interesting exponent of Whig nationalism was Daniel Raymond, a Baltimore lawyer, who in 1820 published *Thoughts on Political Economy*, the first systematic treatise on the subject by an American. This work ran through four editions, the fourth being a condensed academic text with much of the most interesting philosophical commentary eliminated. Raymond not only launched into a vigorous critique of the basic assumptions of Smith's *Wealth of Nations* but also worked out a utilitarian economics such as J. S. Mill might have conceived had he carried his ethics into his economics.[20] Raymond's work provides an excellent philosophical orientation for what has more recently come to be known as "welfare economics." For Raymond political economy is a moral science in the fullest sense, and its proper subject matter is the inquiry into national wealth. National wealth is entirely different from individual wealth, for the nation is a unity, "one and indivisible," and its wealth is not an aggregate of the wealth of its citizens. An individual's wealth or private economy is "such an application of revenue as shall procure the greatest portion of innocent enjoyment." It takes the form of property, and properties, since they can be exchanged, are said to have "value" (exchange value) in relation to each other. The people's collective wealth is not property and has no measurable value; it cannot accumulate through "parsimony"; it is wealth in circulation or consumption. It is the people's collective "capacity for acquiring the

[20] John Neal, Jeremy Bentham's American disciple, received Raymond's work with enthusiasm and tried to gain attention for it among the English writers, but without success.

necessaries and comforts of life." The "source" of these necessaries and comforts is the earth; their "cause" or the capacity for acquiring them is industry or labor. Production is, therefore, wealth only insofar as it is consumed. There is a type of labor which is only indirectly productive, since its effects are not immediately consumable; such "permanent" or "effective" labor, as Raymond calls it, is especially important in public works. The obstacles to an equal distribution of the necessaries and comforts of life are "avarice and luxury."

In short, private economy occupies the middle ground between avarice and parsimony, on the one hand, and luxury and prodigality on the other. If a man steer clear of these, on either hand, he may procure all the enjoyment within the means of his revenue, without infringing upon the most rigid rules of economy.

The rich ought always to bear in mind, that, as they possess all the property, it is their indispensable duty, to consume all the surplus product of the labour of the poor. This is, or this ought to be, the condition upon which they hold their property, and this is a condition favourable enough to them.

The rich must either support the poor in this way, or they must support them as paupers. When all the property belongs to a part of the community, of course, all the product of the earth must, in the first instance, belong to them, and unless that portion of the community, who have no property, can procure the necessaries of life, by their labour, they must either starve, or live upon charity. All cannot find employment in agriculture, and unless the product of manufacturing labour is consumed when produced, it is useless to produce it, for, of itself, it will not support life. If those who have all the necessaries of life, will not exchange a part of them for the product of the labour of the poor, they must maintain these poor without labour. That cannot be economy which, if practised by all men, would cause starvation to one half of the community. If this is economy, then economy is a heinous vice, instead of a virtue.

Nature never planted in the breast of man, a desire for happiness, and gave to wealth the power, or rather made it a means of procuring happiness, without intending that it should be used for that purpose. The legitimate object of wealth, therefore, is to procure happiness, or enjoyment. But, like every other good, it is liable to be abused; and it is always abused, when not so used as to produce innocent enjoyment; and it is always abused, when used for the purpose of gratifying the sordid, selfish, and base passions. . . .

The right of property is therefore a conventional right, and the public grants no title to property in derogation of the public weal. An individual may have a title to property, superior to the title of any other individual, or to any number of individuals, less than the whole, but it cannot be superior to the title of the whole, because the whole includes the title of the individual himself, as well as the title of every body else. Hence the right of the public to take a man's property for the purpose of making public roads, or erecting fortifications, or for any other purpose, which the public good may require.—Hence the right of the government to levy and collect taxes in any manner the public interests may require.—Hence the right to prohibit a man from selling his property to foreigners, or to buy from them those things he may want. The government has a clear and perfect right to make any regulations respecting property, or trade, which the public interests may require.

Every question therefore, respecting a tariff, or protecting duties, must be a question of *expediency*, and not a question of *right*.[21]

Raymond's radical utilitarianism was clearly headed in the direction of economic democracy. He was particularly concerned that each generation should have a new deal, and he stressed the need for regulating inheritance in order to prevent the "accumulation" as private capital of what ought to be consumed as national wealth.

A government should be like a good shepherd, who supports and nourishes the weak and feeble ones in his flock, until they gain sufficient strength to take their chance with the strong, and does not suffer them to be trampled on, and crushed to the earth, by the powerful. The powerful ones in society, however, are not those who are so, by nature, but those who have been made so, by art—by the inheritance or acquisition of enormous wealth; and these are the ones, who ordinarily, engross all the attention and care of the government. These call themselves the nation; and governments are principally occupied in devising means, not for preserving the natural equality of rights, which exists among men; but for producing a still greater inequality in these rights, by augmenting the wealth of the rich: supposing, or pretending to suppose, that by augmenting the wealth of the rich, they augment the wealth of the nation, as if the rich constituted the nation. The inevitable effect of such measures, (as I trust I shall hereafter show,) is to produce poverty, pauperism, and national distress.

The great object of government, as I have said before, should be to preserve as perfect an equality of rights and property, as possible, consistently with the natural inequality of power among men. Laws of primogeniture,

[21] Daniel Raymond, *Thoughts on Political Economy* (Baltimore, 1820), pp. 219-21, 350.

entail, limitation, and every other law, which tends to accumulate wealth, and perpetuate it in particular families, is in direct violation of this principle.[22]

Though this is clearly a philosophy of economic democracy, it does not necessarily imply political democracy. Raymond shared the Whig fears of "a government so popular as ours."

A government like ours, I know, cannot be administered upon such liberal and enlightened principles, and there is no hope that any other form of government will be better calculated to promote national prosperity and wealth. The people always look to their immediate interests, and certain classes will always have an undue influence over the government. . . .

In relation to a government so popular as ours, we may be allowed to ask with an anxiety bordering on fear, where are we to look for that vast amount of political talents and legislative wisdom, of the power of persuasion, and the authority of character, which will be necessary to its energetic and beneficial administration? [23]

Nevertheless, he added in a patriotic vein which ran very deep in him and his fellow-nationalists:

Our country presents the fairest theatre on earth for the acquisition of knowledge in the science of government and political economy. Here experiments may be made with safety.——Here we can see. the operation of the principles of nature in their utmost purity, and here is to be kept alive, that spirit of liberty and equality which is yet to be diffused throughout the world, and is to warm and animate all the nations of the earth.[24]

It is noteworthy that Raymond had little appreciation of the public utility of capital and credit. He regarded banking as essentially industrial pump priming and said of Hamilton's funding of the public debt:

It promotes the circulation of money, and stimulates industry and enterprise. The funding our public debt, in 1790, is a memorable example of the efficacy of such measures, in promoting national wealth.

Without entering at all into the merits of the question, which at that time agitated the public, as to the justice of that measure; it must, at this day, be admitted, that it had a most beneficial influence upon the wealth of the nation, not by adding any thing to the actual property of the nation, but by

---

[22] Daniel Raymond, *Thoughts on Political Economy* (Baltimore, 1820), pp. 231–32.
[23] *Ibid.*, pp. 380–82.   [24] *Ibid.*, p. 469.

stimulating its industry and enterprise. For the matter of the argument, it may be conceded, as was contended by those who opposed the measure, that it was unjust, and took money from one part of the community, to put into the pockets of another part; and the concession will not affect the utility of the measure, in promoting national wealth. Whether unfortunately or not, I shall not attempt to decide; yet, so it is, that the utility of a measure, in promoting national wealth, does not always depend upon its justice.[25]

Admitting the occasional public utility (not the justice) of capitalism, Raymond represents banks as on the whole decidedly "private corporations," the interests of whose stockholders are usually incompatible with public interests.

Every money corporation, therefore, is *prima facie*, injurious to national wealth, and ought to be looked upon by those who have no money, with jealousy and suspicion. They are, and ought to be considered, as artificial engines of power, contrived by the rich, for the purpose of increasing their already too great ascendency, and calculated to destroy that natural equality among men, which God has ordained, and which no government has a right to lend its power in destroying. The tendency of such institutions is to cause a more unequal division of property, and a greater inequality among men, than would otherwise take place; which necessarily bring in their train, as has already been shown, poverty, pauperism, and misery on the rest of the community. The influence of such institutions on national prosperity is precisely the same proportion to their amount of stock, as that of a national debt.[26]

In the second edition (1823) he added a paragraph which indicates that, though he also added several paragraphs on the utility of banking, he became increasingly aware of the dangers of capitalism in general and of Hamilton's public finance in particular.

Hamilton, in his report on a national bank, adopted the theory of Adam Smith, and of course went astray. He took it for granted, that public and private wealth were identical, and that individual profit was public gain, and hence he concluded, that if those who had money, could always keep it at interest, and be enabled also to lend twice or three times as much as they actually possessed, the public would be a gainer. It is, however, a fundamental error to suppose, that the active or productive capital of a country can be augmented in value by substituting a paper for a metallic currency,

[25] *Ibid.*, pp. 304–5.   [26] *Ibid.*, p. 429.

and it is also a gross error to suppose, that individual profit is always public gain.[27]

Though he was in general a protectionist, he was not always in favor of high tariffs. He wrote a detailed criticism of the 1828 tariff for the benefit of the New England merchants who were opposed to it. In general, Raymond was an independent moralist, and his political economy was an expression of his moral philosophy rather than of his political opinions. He had a genuine concern not only for the people's collective interest but also for their individual welfare. Slavery he condemned passionately on both economic and moral grounds. The withdrawal from circulation or consumption of the "surplus" by the propertied classes in the form of capital he regarded as national robbery and impoverishment, for he conceived wealth, not in terms of saving or thrift ("avarice," as he called it), but of happiness or enjoyable consumption. He favored the growth and regulation of public monopolies in order to offset the evils of "money corporations" and of the British "monopoly of the trade of the world."

Though in Raymond's *Political Economy* Whig nationalism received its most adequate philosophical expression, on the technical side a more substantial contribution was made to economics by Henry C. Carey, son of Mathew, whose numerous works became a veritable bible for protectionist politicians from Daniel Webster to Horace Greeley. But the philosophical roots of Carey's system were less integral to the Whig movement than were those of Raymond's system, and they were also a less radical departure from Adam Smith and the classical economists. Carey was much impressed by positivism. He regarded classical economics as the metaphysical stage of "social science" and attempted to put his scheme of the unity of social science on the basis of the general positivist faith in the unity of natural law. Unity of natural law implied unity in man, and Carey criticized eloquently the "metaphysical" abstractions of "the economic man" and "the moral man." Man is a living individual whose labor, capital, morals, laws are all co-operative "instruments in his mastery over nature." Social laws are laws of progress, and progress was for Carey much the same as it was for Herbert Spencer, the process of differentiation or indi-

[27] Daniel Raymond, *Elements of Political Economy* (Baltimore, 1823), 2d ed., II, 136.

vidualization. But, in contrast to Spencer, Carey regarded "association" (in the French sense) as the chief means of such progress. A nation is not primarily a body politic, but an organization of the division of labor. National organization is a form of progress, because it transforms "trade" into "commerce," anarchic or "free" exchange into a decentralized system of responsibilities, in which each member contributes to a self-sufficient whole. Carey regarded the British Empire as "trade" on the largest scale, a highly centralized anarchy, and economic imperialism he regarded as the very antithesis of progress, for it is systematic exploitation, whereas a genuinely national economy is mutual aid through specialization. Similarly, he regarded political democracy as merely an aspect of the general progress toward self-government or "social science," the discovery and application of those "laws which govern man in his efforts to secure for himself the highest individuality and the greatest power of association." [28]

But Carey was more than a philosophical theorist; he was an effective preacher of nationalism. A specimen of his preaching will serve better than any description we might undertake to convey the emotional appeal and moral earnestness behind his version of "the American System."

Two systems are before the world; the one looks to increasing the proportion of persons and of capital engaged in trade and transportation, and therefore to diminishing the proportion engaged in producing commodities with which to trade, with *necessarily* diminished return to the labour of all; while the other looks to increasing the proportion engaged in the work of production, and diminishing that engaged in trade and transportation, with increased return to all, giving to the labourer good wages, and to the owner of capital good profits. . . . One looks to the continuance of that *bastard* freedom of trade which denies the principle of protection, yet doles it out as revenue duties; the other to extending the area of *legitimate* free trade by the establishment of perfect protection, followed by the annexation of individuals and communities, and ultimately by the abolition of custom-houses. One looks to exporting men to occupy desert tracts, the sovereignty of which is obtained by aid of diplomacy or war; the other to increasing the value of an immense extent of vacant land by importing men by millions for their occupation. . . . One looks to increasing the necessity for commerce; the

[28] Henry C. Carey, *Principles of Social Science*, cited in Ernest Teilhac, *Pioneers of American Economic Thought in the Nineteenth Century* (New York, 1936), p. 58.

other to increasing the power to maintain it. One looks to underworking the Hindoo, and sinking the rest of the world to his level; the other to raising the standard of man throughout the world to our level. One looks to pauperism, ignorance, depopulation, and barbarism; the other to increasing wealth, comfort, intelligence, combination of action, and civilization. One looks towards universal war; the other towards universal peace. One is the English system; the other we may be proud to call the American system, for it is the only one ever devised the tendency of which was that of elevating while equalizing the condition of man throughout the world.

Such is the true mission of the people of these United States. . . .

To establish such an empire——to prove that among the people of the world, whether agriculturists, manufacturers, or merchants, there is perfect harmony of interests, and that the happiness of individuals, as well as the grandeur of nations, is to be promoted by perfect obedience to that greatest of all commands, "Do unto others as ye would that others should do unto you,"——is the object and will be the result of that mission.[29]

Among those whom Carey's philosophy of social science inspired was Professor Francis Bowen of Harvard, who in his extraordinary erudition wrote a treatise on political economy (1856) in addition to his works on metaphysics and logic. Though he was a philosopher, his political economy is singularly free from philosophy, except for his restatement of conventional Whig principles. The last page of his *American Political Economy* reads like a summary of Carey's theory that progress leads through differentiation towards industrialization:

The best legislative policy is that which will most effectually develop all the natural advantages of a country, whether mental or material. It is as wasteful, to say the least, to allow mechanical skill and inventive genius to remain unemployed, as it would be to permit water-power to run without turning mills, or mineral wealth to continue in the ore, or forests to wave where cotton and grain might grow luxuriantly. If the rude labor of husbandry is to form the principal employment of the people, the higher remuneration of skilled labor in the arts must be sacrificed; and this would be as bad economy as to turn our richest soils into sheep-pastures, or to feed cattle upon the finest wheat. The dispersion of the inhabitants over vast tracts of territory, in the isolated pursuits of agriculture, the great majority of them being doomed to work which would not tax the mental resources of a Feejee-

[29] Henry C. Carey, *The Harmony of Interests, Agricultural, Manufacturing, and Commercial*, 2d ed. (New York, 1856), pp. 228-29.

Islander, must be fatal; not only to the growth of wealth, but to many of the higher interests of humanity. The hardships and privations of a life in the backwoods are a fearful drawback upon that bounty which confers, as a free gift, a homestead farm with a soil that reproduces the seed a hundred-fold. To give full scope to all the varieties of taste, genius, and temperament; to foster inventive talent; to afford adequate encouragement to all the arts, whether mechanical or those which are usually distinguished as the fine arts; to concentrate the people, or to bring as large a portion of them as possible within the sphere of the humanizing influences, and larger means of mental culture and social improvement, which can be found only in cities and large towns,—these are objects which deserve at least as much attention, as the inquiry where we can purchase calicoes cheapest, or how great pecuniary sacrifice must be made before we can manufacture railroad iron for ourselves. I see not how these ends can be obtained in a country like ours, which is, so to speak, cursed with great advantages for agriculture, emigration, and the segregation of the people from each other, without throwing over our manufacturing industry, at least for half a century longer the broad shield of an effective Protecting Tariff.[30]

— II —

THE COMMON MAN

THE Jeffersonians and the National Republicans between them had prepared the theoretical justification for Jacksonian democracy. It took a severe political struggle in most states for the propertyless citizens to gain the right to vote, which they finally won in the twenties. But it had long been clear that according to Locke's theory a citizen was supposed to have property,[1] and the Whig compromise in both England and America whereby the growing numbers of the unpropertied classes were denied the basic civil rights of representative government, was clearly indefensible in republican theory, though it was maintained as long as possible in practice. The Whig emphasis on "we, the people," coupled with their demand for an energetic executive, was enough to sanction Andrew Jackson's regime. Whig national-

[30] Francis Bowen, *American Political Economy* (New York, 1870), pp. 494–95.
[1] Harrington had defined a commonwealth as a state in which "the whole people are landlords."

ism, too, had provided the American equivalent of Rousseau's "general will." Though it is difficult to find a reasoned defense in America of Rousseau's proposition that the will of the people is always right,[2] it had become since Madison an axiom of American political theory that the will of the people is sovereign. It remained only to educate the sovereign, or, to repeat Madison's phrase, to enlighten public opinion.

It was fear rather than faith that brought in political democracy. James Fenimore Cooper expressed the prevailing sentiment.

the habits, opinions, laws, and I may say principles of the Americans, are getting daily to be more democratic. We are perfectly aware, that while the votes of a few thousand scattered individuals can make no great or lasting impression on the prosperity or policy of the country, their disaffection at being excluded might give a great deal of trouble.[3]

The country slipped from classical republicanism into Jacksonian democracy, without being aware that a theoretical reconstruction was called for. Cooper was an exception, for he made a careful critique of Jacksonian confusions in his *The American Democrat* (1838), trying to cling to his Jeffersonian principles, his aristocratic tastes, and hatred of demagoguery, without betraying his genuine faith in democracy. For the philosophy of democracy, Cooper's work is worth more attention than it receives, and certainly worth more than that of De Tocqueville. Even in his earlier writing he took the trouble to examine the common opinion that property interests should be represented and he stated concisely the more democratic position.

We have come to the conclusion, that it is scarcely worth while to do so much violence to natural justice, without sufficient reason, as to disfranchise a man merely because he is poor. Though a trifling *qualification* of property may sometimes be useful, in particular conditions of society, there can be no greater fallacy than its *representation*. . . . A man may be a voluntary associate in a joint-stock company, and justly have a right to a participation

[2] The nearest approach to the *vox populi vox dei* doctrine is to be found in Edward Everett's "Oration on the First Battles of the Revolutionary War," Concord, April 19, 1825; see his collected *Orations and Speeches*, 4th ed. (Boston, 1856), p. 97.

[3] James Fenimore Cooper, *Notions of the Americans; Picked Up by a Travelling Bachelor* (Philadelphia, 1828), I, 265–66.

in its management, in proportion to his pecuniary interest; but life is not a chartered institution. Men are born with all their wants and passions, their means of enjoyment, and their sources of misery without any agency of their own, and frequently to their great discomfort. Now, though government is, beyond a doubt, a sort of compact, it would seem that those who prescribe its conditions are under a natural obligation to consult the rights of the whole.

The theory of representation of property says, that the man who has little shall not dispose of the money of him who has more. Now, what say experience and common sense? It is the man who has *much* that is prodigal of the public purse. A sum that is trifling in his account, may constitute the substance of one who is poorer. Beyond all doubt, the government of the world, which is most reckless of the public money, is that in which power is the exclusive property of the very rich . . .

We find that our government is cheaper, and even stronger, for being popular. There is no doubt that the jealousy of those who have little, often induces a false economy, and that money might frequently be saved by bidding higher for talent. We lay no claims to perfection, but we do say, that more good is attained in this manner than in any other which is practised elsewhere.[4]

Here the issue between Locke and Rousseau at last comes into the open, and democracy is clearly distinguished from Whiggism.

By 1825 it was a foregone conclusion that the common men would come into power. There remained only to foresee the terrible consequences of that event. The mixture of reverence and condescension toward democracy, which finds its classic expression in De Tocqueville's *Democracy in America,* was shared by many an American gentleman. For though the feudal classes had failed to take root in America and American society was regarded by Europeans as democratic by nature, there was evident in all the Eastern states a growing class consciousness between rich and poor, which undercut and confused the rivalry of sectional interests. On both sides this class consciousness took the form of vilification. The literature of Jacksonian democracy abounds in epithets, but is lacking in philosophy. The nearest one gets to a philosophical formulation of this class struggle is the occasional

[4] *Ibid.,* I, 264–67. The system of property representation is satirized in Cooper's novel *The Monikins.*

assertion of "the right to property." Thomas Skidmore, one of the first labor leaders, wrote in 1829 an effective tract under the title *The Rights of Man to Property*.

Ye proud and rich possessors of the earth, look at this, and see if it be not . . . in your power to consent to a more *honorable* method of obtaining title to possession; say, if ye will not do so? I do not ask you, because it is in your power to confer any favor by giving such consent; for, this community, and every other, whenever they shall understand their rights, will have power enough in their own hands to do what they shall think fit, without seeking for any acquisition from you; but because it will be more agreeable to your own true happiness, to give such consent freely; than, with the ill, but unavailing grace of reluctance. Three hundred thousand freemen, in this State, hold votes in their hands, which no power that you can command can take out; and of these freemen, more than two hundred and fifty thousand are men whom a preceding generation, together with yourselves and their own ignorance of their rights have conspired to place in situations such that they have no property in the State of which they are citizens; although their title to such property is as good as that of any man that breathes.[5]

This went straight to the roots of the real issue in theory and practice. But on the whole the Jacksonian democrats followed the example of their betters and engaged in the most scurrilous vituperation, not as contributions to democratic political economy, but as contributions to democratic political campaigns. The arts of political rhetoric, as De Tocqueville carefully explained, were crowding out the more enlightened arts of argument.

The New England Federalists had set a bad example in this form of controversy. "Squire" Fisher Ames, noted as a dignified gentleman, said: "It [democracy] is an illuminated Hell that in the midst of remorse, horror and torture, rings with festivity; for experience shows, that one joy remains to this most malignant description of the damned, the power to make others wretched." [6] And Noah Webster complained that a bill democratizing the Massachusetts suffrage would prostrate the wealth of individuals "to the rapaciousness of a merciless

[5] Thomas Skidmore, *The Rights of Man to Property! Being a Proposition to Make It Equal among the Adults of the Present Generation* (1829); Chapter VIII, in Thorp, Curti, and Baker, *American Issues* (Philadelphia, 1941), I, 233–34.

[6] Fisher Ames, *Works; the Dangers of American Liberty* (Boston, 1809), p. 432.

gang who have nothing to lose." [7] In the Federalist journals the Democrats were commonly described as "men of desperate fortunes as in morals," "the dregs of mankind," "slaves of vice and indigence," men who can never be reformed, since "their quarrel is with nature and is eternal," etc. To such *ad hominem* remarks the Democrats retorted in kind. The significance of such polemic is clear: the issue in everyone's mind when democracy was mentioned, was not democracy literally, but the clash between rich and poor. Democracy was not a theory of popular government, but a symbol of class conflict. It is, therefore, to the literature of this conflict that we must turn if we wish to understand the spirit of Jacksonian democracy.

In New England the first serious blow to the complacency of the liberals came when some of the respectable (i.e., propertied) Democrats began to speak of "the people," not in the loose, philanthropic way of Jeffersonians, but in a half-romantic, half-prophetic tone, suggesting that even the poor should be trusted. Take, for example, the oration by the democratic historian, George Bancroft, delivered at Williams College, which was suspected of democratic sympathies, in 1835, during the height of Jacksonian politics.

There is a spirit in man: not in the privileged few; not in those of us only who by the favor of Providence have been nursed in public schools: *it is in man:* it is the attribute of the race. The spirit, which is the guide to truth, is the gracious gift to each member of the human family.

If reason is a universal faculty, the universal decision is the nearest criterion of truth. The common mind winnows opinions; it is the sieve which separates error from certainty.

If with us the arts are destined to a brilliant career, the inspiration must spring from the vigor of the people. Genius will not create, to flatter patrons or decorate saloons. It yearns for larger influences; it feeds on wider sympathies.

The public happiness is the true object of legislation, and can be secured only by the masses of mankind themselves awakening to the knowledge and the care of their own interests. Our free institutions have reversed the false and ignoble distinctions between men; and refusing to gratify the pride of

[7] Cited in W. A. Robinson, *Jeffersonian Democracy in New England* (New Haven, 1916), p. 123.

caste, have acknowledged the common mind to be the true material for a commonwealth.

The exact measure of the progress of civilization is the degree in which the intelligence of the common mind has prevailed over wealth and brute force; in other words, the measure of the progress of civilization is the progress of the people.[8]

This might have passed for academic rhetoric and "German" [9] romanticism, had it not been for the cold fact that President Jackson had just vetoed the National Bank Bill, expressing in his message a violent and intensely practical version of the same doctrines, and that the orator had himself favored Jackson's attack on the Bank. He had also been nominated as a state senator by the newly-formed Workingmen's Party; though he declined the nomination, he was tempted to accept in order to defy the warning of his friend Ticknor to keep away from "Jacksonians and Workies." He wrote to his other close friend and associate in German studies, Edward Everett, "the man of letters cannot have brilliant success in politics except on the popular side." He shrewdly calculated that he would be more "popular," if instead of submitting his fortunes to any one of the anti-Whig groups, he labored to unite them—the Workingmen's Party, the Democratic Party, and the Anti-Masonic Party.

Bancroft was typical of Jacksonian democracy in his ability to assert with conviction the reasonableness of the common man and the "common mind" and, at the same time, to engage in the most blatant forms

[8] George Bancroft, "The Office of the People in Art, Government, and Religion," in *Literary and Historical Miscellanies* (New York, 1855), pp. 409, 415, 418–19, 422; in Blau, ed., *American Philosophic Addresses, 1700–1900*, pp. 98–114.

[9] Bancroft was one of those young Harvard men who had imbibed deeply of German romanticism during their postgraduate studies abroad. It appears that Bancroft's distinctive democratic ideas dawned on him as an application of Kantian ethics and Schleiermacher's theology. He formulated them first, not as a theory of politics or interpretation of history, but as a philosophy of education. He noted the following ingenious principles as a program for the school which he and his associates later founded at Northampton: (1) Greek language, first of all the languages; (2) natural history for mental discipline; (3) elimination of classroom competition; (4) abolition of corporal punishment, as degrading; (5) classes to be adapted to individual variability; (6) orphans to be educated as country schoolmasters; (7) a printing establishment for the school. Bancroft's transition from democratic school to democratic politics is amusingly described by his biographer. See Russel B. Nye, *George Bancroft: Brahmin Rebel* (New York, 1944), p. 74.

of demagoguery. Here are his notes for a campaign speech, a perspicu-
ous piece of "social philosophy," half faith, half flattery.

To assert the rights of labor is the mission of the age. Each interest that
has won its rights finds its best friend in Democracy. . . .

Farmers are the true material for a republic, capable of receiving a good
impression, an elegant stamp, the true marble, fit to be wrought into the
likeness of a God. The upright yeomanry is the material; liberty is the soul.

Rewards of labor. Should have the products of labor. He who labors
much should have much and the reverse. The merchant does not produce:
he does but exchange. Hence the city lives on the labor of the manufacturer
and the farmer.

The farmers achieved the Revolution aided by mechanics. The furtherance of our liberty rests on the mechanics.

The people is the sovereign. The man of letters is his counsellor. That is,
in this country the educated men are the privy council to the sovereign.[10]

It is not easy to tell when Bancroft thinks he is telling the truth and
when he is playing politics. Similarly, his *History of the United States*,
or, as it is more accurately called, "history of the American people,"
was both an objective account of the evolution of freedom in America
and also, as his friends said, "a vote for Jackson." Bancroft believed
that history is the history of freedom and the day of judgment. When
he spoke of the "common mind" he meant the collective mind of the
people; his transcendentalism was closer to Hegel's than to Emerson's.
Accordingly, when he wrote to his fellow worker Orestes Brownson,
"the day for the multitude has now arrived," he was both recording
a fact of history and passing judgment.

As Bancroft was a source of embarrassment to Boston, so Brownson
was to Bancroft, for he pushed democracy in both theory and practice
a bit farther than the Democratic Party could afford to go. He had
been inspired to work for institutional reform by Frances Wright.
Typical of her appeal was:

I speak to a public whose benevolence has been long harrowed by increasing pauperism, and whose social order and social happiness are threatened
by increasing vice. . . . I speak to honest men who tremble for their honesty. . . . I speak to human beings surrounded by human suffering, to
fellow citizens pledged to fellow feeling, to republicans pledged to equal

[10] *Ibid.*, p. 109.

rights, and, as a consequent, to equal condition and equal enjoyments; I call them to *unite*.

Look abroad on the misery which is gaining on the land! Mark the strife, and the discord, and the jealousies, the shock of interests and opinions. . . . Go! Mark all the wrongs and the wretchedness with which the eye and the ear and the heart are familiar, and then echo in triumph and celebrate in jubilee the insulting declaration—*all men are free and equal!* [11]

The remedy for existing evils must be found in changing the existing system. Miss Wright braved unpopularity when, as a visiting English-woman, she brought home to American audiences that though there were American features (especially political) in the much-vaunted "American system," its dominant institutions (especially economic) were those of the European system. She forced Americans to face the consequences in terms of happiness and misery of their political econ-omy and to translate the basic problems of morals and education into these terms.

Orestes Augustus Brownson came to Boston in 1836 to organize The Society for Christian Union and Progress; there was enough Universalism left in him to incline him toward Channing's "catholic christianity without a church" rather than toward openly free thought, and there was enough of *The Free Enquirer* in him to make him look among freethinking workingmen for social progress. In upstate New York, where he had worked first with liberal Universalists and then with Robert Owen and Frances Wright (as contributing editor for their *Free Enquirer*), Brownson was a literary genius and a religious radical; in Boston he was a philistine and an agitator. In 1840, in the columns of his pretentious *Boston Quarterly*, there appeared his sensa-tional sermon-article, "The Laboring Classes," which shocked "the middle classes" (to use Brownson's vulgar term) into class conscious-ness.

Now this middle class, which was strong enough to defeat nearly all the practical benefit of the French Revolution, is the natural enemy of the Chartists. . . . Our despair for the poor Chartists arises from the num-ber and power of the middle class. . . . Their only real enemy is in the

[11] From "Lecture on Existing Evils and Their Remedy," June 2, 1819, Phila-delphia; in Frances Wright, *A Course of Popular Lectures* (New York, 1829), pp. 152–53, 157.

employer. In all countries it is the same. . . . Universal education we shall not be thought likely to depreciate; but we confess that we are unable to see in it that sovereign remedy for the evils of the social state as it is, which some of our friends do, or say they do. . . . For God's sake beware how you kindle within the working classes the intellectual spark. . . . If you will doom them to the external condition of brutes, do in common charity keep their minds and hearts brutish. . . . And now commences the new struggle between the operative and his employer, between wealth and labor. Every day does this struggle extend further and wax stronger and fiercer; what or when the end will be God only knows. . . . We are no advocates of slavery . . . but we say frankly that, if there must always be a laboring population distinct from proprietors and employers, we regard the slave system as decidedly preferable to the system at wages. . . . We see no means of elevating the laboring classes which can be effectual without . . . the strong arm of physical force. It will come, if it ever come at all, only at the conclusion of war, the like of which the world as yet has never witnessed.[12]

Bancroft explained hurriedly, "Brownson has played the deuce with us by his visionary doctrines." Brownson himself later confessed (in *The Convert*) that, though he was himself shocked when he reread his "horrible doctrines" of 1840, he was unable "to detect any unsoundness" in his views regarding the relation of capital and labor and the wage system. The immediate consequence of the publication of such views was to make it necessary for him, along with Hawthorne, to seek refuge among the transcendentalists at Brook Farm.

A greater thorn in Bancroft's philosophical side than Brownson was Richard Hildreth, of Deerfield, Massachusetts. A Whig in politics, a lawyer by profession, and a freethinker, Hildreth became a convert to Jeremy Bentham's philosophy and used it very effectively to give expression to democratic ideals. His way of promoting the cause of reform was in every way antithetical to Bancroft's: a radical utilitarian, using the methods of inductive science, relying on economic rather than political measures, Hildreth worked out a systematic social science for social revolution, whereas Bancroft grandly prophesied the advent of the new era while he played the political game. Hildreth was temperamentally as violent and impulsive as Brownson, but his philosophy was the essence of sobriety; Brownson advocated violence, Hildreth advocated what he called "increased productivity" and intel-

[12] Blau, ed., *American Philosophic Addresses, 1700–1900*, pp. 179–83, 203–4.

ligence; neither philosopher, it seems, has been practically effective to date, though the unwitting intellectual descendants of each are now reviving much the same issues that troubled them and advocating similar measures. Hildreth's system is unique in the American tradition and deserves to be revived both for its historical uniqueness, America's only Bentham, and for its intrinsic merit as a system of philosophy.

There had been a little Benthamite philosophy of reform in the efforts of Edward Livingston and in the lectures and projects of Frances Wright during the twenties.[13] The distinctive note, revealing Bentham's influence, was her emphasis on the relation of morals to social conditions and on the impracticality of moral reform without institutional reform. In the forties Richard Hildreth attempted the same thing in a more systematic way. He conceived an elaborate body of doctrines, which he did not live to finish; only the first two of the projected six were published, and the third may still exist somewhere in manuscript. The whole was to be "The Rudiments of the Science of Man"; it was to be carried out "in accordance with the Baconian method, by induction from observed phenomena," and comprised the theories of morals, politics, wealth, taste, knowledge, and education. The *Theory of Morals* (1844) contains the general philosophical orientation, which he summed up admirably elsewhere.

The progress and increase of true morality—that morality which consists in making man happier—depends, first, upon the progress of knowledge, enabling us to form a more correct estimate of the real effect of certain actions, or courses of action, on human happiness; and, secondly and principally, upon an increase in the relative force of the sentiment of benevolence, whereby we are impelled to the performance of good actions. I am also led to conclude, *and this is the most important conclusion in the whole book*, that the relative force of the sentiment of benevolence can be most effectually, if not alone, increased, by diminishing the force of those numerous pains by which the impulses of the sentiment of benevolence are perpetually deadened, or counteracted; that it is contrary to the constitution of human nature to expect those who are perpetually tormented by pains of their own, to be much affected by the pains of other people; that to make men better,

[13] One of Miss Wright's books is dedicated "to Jeremy Bentham, as a testimony of her admiration of his enlightened sentiments, useful labours, and active philanthropy, and of her gratitude for his friendship."

we must begin by making them happier; and that all the preachments of all the priests and professors in the world, will avail nothing for the reformation of mankind, so long as those same priests and professors refuse to do anything for the relief of the enormous pains and evils, under which the mass of men suffer; but, on the contrary, do their utmost to perpetuate those evils, representing them as decrees of nature, and ordinances of God.

We shall yet teach the same lesson in philosophy, which we have taught already in politics,—the lesson, namely, that the people can think for, as well as govern, themselves; and that a pope and a priesthood are just as useless, just as pernicious, as a king and an aristocracy.[14]

This ability of men to think for themselves and to govern themselves grows with experience and intelligence; hence, Hildreth concludes, "Morals is a progressive science." Hence, too, the inductive method is historical method. A large part of his *Theory of Politics* is a historical analysis, and the best known of all his works, his *History of the United States of America*, is an attempt to give a strictly factual, "inductive" account of American progress toward democracy. His theory of progress and of history is summed up in a footnote.

Guizot, in his *History of the Civilization of Modern Europe*, was the first to call particular attention to the fourfold distribution of power in the middle ages, such as it is above described. Finding this distribution of power between monarchs, nobles, clergy, and municipalities coincident with the rise and progress of modern civilization, he somewhat hastily concluded that the continued existence and balance of all these classes was and is essential to that progress. Had he been a little less of a scholar, and somewhat more of a philosopher, or had he even possessed the advantage of our American point of view, a more profound and comprehensive study of history, the history of the present day as well as that of the middle ages, might have convinced him that, in the progress of modern European civilization, the monarchic, aristocratic, and clerical elements have only been so far useful as they have served to counteract and to destroy each other; the whole of the actual progress being due to the municipal element alone.[15]

The analysis of the "municipal element," or civic virtue, then becomes his chief theme. It has nothing to do with rights, either natural or

[14] *A Joint Letter to Orestes A. Brownson and the Editor of the North American Review, in Which the Editor of the North American Review Is Proved to Be No Christian, and Little Better Than an Atheist* (Boston, 1844).

[15] Hildreth, *Theory of Politics* (New York, 1853), p. 121n.

divine. Patriotism or public spirit is simply natural benevolence directed toward "the benefit of the community," and in democracy this spirit "becomes diffused through the whole body of the people." The reason democracy has the best chance of making people happy is simply that it can give the greatest possible number a share in "the pleasure of having power." But it cannot operate at all if the pleasures of power are more than offset by the pains of inequality and poverty. Hence a practical democratic ethics (as distinct from "forensic" ethics) must depend on a "general social revolution," which was begun by Rousseau and the French Revolution. "As things now are, the higher, and even the middle classes, suffer almost as much as the lower . . . and as a necessary consequence, Hatred upon both sides! In the midst of so much suffering, Humanity is hard pressed; and virtue can with difficulty hold her own." [16]

This predicament, that "virtue can with difficulty hold her own" "in the midst of so much suffering," suggested to Hildreth the chief theme for his "Theory of Wealth." His thesis was that the suffering cannot be remedied merely by redistribution.

The good things which the combined efforts of any given community can as yet produce are not enough to give hardly a taste to every body; and the masses have of necessity been kept at hard labor, on bread and water, while luxuries and even comforts have been limited to a few. Labor—the sole resource of the mass of the people—has been of little value, because labor has been able to produce but little; and the proceeds of the labor of production being so small, hence the greater stimulus to substitute in place of it fraud and violence as means of acquisition. . . .

The first great necessity, then, of the human race is the increase of the productiveness of human labor. Science has done much in that respect within the last century, and in those to come is destined to do vastly more. Vast new fields are opening on our American continent, on which labor can be profitably employed. So far from labor being the sole source of wealth, all-sufficient in itself, as certain political economists teach, nothing is more certain than that Europe has long suffered, and still suffers, from a plethora or labor—from being obliged to feed and clothe many for whom it has had nothing remunerative to do. The United States of America have now attained to such a development, that they are able easily to absorb from half a million to a million annually of immigrants from Europe. . . .

[16] Hildreth, *Theory of Morals* (Boston, 1844), pp. 271–72.

The development of productive industry seems then to be at this moment one of the greatest and most crying necessities of the human race. But what is more essential to this development than peace and social order? . . .

This socialist question of the distribution of wealth once raised is not to be blinked out of sight. The claims set up by the socialists, based as they are upon philosophic theories of long standing, having, at least some of them, many ardent supporters even in the ranks of those who denounce the socialists the loudest, cannot be settled by declamations and denunciations, and mutual recriminations, any more than by bayonets and artillery. It is a question for philosophers; and until some solution of it can be reached which both sides shall admit to be conclusive, what the party of progress needs is not action—for which it is at present disqualified by internal dissensions—but deliberation and discussion. The engineers must first bridge this gulf of separation before all the drumming, and fifing, and shouting in the world can again unite the divided column, and put it into effectual motion.[17]

On the engineers depends the hope of the social revolution. This is the note on which Hildreth's *Theory of Politics* closes. In his philosophy the characteristic themes of Whig nationalism and of Jacksonian protest are combined into an impressive and up-to-date theory of social and scientific planning.

In New York City Jacksonian democracy found a peculiarly forceful expression. The editors of the *New York Evening Post*, William Cullen Bryant and William Leggett, in the thirties, and of the *Brooklyn Daily Eagle*, Walt Whitman, in the forties, set a high standard for journalism and gave literary brilliance and political principles to a Democratic Party that needed both in order to be respectable. Both Bryant and Whitman were educated in the principles of free trade and laissez faire, but, under the stimulus of the leftwing leadership of Leggett and Parke Godwin, they applied their classical principles in a novel way.

In 1835 Tammany Hall was split into two factions. The radical, anti-monopoly faction, or Workingmen's Party, finding itself literally in the dark after the conservatives had nominated their candidate and turned out the light, remained in the hall, and by the use of "locofoco" matches and candlelight organized as an independent body. This group gained power and became known nationally as leaders in the cause of labor as well as against the banks, and their type of democracy,

[17] Hildreth, *Theory of Politics*, pp. 271, 272, 273–74.

known popularly as Locofocoism, became the dominant note of Northern Jacksonianism. William Leggett was the most articulate spokesman for its principles, though Bryant did it great service by lending it the wholehearted support of a New Englander. From their editorials in the *Post* the following selections will give the reader a fair idea of the temper of this movement.

Can anything be imagined more abhorrent to every sentiment of generosity or justice than the law which arms the rich with the legal right to fix, by assize, the wages of the poor? If this is not slavery, we have forgotten its definition. Strike the right of associating for the sale of labour from the privileges of a freeman, and you may as well at once bind him to a master, or ascribe him to the soil. If it be not in the colour of his skin, and in the poor franchise of naming his own terms in a contract for his work, what advantage has the labourer of the north over the bondman of the south? Punish by human laws a "determination not to work," make it penal by any other penalty than idleness inflicts, and it matters little whether the task-masters be one or many, an individual or an order, the hateful scheme of slavery will have gained a foothold in the land. . . .

The rich perceive, acknowledge, and act upon a common interest, and why not the poor? Yet the moment the latter are called upon to combine for the preservation of their rights, forsooth the community is in danger! Property is no longer secure, and life in jeopardy. This cant has descended to us from those times when the poor and labouring classes had no stake in the community, and no rights except such as they could acquire by force. But the times have changed, though the cant remains the same. . . .

Of all the countries on the face of the earth, or that ever existed on the face of the earth, this is the one where the claims of wealth and aristocracy are the most unfounded, absurd and ridiculous. With no claim to hereditary distinctions; with no exclusive rights except what they derive from monopolies, and no power of perpetuating their estates in their posterity, the assumption of aristocratic airs and claims is supremely ridiculous. Tomorrow they themselves may be beggars for aught they know, or at all events their children may become so.

.   .   .

But let us ask what and where is the danger of a combination of the labouring classes in vindication of their political principles, or in defence of their menaced rights? Have they not the right to act in concert, when their opponents act in concert? Nay, is it not their bounden duty to combine against the only enemy they have to fear as yet in this free country, monopoly and a great paper system that grinds them to dust? Truly this is strange republican doctrine, and this is a strange republican country, where men cannot unite in one common effort, in one common cause, without rousing the cry of danger to the rights of person and property. Is not this a government of the people, founded on the rights of the people, and instituted for the express object of guarding them against the encroachments and usurpations of power? And if they are not permitted the possession of common interest; the exercise of a common feeling; if they cannot combine to resist, by constitutional means, these encroachments; to what purpose were they declared free to exercise the right of suffrage in the choice of rulers, and the making of laws? . . .

There are some journalists who affect to entertain great horror of combinations, considering them as utterly adverse to the principles of free trade; and it is frequently recommended to make them penal by law. Our notions of free trade were acquired in a different school, and dispose us to leave men entirely at liberty to effect a proper object either by concerted or individual action. The character of combinations, in our view, depends entirely upon the intrinsic character of the end which is aimed at. . . .

There is but one bulwark behind which mechanics and labourers may safely rally to oppose a common enemy, who, if they ventured singly into the field against him, would cut them to pieces: that bulwark is the *Principle of Combination*. We would advise them to take refuge behind it only in extreme cases, because in their collisions with their employers, as in those between nations, the manifold evils of a siege are experienced, more or less, by both parties, and are therefore to be incurred only in extreme emergencies.[18]

The spirit of Locofoco democracy was embodied among New England intellectuals chiefly by Bancroft and Hawthorne, but even Emerson was touched by it. His series of lectures in Boston for 1839–40 carried the title *The Present Age*, and in the course of them Emerson explained how the corrosive progress of reason in human society destroyed the "dread" of tradition, how it then "separated utilities from the labor they should represent," how "the end to be rich infects the whole world," but, Emerson continued, referring to economic democracy, "on the whole, the Movement Party gains steadily, and as by the movement of the world itself. The great idea that gave hope to

---

[18] Bernard Smith, ed., *The Democratic Spirit* (New York, 1941), pp. 210, 214–15, 215–16, 218–19.

men's hearts creeps on the world like the advance of morning twilight." [19] Theodore Parker, who attended the first lecture, reported:

It was *Democratic-Locofoco* throughout, and very much in the spirit of Brownson's article on Democracy and Reform in the last *Quarterly* [Brownson's review]. . . . Bancroft was in ecstasies,—he was rapt beyond vision at the *locofocoism* of the lecture, and said to me the next evening, "It is a great thing to say such things before any audience, however small, much more to plant these doctrines in such minds: but let him come with *us*, before the 'Bay State,' and we will give him three thousand listeners.". . . One grave, Whig-looking gentleman heard Emerson the other night, and said he could only account for his delivering such a lecture on the supposition that he wished to get a place in the Custom-House under George Bancroft.[20]

Walt Whitman's style and thought were more sentimental than either the New York *Post* or Emerson; they resembled Bancroft. His editorials carried on the Locofoco cause for another decade. For example:

The leading spirits of the Democratic faith are always in advance of the age; and they have, therefore, to fight against old prejudices. The contest they engage in does not call for brute courage but moral courage.

No one, we have the authority of Jefferson himself for saying, can realize the afflicting persecutions and insults they had to brook amid that gloomy period, the administration of the older Adams. But resting on their own staunch manly hearts, and defended by the breastplate of a righteous cause, they faltered not. Throwing to the winds all fear, they came out before the people, incessantly teaching and expounding their doctrine, and openly proclaiming the falseness and injustice of their opponents' creed. . . . We stand here the inheritors of their principles and opposed to the same foe— the foe of equal rights. Democracy must conquer again as it did then—and more certainly than it did then. We think so from two simple facts. One is that the great body of workingmen are more powerful and more enlightened now than they were in those days. The other is, that there is a mighty and restless energy throughout the length and breadth of this nation, for going

[19] James Elliot Cabot, *A Memoir of Ralph Waldo Emerson* (New York, 1887), II, 13.

[20] *Ibid.*, II, 18-19. These lectures have apparently never been published as they were delivered. Further information about their content and aim can be gleaned from Emerson's *Journal*, V, 278-350, and his *Letters* (ed. by R. L. Rusk), II, 246-47, 255-56.

onward to the very verge with our experiment of popular freedom. . . .

In less than twenty years from this time, we venture to predict, with every assurance of safety, the nation will find, boldly promulgated in its midst, and supported by numerous and powerful advocates, notions of law, government and social custom, as different from the present day as Leggett's and Jefferson's to those of past ages. We must be constantly pressing onward—every year throwing the doors wider and wider—and carrying our experiment of democratic freedom to the very verge of the limit.

The old and moth-eaten systems of Europe have had their day, and that evening of their existence which is nigh at hand, will be the token of a glorious dawn for the down-trodden people. *Here*, we have planted the standard of freedom, and here we will test the capacities of men for self-government. We will see whether the law of happiness and preservation upon each individual, acting directly upon himself, be not a safer dependence than musty charters and time-worn prerogatives of tyrants. Doctrines that even now are scarcely breathed—innovations which the most fearless hardly dare propose openly—systems of policy that men would speak of at the present day in the low tones of fear, for very danger lest they might be scouted as worse than Robespierrian revolutionists (that hacknied bug-bear theme which has never been presented in its fairness to the people of this Republic) will, in course of time, see the light here, and meet the sanction of popular favor and go into practical play. Nor let us fear that this may result in harm. All that we enjoy of freedom was in the beginning but an experiment.[21]

The experiment of "carrying our experiment of democratic freedom to the very verge of the limit" included, in Whitman's conception of it, the expansion of the labor movement, but it was the very antithesis of socialism. Whitman was what in Europe would be called a syndicalist, and he justified his repudiation of social legislation in favor of direct action on the good old principle of laissez faire. But the kind of social legislation to which he then objected specifically was temperance legislation and "all efforts to legislate men into religion and virtue." In a series of editorials during 1847 he justified these principles as follows.

Although government can do little *positive* good to the people, it may do an *immense deal of harm*. And here is where the beauty of the Democratic principle comes in. Democracy would prevent all this harm. It would have

[21] Walt Whitman, *The Gathering of the Forces* (New York, 1920), I, 7, 8–9, 10–11.

no man's benefit achieved at the expense of his neighbors. It would have no one's rights infringed upon and that, after all, is pretty much the sum and substance of the prerogatives of government. How beautiful and harmonious a system! How it transcends all other codes, as the golden rule, in its brevity, transcends the ponderous tomes of philosophic lore! While mere politicians, in their narrow minds, are sweating and fuming with their complicated statutes, this one single rule, rationally construed and applied, is enough to form the starting point of all that is necessary in government: *to make no more laws than those useful for preventing a man or body of men from infringing on the rights of other men.*

. . .

One of the favorite doctrines of leading Whigs teaches the intricacy and profundity of the science of government. According to them, the most elaborate study and education are required in any one who would comprehend the deep mysteries, the hidden wonders, of the ruling of a nation, and the controlling of a people. . . . The error lies in the desire after *management,* the great curse of our Legislation: everything is to be regulated and made straight by force of statute. And all this while, evils are accumulating, in very consequence of excessive management. . . .

Under the specious pretext of effecting "the happiness of the whole community," nearly all the wrongs and intrusions of government have been carried through. The legislature may, and should, when such things fall in its way, lend its potential weight to the cause of virtue and happiness—but to legislate in direct behalf of those objects is never available, and rarely effects any even temporary benefit. Indeed sensible men have long seen that "the best government is that which governs least." And we are surprised that the spirit of this maxim is not oftener and closer to the hearts of our domestic leaders. . . .

It is all folly to expect from *law,* the popular virtues, worth, and self-denial, which must come from entirely different sources—from the influence and example of home, from well-rooted principles, from a habit of morality. We have therefore little faith in laws that interfere with morals. We have no faith at all in the efforts of law to make men *good.*[22]

[22] Walt Whitman, *The Gathering of the Forces* (New York, 1920), I, 52–53, 53, 54, 56–57, 59.

YOUNG AMERICA

GRADUALLY the Whig program for an energetic government gave way to a faith in the "manifest destiny" of America, and the Democrats transformed the concept of the "American system" into the concept of the natural progress of the American people. After the gloom of 1837 had passed, the rapid expansion westward, the industrial revolution, and the growing political prestige of the United States combined to create a fervid optimism and patriotism; when the excitement of the gold rush and of the 1848 revolutions in Europe were added and the Missouri Compromise of the slavery question had been achieved, the flames of confidence burned into an intense national bonfire of faith in progress and in America's leadership. This glowing optimism of the fifties was the worst possible mental preparation for the tragedy of the sixties.

One of Emerson's lectures epitomizes this transition from Whig to Democratic nationalism; he delivered it in 1844 to the Mercantile Library Association of Boston and entitled it *The Young American*. In the first part he paid his tribute to the cultural significance of the railroad and other "improvements," to the opening up of western land, to the growth of commerce, and called America "the country of the Future . . . a country of beginnings, of projects, of designs, of expectations." He then turned from this Whig picture of human construction and improvement with: "Gentlemen, there is a sublime and friendly Destiny by which the human race is guided." He expanded this "destiny" as a work of nature, not of government.

This beneficent tendency, omnipotent without violence, exists and works. Every line of history inspires a confidence that we shall not go far wrong; that things mend. That is the moral of all we learn, that it warrants Hope, the prolific mother of reforms. Our part is plainly not to throw ourselves across the track, to block improvement, and sit till we are stone, but to watch the uprise of successive mornings, and to conspire with the new works of new days. Government has been a fossil; it should be a plant. I conceive that the office of statute law should be to express, and not to impede the mind of mankind. New thoughts, new things. Trade was one instrument, but Trade is also but for a time, and must give way to somewhat broader and better, whose signs are already dawning in the sky. . . .

In consequence of the revolution in the state of society wrought by trade, Government in our times is beginning to wear a clumsy and cumbrous appearance. We have already seen our way to shorter methods. The time is full of good signs. Some of them shall ripen to fruit. All this beneficent socialism is a friendly omen, and the swelling cry of voices for the education of the people, indicates that Government has other offices than those of banker and executioner. . . .

Look across the country from any hill-side around us, and the landscape seems to crave Government. The actual differences of men must be acknowledged, and met with love and wisdom. These rising grounds which command the champaign below, seem to ask for lords, true lords, *land*-lords, who understand the land and its uses, and the applicabilities of men, and whose government would be what it should, namely, mediation between want and supply. How gladly would each citizen pay a commission for the support and continuation of good guidance. . . . There really seems a progress towards such a state of things, in which this work shall be done by these natural workmen; and this, not certainly through any increased discretion shown by the citizens at elections, but by the gradual contempt into which official government falls, and the increasing disposition of private adventurers to assume its fallen functions. . . .

We must have kings, and we must have nobles. Nature provides such in every society,—only let us have the real instead of the titular. Let us have our leading and our inspiration from the best. In every society some men are born to rule, and some to advise. Let the powers be well directed, directed by love, and they would everywhere be greeted with joy and honour. . . .

I call upon you, young men, to obey your heart, and be the nobility of this land. In every age of the world, there has been a leading nation, one of a more generous sentiment, whose eminent citizens were willing to stand for the interests of general justice and humanity, at the risk of being called, by the men of the moment, chimerical and fantastic. Which should be that nation but these States? Which should lead that movement, if not New England? Who should lead the leaders, but the Young American? . . .

Gentlemen, the development of our American internal resources, the extension to the utmost of the commercial system, and the appearance of new moral causes which are to modify the state, are giving an aspect of greatness to the Future, which the imagination fears to open. One thing is plain for all men of common sense and common conscience, that here, here in America, is the home of man.[1]

This conception of America's destiny created a new type of democratic theory. The guiding hand of nature was not that of natural law, but of natural resources, material and human, a nonpolitical type of common good which guaranteed to the American people as a whole an indefinite progress in every direction. When as sober and cautious a mind as Emerson's could indulge in these extravagant hopes, the boundless, fanatical optimism and jingoism of the young "aristocrats" to whom Emerson appealed can readily be imagined. One of them, the ever-young Walt Whitman, "yawped" in his *Daily Eagle*:

While the foreign press—a good portion of it, at least—is pouring out ridicule on this Republic and her chosen ones—Yankeedoodledom is going ahead with the resistless energy of a sixty-five-hundred-thousand-horsepower steam engine! It is carrying everything before it South and West, and may one day put the Canadas and Russian America (Alaska) in its fob pocket! Whether it does these things in a conventionally "genteel" style or not, isn't the thing: but that it will tenderly regard human life, property and rights, whatever step it takes, there is no doubt. At all events, Yankeedoodledom will never *never* be guilty of furnishing duplicates to the Chinese war, the "operations of the British in India," or the "extinguishment of Poland." Let the Old World wag on under its cumbrous load of form and conservatism; we are of a newer, fresher race and land. And all we have to say is, to point to fifty years hence and say, Let those laugh who win! [2]

This fanaticism was certainly as great as our own, in fact, it was at bottom the same fanaticism with which we are still afflicted. It soon took practical shape in a political movement. The ambitious Democrats, eager for a more aggressive foreign policy, eager to "make progress," as they called it, in all fields, began ridiculing the "old fogies" in the party and began to groom a leader for "Young America," the name they adopted for their "movement." They chose Stephen A. Douglas, and for a brief time it looked as if this "little giant" of the Midwest would devote himself to the cause of insur-

[1] Ralph Waldo Emerson, *The Works*. Bohn's Standard Library (London, 1885), II, 300–6 *passim*.
[2] Walt Whitman, *The Gathering of the Forces* (New York, 1920), I, 32–33.

gency; but, being an experienced politician, he committed himself to
no faction, while encouraging all; and, being intelligent, he could not
agree that the slavery question had been solved. When Franklin Pierce
was chosen the Democratic candidate for President in 1852, the Young
Americans immediately hailed *him* as their man. They did succeed in
getting into the platform their chief slogan.

With the recent development of this grand political truth,—of the sovereignty of the people and their capacity and power for self-government,
which is prostrating thrones and erecting republics on the ruins of despotism
in the Old World,—we feel that a high and sacred duty is devolved, with
increasing responsibility, upon the Democratic party of this country . . . to
sustain and advance among us constitutional liberty, . . . and uphold the
Union as it was, the Union as it is, and the Union as it shall be.[3]

The chief political spokesman of the group was George N. Sanders of
Kentucky, then editor of the New York *Democratic Review*, but
Sanders's campaign literature and editorials were so ridiculously ex-
travagant that it would be an insult to philosophy to discuss them here.
Suffice it to quote a bit of verse from this magazine, which will serve
to illustrate the general level of its "thought" and taste.

> Action, like the Sun is fruitful, ever glorious, ever young,
> Building up collossal structures to outlive the pen and tongue—
> Whose broad shadows sweep the future till the sun-rays o'er them find
> Congenial base to build upon—the granite of the mind.
>
> . . .
>
> Age don't measure manhood's stamen: only labor's young and bold,
> And inaction, loathsome hecatomb of God's abortions, old
> Thought is labor, and the progress or the death of mind, marks time,
> "Life is labor," labor's progress!—is vitality a crime?
>
> . . .
>
> Wherever Action leaves the past, and brings the future near—
> Where'er electric progress leaps from customs cloudy sphere—
> Wherever Thought, like nature, yearly fruits progressive bloom,
> And where Free-Will, like Christ, escapes all living from earth's tomb—
>
> . . .

[3] Lawrence Sargent Hall, *Hawthorne: Critic of Society* (New Haven, 1944), p.
102.

Oh! *there* is Young America—the "Star of Empire" West—
Its seventy years of glory rolling round it like a vest
Of light—as round Uranus farthest star *old* earth above
Its satellites triumphant roll in honor to their love.

. . .

There! there is Young America in youthful thought sublime,
Its starry beacon flung out as a hope to every clime,
E'en as the starry flag of God, the world's dark chaos o'er,
Invites each man that will be saved to an immortal shore! [4]

It is difficult to characterize this progressive group of the fifties. Sanders was a Jacksonian Democrat fighting primarily the Jeffersonian Virginia aristocracy that had controlled Kentucky politics for two generations. In the House of Representatives Young America had members from Ohio, Mississippi, Alabama, Tennessee, and California. There was a scattered band of Kossuth enthusiasts throughout the country, led by Senator Soulé of Louisiana, who were willing to intervene in the Hungarian revolt and in the struggles of European liberals in general. There were businessmen who hoped an expanded merchant marine would bring a boom in the export trade, etc.—a great variety of interests led to a variety of emphases, but they were all agreed that the slavery issue should be regarded as settled by the Missouri Compromise and that the Union must go "forward" in confidence. President Pierce, who voiced this sentiment in his inaugural address, apparently believed quite firmly that the worst danger to the Union had passed.

Among this motley group one member should especially hold our attention, for to him, even more than to Emerson, this movement represented a great crisis in history, and he devoted himself wholeheartedly to it both in thought and action. Nathaniel Hawthorne's "Young Americanism" was a distinctive brand of democracy, and it expressed one of the deepest of his ideals. In him it was primarily neither political nor economic democracy, but social—a love of social equality and a preference for classless society. He was a "pure" democrat, a man of the people.

Even as a youth in Salem and at Bowdoin College, in Maine, he

[4] "Young America!" *Democratic Review*, XXXI (1852), 86–87, Stanzas I, VI, XII, XIII, XVIII.

was conscientiously shy, that is, he made it a habit and an ideal *not* to be distinguished, at a time when all about him were cultivating individuality. He refused to mount a platform, and in other ways he gave his fellows to understand that even his chosen career as a writer was to be humble. "I shall never make a distinguished figure in the world, and all I hope or wish is to plod along with the multitude." [5] He was not ambitious and even loathed working for a living. "Labor is the curse of the world, and nobody can meddle with it, without becoming proportionably brutified," he wrote to his sweetheart after his disillusionment over Brook Farm. He had hoped to have a maximum of leisure there with a minimum of labor, and the nearest he could come to this ideal state was during the years when he enjoyed Democratic political patronage at the Salem customhouse and at the Liverpool consulate. But his hatred of labor was neither indolence nor snobbery; it was, as in the case of Thoreau, a discriminating sense of values. Hawthorne's Puritan conscience took the secular form of a lifelong preoccupation with moral criticism; he criticized carefully himself, his family, his neighbors, his British hosts, and his American government, and always with kindly humor and sincere patriotism. Hawthorne seemed a Puritan ghost in transcendentalist Concord, to say nothing of aristocratic Rome and England, yet in his own mind, his religious, somber democracy had more life in it and a more certain future than did that of the distinguished "dreamers." He understood democracy to be the sober, realistic enterprise of common men, in opposition to the romantic, irresponsible "egotism" of transcendentalist reformers. After his experience at Brook Farm he was particularly caustic in his analysis of such philanthropists.

They have no heart, no sympathy, no reason, no conscience. They will keep no friend, unless he make himself the mirror of their purpose; they will smite and slay you, and trample your dead corpse under foot, all the more readily, if you take the first step with them, and cannot take the second, and the third, and every other step of their terribly strait path. They have an idol to which they consecrate themselves high-priest, and deem it holy work to offer sacrifices of whatever is most precious; and never once seem to suspect—so cunning has the Devil been with them—that this false deity, in

[5] Hawthorne, *The Complete Works;* with introductory notes by George Parsons Lathrop (Cambridge, 1886), Riverside edition, XII, 466; from letter to Bridge, October 13, 1852.

whose iron features, immitigable to all the rest of mankind, they see only benignity and love, is but a spectrum of the very priest himself, projected upon the surrounding darkness. And the higher and purer the original object, and the more unselfishly it may have been taken up, the slighter is the probability that they can be led to recognize the process by which godlike benevolence has been debased into all-devouring egotism. . . .

I felt myself (and, having a decided tendency towards the actual, I never liked to feel it) getting quite out of my reckoning, with regard to the existing state of the world. I was beginning to lose the sense of what kind of a world it was, among innumerable schemes of what it might or ought to be. It was impossible, situated as we were, not to imbibe the idea that everything in nature and human existence was fluid, or fast becoming so; that the crust of the earth in many places was broken, and its whole surface portentously upheaving; that it was a day of crisis, and that we ourselves were in the critical vortex. Our great globe floated in the atmosphere of infinite space like an unsubstantial bubble. No sagacious man will long retain his sagacity, if he live exclusively among reformers and progressive people, without periodically returning into the settled system of things, to correct himself by a new observation from that old standpoint.

It was now time for me, therefore, to go and hold a little talk with the conservatives, the writers of *The North American Review*, the merchants, the politicians, the Cambridge men, and all those respectable old blockheads who still, in this intangibility and mistiness of affairs, kept a death-grip on one or two ideas which had not come into vogue since yesterday morning. . . .

Admitting what is called philanthropy, when adopted as a profession, to be often useful by its energetic impulse to society at large, it is perilous to the individual whose ruling passion, in one exclusive channel, it thus becomes. It ruins, or is fearfully apt to ruin, the heart, the rich juices of which God never meant should be pressed violently out and distilled into alcoholic liquor by an unnatural process, but should render life sweet, bland, and gently beneficent, and insensibly influence other hearts and other lives to the same blessed end.[6]

It was Hawthorne's attempt to be morally realistic in the face of the fanatical, professional philanthropy of the abolitionists, that led him to underestimate the seriousness of the slavery issue. In his campaign biography of Franklin Pierce he describes Pierce's ideas on slavery as obviously his own.

[6] Hawthorne, *The Blithedale Romance.*

He fully recognized, by his votes and by his voice, the rights pledged to the South by the Constitution. This, at the period when he so declared himself, was comparatively an easy thing to do. But when it became more difficult, when the first imperceptible movement of agitation had grown to be almost a convulsion, his course was still the same. Nor did he ever shun the obloquy that sometimes threatened to pursue the northern man who dared to love that great and sacred reality—his whole, united, native country—better than the mistiness of a philanthropic theory. . . .

If the work of antislavery agitation, which it is undeniable leaves most men who earnestly engage in it with only half a country in their affections, —if this work must be done, let others do it. . . .

There is still another view, and probably as wise a one. It looks upon slavery as one of those evils which divine Providence does not leave to be remedied by human contrivances, but which, in its own good time, by some means impossible to be anticipated, but of the simplest and easiest operation, when all its uses shall have been fulfilled, it causes to vanish like a dream. There is no instance, in all history, of the human will and intellect having perfected any great moral reform by methods which it adapted to that end; but the progress of the world, at every step, leaves some evil or wrong on the path behind it, which the wisest of mankind, of their own set purpose, could never have found the way to rectify.[7]

Thus, on the basis of what proved to be a very unrealistic analysis of the moral state of the nation, Hawthorne and the Young Americans confidently expected nationalism to overcome party antagonisms:

Both parties, it may likewise be said, are united in one common purpose,— that of preserving our sacred Union, as the immovable basis from which the destinies, not of America alone, but of mankind at large, may be carried upward and consummated. And thus men stand together, in unwonted quiet and harmony, awaiting the new movement in advance which all these tokens indicate.[8]

When the Civil War came, Hawthorne adapted his mind to it better than Pierce did, who continued to oppose it. Hawthorne quickly jumped to the conclusion that "the old union" was an impossible one and that the sooner we had a genuine union, though a smaller one, the better. He was, therefore, in favor of beating the South and then let-

[7] Hawthorne, *The Complete Works*, Riverside edition, XII, 370–71, 416, 417.
[8] *Ibid.*, XII, 436.

ting it drift for itself. Not long after the outbreak of the war he wrote to an English friend this astonishing letter:

Cannot an Englishman's common sense help you to see that this is so? Cannot your English pride of country win any sympathy from you for a people who have all their moral inheritance at stake? Who cares what the war costs in blood or treasure? People must die whether a bullet kills them or no; and money must be spent, if not for gun-powder, then for worse luxuries. My countrymen choose to spend themselves and their property in war; and they find, at this very moment, an enjoyment in it worth all their sacrifices. I never imagined what a happy state of mind a civil war produces, and how it invigorates every man's whole being. You will live to see the Americans another people than they have hitherto been; and I truly regret that my youth was not cast in these days, instead of in a quiet time.

When we have established our boundary lines to our satisfaction, and demonstrated that we are strong enough to subjugate the whole South, I trust we shall cast off the extreme Southern States, and, giving them a parting kick, let them go to perdition in their own way. I want no more of their territory than we can digest into free soil; but now that we have actually come to swords' points, it would be a sin and shame to take less. . . .

. . . Lowell had a nephew (whom he dearly loved) killed, and another wounded, in one battle; and a son of Holmes received two wounds in the same. The shots strike all round us, but even the mothers bear it with wonderful fortitude.

Emerson is breathing slaughter, like the rest of us; and it is really wonderful how all sorts of theoretical nonsense, to which we New Englanders are addicted in peaceful times, vanish in the strong atmosphere which we now inhale. The grim endurance of the merchants, and even of the shopkeepers, surprises me. The whole world, on this side of the Atlantic, appears to have grown more natural and sensible, and walks more erect, and cares less about childish things. If the war only lasts long enough (and not too long) it will have done us infinite good.[9]

This letter leaves no doubt as to the intensity of Hawthorne's Young Americanism and his ability to carry its point of view into the thick of battle. For him this faith was never an easy optimism; it was essentially a moral struggle, apt to end in tragedy.

What made Hawthorne's personal tragedy all the deeper was that during his residence in England, he had learned to enjoy the mellow,

[9] Quoted in Edward Mather, *Nathaniel Hawthorne* (New York, 1940), pp. 316-17.

"superior" standards and morals of the British aristocracy, which he called affectionately "our old home," and on returning to America he was shocked at the rudeness of our culture. The conflict that raged within him between the love of the beauties of old aristocracy and the devotion to the ideals of young democracy preoccupied him during his last years. He made a profound exposition of this inner conflict and its generalized dialectic in *Dr. Grimshawe's Secret.*

I do aver that I love my country, that I am proud of its institutions, that I have a feeling unknown, probably, to any but a republican, but which is the proudest thing in me, that there is no man above me,—for my ruler is only myself, in the person of another, whose office I impose upon him,—nor any below me. If you would understand me, I would tell you of the shame I felt when first, on setting foot in this country, I heard a man speaking of his birth as giving him privileges; saw him looking down on laboring men, as of an inferior race. And what I can never understand, is the pride which you positively seem to feel in having men and classes of men above you, born to privileges which you can never hope to share. It may be a thing to be endured, but surely not one to be absolutely proud of. And yet an Englishman is so.[10]

What we find it hardest to conceive of is, the satisfaction with which Englishmen think of a race above them, with privileges that they cannot share, entitled to condescend to them, and to have gracious and beautiful manners at their expense; to be kind, simple, unpretending, because these qualities are more available than haughtiness; to be specimens of perfect manhood;—all these advantages in consequence of their position. If the peerage were a mere name, it would be nothing to envy; but it is so much more than a name; it enables men to be really so superior. The poor, the lower classes, might bear this well enough; but the classes that come next to the nobility,—the upper middle classes,—how they bear it so lovingly is what must puzzle the American. . . .

I, who feel that, whatever the thought and cultivation of England may be, my own countrymen have gone forward a long, long march beyond them, not intellectually, but in a way that gives them a further start. If I come back hither, with the purpose to make myself an Englishman, especially an Englishman of rank and hereditary estate, then for me America has been discovered in vain, and the great spirit that has been breathed into us is in vain; and I am false to it all!

[10] Nathaniel Hawthorne, *Dr. Grimshawe's Secret*, in *Works*, XI, 200.

But again came silently swelling over him like a flood all that ancient peace, and quietude, and dignity which looked so stately and beautiful as brooding round the old house; all that blessed order of ranks, that sweet superiority, and yet with no disclaimer of common brotherhood, that existed between the English gentleman and his inferiors; all that delightful inter-course, so sure of pleasure, so safe from rudeness, lowness, unpleasant rubs, that exists between gentleman and gentleman, where in public affairs all are essentially of one mind, or seem so to an American politician, accustomed to the fierce conflicts of our embittered parties; where life was made so en-ticing, so refined, and yet with a sort of homeliness that seemed to show that all its strength was left behind; that seeming taking in of all that was desirable in life, all its grace and beauty, yet never giving life a hard enamel of overrefinement. What could there be in the wild, harsh, ill-conducted American approach to civilization, which could compare with this? What to compare with this juiciness and richness? [11]

Even more general than this conflict between class society and class-less society was a conflict related to it, a conflict that haunted Haw-thorne throughout his life and in all his "romances," the conflict be-tween conscientiousness and practical achievement, the conflict between Puritan and Yankee. In *Dr. Grimshawe's Secret* there appears an absolutely conscientious gardener, whose scrupulousness compels him to lead a very restricted life; he is confronted by a young, would-be statesman, Redclyffe, in whose mind the conflict between democracy and aristocracy is raging.

"I question," said Redclyffe, smiling, "whether . . . we need trouble our consciences much with regard to what we do. . . . So highly cultivated a conscience as that would be a nuisance to one's self and one's fellows."

"You say a terrible thing," rejoined the old man. "Can conscience be too much alive in us? Is not everything, however trifling it seems, an item in the great account, which it is of infinite importance, therefore, to have right? A terrible thing is that you have said."

"That may be," said Redclyffe; "but it is none the less certain to me, that the efficient actors—those who mould the world—are the persons in whom something else is developed more strongly than conscience. There must be an invincible determination to effect something; it may be set to work in the right direction, but after that it must go onward, trampling down small ob-stacles—small considerations of right and wrong—as a great rock, thunder-

[11] *Ibid.*, pp. 282–83, 331–32.

ing down a hillside, crushes a thousand sweet flowers, and ploughs deep furrows in the innocent hillside."

As Redclyffe gave vent to this doctrine, which was not naturally his, but which had been the inculcation of a life hitherto devoted to politics, he was surprised to find how strongly sensible he became of the ugliness and indefensibleness of what he said. He felt as if he were speaking under the eye of Omniscience, and as if every word he said were weighed, and its emptiness detected, by an unfailing intelligence. He had thought that he had volumes to say about the necessity of consenting not to do right in all matters minutely, for the sake of getting out an available and valuable right as the whole; but there was something that seemed to tie his tongue. . . .

He was surprised to find how he had to struggle against a certain repulsion within himself to the old man. He seemed so nonsensical, interfering with everybody's right in the world; so mischievous, standing there and shutting out the possibility of action. . . . You must either love him utterly, or hate him utterly; for he could not let you alone. Redclyffe, being a susceptible man, felt this influence in the strongest way; for it was as if there was a battle within him . . .[12]

In this conflict, according to Hawthorne, democracy and the Puritan conscience are partners against political traditions. The revolt of the Young Americans appealed both to his conscience and to his realism. He became an ardent partisan, not knowing that his party was much more romantic than were his own realistic "romances," and that his own inner conflict was a symptom of national tragedy.

— 13 —

FRONTIER FAITHS AND COMMUNITIES

THE youngest part of America, the ever-receding frontier, generated a type of social philosophy quite different from either nationalism or individualism; it might be labeled communalism. Ever since the hunting, nomadic tribes of mankind began to dream of settling down in some eternally happy hunting ground, or some garden

[12] Hawthorne, *Dr. Grimshawe's Secret*, pp. 268–71.

of Eden, or even a farm, they have conceived of these "promised lands" as the "inheritance" of a clan or large family, which for one reason or another had been condemned for generations to a pilgrim existence. It was, therefore, no accident that when the Great West was opened little bands of pioneers felt "called" by God or fortune to leave the old, decaying world and its institutions and to venture upon a new life, a new society in a new world. The story of the stream of pilgrim communities, congregations, and families that left Europe for America with the vision of a promised land guiding them is a familiar theme of American history. But it was the continuation of the same pathetic story that the westward trekking tells when wars, depressions and persecutions began to make themselves felt on the eastern seaboard of the supposedly "new" world. Only too soon the European pattern showed itself here, and the children of pilgrims once more took to pilgrimage. Especially after 1808, after 1812, and after 1837 there were thousands of Americans who heard voices calling them westward and who banded together to find what Edward Everett called "a land of equal laws and happy men."

It is not the irruption of wild barbarians, sent to visit the wrath of God on a degenerate empire. . . . It is the human family, led out by Providence to possess its broad patrimony.

The embodiment of a vision, which the ancients, from the earliest period, cherished of some favored land beyond the mountains or the seas; a land of equal laws and happy men. . . . Atlantis hath arisen from the ocean; the farthest Thule is reached; there are no more retreats beyond the sea, no more discoveries, no more hopes.[1]

Here in the Great West if anywhere must arise the kingdoms of God foretold by ancient prophets and foreseen by countless generations of seekers and wanderers. These were the latter days, the end of man's pilgrimage on earth.

The hope of building perfect little societies took both secular and religious forms. The secular forms were usually conceived in terms of Platonic republics; "phalansteries" of "associated" men were to put "socialism" into practice. The religious forms were extremely

[1] From Edward Everett's oration on "The Circumstances Favorable to the Progress of Literature in America" (Boston, 1824), in Blau, ed., *American Philosophic Addresses, 1700–1900*, pp. 89, 92–93.

diversified: pilgrim congregations, missions, "millennial dawn" groups, "latter day saints," etc.—all more or less theocratic and apocalyptic.

The first form of frontier philosophy to become established in America was that of pilgrim congregations. The story of the Plymouth Pilgrims, their attempts to understand themselves literally as a new Israel called from a wilderness to a promised land, and their building of congregational towns on the basis of this theory has often been told. But there were other pilgrim congregations with other more elaborate and original theories to guide them. Most conspicuous, after the New England separatists, were the Moravians, whose settlements like those of New England were gradually transformed from little kingdoms of God to American towns. When they began to immigrate, these Czechs and Germans, forced successively out of Bohemia, Moravia, and Saxony, were organized as nomadic congregations, their theory being that God had intended them to combine the life of a communion of saints with a perpetual missionary enterprise. The settlements of Bethlehem, Pennsylvania, of Salem, North Carolina, of Barbadoes, and others were, therefore, theoretically headquarters for missions to the Indians. The attempt to organize each community as a single family and to develop a "general economy" or communism, was subordinate to the prime purpose of maintaining a continuous flow of trained missionaries to the Indians, who were the advance scouts of the communal, worldwide pilgrimage to which the congregations were dedicated. So thoroughly were they absorbed in the communal nature of their task that they resisted energetically for two generations the natural temptations of the members to remove their private families from the family of God and to take their chances in the competitive economy of a free country. The missionaries carried the communal ideal even to the Indians and succeeded in organizing several "Christian villages," part white and part Indian, whose economic life was made an integral part of the general economy of the fraternal union.

In this conception of the nature of the missionary enterprise the Moravians had been anticipated by the Jesuits and the Franciscans, who in the far Southwest had constructed self-sustaining mission communities among and with the Indians. In their prime the great California missions were more monastic than democratic, but their communal economy was not very different from that of the Moravians. For that matter, some of the German Protestant communities in Pennsylvania were definitely monastic, notably the Ephrata community.

Most of these little communions of saints had European origins. Pennsylvania and Missouri were full of German sects of Old World origin, too numerous to mention. Among the more extreme and venturesome groups were the Rappites from Württemberg, who founded Harmony, Ind., in 1814—an anticlerical, pietist, austere, kindly, celibate, hard-working community. Another branch of this same group founded Zoar, Ohio, in 1817. In 1842 the Community of True Inspiration, or the Ebenezer Society, a pietist group similar to the Rappites, emigrated from Germany; they finally (1854) found a permanent home in Amana, Iowa—a communist society of peasants, without professional clergy or professional entertainment, sharing in very simple religious sacraments and services, each member subject to receiving inspiration direct from God. The Amana community still exists, though in modified form. There was a persecuted congregation of Swedish pietists, which emigrated under the leadership of its prophet, Eric Janson, and finally came to rest as a pioneering colony in northern Illinois (1846–62). And in the sixties large numbers of Mennonite communists, or Hutterites, emigrated from southern Russia and formed colonies in South Dakota, known as Bruederhof communities.

The story of the Society of Friends, or Quakers, would properly belong to this sketch of frontier faiths, but like the New England Puritans the Pennsylvania Quakers rapidly lost their otherworldly aspects and became founding fathers of our secular state. A branch of this society, however, the Shaking Quakers, or Shakers, is an excellent example of a frontier communion. These followers of the prophetess, Mother Ann Lee, are more properly known as the Millennial Church, or United Society of Believers. Shortly after her death, the scattered believers in the Hudson and Connecticut River valleys were "gathered in gospel order" (1787) into several large families. The members took the following vows:

It . . . is our faith, being confirmed by our experience, that there can be no Church in complete order according to the law of Christ, without a joint-interest and union, in which all the members have an equal right and privilege according to their calling and needs, in things spiritual and temporal. . . .

All the members who were received into the Church were to possess one joint-interest as a religious right; that is, all were to have just and equal rights and privileges according to their needs in the use of all things in the church—without any difference being made, on account of what any of us brought in, so long as we remained in obedience to the order and government of the Church, and were holden in relation as members. All the members were, likewise, equally holden, according to their abilities, to maintain and support one joint-interest in union and conformity to the order and government of the Church. . . .

As it was not the duty nor purpose of the Church in uniting into Church-order to gather and lay up an interest of this world's goods, but what we became possessed of by honest industry, more than for our own support, was to be devoted to charitable uses, for the relief of the poor and such other uses as the gospel might require. Therefore, it was and still is our faith never to bring debt or blame against the Church or each other for any interest or services which we have bestowed to the joint-interest of the Church, but freely to give our time and talents, as Brethren and Sisters, for the mutual good one of another and other charitable uses, according to the order of the Church.[2]

Their aim was to carry forward the spiritual regeneration of the world, or the process of the last judgment, the separation of good and evil. This process had begun with the second coming or "female incarnation" of Christ in Mother Ann and would continue throughout the "millennial age."

God has begun to judge the nations of the earth, who have long been erring in judgment and straying from the paths of justice and truth; and this righteous judgment will never cease until the work of God shall be fully accomplished.

It will prove efficacious in its operations, and will be made manifest in the conviction of evil of every description, and in the full developement of error of every kind, whether in judgment, opinion or practice. It will produce in the willing and obedient, the effectual destruction of all kinds of vice and

[2] Marguerite Fellows Melcher, *The Shaker Adventure* (Princeton, 1941), pp. 89, 90–91.

immorality, and every principle of evil. It will enlighten mankind in the knowledge of the truth, and widely extend the benign principles of peace and good will to man. It will greatly increase the practical duties of humanity, benevolence and charity, and produce a universal diffusion of divine light, and the knowledge of salvation; and in the end it will effect the final decision and termination of the probationary state of all souls.

This Day of Judgment will be gradual and progressive, but certain and effectual; and will continue until a full and final separation shall be made between good and evil. Then shall the righteous no longer suffer under the oppressive hands of the wicked; nor shall the wicked any more shelter himself under the banners of the righteous; but each shall reap the reward of his own doings, whether they be good or evil: for God will search the heart and try the reins of every creature.

Then shall the covering be taken off from all people, and the veil be removed from all faces. Then shall Antichrist no longer beguile mankind with the mere name of religion in which there is no reality; nor his ministers any more deceive souls with the hope of salvation in their sins. Fraud and violence, theft and robbery, pride and ambition, malice and envy, falsehood and deception, and every species of wickedness will be completely uncovered, and appear in all their naked deformity; nor will it be in the power of man to conceal the smallest crime: for every secret sin will be fully brought to view. . . .

Let all lay aside the false doctrines of Antichrist, and consider and rightly appreciate this important truth; That man is a free agent, capable of thinking, believing and acting for himself; and therefore he is accountable to God for the use and improvement he makes of his free agency, and must be judged and rewarded according to his works. The important period is fast approaching when the dividing line must be fully drawn, when the decisive sentence shall be pronounced: "He that is unjust, let him be unjust still; and he that is filthy, let him be filthy still; and he that is righteous let him be righteous still; and he that is holy let him be holy still. And behold I come quickly; and my reward is with me, to give every man according as his work shall be."

Tho' thousands in past ages, who conscientiously lived up to the best light they were able to obtain, were so far enlightened by the Spirit of God, as to see the natural tendency of indulging those inordinate desires which led to these baleful corruptions, and honestly took up their crosses, and, for a season, maintained a principle of continency; yet the fountain of iniquity was not discovered; the veil of the flesh, which is the covering that darkened the sight, was not yet removed. So great indeed has been the darkness which has covered the earth, and so benighted were the minds of the great mass of the professors of Christianity, that those souls who were thus partially enlightened, have generally been stigmatized as heretics, and have suffered great persecutions on account of their faith. And tho' such souls, like stars in the night, might shine in the midst of surrounding darkness; yet they could not dispel the darkness, nor enlighten the earth. This remained to be accomplished by the Spirit of Christ in the female. The dawning of the millennial day, and the rising of the Sun of Righteousness, having now commenced, will gradually disperse these clouds of darkness, and open the eyes of a benighted world.[3]

The distinctive "moral principles" governing the members of "the Kingdom of Christ" were "separation from the world, practical peace, simplicity of language, right use of property, and a virgin life." By "separation from the world" and "practical peace" the members were forbidden to participate not only in wars but also in "contentions of the world, so as to feel for one political party more than for another." They were strict isolationists in politics and regarded themselves as literally citizens of another world.

Less communistic than the Shakers, but even more definite in their millennial hope were the numerous Adventist sects. In 1818 a New York farmer, William Miller, announced that

in about twenty-five years from that time (1818) all the affairs of our present state would be wound up; that all its pride and power, pomp and vanity, wickedness and oppression, would come to an end; and that, in the place of the kingdoms of this world, the peaceful and long-desired kingdom of the Messiah would be established under the whole heaven.[4]

Though the Millerite and subsequent anticipations of the Day of Judgment seem to be merely fanatical exercises in the interpretation of Scripture, the persistence of the millennial faith in spite of the failures of the detailed predictions is eloquent testimony that it had deep social roots. It was especially marked on the American frontier and among the agricultural population. There is abundant evidence that many a pioneer justified his toils not by the hope that he was expand-

---

[3] *A Summary View of the Millennial Church; or, United Society of Believers, Commonly Called Shakers* (Albany, 1848), 2d ed., rev. and improved, pp. 368–69, 371, 266–67.

[4] Elmer T. Clark, *The Small Sects in America* (Nashville, 1937), p. 45.

ing an enduring civilization but by the pathetic confidence that his and all other troubles would soon come to an end and that he would at least have the satisfaction of seeing the oppressor found out and punished.

Most spectacular of all those latter-day saints were the Mormons. In 1823 another New York farmer, Joseph Smith, received a revelation that he was to gather the remnants of God's chosen people to build a new Zion. That dissatisfaction with existing faiths was an important motive in his quest is clear from his own account of one of his youthful revelations.

My object in going to inquire of the Lord was to know which of all the sects was right, that I might know which to join. No sooner, therefore, did I get possession of myself, so as to be able to speak, than I asked the Personages who stood above me in the light, which of all the sects was right—and which I should join.

I was answered that I must join none of them, for they were all wrong; and the Personage who addressed me said that all their creeds were an abomination in his sight; that those professors were all corrupt; that: "they draw near to me with their lips, but their hearts are far from me; they teach for doctrines the commandments of men, having a form of godliness, but they deny the power thereof."

He again forbade me to join with any of them; and many other things did he say unto me, which I cannot write at this time. When I came to myself again, I found myself lying on my back, looking up into heaven. When the light had departed, I had no strength; but soon recovering in some degree, I went home. And as I leaned up to the fireplace, mother inquired what the matter was. I replied, "Never mind, all is well—I am well enough off." I then said to my mother, "I have learned for myself that Presbyterianism is not true." [5]

The trek of the Mormon congregation by stages (1831–48) to Utah is an epitome of the general migration westward, and the *Book of Mormon* is a classic illustration of how preposterous nonsense can be sanctified and hallowed by the sufferings and labors of an heroic people.

In general, it is important in studying these frontier faiths not to interpret them too literally by their creeds and verbal symbols, but to see their social substance. The exclusive theocracy and co-operative

[5] Joseph Smith, *The Pearl of Great Price* (Salt Lake City, 1929), p. 48.

commonwealth attempted, never completely realized, in the "Land of Deseret" are the best measure of the motives and ideals of its settlers and of their desires to escape socially and intellectually from what they felt to be a doomed world. Perhaps the most significant aspect of the social ideals of the frontier was the intense desire of relatively small societies for complete independence; but this independence was seldom sought in its own right, in the name of liberty, but as a consequence of each group's feeling itself religiously privileged. In other words, the intense religious and social ferment of the period produced in the East the confusion and contentions of rival churches; in the West it produced a profusion of voluntary societies, each brightening its own little corner with its own holy light.

The community of perfectionists at Oneida, New York, had a somewhat different orientation from those mentioned. It was founded by John Humphrey Noyes in 1847. He had organized a community in 1845 at Putney, Vermont, but it was not tolerated there. These perfectionists and communists sought to demonstrate that they were above the law, above conventions, above self-seeking. They had all things and each other in common and were governed exclusively by love—and by certain strict regulations formulated by Noyes. The experiment would have perished within a few years for lack of love and food (its agriculture proved unprofitable), but it was saved, almost accidentally, by being transformed into an industrial community on a joint stock company basis.

The most pretentious of these many frontier communities, and philosophically the most erudite, was a brotherhood founded by Thomas Lake Harris and Lawrence Oliphant at Amenia, New York, about 1860. Harris was a Universalist, Swedenborgian, Spiritualist, and a poet, who on a visit to England became convinced that the Christian church must give way to a Christian society. Oliphant was a British aristocrat, diplomat, and adventurer, who, with his mother, sought an escape from the vices of the Old World. Together, Harris and the Oliphants gathered a heterogeneous community for agriculture, first at Amenia, then on the shores of Lake Erie, and still later in California. This community was to serve as the pivot of "archnatural" forces for the regeneration of the world, a "vortex" of salvation. The redeeming energy which was to spread from this vortex was to be generated by "the divine breath in human society." The members were, in their work, worship, love, and dancing, supposed to inhale the Holy Spirit and to become literally spiritualized. Harris himself, the "father" and "pivotal man," became, through a series of intense sufferings and revelations, an "arch-natural" or divine person, technically immortal. His chief office was to open a path to heaven for the descent of the spirits to earth, which would make possible the ultimate brotherhood of all men and the union of heaven and earth. This union he conceived in terms of a "new republic" based on Christian socialism.

The most representative and moderate form of religious frontier democracy is found in the Disciples of Christ, or Campbellites. This movement really began among the Baptists of the Ohio Valley, where, in 1829, Alexander Campbell (of Scotland) began to publish the *Millennial Harbinger*. He urged a strict congregational, democratic church government, without centralized boards or missionary activities. "Money and power are the two principal members of the old beast." He repudiated an educated and salaried clergy, creeds, organ music, and anything that inclined toward "money and power." An interesting, though small, branch of the Campbellite movement was the work of an English physician and Unitarian, John Thomas, who in 1850 organized several congregations of Christadelphians. They have most of the features of the Disciples, except that they are Unitarian, and in addition they emphasize millenarianism. They do not vote, hold office, participate in war, and they refuse to consider themselves members of any "worldly" state; they "have no kingdom until the kingdom shall be given to them at the coming of Christ."

The democratic tendencies so thoroughly embodied in the Disciples of Christ made themselves felt to a greater or lesser extent in all the popular churches of the frontier. The typical Baptist and Methodist clergymen of the early days were three-quarters farmers, and their salaries as ministers were negligible. The Methodist circuit riders were theoretically, as well as practically, pilgrims, and the theory of the itinerant ministry, which forbids a minister to "settle" in a congregation, is still maintained. The churches in frontier settlements functioned, as Professor Sweet has shown, not merely as community centers of religious comfort and inspiration, but also as courts, schools, and clubs. They represented informal attempts at local self-govern-ment and self-education.

The churches once organized held business meetings once each month with the minister as moderator, and a large share of the business had to do with the disciplining of members. A random turning of the pages of any of the old record books of the early frontier churches will soon convince one that the church was a large factor in maintaining order in these raw com-munities. Discipline was meted out to members for drinking, fighting, harmful gossip, lying, stealing, immoral relation between the sexes, gambling and horse racing. Even business dealings and intimate family affairs, such as the relation between parents and children, were considered matters for church discipline. . . .

The frontier Methodist preachers brought home to the pioneers the fact that they were the masters of their own destiny, an emphasis which fitted in exactly with the new democracy rising in the West, for both emphasized the actual equality among all men.[6]

It was natural, under these circumstances, that the Bible should be the frontier library and encyclopedia; whatever happened had to be explained biblically. The erudition displayed by laymen, as well as by their otherwise uneducated, local preachers, is a testimony to the seriousness of their philosophical reflection. Even today, where frontier conditions have disappeared (and they have certainly not disappeared entirely) there are many survivals of biblical philosophy. In our colleges, too, there are remnants of the unsecularized philosophical imagination which bear a tawdry testimony to the early days when each sect established a "seminary" largely to promote expertness in Bible interpretation. A close examination of what is dismissed today in philosophical circles as dogmatism, authoritarianism, and super-naturalism reveals the skeletons of a "Bible learning" which in frontier societies, when it was in its prime, enjoyed the living context of a cul-ture for which it was the most important and genuine philosophical criticism, speculation, and system-building,—all in an idiom and per-spective which is now practically unintelligible, but which was the only historical background and semantic equipment available to these

[6] William Warren Sweet, The Story of Religions in America (New York, 1930), pp. 315, 317.

wilderness men. John Humphrey Noyes expressed the spirit of this democratic "Bible science" when he exclaimed: "Never will I be whipped by ministers or anybody else into views that do not commend themselves to my understanding as guided by the Bible and enlightened by the Spirit."

One secular enthusiast for communal living and student of the careers of American communal experiments was disgusted when he learned that most of them failed because the members discovered that they could make larger profits in competitive business; he concluded his criticism of such "selfishness" with the remark that communism depends on the sentiment "that the sweetest joy in this world comes, not from riches and what riches can procure, but from sharing life's burdens with others." [7] This kind of joy in sharing burdens is basic in religious experience and imagination; it is, therefore, natural that the hardships of pioneering strengthened the bonds of religious fellowship. But the secular communities, whose motives and ideas were derived from utilitarian doctrines, expected to achieve by association the greatest happiness of the greatest number. When these secular socialists began to experience less happiness, in the sense of prosperity, and more "joy," in the sense of sharing burdens, they were inclined to feel disillusionment. There was one other advantage which the religious communities had over the secular: in them the autocratic or paternalistic form of government, which was the rule in most of the communities, both secular and religious, could be justified as a form of theocracy, whereas the secular associations were seriously embarrassed by attempts at democratic management. As long as a benevolent capitalist, like Robert Owen, or a small group of investors owned the property "in trust" for the community, there was usually "businesslike" management, but when, in the interests of communist theory the assets and responsibilities were more equally shared, troubles arose. In fact, there is considerable irony in our considering these communities under the heading "democracy." Insofar as they were symptomatic of revolt against oppression, insofar as they sought freedom for minorities, and insofar as they promoted co-operative enter-

[7] William A. Hinds, *American Communities and Co-operative Colonies* (Chicago, 1908), 2d rev., p. 275.

prise, they undoubtedly deserve attention as frontier democracy; but their inner structure and politics were often specimens of petty tyranny and revealed anything but a love of equality.

The experience of the secular communities is instructive for the study of practical democracy, but what concerns us here is their contribution to social theory. We must exclude from consideration here some of the most substantial and noted communities, such as Brook Farm, Fruitlands, North American Phalanx, the Northampton Association, and the Positivist village of Modern Times, L.I., as not properly speaking frontier communities; they were experiments in the solution of problems of labor and co-operative industry within a settled social order and attempts at reconstructing that order. The frontier communities were less ambitious; they were escape mechanisms, experiments in co-operative pioneering. The New Harmony (1825–28) and Yellow Springs (1824–25) communities of Robert Owen were not conceived as frontier settlements, but as examples of industrial reconstruction on the plan which had worked successfully in Scotland. The "reformers" whom Owen imported soon made fools of themselves under frontier conditions, and Owen himself realized that being surrounded by "free land" his whole enterprise was inappropriate. The Harmony colony of the Rappites, on the other hand, had better success, not merely because of its religious inspiration, but because it had been planned for the frontier. The Fourierist colonies were divided in this respect. The best-known community, the North American Phalanx at Red Bank, New Jersey, was not a pioneering venture, but a fairly successful experiment in co-operative truck farming for a settled market in an industrial environment. There were about a score of Fourierist attempts at pioneering in the West, only one of which had any measure of success; in Wisconsin a Phalanx was begun in 1844 (near where Ripon now stands) which lasted for about six years. Following a lyceum lecture at Kenosha, Wisconsin, there was a protracted discussion of the subject "Does the system of Fourier present a practical plan for such reorganization of society as will guard against our social evils?" Instead of trying the plan within the world of "social evils," these citizens agreed to move out into the woods and begin afresh. They took a tract of unimproved government land and under typical frontier conditions built a village on the Fourierist model

—free discussion, religious toleration, no intoxicating beverages, labor credits, joint stock, etc. At first progress was steady, and compared with other frontier settlements it was a decided success. What ruined it was the rapid disappearance of frontier conditions.

It was a social failure, largely because we could not at the time make the home attractive and pleasant. Many thought they could do better with their means outside. We could not induce others with means to join us and purchase the stock of the discontented, as their desire to get out discouraged others from coming in, and finally the discontented obtained a majority and voted to dissolve. The little town of Ripon, which had grown up near us with whisky-shops, etc., became a great annoyance, and with its prejudice, falsehoods and abuse, greatly aided in the dissolution of the Phalanx.[8]

Another famous experiment in "rational, democratic communism," closely related to the Fourier system, was the Icarian adventure of the French reformer Étienne Cabet. The genuine pioneering adventure in Texas proved too much of a hardship for these French immigrants; but when they had the good fortune to take over ready made the town of Nauvoo, Illinois, which the Mormons had left behind them, they prospered and lived the life of French villagers. They immediately engaged in French politics, quarreled bitterly about a constitution, and split hopelessly into factions. In short, this experiment was less an illustration of frontier democracy than it was an importation of French local politics.

A small, but theoretically significant venture, was an agricultural community conducted for two years (1844–46) in Skaneateles, New York, by an antislavery enthusiast, John A. Collins. It was intended to "work a perfect regeneration of the race, by bringing man into harmony with the physical, moral and intellectual laws of his being." These principles included communism of property, communal care of children, vegetarianism, anarchism, and nonresistance.

We repudiate all creeds, sects, and parties, in whatever shape and form they may present themselves. Our principles are as broad as the universe, and as liberal as the elements that surround us. We estimate a man by his acts rather than by his peculiar belief, and say to all, "Believe what you may, but act as well as you can." [9]

[8] *Ibid.*, p. 285.   [9] *Ibid.*, p. 295.

The community was economically successful, but Mr. Collins's belief in nonresistance was exploited by a "long-headed, tonguey, Syracuse lawyer," who secured title to a large portion of the society's funds. In other words, it was not pioneer conditions that ruined this experiment in radical freedom; it was the proximity of Syracuse.

A pathetic attempt was made by the English reformer Frances Wright to "regenerate" slaves and make them fit for self-government. To a forest tract in Tennessee she took nine adult slaves, a few negro children, and an "overseer," who had been a Shaker. This group, "released from the fear of the lash," succeeded in clearing a few acres and erecting a few cabins. Miss Wright then expounded her more ambitious plans for Southern democracy—a mixed white and black co-operative community, in which there would be social equality, but the blacks would do all the manual labor. She was obliged to ship her few slaves to Haiti and to take up her residence in New Harmony.

It is difficult to generalize about frontier philosophy on the basis of such diversified and scattered experiences and experiments. I am inclined to think, however, that what Alice Felt Tyler writes about Icaria is true in general.

Once more the American frontier had received a peculiar people whose desire it was to live apart and according to its own theories and ideals, and once more it had slowly added its pressures of individualism and opportunity to the stresses of internal friction to bring about the end of the experiment.[10]

In other words, the function of the frontier in the minds of the discouraged exiles from "the world" was to provide a place of isolated peace and freedom for congenial groups. But this kind of frontier disappeared only too quickly; interference from without and discontent from within shattered the dreams men had of oases of brotherhood in a world of conflict. A Mormon sociologist once pointed out to me how frontier history proves that no people can long expect to remain a chosen people in America.

In the face of such radical disillusionment, in the knowledge that when one flees to the frontier one flees from cruelty to hardship the frontier philosopher in his search for a union of freedom, peace, and happiness seldom understood his life, either realistically or romantically. He composed neither the *Song of the Broad-Axe* nor *Pioneers!*

[10] Alice Felt Tyler, *Freedom's Ferment* (Minneapolis, 1944), p. 224.

O Pioneers!; such poems picture the frontier in perspective and from a distance. The more typical response of the weary frontiersman is to escape into the future, expecting his hopes to be realized in God's time and in ways past understanding.

Sing to my soul, renew its languishing faith and hope,
Rouse up my slow belief, give me some vision of the future,
Give me for once its prophecy and joy.

O glad, exulting, culminating song!
A vigour more than earth's is in thy notes,
Marches of victory—man disenthrall'd—the conqueror at last,
Hymns to the universal God from universal man—all joy!
A reborn race appears—a perfect world, all joy!
Women and men in wisdom innocence and health—all joy!
Riotous laughing bacchanals fill'd with joy!
War, sorrow, suffering gone—the rank earth purged—nothing but joy
    left!
The ocean fill'd with joy—the atmosphere all joy
Joy! joy! in freedom, worship, love! joy in the ecstasy of life!
Enough to merely be! enough to breathe!
Joy! joy! all over joy! [11]

The enjoyment of such visions has always been open to philosophers as well as to poets and to mystics, for in expressing such elemental passion and hope and in portraying such ideal society, though totally unrelated to present possibilities and, probably, to any real future state, the philosophical imagination prolongs moral courage and even now transfigures the wilderness.

— 14 —

LIBERTY AND UNION

DURING the fifties the compromises between democracy and nationalism ran their course and finally exhibited the stark contradictions in both theory and practice by which Americans were attempting to keep the peace. Compromise gave place to evasion, and

[11] Walt Whitman, *Leaves of Grass* ("The Mystic Trumpeter").

evasion to secession. The platform on which the National Republicans had succeeded in getting an unknown, elusive, Midwesterner elected as President in 1860 was an absurd bundle of evasions, and Lincoln's supporters knew that they were obliged to make sectional promises in their sectional campaigns, which, when put together as a national program were completely incompatible. But this egregious piece of politics was merely a culmination of the degradation of American democracy since party politics had frankly built upon demagogic appeals and the spoils system as its foundation. The political leaders of the country were disgusted with each other, and the country was disgusted with all of them and their political game. It was well enough to orate about "liberty and union, one and inseparable" and to insist that the government of the people must be both *for* and *by* the people. But such conceptions of "national democracy" seemed utopian, if not illusory. How could democratic ideals be achieved in the face of democratic politics?

The New England abolitionists and the Southern nullificationists were agreed to sacrifice union to liberty, but between these extremists the great majority of citizens and the political leaders of the middle and western states were willing to subordinate liberty to union. It was Jackson who had first declared, "The union must and shall be preserved," and Jacksonian Democrats now tried desperately to hold the country together by strategy, while their own principles were pulling it apart.

The Southern theorists were inclined to defend themselves on the Jeffersonian principles of natural rights, social contract, and merely federal union of states. They evaded the problem of civil liberty and equality for slaves by the doctrine, incorporated into the law by Chief Justice Taney's famous decision, that slaves are property, not persons. As the controversy narrowed down to the slavery issue, however, the majority of controversialists dropped moral theory entirely and defended the institution on utilitarian, economic grounds. Occasionally the economics became moralistic, for example, in the case of the Charleston (South Carolina) Baptist Association, which in 1856 passed a resolution to the effect that "slavery is really a matter of political economy. It is simply a question whether we shall buy the whole time of the laborer, with an obligation to care for and support him in sickness and old age, or whether we shall buy only part of his time, with no such obligation."

Albert Taylor Bledsoe was one of the few exceptions and deserves some consideration here for his attempt to clarify the general moral issues. He followed Calhoun in repudiating the literal doctrine of natural rights and social contract. In the classical theories, he said, "the natural rights of mankind are first caricatured, and then sacrificed."

The original right is in those who compose the body politic, and not in any individual. . . . Civil society . . . is no accidental or artificial thing . . . it is a decree of God; the spontaneous and irresistible working of that nature which . . . manifests itself in social organizations.[1]

Individual rights are fictitious, but society has the inalienable right and duty to "make such laws as the general good demands." Equality means only that in civil society all men are equally subject to "the general good." Such doctrine was an unconventional defense of slavery and was disconcerting to the South, since it seemed to yield too much to nationalism. The real temper of Bledsoe's tract, however, and of Southern sentiment in general, appears less in this theory of the general good than in the militant, uncompromising assertion: "The inalienable rights are neither liberty nor life . . . but conscience, truth, honor may not be touched by man." [2]

In general, both the North and the South were relieved, as well as awed, when the political debates gave way to civil war. The air was cleared for "a new birth of freedom" and a new theory of union. Lincoln, on whom fell the practical burden of defending emancipation and union, made a substantial beginning in the philosophical reconstruction, though his theories suffered martyrdom with him. He had personally inherited frontier democracy, Whig principles, and the compromising tactics of the moderate Republicans. After war had been declared, he was free to abandon his party tactics and to formulate, as best he could, a militant but conciliatory program for liberty and union. He discarded the partisan slogans of the time based on the

[1] Albert Taylor Bledsoe, *An Essay on Liberty and Slavery* (Philadelphia, 1856), p. 30.
[2] *Ibid.*, p. 111.

constitutional rights of the slave states and on the notion that there could be "free-soil" and slave states, and rested his conviction (expressed as early as 1858) that the nation cannot be "half slave and half free" on a reinterpretation of the Declaration of Independence. The principles of that Declaration, he claimed, implied a classless society, in which independence is the right of all men severally, and whose union is indissoluble. He applied his theory of independence not merely to the emancipation of slaves but also to the promotion of economic independence among free laborers. His ideal was that of the independent farmer, and he regarded all employment by and for others as an apprenticeship or temporary servitude, which would naturally terminate in the laborer's setting up his own business or shop as an independent property owner. In this way Lincoln hoped that the ideal of a classless society might be realized both politically and economically. Though these ideas had some relevance to conditions in the West, they proved quite inapplicable in the plantation economy of the South and the growing industrial capitalism of the North. As a consequence, Lincoln's eloquent formulation of a national democracy of free men has remained a popular ideal, whose power as a sentiment and absolute standard grows with each generation that finds itself farther from its realization.

Another sentimental reconciliation of liberty and union was lived (one can hardly say, expounded) by Walt Whitman. This extraordinary poet deserves as little as does Lincoln, the prophet, to be put down among the philosophers. He attempted to reconcile all men personally without attempting to reconcile any of their ideas, and when someone complained to him that he offered men no consistent philosophy, he replied, "I guess I don't, I should not desire to do so." [3] He had an uncanny ability to sympathize with everything, without troubling to analyze anything. "Whoever you are, to you endless announcements!" He appropriated everything, pretended to be a representative American, and imagined that in singing *The Song of Myself* he was expressing not merely the individualism of the transcendentalists, but the "divine average" of the democrat. His liberty, too, as well as his "merging," was practically boundless and more natural than civil. Whitman's sentimental democracy was, how-

[3] Newton Arvin, *Whitman* (New York, 1928), p. 219.

ever, not mere sentimentality, but like Lincoln's, a product of the collapse of his democratic politics. He lost his faith in the Democratic Party when, in the fifties, it turned its back on the "barn-burning," "Locofoco" type of Jacksonianism which he had sponsored in the forties. He tried to be a Free-Soiler, but this venture proved impractical, and he finally gave up his "national democracy" to become an ardent supporter of Lincoln. But he regarded the war as the culmination of the corruption of the party system. "America has outgrown parties; henceforth it is too large, and they too small." "I place no reliance upon any old party nor upon any new party." [4] In place of party politics he had faith in "personal leaders" on the one hand, and on the other, in comradeship or "calamus politics." He hoped that with the gradual breaking down of parties, sects, classes, and prejudices, a natural human sympathy would spread and that this would ripen into civic friendship and manly love.

Other states indicate themselves in their deputies . . . but the genius of the United States is not best or most in its executives or legislatures, nor in its ambassadors or authors or colleges or churches or parlors, nor even in its newspapers or inventors . . . but always most in the common people. . . .

The largeness of nature or the nation were monstrous without a corresponding largeness and generosity of spirit of the citizen. Not nature nor swarming states nor streets and steamships nor prosperous business nor farms nor capital nor learning may suffice for the ideal of man . . . nor suffice the poet. No reminiscences may suffice either. A live nation can always cut a deep mark and can have the best authority the cheapest . . . namely from its own soul. This is the sum of the profitable uses of individuals or states and of present action and grandeur and of the subject of poets. . . . The pride of the United States leaves the wealth and finesse of the cities and all returns of commerce and agriculture and all the magnitude of geography or shows of exterior victory to enjoy the breed of full-sized men or one full-sized man unconquerable and simple. [5]

On the economic side he shared Lincoln's hope for "the creation of a large, independent, democratic class of small owners," [6] and retained throughout his life a burning hatred of inequalities and class oppression. But he took little interest after 1860 in schemes of reform.

[4] *Ibid.*, p. 48.
[5] Walt Whitman, *Leaves of Grass*, 1st edition, author's Preface.
[6] Newton Arvin, *Whitman*, p. 103.

His faith in natural law and human nature was not the principled faith of economic theory, but a childlike faith in which he had been religiously reared—a combination of Hicksite Quakerism and deism. The natural order was not so much social as it was theological [7]— the law of divine freedom.

The whole Universe is absolute Law. Freedom only opens entire activity and license *under the law.* . . . Can we attain such enfranchisement—the true Democracy, and the height of it? While we are from birth to death the subjects of irresistible law, enclosing every movement and minute, we yet escape, by a paradox, into true free will. Strange as it may seem, we only attain to freedom by a knowledge of, and implicit obedience to, Law. Great —unspeakably great—is the Will! The free Soul of man! At its greatest, understanding and obeying the laws, it can then, and then only, maintain true liberty. For there is to the highest, that law as absolute as any—more absolute than any—the Law of Liberty. The shallow, as intimated, consider liberty a release from all law, from every constraint. The wise see in it, on the contrary, the potent Law of Laws, namely, the fusion and combination of the conscious will, or partial individual law, with those universal, eternal, unconscious ones, which run through all Time, pervade history, prove immortality, give moral purpose to the entire objective world, and the last dignity to human life.[8]

From this point of view the "organic compacts" of states and nations, and the democratic solidarity of mankind itself, to which Whitman became converted late in life, are but reflections of a metaphysical pattern that governs the universe. He was not so much an optimist as he was a conscientious liberal, thinking it his duty to welcome with open arms whatever experience, history, or science showed to be real. In his *ungrudging* yielding to the verdict of time, he changed his opinions as freely as though he had never "made up his mind." He enjoyed the freedom of one who is "both in and out of the game and watching and wondering at it."

The "watching and wondering" aspect of Whitman became more marked during the years that followed the "victory" of the Union, as he became increasingly aware that his "democratic vistas" were

[7] Cf. his poem, "Chanting the Square Deific," which adds a fourth person to the Trinity, viz., Satan, the tempter, "plotting revolt"; and changes the Holy Spirit to "Santa Spirita," the breath of life, "essence of forms, life of the real identities."

[8] Walt Whitman, *Prose Works* (New York, 1892), pp. 336–37.

visionary in the face of the dominant tendencies and standards of American life. His philosophy of life became also a philosophy of death and resurrection—a tragic democracy. The depth of his tragic attitude, his complete renunciation of democratic politics, appeared most conspicuously when the rise of populist democracy failed to arouse him in the slightest. He nourished from beginning to end his religious, hopeless devotion to the "barn-burning" tradition.

Then courage European revolter, revoltress!
For till all ceases neither must you cease.

I do not know what you are for, (I do not know what I am for myself, nor
   what any thing is for,)
But I will search carefully for it even in being foil'd,
In defeat, poverty, misconception, imprisonment—for they too are great.

Did we think victory great?
So it is—but now it seems to me, when it cannot be help'd, that defeat is
   great,
And that death and dismay are great.[9]

Whitman and Lincoln were the exceptions; the general run of Union philosophers abandoned the cause of radical democracy, to expound less popular versions of freedom. One of the most pretentious and pedantic attempts to pull the country together was made by Francis Lieber, a garrulous German professor who regarded himself as half national hero, half moral scientist. He came to America in 1827, fresh from the campaigns against Napoleon and the uprisings of German youth against the feudal aristocracy. An exile for liberalism's sake, an ardent fighter for German unity, with a smattering of Niebuhr's world-history and of idealistic philosophy, he devoted himself whole-heartedly to the task of adapting his German, bourgeois, national liberalism to American political theory and constitutional law. He had the misfortune to arrive during the rise of Jacksonian democracy and to be obliged to teach at the University of South Carolina. His idea was to teach love of union and respect for civil liberties to Southern "gentlemen" (whom he pictured romantically as America's noble-

---

[9] Walt Whitman, *Leaves of Grass*, "To a Foil'd European Revolutionaire."

men). His doctrine that man is by nature a social animal, his repudiation of social contract theory and natural rights, were no news to followers of Calhoun; and his emphasis on civil liberty, or, as he preferred to call it, institutional liberty (constitutional guarantees), gave a new birth to the Jeffersonian faith in bills of rights. But when he discussed popular sovereignty and the will of the people, he was clearly no Jacksonian Democrat.

The true and stanch republican wants liberty, but no deification either of himself or others; he wants a firmly built self-government and noble institutions, but no absolutism of any sort—none to practise on others, and none to be practised on himself. He is too proud for the *Vox populi vox Dei.* He wants no divine right of the people, for he knows very well that it means nothing but the despotic power of insinuating leaders. He wants the real rule of the people, that is, the institutionally organized country, which distinguishes it from the mere mob. For a mob is an unorganic multitude, with a general impulse of action. Woe to the country in which political hypocrisy first calls the people almighty, then teaches that the voice of the people is divine, then pretends to take a mere clamor for the true voice of the people, and lastly gets up the desired clamor. The consequences are fearful and invariably unfitting for liberty. . . .

A degree of shame seems there to be attached to a person that does not swim with the broad stream. No matter what flagrant contradictions may take place, or however sudden the changes may be, there seems to exist in every one a feeling of discomfort, until he has joined the general current. To differ from the dominant party or the ruling majority, appears almost like daring to contend with a deity, or a mysterious, yet irrevocable destiny. To dissent is deemed to be malcontent; it seems more than rebellious, it seems traitorous; and this feeling becomes ultimately so general, that it seizes the dissenting individuals themselves. They become ashamed, and mingle with the rest. Individuality is destroyed, manly character degenerates, and the salutary effect of parties is forfeited. He that clings to his conviction is put in ban as unnational, and as an enemy to the people. Then arises a man of personal popularity. He ruins the institutions; he bears down everything before him; yet he receives the popular acclaim, and the voice of the people being the voice of God, it is deemed equally unnational and unpatriotic to oppose him.[10]

All absolutism, whether monarchical or democratic, is in principle the

---

[10] Francis Lieber, *On Civil Liberty and Self-Government* (Philadelphia, 1859), pp. 414–16.

same, and the latter always leads by short transitions to the other. We may go farther; in all absolutism there is a strong element of communism. . . . There is no other civil liberty than institutional liberty, all else is but passing semblance and simulation. It is one of our highest duties, therefore, to foster in the young an institutional spirit . . .[11]

The only effective way to prevent absolutism, according to Lieber, is to promote self-government; and the only way to promote self-government is to have in the people's culture a large number of relatively independent institutions. In place of checks and balances within the government, there should be many self-governing bodies *organically* related and legally constitutional, but each enjoying liberty. Within this broad concept of institutional decentralization Lieber included not only state and local governments, but family, church, exchange, science, etc.—institutions that, like the state, were necessary to the organic life of a civilized society.

By institutional self-government is meant that popular government which consists in a great organism of institutions or a union of harmonizing systems of laws instinct with self-government. It is essentially of a co-operative character, and thus the opposite to centralism. It is articulated liberty, and thus the opposite to an inarticulated government of the majority. It is of an inter-guaranteeing, and consequently, inter-limiting character, and in this aspect the negation of absolutism. It is of a self-evolving and genetic nature, and thus is contradistinguished from governments founded on extra-popular principles, such as divine right. Finally, institutional self-government is, in the opinion of our race, and according to our experience, the only practical self-government, or self-government carried out in the realities of life, and is thus the opposite of a vague or theoretical liberty, which proclaims abstractions, but, in reality, cannot disentangle itself from the despotism of one part over another, however permanent or changing the ruling part may be.

Institutional self-government is the political embodiment of self-reliance and mutual acknowledgment of self-rule. It is in this view the political realization of equality.[12]

This idea was Lieber's one claim to fame, for it was not only a good idea, well-conceived, but it happened to suit admirably the character

---

[11] Lieber, *Reminiscences, Addresses, and Essays* (Philadelphia, 1881), in his *Miscellaneous Writings*, I, 343.
[12] Lieber, *On Civil Liberty and Self-Government*, pp. 323–24.

of American society and liberty. It is an idea that is being continually revived and re-applied. It is true that Lieber's own application of it was not very original or helpful. In general, like the historical sociologists of his time, he relied on time and history to produce the proper institutions for a people. To his credit it must be said that he did not use this theory to justify slavery, as there was great temptation to do; for slavery, to him, was by its nature opposed to civil liberty, and Lieber said so even in South Carolina. Not content with a purely historical foundation for his institutionalism, he tried to name those institutions which were universal and basic to civilization and might be said to grow out of human nature.

1. Language, that is, the conscious conveyance of ideas to others by articulate sounds, and not mere communion by impulsive utterances; 2. Individual Property and consequent mutual acknowledgment of rights; 3. Exchange, which is the necessary effect of the former combined with man's judgment; 4. Sexual Shame; 5. The Family, Authority, Government, or Superiors and Inferiors, independent upon physical force or instinct; 6. Religion, that is, some fear at least of superior and invisible powers, and a desire of propitiating them; 7. Taste or the Love of the Beautiful, though it manifest itself only in the rudest tattooing, painting, or other attempts at ornament, and Rhythm in language, step, or tune, which is connected with man's universal love of symmetry; 8. Punishment, or the intentional infliction of some sufferance for some committed wrong, which proves the existence of conscience; that is, a consciousness that there are such things as right and wrong acts, and also of the universal intuitive conviction that it exists alike in all men. In other words, man is always, and the animal never, an ethical, religious, jural, speaking, aesthetical, and exchanging being.[13]

There was nothing startling in this, to be sure, but it gave Lieber an excellent formula for solving the dilemma of individualism [14] versus socialism: for individuality is the historical *product* of these self-governing institutions.

Both, individualism and socialism, are true and ever-active principles, and . . . the very idea of the state implies both; for, the state is a society, and a society consists of individuals who never lose their individual character,

---

[13] Lieber, *Reminiscences, Addresses, and Essays* in his *Miscellaneous Writings*, I, 209-10.
[14] Lieber claimed that the term "individualism" was his invention.

but are united by common bonds, interests, organizations, and a common continuity. . . .

The two principles of humanity, individualism and socialism, show themselves from the very beginning in their incipient pulsations, and as mankind advance they become more and more distinct and assume more and more their legitimate spheres. Individualism is far more distinct with us than in antiquity, in property and in the rights of man, with all that flows from them; and socialism is far more clearly developed with us than with the Greeks or Romans, in primary education, charity, intercommunion, by the liberty of the press or the mail, the punitory systems, sanitary measures, public justice, and the many spheres in which the united private wants have been raised to public interests, and often passed even into the sphere of international law.[15]

This historical development suggested to Lieber the possibility and practicability even in our own time of international institutions:

In antiquity history coursed in the narrow channel of single countries; in modern times history resembles our own broad ocean where the flags of many nations meet. It is Christianity and the broad universal character of modern knowledge, closely connected with Christianity, which have rendered possible this striking phenomenon. With the ancients everything was strictly national; religion, polity, knowledge, literature, art, acknowledgment of right, all were local; with us, the different colors on the map do not designate different districts of religion, knowledge, art, and customs. There are wires of mental telegraphs which cross all those red and blue and yellow lines. And who will say that the time cannot arrive when that broad sea of history, as we just called it, this commonwealth of active and polished nations, shall extend over the face of our planet? [16]

In 1868 he wrote a pamphlet entitled *Nationalism and Internationalism*, which made him famous as an exponent of the theory of American nationality, because he proved that the Americans were a nation even before they were a state; but in Lieber's own mind the chief point of the pamphlet seems to have been the gradual growth of a "commonwealth" of "interdependent" nations. It may be important to stress this internationalism in Lieber, for he has been frequently represented as a fanatical nationalist, whereas he explicitly repudiated the extreme nationalism of the Hegelians and of his otherwise admired Prussians. Lieber's defense of the Union during the Civil

[15] *Ibid.*, pp. 363, 364–65.   [16] *Ibid.*, pp. 214–15.

War, his glowing patriotism, and his belief in the indissolubility of our constitutional (institutional) government brought him national recognition. He became quite unpopular in South Carolina and was delighted when in 1858, after much anxious wire-pulling, he was inaugurated as professor of history and political science in Columbia College, New York. But Lieber's heart was less than half in his college teaching; his ambition was to be a great pioneer in international jurisprudence. In 1870, as a reward for his services to the Union cause, he hoped to be rewarded by a diplomatic post, and he wrote to Hamilton Fish, "I much desire to wind up my active life with some high mission in the center of Europe. . . . I would do something for the promotion of the law of nations, the jural church of good will among men." [17] He was offered instead the post of umpire under the Mexican convention for settling claims! The poor, much unappreciated professor had the great joy of living to see Germany unified, and in his enthusiasm for Bismarck his youthful opposition to Napoleon was revived to such an extent that he almost forgot his love for the "Anglican race" and wrote to Franz von Holtzendorff that in America "so much has gone wrong while in Germany so many glorious changes have taken place," that a professorship at the University of Strassburg would be appreciated.

A Catholic, curious reconciliation of liberty and nationalism came from Orestes A. Brownson, who published in 1865 *The American Republic: Its Constitution, Tendencies, and Destiny.* Brownson's intellectual career since the election of 1840, when he became embittered toward democratic politics, had been tortuous in the extreme. He had turned traitor to his party, joined the ranks of Calhoun, preached states' rights, and had then gradually become "a conservative Whig with a dash of federalism." He continued to fulminate against the progress of industrialism and capitalism, but he lost completely his faith in the intelligence and integrity of the common people along with his faith in their leaders. Gradually he saw that the basic issue was between republicanism and democracy; republicanism was a respect for natural law, constitutional order, and a pursuit of the general welfare of the people, but not *by* the people. He now became convinced

[17] Quoted in J. Dorfman and R. G. Tugwell, "Francis Lieber," *Columbia University Quarterly,* XXX (December, 1938), 290.

that true freedom in both government and morals is to be found in conformity to the Divine Order or Providential Constitution rather than in claiming private independence or individual rights. His conversion to a republican Catholicism (under the influence successively of Channing, Leroux, and Gioberti) gave him a new social philosophy and an iconoclastic form of orthodoxy.

He combined two doctrines to form a new conception of "the church of the future," to replace his democratic Society for Christian Union and Progress, in which he had lost faith: one of these doctrines came from the St. Simonian writer Pierre Leroux, who had developed a collectivist doctrine of the communion of mankind with Christ; the other came from William Ellery Channing, whose emphasis on the mediatorial office of Jesus now seemed to Brownson the very essence of Christianity. He attempted to maintain Channing's conception of "Catholic Christianity," for the theory of salvation seemed to Brownson all the more important now that he, unlike Channing, had rediscovered the corruption of human nature. This faith in the Mediator was strengthened in Brownson by Leroux's idea that mankind is redeemed collectively by a universal communion of men *with each other* in Christ, a type of catholic "association" which is the divine life or constitution underlying the Catholic Church. This doctrine of communion Brownson never abandoned, regarding it, after his conversion to the Catholic Church in 1844, as the central truth in the sacramental system.

From Gioberti he learned also to think of a people collectively as "catholic" and to speak of the collective "redemption" of its "civilization." This redemption must follow the general pattern of creation; in communion the free, absolute being communicates its freedom to its dependent *members*. This is the cosmic republic of God, which it is America's "mission" to realize.

Human society, when it copies the Divine essence and nature either in the distinction of persons alone, or in the unity alone, is sophistical, and wants the principle of all life and reality. It sins against God, and must fail of its end. The English system, which is based on antagonistic elements, on opposites, without the middle term that conciliates them, unites them, and makes them dialectically one, copies the Divine model in its distinctions alone, which, considered alone, are opposites or contraries. It denies, if Englishmen could but see it, the unity of God. The French, or imperial system, which excludes the extremes, instead of uniting them, denies all opposites, instead of conciliating them—denies the distinctions in the model, and copies only the unity, which is the supreme sophism called pantheism. The English constitution has no middle term, and the French no extremes, and each in its way denies the Divine Trinity, the original basis and type of the syllogism. The human race can be contented with neither, for neither allows it free scope for its inherent life and activity. The English system tends to pure individualism; the French to pure socialism or despotism, each endeavoring to suppress an element of the one living and indissoluble truth. . . .

The special merit of the American system is not in its democracy alone, as too many at home and abroad imagine; but along with its democracy in the division of the powers of government, between a General government and particular State governments, which are not antagonistic governments, for they act on different matters, and neither is nor can be subordinated to the other.

Now, this division of power, which decentralizes the government without creating mutually hostile forces, can hardly be introduced into any European state. . . .

Nowhere else than in this New World, and in this New World only in the United States, can this problem be solved, or this contribution be made, and what the Graeco-Roman republic began be completed.

But the United States have a religious as well as a political destiny, for religion and politics go together. Church and state, as governments, are separate indeed, but the principles on which the state is founded have their origin and ground in the spiritual order—in the principles revealed or affirmed by religion—and are inseparable from them. There is no state without God, any more than there is a church without Christ or the Incarnation. . . .

The religious mission of the United States is not then to establish the church by external law, or to protect her by legal disabilities, pains, and penalties against the sects, however uncatholic they may be; but to maintain catholic freedom, neither absorbing the state in the church nor the church in the state, but leaving each to move freely, according to its own nature, in the sphere assigned it in the eternal order of things. . . .

Logic and historical facts are here, as elsewhere, coincident, for creation and providence are simply the expression of the Supreme Logic, the Logos, by whom all things are made. Nations have originated in various ways, but history records no instance of a nation existing as an inorganic mass organizing itself into a political community. . . .

The life that man derives from God through religion and property, is not derived from him through society, and consequently so much of his life he holds independently of society; and this constitutes his rights as a man as distinguished from his rights as a citizen. In relation to society, as not held from God through her, these are termed his natural rights, which she must hold inviolable, and government protect for every one, whatever his complexion or his social position. These rights—the rights of conscience and the rights of property, with all their necessary implications—are limitations of the rights of society, and the individual has the right to plead them against the state. Society does not confer them, and it cannot take them away, for they are at least as sacred and as fundamental as her own.

But even this limitation of popular sovereignty is not all. The people can be sovereign only in the sense in which they exist and act. The people are not God, whatever some theorists may pretend—are not independent, self-existent, and self-sufficing.[18] .

America is thus providentially blessed because she is a unity of states, a sovereign union of collective wills, by virtue of which national "constitution" she was able to draw up a Federal Constitution for government. This idea was similar to Lieber's, but it seems to have been suggested to Brownson by the legal theory of John C. Hurd. The aim of this fine-spun theory of states-in-union was, as Brownson expressed it, to do away with states' sovereignty, but maintain states' rights, to make secession treason, but to treat the defeated states as jural persons (collective peoples) in their own spheres or territories. Brownson's treatise, was, in fact, written as a warning to the rabid reconstructionists. Individualism had been defeated, he said, but

There is some danger that for a time the victory will be taken as a victory for humanitarianism or socialism, . . . It is so taken now, and the humanitarian party throughout the world are in ecstasies over it. The party claim it. The European Socialists and Red Republicans applaud it, and the Mazzinis and the Garibaldis inflict on us the deep humiliation of their congratulations. A cause that can be approved by the revolutionary leaders of European Liberals must be strangely misunderstood, or have in it some infamous element. It is no compliment to a nation to receive the congratulations of men who assert not only people-king, but people-God; and those Americans who are delighted with them are worse enemies to the American democracy

[18] O. A. Brownson, *The American Republic; Its Constitution, Tendencies, and Destiny* (New York, 1865), pp. 401-2, 403, 409, 428, 144, 82-83.

than ever were Jefferson Davis and his fellow conspirators, and more contemptible, as the swindler is more contemptible than the highwayman.

But it is probable the humanitarians have reckoned without their host. Not they are the real victors. When the smoke of battle has cleared away, the victory, it will be seen, has been won by the Republic, and that that alone has triumphed. The abolitionists, in so far as they asserted the unity of the race and opposed slavery as a denial of that unity, have also won; but in so far as they denied the reality or authority of territorial and individual circumscriptions, followed a purely socialistic tendency, and sought to dissolve patriotism into a watery sentimentality called philanthropy, have in reality been crushingly defeated, as they will find when the late insurrectionary States are fully reconstructed.[19]

Brownson's *American Republic* was aimed not merely at the Protestant humanitarian democrats or "barbarians," as he called them, but equally at the Jesuits and Catholic monarchists. He was an implacable enemy of Louis Napoleon and attacked his alliance with the Church so bitterly that this was one of the prime reasons for the Church's condemnation of Brownson's belated "liberalism." The Italian republican ideal of a free church in a free state soon met with papal condemnation. Hence Brownson's attempt to assert as essentially Catholic doctrines the separation of church and state, which had been effected in the United States Constitution, and the faith in the sovereignty of justice and natural law (versus political absolutism), which was a commonplace of common law, proved to be unwelcome to the Church, and would no doubt appear anachronistic even today, were it not being seriously revived by both French and American Catholic writers.

The particular predicament in the theory of sovereignty which was the immediate occasion of Brownson's theory of the American constitution was also the occasion for the growth of an important school of American jurisprudence. Into the technical legal problems of this "science" we cannot enter here, but several general issues in social philosophy, especially in the theory of national government, arose in the legal context, which are still of major significance in American philosophy.

The foundations of constitutional law were laid by the great Virginians, James Wilson, James Madison, and John Marshall. Federal-

[19] O. A. Brownson, *The American Republic; Its Constitution, Tendencies, and Destiny* (New York, 1865), pp.366–67.

ism was comparatively intelligible as a political principle, but when it came to translating federal politics into the terms of English law there were serious difficulties. Madison's doctrine of "divided sovereignty" was generally accepted.

> The sovereignty of the people of the States was in its nature divisible, and was, in fact, divided, according to the Constitution of the U. S. . . . As the States in their highest sovereign character, were competent to surrender the whole sovereignty and form themselves into a consolidated State, so they might surrender a part and retain, as they have done, the other part, forming a mixed Government.[20]

But Calhoun appropriated this doctrine for the cause of nullification, and John Quincy Adams, Daniel Webster, and Joseph Storey, who came to the defense of the Union, were hard pressed to challenge him on strictly legal ground. They had to rely all too heavily on the clause in the preamble, "We the people of the United States," sometimes asserting that the individual citizens of the United States were the source of sovereignty, sometimes asserting that the people was a collective whole before the Constitution was framed.

The first lawyer to make a thoroughgoing attempt at a defensible Unionist theory of sovereignty was John Codman Hurd, of Columbia College and Yale Law School. He describes clearly how he came to sense the basic problem.

> As for my earliest notions—I suppose the doctrine which I must have heard inculcated and have received from my reading was that commonly accepted by the Whig party (1830–1850). This I understood as taking the Constitution for record-evidence of a grant, transfer or cession, absolute or irrevocable, by each State, severally, to an administrative government organized under the Constitution as a written law, or to some person or persons represented by that government, of certain powers originally inherent in each State, severally, as a sovereign nationality.
>
> After my earliest reflections on this subject, I must have abandoned the conception of each of the thirteen colonies as having simultaneously acquired a severally sovereign existence by its several force and will; if indeed I had ever so conceived it. I probably came to regard the several force and will of the colony as acquiring for it the power which was exercised severally and internally in the ensuing condition of union, and the joint force and will

[20] James Madison, *Works*, IV, 390–91.

of all the colonies as acquiring, for all the States, as composing one political person, the powers manifested externally and internally as a recognized national State.

This condition of things I then regarded as an intrinsic fact in the genesis of each State and of the Union; a political fact in their history, distinct from the establishment of any particular instrument of government. It was not merely older than the Constitution and the Articles of Confederation, but was the political fact, from which alone they, as being legislative effects, derived their existence and authority.

But this view was founded on the assumption, which I had accepted as sound in theory, it being generally affirmed by Northern historians and jurists as having been actually realized in our case by the adoption of the Constitution, that what is called sovereignty is capable of being held in division.

It was the civil war which led me to question whether this theoretical separation of sovereign powers had been exhibited in our political system.[21]

Shortly before the Civil War, in a work on the "jurisprudence of conditions of freedom and bondage," Hurd went to the bottom of the issues raised by the Dred Scott Decision and undertook a major theoretical inquiry into the nature of legal persons and property. His sympathies were in general with the Austinians in their impatience with metaphysics, in their preference for positive law and legal facts over moral principles. He sought strenuously, as our contemporary legal realists do, to avoid mythological concepts and needless hypotheses. Accordingly, he rejected the whole doctrine of popular consent as the basis for authority and analyzed law in terms of "the will of the state" or "the power of society" or, more plainly, "force." From the point of view of will or power, it was clear to him that sovereignty could not be divided within the national domain. "The power of every state, or nation, is absolute, self-dependent, or supreme, within that space, or territory, which it possesses or occupies, as its own domain, and over all persons and things therein." [22] In his later works Hurd attempted to demonstrate that "the national existence" prior to the adoption of the Constitution was not one in which the several

[21] John C. Hurd, *The Union-State; a Letter to Our States-Rights Friend* (New York, 1890), pp. 7–9.

[22] Hurd, *Topics of Jurisprudence Connected with Conditions of Freedom and Bondage* (New York, 1856), p. 55.

states were sovereign, but that there was even then "a single possessor of the entire sum of sovereign powers . . . in the person of thirteen states manifesting the will and force to hold such power as one national State within all the territory known as that of the United States." [23] Hence the United States is a *Bundes-staat*, not a *Staatenbund*, a sovereign "union-state," not a federation of sovereigns.

At about the same time that Brownson developed a similar thesis in his *American Republic*, J. A. Jameson developed this idea of national union as a "political fact" behind the legal authority. "Back of all the states, and of all forms of government either the states or the Union, we are to conceive of the nation; a political body, one and indivisible." [24]

This conception of the sovereign power of the united people was further developed by a group of political scientists, who added to the Austinian analysis of Hurd and the idealistic liberalism of Lieber, a direct study of the German nationalists, especially Bluntschli. President Theodore Dwight Woolsey, of Yale, Professor John W. Burgess, of Columbia, Professor W. W. Willoughby, of Johns Hopkins, and Professor Woodrow Wilson, of Princeton were the leaders in developing a systematic theory of the national state in America. In general this development of nationalist theory paid more attention to the concept of organic unity than it did to liberty. It was not until Wilson began preaching "the new freedom" that liberty and union were reunited.

— 15 —

IDEALISTIC DEMOCRACY

THE impact of Hegel on democratic theory in America was greater than is generally believed, and it is scarcely an exaggeration to claim that it was primarily the Hegelian influence which prevented national collectivism, as outlined in our last chapter, from taking a decidedly undemocratic turn and gave America an appropriate

[23] Hurd, *The Union-State; a Letter to Our States-Rights Friend*, p. 48.
[24] J. A. Jameson, *The Constitutional Convention* (Chicago, 1867), p. 54.

ideology for understanding the growth after 1880 of national social-ism and economic democracy.

The most extravagant democratic enthusiast for Hegel was Walt Whitman, who, though he never read [1] Hegel and could scarcely be said to have understood him, wrote the following extraordinary com-mentary on "J. Gostick's abstract" of Hegel's philosophy.

The most profound theme that can occupy the mind of man—the prob-lem of whose solution science, art, the bases and pursuits of nations, and everything else, including intelligent human happiness . . . depends for competent outset and argument, is doubtless involved in the query: What is the fusing explanation and tie—what the relation between the (radical, democratic) Me, the human identity of understanding, emotions, spirits, etc., on the one side, of and with the (conservative) Not Me, the whole of the material objective universe and laws, with what is behind them in time and space, on the other side? . . . G. F. Hegel's fuller statement of the matter probably remains the last best word that has been said upon it, up to date . . .

According to Hegel the whole earth . . . with its infinite variety, the past, the surroundings of to-day, or what may happen in the future, the contrarieties of material with spiritual, and of natural with artificial, are all, to the eye of the *ensemblist,* but necessary sides and unfoldings, different steps or links in the endless process of creative thought. . . .

To politics throughout, Hegel applies the like catholic standard and faith. Not any one party, or any one form of government, is absolutely and ex-clusively true. Truth consists in the just relations of objects to each other. A majority or democracy may rule as outrageously and do as great harm as an oligarchy or despotism—though far less likely to do so. But the great evil is either a violation of the relations just referr'd to, or of the moral law. The specious, the unjust, the cruel, and what is called the unnatural, though not only permitted but in a certain sense, (like shade to light,) inevitable in the divine scheme, are by the whole constitution of that scheme, partial, in-consistent, temporary, and though having ever so great an ostensible major-ity, are certainly destin'd to failure, after causing great suffering. . . .

---

[1] Whitman's poem, "Roaming in Thought," bears the subtitle, "After Reading Hegel," but there is abundant evidence that he wrote it *before* reading Hegel; in fact, the poem is itself the best evidence.
"Roaming in thought over the Universe, I saw the little that is Good steadily hasten-ing towards immortality,
And the vast all that is call'd Evil I saw hastening to merge itself and become lost and dead."

In short (to put it in our own form, or summing up,) that thinker or
analyzer or overlooker who by an inscrutable combination of train'd wisdom and natural intuition most fully accepts in perfect faith the moral unity
and sanity of the creative scheme, in history, science, and all life and time,
present and future, is both the truest cosmical devotee or religioso, and the
profoundest philosopher. While he who, by the spell of himself and his
circumstance, sees darkness and despair in the sum of the workings of God's
providence, and who, in that, denies or prevaricates, is, no matter how much
piety plays on his lips, the most radical sinner and infidel.

I am the more assured in recounting Hegel a little freely here, not only
for offsetting the Carlylean letter and spirit—cutting it out all and several
from the very roots, and below the roots—but to counterpoise, since the
late death and deserv'd apotheosis of Darwin, the tenets of the evolutionists. Unspeakably precious as those are to biology, and henceforth indispensable to a right aim and estimate in study, they neither comprise nor
explain everything—and the last word or whisper still remains to be
breathed, after the utmost of those claims, floating high and for ever above
them all, and above technical metaphysics [have been made].

[Whitman's footnote] I have deliberately repeated it all, not only in
offset to Carlyle's everlurking pessimism and world-decadence, but as presenting the most thoroughly *American points of view* I know. In my opinion
the above formulas of Hegel are an essential and crowning justification of
New World democracy in the creative realms of time and space. There is
that about them which only the vastness, and multiplicity and the vitality of
America would seem able to comprehend; to give scope and illustration to,
or to be fit for, or even originate. It is strange to me that they were born in
Germany, or in the old world at all. While a Carlyle, I should say, is quite
the legitimate European product to be expected.[2]

It is clear that Hegel came to Whitman as the revelation of a complete faith—philosophy, theology, history, and politics combined. It
integrated natural and social philosophy in a way which no one in
America had succeeded in doing. Above all, it provided a pattern in
which conflict could be understood and accepted as "dialectic" or as an
inherent part of "the moral unity and sanity of the creative scheme."
It was the perfect philosophy for Whitman's concept of democratic
"merging."

It was, therefore, no accident that the first center of American
Hegelianism was Missouri, the storm center of pre-Civil War com-

[2] Walt Whitman, *Specimen Days in America* (Oxford, 1931), pp. 276–79.

promise—the place where North, South, West, and Germans met in struggle and in synthesis. In St. Louis a young German, Henry Brokmeyer, fleeing his country during the Revolution of 1848, found himself suddenly caught in the center of the struggle between the Northern and Southern states. Was this another revolution? Though he was not an academic philosopher, but a businessman, he attempted to find a general significance in this national strife. He had learned a little of Hegel at Brown University, especially from F. H. Hedge, who was then Unitarian minister at Providence.

As Hegel had fought for a united Germany, Brokmeyer saw in his philosophy the rationale of a reunited America. In the Hegelian dialectic as applied to the state, "abstract right" is opposed by an equally "abstract morality," and the two are reconciled in the culminating "ethical state." To Brokmeyer and his followers, the southern secessionists represented "abstract right," the northern abolitionists represented "abstract morality," and the new union that was to emerge from the tragic conflict was the "ethical state." [3]

He shared this insight and enthusiasm with two educators, William Torrey Harris and Denton J. Snider, who set to work to study and translate Hegel. When they found little outlet for their philosophy in academic and literary circles, they published their own *Journal of Speculative Philosophy* (1867). In the first number of this journal the editors addressed themselves "To the Reader" as follows:

The national consciousness has moved forward on to a new platform during the last few years. The idea underlying our form of government had hitherto developed only one of its essential phases—that of brittle individualism—in which national unity seemed an external mechanism, soon to be entirely dispensed with, and the enterprise of the private man or of the corporation substituted for it. Now we have arrived at the consciousness of the other essential phase, and each individual recognizes his substantial side to be the State as such. The freedom of the citizen does not consist in the mere Arbitrary, but in the realization of the rational conviction which finds expression in established law. That this new phase of national life demands to be digested and comprehended, is a further occasion for the cultivation of the Speculative. [4]

[3] Paul Russell Anderson and Max Harold Fisch, *Philosophy in America; from the Puritans to James* (New York, 1939), p. 473.
[4] *Journal of Speculative Philosophy*, I (1867), 1.

The general pattern for "digesting and understanding the national life" was expounded by Brokmeyer as follows:

In the genesis of spirit we have three states,—manifestation, realization and actualization. The first of these, upon which the other two are dependent and sequent, falls in the individual man. For in him it is that reason manifests itself before it can realize, or embody itself in this or that political, social or moral institution. And it is not merely necessary that it should so manifest itself in the individual; it must also realize itself in those institutions before it can actualize itself in art, religion and philosophy.[5]

Snider constructed an elaborate and ingenious system of dialectic, which he entitled "Universal Psychology." Of the many volumes in which this system is expounded, three are particularly relevant to the interpretation of American history: *Social Institutions* (1901), *The State, Especially the American State, Psychologically Treated,* (1902), and *The American Ten Years War, 1855–1865* (1906). His theory of the dialectical structure of the American Constitution was that:

In this country not one single state is the governing state, but each is through all, and all through each; and the member of Congress is to represent all through his own district or state, and the latter through all. His basic thought should be to legislate for the Union as state-producing in its widest and deepest sense, and not for his state or group of states to the injury or destruction of the total Union. The "state-producing" Union through the Union-producing state is the soul of the Constitution, which the legislator is to be perpetually incorporating in the law.[6]

As Snider goes through the dialectic of American history (largely in terms of Hegel's *Philosophy of Right*) he comes at last to the great crisis, which he analyzes into three dialectically conceived periods and then summarizes as follows:

The American folk-soul, so we may name it, is in great distress, which is growing greater, quite beyond the point of further endurance. It is divided within itself into two antipathetic, if not warring halves, which get to downright battle in Kansas. It is becoming a cleft folk-soul, cleft into north and south, or into free-states and slave-states. The question is burning in every

[5] Frances B. Harmon, *The Social Philosophy of the St. Louis Hegelians* (New York, 1943), pp. 7–8.

[6] *Ibid.*, p. 58.

heart: Shall this so-called Union remain dual, in an eternal wrangle or shall it be made one and a real Union? The spirit of the age, the genius of history, may be heard commanding first in a whisper which is soon to break out into thunder tones. The strain of destiny woven into the Constitution at its birth and burdening it with its own deepest self-contradiction must now be eliminated; it can no longer remain half-slave, half-free in the prophetic words of the coming leader.[7]

Harris added an interesting comment to Snider's interpretation of the Civil War.

The French Revolution was a gigantic object lesson of the dialectic in human history and it seems to me that Hegel has a wondrous insight into the self-contradictions of that movement though I doubt whether Hegel saw any more than Carlyle the positive import of the *Aufklärung* which began to appear in the world-history in such a form that it could not be mistaken only in the career of the United States. Perhaps we might say that it was only after the "American Ten Years War" of which you have written so ably, that any of us could be sure that the *Aufklärung* had found at last a positive content. Spanish and Portuguese colonization, revolutions and experiments at democratic governments in France and Spain and Italy, are only *reductiones ad absurdum*. In fact it almost looks as though our trade unionism, our free silver, our Wall Street trusts and a long series of portents of the same kind are already on us or looming up out of the future, like Banquo's train of ghosts which grieved the sight of Macbeth, threaten the stability of democratic government. The only thing that settles our faith is the desperate thought that there is no possible return to monarchy in its old form.

Well, Hegel devoted nearly one-third of his Phenomenology to the French Revolution.[8]

These illustrations must suffice to give the reader an idea of how Hegel was applied to American politics. The economic dialectic is even more interesting and quite novel for America. After Snider has surveyed the dialectic of institutions—family (thesis), individual property (antithesis), state (synthesis)—he makes the following application to his own times and environment.

There is no doubt that wealth can become and does become grasping, tyrannical, negative to the very social order whence it sprang. The free indi-

---

[7] *Ibid.*, p. 62.   [8] *Ibid.*, pp. 63–64.

vidual, unfolding through his freedom and amassing vast properties can and does use them not infrequently to the detriment of the freedom of others. At this point Individual Ownership has become self-destructive; the free individual, in the untrammeled pursuit of private gain, uses the liberty which he has enjoyed and employed, to assail and destroy that same liberty in others. That is, Free-Will, instead of securing Free-Will, has become negative to Free-Will and thus is anti-institutional. For, as we may recollect, the positive Institution is actualized Free-Will, which returns and secures itself.

Thus Individual Ownership must be followed or transformed and corrected by another institutional form which we have here called Civic Communism. . . . The Community must again hold property, especially must it take possession of its own property, determining slowly, carefully, justly what is its own property. For the free Individual in exploiting his freedom of acquisition, has also appropriated the Community's wealth. Still Individual Ownership in its rightful sphere is not to be jeoparded, but is to be the more carefully confirmed and secured because of this limitation put upon it in new social arrangements. But where it has become destructive of freedom, and indeed self-destructive, it must be saved from itself. . . .

Society turns upon *the willed Product* with its manifold development and transformation, culminating in the universal middleman (not yet quite universal but rapidly tending thitherwards). This willed Product, becoming more and more complicated, is finally the all-willed Product, which Society is to mediate both in its production and its distribution. With this mediation of the willed Product all the great social conflicts of the time are connected —round it move social revolution as well as social evolution. . . .

The social Monocrat, is the most interesting figure in the civilized world to-day. The people of both continents are looking at him with a kind of awe, wondering what will develop out of him next. No President of a Republic, no King or Emperor attracts the gaze and provokes the speculation of mankind like our Monocrat. Three or four of them have attained colossal proportions which are beginning to reach around the globe. And the curious fact about this matter is that he is the product of Democracy, to which Monocracy seems to be the rising counterpart and fulfillment. . . .

As yet the social Monocrat is purely individual in his work, is seeking his own personal gain. Is this the end of him, or is he being evolved for another and higher social purpose? We think that he is in training for becoming the recognized institutional administrator of the Social Whole, which is finally to choose him in some way. At present he seizes his power through his talent and uses it for himself autocratically; but he is to rise out of this individualistic condition, and work for all socially, and not simply for himself. He will administer the social Institution, not from the outside, but from the inside, being an organic constituent thereof, and as such his end will be the ultimate end of all Institutions, the actualizing of freedom in the world. His authority will no longer be capricious or even patriarchal, but institutional, perchance constitutional, like the President of the United States. A federated social world might make him its chief. For such exalted service he would receive adequate compensation, which, however, is not to be altogether settled by himself for himself. It would seem that the coming communal ownership is already calling for him, and he is now in the process of preparation for his future institutional vocation.[9]

For Snider, in other words, state socialism, or as he called it, "monocratic democracy," was conceived as the final form of institutionalized free-will. He and Brokmeyer both took an active part in local politics. Brokmeyer was lieutenant governor of Missouri (1876–80).

Harris, on the other hand, turned to national education to make his chief contribution. As United States Commissioner of Education (1889–1906) he attempted to put the St. Louis philosophy in practice by expounding it as a theory of education and by representing the institution of national, public education as the culminating embodiment of freedom. "Education is the process of the adoption of the social order in place of one's mere animal caprice. It is a renunciation of the freedom of the moment for the freedom of eternity." [10]

When Bronson Alcott learned of all this, during his visit in St. Louis, he was stunned. This was a far cry from the New England transcendentalism in which he was bred; and yet it appealed to him, for he realized at once that his own interest in "spiritual association" could be harmonized with this Hegelian version of democracy. Behind the Concord Summer School of Philosophy (1877–87), which Alcott and Harris organized, there was this hope and plan to bring New England transcendentalism and the Western democratic idealism together. But East and West merely met at Concord, for by this time neither movement had enough vitality left to launch a major philosophic tradition.

A fresh impetus came to Hegelian democratic idealism from a

[9] Denton J. Snider, *Social Institutions* (St. Louis, 1901), pp. 319–20, 331, 332, 333–34.

[10] Quoted in Payson Smith, "In Appreciation of William T. Harris," *The Educational Record*, XVII (1936), 134.

rather unlikely quarter. The Reverend Dr. Elisha Mulford, an Episcopalian rector and during his last years (1880–85) a lecturer at the Cambridge Theological Seminary, was more of a scholar than a preacher. He spent several years of study in Germany and then became a personal friend of Frederick Denison Maurice, the Anglican Hegelian and reformer. On his return to the United States he published (1870) *The Nation,* a book which enjoyed great prestige among both philosophical and theological readers. It was followed in 1881 by *The Republic of God,* in which the religious implications of his nationalism were made more explicit. Mulford's *The Nation* was in many ways a Protestant companion piece to Brownson's *The American Republic,* which, incidentally, is frequently cited in Mulford's work. But its influence and aim were different: instead of throwing a halo over the American Constitution, it served to shift the focus of attention from the politics of democracy to the religious expression of the ideals of democracy, and thus to give added incentive to the social gospel. Christian socialism in the United States, unlike that of England, was first promulgated among utopian communities; Mulford introduced into America the nationalist conception of "the Kingdom of God" which Coleridge and Thomas Arnold had preached so effectively in England.

In the Preface the author acknowledges his obligation to "the Rev. Mr. Maurice of London, and to Hegel and Stahl, to Trendelenburg and Bluntschli," but even without this explicit statement of his sources, the Hegelian nature of the work would be obvious. It begins:

> There is moving toward its realization in national laws and institutions, the necessary being of the nation itself. The nation thus becomes an object of political knowledge. . . .
> It is this conception of the state as involving unity and continuity which is the condition of political science, that is to be set forth alike against the political empiric and the political dogmatist. . . . It is a logic which is presumed in politics,—if politics be an object of knowledge,—but a logic formed in the necessary conception and manifest in the realization of the nation, not the barren forms of logic as it is held in the notions of the schools. In this conception that certainly is to be retained which works well, but political science is to apprehend the law and condition of its working. . . .
> *The nation is a moral organism.* . . .

Its members are persons who subsist in it, in relations in the realization of personality. It is the condition in which a person exists in the fulfillment of the relations of life with those who are persons. . . .

The process of the nation is only as a moral organism. It is not constituted in the necessary process of the physical world, but it is constituted in the order of a moral world. Its course is defined in law, and in law as prescribing the actions and relations of men as moral agents. Its attainment is in freedom. Its goal is peace, and that not in the barren conception in which there is the negation of purpose and energy, but peace as the conquest of man, in which there is the satisfaction of his spirit and the achievement of his aim.

The conditions of history presume the being of the nation as a moral organism. History is not a succession of separate events and actions, but a development in a moral order, and in the unity and continuity of a life which moves on unceasingly, as some river in its unbroken current. . . .

Those who have been the masters of political science, and it has perhaps fewer great names than any other science, all repeat this conception. Milton says, "A nation ought to be but as one huge Christian personage, one mighty growth or stature of an honest man, as big and compact in virtue as in body, for look, what the ground and causes are of single happiness to one man, the same ye shall find them to a whole state." Burke says, "The state ought not to be considered as a partnership agreement to be taken up for a little temporary interest and dissolved at the fancy of the parties. It is to be looked on with other reverence, because it is not a partnership in things subservient to the gross animal existence of a temporary and perishable nature. It is a partnership in all science; a partnership in all art; a partnership in every virtue and in all perfection." Shakespeare says,—

> "There is a mystery—with whom relation
> Durst never meddle—in the soul of state;
> Which hath an operation more divine
> Than breath or pen can give expressure to." [11]

Mulford then engages in a careful critique of the current themes of the Constitution, of sovereignty, and of representation, pointing out how these theories must be modified to fit the idea of "the moral organism." He represents the organic will of the people, which is sovereign, as the realization of the persons of its members. Each individual has "rights of human nature," since "man is made in the image

[11] Elisha Mulford, *The Nation; the Foundations of Civil Order and Political Life in the United States* (Boston, 1881), pp. v–vi, 16, 17, 23.

of God." The realization of these natural [12] rights is through positive or civil rights, which means that right must be "institutionalized." The sovereign or "real" constitution of the nation "formalizes" itself by enacting a legal constitution and formulating constitutional rights. The legal order is, therefore, not an end in itself; "its worth is derivative only from the life it conserves." The process of government leads inevitably to representation, and it is with reference to the theory of representation that the problem of sovereignty is most acute. In whom does the nation's sovereignty find formal expression? In "each and every individual in the nation?" No; "this is indefinite and can admit of no actualization." Is it in "the qualified electors?" No; for "the nation alone has the right to define the qualifications of its electors." Is it in the interests represented?

This is the postulate of Mr. Calhoun. . . . This identifies the nation with the commonwealth or the civil corporation. . . . There is no combination of private interests or private rights which can attain to the conception of public rights or duties, or create a public spirit. . . . The nation is constituted in its normal political order, in the representation of persons. . . . The nation is formed in the realization of personality. . . . In this the nation is constituted in conformance to its necessary conception, as the realization of freedom. The real education of the people is to be provided for in the organization of political power. They for whom, in the want of a realized personality, the exercise of electoral power is not possible, yet have a right to the aid of all in the nation that may tend to its development. They are not to be left in political indifference because destitute of the capacity for political power. They have the right to be educated by the state for the state.[13]

The representative of the people is, therefore, responsible to no particular constituency or interest, but "only to the nation and to God" for the personal development of each member of the nation.

[12] "Mr. Hurd describes these rights, while limiting them to the civil sphere, as individual rights, and Dr. Lieber, as primordial rights. But neither phrase is comprehensive of them, and neither has passed into common use. They have no historical justification, and the assertion of these rights in history has not been from academies or courts, but from the common people. The term natural rights is the more simple and the more exact."—*Ibid.*, p. 75.

[13] *Ibid.*, Chapter XIII *passim.*

Subordinate to the nation is the commonwealth or civil corporation. The function of the civil or jural order, as distinct from the political or moral organism, is to look after the material interests of the people and the administration of justice. In the United States the commonwealth is a union of many commonwealths. The several states in the union are not truly political bodies, but economic and legal corporations for carrying on the people's business. It is the primary duty of the nation as a theocracy to see to it that its business be conducted as an instrument of its freedom.

There has been in the historical course of the United States the higher development of the civil and political organization of society,—the commonwealth and the nation. Their sequence is not the mere accident of history, nor the induction of an arbitrary theory, nor the assumption of a legal formula; but it has been justified in the reason of the state. It is an organization ampler and nobler than they who in the generations have builded in it, could wholly comprehend; and working steadily and faithfully in their own day, they have wrought in the ages, building better than they knew. It has been vindicated in political science in the pages of its few masters. It fills the almost prophetic conception of Milton,—"not many sovereignties united in one commonwealth, but many commonwealths in one united and intrusted sovereignty."

The commonwealth is poor and empty, as are all things else, in seeking to be something other than itself. When it assumes a national place and national relations, it is severed from its consistent strength and its symmetric order, and is weak in the assumption of unreal powers. It becomes the caricature of the state, moving with a deceptive pomp in a disastrous pageant. In the building of a false civilization, in the accumulation of merely material interests, it bears with it the ruin of a people. The family has its own place, and the commonwealth has its own dignity; but the worth of each is in the fulfillment of its own law. And if the commonwealth, instead of its maintenance in the unity of the nation in which its interests alone have a moral ground, and are formed in the spirit of a moral interest, is broken and dissevered from it, it is when material possessions are counted as beyond freedom, and gold is more precious than humanity . . .[14]

Internally, therefore, the spirit of "confederacy" is the spirit of business or of private interests seeking to dominate. The national spirit is the antithesis of the spirit of the commonwealths when they seek

[14] *Ibid.*, pp. 319–20.

independence. Freedom demands their dependence on the nation. Externally, the antithesis of nationalism is imperialism, for an empire is a people devoted to aggrandizement rather than to freedom.

The close of the history of two of the great nations, in the ancient world, is the warning of the evil. The life of the nation perished,—in Greece, in the confederacy, in Rome, in the empire. The nation has always to contend with the dissolution of a confederate principal, and the domination of an imperial principal. . . .

The nation can meet the forces with which it has to contend only as it realizes its own moral being, and recognizes its origin and end in God. If it be held in a merely material conception, it can bring no strength to the real battle of history, where moral forces contend. If it be regarded as only formal, it will be broken by that held in a subtler bond. The nation is called to a conflict in every age, where the result does not depend upon the strength of its chariots, nor the swiftness of its horses. It is to contend with weapons wrought not alone in earthly forges—it is to go forth clothed with celestial armor, and of celestial temper. It is to fulfill a divine calling. It is to keep a holy purpose. It is to enter the battle for righteousness and freedom. It is to contend through suffering and sacrifice, with faith in the redemption of humanity, . . .

The nation in its historical life and calling moved toward the coming of Him in whom there was the manifestation of the real—the divine life of humanity. The work of Judaea and Greece and Rome had its unity in the Christ, who is the centre of history. The title written of Him in his perfected sacrifice, was the King of the Jews, and the words to which history was to bear witness in the ancient nations, were written in Hebrew, and Greek, and Latin. And as the life of the first nations was, so also shall that of the last nations be. As it was toward his coming that the nations of the ancient world moved, so toward Him, and still in his coming, do all the nations move.[15]

In *The Republic of God* Mulford developed this last theme as a theory of the church universal. Nations are called by God, they are all holy, chosen peoples, whose mission is one, namely, the redemption of humanity. "The Christ" as redeemer is the "physically departed," wholly spiritual Christ, present as the Holy Spirit, "the head of the human race in its real and eternal life." "The ethical relation of man is that which gives to social law and the development of history an ele-

[15] *Ibid.*, pp. 354, 381, 411.

ment that is universal." [16] Mankind in Christ is, therefore, a universal moral organism. Christ's second coming is in history.

It will not verify itself by external pageants. It will verify itself through the life of the Spirit in the history of the world; and as the skepticism of men must meet it there, so the faith of men shall there have its strength. . . . There is henceforth the conviction of the world. There is henceforth the realization of the kingdom of heaven on earth.[17]

The "gospel of the kingdom," Mulford points out, is addressed to "the common political life of men." The church is not a separate corporation or power; it is merely "the witness to the life of the spirit in humanity." "The Spirit is not the gift of the church, but the church of the Spirit." [18] "The sacraments are the evidence of the presence with the nation of the Lord of Hosts," [19] and they serve to interpret "those events in which the unity and freedom of the nation is conserved." This spiritual life is the reality of human freedom, "the consummation of life." It is "self-determined life" or the power of freedom. Mulford gives an extraordinary and eloquent picture of this free life of holy nations.

Henceforth the law of sacrifice becomes the law of power. In this world of forms the symbols of sacrifice become the symbols of power. The Lamb that was slain from the foundation of the world becomes, in the mystic vision of S. John the Divine, the Lamb that sits in the midst of the throne. This type is not lost in history. The manifestation of power is not in a separation from men, nor in the assertion of a dominion over men, but in the service of men. It is not the Caesar that becomes the enduring power with men. The nation, which in this last age, is the exponent of the highest historical forces, has its foundations, its unity and order and freedom, laid in sacrifice. But it is through sacrifice, as through the negation of this finite world, that there is the coming of the life that is eternal, the realization of the life that is infinite.[20]

This fusion of religious language and emotion with democratic nationalism proved to be a powerful force in American society no less than in European. It obviously gave a religious incentive to secular reform, thus robbing the churches of their pretended monopoly of

[16] Elisha Mulford, *The Republic of God* (Boston, 1881), p. 128.
[17] *Ibid.*, pp. 131–32.   [18] *Ibid.*, p. 216.
[19] *Ibid.*, p. 231.   [20] *Ibid.*, p. 189.

"spirituality." In fact, it enlisted the churches themselves in the social cause. But it had a further significance, for it gave to what seemed an excessively academic system a general social meaning. To many academic idealists this version of Hegelian philosophy came as a faith and gave them a field for religious devotion which the churches had failed to give them. There came a generation of philosopher-statesmen in both academic and national politics.

There came, too, out of this idealism a philosophy of education and a social ethics which had a revolutionary effect on American culture and provided democracy with a comprehensive system of thought and action. To conceive national freedom as a positive goal to be achieved through the "realization" of the capacities of all citizens, gave the public school system an enlarged significance and related it directly to social experience outside the school. Said one of these teachers of idealism:

We need not exclaim "Lord, Lord," to Hegel, yet we cannot but acknowledge the reasons for his sway. The absolutism, out of which so many fashion a convenient bogy, has after all little to do with man's making himself in God's image. Rather, it relates to certain contributions to the conditions of philosophic and theological progress, in the absence of which a theory of things would be incoherent or impossible. Experience must be its own judge. This, in a word, is Hegel's epoch-making discovery.[21]

This faith that "experience must be its own judge" became a basic proposition for both American philosophy and American Democracy. Two statements by two of its leaders will serve to suggest how it achieved systematic, technical elaboration.

Mind is an organic whole made up of coöperating individualities, in somewhat the same way that the music of an orchestra is made up of divergent but related sounds. No one would think it necessary or reasonable to divide the music into two kinds, that made by the whole and that of particular instruments, and no more are there two kinds of mind, the social mind and the individual mind. . . .

The unity of the social mind consists not in agreement but in organization, in the fact of reciprocal influence or causation among its parts, by virtue of which everything that takes place in it is connected with everything else, and so is an outcome of the whole. Whether, like the orchestra, it gives

[21] R. M. Wenley, *Contemporary Theology and Theism* (New York, 1897), p. 187.

forth harmony may be a matter of dispute, but that its sound, pleasing or otherwise, is the expression of a vital coöperation, cannot well be denied.

Social consciousness, or awareness of society, is inseparable from self-consciousness, because we can hardly think of ourselves excepting with reference to a social group of some sort, or of the group except with reference to ourselves. The two things go together, and what we are really aware of is a more or less complex personal or social whole, of which now the particular, now the general, aspect is emphasized. . . .

Self and society are twin-born, we know one as immediately as we know the other, and the notion of a separate and independent ego is an illusion. . . .

Our democratic system aims to be a larger organization of moral unity, and so far as it is so, in the feeling of the individual, it fosters this open and downright attitude toward his fellows. In idea, and largely in fact, we are a commonwealth, of which each one is a member by his will and intelligence, as well as by necessity, and with which, accordingly, the human sentiment of loyalty among those who are members one of another is naturally in force. . . .

The very fact that our time has so largely cast off all sorts of structure is in one way favorable to enduring production, since it means that we have fallen back upon human nature, upon that which is permanent and essential, the adequate record of which is the chief agent in giving life to any product of the mind.[22]

Since a democratic society repudiates the principle of external authority, it must find a substitute in voluntary disposition and interest; these can be created only by education. But there is a deeper explanation. A democracy is more than a form of government; it is primarily a mode of associated living, of conjoint communicated experience. The extension in space of the number of individuals who participate in an interest so that each has to refer his own action to that of others, and to consider the action of others to give point and direction to his own, is equivalent to the breaking down of those barriers of class, race, and national territory which kept men from perceiving the full import of their activity. These more numerous and more varied points of contact denote a greater diversity of stimuli to which an individual has to respond; they consequently put a premium on variation in his action. They secure a liberation of powers which remain suppressed as long as the incitations to action are partial, as they must be in a group which in its exclusiveness shuts out many interests.

[22] Charles Horton Cooley, *Social Organization; a Study of the Larger Mind* (New York, 1912), pp. 3, 4, 5, 182, 176.

The widening of the area of shared concerns, and the liberation of a greater diversity of personal capacities which characterize a democracy, are not of course the product of deliberation and conscious effort. On the contrary, they were caused by the development of modes of manufacture and commerce, travel, migration, and intercommunication which flowed from the command of science over natural energy. But after greater individualization on one hand, and a broader community of interest on the other have come into existence, it is a matter of deliberate effort to sustain and extend them. Obviously a society to which stratification into separate classes would be fatal, must see to it that intellectual opportunities are accessible to all on equable and easy terms.[23]

— 16 —

EQUALITY AND SOLIDARITY

A corrupt democratic government must finally corrupt the people, and when a people become corrupt there is no resurrection. The life is gone, only the carcass remains; and it is left but for the plowshares of fate to bury it out of sight.

Now this transformation of popular government into despotism of the vilest and most degrading kind, which must inevitably result from the unequal distribution of wealth, is not a thing of the far future. It has already begun in the United States, and is rapidly going on under our eyes. That our legislative bodies are steadily deteriorating in standard; that men of the highest ability and character are compelled to eschew politics, and the arts of the jobber count for more than the reputation of the statesman; that voting is done more recklessly and the power of money is increasing; that it is harder to arouse the people to the necessity of reforms and more difficult to carry them out; that political differences are ceasing to be differences of principle, and abstract ideas are losing their power; that parties are passing into the control of what in general government would be oligarchies and dictatorships; all are evidences of political decline.[1]

CRITICAL democrats were becoming increasingly aware that it was not only the party system which was not working properly but the economic system as well. Especially after the severe depression of the seventies, it was impossible to maintain the faith in progress as

---

[23] John Dewey, *Democracy and Education; an Introduction to the Philosophy of Education* (New York, 1916), pp. 101–2.

[1] Henry George, *Progress and Poverty* (Modern Library ed., New York, 1929), pp. 532–33.

it was being preached. As Henry Demarest Lloyd proved conclusively, wealth was not producing commonwealth; a plutocracy had captured control, and the issue now was *Wealth against Commonwealth.* If democracy were to survive, equality must be regained. The problem was intensely real and practical; its theoretical solutions were likewise suggested by practical experience and intended to be useful. To the learned political scientists the homespun theories of Henry George's *Progress and Poverty* (1879), of Edward Bellamy's *Equality* (1897), and of the intervening volumes that constituted the bible of the Populist faith were full of technical blunders and uncritical assumptions. Nevertheless, these works cannot be dismissed as unphilosophical; for they diagnosed American society more drastically than any of their more scientific contemporaries. Their authors succeeded in making these criticisms from the point of view of their own democratic faith, so that their arguments appealed to the society which they criticized, but of which they were common specimens. Such democratic philosophers can "completely change the character of political economy, give it the coherence and certitude of a true science, and bring it into full sympathy with the aspirations of the masses of men, from which it has long been estranged." [2] Works like these are ever ready helps in time of trouble and are still kept on the great American bookshelf, to be dusted off whenever a major crisis or a periodic depression causes episodic introspection.

The power of Henry George's *Progress and Poverty* can be explained in part by the fact that it grew directly out of his own sufferings and observations. As a struggling young printer and reporter in California during the boom days, he was baffled by his own poverty in the midst of one of nature's most lavish displays of wealth. He had migrated from Philadelphia and was very conscientiously trying to become wealthy and wise by the Benjamin Franklin prescription of prudence, thrift, and virtue. As he worked away, a typical pioneer, he began to see visions and dream dreams. He wrote to his sister back East:

How I long for the Golden Age, for the promised Millennium, when each one will be free to follow his best and noblest impulses, unfettered by the restrictions and necessities which our present state of society imposes

[2] *Ibid.,* p. xvi.

upon him; when the poorest and the meanest will have a chance to use all his God-given faculties and not be forced to drudge away the best part of his time in order to supply wants but little above those of the animal. . . .

Is it any wonder that men lust for gold and are willing to give almost anything for it, when it covers everything,—the purest and holiest desires of their hearts, the exercise of their noblest powers! What a pity we can't be contented! Is it? Who knows? Sometimes I feel sick of the fierce struggle of our highly-civilized life, and think I would like to get away from cities and business, with their jostlings and strainings and cares, altogether, and find some place on one of the hill-sides which look so dim and blue in the distance, where I could gather those I love, and live content with what Nature and our own resources would furnish; but alas, money, money is wanted even for that.[3]

Puzzled and discouraged by this paradox of poverty amid *natural* abundance, he was shocked and horrified when he went to New York (on business) and saw there the extremes of *social* inequality, rich and poor side by side. It was basically the same problem as his own, and he "vowed" to solve it. He was convinced both by childhood faith and later experience that God is generous and that the Malthusian attempts to charge misery to lack of food were "blasphemous." He spoke continually of "the bounty of the Creator." What is more, he believed in divine justice, in a "natural order" or social system according to the Will of God. Among other natural rights man has a "natural right to property," a sacred right, based on God's care for all equally. A denial of such rights George regarded as an irreverent denial of God's order.

This faith was quite different from the Hegelian faith in the socialized Kingdom of God. For state socialism and communism were both associated in George's mind with utopian communities. "Socialism in anything approaching such a form, modern society cannot successfully attempt. The only force that has ever proved competent for it—a strong and definite religious faith—is wanting and is daily growing less." [4]

Along with George's belief in private property went his belief that there is no inherent conflict between capital and labor.

[3] George Raymond Geiger, *The Philosophy of Henry George* (Grand Forks, N.D., 1931), pp. 30–31, quoting a letter to George's sister dated Sept. 16, 1861.
[4] Henry George, *Progress and Poverty* (Modern Library ed.), p. 320.

Labor and capital are but different forms of the same thing—human exertion. Capital is produced by labor; it is, in fact, but labor impressed upon matter. . . . Hence the principle that, under circumstances which permit free competition, operates to bring wages to a common standard and profits to a substantial equality . . . operates to establish and maintain this equilibrium between wages and interest. . . . Interest and wages must rise and fall together.[5]

This much he had learned from J. S. Mill's *Political Economy*, and he regarded the "principle" as part of a just, natural order. Similarly, he took for granted that the division of labor is beneficial; he called it the "process of integration, of the specialization of functions and powers," which draws men together into a social organization.

On the basis of these principles he formulated what he called "the law of progress," by which he meant a prescription for a system of production which enables men to spend a maximum of human energies in making improvements, and a minimum in "merely maintaining existence."

Men tend to progress just as they come closer together, and by co-operation with each other increase the mental power that may be devoted to improvement, but just as conflict is provoked, or association develops inequality of condition and power, this tendency to progression is lessened, checked, and finally reversed.[6]

This formula is not so much a law of history as a prescription for happiness. It is a *moral* law. For the philosophy of history George had a Schopenhauerean [7] scorn. History is not progress; it is a succession of cycles of progress and decline.

If progress operated to fix an improvement in man's nature and thus to produce further progress, though there might be occasional interruption, yet the general rule would be that progress would be continuous—that advance would lead to advance, and civilization develop into higher civilization. Not merely the general rule, but *the universal rule*, is the reverse of this. The earth is the tomb of the dead empires, no less than of dead men. Instead of progress fitting men for greater progress, every civilization that

---

[5] Henry George, *Progress and Poverty* (Modern Library ed.), pp. 198–99.

[6] *Ibid.*, p. 508.

[7] George Raymond Geiger, *The Philosophy of Henry George* (New York, 1933), pp. 330–31, for a discussion of George's preference for Schopenhauer over both Hegel and Spencer.

was in its own time as vigorous and advancing as ours is now, has of itself come to a stop.[8]

The problem of progress was, therefore, not an historical problem, but a moral and economic problem. Under what conditions is "the law of progress" violated?

George's answer was quite simple. Association produces crowding; crowding raises rent; inequalities of rent produce "unearned income" for those who have a monopoly of valuable land. If the profits of the landlord were taken from him, equality would be restored and progress could again proceed.

Unfortunately for Henry George, the thousands of American farmers who were convinced that he had discovered the cause of poverty had no enthusiasm for his remedy, and the thousands of urban workers who were enthusiastic for his remedy could not convince him of the beauties of socialism. Philosophically, however, he achieved his basic aim. He awakened his countrymen to the "non-progressive" uses to which the nation's wealth, especially its wealth in land, was being put and to the natural resources available "in God's bounty" if men would only "associate in equality."

What Henry George did to awaken in Americans a hope for the abolition of poverty through public control of natural resources, Edward Bellamy did to awaken in them a sense of the progress which might be realized through a more equitable and systematic use of industrial resources and invention. His novel *Looking Backward* (1888) created a socialist nationalist movement that captured the imagination and energies of large sections of the middle classes in all parts of the country. "Bellamy clubs" were formed in most of the large cities, and some of them still exist. Through the activities of these clubs the public ownership of public utilities was promoted, and an additional impetus was given to the general Populist uprising of the nineties.

The philosophical orientation of Bellamy's nationalism is extraordinary. As a youth he composed a tract entitled *The Religion of Solidarity,* which developed into a philosophical scheme the then-current and popular notion that there are centripetal and centrifugal forces in man. Both nature and society are essentially a balance of

[8] Henry George, *Progress and Poverty* (Modern Library ed.), p. 485.

centripetal and centrifugal forces, and this balance is the essence of solidarity. Man, both as a physical and as a social being, is part of an organic whole. Though this conception was a commonplace of democratic nationalism, Bellamy took it more seriously than most of his fellow democrats. He developed particularly a theory of human nature according to which the ordinary personality with its self-centeredness, its segregation, and its apparent independence is supplemented by an "impersonal consciousness" which binds it to the "universal soul." Solidarity thus has a psychological foundation, man being at once individual and part of "the all-identical life of the universe within us."

Nor is this tendency of the human soul to a more perfect realization of its solidarity with the universe, by the development of instincts partly or wholly latent, altogether a theory. It is already an observed fact, a matter of history. Sentimental love of the beautiful and sublime in nature, the charm which mountains, sea, and landscape so potently exercise upon the modern mind through a subtle sense of sympathy, is a comparatively modern and recent growth of the human mind. The ancients knew, or at least say, nothing of it. It is a curious fact that in no classical author are to be found any allusions to a class of emotions and sentiments that take up such large space in modern literature. It is almost within a century, in fact, that this susceptibility of the soul seems to have been developed. It is not therefore surprising that its language should still be vague. I am sure that much of the unrest and reaching out after the infinite, which is the peculiar characteristic of this age, is the result of this new sense. If culture can add such a province as this to human nature within a century, it is surely not visionary to count on a still more complete future development of the same group of subtle psychical faculties.[9]

Bellamy played with such ideas in a series of psychological stories which he wrote to illustrate the possibilities of development in the human personality, which show interesting anticipation of more recent psychology. He began to write "romances" similar to those of Hawthorne, his philosophical interest being not unlike Hawthorne's, too—an analysis of the "economy of happiness" in a democratic environment. His studies were extremely sensitive presentations of the social psychology of conscience. He then began playing with the idea

[9] Arthur E. Morgan, *The Philosophy of Edward Bellamy* (New York, 1945), pp. 12–13.

of a "romance" of society as a whole. Meanwhile, he had seen Europe, had felt the urgency of "the social problem," and had learned a little of state socialism (*not* Marxian). His journalism and lectures at Chicopee Falls, Massachusetts, his home town, showed the effects of his concern with economic problems.

The great reforms of the world have hitherto been political rather than social. In their progress classes privileged by title have been swept away, but classes privileged by wealth remain. A nominal aristocracy is ceasing to exist, but the actual aristocracy of wealth, the world over, is every day becoming more and more powerful. The idea that men can derive a right from birth or name to dispose of the destinies of their fellows is exploded, but the world thinks not yet of denying that gold confers a power upon its possessors to domineer over their equals and enforce from them a life's painful labors at the price of a bare subsistence. . . . What is the name of an institution by which men control the labor of other men, and out of the abundance created by that labor, having doled out to the laborers such a pittance as may barely support life and sustain strength for added tasks, reserve to themselves the vast surplus for the support of a life of ease and splendor? This, gentlemen, is slavery. . . .

Let not any one falsely reply that I am dreaming of a happiness without toil, of abundance without labor. Labor is the necessary condition, not only of abundance but of existence upon earth. I ask only that none labor beyond measure that others may be idle, that there be no more masters and no more slaves among men. Is this too much? Does any fearful soul exclaim, impossible, that this hope has been the dream of men in all ages, a shadowy and Utopian reverie of a divine fruition which the earth can never bear? That the few must revel and the many toil; the few waste, the many want; the few be masters, the many serve; the toilers of the earth be the poor and the idlers the rich, and that this must go on forever? . . .

Not so, for nothing that is unjust can be eternal, and nothing that is just can be impossible.[10]

Then an inspiration of an extraordinary sort came to him: socialized labor is conspicuous in military service, why not organize national industrial service on a military basis? Let him tell of his new enthusiasm himself.

[10] Arthur E. Morgan, *Edward Bellamy* (New York, 1944), pp. 225–26, quoting Bellamy's article "How I Wrote *Looking Backward,*" *Ladies' Home Journal*, II (April, 1894), 1–3.

In undertaking to write *Looking Backward* I had, at the outset, no idea of attempting a serious contribution to the movement of social reform. The idea was a mere literary fantasy, a fairy tale of social felicity. There was no thought of contriving a house which practical men might live in, but merely of hanging in mid-air far out of reach of the sordid and material world of the present, a cloud-palace for an ideal humanity.

The idea of committing the duty of maintaining the community to an industrial army, precisely as the duty of protecting it is entrusted to a military army, was directly suggested to me by the grand object lesson of the organization of an entire people for national purposes presented by the military system of universal service for fixed and equal terms, which has been practically adopted by the nations of Europe . . . It was not till I began to work out the details of the scheme . . . that I perceived the full potency of the instrument I was using and recognized in the modern military system not merely a rhetorical analogy for a national industrial service, but its prototype, furnishing at once a complete working model for its organization. . . .

Something in this way it was that, no thanks to myself, I stumbled over the destined corner-stone of the new social order. It scarcely needs to be said that having once apprehended it for what it was, it became a matter of pressing importance to me to show it in the same light to other people. This led to a complete recasting, both in form and purpose, of the book I was engaged upon. Instead of a mere fairy tale of social perfection, it became the vehicle of a definite scheme of industrial reorganization.[11]

Thus Bellamy put labor on a basis of national *duty*:

Nationalists . . . [would make] equal provision for the maintenance of all an incident and an indefeasible condition of citizenship, without any regard whatever to the relative specific services of different citizens. The rendering of such services, on the other hand, instead of being left to the option of the citizen with the alternative of starvation, would be required under a uniform law as a civic duty, precisely like other forms of taxation or military service, levied on the citizen for the furtherance of a common-weal in which each is to share equally.[12]

In order to achieve the organization of labor as a national service, Bellamy and his nationalist clubs relied largely on nationalization of

[11] *Ibid.*
[12] Bellamy, "Introduction to the American Edition," in G. B. Shaw, ed., *The Fabian Essays in Socialism*, p. xvii.

utilities. Competition was to be completely destroyed as the root of all evil. This "brotherhood" was to include all mankind. It is significant that the program of nationalization did not imply a nationalistic conception of solidarity. The ethics of the movement was humanitarian and cosmopolitan. All men are equal because each man has "the worth and dignity of the individual." "That dignity, consisting of the quality of human nature, is essentially the same in all individuals, and therefore equality is the vital principle of democracy." [13] In *Equality* Bellamy attempted to defend this conception of a "Brotherhood of Humanity" and to outline an economic system in which "all material conditions" are made subservient to "this intrinsic and equal dignity of the individual." Thus, while sacrificing the Yankee ideal of individual independence, Bellamy reasserted the traditional American faith in the moral qualities of the individual and in general adapted his collectivist program to the middle-class, Protestant conscience of his environment.

More typical of later American socialism than Bellamy's utopianism, was the Fabian type of socialist doctrine introduced into America by the Danish liberal, Laurence Gronlund. His book *The Co-operative Commonwealth* (1884) went through several editions, and though it never enjoyed the spectacular success of *Looking Backward,* it remained even after the decline of the Bellamy enthusiasm a standard exposition of democratic socialism.[14] He argued that it was a principle of political economy that capital and labor are partners in production, but that in fact capitalists and laborers do not co-operate. The state (or "organized society") must compel these rival classes to perform their natural duties by taking over the ownership of the means of

---

[13] Bellamy, *Equality* (New York, 1934), p. 26.

[14] In the Introduction to the 1890 edition, Gronlund remarked pointedly: "The happiest effect of my book is that it has led indirectly, and probably unconsciously, to Mr. Bellamy's 'Looking Backward,' the novel which without doubt has stealthily inoculated thousands of Americans with socialism, just because it ignored that name and those who had written on the subject. It should, however, in justice to the cause, be stated, that there are three ideas in that novel for which socialism should not be held responsible, as has been done by Prof. Francis A. Walker, in a criticism. These are a love for militarism, equal wages, and appointments by the retired functionaries. They are decidedly unsocialistic notions, belong exclusively to Mr. Bellamy, and will be further noticed in the course of this volume."—Laurence Gronlund, *The Co-operative Commonwealth* (Boston, 1893), p. viii.

production and transportation. Gronlund, unlike Bellamy, had an idealistic theory of the national state, derived largely from Hegel.

To the State we owe our freedom. . . . It gives us all the rights we have. . . . As against the State . . . even Labor does not give us a particle of title to what our hands and brain produce. . . . The Public Welfare means more than the welfare of all the living individuals composing it. Since the State is an organism, it is more than all of us collectively.[15]

Gronlund admits that in all states,

our own country included, classes exercise the authority and direct all social activity. Do not bring forward the insipid commonplace that, properly speaking, we have no "classes" in our country and that the "people" govern here! No classes? Indeed! . . .

The autocrats of our industrial affairs dictate the policy of the government.[16]

This class-state will develop into a *Commonwealth*—bless the Puritans for that splendid English word! It will develop into a state that will know of no "classes" either in theory or practice. . . . This Commonwealth will be a society all of whose units have a sense of belonging together . . . pervaded by a feeling of what we, using a foreign word, call *Solidarity*, but what we not inaptly may in English term *corporate responsibility*.[17]

To achieve this corporate responsibility Gronlund recommends abandoning the present Constitution and the system of party government, whereby "the whole" is turned over successively to rival parties, and instituting a "social economy" or civil service for the *administration* (not government) of public affairs. "That is what Democracy means; it means administration by the competent." [18]

Gronlund believed that this "German type" of socialism, which, he maintained, persuaded Germans to embrace it simply because it was logical, would have to be preached to Anglo-Saxons as a religious duty. He therefore published in Bellamy's periodical, *The Nationalist*, a series of sentimental appeals which he later expanded and published in book form under the title *Our Destiny; the Influence of Nationalism on Morals and Religion* (1890). His thesis was that "a construc-

---

[15] *Ibid.*, pp. 82–88.   [16] *Ibid.*, pp. 89, 91.
[17] Gronlund, *The Co-operative Commonwealth* (New York, 1884), pp. 94–95.
[18] Gronlund, *The Co-operative Commonwealth* (Boston, 1893), p. 181.

tive form of socialism" was naturally "evolving" among American working men, that the "conscience of the country" was being aroused by the Nationalist and Christian Socialist movements, so that "our comfortable classes are becoming conscious of being part of a living organism that suffers," and that these "comfortable classes" are now ready to recognize their "duty to put their shoulders to the wheel of progress . . . to cooperate with the Power behind Evolution." The fervor of his apocalyptic faith is extravagantly expressed near the end of the volume.

And now the most solemn moment has arrived for me. When I reflect that what remains to be said may prove the spark that, applied to the will of some of my readers, may turn them into leaders of men whom we so much need, I almost tremble from the excitement that masters me. How blessed life then would be! For everything else is ready—only leaders are wanting. . . .

I have a firm conviction that the leaders wanted now must come out from profoundly religious minds. Only such can be inflamed with the needed enthusiasm (and the age will rival that of the first crusades in enthusiasm) and inaugurate the great change in love and not in hate. You must feel within yourself that God needs you, that he cannot do without you. . . . We must act out our own destiny, or nothing will be done—that is the meaning of being God's co-workers, and of free-will. Oh! if it were written in letters of fire on every heart: we carry out God's thoughts.[19]

Gronlund was preoccupied during his last years in organizing an American socialist fraternity among college students. This secret society was to have the emotional and philanthropic values of a fraternity or lodge and was to train labor leaders, on whom his hopes depended.

This faith in conscientious co-operation was the gospel not only of the middle-class reformers, but of the labor leaders, too. Conspicuous among them was Terence V. Powderly, General Master Workman of the Knights of Labor until 1893 and under President McKinley Commissioner-General of Immigration. His pathetic "destiny," to close his career as labor leader with a political spoils office under the Mark Hanna regime, is eloquent testimony to the failure of this populist movement for economic democracy to achieve its aims. Powderly's

[19] Gronlund, *Our Destiny; The Influence of Nationalism on Morals and Religion* (Boston, 1891), pp. 214–15.

appeals to the chivalrous and religious sentiments of the hundreds of
thousands of members of the Noble Order of the Knights of Labor,
and his constant championing of the idea of solidarity ("An injury to
one is the concern of all") make him an excellent example of a deep-
seated American faith that still survives its many defeats and gains in
religious intensity as it loses in practical success. Though the philosophy of solidarity was no doubt a middle-class theory based on middle-
class prejudices and interests, it is not true that it was confined to these
classes or that it functioned primarily as a class ideology. The faith in
co-operation as essential to democracy was, and still is, a determination on the part of the overwhelming majority of Americans that the
issue of wage slavery shall not, like that of negro slavery, lead to
civil war and violence. Generation after generation has exhibited this
religious devotion to the cause of peaceful democracy, and the following words of Powderly may serve as a summary statement of this
enduring faith.

During the greater part of nineteen hundred years, men were as neighbors and enemies engaged in commerce and trade. Finally nations as well
as individuals began to buy from and sell to each other. International com-
mercialists began to strive for as much of the "root of all evil" as they could
honestly get or dishonestly gouge each other out of, and Churchianity,
which largely supplanted Christianity and is often mistaken for it, has not
stayed the grasping hand of an individual trader, a national commercialist,
or an international murderer whose greed prompted him to reach out for
the market of neighbor and enemy and gather in all that could be gained.
. . . Striving for the world's trade, or the international "root of all evil,"
brought on a war that slaughtered men, violated women, starved children,
and spread disease, want, and famine where God had blessed with sufficiency
for every need. . . .

We must teach our members, then, that the remedy for the redress of
the wrongs we complain of does not lie in the suicidal strike; but in thorough,
effective organization. Without organization we cannot accomplish anything; through it we hope to forever banish that curse of modern civilization
—wage slavery . . .

Organization once perfected, what must we do? I answer, study the best
means of putting your organization to some practicable use by embarking in
a system of COÖPERATION.

Powderly then insisted that labor unions should be kept entirely voluntary, and he explained that the voluntary or coöperative system of organization is a system

which will eventually make every man his own master—every man his own employer; a system which will give the laborer a fair proportion of the products of his toil. It is to coöperation, then, as the lever of labor's emancipation, that the eyes of the workingmen and women of the world should be directed, upon coöperation their hopes should be centered. . . .

I can imagine nothing worse happening to organized labor than to make membership in it a condition of employment. To promulgate such a decree and to enforce it through the strike would be suicidal. For a union to demand that the man entering the shop shall first apply for admission and then raise the initiation fee so high that he cannot afford to pay it is to resort to might and not right. The closed shop through coercion would not survive the storm of opposition it would encounter among workingmen themselves. . . .

When it is admitted that the individual shall not be allowed to follow the calling of his choice except by joining a union or any other organization, we shall have to admit that the industry of which that union is a part shall flourish only as the union shall have become that which the unions I knew strenuously objected to—monopoly. . . .

Here we are of all races, we come from everywhere to make a family that has no family tree, a family with no common ancestor, and yet a family that may be traced back to the greatest of all common ancestors—God the Father. We are all children of Him who gave us birth and everything following it to make us happy, contented, prosperous, if we but use His gifts wisely and intelligently. It is because we allowed some to monopolize all the gifts, that there is dissatisfaction, distrust and want in the land. We affect reverence for and belief in God, yet sneer at him who tells us that God gave this earth to all His children, to be used for the benefit of all. . . .

The term "master and servant" is dead. The world is accustoming itself to know all as servants, and the word service shall soon take on its real meaning and significance. Out of all the marching and countermarching, out of all the contentions and transitions, will come a fuller, clearer realization of our duty to each other, and our highest duty to each other is service to each other. How this service may best be performed shall constitute the real problem of the future; in its solution toleration must take the place of intolerance, moderation must supplant excess, secret scheming and underhand dealing must give way to open and aboveboard business methods, and the term "love your neighbor" must be clothed anew with the meaning intended when the words were first spoken.[20]

I know that many readers will think such sermons out of place in a history of philosophy, and for their benefit I should explain why Mr. Powderly's preaching seems to me historically very important and quite philosophical. In the first place, his thinking is more critical than it appears to be to us who in our sophistication look back on the Knights of Labor, the Nationalists, the Populists, and the Christian Socialists as "the last important manifestation of middle-class reform philosophies in the American labor movement." The end is not yet, not even for middle-class reform philosophies; and such social gospels, even if they do mark the end of an era, are significant less as a conclusion than as a center for democratic thought. From the point of view of the social theory of today the gospel of co-operation seems antique indeed, and worthy only of pulpits. But from the point of view of the general course of popular reflection on social problems that gospel is central. And it is central not merely socially, as are the so-called middle classes, but intellectually, as a norm to which democrats of all ages appeal when they find it necessary to make appeals. Mr. Powderly's faith in co-operation was not merely the outcome of his long experience with labor problems, it was the substance of the faith of the common people. The philosophy of the common man is very apt to be commonplace, but it is not for that reason uncritical. It reflects the kind of thinking which democratic society invariably generates, and which therefore will find future expressions in the democracies of the future. It defines the essential meanings of democracy; the other versions which we have surveyed are largely variations on this central theme.

But the gospel of co-operation is not merely the least common denominator of democratic theories, it is also an enduring type of sentimentality and enthusiasm, which no account of American thought can afford to ignore. It was good fortune rather than good judgment which gave to the United States its national socialism before it received its Marxism. As a result our fanatics for solidarity and for a

[20] Terence V. Powderly, *The Path I Trod* (New York, 1940), ed. by Harry J. Carman, Henry David, and Paul N. Guthrie, pp. 264, 265–66, 269, 278–79, 314, 315, 423, 426, 427.

compulsory national service (in Bellamy's case, for an industrial militia) were on the whole a genial, unambitious, scattered lot of poor philanthropists. They were neither class-conscious nor internationally militant; the same gospel if believed by an organization of aggrieved veterans could easily be given a revolutionary power.[21] American national socialism was pre-Marxian, but it was post-revolutionary. It was a commentary on the experience of previous generations of struggle. There was more recognition of class struggle in the politics and theories of James Madison, of Calhoun, and of Webster, before the industrial revolution had reached its height, than in the days of Bellamy, Bryan, Powderly, and Carnegie, when there was a conscious effort to avoid further struggle. The preaching of co-operation had *behind* it the bitter memories of conflict; it was a philosophy of industrial innocence, but of political maturity. These circumstances of American bourgeois socialism require that we interpret it as indigenous and not merely as an extension of European movements; and they require that we evaluate its utopian and religious qualities in a way which to Europeans may seem childish. In America such religion was neither an opiate of the people nor a prescientific mythology; it was a carefully constructed mythology for wakening Puritans out of their false sense of security.

GUIDE TO THE LITERATURE FOR PART III

The Whig tradition has received inadequate treatment as an intellectual system. There are scattered but sympathetic treatments of its general themes in the recent writings of Charles A. Beard, especially *The Idea of National Interest* (New York, 1934) and *The American Spirit* (New York, 1942), as well as in Merle Curti, *The Growth of American Thought* (New York, 1943). There is a brief but excellent statement of its chief ideas in Ralph W. Gabriel, *The Course of American Democratic Thought* (New York, 1940), pp. 78–87. Under the heading "Particularism versus Nationalism"

[21] We can still look forward to the year 2000 from which Bellamy was looking backward and at this half-way station it seems by no means certain that American national socialism is dead and gone. It seems probable, however, that the national socialists of 2000 A.D. will not look backward far enough to discover Bellamy's kinship to them.

there are good general surveys of the movements and issues in J. Mark Jacobson, *The Development of American Political Thought* (New York, 1932), Chapter VI, and in John W. Burgess, *The Middle Period* (New York, 1897), Chapters I, V–VIII. Joseph Dorfman, *The Economic Mind in American Civilization* (New York, 1946) contains a good general account of Whig economic theory, I, 362 ff., and discussions of Alexander Hamilton, I, 404–17, and Verplanck, I, 394; Volume II is largely devoted to the movements covered here, and especially should be read for its discussions of Colwell, Bowen, Cooper, Raymond, Cardozo, Lieber, Galloway, G. Tucker, Dew, N. B. Tucker, Holmes, and Ware.

The most recent, and in many ways the best attempt to write the history of American democratic thought is Ralph W. Gabriel, *The Course of American Democratic Thought* (New York, 1940). It does more justice to the philosophic aspects of democracy than any other history. Parts I and II give excellent critical statements of the chief ideas associated with democracy from the rise of Jacksonianism to the Civil War. Unfortunately the book does not give a connected account of the *course* of the history of American democracy. Vernon L. Parrington, in *Main Currents in American Thought*, Volume II, "The Romantic Revolution in America 1800–1860" (New York, 1927), treats democratic ideas very sympathetically; this account has the additional merit of including much Southern material which, though not in the strict sense democratic theory, is an important element in democratic politics. Arthur M. Schlesinger, Jr., *The Age of Jackson* (Boston, 1945), is an excellent treatment of the intellectual currents of the period and a re-appraisal of some traditional fallacies. It appeared, unfortunately, too late to be used in the preparation of this part. William Sumner Jenkins, *Pro-Slavery Thought in the Old South* (Chapel Hill, N.C., 1935) contains an excellent account of the various Southern defenses of the "peculiar institution" as the basis for an "Athenian democracy"; notable are the approaches of Thomas R. Dew, James Henry Hammond, George N. Fitzhugh, and Edmund Ruffin. Chapters XII–XVI in the Beards's *Rise of American Civilization* (New York, 1928), entitled "Jacksonian Democracy," gives an excellent account of the general course of American democracy to the Civil War. For the economic history of the period an even more illuminating account may be found in Harry J. Carman and Samuel McKee, Jr., *A History of the United States* (Boston, 1931), Volume I. The political theories of democracy are sketched in Raymond G. Gettell, *History of American Political Thought* (New York, 1928), Chaps. VIII and X, and in Charles E. Merriam, *A History of American Political Theories* (New York, 1903), Chaps. V–VIII. Arthur A. Ekirch, Jr., *The Idea of Progress in America 1815–1860* (New York, 1944), should also be consulted. The relevant selections in Bernard Smith, ed., *The Democratic Spirit* (New York, 1941), are especially good for this period. Francis W. Coker, ed., *Democracy, Liberty, and Property: Readings in the American Political Tradition* (New York, 1942), also contains good and relevant selections.

CHAPTER 10

Hamilton's National Capitalism

Hamilton's complete *Works*, edited by H. C. Lodge, were published in 1904, in 12 volumes, and a representative selection will be found in the American Writers Series, edited by Frederick C. Prescott. The editor's introduction to these selections gives an excellent general portrait, but an inadequate idea of Hamilton's political economy. *Industrial and Commercial Correspondence of Alexander Hamilton* (Chicago, 1928), edited by A. H. Cole, and Alexander Hamilton, *Papers on Public Credit, Commerce and Finance* (New York, 1934), edited by Samuel McKee, Jr., make available Hamilton's economic writings. The best exposition of Hamilton's economics is William S. Culbertson, *Alexander Hamilton; an Essay* (New Haven, Conn., 1916). An excellent critical sketch of Hamilton's career, emphasizing his capitalistic doctrines and practices, will be found in Rexford Guy Tugwell and Joseph Dorfman, "Alexander Hamilton: Nation-Maker," *Columbia University Quarterly*, XXIX (1937), 209–26; XXX (1938), 59–72. For the *Report on Manufactures* see E. G. Bourne, "Alexander Hamilton and Adam Smith," *Quarterly Journal of Economics*, VIII (1894), 328. In Herbert Croly, *The Promise of American Life* (New York, 1910), there is an unusual exposition of the significance of Hamilton's nationalism, and in Nicholas Murray Butler, *Building the American Nation* (Cambridge, Eng., 1923), the suggestion is made that Hamilton and Jefferson should not be regarded as antithetical, but as complementary "Founding Fathers." There are several editions of the *Federalist Papers*, the most convenient being the Sesquicentennial edition (Washington, 1937), with an introduction by Edward M. Earle, which is worth reading. For Hamilton's general philosophy the following numbers of the *Federalist Papers* are of most value: Nos. 6, 11, 16, 17, 22, 27, 28, 36, 70, 71. F. S. Oliver, *Alexander Hamilton* (London, 1906), and H. J. Ford, *Alexander Hamilton* (New York, 1931), are the best biographies.

The American System as a Whig Party Platform

For an exposition of the American system by the Whig political leaders, it is necessary to search in odd places in the diary of John Quincy Adams and among the speeches of Adams, Henry Clay, and John C. Calhoun. John

Quincy Adams, *The Jubilee of the Constitution; a Discourse Delivered at the Request of the New York Historical Society . . . the 30th of April, 1839* (New York, 1839), lays great emphasis on the unity of the American people even before the Declaration of Independence and develops his whole interpretation of the Constitution on the basis of "one people."

Charles M. Wiltse, *John C. Calhoun, Nationalist, 1782–1828* (Indianapolis, Ind., 1944), aims to present Calhoun as a wholehearted nationalist until he was suddenly and bitterly disillusioned in 1828 and also refers to him as primarily a "metaphysician" rather than a politician. Unfortunately, it is impossible to find Calhoun's metaphysics, and it is doubtful, in view of other biographies, whether Calhoun was as free from sectionalist interests as he is here represented. But this volume is a valuable account of Whig history and also has value as a biography of Calhoun. There is a "Footnote on John C. Calhoun" on pp. 103–10 of Gabriel's *Course of American Democratic Thought*, but this deals almost exclusively with the later Calhoun. It gives an excellent summary of Calhoun's political philosophy as found in his *Disquisition on Government*, but Gabriel's attempt to show the originality of these ideas leaves me unconvinced. He is quite right in representing Calhoun as an unconventional thinker and as an uncompromising champion of liberty. It seems to me that in this respect Calhoun was the last stand of Jeffersonianism, for the "fundamental law" which Gabriel and Calhoun celebrate was a commonplace of Deism.

Nationalist Political Economy

The descriptions of nationalist political economy are very inadequate from the philosophical point of view, except as they are included in Joseph Dorfman's comprehensive work, referred to above. There is a general statement in Sidney Sherwood, *Tendencies in American Economic Thought* (Baltimore, 1897), and a cumbersome analysis in Ernest Teilhac, *Pioneers of American Economic Thought in the Nineteenth Century* (New York, 1936).

There is a fairly good account of Daniel Raymond by C. P. Neill, *Daniel Raymond; an Early Chapter in the History of Economic Theory in the United States* (Baltimore, 1897), but Raymond's own works are decidedly the most interesting literature in the field. The first edition, *Thoughts on Political Economy* (Baltimore, 1820), and the second edition, *Elements of Political Economy*, two volumes (Baltimore, 1823), are philosophically more interesting than the later, more condensed editions. The fourth edition (Baltimore, 1840) includes "The Elements of Constitutional Law," but since this was a text for college students, it is confined strictly to legal history.

On Mathew Carey see E. L. Bradsher, *Mathew Carey* (New York, 1912). Carey's *Autobiography* was reissued as Research Classic No. 1 (Brooklyn, N.Y., 1942); it was originally published as a series of letters in the *New England Magazine*, 1833–37. It is entertaining reading, but throws little light on Carey's economic theories.

Henry C. Carey's chief works are: *Principles of Political Economy*, three volumes (Philadelphia, 1827–40); *The Past, the Present, and the Future* (Philadelphia, 1843); *Principles of Social Science*, three volumes (Philadelphia, 1858–59); and *The Unity of Law; as Exhibited in the Relations of Physical, Social, Mental and Moral Science* (Philadelphia, 1872). His tract *Commerce, Christianity, and Civilization versus British Free Trade; Letters in Reply to the London Times* (Philadelphia, 1876) is less ambitious philosophically than the title would lead the reader to believe. Christianity appears in the work only when the author complains that free trade is driving commerce from Christian neighbors to Hindu heathen.

Charles Jared Ingersoll followed his *View of the Rights and Wrongs, Power and Policy, of the United States of America* (Philadelphia, 1808), with a series of discussions of economic and cultural nationalism, of which the best known was his *Inchiquin, the Jesuit's Letters* (Philadelphia, 1810). His address before the American Philosophical Society in 1823, *The Influence of America on the Mind* (Philadelphia, 1823), which has been called the American declaration of cultural independence, is reprinted in Blau, ed., *American Philosophic Addresses, 1700–1900*, pp. 20–59. He also wrote, and published between 1845 and 1852, a *History of the War of 1812* in four volumes, giving expression to his nationalism and his feeling against Britain.

Francis Bowen published his *Principles of Political Economy* (New York, 1856). He revised it under the title *American Political Economy* (New York, 1870) to include a critique of national finance since 1861.

Among the many American formulations of classical political economy two should be mentioned: Thomas Cooper, *Lectures on the Elements of Political Economy* (Columbia, S.C., 1826), of which a second edition was published in 1831, because it was an important item in the controversy of the day; and Henry Vethake, *The Principles of Political Economy* (Philadelphia, 1838), because it takes for granted that as early as 1838 the American system was passé and that economic nationalism would probably never be revived.

Gulian C. Verplanck's *Letter to Col. William Drayton of South Carolina, in Assertion of the Constitutional Power of Congress to Impose Protecting Duties* (New York, 1831) reveals clearly the interest of commercial and manufacturing groups in stability of policy and in the maintenance of the Union. Though the author is on principle opposed to protectionism, he pleads for a policy of "prudent and expedient" compromise in order to stave off the greater evils of periodic depressions and nullifications. Verplanck's position with respect to cultural nationalism is revealed in his address on "The Advantages and Dangers of the American Scholar," reprinted in Blau, ed., *American Philosophic Addresses, 1700–1900*, pp. 119–50.

CHAPTER 11

Arthur M. Schlesinger, Jr., has written by far the best account of this theme in his *The Age of Jackson* (Boston, 1945) but unfortunately ch. xxiv, which seeks to define the philosophical characteristics of Jacksonian democracy, is inadequate and misleading. The transition from Jeffersonian to Jacksonian democracy is illustrated in William B. Hatcher, *Edward Livingston—Jeffersonian Republican and Jacksonian Democrat* (Baton Rouge, La., 1945). The democracy of James Fenimore Cooper is still a polemical subject. The reader will get an idea of the problems involved in Dorothy Waples, *The Whig Myth of James Fenimore Cooper* (New Haven, 1938). Van Wyck Brooks's account of Cooper in *The World of Washington Irving* (New York, 1944) is judicious.

Russell B. Nye, *George Bancroft, Brahmin Rebel* (New York, 1944), gives a vivid picture of New England democracy. A. J. G. Perkins and Theresa Wolfson, *Frances Wright: Free Enquirer* (New York, 1939), Richard W. Leopold, *Robert Dale Owen, a Biography* (Cambridge and London, 1940), and Arthur M. Schlesinger, Jr., *Orestes A. Brownson; a Pilgrim's Progress* (Boston, 1939), tell the story of the philosophical leaders of working-class democracy. What little literature there is on Richard Hildreth discusses him as a historian; see A. M. Schlesinger, Jr., "The Problem of Richard Hildreth," *The New England Quarterly*, XIII (1940), 223–45. However, a biography by D. E. Emerson will be published soon, and some of his philosophical papers are being edited by Martha M. Pingel. Other aspects of the subject are treated in Paul A. Palmer, "Benthamism in England and America," *The American Political Science Review*, XXXV (1941), 855–71. For Locofoco and Barnburning democracy see Allan Nevins, *The Evening Post; a Century of Journalism* (New York, 1922), chap. v and vi. For Whig denunciation of Locofoco democracy see Dallas C. Dickey, *Seargent S. Prentiss* (Baton Rouge, La., 1945), pp. 254 ff.

CHAPTER 12

On Young America see Merle Curti, " 'Young America,' " *The American Historical Review*, XXXII (1926–27), 34–55, which emphasizes the foreign policy of Young America rather than its general theory of progress; Merle Curti, "George N. Sanders—American Patriot of the Fifties," *The South Atlantic Quarterly*, XXVII (1928), 79–87; Lawrence S. Hall, *Hawthorne, Critic of Society* (New Haven, 1944), chap. v, and Randall Stewart, ed., "Hawthorne and Politics; Unpublished Letters to William B. Pike," *The New England Quarterly*, V (1932), 237–63. Hall's work on Hawthorne as a social critic is far and away the most illuminating account of Hawthorne as a Democrat; it should be supplemented, however, by Lloyd Morris, *The Rebellious Puritan* (New York, 1927), Newton Arvin, *Hawthorne* (London, 1930), and Edward Mather, *Nathaniel Hawthorne; a Modest Man* (New York, 1940).

A sympathetic but warning criticism on the part of an historically minded idealist is Caleb Sprague Henry's "piece" "Young America—the True Idea of Progress," which was first published in the *New York Daily Times*, May 2, 1854, and is reprinted in Caleb S. Henry, *Considerations on Some of the Elements and Conditions of Social Welfare and Human Progress* (New York, 1861), pp. 199–206.

A chronological list of major works of democratic theory to supplement the last two sections of this bibliographical guide follows.

1824   Edward Everett, "The Circumstances Favorable to the Progress of Literature in America," in Blau, ed., *American Philosophic Addresses, 1700–1900*, pp. 64–93.

1828   James Fenimore Cooper, Notions of the Americans.

1828–31   Robert Dale Owen, Frances Wright, and Orestes A. Brownson, editorials and articles in the *Free Enquirer*.

1829   Frances Wright, Course of Popular Lectures; "On Existing Evils and Their Remedy," reprinted in Blau.

1829   Thomas Skidmore, The Rights of Man to Property!

1829–40   W. C. Bryant and William Leggett, editorials in the New York *Post*. Selections in Smith, The Democratic Spirit.

1832   Andrew Jackson, "Bank Veto Message." Selection in Thorp, Curti, and Baker, American Issues.

1834   George Bancroft, Preface to Vol. I of the History of the United States, and "The Office of the People in Art, Government and Religion," in Blau, ed., *American Philosophic Addresses, 1700–1900*, pp. 94–114.

1835   James Fenimore Cooper, The Monikins.

1835–40   Alexis de Tocqueville, Democracy in America.

1836   George Sidney Camp, Democracy.

1838   James Fenimore Cooper, The American Democrat.

1840   Orestes A. Brownson, "The Laboring Classes," in Blau, ed., *American Philosophic Addresses, 1700–1900* pp. 174–204.

1840   Richard Hildreth, "Introduction" to Jeremy Bentham's Theory of Legislation.

1844   Richard Hildreth, Theory of Morals, and An Open Letter to Orestes A. Brownson and the Editor of the *North American Review*.

1844   Ralph Waldo Emerson, "The Young American."

1845   Edwin de Leon, The Position and Duties of Young America.

1846–47   Walt Whitman, editorials in the Brooklyn *Daily Eagle*, collected in The Gathering of the Forces, 2 volumes (New York, 1920).

1852   *The Democratic Review,* Vols. XXX–XXXI (new series, Vols. I–II), expressing the ideas of the Young America movement.

1852   Nathaniel Hawthorne, The Blithedale Romance, and "The Life of Franklin Pierce" (in Volume XII of Collected Works, which also contains a sketch of the Life of Hawthorne).

1853   Richard Hildreth, Theory of Politics.

1853–58   Nathaniel Hawthorne, English Note Books.

1854   George Bancroft, "The Necessity of Progress," in Literary and Historical Miscellanies, 1855.

1856   Albert T. Bledsoe, An Essay on Liberty and Slavery.

c. 1860   Nathaniel Hawthorne, Dr. Grimshawe's Secret.

1862   Nathaniel Hawthorne, "Chiefly about War Matters," in his Works, Vol. XII.

1863   Nathaniel Hawthorne, Our Old Home.

1876–77   George Ticknor, Life, Letters and Journals, 2 vols.

CHAPTER 13

The literature on frontier philosophy is misleading, for it is usually either a philosophizing about the frontier or an exposition of what the frontier meant to the East. Philosophizing under frontier conditions or in explanation of pioneering was, in the nature of things, not apt to take literary form and consequently the available evidence is often quite circumstantial. It is customary to emphasize the individualism of the frontier, and, properly understood, there is no attempt here to deny this generalization, but it is important to distinguish between the individualistic mode of life and the communal mode of thought. It is undoubtedly true that in most frontier communities there grew very early the ordinary institutions and habits of the older centers of civilization. No attempt is made here to survey such contributions from frontier communities to the more general and settled traditions of the country. We have singled out the theories of local independence as the most distinctive contribution of a frontier environment to the theory of democracy, in order to counteract the common impression that philosophical individualism was prevalent.

For the general description of the frontier and its meaning in American history the classic work is Frederick Jackson Turner, *The Frontier in American History* (New York, 1920). There are numerous critiques of his theories which are scarcely relevant to our subject here. The most recent and also the most judicious interpretation of frontier thought is Alice Felt Tyler, *Freedom's Ferment: Phases of American Social History to 1860* (Minneapolis, Minn., 1944), especially Part II, "Cults and Utopias"; this work has the merit of adding to a vivid description of the varieties of frontier speculation and enthusiasm a critical examination of their relation to freedom and democracy. Another good treatment is Ernest Sutherland Bates, *American Faith, Its Religious, Political, and Economic Foundations* (New York, 1940), Book IV, "The Faith Romanticized." H. Richard Niebuhr, *The Social Sources of Denominationalism* (New York, 1929), Chapter VI, "Sectionalism and Denominationalism in America," emphasizes the gregarious values of evangelistic religion for the impoverished life of the frontier.

William A. Hinds, *American Communities and Co-operative Colonies* (second revision, Chicago, 1908), is the most convenient survey of the chief religious and secular experiments in communal organization. It is supplemented by John Humphrey Noyes, *History of American Socialisms* (Philadelphia, 1870). Charles W. Ferguson, *The Confusion of Tongues* (New York, 1929), and Gilbert Seldes, *The Stammering Century* (New York, 1928), have relevant chapters. More recent guides to the religious groups will be found in the 1926 United States census of religious bodies, in Elmer T. Clark, *The Small Sects in America* (Nashville, Tenn., 1937), and in M. Phelan, *Handbook of All Denominations* (fifth edition, Nashville, Tenn., 1929).

The relation of the frontier to the major evangelical churches has been treated most adequately by W. W. Sweet, in *The Rise of Methodism in the West* (New York, 1920), *Religion on the American Frontier*, Vol. I, "The Baptists" (New York, 1931), and *The Story of Religion in America* (New York, 1930), Chapters XIV–XVII, and by Peter G. Mode, *The Frontier Spirit in American Christianity* (New York, 1923). To these accounts should be added the vivid description in W. E. Garrison, *Religion Follows the Frontier; a History of the Disciples of Christ* (New York, 1931). The *Autobiography of Peter Cartwright* (New York, 1856, and later editions) is an unusually interesting life of a circuit rider.

The literature of the particular sects and communities is too voluminous to mention in detail; there is a convenient bibliography at the end of the above-mentioned work by Elmer T. Clark. A few works are selected for mention here which have special philosophical interest: Jacob John Sessler, *Communal Pietism among Early American Moravians* (New York, 1933); Marguerite Fellows Melcher, *The Shaker Adventure* (Princeton, N.J., 1941); Ruth and R. W. Kauffman, *The Latter Day Saints* (London, 1912); Ephraim E. Ericksen, *The Psychological and Ethical Aspects of Mormon Group Life* (Chicago, 1922); William J. McNiff, *Heaven on Earth; a Planned Mormon Society* (Oxford, Ohio, 1940); Fawn M. Brodie, *No Man Knows My History; the Life of Joseph Smith* (New York, 1945); Richard W. Leopold, *Robert Dale Owen; a Biography* (Cambridge, Mass., 1940); A. J. G. Perkins and Theresa Wolfson, *Francis Wright; Free Enquirer* (New York, 1939); Marguerite Beck Block, *The New Church in the New World* (New York, 1932); Herbert W. Schneider and George Lawton, *A Prophet and a Pilgrim* (New York, 1942); Robert A. Parker, *A Yankee Saint; John Humphrey Noyes and the Oneida Community* (New York, 1935); Shirley Jackson Case, *The Millennial Hope* (Chicago, 1918); and E. L. Eaton, *The Millennial Dawn Heresy* (New York, 1911).

CHAPTER 14

The literature of the Southern defenses of liberty against union after Calhoun have only recently been restudied and brought to the attention of students. There is a representative anthology in W. Thorp, M. Curti, and C. Baker, *American Issues* (Chicago, 1941), under the heading "The Southern Cause, 1800–1860." V. L. Parrington, *Main Currents in American Thought*, Vol. II, "The Romantic Revolution in America," under the heading "The Mind of the South," Avery Craven, *The Coming of the Civil War* (New York, 1942), and Gettell, *History of American Political*

Thought (New York, 1928), Chapter IX, "Political Theory of Slavery," are suggestive and provocative discussions. It is unfortunate, though intelligible, that the literature of the slavery controversy should crowd out the discussion of other theoretical issues. We know that there was a considerable body of philosophical speculation in the South, but just what it was we cannot tell as yet. A case in point is Albert Taylor Bledsoe's *An Essay on Liberty and Slavery* (Philadelphia, 1856), in which there is a general discussion of social theory only indirectly related to slavery. The writings of George Tucker are worth mentioning in this connection, especially his elusive satire *A Voyage to the Moon* (New York, 1827). See also the accounts by Dorfman, in his *Economic Mind in American Civilization*, of Condy Raguet, J. N. Cardozo, M. R. H. Garnett, T. R. Dew, N. B. Tucker, G. F. Holmes, and G. Fitzhugh.

From the Northern point of view the issues of this period are usually described under the heading "Particularism vs. Nationalism." A typical outline, together with a useful anthology, is Jacobson, *The Development of American Political Thought*, Chapter VI. John W. Burgess's nationalistic history, *The Middle Period* (New York, 1897), is worth reading to give the political narrative of the period as well as the Unionist interpretation of the theoretical issue. The interpretation of the Civil War as "the second American Revolution" is stated very well in Chapters XVII–XVIII of the Beards's *The Rise of American Civilization*, and in A. C. Cole, *The Irrepressible Conflict, 1850–1865*, which is Volume VII of *A History of American Life*, edited by A. M. Schlesinger and D. R. Fox. Parrington has a succinct, judicious chapter on Lincoln as a theorist of democracy. Herbert Croly, *The Promise of American Life* (New York, 1910), has an interesting interpretation of Lincoln.

The political side of Whitman is most adequately discussed in Newton Arvin, *Whitman* (New York, 1938). This should be supplemented by F. O. Matthiessen's excellent review of *The Portable Walt Whitman*, ed. by Mark Van Doren, in the New York *Times* Book Review Section, July 29, 1945, p. 1. Van Doren's chronological arrangement of the major poems and his generous selections from the prose make an exceptionally useful anthology for the political philosophy and career of Whitman. There is a treatment of Whitman's democratic ideals in Jerome Nathanson, *Forerunners of Freedom: the Re-creation of the American Spirit* (Washington, D.C., 1941), Chapter II.

The chief philosophical writings of Francis Lieber are, in the order of their composition: *The Manual of Political Ethics* (Philadelphia, 1838–39); *Essays on Property and Labor* (New York, 1841); *On Civil Liberty and*

Self-Government (Philadelphia, 1853); "Inaugural in Columbia, S.C." (1835) in *The Miscellaneous Writings of Francis Lieber* (Philadelphia, 1881) I, 179; "First Constituents of Civilization" (1845), in *Miscellaneous Writings*, I, 205; "Inaugural in Columbia College, N.Y." (1858), in *Miscellaneous Writings*, I, 329; "On Nationalism and Internationalism" (1868), in *Miscellaneous Writings*, II, 221; "On the Rise of the Constitution of the United States" (1872), in *Miscellaneous Writings* II, 15.

The standard secondary works on Lieber are Thomas S. Perry, ed., *The Life and Letters of Francis Lieber* (Boston, 1882), and L. R. Harley, *Francis Lieber; His Life and Political Philosophy* (New York, 1899). The best recent articles on Lieber are Joseph Dorfman and Rexford Guy Tugwell, "Francis Lieber: German Scholar in America," *Columbia University Quarterly*, XXX (1938), 159–90; 267–93, and Merle Curti, "Francis Lieber and Nationalism," *The Huntington Library Quarterly*, IV (1940–41), 263–92.

The chief philosophical writings of Orestes A. Brownson after his conversion to the Roman Catholic Church are: *Charles Elwood; or, The Infidel Converted* (Boston, 1840); *Essays and Reviews, Chiefly on Theology, Politics and Socialism* (New York, 1852), of which the most significant are "Authority and Liberty" (1849), "Political Constitutions" (1847), "The Higher Law" (1851), "Catholicity Necessary to Sustain Popular Liberty" (1845), "Legitimacy and Revolutionism" (1848), "Labor and Association" (1848), "Socialism and the Church" (1849); *The Convert; or, Leaves from My Experience* (New York, 1857); *The American Republic; Its Constitution, Tendencies, and Destiny* (New York, 1866); *Conversations on Liberalism and the Church* (New York, 1870). Brownson's *Collected Works* in 20 volumes were edited by his son Henry F. Brownson (Detroit, 1882–1887). Henry F. Brownson's informative biography of his father was published in three volumes (Detroit, 1898, 1899, 1900). Of recent biographies the most useful for philosophical purposes are Arthur M. Schlesinger, Jr., *Orestes A. Brownson: a Pilgrim's Progress* (Boston, 1939), and Theodore Maynard, *Orestes Brownson: Yankee, Radical, Catholic* (New York, 1943), the former most informative on his early life and the latter on his "ontologism" and anti-Jesuit liberalism. Thomas I. Cook and Arnaud B. Leavelle, "Orestes A. Brownson's *The American Republic*," *The Review of Politics*, IV (1942), 77–90, 173–93, is a rather pedestrian discussion, but the footnotes contain useful references. A scathing criticism of Brownson as an interpreter of Cousin was published in *The American Quarterly Church Review and Ecclesiasti-*

cal Register, XIX (1867–68), 532–47. Whether or not the author was C. S. Henry, as I suspect, the article brings out the contrast between Cousin's influence on Rosminian and transcendentalist thinking.

John C. Hurd's works are: *Topics of Jurisprudence Connected with Conditions of Freedom and Bondage* (New York, 1856); *The Law of Freedom and Bondage in the United States,* 2 volumes (Boston, 1858–62); *The Theory of Our National Existence* (Boston, 1881); *The Union-State: a Letter to Our States-Rights Friend* (New York, 1891).

Brief accounts of the development of the theory of American nationality are given in Thomas I. Cook and Arnaud B. Leavelle, "German Idealism and American Theories of the Democratic Community," *The Journal of Politics,* V (1943), 213–36, in Gettell, *A History of American Political Thought,* pp. 397–411, in C. E. Merriam, *American Political Ideas 1865–1917* (New York, 1920), *passim,* and in Carpenter, *The Development of American Political Thought,* Chapter VI, "Some Recent Tendencies."

The chief works of this school of political theory in addition to those of Hurd and Brownson are:

John A. Jameson, The Constitutional Convention (Chicago, 1867).

John N. Pomeroy, An Introduction to the Constitutional Law of the United States (New York, 1868).

Theodore D. Woolsey, Political Science; or, The State Theoretically and Practically Considered, 2 volumes (New York, 1877).

Philemon Bliss, Of Sovereignty (Boston, 1885).

Woodrow Wilson, The State (Boston, 1889).

John W. Burgess, Political Science and Constitutional Law (Boston, 1890).

Westel W. Willoughby, An Examination of the Nature of the State (New York, 1896).

—— Social Justice (New York, 1900).

—— Ethical Basis of Political Authority (New York, 1930).

Bliss and Wilson began a more critical discussion of sovereignty, which has continued to the present day.

CHAPTER 15

The relation of Walt Whitman to Hegel is discussed by Mody C. Boatright, "Whitman and Hegel," University of Texas *Studies in English,* IX (1929), 134–50, Robert P. Falk, "Walt Whitman and German Thought," *Journal of English and Germanic Philology,* XL (1941), 315–30, and W. B. Fulghum, Jr., "Whitman's Debt to Joseph Gostwick," *American Literature,* XII (1940–41), 491–96. These students agree that

Whitman's knowledge of Hegel (and of other German thinkers) was derived from Joseph Gostwick's popular handbook, *German Literature* (Philadelphia, 1854); they assign various dates to his study of this book, as they find more or fewer traces of Hegelian ideas in the early poems. The view of Falk, which sets the date just before 1870, seems to us the best authenticated.

There is an excellent satire of Whitman's philosophy of "merging" from the point of view of a radical individualism in D. H. Lawrence, *Studies in Classic American Literature* (New York, 1923). The St. Louis school has been described by Charles M. Perry, *The St. Louis Movement in Philosophy: Some Source Material* (Norman, Oklahoma, 1930). At the end of this work there is an extensive bibliography, including lists of the works of Brokmeyer, Harris, and Snider. For a narrative account of the movement, special attention should be paid to Denton J. Snider, *The St. Louis Movement in Philosophy, Literature, Education and Psychology; with chapters of autobiography* (St. Louis, 1920), and to Chapter IV of Snider's autobiography *A Writer of Books in His Genesis* (St. Louis, 1910). Edward L. Schaub, ed., *William Torrey Harris 1835–1935* (Chicago, 1936), a collection of essays, papers, and addresses in commemoration of the Harris centennial, includes H. G. Townsend, "The Political Philosophy of Hegel in a Frontier Society"; Charles M. Perry, "William Torrey Harris and the St. Louis Movement in Philosophy"; and George Rowland Dodson, "The St. Louis Philosophical Movement." An account of the social philosophy of this group, emphasizing the theories of Snider, has been written by Frances B. Harmon, *The Social Philosophy of the St. Louis Hegelians* (New York, 1943). Another aspect of the movement has been discovered and described by Paul Russell Anderson, "Hiram K. Jones and Philosophy in Jacksonville," *Journal of the Illinois State Historical Society*, XXXIII (1940), 478–520, and "Quincy, an Outpost of Philosophy," *Journal of the Illinois State Historical Society*, XXXIV (1941), 50–83. Unfortunately some of his material is still unpublished. Kurt F. Leidecker, *Life and Letters of William Torrey Harris* (New York, 1946), gives the most complete account of Harris's mind and supplements the same author's previously published bibliography of Harris in the centennial volume.

Elisha Mulford published *The Nation* (Boston, 1870) and *The Republic of God; an Institute of Theology* (Boston, 1881). There is practically no literature about Mulford; there are, however, two notices by Theodore T. Munger which are of some value: "The Works of Elisha Mulford," *Century Illustrated Monthly Magazine*, n.s., XIII (1887–88), 888–95; and "Personal Impressions of Dr. E. Mulford," *The Independent* (New

York), XXXVIII, No. 1936 (January 7, 1886), 2. A manuscript appreciation of Mulford by A. V. G. Allen is available in the Wright Memorial Library, Cambridge, Mass. An anonymous obituary notice in the Boston *Transcript* for December 10, 1885, contains biographical information. President Buckham of the University of Vermont, sometime about 1900, led Sho Nemoto, a Japanese, to the study of Mulford. In 1905, Nemoto requested the consent of Mulford's publishers to prepare Japanese translations of both *The Nation* and *The Republic of God*. His translation of *The Nation* was published at Tokyo, 1914.

CHAPTER 16

For the general history of the agrarian and populist movements of the last part of the nineteenth century, see Louis M. Hacker and Benjamin B. Kendrick, *The United States since 1865* (New York, 1932), Section five, "Agrarian Discontent." Gabriel, *The Course of American Democratic Thought*, Chapter XVII, "Neo-Rationalism, the Evolution of the Philosophy of the General Welfare States," is a good discussion of the intellectual qualities of the movement, although the title is misleading. Detailed treatments are to be found in John D. Hicks, *The Populist Revolt* (Minneapolis, 1931), A. M. Arnett, *The Populist Movement* (New York, 1922), Solon J. Buck, *The Granger Movement* (Cambridge, Mass., 1913), and *The Agrarian Crusade* (New Haven, 1920), James A. Dombrowski, *The Early Days of Christian Socialism in America* (New York, 1936), and Charles H. Hopkins, *The Rise of the Social Gospel in American Protestantism, 1865–1915* (New Haven, 1940). There is also a good brief account of Christian Socialism in America in Gabriel, *Course of American Democratic Thought*, Chapter XXIV, "Protestantism Moves toward Humanism and Collectivism."

For Henry Lloyd see *Wealth against Commonwealth* (Washington, D.C., 1936) and C. A. Lloyd, *Henry D. Lloyd*, 2 volumes (New York, 1912).

Henry George's *Progress and Poverty* is available in many editions. The most adequate treatment of his philosophical ideas is in G. R. Geiger, *The Philosophy of Henry George* (New York, 1933).

Edward Bellamy's *Looking Backward* is readily available. His *Equality* was reissued New York, 1934. These should be supplemented by Bellamy's early work "The Religion of Solidarity," reprinted in Arthur E. Morgan, *The Philosophy of Edward Bellamy* (New York, 1945). Bellamy's early novels and his contributions to the *Nation* throw further light on his ideas. A critical study of the nationalist movement has been undertaken by Edward

McNair, but is as yet not published. Arthur E. Morgan, *Edward Bellamy* (New York, 1944), is the only comprehensive study of Bellamy and contains many interesting quotations from Bellamy manuscripts.

For Gronlund see Laurence Gronlund, *The Co-operative Commonwealth* (New York, 1884), and *Our Destiny: the Influence of Nationalism on Morals and Religion; an Essay in Ethics* (Boston, 1891).

Terence V. Powderly's autobiography *The Path I Trod* was edited by Harry J. Carman, Henry David, and Paul N. Guthrie (New York, 1940).

— IV —

ORTHODOXY

It is the property of good and sound knowledge to putrify and dissolve into a number of subtle, idle, unwholesome, and (as I may term them) vermiculate questions.[1]

TO recognize wormy knowledge when one sees it is not difficult, but to explain critically what causes philosophy to putrify and why it continues to exist in a decayed state is a difficult and disagreeable task, for it is not easy to define the life of an idea and it is not pleasant to look for signs of life among skeletons. Following Bacon, we shall distinguish living philosophy from dead by noting whether philosophy is being practiced and pursued in "the advancement of learning" among all the arts and sciences or whether it is being taught and refined as a particular body of knowledge. It is a conspicuous fact that in the traditions of both puritanism and the Enlightenment there was no specialized discipline labeled "philosophy." Theology, science, government, philanthropy were all philosophical. There was a current distinction between natural and moral philosophy, analogous to the distinction we now make between the natural and the social sciences. But philosophy did not exist as a special field of inquiry or body of doctrine. The pursuit of truth everywhere, whether encyclopedic or specialized, was recognized as a philosophical enterprise. Thus philosophy flourished without being taught; it was the spirit of the arts and sciences, without being itself distinguished as a particular article of faith or doctrine. We must now observe how philosophy lost its living connections with the general culture of the American people and became a technical discipline in academic curricula. At the same time we must observe how religion and morals gradually severed their philosophical bonds, and, as the philosophers would say, became unenlightened.

Religious and academic orthodoxies should be distinguished from conservatism. Conservatism may or may not be philosophical, and orthodoxy may or may not be conservative. Orthodoxy as a philosophical ideal has nothing directly to do with moral conservatism; it indicates merely that philosophy has shifted its interest from specu-

[1] Francis Bacon, *Advancement of Learning*, Bk. I, sec. 5.

lative inquiry to systematic instruction. Philosophers, in the eighteenth-century meaning of the term, were investigators (either natural or moral); in the nineteenth century, however, there grew up a species of educator known as professors of philosophy. They were primarily teachers, and their ambition was to be orthodox, to teach the truth, i.e., to instruct their students in correct doctrine by relying on the best authors, by using systematic texts, and by inventing precise termi-nologies. Similarly the theologians lost most of their speculative or philosophical interest and were content to refine their systems for the edification of the faithful and the confounding of rival theologians. In short, our history of American philosophy now takes us into the school-rooms of colleges and seminaries. What President Francis Wayland said of his own famous textbook in moral science states the ideal of orthodoxy in general: "Being designed for the purposes of instruction, its aim is to be simple, clear, and purely didactic." [2]

— 17 —

ORTHODOXY AMONG THE LIBERALS

WE have noted the native roots of New England religious liberalism and its flowering in William Ellery Channing. We have now to observe how this liberalism, which was largely inspired by Platonic idealism and republican philosophy, gradually became a Unitarian orthodoxy, which increasingly alienated its philosophical friends and became increasingly irrelevant to American moral issues.

In England the liberalism of the Unitarians, such as Richard Price and Joseph Priestley, was less significant than in America, because it was overshadowed both socially and intellectually by the secular liberalism of the utilitarians. But the reverse situation prevailed in America, where the Unitarian liberals maintained their leadership during and after the Enlightenment. After the decline of the Jeffer-sonian Republicans there was no secular philosophical liberalism in America to compare with that of Jeremy Bentham and the Mills in

[2] Francis Wayland, *The Elements of Moral Science* (Boston, 1849), p. 4.

England. Both within and without academic walls it was the clergy who for several generations read, wrote, taught, and preached what little philosophy survived the Enlightenment. Though this fact is not easy to explain, it accounts in large measure for the decline of criticism and the vogue of exhortation—the tendency to glorify reason rather than to use it.

After Priestley's emigration to Pennsylvania, he became the leader of the Unitarians in the middle Atlantic states, and these Unitarians were much more "rationalistic" than the New England liberals. That is, Priestley and his associates were more influenced by natural science and materialism than were the New England humanitarians, and their polemic was on that account more negative, anti-revelation, anti-miracle, anti-trinitarian. When these two religious groups fused, in 1819, following Channing's famous Baltimore address on *Unitarian Christianity,* and formed the Unitarian Association, the differences between the Priestley type and the Channing type of Unitarianism came to the fore. Even in New England the individualism of the clergy waned, and the demand increased for a Unitarian church with creed, offices, and all the other institutions of a conventional Christian denomination. Channing opposed this tendency and even went so far as to repudiate the label "Unitarian," preferring to remain a "liberal" or "catholic" Christian, instead of being forced into something too much like a deistic church. When Theodore Parker and other students of the "higher criticism" of the Bible added their "negative" note to Priestley's, the more humanitarian and Christian Unitarians complained that their movement was degenerating into a sect, and the sect into a rationalistic orthodoxy. This was one of the major reasons why both social reformers and transcendentalists among the Unitarians turned against "rationalism" and materialism, if not against Unitarianism itself.

Channing's liberalism had found its inspiration in the dignity of human nature and had turned its back on the threadbare themes of the design argument and on natural religion generally. Early New England Unitarianism was above all humane and humanitarian, preoccupied with self-culture and social progress. Unitarian orthodoxy, on the other hand, with its emphasis on rational theology, its antipathy for revelation and lesser miracles, its cool enthusiasm for higher criti-

cism, and its increasingly smug use of reason at the expense of liberality, became too sectarian to hold the philosophic interests and practical devotion of those liberals in whom the love of freedom was both
a political heritage and a transcendental passion. When Unitarianism
lost the leading transcendentalists, it lost most of its intellectual vigor
and moral liberalism. It continued to exist for several generations as
a fertile soil for growing minds, but these minds usually sought the
light above and looked down in scorn upon their roots.

A similar degeneration took place among the freethinkers, who
dwindled from being among the major prophets of the American
Rebellion and the Jeffersonian revolution to being a small sect of
militant "rationalists." When the enthusiasm for the French Revolution waned and Jacobinism was no longer an important issue, the freethinkers followed Paine's example in concentrating fire on the bigotry
of the clergy and on ecclesiastical privileges. For several decades (i.e.,
until the 1830's) a lively battle ensued, centering about the Presbyterian attempts to gain political power and the attacks by orthodox
enthusiasts (such as Jedidiah Morse) on infidelity generally. During
these years free thought received no new philosophical inspiration.
Abner Kneeland was an ex-Universalist, and Samuel Underhill an
ex-Quaker; both became increasingly skeptical of the evidences of
Christianity, and Underhill's medical studies inclined him to materialism. Frances Wright attempted, during her American lecture-tours,
to introduce Bentham's ideas; O. A. Brownson preached a combination
of French and English Universalism. Despite these able leaders
nothing significant developed, nothing comparable to the rise of
British liberalism. Not until the 1840's did German freethinkers,
with fresh sources and motives, emigrate in large numbers, whereas
the labor movement in America never did make much use of atheism
as an ally. And not until the works of Huxley and Spencer arrived
was there any significant stimulus for the small bands of radicals who
were still carrying on the rationalism of the Enlightenment.

Typical of this latter-day rationalism was the philosophy of Joseph
Buchanan (1785–1829), of Kentucky, a student of Benjamin Rush,
an ardent Jeffersonian, who as a journalist and an educator fought an
energetic though losing fight against the rising forces of Jacksonian
democracy and evangelical religion. His *Philosophy of Human Nature* (1812) is a well-constructed argument for rationalistic (if not

materialistic) psychology, based largely on the medical psychology current in Scotland and embodying the ideas of Hume, Hartley, Thomas Brown, and Erasmus Darwin. He treats the mind as an integral part of the material organism of man and as a consequence of man's "excitability" (as Rush had called it). Through education and habit formation, Buchanan thought, man's natural "unity of excitement" is extended artificially, and "sentiments" become associated with actions. His interest in the control of sentiments through education led him to devote his later years to educational reform. He enlarged on Pestalozzi's methods and hoped by his system to produce genius almost at will.

In human nature, sentiment is the only spring of action—the sole power which puts the whole man in motion, and determines in a great degree the measure of his abilities. There is nothing more essential to genius itself, than strength and durability of intellectual feeling. The success of the educator in cultivating the understanding itself must depend very much on the plastic influence and rational control which he is able to exercise over the sentiments of his pupils. By instituting an ardent perseverence of temper he may generate capacity, talents, genius.[1]

Similarly, Buchanan in his last years outlined "The Art of Popularity" (1820) by which he hoped to generate political leaders.

Buchanan's career is typical of the fate of early nineteenth-century religious and scientific radicalism: it began in public affairs and medical research; it ended in an educational system which failed in practice, but served incidentally to formulate a genuine science of psychology.

— 18 —

ORTHODOXY AMONG THE NEW LIGHTS

WHILE various types of liberals were thus drifting into various little orthodoxies, a similar fossilization was taking place among the followers of Jonathan Edwards. The "new light" theology, as it was conceived by Edwards, was certainly a major philosophical con-

---

[1] *Kentucky Gazette,* Feb. 2, 1813.

struction as well as a powerful religious stimulus. The story of its decline and sectarianization is one of the clearest illustrations of the way in which a classical philosophical theology can lapse into a merely theological orthodoxy.

Jonathan Edwards and his pupils Joseph Bellamy and Samuel Hopkins developed their theory of God's moral government to fit the current theories of moral and natural law, emphasizing the constitutional principle of disinterestedness as essential to justice and morality. Edwards had the good sense to rest his case on the theory of man's disinterested benevolence, or "holy love," toward Being in general, but Bellamy was forced by the "old light" Calvinists, who believed that God's sovereignty was absolute and his decrees inscrutable, to defend God's constitutional government by insisting on God's disinterested love of justice, which he uncompromisingly termed "God's vindictive justice"; and Hopkins wrote still more offensively when he expounded and glorified God's "disinterested malice" toward sin, and argued that in every natural man there must reside a "disinterested malice" toward God. God, in order to make a public exhibit of his infinite hatred of infinite sin, had appointed Christ, though he was innocent, to be a public representative of man's sinfulness in Adam (Adam being the "federal head" or representative of all sinners), and had demanded Christ's atonement in order that thereafter the divine sense of justice would not interfere with God's granting grace freely to whom he chose. Such "moral government" was obviously shocking to liberals and humanitarians, who, like Channing, took for granted that not even the authors of such arguments for orthodoxy could really believe that they were true. Edwardeanism was on the way to becoming the "one-hoss shay" which Oliver Wendell Holmes ridiculed. Hopkins, especially, gave the impression that he himself realized the paradox in which his theology was involved when he entitled his very first published work *Sin, through Divine Interposition an Advantage to the Universe: and Yet, This No Excuse for Sin or Encouragement to It.* Hopkins had the candor to face openly the basic difficulties not only of his particular theology but also of all natural theology in general, but he allowed his theological logic to get the better of his philosophical good sense. In the most benevolent manner he would preach the most incredible ferocities. His followers, lacking his benevolence and insisting on his doctrines, made a burlesque of the whole Edwardean philosophy. In fact, theologians like Nathanael Emmons, Nathanael Whitaker, John Smalley, and Stephen West can scarcely be called philosophers at all, since they lost all sense of the general theory of natural law and moral government underlying their theologies and engaged in the most grotesque refinements of theological distinctions to save their absurdly involved systems.

To take but one illustration: the Edwardeans had made a basic distinction between secular morality and piety (holiness) and had attempted to keep apart on the basis of this distinction civil society (based on moral relations) and the communion of saints (based on holy love). Bellamy preached this doctrine in the negative form: "The more unable to love God we are, the more are we to blame." Hence, the more reliance we put on moral effort, "strivings," the more hopeless are our chances of obtaining grace. It follows that "the secure, unawakened sinner does not sin so directly and immediately against God as the awakened, convinced sinner." Hopkins, to avoid so discouraging a conclusion, then argued that moral striving *may* be not an obstacle *to* grace but evidence *of* grace. The moral man *may* have been imperceptibly regenerated and his virtues are not "unregenerate workings" but "holy exercises" in grace. Nathanael Emmons then distinguished between such moralistic, or as he called it "external," evidence of regeneration and the "internal reality" of grace which God alone could judge. For practical purposes, therefore, he encouraged the view that the evidence of regeneration is gradual, though real regeneration is instantaneous, and urged church members to give their fellow members the benefit of the doubt. Nathanael Whitaker then retorted that "such a way of flattering sinners may engage their affections to their minister, but does not lead them to a sense of their entire wretchedness without Jesus Christ." [1] Emmons thought it was sensible to define "visible saints" as "those who appear to profess real holiness." [2] But who is to tell who is merely appearing to profess, who is really professing, who is apparently professing real holiness, and who is really professing apparent

---

[1] Nathanael Whitaker, *Two Sermons on the Doctrine of Reconciliation* (Salem, 1770), p. 117.

[2] Nathanael Emmons, *A Dissertation on the Scriptural Qualifications for Admission and Access to the Christian Sacraments; Comprising Some Strictures on Dr. Hemmenway's Discourse concerning the Church* (Worcester, Mass., 1793), p. 51.

holiness? By trying to be practical these theologians became deeper and deeper involved in the net of epistemology. It became increasingly necessary to defend dialectically doctrines which were losing credibility. Practical churchmen like Timothy Dwight and Nathanael W. Taylor, of Yale, came to the rescue; they "moderated," softened, and simplified orthodoxy for church purposes, but they abandoned the attempt to give it a philosophical foundation.

— 19 —

FACULTY PSYCHOLOGY

THE more philosophical clergymen discovered a new way with Edwards and developed a new psychology to serve their new orthodoxy. One after another the contenders had learned that it was difficult to refute Edwards's analysis of "moral necessity" in his own terms.[1] Using the Lockean concepts of mind, understanding, affections, motive, power, and will, Edwards had constructed a convincing argument for the belief that all acts are motivated, that the will is hence not independent of the affections, and that "the understanding" supplies the motives for "the will." But as early as 1793 the Reverend Samuel West published *Essays on Liberty and Necessity*, in which he suggested that Locke and Edwards were working with an oversimplified account of "the faculties of the mind."[2] There are really three of these faculties: perception, propension, volition. In perception (including apprehension, judgment, and memory) the mind is impressed; in propension the mind is moved or affected; but in volition the mind is an agent, self-determining its acts. Most significant is West's empirical argument for this self-determination: "If any one dislike this account of the matter, let him inform me how we came by the ideas of independence, efficiency, etc. If these ideas be not on consequence of experiencing in ourselves, that, in willing and choosing, we act independently of any extrinsic cause, from what quarter do they arise?"[3] This appeal to consciousness embarrassed Jonathan Edwards, Jr., who undertook to

---

[1] See J. Haroutunian, *Piety versus Moralism.*   [2] *Ibid.*, pp. 243–44.
[3] Samuel West, *Essays on Liberty and Necessity* (Boston, 1793), p. 26.

defend his father's position, and he confessed he had no consciousness of acting (i.e., of making acts): "The existence of the mind and of its powers, is *inferred* from the acts, and we are not properly conscious of them."[4] To deny the consciousness of freedom was easy, and Calvinists had repeatedly pointed out that whether such consciousness exists or not is irrelevant, since feeling free does not make one free. But to deny the consciousness of activity seemed less tenable and too timid. In any case, the appeal to consciousness itself had now been made forcefully, and this appeal became the dominant note of philosophizing in the nineteenth century. Edwards was now attacked by one philosopher after the other for failing to take consciousness, emotion, or feeling into account as a distinct mental faculty; the criticism of Edwards in America paralleled the criticism of Locke in Scotland.

The first serious formulation of the new "mental philosophy" came from the Reverend Asa Burton of Thetford, Vermont. His *Essays on Some of the First Principles of Metaphysicks, Ethicks, and Theology* were not published until 1824, but were composed "as an introduction to divinity" about twenty years earlier in the isolation of a frontier town, with a meager library and after only a little schooling at Dartmouth College. The work seems to indicate the general influence of Reid and the Scottish school, but there is evidence to show that Burton relied chiefly on "reasoning, writing, and a close application of mind."

I studied with a view of becoming acquainted with the intellectual and active powers of the mind. I accordingly read every author who had made the mind the subject of his investigations, which was then in print. I read every English, Scottish, French and German author, and the more I read, the more my mind was confused. . . . Being unable to form any consistent scheme by reading, I concluded to lay aside books, and ascertain, if possible, the truth by reasoning, writing, and a close application of mind.[5]

Burton distinguished three faculties of the mind: understanding, taste, and will. Unlike the liberals who expounded a similar tri-faculty psychology, Burton was not trying to free the will; he was a rigorous Calvinist, but he entered the Edwardean controversy by maintaining

---

[4] Jonathan Edwards, Jr., *A Dissertation concerning Liberty and Necessity* (1797), *Works*, I, 421; quoted in Haroutunian, *op. cit.*, p. 244.

[5] Thomas Adams, "Memoir of Rev. Asa Burton, D.D.," *American Quarterly Register*, X (1838), 328.

that it is not the faculty of volition that makes us moral agents, but the faculty of taste, and he became known as the champion of "the taste scheme" in opposition to Emmons's "exercises scheme."

> The will is only an *executive* faculty. It is no more than a servant of the heart, to execute its pleasure. The will is no *primary* principle of action; its office is to obey the commands of the heart. Accordingly, for all the good or evil produced by the will, the heart only is praise or blame worthy; or every moral agent is to be blamed or praised, on account of the good or evil heart in him.[6]
> Hence the heart, or the faculty of taste, being the only property of the mind which is susceptible of pleasure and pain, is the principle of action in moral agents . . .[7]

As the new three-faculty psychology became familiar during the 1830's, being expounded in both American and Scottish texts, and as it was re-enforced by the transcendentalist psychology coming in from Coleridge, Cousin, and the Germans, the criticism of Edwards and of necessitarianism in general gained momentum rapidly. Jeremiah Day, president of Yale, published *An Inquiry Respecting the Self-Determining Power of the Will or Contingent Volition* (1838) and *An Examination of President Edwards's Inquiry on the Freedom of the Will* (1841). He used the new psychology, which he had apparently learned by reading Henry's translation of Cousin, to bolster the moderate orthodoxy of the Presbyterians and Congregationalists, and in general defended Edwards. He made a special point of warning against interpreting the faculties as distinct agents. "They are different powers of one and the same agent. It is the *man* that perceives, and loves, and hates, and acts; not his understanding, or his heart, or his will, distinct from himself." [8]

At about the same time (1839–41) Henry P. Tappan, professor of intellectual and moral philosophy at New York University, wrote several treatises on the will, "appealing to consciousness" from the

---

[6] Asa Burton, *Essays on Some of the First Principles of Metaphysicks, Ethicks, and Theology* (Portland, Me., 1824), p. 91; quoted in Haroutunian, *op. cit.*, p. 251.

[7] *Ibid.*, p. 97; quoted in *op. cit.*

[8] J. Day, *An Inquiry respecting the Self-Determining Power of the Will* (New Haven, 1836), p. 40; quoted in J. W. Fay, *American Psychology before William James* (New Brunswick, 1939), p. 112.

transcendentalist point of view, and he used Edwards's *Treatise* as the object of his attack.

> In the consciousness, and in the consciousness alone, can a doctrine of the will be ultimately and adequately tested.[9]

> The great point,—whether will and desire are one,—whether the volition is as the most agreeable,—he takes up at the beginning as an unquestionable fact, and adheres to throughout as such; but he never once attempts an analysis of consciousness in relation to it, adequate and satisfactory. His psychology is an assumption.[10]

> Now, if the will and the affections or sensitivity are one, then, as a mere psychological fact, we must grant that volition is necessary; for nothing can be plainer than that the desires and affections necessarily follow the correlation of the sensitivity and its objects. But if we can distinguish in the consciousness, the will as a personal activity, from the sensitivity,—if we can distinguish volition from the strongest desire or the sense of the most agreeable,—then it will not follow, because the one is necessary, the other is necessary likewise, unless a necessary connexion between the two be also an observed fact of consciousness.[11]

Tappan's critique was intended to establish the belief in a self-determining or contingent will as the basis for moral responsibility and "evangelical religion," but he had no interest in saving Calvinist orthodoxy. He remained a Presbyterian socially,[12] though he early repudiated even the moderate, fashionable form of Presbyterian doctrine, and had become an enthusiastic disciple of Cousin.

Another "review" of Edwards came in 1845 from a southern lawyer

---

[9] Henry Philip Tappan, *A Review of Edwards's "Inquiry into the Freedom of the Will"* (New York, 1838), p. xiii.

[10] *Ibid.*, pp. 173–74.   [11] *Ibid.*, pp. 197–98.

[12] "If any one ask me, why I am a Presbyterian? I cannot answer, that it is on account of doctrine; for other denominations hold the same system of doctrine. Nor can I say it is on account of Polity; for other denominations have polities which appear to accomplish the same ends. I dare not say I am a Presbyterian because I believe my Church to be the only true church, or even better than others; for I find the most perfect forms of Christian character developed elsewhere. I am a Presbyterian from taste, association, habit, and education; and, because, being this, I can see no sufficient reason for changing to anything else. I suppose most of us of the different denominations, to be candid, would say about the same thing."—Tappan, sermon on the text Matthew 13:3–4 and 24–30, MSS., pp. 60–61, in the General Library, University of Michigan; quoted in C. M. Perry, *Henry Philip Tappan* (Ann Arbor, Mich., 1933), p. 67.

and professor of mathematics, Albert Taylor Bledsoe, and his criticism, too, was independent of an interest in religious orthodoxy. He, like Tappan, was interested primarily in psychological orthodoxy—the appeal to consciousness. But he is more critical than Tappan in his use of this appeal.

If the will is not distinguished from the affections, we shall have the will acting upon itself; a doctrine to which the necessitarian will not listen for a moment. And if they are distinguished from the will, we shall have two powers of action, two forces in the mind, each contending for the mastery. But what do we mean by a will, if it is not the faculty by which the mind acts, by which it exerts a *real force?* And if this be the idea and definition of a will, we cannot distinguish the will from the affections, and say that the latter exerts a real force, without making two wills. . . .

The truth is, that in feeling the mind is passive; and it is absurd to make a passive impression, the active cause of any thing. The sensibility does not *act*, it merely *suffers*. The appetites and passions, which have always been called the "active powers," the "moving principles," and so forth, should be called the passive susceptibilities. Unless this truth be clearly and fully recognized, and the commonly received notion respecting the relation which the appetites and passions sustain to the will, to the *active power*, be discarded, it seems to me, that the great doctrine of the liberty of the will, must continue to be involved in the saddest perplexity, the most distressing darkness.[13]

The phenomena exhibited by these two faculties of the soul, the sensibility and the will, are entirely different from each other; and there is not the least shadow of evidence going to show that the faculties themselves are one and the same. On the contrary, we are compelled by a fundamental law of belief, to regard the susceptibility of our nature, by which we feel, as different from that power of the soul, by which we act or put forth volitions. . . . And yet, in the face of all this, President Edwards has expressly denied that there is any difference between these two faculties of the soul. It is in this confusion of things, in this false psychology, that he has laid the foundation of his system.[14]

Whether our volitions come to pass in the manner we call freely, or are brought to pass by the operation of necessary causes, is a question of fact, which should be referred to the tribunal of consciousness. If we ever hope to settle this question, we must occasionally turn from the arena of dialectics,

[13] Albert Taylor Bledsoe, *An Examination of President Edwards' Inquiry into the Freedom of the Will* (Philadelphia, 1845), pp. 101–2.
[14] *Ibid.*, p. 127.

and unite our efforts in the cultivation of the much-neglected field of observation. We must turn from the dust and smoke of mere logical contention, and consult the living oracle within. . . .

This appeal is not declined by the necessitarian. He consents to the appeal; and the dispute is, as to the true interpretation of the decision of the tribunal in question.[15]

He reasons not from the observed, but from the assumed, nature of a volition. It must be an effect, says he, and though I do not see "the effectual power by which it is produced"; yet there must be such a power.[16]

We are merely conscious of the existence of thought, of feeling, of volition; and we are so made, that we are compelled to believe that there is something which thinks, and feels, and wills. It is thus, by what has been called a fundamental law of belief, that we arrive at the knowledge of the existence of our minds. In like manner, from the fact of consciousness that we do act, or put forth volitions, we are forced, by a fundamental law of belief, to yield to the conviction that we are free.[17]

At about the same time as Bledsoe's *Examination* appeared, President Asa Mahan, of Oberlin College, an Andover Seminary alumnus, published his *Doctrine of the Will*, repeating what had by now become a commonplace: "Edwards had confounded the Will with the Sensibility. . . . His whole work is constructed without an appeal to Consciousness, the only proper and authoritative tribunal of appeal in the case." [18] But Mahan, like Burton and Day, was writing as an orthodox minister defending the essentials of the Calvinist faith, and he coupled his argument for the freedom of the faculty of the will with a plea for centering the analysis, not on the will, but on "the religious affections." Thus, he came round in the end to Jonathan Edwards's original interest.

The important outcome for philosophy of this psychological critique of Edwards was not the argument for free will or the defense of orthodoxy, but the founding of a faculty psychology and of an appeal to introspection. This method of approach to "mental philosophy" dominated at least two generations of philosophers, created a new "science," and profoundly affected the course of academic studies in philosophy.

[15] *Ibid.*, p. 224. [16] *Ibid.*, p. 227.
[17] *Ibid.*, pp. 229–30. [18] J. W. Fay, *op. cit.*, p. 118.

THE RISE OF MENTAL PHILOSOPHY

UNTIL about 1820 it had been customary to divide philosophy into natural and moral; the curricula of our colleges reflected this division. Logic, metaphysics, and natural theology, like rhetoric and criticism, were usually taught as independent subjects and seldom included under philosophy. In courses of natural philosophy the students studied the natural sciences (as they then existed). Favorite texts were Benjamin Martin's *Philosophia Brittanica*, William Enfield's *Institutes of Natural Philosophy*, William Nicholson's *Natural Philosophy*, and William Smellie's *Philosophy of Natural History*. The lectures and recitations were usually accompanied by a course of laboratory exercises, called "experimental philosophy" and held in what was often referred to as "the philosophy chamber." Moral philosophy included political philosophy, natural law and political economy. In this field favorite texts were Hutcheson, Paley, Ferguson, Vattel's *Principles of Natural Law* (1723), Pufendorf, Grotius, and Cicero. Frequently there would be in the curriculum, along with "Kames' criticism" a course labeled simply "Locke" or "Locke on the Understanding."

About 1820, however, there occurred a significant revolution in the very idea of what constitutes philosophy, as well as in its instruction. The Scottish philosophy invaded the country and rapidly crowded out the older eighteenth-century texts. Thomas Reid's *Intellectual and Active Powers* (as his two works were usually called for short) and Dugald Stewart's *Elements of the Philosophy of the Human Mind* (often referred to as *Intellectual Philosophy*) and *The Active and Moral Powers* set the pattern for the new division of philosophy into mental and moral.

The study of Locke, Berkeley, and Hume was now absorbed into a course called mental or intellectual philosophy or science of the human mind. With it went a course in moral philosophy or science of morals. Natural philosophy broke up into a number of physical sciences; natural theology (i.e., Paley) was usually discarded completely and replaced by "Christian evidences"; and the political and economic sciences either became entirely independent of the course in moral philosophy, which was devoted to the "moral and active" faculties of the mind, or they were appended to the psychological ethics in the form of practical ethics or theory of duties. In the center of attention was the new faculty psychology or theory of the powers of the mind, so that it is not a great exaggeration to say that for academic purposes philosophy became mental philosophy, subdivided into intellectual and moral.

Though the Scottish texts furnished the models and inspiration for the new American academic orthodoxy, a flood of American texts appeared, all on the same general pattern. Curiously enough, this academic pattern had been anticipated by Samuel Johnson's *Elementa Philosophica* (1752), which was composed of "Noetica" and "Ethica." But neither his text nor his attempt to popularize Berkeley was successful.

Another work which anticipated the trend was Frederick Beasley's *A Search of Truth in the Science of the Human Mind* (1822). The Reverend Dr. Beasley was provost of the University of Pennsylvania and an Episcopalian, but he had attended Princeton during the days when the vestiges of Edwards's influence were being submerged by the Scottish tide. His account of what happened at Princeton and of his reaction against it is worth reading, since it illustrates the kind of interest which mental philosophy (or "pneumatology" as Beasley terms it) was kindling.

In the College of Princeton, to which we were attached, after the fanciful theory of Bishop Berkeley, as a kind of philosophical daydream, had maintained its prevalence for a season; the principles of Reid, and the Scottish metaphysicians superseded it, and during the period of our residence in the seminary, acquired and maintained undisputed sway. At that time, I, together with all those graduates who took any interest in the subject, embraced without doubt or hesitation the doctrines of the Scottish school. Since, however, I came in possession of the station, which I at present occupy in the College of Philadelphia, my duty as well as inclination, led me to renew my inquiries into this branch of science. The farther I proceeded, the more interesting the subject became, and I determined, if possible, to compass the whole ground, by consulting every author who had written upon it, both in ancient and modern times. I had advanced but a short distance upon this extended plan, before I thought I perceived, that the Scottish metaphysicians had either inadvertently or wilfully, done their predecessors very great injustice, in their animadversions upon their writings, ascribed to them opinions which they never held, assumed to themselves the merit of broaching and promulging the very doctrines which they taught, and, at the same time, had fallen into the grossest errors in that new system of pneumatology, which they claimed the credit of introducing.[1]

I trust, I shall be able to show to your entire satisfaction, and that of the learned world, that, instead of scepticism being inlaid in the old theory . . . there is no kind of connection, between the premises of Mr. Hume or Berkeley, and the principles of Mr. Locke. And, should I be so fortunate as to succeed in accomplishing this task, I doubt not you will perceive, not only will Mr. Locke and other philosophers, be restored to those well-merited honours, from which, for a time, at least, they have been degraded; but no inconsiderable service will have been rendered also, to the interesting science of human nature. No small part of that task, which we have to perform in the cultivation of science, consists in the detection and exposure of errors; and the very first step, which we make in our attempts to advance still farther towards perfecting any of the branches of philosophy, is to ascertain with precision and accuracy, the limits to which it has been already extended, and nicely to mark, in all cases, the lines of separation between what is true and false in the received doctrines about it; or in other words, determine whether philosophers have succeeded or failed, in their attempts to furnish solutions of the various phenomena of nature.[2]

Beasley introduced a course in "philosophy of the human mind" into the University of Pennsylvania as early as 1817, but when the curriculum was revised in 1826, it was discontinued, and Beasley himself left in 1828.

The first great American textbook writer in mental philosophy was Thomas C. Upham, professor of mental and moral philosophy at Bowdoin College, who in 1827 published *Elements of Intellectual Philosophy*. This work he expanded into a two-volume work by 1831, *Elements of Mental Philosophy*, classifying his subject under the two general heads "intellectual" and "sentient." In 1834 this was supplemented by *A Philosophical and Practical Treatise on the Will*. By this time he had discovered Burton's three-faculty psychology, and

---

[1] Frederick Beasley, *A Search of Truth in the Science of the Human Mind*, Part 1 (Philadelphia, 1822), Dedication, pp. ii–iii.
[2] *Ibid.*, pp. iv–v.

in the second edition of his *Elements of Mental Philosophy* (1843) he added the subtitle *Embracing the Two Departments of Intellect and Sensibilities*. Upham followed what he called "the principles of eclecticism and induction"; though his basic ideas came from Reid and Stewart, he soon embodied others from such a great variety of sources that his carefully constructed and revised texts took on the appearance of what even today would be called empirical psychology rather than a philosophical system. A noteworthy instance of his scientific interest is a small volume published in 1840 under the title *Outlines of Disordered Mental Action,* which is the first American text in abnormal psychology. Though he carried on some of Benjamin Rush's interests in the effects of bodily states on the emotions, he conceived of the whole field of mental pathology systematically; for every faculty expounded in his "philosophy of sanity," he now attempted an account of its "insane" functioning, collecting examples of each disorder from medical sources. He describes in order the derangements of "external intellect" (including "deranged sensibilities"), "idiocy of conscience," and "imbecillity of the will."

Between 1837 and 1857 American textbooks on mental philosophy appeared at the rate of about one a year. The culmination of this production was reached in Noah Porter's *Human Intellect* (1868) and James McCosh's *Psychology* (1886). Of the chief writers in this field (Asa Mahan, Frederick Rauch, Francis Bowen, Laurens P. Hickok, Joseph Haven, Henry N. Day, Noah Porter, James McCosh) McCosh is almost the only one who adhered closely to the Scottish school; Bowen, at Harvard, was for years a champion of the Scottish philosophy, but he became increasingly absorbed in criticizing transcendentalist innovations, making historical studies, and contributing to the more general task of "Christian evidences." German and French influences, to say nothing of British empiricism, made serious inroads on orthodoxy and on the theory of the mental faculties, and the writings of Sir William Hamilton, which gained enormous prestige, encouraged criticism of the earlier versions of Reid and Stewart. It is, therefore, a serious mistake to regard the whole period of academic philosophy until James as under the dominance of the Scottish school and of orthodoxy. True, with few exceptions the clergy were the professors of philosophy and the college presidents, but within the ranks of the clergy there grew rapidly a genuine cultivation of philosophy for its own sake, a hospitality for unorthodox ideas, especially for the unorthodoxies of German idealism, and a writing of obscure, unconventional works, which can hardly be called texts. This development of academic idealism out of academic orthodoxy will be described in a later section. The important texts in psychology and moral philosophy by Laurens P. Hickok, John Bascom, Henry N. Day, Julius H. Seelye, J. M. Baldwin and John Dewey, represent on the one hand the outcome of this long enterprise of academic systematization and on the other the beginnings of the critical movement which established itself during the eighties and nineties in a score of colleges and universities.

— 21 —

THE EXPLOITATION
OF THE MORAL FACULTIES

A SIMILAR story could be told of academic moral philosophy in the nineteenth century as it became subjected to the faculty psychology. The first influential American texts in this field were written by Francis Wayland, president of Brown University. Wayland, though a Baptist preacher, had something of a medical education, had studied under Moses Stuart at Andover Seminary, had attended Union College, and in general had freed himself and his textbooks of the limitations of denominational theologies. His *Elements of Moral Science* (1835) had a spectacular success: up to 1890 it had sold 200,000 copies. He had been teaching Paley and Butler with increasing discontent, and finally abandoned the whole enterprise of natural theology to which those authors were committed. He retained Butler's theory of conscience and attempted to put this theory on a more scientific basis. In his striking Phi Beta Kappa oration of 1831, entitled "The Philosophy of Analogy," he outlined his methodology. By "the science of analogy" he meant the art of hypothesis, learning to ask questions of nature; and he expounded this method as a necessary supplement to induction and deduction. Its value for natural science is obvious; its value for natural theology lies merely in that it provides an argument against the validity of any disproof of God's existence and immortality. Natural theology is possible, he thought, only in the negative sense that nature answers only with a "simple yea or nay," and is more likely to deny the dogmatic denials of atheists than to confirm modest positive hypotheses based on the faith in the intelligence of nature. He seems thus to have separated early in his career the problems of natural science from those of moral science. Though he wrote a text in 1854 on intellectual philosophy, he made no significant contribution in that field. He devoted himself almost wholly to moral philosophy. Disgusted with Paley's attempts to prove that man is by nature intended for eternal happiness, he adopted a radically anti-utilitarian ethics, emphasizing with Bishop Butler the intentions rather than the consequences of conduct, and basing both his individual and social ethics on a system of conscience and duty, rather than on prudence and policy. One source of the text's popularity was undoubtedly the fact that almost two-thirds of the book is devoted to "Practical Ethics," the theories of conscience and virtue in the first third being as brief and simple as possible. Another reason for the book's wide use was that it was not contentious; its judgments were judicious, and its principles simple. There was in it a minimum of philosophical debate on volition, moral sense, and mental faculties, and little account of the history and variety of ethical systems. It clearly aimed to be moral "science," not philosophy. In his *Political Economy* (1837) Wayland argued for free trade. On the slavery issue he met with disfavor in both the North and the South; he attempted to conciliate the North by being a "conscientious" objector to slavery and to conciliate the South by refusing to regard slavery as a "political" issue.

After Wayland, probably the most influential teacher of moral philosophy in America was Mark Hopkins, president of Williams College. He was more important for his oral teaching than for his writings. Nevertheless, his Lowell Institute Lectures entitled *Lectures on Moral Science*, published in 1862, but composed as early as 1830, were a useful and distinctive text. Hopkins's approach to ethics is an interesting contrast to Wayland's. Both men became critical of Paley, and Hopkins felt obliged to substitute for Paley an analysis of the ends for which "the human constitution" is designed. In turning thus to the human "constitution" (a term and an idea which he may have borrowed from the phrenology of Combe) Hopkins was consciously abandoning mere "mental philosophy" for a wider orientation. He had a medical, not a theological education, and he was unwilling to assert the existence of mental faculties or powers without giving them a working relation to physical forces. So he formulated what he called "the law of limitation," according to which the conditioning and the conditioned forces have their natural spheres or limitations, and according to which there is an ascending order of levels of conditioning in nature. When he comes to man, he finds that since man has both sensibility and will (in addition to reason) he is capable of being "morally conditioned," i.e., he can be moved by the rational choice of ends. Mark Hopkins presents this "constitution" of forces (from gravitation to conscience and worship), not merely as a natural order, but as a natural growth, and beautifully summarizes what later became known as emergent evolution:

In worshipping God man does not act for himself alone. He is the priest of nature. Standing at its head, and he alone recognizing the Creator, it is only through him that the praise that goes up from all parts of the works of God can find intelligent expression. From the beginning of time those works have been an expression of the perfections of God. As we now look at the march of the creation that expression was relatively feeble at first, but has become more full and pronounced at every new epoch. With the progress in time there has also been progress upward in the manifestation of those forces and products which we have in the series before us, but until man came the expression of praise did not become conscious and articulate. It was for him to gather it up and give it voice, and it is one of his high and peculiar prerogatives to do this. He needs but to have an ear rightly attuned, as was that of him who heard the heavens declaring the glory of God, or that of the Apostle John, in Patmos, and to put it to the universe as God has made it, to hear a low voice coming up from gravitation giving praise to God. And then he would hear that voice rising as he should go up through Cohesion, and Chemical Affinity, and Vegetable Life, and Animal Life, and Rational Life, and the provision made for every living thing, until he would come into full sympathy with the Apostle, and, with him, be ready to say in regard to the whole universe of God, "And every creature which is in heaven, and on the earth, and under the earth; and such as are in the sea, and all that are in them, heard I saying, blessing, and honor, and glory, and power, be unto Him that sitteth upon the throne, and unto the Lamb, for ever and ever." [1]

Hopkins labored long on his analysis of human nature, finding through it a rational teleology.

When the Lectures were first written, the text-book here, and generally in our colleges, was Paley. Not agreeing with him, and failing to carry out fully the doctrine of ends, I adopted that of an ultimate right, as taught by Kant and Coleridge, making that the end.[2]

The fruit of this inquiry into the natural powers and ends of man was a series of lectures which have an Aristotelian beginning and a Platonic ending; Hopkins had been led by Coleridge to rediscover not only Cambridge Platonism but more particularly Edwards's theory of holy love. The lectures are truly poetic and by far the most rewarding literature among the dreary waste of textbooks. Later (1868–70) Hopkins unfortunately reconstructed his arguments in another series of lectures, entitled *The Law of Love and Love as a Law*, in order to put its orthodox basis (i.e., that man's chief end is to love and enjoy God) at the beginning instead of at the end, and this later version is quite academic and overly formal.

Mark Hopkins is the only important exception to the fashion of regarding mental and moral philosophy as complementary to each other. The text-books usually went in pairs: the psychology laid the foundation for the ethics. The culmination of such pairs was Noah Porter's *The Elements of Intellectual Science* (1871) and *The Elements of Moral Science* (1885). These texts, by the president of Yale University, were pre-eminent for a whole generation. They were comprehensive, clear, systematic and irenic. Noah Porter was in many ways the greatest and most erudite of the professors of philosophy. He began as a theological student of Nathaniel Taylor's moderate Calvinism, and hence studied the Scottish classics. He then spent two years in Berlin and became much better acquainted with German thought than most of his contemporaries and succeeded in appropriating much

---

[1] Mark Hopkins, *An Outline Study of Man* (New York, 1873), pp. 300–1.
[2] Mark Hopkins, *Lectures on Moral Science* (Boston, 1862), p. viii.

of it in his texts. Though he adhered to the faculty psychology, he undertook a serious study and criticism of the English empiricists,[3] especially Mill, Spencer, and Bain; in general, he introduced into his texts a wealth of historical orientation and clarification. Above all, he gave the appearance of scientific objectivity and, indeed, had little speculation of his own wherewith to encumber his texts.

— 22 —

SCOTTISH COMMON SENSE AS AMERICAN REALISM

THE Scottish Enlightenment was probably the most potent single tradition in the American Enlightenment. From Hutcheson to Ferguson, including Hume and Adam Smith, came a body of philosophical literature that aroused men from their dogmatic slumbers on both sides of the Atlantic. The Scotch-Irish in America were peculiarly receptive to enlightenment from this source, for being both religiously and socially uprooted they were relatively free to listen to "reason" and "moral sense" from their countrymen. It is important to remember that the school of Edinburgh, as it was commonly called, owed its appeal to its systematic exposition of both reason and moral sentiment as supplementary factors in human life, and as substitutes for supernatural grace and revelation. The Edinburgh school was not grounded on "common sense," but on Platonism. When the reaction set in, when, to speak of both Scotland and America, the Presbyterians came into academic power, their exploitation of "common sense" made the schools of Aberdeen and Princeton as extreme centers of traditionalism as Edinburgh and Harvard had been centers of secularism and criticism.

For America, at least Dugald Stewart and Thomas Brown still be-

---

[3] At least one of his references, to be sure, is condescending: "The Associational Philosophy has never attained the predominance in this country which might have been anticipated from the absorbing interest of the people in material enterprises." (Ueberweg, *History of Philosophy*, translated by G. S. Morris, with an appendix on English and American philosophy by Noah Porter, New York, 1889, II, 455).

longed to the Enlightenment, whereas Thomas Reid (of Glasgow) definitely marked the reaction. It is true that an extreme materialist such as Thomas Cooper could lump them all together, for to a medical student at Edinburgh all the theologians and metaphysicians appeared benighted; they didn't know the "elements of physiology," he complained. But, apart from such scientists and medical specialists, men like Thomas Jefferson and Channing found Stewart "enlightening." Thomas Brown was more nearly on the borderline of academic "science." He became the chief object of opposition among theologians, because they felt that his "rationalism," as they usually labeled Brown's attempt at a thoroughly mechanistic or associationist psychology, was headed for materialism. The heart of the Enlightenment, as we have repeatedly said, was the marriage of natural science with morals and religion. The systems of Brown and Erasmus Darwin were foundations for scientific work in physiological psychology and biology, but they had no contribution to make toward moral and religious knowledge. Now there came a parting of ways. Reid, Beattie, and the common-sense school restored the grounds of moral and religious certainty, but alienated more critical scientists.[1] In short, what made Scottish common sense so "vermiculate" was the use of philosophical reason as a moral sedative, which was administered in our colleges in excessive doses by the clergy in the hope that it would be an antidote to the powerful stimulants of the experimental sciences.

What makes the literature of Scottish common sense in America so dull is not merely that it is academic, for after all the Edinburgh lectures were academic, too, but that it is pedantic. It is not good sense to dress up common sense in the academic garb of science, and it is even worse pedantry to dress up antiquated dogmas in the garb of common sense.

To give a specific illustration of these generalities, when John Witherspoon came to Princeton, he brought with him a mild dose of Edinburgh Enlightenment. It was mild, that is, in Edinburgh, and would have been so at Harvard; but at Princeton and Yale, where the Presbyterians were beginning to fear "the triumph of infidelity," even

---

[1] Cf. Benjamin Rush, "Thoughts on Common Sense," in *Essays Literary, Moral and Philosophical*, pp. 249–56, written in 1791. The doctor here ridicules "common sense" as a supposed faculty and specifically criticizes Reid's use of it.

Witherspoon's relatively pious recension of the typical Edinburgh course in moral philosophy was looked upon by some of the Edwardean pietists as "infidelity reduced to a system." And Witherspoon's vigorous participation in the American rebellion made him, on the whole, a representative of the American Enlightenment. But by the time his son-in-law Samuel Stanhope Smith became professor of moral philosophy at Princeton (1779) and published in 1812 *The Lectures, Corrected and Improved, Which Have Been Delivered for a Series of Years in the College of New Jersey; on the Subjects of Moral and Political Philosophy,* his elaborate exposition of scientific methods served merely as an academic apology for reviving ancient arguments for the immateriality and immortality of the soul. His painfully conscientious attempt "to avoid the dangers of a weak and suspicious skepticism, as of a bold and positive dogmatism" makes it plain to the student that he is avoiding the lively issues of contemporary thought as well. In any case, it is clear that Scottish philosophy had ceased to be a critical stimulant in society and was serving as a purely pedagogical discipline. President James McCosh, of Princeton, attempted to explain the prestige of Scottish realism as follows:

America has arrived at a stage at which there is a body of men and women who have leisure and taste to cultivate the liberal arts and advance the higher forms of civilization. She does not claim to have accomplished in a century or two what Europe has done in twice that time. . . . Still, she now ranks with any other one nation in literature, science, and art. . . . She has had a considerable number of able philosophic thinkers. It may be doubted whether any country has had a more acute metaphysician than Jonathan Edwards, whose views were restricted, and who was kept from doing more, simply by his want of books, and of collision with other thinkers. The theologians of America have made constant use of philosophic principles in defending their doctrinal positions; but the thinking people have not formed a separate school, as the French, the English, the Scotch, and the Germans have. In the last century and the earlier part of this, they followed Locke or Reid, one or both, always making an independent use of what was good, and carefully separated themselves from his sensational tendencies. In this past age our thinking youth have been strongly attracted by Kant and his school, some of them being caught in the toils of Hegel. In the present age a number are following John S. Mill, Bain, and Herbert Spencer. All this, while we never have had a distinctive American philosophy.

The time has come, I believe, for America to declare her independence in philosophy. . . . She should require that her philosophy have a character of its own. She had better not engage in constructing new theories of the universe spun out of the brain. The world has got sick of such. . . .

If a genuine American philosophy arises, it must reflect the genius of the people. Now, Yankees are distinguished from most others by their practical observation and invention. They have a pretty clear notion of what a thing is, and, if it is of value, they take steps to secure it.

It follows that, if there is to be an American philosophy, it must be Realistic . . . opposed to idealism on the one hand and to agnosticism on the other.[2]

This proud explanation of "what an American philosophy should be" is ridiculous as an exhibition of a man of "leisure and taste" cultivating the liberal arts and advancing "the higher forms of civilization." The boast of "common sense" professors like McCosh that they had inherited the Enlightenment and were using it as intellectual capital for American philosophical independence is not to be taken seriously, except as an exhibition of Yankee "invention." But it is an excellent definition of realism in the sense of orthodoxy. Idealism and agnosticism were both powerful forces in American thought, but neither had an academic foothold. The safe and sane system of Scottish realism, on the other hand, was an ideal pattern for preventing youth from indulging in speculative extremes.

There is another side to the picture, however, for McCosh and his Presbyterian colleagues restored to the evangelical churches a philosophical grounding for their faith which they had lost since Edwards. These churches had founded an enormous number of colleges and seminaries in which philosophy had no place and to which the whole philosophical enterprise was meaningless. For them educators like McCosh, who could expound as a reasoned metaphysics the "first and fundamental truths" of orthodox theology and at the same time showed some sympathy for science, even for evolution, and who would try to meet positivism and agnosticism on their own ground, were a "revelation" and filled a desperate need.[3] If this was true for the Congregationalists and Presbyterians, it was even more true of the

[2] James McCosh, *Realistic Philosophy* (London, 1887), I, 1–4.

[3] The vindication of philosophy and reason from the point of view of a Christian preacher is clearly exhibited in Thomas C. Upham's *Absolute Religion*, pp. 15–18.

personalists among the Methodists, whom we shall discuss later, but who are also part of the story of academic orthodoxy. For it was characteristic especially of the teaching of McCosh at Princeton and of Bowne at Boston that they did not take the conventional attitude of "apologetics"; they expounded "metaphysical truth" with clear and secular arguments, making theological considerations a decidedly secondary matter. Their orthodoxy was strictly philosophical. As churchmen they were decidedly liberal. McCosh, particularly, was shrewd in changing his teaching when he came to America from common sense to realism, from "intuitions of the mind" to "first and fundamental truths."

McCosh, with his Scottish philosophy, failed in America insofar as he attempted to lay the foundations of realism. His own drift in his exposition of realism from psychological arguments for immediate perception of reality to the logical arguments for a priori truths is indicative of the way Scottish realistic intuitionism, even before the arrival of McCosh, was rapidly paving the way for objective idealism. Instead of establishing orthodoxy, this Scottish "pneumatology" displaced French "ideology" only to usher in German psychology and transcendentalism.

GUIDE TO THE LITERATURE FOR PART IV

The historical accounts of this theme are very meager and misleading. The general remarks which I. Woodbridge Riley makes on the character of academic philosophy, in his *American Philosophy from Puritanism to Pragmatism* (New York, 1915), pp. 118–39, are worth reading. There are expositions of some of the important Scottish and American authors in A. K. Rogers, *British and American Philosophy since 1800* (New York, 1922). By far the most informative account is by Noah Porter in his appendix "On English and American Philosophy" to the translation of the 4th edition of Ueberweg, *History of Philosophy*, II, 450–60. Porter, however, was not writing a history, but rather notations on his contemporaries. The description of *The Old Time College President*, by George P. Schmidt (New York, 1930), gives a general view of the academic setting and personnel of philosophy at this time, and the biographies of McCosh, Wayland, Hopkins, and other leading educators, who were also professors of philosophy, supply more detail. A. C. Armstrong's two articles, "Philosophy in the United States," *Educational Review*, X (1895), 1–11, and "Philosophy in American Colleges," *Educational Review*, XIII (1897), 10–22, are primarily concerned with the 1890's, but there are several excellent pages on the development of the academic tradition. The second part of Benjamin Rand's history of "Philosophical Instruction in Harvard University from 1636 to 1906," *Harvard Graduates' Magazine*, XXXVII (1928–29), 188–200, describes this period. G. Stanley Hall's "Philosophy in the United States," *Mind*, IV (1879), 89–105, gives a graphic, though somewhat satirical, picture of philosophical instruction in the colleges.

CHAPTER 17

The Unitarians

George W. Cooke, *Unitarianism in America* (Boston, 1902), is the standard history. There is a general description of Unitarianism in relation to the more radical liberalism of the Enlightenment in G. A. Koch, *Republican Religion* (New York, 1933), Chapter VII. Thomas Belsham's early *American Unitarianism; or, A Brief History of the Progress and Present State of the Unitarian Churches in America* (Boston, 1815) gives valuable information. Octavius B. Frothingham, *Boston Unitarianism 1820–1850* (New York, 1890), reveals the dissatisfaction of one of the liberal leaders in the movement with its orthodox wing. For the differences between the Channing and Priestley types of Unitarianism the reader may profitably consult George E. Ellis, *A Half Century of Unitarian Controversy* (Boston, 1856), and scattered criticisms in the writings of Channing and Parker. An excellent diagnosis of the trends in Unitarianism is made by C. H. Faust in "The Background of the Unitarian Opposition to Transcendentalism" in *Modern Philology* (XXXV, 1938), pp. 297–324.

For Joseph Priestley's philosophical and religious views see his *Free Discussion of the Doctrines of Materialism, and Philosophical Necessity, in a Correspondence between Dr. Price and Dr. Priestley* (London, 1778), *Discourses on the Evidences of Revealed Religion* (London, 1794), *A General View of the Arguments for the Unity of God* (Birmingham, Eng., 1780), *The Corruptions of Christianity* (Birmingham, Eng., 1782), and Anne Holt, *Life of Joseph Priestley* (London, 1931).

Free Thought

The free-thought literature of this period is surveyed in detail by Albert Post, *Popular Free Thought in America, 1825–1850* (New York, 1943);

Chapters II, "The Rise of the Freethought Press," and IX, "The Creed of the Freethinker," give a general picture of the movement's philosophical outlook and tendency. An outline of a more analytical interpretation will be found in Joseph L. Blau's review article, " 'The Freeborn Mind,' " *Review of Religion*, IX (1944), 31–41. See also Henry Steele Commager, "The Blasphemy of Abner Kneeland," *New England Quarterly*, VIII (1935), 29–41, which contains an account of the communal experiment at Salubria, Iowa, as well as a discussion of Kneeland. The most typical literature is in the form of periodical articles, pamphlets, and addresses. Among the more interesting periodicals were the *Free Enquirer* (New York, 1829–35), edited by Robert Dale Owen, Francis Wright, and others, among them O. A. Brownson, which was a continuation of the *New-Harmony Gazette* (1825–29), the *Beacon* (New York, 1836–49), edited chiefly by Gilbert Vale, and Abner Kneeland's *Boston Investigator* (1831–50). Kneeland's *Review of the Evidences of Christianity* (Boston, 1831, 3d edition), Miss Wright's *Course of Popular Lectures* (New York, 1829), and Robert Dale Owen's autobiographical *Threading My Way* (New York, 1874) are books by outstanding leaders of the movement. On Joseph Buchanan see Niels H. Sonne, *Liberal Kentucky, 1780–1828* (New York, 1939), which gives an account of Buchanan's career and philosophy and a complete bibliography. I. Woodbridge Riley was the first historian to call attention to Buchanan in his *American Philosophy; the Early Schools* (New York, 1907), but his account of him as a materialist is inadequate and misleading; nevertheless, he quotes large sections of Buchanan's *Philosophy of Human Nature* (Richmond, Ky., 1812), a book which is very difficult to obtain.

CHAPTER 18

This theme is treated most adequately by Joseph Haroutunian, in his *Piety versus Moralism; the Passing of the New England Theology* (New York, 1932), in which there is an extensive bibliography of the controversial literature. An older and somewhat more detailed account is given in Frank Hugh Foster's *A Genetic History of the New England Theology* (Chicago, 1907). Haroutunian's critical comment on Foster's point of view, pp. 256–57, will aid the reader in making allowances for Foster's interpretations. Two aspects of the movement (the decline of the church covenant and the theory of God's moral government) are sketched in H. W. Schneider's *Puritan Mind* (New York, 1930), chapter VII, "Decline and Fall." Oliver Wendell Elsbee, "Samuel Hopkins and his Doctrine of Benevolence," *New England Quarterly*, VIII (1935), 534–50, gives further information. The most rewarding reading among the numerous writings of the Edwardean theologians is to be found in Joseph Bellamy, *True Religion Delineated; or, Experimental Religion, as Distinguished from Formality on the One Hand, and Enthusiasm on the Other, Set in a Scriptural and Rational Light* (1750), *Four Sermons on the Wisdom of God in the Permission of Sin* (1758), and *A Careful and Strict Examination of the External Covenant. . . . a Vindication of the Plan on Which the Churches in New England Were Originally Founded* (1769), Samuel Hopkins, *An Inquiry into the Nature of True Holiness* (1773), and *A Dialogue between a Calvinist and a Semi-Calvinist*, Samuel Webster, *A Winter Evening's Conversation upon the Doctrine of Original Sin* (New Haven, 1757), and Peter Clark's reply, *The Scripture Doctrine of Original Sin, Stated and Defended, in a Summer Morning's Conversation* (Boston, 1758). Ezra Stiles Ely's *Contrast of Hopkinsianism and Calvinism* (1811) makes a detailed theological analysis of the new light "departures" from Orthodoxy, and Horace Holley, in his review of this work (*General Repository and Review*, III [1813], 352 ff.), discusses the contrast from the liberal point of view. The works of Moses Stuart contain the last impressive defense of orthodoxy in view of the rise of the new criticism. The most authoritative expositions of moderate Calvinism, or "Orthodoxy," are to be found in Timothy Dwight's *Theology* (Middletown, Conn., 1818), 5 volumes, and Nathaniel W. Taylor's *Essays on the Means of Regeneration* (New Haven, 1829) and *Lectures on the Moral Government of God* (New York, 1859). The theology of Edwards A. Park marks the turning point at Andover; a good expression is his famous sermon *The Theology of the Intellect and That of the Feelings* (Boston, 1850), reprinted in Blau, ed., *American Philosophic Addresses, 1700–1900*, pp. 627–58.

CHAPTER 19

The most extensive collection of titles and quotations on this subject has been made by Jay Wharton Fay, *American Psychology before William James* (New Brunswick, N.J., 1939). His chronological table, bibliography, and biographical notes are particularly useful, though not always accurate. G. S. Brett, *A History of Psychology*, III (London, 1921), 255–61, is worth consulting in spite of Fay's strictures. There are scattered references in other histories of psychology, but no adequate account in any. Most of the primary sources are listed in Fay's work and need not be given here. Many of them will be listed as textbooks in the next section. Suffice it here to give in chronological order the chief items in the criticism of Jonathan Edwards's psychology.

1793 and 1795, Samuel West, Essays on Liberty and Necessity.
1797, Jonathan Edwards, Jr., A Dissertation concerning Liberty and Necessity; Containing Remarks on the Essays of Dr. Samuel West.
1820, Nathaniel Baylies, An Essay concerning the Free Agency of Man.
1824, Asa Burton, Essays on Some of the First Principles of Metaphysicks, Ethicks, and Theology.
1832, Nathaniel W. Taylor, Reply to Dr. Tyler's Examination.
1838, Jeremiah Day, An Inquiry Respecting the Self-determining Power of the Will; or, Contingent Volition.
1841, —— An Examination of President Edwards's Inquiry on the Freedom of the Will.
1839, Henry P. Tappan, A Review of Edwards's "Inquiry into the Freedom of the Will."
1845, Albert T. Bledsoe, An Examination of President Edwards' Inquiry into the Freedom of the Will.
1846, Asa Mahan, The Doctrine of the Will.
1864, Rowland G. Hazard, Freedom of the Mind in Willing.
1864, Daniel D. Whedon, The Freedom of the Will as a Basis of Human Responsibility and a Divine Government.

CHAPTERS 20–21

In addition to the secondary literature mentioned previously, G. Stanley Hall, "On the History of American College Text-books and Teaching in Logic, Ethics, Psychology and Allied Subjects," *Proceedings of the American Antiquarian Society*, n.s., IX (1893–94), 137–94, and Louis F. Snow, *The College Curriculum in the United States* (privately printed, 1907), should be consulted. William G. Roelker, "Francis Wayland; a Neglected Pioneer of Higher Education," *Proceedings of the American Antiquarian Society*, Vol. LIII (1944), Part I, attempts to appraise the educational contributions of one of the outstanding college presidents. In 1819 Ezra Stiles Ely published *Conversations on the Science of the Human Mind*, in which he pointed out that a "systematic treatise" was needed and reviewed the works of Reid and Steward from this point of view. We give here a chronological listing of the chief texts concerning both mental and moral philosophy.

1822, Frederick Beasley, A Search of Truth in the Science of the Human Mind.

1824,   Asa Burton, Essays on Some of the First Principles of Metaphysicks, Ethicks, and Theology.

1834,   Caleb S. Henry, ed. and tr., Victor Cousin's Elements of Psychology: Included in a Critical Examination of Locke's Essay.

1835,   Francis Wayland, The Elements of Moral Science.

1837,   Jasper Adams, Elements of Moral Philosophy.

1839,   Thomas C. Upham, Elements of Mental Philosophy, Embracing the Two Departments of the Intellect and the Sensibilities.

1840,   Frederick A. Rauch, Psychology; or, a View of the Human Soul, including Anthropology.

1842,   Samuel S. Schmucker, Psychology; or, Elements of a New System of Mental Philosophy, on the Basis of Consciousness and Common Sense.

1845,   Asa Mahan, A System of Intellectual Philosophy.

1846,   James R. Boyd, Eclectic Moral Philosophy.

1846,   Leicester A. Sawyer, Elements of Mental Philosophy; Containing a Critical Exposition of the Principal Phenomena and Powers of the Human Mind.

1848,   Laurens Perseus Hickok, Rational Psychology; or, the Subjective Idea and Objective Law of All Intelligence.

1848,   Asa Mahan, The Science of Moral Philosophy.

1849,   Francis Bowen, On the Application of Metaphysical and Ethical Science to the Evidences of Religion.

1852,   Archibald Alexander, Outlines of Moral Science.

1852,   Hubbard Winslow, Elements of Intellectual Philosophy.

1853,   Laurens Perseus Hickok, A System of Moral Science.

1854,   —— Empirical Psychology; or, The Human Mind As Given in Consciousness.

1854,   Francis Wayland, Elements of Intellectual Philosophy.

1856,   Hubbard Winslow, Elements of Moral Philosophy; Analytical, Synthetical, and Practical.

1857,   Joseph Haven, Mental Philosophy; Including the Intellect, Sensibilities, and Will.

1859,   —— Moral Philosophy; Including Theoretical and Practical Ethics.

1862,   Mark Hopkins, Lectures on Moral Science Delivered before the Lowell Institute.

1866,   Joseph Alden, Christian Ethics; or, The Science of Duty.

1866,   —— Elements of Intellectual Philosophy.

1868, Noah Porter, The Human Intellect; with an Introduction upon Psychology and the Soul.

1869, John Bascom, The Principles of Psychology.

1869, James H. Fairchild, Moral Philosophy; or, The Science of Obligation.

1869, Mark Hopkins, The Law of Love, and Love as a Law: or, Moral Science, Theoretical and Practical.

1871, William D. Wilson, Lectures on the Psychology of Thought and Action, Comparative and Human.

1873, Mark Hopkins, An Outline Study of Man; or, The Body and Mind in One System.

1876, Henry N. Day, Elements of Psychology.

1876, —— The Science of Ethics; an Elementary System of Theoretical and Practical Morality.

1878, John Bascom, Comparative Psychology.

1879, —— Ethics; or, Science of Duty.

1880, James McCosh, The Emotions.

1882, Edward J. Hamilton, The Human Mind: a Treatise in Mental Philosophy.

1885, Noah Porter, The Elements of Moral Science; Theoretical and Practical.

1886, Borden Parker Bowne, Introduction to Psychological Theory.

1886, John Dewey, Psychology.

1886, James McCosh, Psychology: Vol. I. The Cognitive Powers. Vol. II. The Motive Powers.

1891, John Dewey, Outlines of a Critical Theory of Ethics.

1892, Borden Parker Bowne, Principles of Ethics.

1892, Noah K. Davis, Elements of Psychology.

1892, James McCosh, Our Moral Nature.

CHAPTER 22

American editions of the Scottish philosophy are too numerous to mention. Chief among their editors were Levi Hedge, James Walker, and Francis Bowen, all of Harvard. Bowen made a developed statement of Sir William Hamilton's logic in his *Treatise of Logic* (Cambridge, Mass., 1865). Professor Joseph Haven, of Amherst College, was next to McCosh the most persistent exponent of the Scottish tradition. Samuel Tyler, of the Maryland Bar, in 1844 published *A Discourse of the Baconian Philosophy*, which attempts in an ingenious manner to treat Scottish orthodoxy and natural theology as an application of inductive method as it was preached in Bacon's *Novum Organum.*

McCosh's chief philosophical work had been done before his arrival in this country. He was one of the leaders in the Free Church revolt in Scotland. His first work to attract attention, *The Method of the Divine Government, Physical and Moral,* appeared in Edinburgh, 1850; it went through ten editions and contained an ingenious theory of theistic evolution, which he developed in two other works, *Typical Forms and Special Ends in Creation* (London, 1855) and *The Supernatural in Relation to the Natural* (Cambridge, Eng., 1862). During his professorship at the University of Belfast, 1852–68, he published works which established his philosophical reputation: *Intuitions of the Mind Inductively Investigated* (London, 1860) and *An Examination of J. S. Mill's Philosophy, Being a Defense of Fundamental Truth* (London, 1866). His chief American works are: *Christianity and Positivism* (New York, 1871), *The Scottish Philosophy, Biographical, Expository, Critical, from Hutcheson to Hamilton* (London, 1874), *Psychology* (New York, 1886–87), *Realistic Philosophy Defended in a Philosophic Series,* 2 volumes (New York, 1887), *The Development Hypothesis—Is It Sufficient?* (New York, 1876), *The Religious Aspect of Evolution* (New York, 1887), *First and Fundamental Truths, Being a Treatise on Metaphysics* (New York, 1889), *The Tests of the Various Kinds of Truth, Being a Treatise of Applied Logic* (New York, 1889), and *Our Moral Nature, Being a Brief System of Ethics* (New York, 1892). *The Life of James McCosh,* edited by William Milligan Sloane (New York, 1896), contains considerable autobiographical material, an outline of his philosophy, and an extensive bibliography by Joseph H. Dulles.

—V—

THE TRANSCENDENTAL TEMPER

THE FLOWERING OF THE ENLIGHTENMENT

EUROPE felt the power of political and intellectual reaction after Napoleon more than did America, whose expanding power and territory during the Napoleonic struggle gave it not merely an "era of good feeling" but also a sense of possessing resources for indefinite development. The romantic character of American material progress stood in evident contrast to the sordid class struggles of European powers and to the persistence of feudal ideas and institutions. America also felt little of the force of the Benthamite reaction against the principles of the Enlightenment and little of the bourgeois and hedonistic variety of utilitarianism. Hence the faith in the creative power of reason and the principles of secular moralism were taken over from the Enlightenment and embodied into transcendentalism without shock or reaction; romantic idealism was able to "build its universe" on the foundations, rather than on the ruins, of the romantic faith in reason. In short, the intellectual and moral situation of America after 1815 resembled that of Scotland and Prussia more than that of France, England, or Austria. Emerson was not fighting Burke's battles, but like the German Kantians, like Ferguson, Carlyle and Erasmus Darwin in Scotland, could readily transform the faith of the Enlightenment into a gospel of self-culture and self-reliance, both national and individual.

Even Orestes Brownson, whose disillusionment over the Enlightenment and flight to Catholicism most closely resembled the pattern of European reaction, was by no means a typical reactionary. For him conversion to the Church of Rome was not a return home, but a new adventure, conceived in a thoroughly romantic spirit. To his mind he was advancing from sectarian Universalism to the genuinely universal, the cosmopolitan, the eternal. The French romanticists, Constant, Cousin, and Leroux, to say nothing of the Italian patriot Gioberti, helped him to rise above American and Protestant provincialisms and to feel in the embrace of authoritative truth the most perfect freedom. For him the enjoyment of authority was a means of self-assertion, and in submitting to the pope alone he felt free to condemn all others as heretics. He was the most contentious, confident, and unpredictable of all the New England romanticists. And he never lost the faith of his youth in independence of spirit, though he carried on his protestations in the name of orthodoxy.

Brownson was never an idealist in the technical sense and should not be reckoned among the transcendentalists except as that term is used to describe romanticism in general. A reviewer (probably C. S. Henry) in the *American Church Quarterly* for 1868, reviewing his article in the *Catholic World* on "Victor Cousin and His Philosophy," makes it quite clear that Brownson did not understand Cousin, and Professor Wellek has recently [1] shown that, though he knew some of the writings of the German idealists, he early repudiated them as too subjective. Hawthorne, by the way, was in no sense a transcendentalist, and Parker, as we shall see, only to a very limited degree.

A more representative, less paradoxical, romanticist than Brownson, one who kept the faith of the Enlightenment and preached it with power, was Theodore Parker. He understood better than any of his American contemporaries how to interpret the critical philosophy of Kant as a flowering of the Enlightenment, for that philosophy opened his eyes to the nature of practical reason, and to the limitations of natural science. Armed with a double-barreled reason, one aimed at nature and the other at human nature, he could bring down the Absolute from heaven to earth. His faith transcended natural theology without renouncing natural religion, and his reason roamed critically over the prejudices and vices of his times. Parker's conception of absolute religion embodied both the principles of critical observation and of transcendental criticism, and he therefore preached, as Kant did, the gospel of criticism as a reconciliation of reason and faith. Though he crossed the threshold of transcendentalism,

He lived in the wonderful afterglow of the Enlightenment, reason tinged with humanitarianism, realism with romanticism. He lived in an age of faith and of hope, in a country where all things seemed possible. He was the

[1] In the *New England Quarterly*, XV (1942), 670–77.

heir of the rationalists, but their skepticism seemed irrelevant, here, in America. He was the heir of the idealists, and their abstractions seemed concrete, here in this brave new world. He was warmed by the first generous winds of science, and they brought certainty, not doubt. He knew that reason would triumph over unreason.[2]

From the Enlightenment Parker took over his basic idea of "the infinity of God," which he regarded as "*the* philosophical idea of God."[3]

He is perfect Cause of all that He creates, making every thing from a perfect motive, of perfect material, for a perfect purpose, as a perfect means;— that He is perfect Providence also, and has arranged all things in his creation so that no ultimate and absolute evil shall befall any thing which He has made;—that, in the material world, all is order without freedom, for a perfect end; and in the human world, the contingent forces of human freedom are perfectly known by God at the moment of creation, and so balanced together that they shall work out a perfect blessedness for each and for all his children.[4]

Elsewhere he calls this theory of immanent divine perfection the idea of "solidarity between the creation and the Creator." He distinguishes his idea of God from that of deism on the ground that since natural theology "derives its idea of God solely by induction from the phenomena of material nature, or of human history, leaving out of sight the intuition of human nature and . . . consciousness," it must present God as "finite and imperfect." This statement is, of course, historically false, and there is really no important difference between the God of Parker and of Leibniz. Critics of his *Discourses on Religion* who called them "vehemently deistical" were justified, for Parker regarded all the distinctive institutions of the Christian religion, including its Bible, doctrines, and sacraments, as "transient," claiming that there is only one, absolute, true religion based on the eternal word and law of God and that this religion is found wherever there is sincere piety and rational morality. His position here is distinguished from natural religion only in that he is still more extreme than the deists,

---

[2] Henry Steele Commager, *Theodore Parker* (Boston, 1936), pp. 195–96.

[3] See his sermon by that title, reprinted in Blau, ed., *American Philosophic Addresses, 1700–1900*, pp. 663–79.

[4] Theodore Parker, *Additional Speeches, Addresses, and Occasional Sermons* (Boston, 1867), II, 301.

for he denies the permanence and universality even of natural theology. No theology is absolute, for absolute religion is piety, and piety is independent of any theology and basic to all.

Even man's "consciousness" of God and of immortality, on which Parker lays so much stress, turns out on examination to be not an intellectual intuition or definite idea, but a feeling or "affectional fact," sometimes called also an "intuitive perception," instinct, or innate idea.[5] In his psychology of religion Parker is not clear or consistent. When he is most explicit he lists "the religious faculty" as a distinct capacity of human nature in addition to intellect, conscience, and the affections, regarding it as "the highest faculty."

I have always taught that the religious faculty was the natural ruler in all this Commonwealth of man; yet I would not have it a tyrant, to deprive the mind or the conscience or the affections of their natural rights. But the importance of religion, and its commanding power in every relation of life, that is what I have continually preached . . .[6]

Occasionally, however, he refers to religion as an expression of the affections in general, and he is content to name only the conventional three faculties. Religion is the primary expression of "soul" or "spirit," but precisely what he means by these terms is not stated. Similarly, immortality sometimes refers to the "eternal" life of the spirit here and now, sometimes to a future life. However, his central idea is clear enough. Religion is piety; piety is love of God. This type of love is a perfectly natural [7] want or desire in human nature, and there must be a natural object that satisfies this want. Parker is inclined to take the existence of God for granted, but insofar as he has an argument at all, it is a version of the ontological argument. He begins with the felt need and love for God and concludes that since this need is a basic faculty of man it must imply the existence of an object that satisfies it. He cites Schleiermacher's formula "the sense of dependence" and defines God as the absolutely self-contained, hence infinite, being; but

---

[5] Charles Follen, Parker's contemporary, was in the habit of referring to Kant's categories as "innate ideas." See René Wellek, "The Minor Transcendentalists and German Philosophy," *The New England Quarterly*, XV (1942), 658.

[6] Parker, *Additional Speeches, Addresses, and Occasional Sermons*, II, 304.

[7] Contrast Edwards's theory of the supernatural sense.

he omits the "absolute" before "dependence," and obviously prefers his own formula "absolute *love* of God" as a definition of piety.

Religion, strictly speaking, has two basic forms, piety and morality, respectively the subjective and the objective forms of love. Though Parker thus combined the approaches of Schleiermacher and Kant, he followed Kant in emphasizing morality or "practical holiness" as the most important part of religion. In social morality and philanthropic reform his faith and his preaching found their most vigorous expression, and it was this practical type of religion that appealed to him as the very essence of "manliness," for in it all the faculties of man were united in concentrated and constructive effort.

The preaching of the churches is not adapted to produce the higher kinds of morality. Certain humble but needful forms thereof the church helps, and very much indeed. On the whole it blocks the wheels of society backwards, so that society does not run down hill; but, on the other hand, it blocks them forward, so that it is harder to get up; and, while you must run over the church to get far down hill, you must also run over it to get up. It favors certain lower things of morality: higher things it hinders. . . .

I confess, that, while I respect the clergy as much as any class of men, I hate the false ideas of the popular theology, and hate them with my body and with my spirit, with my mind and my conscience, with my heart and my soul; and I hate nothing so much as I hate the false ideas of the popular theology. They are the greatest curse of this nation. . . .

Now, I must confess that I hate Slavery; and I do not hate it any the less since it has become so popular in Boston, and, after a belief in the finality of the Compromise Measures has been made the *sine qua non* of a man's social, political, and ecclesiastical respectability. I always hated it, and hate it all the worse to-day for what it has done.

Then I have preached against Oppression in every form: the tyranny of man over woman; of popular opinion over the individual reason, conscience, and soul. I have preached against the tyranny of public law, when the law was wicked. Standing in a pulpit, preaching in the name of God, could I call on you to blaspheme the name of God for the sake of obeying a wicked statute which men had made? When I do that, may my right arm drop from my shoulder, and my tongue cleave to the roof of my mouth! I have preached against the tyranny which takes advantage of men's misfortunes, and with the sponge of illegal usury sucks up the earnings of honest men; against the tyranny of the few over the money in Europe, and of the many over the few in America. I love freedom of thought and of action; and I claim for every man the right to think, not as I do, but as he must or may. . . .

Since intemperance has become so popular in Boston; since it has got the mayor and aldermen on its side, and while every thirty-fifth voter in Boston is a licensed seller of rum; when it is invested with such strength, and gets possession of the House of Representatives,—I have preached against it all the more. I know, from the little town where I was born, as well as this large one, what a curse and blight drunkenness is.

Then I have preached against War, and I suppose, before long, I shall have a new occasion to lift up my voice against it once more.

Now, with such ideas, and such a style of preaching, I could not be popular. Hated I must needs be.[8]

This is typical of Parker's "manliness." He assumed that since man naturally loves infinite perfection, he has "the desire for a perfect manly character." It is, therefore, natural for man to make progress indefinitely, both individually and socially. Progress he conceived religiously: it begins in man helping man, through education and philanthropy; it culminates in God helping man through "inspiration" to become "perfectly manly," or possibly to become a genius. Since progress in general begins in social co-operation and ends in individual perfection, so, according to Parker, American history, too, should be interpreted as a progress with two phases, the earlier collectivist or "organizational," the later individualist or "the attempt to re-establish the personal freedom which had been denied in collectivism." However, he refused to drag God into the theory of historical progress. God, the infinite, cannot be "an improvable and progressive Deity." "That is a fatal error with Hegel and his followers in England and America." God, though immanent in both matter and spirit, transcends history. So, also, the principles of morals or the laws of God are eternal. In history we see their manifestation, but they can be discovered unhistorically or by an appeal to the moral consciousness and the "intuition of human nature." Parker, like the deists, believed the ideas of God, immortality, and right to have an a priori foundation; he even called them "innate" ideas. But he appealed, strictly speaking, less to the intuitions as evidence of particular, immediate truths

[8] *Ibid.*, II, 317, 320, 322–23, 324.

(as did the transcendentalists) and more to the "intuition of [i.e., into] human nature," which reveals man's basic wants and capacities. There were really only three of these "intuitions of human nature," according to Parker.

[Kant] gave me the true method, and put me on the right road. I found certain primal intuitions of human nature, which depend on no logical process of demonstration, but are rather facts of consciousness given by the instinctive action of human nature itself: the instinctive intuition of the divine, the instinctive intuition of the just and right, the instinctive intuition of the immortal. Here, then, was the foundation of religion, laid in human nature itself.[9]

There is another side to Parker's character, no less philosophical and more academic: he was devoted to the advancement of learning for its own sake. He was the first American scholar to have an appreciation of the far-reaching importance of historical criticism, especially in the Biblical field. To some extent his philological and historical erudition was an instrument of reform in theology and morals, but basically it was sheer enjoyment of criticism. He studied history as a moralist studies human experience: history, he said, is "philosophy teaching by experience." Partly to become acquainted with as much of human experience as possible, partly for the sheer love of philology, he studied many languages and read voluminously in their literatures. He displayed his encyclopedic learning freely and proudly to his friends, but he made little constructive or systematic use of it. So that, for all his love of learning, his understanding was not so critical as it was extensive. He was a prophet of criticism rather than a critical scholar.

His transcendentalism was, on the whole, more critical than ro-

[9] René Wellek, "The Minor Transcendentalists and German Philosophy," *The New England Quarterly*, XV (1942), 669; from "My Experience as a Minister," in J. Weiss, *The Life and Correspondence of Theodore Parker* (Boston, 1864), II, 454–55. Professor Wellek, who cites this passage in the article referred to above, adds: "There is little point in stressing that this is a false interpretation of Kant. It . . . is in perfect harmony with the intuitive philosophy of Jacobi or Schleiermacher, of the French eclectics, and even of the Scottish common-sense school." But certainly these intuitive schools of thought made a more extensive use of intuitive knowledge than Parker does. The abuse of the principle of "instinctive action" in the realm of belief was certainly prevalent among Parker's friends, and relatively Parker shows critical restraint.

mantic. With the exception of the few ideas which he regarded as innate and irrefutable, he expounded his thoughts in an orderly, argumentative fashion and consciously refrained from reliance on epigrams and "insights" as did the other American transcendentalists. Though he welcomed the movement and enjoyed its freedom of expression, he tried without success, both in his own writing and in his editorship of the *Massachusetts Quarterly Review,* to emphasize contributions to scholarly inquiry. He did not indulge in, and probably did not believe in, the reason that passeth understanding. He believed ardently that life transcends knowledge and seems to have regarded this fact as the chief of transcendentalism's discoveries. Religion (piety, love) transcends theology; "the feeling of immortality" is "lived as life" before it is formulated as belief; the doing of right and wrong and the "spontaneous" moral consciousness are prior to moral knowledge. He sometimes refers to this realm of transcendental life or fact as the realm of truth, but he seldom bases his arguments on transcendental truths, i.e., beliefs or propositions. In short, he gives a fairly critical account of the facts of transcendence. In his essay on *Transcendentalism* he uses the term very loosely, indeed, to embrace practically anything that is not sensationalism and materialism. This essay makes it quite clear that his chief aims were to free natural religion from any taints of sensationalism, materialism, and pantheism that might be charged to it, to free it from dubious cosmology, and to rest it on the absoluteness of the moral law and the religious consciousness. Having given this "intuitive" status to his own faith, he then turned in the most rationalistic fashion to demolish all others.

— 24 —

SPIRITUALITY AMONG CHRISTIANS

Whence do we derive our knowledge of the attributes and perfections which constitute the Supreme Being? I answer, we derive them from our own souls. The divine attributes are first developed in ourselves, and thence transferred to our Creator. The idea of God, sublime and awful as it is, is the idea of our own spiritual nature, purified and enlarged to infinity. In ourselves are the elements of the Divinity. God, then, does not sustain a figurative resemblance to man. It is the resemblance of a parent to a child, the likeness of a kindred nature.

. . .

I am aware that it may be objected to these views, that we receive our idea of God from the universe, from his works, and not so exclusively from our own souls. The universe, I know, is full of God. The heavens and earth declare his glory. In other words, the effects and signs of power, wisdom, and goodness, are apparent through the whole creation. But apparent to what? Not to the outward eye; not to the acutest organs of sense; but to a kindred mind, which interprets the universe by itself. It is only through that energy of thought by which we adapt various and complicated means to distant ends, and give harmony and a common bearing to multiplied exertions, that we understand the creative intelligence which has established the order, dependencies, and harmony of nature. We see God around us because He dwells within us.[1]

THIS passage from Channing's famous sermon is usually cited as the first clear expression of transcendental theology in America. Taken out of its context in the sermon it sounds like the impieties charged against Theodore Parker, but coming from Channing it was accepted without alarm as merely another expression of the current reaction against Calvinism. It was really a symptom of the radical shift that was taking place not only in theology but also in philosophy generally from the study of nature to the study of the soul. Mental philosophy and "spiritual" religion added a new dimension to speculative inquiry and soon became exciting concepts, promising a new type of liberalism and liberation.

The first enthusiasm for this sophisticated form of spirituality came not from the Unitarians, who were as a group rather smug and content with their reasonableness. It came from those enlightened churchmen who, despite their critical theology, felt the power of the traditional symbols and sacraments of Christianity, who witnessed with envy the evangelical revival of piety among the illiterate, and who cherished what they were unable to defend. There must be some way to justify philosophically a faith that possessed so much power in practice! To them came Coleridge's very timely Aids to Reflection.

[1] "Likeness to God": discourse at the ordination of the Reverend F. A. Farley, Providence, R.I., 1828, in William E. Channing, The Works (Boston, 1898), pp. 293–94; in Joseph Blau, ed., American Philosophic Addresses, 1700–1900 (New York, 1946), pp. 566–85.

The first American editor, the Reverend James Marsh, of the University of Vermont, explained that the reader of the *Aids*

will appreciate them more and more, as consistent with, and guiding to, the reception of the whole truth as it is in Christ;—guarding him, on the one hand, against the self-deceiving humility of those, who disparage the authority of reason and conscience, while they "lean to their own understanding," and "trust in their own devices"; and, on the other, against that pride, which discourses of the "higher nature of man," and arrogates to every man, as inherent in that nature, the power of spiritual life, which we can receive only "through the redemption that is in Christ Jesus." Thus, as the author showed himself both living and dying to be eminently, in his speculative views a philosopher, and in spirit a christian, there will be found in his writings a philosophy that is religious, and a religion that is philosophical.[2]

Coleridge's appeal to "spiritual" reflection was a gospel for those who had repudiated the truths of revelation and the influx of divine grace, but needed some kind of saving grace nonetheless. Inspiration was to take the place of regeneration, and intuition of "the written Word." For Coleridge personally and for most of his readers his *Aids to Reflection* served this purpose. Philosophical reflection was a new form of religion, and this use of reason was called "spiritual" to distinguish it from secular intelligence and science. The technique of meditation for inspiration, insight or wisdom was dignified by Coleridge, following Schelling, as a separate and unique human faculty, called "reason" to distinguish it from the discursive or demonstrative "understanding." Thus "spiritual religion" was qualitatively different from both "natural religion" and "revealed religion." Here was piety without superstition and spirituality without creed. Marsh set to work at once to adapt Coleridge to American needs, adding to his edition (1829) a long introductory essay and copious notes. Marsh was a professor of classics and had a good background in Greek philosophy as well as in Cambridge Platonism. He readily used Coleridge's aids and hints to outline to his classes not merely a spiritual religion but also an idealistic physics, aesthetics, and metaphysics. These innovations gradually transformed his lectures in theology, ethics, and

[2] James Marsh, "Advertisement," in Samuel Taylor Coleridge, *Aids to Reflection;* with a Preliminary Essay by James Marsh (Burlington, Vt., 1829).

the pagan classics, so that Marsh was able to establish an enduring reform in the curriculum and methods of instruction, which, added to his personal influence, made Coleridge's philosophy an academic tradition at the University of Vermont. Marsh explained that the analysis of the mind as an object in itself was too foreign to the interests and conventional studies of most men and that "the most effectual method of instruction" is, therefore, to associate reflection upon man's "inward being . . . and upon the mysterious powers and agencies of reason, and conscience, and will" with the study of morals and religion. Thus, courses in moral and religious philosophy became handmaidens to psychology. Beyond academic walls, however, it was the other way around: the new psychology was an instrument of religious reflection and created a new theology. It was among the clergy that the "distinctions" of Coleridge came with a message of relief.

It is yet a special object of the Author of this Work to show that the spiritual life, or what among us is termed experimental religion, is, in itself, and in its own proper growth and development, essentially distinct from the forms and processes of the understanding; and' that, although a true faith cannot contradict any universal principle of speculative reason, it is yet in a certain sense independent of the discursions of philosophy, and in its proper nature beyond the reach "of positive science and theoretical insight." "Christianity is not a theory, or a speculation; but a life. Not a philosophy of life, but a life and a living process." It is not, therefore, so properly a species of knowledge, as a form of being.[3]

"Experimental religion" had at last achieved a philosophy to take the place of Edwards.

The philosophy of life as a creative process became the dominant interest in Marsh's own exposition of transcendentalism. The objective reason which controls our "spontaneous" consciousness, as distinct from our "voluntary understanding," is an "organific power of life." "The power of life, then, does not come from beneath, out of the inferior elements, but from above." [4] We are, strictly speaking, supernatural creations. The self-conscious individual

is a higher birth, a principle of higher and spiritual energy, and having its

[3] James Marsh, "Preliminary Essay," in *ibid.*, p. 26.
[4] James Marsh, *The Remains of the Rev. James Marsh*, ed. by Joseph Torrey (Boston, 1843), p. 373.

proper relations to a world of spirit. It enters into the life of nature, in some sense, as the power of organic life enters into the lower sphere of inorganic matter. In its own essence, and in its proper right, it is supernatural, and paramount to all the powers of nature. . . . The understanding, reflecting and reproducing, in its own abstract forms, the fleeting experiences of the life of nature . . . seduces the will into the pursuit of the ends thus determined; and thus the spiritual principle is brought into bondage to the life of nature.[5]

It is only by freeing the spiritual principle from the limitations of that narrow and individual end which the individual nature prescribes, and placing it under that spiritual law which is congenial to its own essence, that it can be truly free. When brought into the liberty with which the Spirit of God clothes it, it freely strives after those noble and glorious ends which reason and the Spirit of God prescribe.[6]

These passages may be enough to suggest that Marsh found here a philosophy of sin and grace (an emergent evolutionism in reverse, so to speak) which enabled him to give a new, "inner" meaning to the old Puritan doctrine of redemption and to the truths of "experimental religion." He preached this spiritual art of reflection as an educated form of spirituality, condemning at the same time the popular, emotional revivals. He edited some of the works of the Cambridge Platonists, and in general attempted to revive Puritan idealism.

Meanwhile, an Anglican, a professor of philosophy at New York University, was introducing the system of Victor Cousin into America, for much the same reasons that Marsh introduced Coleridge. Caleb Sprague Henry realized that in Cousin's idealism, the intuitionist element of the Scottish tradition, which was familiar in America, had been freed from its "common sense" associations and allied to the doctrines of the German romanticists. In the introduction to his edition of Cousin's *Elements of Psychology* (1834) he summarized the transcendental argument for absolute knowledge.

M. Cousin thinks he finds the true solution in the distinction between the spontaneous and reflective reason. In the intimacy of consciousness, at a depth to which Kant had not penetrated, and beneath the apparently relative and subjective character of the necessary principles of the intelligence, may be found, according to him, the instantaneous but real fact of a spon-

---

[5] *Ibid.*, pp. 382–83.   [6] *Ibid.*, p. 389.

taneous apperception of truth, a cognition which, not instantly reflecting itself, takes place unnoticed in the depths of consciousness, but yet is there, and is the true basis of that which, subsequently, under a logical form, by reflection, becomes a necessary truth. The subjective, along with the reflective, altogether expires in the spontaneous apperception. Reason indeed becomes subjective in its relation to reflection, to the free and voluntary self, the seat and type of all personality; but in itself, and in spontaneity, it is impersonal, exempt from individuality; it does not even belong to humanity; consequently, its laws rest upon no basis but themselves; they appear in, preside over, and govern humanity, but belong not to it. Nothing is less personal than reason, particularly in spontaneous, pure affirmation; nothing therefore is less subjective; and the truths which are thus given us, are absolute truths.[7]

Translated into Christian theology, this doctrine becomes the insistence that religious experience must precede religious knowledge. By a "preliminary discipline" that is "not speculative, but practical and spiritual," a Christian achieves the "Spiritual consciousness of the regenerate soul, by its entrance through Christ, into the new life and reality of the spiritual world." [8]

Henry resembled Parker more than he resembled Marsh in conceiving "spiritual" discipline as "practical" in the secular, moral sense. Spirituality meant morality to Henry, and the chief deliverance of the absolute voice of reason is the "simple, ultimate, and absolute conception" of right and obligation.

In common with all our necessary principles, the conception of right and wrong has, logically speaking, no origin. Being a simple and ultimate conviction of the reason, it is neither produced by nor resolvable into any other conception; and the question concerning its origin can, in propriety, relate only to the psychological conditions under which the conception is evolved.[9]

Morality or "virtuous desire" is spiritual, not because it is a consequence of the love of God or subjective to the will of God, but because it is logically primitive and psychologically spontaneous. It requires

---

[7] Cited in Ronald Vale Wells, *Three Christian Transcendentalists: James Marsh, Caleb Sprague Henry, Frederic Henry Hedge* (New York, 1943), pp. 56–57.

[8] Cited in *ibid.*, p. 60.

[9] William Whewell, *On the Foundations of Morals;* with additional discourses and essays by C. S. Henry (New York, 1839), pp. 208–9.

no further motivation or justification either of Divine Will or of self-interest. This absoluteness of morality Henry discovers in both reason and true Christianity. Like Parker he was above all a social reformer and preacher of public morals. He took an active part in the peace movement, in abolitionism, but more especially in fighting the corruption of New York City politics. Public corruption gave him his chief theme for preaching the necessity of regeneration, and his social version of the gospel of redemption is worth noting, for it was a vigorous revival of the Augustinian philosophy of history and a thoroughgoing attack on the complacency of the current theories of progress.

He studied carefully and translated Guizot's *History of Civilization*, and it suggested to him that the spirit of civilization is the spirit of "the understanding" and that this principle is continually at war with the spirit of reason and Christianity. God, "the Genius of human history," is using this conflict between civilization and Christianity, between understanding and reason, between nature and spirit, providentially to bring about the eventual perfection of human society. Meanwhile, human corruption manifests itself in its faith in civilization as the source of progress.

The present age, above all others that have ever preceded it, is the age of the understanding—the faculty of adapting means to ends in the sphere of time and sense. Never, in all former ages together, has the understanding achieved such stupendous triumphs as in the last fifty years. And the end which all these achievements—discoveries, inventions, conquests over nature—are made to serve: what are they? Mainly wealth and the multiplication of the means and refinements of enjoyment or other material or worldly ends.[10]

He wrote a scathing attack on Bancroft's famous *Oration on Human Progress* (1854) [11] from this point of view and then developed his own theory of history as follows:

I humbly presume to think, that neither the theoretical possibility of the social perfectionment of the human race; nor the necessity and universality of the idea and of the impulse to realize it; nor the actual progress of civilization; nor the universal spread of civil liberty and free institutions; nor any

[10] C. S. Henry, *Considerations on Some of the Elements and Conditions of Social Welfare and Human Progress* (New York, 1861), p. 290.
[11] See above, pp. 121 and 214.

advancement of science, or widest diffusion of knowledge, contain in them-selves—either separately or combined—any absolutely certain warrant that this ideal perfection of human society will ever be actually realized, or per-petually approached, in the lifetime of humanity on the globe. . . .

On the contrary, *the progressive development of such a civilization in the same line, would be the intensification of all the irrational aspects it now presents*—wealth more and more regarded as the great good and the limits to its desire and pursuit more and more extended, with a corresponding in-crease in the strength of the temptations to frauds, dishonesties and other wrongs and crimes peculiarly incident to such a state of society—and, with the increase of wealth, a greater and greater increase in the number, variety and ingenious refinements of luxurious enjoyment and gratifications of vanity and worldly pride—and, by the inevitable laws of such a civilization, all this tending, not to equalize among the laboring masses the conditions of comfort and welfare, but to make the poor poorer, and more poorly off in physical comforts, in the leisure and means for rational development and true domestic life, and so to increase the causes of degradation and the temptations to vice and crime.

Besides: the perfection of human society on the earth implies not only the advancement of individuals and communities, but also of nations and the community of nations, to a true rational life. It implies the pacification of the world, the union of the nations in a true brotherhood of justice, love and peace. But if mere civilization does not and cannot make individual men in society live together as brethren, how is it to effect the pacification of the world? The widest extension of commercial relations is no certain guaranty for the universal reign of peace, though it tends that way. But as in the past, so in the future, there is no security against collisions of interest; and ambition, pride and passion may still be stronger than the dictates of pru-dence and enlightened self-love. . . .

In Christianity—not, indeed, considered merely as a body of doctrines and ethical precepts, and a visible institute of worship and moral discipline, but in Christianity considered as an historical organization of supernatural Divine powers—I see propounded the only adequate cure for the corruption of the human race.

I speak not now as a theologian, but as a philosopher, when I say, the corruption of the human race. For this corruption is simply a matter of fact, of which all history is the undeniable demonstration; a fact of universal observation; a fact testified in the inmost consciousness of every one of us —who know and feel that we are not, and of our own unaided power shall never become, what we know and feel we ought to be. It is this fact which contains the reason why the history of humanity has been ever a history of abortive strivings after a perfection never reached—the reason why the progress of civilization, why education, science, knowledge, and civil liberty afford in themselves no guaranty that this perfection ever will be reached. As a philosopher I see—what every genuine philosopher must see—that no creed, however sublime, no ethical teachings, however divine, no institutes of worship and discipline, however pure and ennobling, can work the regeneration of the human race; because that is something which no merely moral influences can accomplish. As a philosopher, too, I am bound to look at Christianity in the character in which it undeniably propounds itself to the world—and that is not merely as a creed, a code, and a worship, but also as the incorporation into the life of humanity of Divine restoring powers . . .

The union of God and Man in the person of Christ, is the central fact in the history of the world, and of the universe, too. It is the central principle of the unity of the human race, and of all rational creatures. This truth the Infinite Father announces in these stupendous words: *"that in the dispensation of the fulness of time, He might gather together IN ONE all things in Christ, both which are in heaven and which are on earth, even in Him."* What words can be more express and clear? You see that the everliving Divine-human Person of Christ, is the centre of the unity of the human race, of its union with God, with itself, and with the rational universe.[12]

With this philosophical faith in Christ as the historical redeemer of mankind, Henry was prepared to oppose the Unitarian version of Christianity on transcendentalist principles. Immediately after Emerson's *Divinity School Address* and while Parker was writing his *Levi Blodgett Letter* Henry delivered a vigorous sermon against the current attempts to rob Christianity of its living (historical) powers.[13]

Judged from this point of view the Reverend Frederic H. Hedge should, perhaps, not be listed here as a Christian transcendentalist, for he was certainly closer to Parker's than he was to Henry's position, but both Christian charity and historical fact compel us to acknowledge his importance as a stanch defender of the church among the other, more "emancipated" members of the Transcendental Club. He was

[12] C. S. Henry, *Considerations on Some of the Elements and Conditions of Social Welfare and Human Progress* (New York, 1861), pp. 220–21, 238–39, 225–26, 241–42, 250–51.
[13] William Whewell, *On the Foundations of Morals* (New York, 1839), with additional discourses and essays by C. S. Henry.

successively minister to Unitarian congregations in Bangor, Maine, Providence, Rhode Island, and Brookline, Massachusetts. During the years 1857 to 1884 he taught at Harvard, first ecclesiastical history, then German literature. His chief philosophical inspiration came from the study and translation of German romantic literature. He studied in Germany during the years 1810–22 and was probably the best informed of the native New Englanders on the subject of German philosophy. The other three Harvard men who went to Germany for study during the same decade failed to become seriously interested in the more technical aspects of German idealism, though they were captivated by its romantic spirit.

Edward Everett, who was to procure that copy of Kant's philosophy for Moses Stuart, studied classical philology in Göttingen. Everett was President of Harvard from 1846 to 1849, but no interest in German philosophy is recorded in his life except an abortive plan to give an address on "the influence of German thought on the contemporary literature of England and America," in 1837. George Ticknor came as early as 1816 to the conclusion that the present "barrenness" of German literature was to be charged to the philosophy of Kant, which "absorbed and perverted all the talents of the land." It was a vast "Serbonian bog where armies whole have sunk." After his return to Harvard, Ticknor lectured on French and Spanish literature. George Bancroft, who kept up an interest in German *belles lettres* and later wrote several valuable studies, went to hear Hegel in Berlin, but thought the lectures merely a "display of unintelligible words." He admired Schleiermacher, however, whom he heard lecture on education, largely because "he has never suffered himself to be moved by any one of the many systems which have been gaining admirers and losing them successively for thirty years past." [14]

Karl T. C. Follen, too, who had come to New England from the headquarters of idealism in Germany, knew little philosophy and had little sympathy for the post-Kantians. Even Hedge, who had made a special study of the philosophers and had translated a volume of selections, brought them out under the title *Prose Writers of Germany* (1848) and gave preference to the literary authors. But Hedge at least knew German idealism from Kant to Hegel at first hand and was

---

[14] René Wellek, "The Minor Transcendentalists and German Philosophy," *The New England Quarterly*, XV (1942), 656.

the most reliable source for the American transcendentalists in their search for German inspiration. Curiously enough, though he had a scholarly interest in idealism and believed in it as an academic system, he had little of the *Sturm und Drang*, the romantic enthusiasm which infected his friends around Boston. He was sober and conservative; he was above all a churchman.

Some thirty years ago, a club was formed of young men, mostly preachers of the Unitarian connection, with a sprinkling of elect ladies,—all fired with the hope of a new era in philosophy and religion, which seemed to them about to dawn upon the world. There was something in the air,—a boding of some great revolution,—some new avatar of the Spirit, at whose birth these expectants were called to assist. . . . For myself, though I hugely enjoyed the sessions, and shared many of the ideas which ruled the conclave, and the ferment they engendered, I had no belief in ecclesiastical revolutions to be accomplished with set purpose; and I seemed to discern a power and a meaning in the old, which the more impassioned would not allow. I had even then made up my mind, that the method of revolution in theology is not dissension, but development. My historical conscience, then as since, balanced my neology, and kept me ecclesiastically conservative, though intellectually radical. . . . Others judged differently; they saw in every case of dissent, and in every new dissentient, the harbinger of the New Jerusalem. "The present church rattles ominously," they said: "it must vanish presently, and we shall have a real one." . . .

There have been some vanishings since then . . . but the Church that was present then, and was judged moribund by transcendental zeal, and rattled so ominously in transcendental ears, is present still. . . . What is the lesson of history and private experience concerning revolutions in religion? Ecclesiastical continuity,—that we are under tutelage. The Church does not exist by the will of man, but by his constitution. It cannot be abolished by the will of man; it cannot perish by disaffection. Only a new Church can supplant the old. And the new Church will not be an association of thinkers and critics, with correct and rational theories of God, discarding supernaturalism, and planting themselves on abstract theism. Such associations exist under all dispensations; but they have never succeeded in planting a Church, or supplanting one.[15]

Hedge clearly did not share the transcendental temper, and it is ironical that his name should be so closely associated with the Transcenden-

[15] Cited in Ronald Vale Wells, *Three Christian Transcendentalists: James Marsh, Caleb Sprague Henry, Frederic Henry Hedge* (New York, 1943), pp. 103-4, 104n.

tal Club, or "Hedge Club," as it was sometimes called, because it met whenever Hedge happened to come to town.

Nevertheless, his sermons and essays contain many representative expositions of the central transcendentalist themes. He was closest to Schelling in his thinking. His favorite theme was the unity of nature and spirit: "matter is nature at rest; spirit is nature in action." Natural history and human history are but phases of the growth of nature's self-consciousness. "All that is natural is spiritual in its ascent and cause; all that is spiritual is natural in its descent and being." In mythological terms:

In becoming spiritual, man receives a new natural birth, which means that he enters into conscious communion with the God by whom his spirit has been unconsciously nourished. The former stage is Adam, the latter, Christ; "but both are one and the same man,—the same human nature in different stages of development. First that which is animal; then that which is spiritual." [16]

In this emergent evolution, as we may well call it, there are three stages: nature, governed by the laws of motion; morals, governed by the law of duty; and spirit, governed by the law of love.

The realm of spirit, in which religion dominates, is according to Hedge not sharply distinguished from practical morality. Love and duty shade into each other. Hedge's chief concern was that the spirit of reform in both morals and religion should be constructive rather than negative. He preached social and intellectual liberalism as the basis of what he called his "broad church" program, and was one of the leaders among Unitarians in striving to avoid exclusiveness and sectarianism.

There is a spirit at work in the affairs of men, mightier than all ecclesiastical establishments and sectarian combinations. The old lines are everywhere disappearing, old sects are breaking up. The tide of humanity is sweeping away these petty barriers, and bearing us and our institutions on to a higher mark and a better day. A time is coming, when the only Christianity that shall pass current shall be the practical Christianity, which believes in a heavenly kingdom to be realized on earth, in the social perfection of man, and which labors, in the spirit of Christ, to promote it. . . . A time is coming, when there shall be but one Church—the Catholic Protestant Church

[16] *Ibid.*, pp. 106–7. The quotation from Hedge in this excerpt from Dr. Wells's exposition is taken from *Reason in Religion*, p. 29.

of Christian union and Christian progress; but one order of priesthood—
the hierarchy of the wise and good; but one standard and law—the law of
the spirit of life in Christ Jesus.[17]

— 25 —

EMERSON

THERE were several tendencies in American culture against
which transcendentalism set itself; some of them were products
of the Enlightenment, others were reactions against it; some were
common enemies of any idealism, others were specific circumstances
which serve to explain some of the peculiar traits of the American
movement.

We have noted the growth of natural science which accompanied the
Enlightenment's glorification of natural law. As the study of nature
lost its romance and became a laboratory task, the moralists not only
lost interest in it but also asserted that "the kingdom of man over
nature cometh not with observation." This motto and cliché of the
transcendentalists reflected, not a repudiation of science as such, but a
realization that science could not be a substitute for either philosophy
or religion, as the Enlightenment had led men to believe it might
become. The conquest of man was *over-and-above* nature rather than
through nature, and the transcendentalists took on a lordly air, "using"
nature for what it was worth to them morally, but showing little interest in detailed natural knowledge or experimental progress. Accordingly, they interpreted the progress of man as a growth out of nature
into a higher and purer environment. Their chief objection to the
attitude of "observation" and the discovery of nature's powers and
laws was that they imply a servile, obedient spirit, which can never
lead man to assert his proper freedom. The transcendentalists were
independents and Antinomians; they recognized no laws that were
not their laws or, for that matter, any worlds that were not "built" for
and by individual spirits as expressions of their sovereignty over ex-

[17] Cited in *ibid.*, p. 138. Taken from an article by Hedge, "The Churches and the
Church," in *Christian Examiner*, XLI (1846), 204.

ternal forces. Though they recognized God as an "over-soul," they made it clear that He is no over-lord and that His Spirit is continuous with and expressive of the discipline that free wills exhibit of themselves. Or, to put the doctrine more technically, God is transcendent over nature precisely because he is immanent in man's spirit.

The transcendentalists' attitude toward history was like their attitude toward nature. They felt above it. New England in the 1820's and 1830's was producing its first crop of historians—Bancroft, Prescott, Motley, Parkman, Hildreth, and many lesser ones. The look backward was symptomatic of the feeling of having arrived. Boston was resting on the founders' oars a bit and surveying the progress of two centuries. Puritanism was in the past, no longer a virtue or a danger, and there was already discernible a feeling for the antique, if not a love of it. Hawthorne, for example, reveled in the Puritan past and in its conscience as in a land of romance. Toward such rummaging in the attics and errors of ancestors, the transcendentalists showed scorn. They read history, of course, the more ancient and remote the better, but they merely "appropriated" it to kindle their imagination or to furnish texts for spiritual lessons. Some looked forward in the spirit of utopian reform, some looked inward to the eternal, but few looked backward with a historian's interest. They still felt the impetus of the eighteenth century and were confident that they were still in the center of creative activity, too busy for reminiscence and too hopeful for regrets.

They were opposed to common sense and to vulgarity. Individuality they respected to the point of eccentricity, but not just any old individual; they were the flowering of gentility and "culture." They have been called philosophers of democracy, and in a loose sense their love of independence, contempt for tradition, and cultivation of their own resources can be linked to the democratic ideal of life. But historically speaking they belonged to the era of liberals, not of democrats. They were not representative men, certainly not political Democrats. Their speech and manners were studied and stilted. What freedom they exhibited was conscientious, not spontaneous. They indulged excessively in diaries and journals. They used philosophy for literary purposes, and their pompous language often ill concealed commonplace ideas. They were Yankees studying to be Victorians. They were too "cultivated," to be cultured. What culture they had was amazingly cosmopolitan and eclectic; classical, German, French, Italian, Confucian, Vedic, Buddhist literatures were all grist for their mill, and they could have felt at home (when not lecturing) in heaven itself, for they eagerly embraced any and all forms of the spirit. In this receptivity they certainly outdid both their German and their English comrades in transcendental philosophy, possibly because their provincial limitations made them more dependent on imported goods. Be that as it may, their industry and sympathy in appropriating the most diverse faiths and idioms is a monument to their erudition as well as a contribution to American literacy.[1] Nevertheless, this industrious reading of books was scorned by them as a betrayal of self-reliance and was justified only insofar as it taught the reader to see himself in a reflected light.

Perhaps the deepest antipathy of the transcendentalists was toward institutions. Organization was inherently a confession of dependence or of the pursuit of material power, both of which were foreign to the life of the spirit. They carried the individualism of the Enlightenment to fanatical extremes. Government should be literally self-government, they taught, and no man should seek to govern his fellowman. On the lower, or "material," plane organization and institutions could be justified, but the predicaments of physical existence were not to be confused with the concerns of the spirit and were to be accepted as the necessary "conditions," but not the "ground" of real being. Of all institutions the churches were the least justified, since they brought government and authority into the realm of spirit where freedom reigns. It was needless, at least in New England, to combat Calvinism,

[1] Mr. Frederic I. Carpenter has pointed out that this New England humanism produced not only the transcendentalist romanticism but also the gentility of Longfellow, Lowell & Co. "Puritan humanism now expanded to become classical humanism; the religion of the Bible became the religion of Books. Lowell felt this continuity when he prophesied, with characteristically heavy humor, that 'the broad foreheads and the long heads will win the day at last . . . and it will be enough if we feel as keenly as our Puritan founders did that those organs of empire may be broadened and lengthened by culture.' Although it is significant that he described culture as a means to empire, it is even more significant that he traced it to the Puritan past and that he made it a continuing means to salvation . . ."—Frederic I. Carpenter, "The Genteel Tradition; a Reinterpretation," *The New England Quarterly*, XV (1942), 436.

for the Unitarians had attended to that. The transcendentalists turned on the Unitarians themselves, their own mother church, with some of their most barbed criticism. Fortunately for the Unitarians and the churches, the politics of slavery made the state so obnoxious to the transcendentalists that they ceased their anticlericalism and themselves often took to the pulpit in denouncing the government. In them the theory and practice of independence reached their high-water mark.

Denton J. Snider, the St. Louis Hegelian, in working out his dialectic of American history, explained that in the interests of freedom Emerson "negated" institutions, but realized his own objective or synthetic freedom in becoming an institution himself. This remark is incisive, empirical truth, regardless of the dialectic, and calls attention to the important fact that the history of American philosophy must interpret not only the mind of Emerson the individual but also Emerson institutionalized in American culture. Transcendentalism, insofar as it was an organized movement and remains a social force, is the anti-institutional institution.

Emerson literally saved himself by transcendental self-reliance. Having emancipated himself in 1832 from the restrictions and obligations of the Unitarian ministry, only to find in freedom greater burdens, he turned, sick in body and mind, to travel in Europe. Though the rest was beneficial and though he was no doubt encouraged and instructed by his visits with the British transcendentalists, he owed the renewal of his strength and mission primarily to neither of these facts, but to the discovery during his year abroad of the art of self-reliance, both socially and intellectually. He learned to think and act for himself, finding his own meanings in things, and though he usually found no new meanings, the significant fact to him was that they were appropriated and were literally *his* meanings. With this discovery as a clue, he turned to nature, history, books, friends, experience, etc. to find out what each meant to him. And when he had succeeded in generalizing this procedure, he not only had a series of lectures but a philosophy as well. He had "built his own world" and could now tell his fellow Americans each to build his own. The fact that this subjective method was a personal salvation to him explains much of the vitality of Emerson's writing and speaking. He always seemed to be speaking from experience, even when he was merely repeating what he had read. It was a natural consequence of this method that his thinking never achieved clarity or system; each utterance came as an authentic revelation of Spirit and could be used by him and other preachers as a text, almost Biblical, for numberless sermons.

These two basic traits of his thought account for much of Emerson's power as an American institution: (1) he invented a secular pulpit, a secular technique of sermonic commentary, and a secular "wisdom literature" which gave his sentences an oracular quality; (2) he spoke as man to man, appealing from experience to experience. Thus, both his manner and his message were peculiarly welcome to a public bred and bored by pulpits and brought to other American thinkers (if not scholars) the same confidence, self-cultivation, and individuality which he had achieved.

Emerson's idealism was neither Platonic nor Berkeleyan, though he knew a little of both. Things interested him neither in terms of their universal patterns nor in terms of their natural existence, but in terms of their ability to stimulate the poetic imagination, which he and his fellow transcendentalists called reason or spirit.

Such "spirit" was doubly subjective: it was imagination rather than knowledge—poetry not science—and it had self-knowledge as its avowed object. It was a synthesis of introspection and reflection, and it created a self-esteem, now heroic, now pathetic.

The very time sees for us, thinks for us; it is a microscope such as philosophy never had. Insight is for us which was never for any. And doubt not the moment and the opportunity are divine. He who shall represent the genius of this day, he who shall, standing in this great cleft of Past and Future, understand the dignity and power of his position so well as to write the laws of Criticism, of Ethics, of History, will be found, an age hence, neither false nor unfortunate, but will rank immediately and equally with all the masters whom we now acknowledge. . . .

Certainly we concede that nothing has yet been greatly done, but we will not therefore distrust this great faith. Its boundlessness is already a grandeur. The greatness of this age is in its Prayer. . . . The problem which belongs to us to solve is new and untried. Born in the age of calculation and criticism, we are to carry it, with all its triumphs, and yield it captive to the universal Reason. Educated in the very shop and the mill, taught that nature exists for use and the raw material of art, conveyed, clothed, fed by steam, educated in traditions, and working in state, in church, in education, and in charities by mechanical methods, we are yet made to hear the auguries and prophecies of the Soul, which makes light of all these proud mechanisms, breathes on them and they become ashes and shadows, and calls us to the Holy and the Eternal, not by the Past, but by the Present, not by men, but alone, not by Bibles, but through thought and lowliest submission of heart. I see already this effort in eminent individuals. They are renouncing that which had been their pride: they encounter scorn and live with scorned men. They acquire a serener, heavenlier eye and brow.[2]

Emerson felt the lack in himself and in his society of the poetic uses of the intellect. Science and morals were commonplaces and were regarded, in the tradition of the Enlightenment, as the two foci of the life of reason. The cultivation of *aperçu*, of intuitive insights, poetic perspectives, and visionary ideas, was needed. "Culture inverts the vulgar views of nature, and brings the mind to call that apparent which it uses to call real, and that real which it uses to call visionary."[3]

The invariable mark of wisdom is to see the miraculous in the common. . . . The immobility or bruteness of nature, is the absence of spirit; to pure spirit, it is fluid, it is volatile, it is obedient. Every spirit builds itself a house; and beyond its house a world; and beyond its world a heaven. Know then, that the world exists for you. For you is the phenomenon perfect. . . . Build, therefore, your own world. As fast as you conform your life to the pure idea in your mind, that will unfold its great proportions. A correspondent revolution in things will attend the influx of the spirit. . . . The Kingdom of man over nature, which cometh not with observation,— a dominion such as now is beyond his dream of God,—he shall enter without more wonder than the blind man feels who is gradually restored to perfect sight.[4]

Shifting the focus of the mind from nature as existence to nature as food for spirit, was Emerson's primary aim and his chief argument

[2] Ralph Waldo Emerson, *Journals;* with annotations, edited by Edward Waldo Emerson and Waldo Emerson Forbes, 1820–1872 (Cambridge, 1911), V, 293, 295, 311. Thoreau made the same point more lightheartedly.
> There is such health and length of years
> In the elixir of thy note,
> That God himself more young appears,
> From the rare bragging of thy throat.
From "Upon the Bank at Early Dawn," in Thoreau, *Collected Poems;* edited by Carl Bode (Chicago, 1943), p. 204.
[3] Chapter on "Idealism," in *Nature.*   [4] *Nature.*

for idealism. He felt the liberation which poetic imagination brings, but in his eagerness to welcome the achievements of the mind in disregard of matter, he (and most of his friends) went to the absurd lengths of welcoming almost anything that revealed extraordinary power. Note, for example, the following list:

the traditions of miracles in the earliest antiquity of all nations; the history of Jesus Christ; the achievements of a principle, as in religious and political revolutions, and in the abolition of the slave-trade; the miracles of enthusiasm, as those reported of Swedenborg, Hohenlohe, and the Shakers; many obscure and yet contested facts, now arranged under the name of Animal Magnetism; prayer, eloquence; self-healing; and the wisdom of children.[5]

The transcendentalists shared and abetted the fashion of their day in extending an uncritical sympathy toward almost anything that was unscientific, in their effort to emancipate the spirit from the habits of natural understanding. In this trait, and in general, Emerson represents the golden mean of New England transcendentalism. Though he patronized and sympathized with the reformers and mystics surrounding him, he himself yielded in neither direction; he kept himself aloof, using these ideas and enthusiasms as themes for critical self-cultivation. Not only as a person, but also as an institution, Emerson was both the genial critic and the constructive idealist, combining Yankee humor and sobriety with poetic imagination and freedom. His ability to keep on friendly terms with his intellectual and social environment and tradition made him a great American mediator; his public accepted from him as gospel what in other tones and idioms it repudiated as heresy or humbug.

— 26 —

SPIRITUAL ASSOCIATION

MOST of the humanitarian reform movements in New England arose out of the Enlightenment and were related to transcendentalism only indirectly. Channing, Brownson, Parker, Garrison all

[5] *Ibid.*

received their impetus and early ideals from the Age of Reason. This is true in a measure even of the Fourierist enthusiasm and utopian schemes for regenerating society. W. H. Channing, Ripley, Brisbane, and the others derived their theories of association from sources which reflected social contract theories and when they learned transcendentalist philosophy they regarded their social schemes as opportunities to give transcendental conversation a more congenial environment. Though Brook Farm was largely a community of transcendentalists, it was not literally a transcendentalist society. Nevertheless, utopian socialism was significantly affected by transcendentalist doctrine, for the communities, originally conceived as schemes of reform, to dignify labor, equalize property, and purify morals, were justified by the transcendentalists as escapes of the spirit from the slavery of material concerns. They became in the end socialized expressions of romantic idealism.

The case of Bronson Alcott, however, is somewhat different; his social theory was transcendentalist to begin with. His work as an educator and his social experiment of Fruitlands were practical applications of an idealist philosophy. He began in his Temple School at Boston to encourage children in the habits of self-expression and moral reflection, using conversation and diaries (two basic habits in his own life) as foundations for educational discipline. He was a Pestalozzian reformer, but he added to his educational ideas his own personal interest in idealism as he discovered it by reading Marsh's edition of Coleridge, then Wordsworth, Herder, Plato, Plotinus, and then more and more of the mystics of East and West. Though his Boston school failed, it achieved fame in England and led to Alcott's acquaintance with a group of British "integralist" reformers, who met as "the friends of human progress," discussed "Reformation, Transition, and Formation," and resolved to "select a spot whereon the new Eden may be planted and man may, untempted by evil, dwell in harmony with his Creator, with himself, his fellows, and with all external natures." [1] The result was the experiment of "Fruitlands," Harvard, Mass., in 1843, financed and "managed" by Alcott's English friend Charles Lane. For Alcott this meant primarily an attempt to combine the "Pythagorean" asceticism with a "consociate family" life. In the new

[1] O. Shepard, *Pedlar's Progress*, p. 326.

Eden of Fruitlands the apple was a principal food, not a temptation; men, animals, and even the soil were to be spared all unnecessary bondage and pollution. The purified "family" was to vindicate itself as the basic institution of all society. It was to be even more, it was to illustrate the creative power of spiritual generation. Alcott believed literally that spirit came before matter and that all "genesis" is of the spirit. God created man's spirit, and man, as he became increasingly debased or animalized, created the lower and material corruptions of being. Alcott's idealism, in short, was corrupted by mysticism. His *Orphic Sayings*, which were at first in the manner and spirit of Coleridge, became increasingly esoteric.

There is an amusing description by Denton J. Snider of Alcott delivering his Orphic sayings in St. Louis.

The old prophet would read his oracular message in a rather sepulchral voice, as if it were issuing from the sacred cave of Trophonius himself; then he would throw down the written slip and cry out: "What say you to it, gentlemen?" The Orphic utterance was often dark, tortuous and riddle-some, yet certainly with a content of some kind. I was interested in seeing how diversely the same thought or perchance the same oracle would mirror itself in those different minds. Some twenty men—only men were present—had gathered into a kind of circle before the new Orpheus, while directly in front of him sat Brockmeyer, with alert, probably mischievous eyes, acting as chief interpreter or perchance as hierophant, though others would add their mite of a word. The conduct of the hierophant that evening had more mystery in it than even the Orphic sayings. To some of them he would give an easy, sober significance, which we all understood; but others he seemed to turn inside out and then to shiver into smithereens. Finally he picked up one which had just been read, and at the fiery touch of his dialectic, set off with his Mephistophelean chuckle, he simply exploded it into mist with a sort of detonation, as if it were a soap bubble filled with explosive gas. Mr. Alcott, who had already begun to suspect that his oracles were made to contradict themselves by some Hegelian process which he did not understand, now grew testy and actually lost his temper, raising his voice to a loud raucous tone: "Mr. Brockmeyer, you confound us by the multiplicity of your words and the profusion of your fancy." This was the first wholly intelligible saying of Orpheus that evening, and certainly the most impressive. Mr. Brockmeyer restrained himself and calmly replied, "Perhaps I do." . . .

After this stirring interlude Mr. Harris, always the reconciler in any fight but his own, stepped into the breach and took up the interpretation while the reading went on, though not with its pristine vigor. Still one of these later sayings caused a good deal of comment as well as surmise: It ran thus, as I recollect: "It requires a Christ to interpret a Christ." Ten o'clock struck, and the discussion had zigzagged about in all sorts of twists and turns above and below the surface. I was quizzing with myself: Has the foxy Yankee prophet just coined this little oracle on Brockmeyer, or on Harris, or on all of us together, with himself visible in the background? I rose to my feet and gave expression to the only remark I made during the evening: "Gentlemen, I may be permitted to state my interpretation of this last saying: its hidden meaning is, in my judgment, that only an Alcott can rightly interpret an Alcott. That being the case, we all had better now go home." At this rather un-Orphic deliverance little tidbits of tee-hees fluttered round the circle as the people sprang up and began to take their hats, while Orpheus himself looked at me somewhat oracularly, I thought, and shut impatiently his map of oracles.[2]

He was rescued in part from his vagaries by W. T. Harris and the St. Louis Hegelians, who forced him to define his idealism more precisely. Under Howison's influence he then represented himself as a personalist. By this type of idealism he intended to repudiate the vague "over-soul" of Emerson and deism. He also repudiated, under Hegelian influence, his earlier individualism and even interpreted the failure of Fruitlands as a consequence of his too "individualistic" emphasis on the family, to the exclusion of economic and political institutions. Out of Alcott's acquaintance with the St. Louis Hegelians grew the Concord Summer School of Philosophy (1879–87), which was an important event in the history of American idealism and of which we shall have more to say later.

— 27 —

SPIRITUAL SOLITUDE

HENRY THOREAU was a vigorous, good-natured rebel. He repudiated not only the Puritan conscience but the transcendental conscience as well and gave expression to paganism as a principle of

---

[2] Denton J. Snider, *A Writer of Books in His Genesis*, pp. 335–37.

self-culture. He was the Nietzsche of New England. His doctrine of "civil disobedience" was merely the conscientious and philosophical justification of his wholehearted scorn for society, especially his society. He discovered a critical, practical scheme for private rebellion. It was not that he loved nature more, but that he found his spirit (i.e., his reflections on reading) to be freer in solitude and open air. He was not a naturalist except incidentally; he was a poet who felt no need for institutional morals.

> I am a parcel of vain strivings tied
>   By a chance bond together,
> Dangling this way and that, their links
>   Were made so loose and wide,
>   Methinks,
>   For milder weather.[1]

He gave picturesque expression to the most pervasive theme of New England transcendentalism, i.e., the danger to the life of the free spirit from absorption in economic and political concerns.

For six days shalt thou labor and do all thy knitting, but on the seventh, forsooth thy reading. Happy we who can bask in this warm September sun, which illumines all creatures, as well when they rest as when they toil, not without a feeling of gratitude. . . . It is remarkable, that notwithstanding the universal favor with which the New Testament is outwardly received, and even the bigotry with which it is defended, there is no hospitality shown to, there is no appreciation of, the order of truth with which it deals. I know of no book that has so few readers. There is none so truly strange, and heretical, and unpopular. To Christians, no less than Greeks and Jews, it is foolishness and a stumbling block. There are, indeed, severe things in it which no man should read aloud but once.—"Seek first the kingdom of heaven."—"Lay not up for yourselves treasures on earth."—"If thou wilt be perfect, go and sell that thou hast, and give to the poor, and thou shalt have treasure in heaven."—"For what is man profited, if he shall gain the whole world, and lose his own soul? or what shall a man give in exchange for his soul?"—Think of this, Yankees! . . . I have not the most definite designs on the future. Absolutely speaking, "Do unto others as you would that they should do unto you" is by no means a golden rule, but the best of current silver. An honest man would have but little occasion for it.

[1] Henry David Thoreau, "I Am a Parcel of Vain Strivings Tied," in his *Collected Poems*, edited by Carl Bode (Chicago, 1943), p. 81.

It is golden not to have any rule at all in such a case. . . . A healthy man, with steady employment, as wood chopping at fifty cents a cord, and a camp in the woods, will not be a good subject for Christianity. The New Testament may be a choice book to him on some, but not on all or most of his days. He will rather go a-fishing in his leisure hours. The apostles, though they were fishers too, were of the solemn race of sea-fishers, and never trolled for pickerel on inland streams. Men have a singular desire to be good without being good for anything, because, perchance, they think vaguely that so it will be good for them in the end. . . . Everywhere "good men" sound a retreat, and the word has gone forth to fall back on innocence. Fall forward rather on to whatever there is there. Christianity only hopes. It has hung its harp on the willows, and cannot sing a song in a strange land. It has dreamed a sad dream, and does not yet welcome the morning with joy.[2]

> Great God, I ask thee for no meaner pelf
> Than that I may not disappoint myself,
> That in my action I may soar as high,
> As I can now discern with this clear eye.
>
> And next in value, which thy kindness lends,
> That I may greatly disappoint my friends,
> Howe'er they think or hope that it may be,
> They may not dream how thou'st distinguished me.
>
> That my weak hand may equal my firm faith,
> And my life practice more than my tongue saith;
> That my low conduct may not show,
> Nor my relenting lines,
> That I thy purpose did not know,
> Or overrated thy designs.[3]

But this religious and moral rebellion is very unlike Nietzsche's paganism in that it is genial, unpretentious, and pious.

> Always the general show of things
>   Floats in review before my mind,
> And such true love and reverence brings,
>   That sometimes I forget that I am blind.

[2] Thoreau, "Sunday," in *A Week on the Concord and Merrimack Rivers.*
[3] Thoreau, "Great God, I Ask Thee for No Meaner Pelf," in *Collected Poems,* edited by Carl Bode, p. 10.

But now there comes unsought, unseen,
    Some clear, divine electuary,
And I who had but sensual been,
    Grow sensible, and as God is, am wary.

I hearing get who had but ears,
    And sight, who had but eyes before,
I moments live who lived but years,
    And truth discern who knew but learning's lore.

I hear beyond the range of sound,
    I see beyond the range of sight,
New earths and skies and seas around,
    And in my day the sun doth pale his light.

A clear and ancient harmony
    Pierces my soul through all its din,
As through its utmost melody,—
    Farther behind than they—farther within.[4]

Despite Thoreau's moral individualism, there grew in him a sense of the unity of all life, a nature-mysticism, an awareness of breathing with the universal breath of life. "I see, smell, taste, hear, feel, that everlasting Something to which we are allied." Derived in part from his reading of Buddhist philosophy and the *Bhagavadgita,* in part from his habit of reporting his life in the woods, he became more than a solitary outcast from society; he became an authentic brahman, finding his bliss in the least articulate but most pervasive communion with the eternal life. If we may be guided by his *Journal,* we must picture him as becoming what the orientals call a "forest ascetic" writing "forest treatises."

I go and come with a strange liberty in nature. . . . Shall I not have intelligence with the earth? Am I not partly leaves and vegetable mold myself? (Walden) [5]

This absorption into nature was not a Spinozistic worship of the order in nature or a love of observing natural creatures and processes, but a

---

[4] Thoreau, "Inspiration," in his *Collected Poems,* ed. by Carl Bode, pp. 230–32.
[5] Thoreau, *Writings* (Boston and New York, 1906), II, 143, 153.

sense of the endlessness of the life in which man participates. Thoreau could as spontaneously merge himself in nature as Whitman could in Brooklyn.

— 28 —

AT SEA

HERMAN MELVILLE (1819–91), the most rebellious temperament among the mid-century rebels, came both geographically and philosophically from the borderland of the New England transcendentalists. He spent his first and last years in New York City, was familiar with the Hudson Valley as far as Albany and lived for a time on his farm in western Massachusetts. At the age of seventeen he took to sea "as a substitute for pistol and ball." "Talk not of the bitterness of middle age and after life, a boy can feel all that. . . . Before the death of my father I never thought of working for my living, and never knew there were hard hearts in the world . . . I had learned to think much, and bitterly, before my time." [1] His life at sea was really more a substitute for work than for "pistol and ball." His romanticism was likewise a flight from routine work to lonely wanderings of mind. In describing a paper mill, "Tartarus of Maids," he wrote: "At rows of blank-looking counters sat rows of blank-looking girls, with blank, white folders in their blank hands, all blankly folding blank paper." [2] He was never able to endure the insensitivity of so-called civilized men and relations, nor was he ever able to accept the practical ideals of his practical neighbors. What principles he could understand were transcendental absolutes, perfect in themselves, but of no utility. Physical adventure he understood, and the play of natural powers he enjoyed, but the invisible world, both of speculation and of morals, filled him with terror. "Though in many of its visible aspects the world seems formed in love, the invisible spheres were

[1] Raymond Weaver, *Herman Melville, Mariner and Mystic* (New York, 1921), p. 75.
[2] "The Tartarus of Maids," quoted by F. O. Matthiessen, in *American Renaissance*, p. 401.

formed in fright." [3] Melville, being thoroughly infected with the transcendental temper, was therefore haunted by the realm of absolutes. He was tempted, like Jonah, to flee from God, but determined, like Captain Ahab of *Moby Dick*, to face Him defiantly. "The reason the mass of men fear God and *at bottom dislike* Him, is because they rather distrust His heart, and fancy Him all brain like a watch." [4] Melville's basic intellectual program was to approach God by means of the "heart" rather than the "head," imagining that though both men and God are eternal mysteries to themselves and each other, they enter together into a tragedy which both can feel and act. "The tragedy of mind," as Mr. Sedgwick has well named this theme, is a combination of the tragedies of Prometheus, Job, and Jonah. The fear that God is really frightful is no mere "evil monomania," as Captain Ahab's madness and hate seem to be to the thoughtless reader; it is the fearless facing of the consequences of philosophical adventure into the boundless.

It was Hawthorne's understanding of this tragedy that interested Melville in him particularly. The two men were neighbors for a time (near Pittsfield, Mass.), and Melville made persistent attempts to win Hawthorne's friendship and sympathy, without much success. The following comment made in his review of *The House of the Seven Gables* explains at once his interpretation of Hawthorne and his own philosophy.

A certain tragic phase of humanity, . . . in our opinion, was never more powerfully embodied than by Hawthorne. We mean the tragedies of human thought in its own unbiassed, native, and profounder workings . . . [Man] may perish: but so long as he exists he insists upon treating with all Powers upon an equal basis. If any of those other Powers choose to withhold certain secrets, let them; that does not impair my sovereignty in myself; that does not make me tributary. And perhaps, after all, there is *no* secret. . . . We incline to think that God cannot explain His own secrets, and that He would like a little information upon certain points Himself. We mortals astonish Him as much as He us. But it is this *Being* of the matter; there lies the knot with which we choke ourselves. As soon as you say *Me*, a *God*, a *Nature*, so soon you jump off from your stool and hang from the

---

[3] Weaver, *op. cit.*, p. 26.
[4] From a letter to Hawthorne, quoted by Weaver, *op. cit.*, p. 322.

beam. Yes, that word is the hangman. Take God out of the dictionary, and you would have Him in the street.[5]

Hawthorne, in turn, failed to understand Melville's "endless questioning of providence and futurity, and of everything else that lies beyond human ken." [6] It was precisely this hopeless interest in the things "beyond human ken" that chiefly fascinated Melville and kept alive in him an *amor intellectualis* for "the infinite cliffs and gulfs of human mystery and misery." [7]

Any attempt to identify transcendental principles with "civilized" standards, seemed to Melville diabolical. He had only contempt for thinkers like Emerson, who, he said, are "cracked right across the brow" when they believe in compensations and "correspondences." Nevertheless, he had, if not contempt, at least only pity for those who on the contrary ignored transcendentals entirely and who were resigned too readily and fatalistically to saying "Sinner, sin out life's petty lease." [8] He took quite seriously Christ's suggestion that the only real remedy would be to "be born anew," but he thought it of fundamental importance to appreciate in *this* birth the principles of a *new* one. And his chief transcendental insight consisted precisely in his realization that absolute and relative standards are necessary to each other, neither being intelligible in itself.

This point he makes very characteristically in the supposed "pamphlet" by "Plotinus Plinlimmon," which was intended to explain the "ambiguities" to Pierre. Since this "lecture" is the nearest Melville ever came to making a technical, academic formulation of what might be called his philosophy, and since *Pierre* is difficult of access to many readers, I shall quote at length.

CHRONOMETRICALS AND HOROLOGICALS

(Being not so much the Portal, as part of the temporary Scaffold to the Portal of this New Philosophy.)

[5] Quoted in Weaver, *op. cit.*, pp. 316–17. I cite this passage for the particular benefit of our German friends who may wish to find an American representative of *Existenzphilosophie* and a disciple of Kierkegaard.

[6] Quoted in Weaver, *op. cit.*, p. 318.

[7] From *Pierre*, quoted by Weaver, *op. cit.*, p. 338. Melville states that Dante inspired and later Schopenhauer reenforced his sense of the abyss of misery.

[8] Herman Melville, *Clarel*, II, 253.

Now in an artificial world like ours, the soul of man is further removed from its God and the Heavenly Truth, than the chronometer carried to China, is from Greenwich. And as that chronometer, if at all accurate, will pronounce it to be 12 o'clock high-noon, when the China local watches say, perhaps, it is 12 o'clock midnight; so the chronometric soul, if in this world true to its great Greenwich in the other, will always, in its so-called intuitions of right and wrong, be contradicting the mere local standards and watch-maker's brains of this earth. . . .

And thus, though the earthly wisdom of man be heavenly folly to God; so also, conversely, is the heavenly wisdom of God an earthly folly to man. Literally speaking, this is so. Nor does the God at the heavenly Greenwich expect common men to keep Greenwich wisdom in this remote Chinese world of ours; because such a thing were unprofitable for them here, and, indeed, a falsification of Himself, inasmuch as in that case, China time would be identical with Greenwich time, which would make Greenwich time wrong.

But why then does God now and then send a heavenly chronometer (as a meteoric stone) into the world, uselessly as it would seem, to give the lie to all the world's time-keepers? Because He is unwilling to leave man without some occasional testimony to this:—that though man's Chinese notions of things may answer well enough here, they are by no means universally applicable, and that the central Greenwich in which he dwells goes by a somewhat different method from this world. And yet it follows not from this, that God's truth is one thing and man's truth another; but—as above hinted, and as will be further elucidated in subsequent lectures—by their very contradictions they are made to correspond. . . .

To any earnest man of insight, a faithful contemplation of these ideas concerning Chronometricals and Horologicals, will serve to render provisionally far less dark some few of the otherwise obscurest things which have hitherto tormented the honest-thinking men of all ages. What man who carries a heavenly soul in him, has not groaned to perceive, that unless he committed a sort of suicide as to the practical things of this world, he never can hope to regulate his earthly conduct by the same heavenly soul? And yet by an infallible instinct he knows that that monitor cannot be wrong in itself.

And where is the earnest and righteous philosopher, gentlemen, who looking right and left, and up and down through all the ages of the world, the present included; where is there such an one who has not a thousand times been struck with a sort of infidel idea, that whatever other worlds God may be Lord of, he is not the Lord of this; for else this world would seem to give the lie to Him; so utterly repugnant seem its ways to the instinctively known ways of Heaven. But it is not, and cannot be so; nor will he who regards this chronometrical conceit aright, ever be more conscious of that horrible idea. For he will then see, or seem to see, that this world's seeming incompatibility with God, absolutely results from its meridional correspondence with Him. . . .

This chronometrical conceit does by no means involve the justification of all the acts which wicked men may perform. For in their wickedness downright wicked men sin as much against their own horologes, as against the heavenly chronometer. That this is so, their spontaneous liability to remorse does plainly evince. No, this conceit merely goes to show, that for the mass of men, the highest abstract heavenly righteousness is not only impossible, but would be entirely out of place, and positively wrong in a world like this. To turn the left cheek if the right be smitten, is chronometrical; hence no average son of man ever did such a thing. To give *all* that thou hast to the poor, this too is chronometrical; hence no average son of man ever did such a thing. Nevertheless, if a man gives with a certain self-considerate generosity to the poor; abstains from doing downright ill to any man; does his convenient best in a general way to do good to his whole race; takes watchfull loving care of his wife and children, relatives and friends; is perfectly tolerant to all other men's opinions, whatever they may be; is an honest dealer, and honest citizen, and all that; and more especially if he believe that there is a God for infidels, as well as for believers, and acts upon that belief; then, though such a man falls infinitely short of the chronometrical standard, though all his actions are entirely horologic;—yet such a man need never lastingly despond, because he is sometimes guilty of some minor offense.

In short, this chronometrical and horological conceit, in sum, seems to teach this:—That in things terrestrial (horological) a man must not be governed by ideas celestial (chronometrical); that certain minor self-renunciations in this life his own mere instinct for his own everyday general well-being will teach him to make, but he must by no means make a complete unconditional sacrifice of himself in behalf of any other being, or any cause, or any conceit. . . .

A virtuous expediency, then, seems the highest desirable or attainable earthly excellence for the mass of men, and is the only earthly excellence that their Creator intended for them. When they go to heaven, it will be quite another thing. There, they can freely turn the left cheek, because there the right cheek will never be smitten. There they can freely give all to the poor, for ~~there~~ there will be no poor to give to. A due appreciation of this matter will do good to man. For, hitherto, being authoritatively taught by his dogmatical teachers that he must, while on earth, aim at heaven, and attain it, too, in all his earthly acts, on pain of eternal wrath; and finding by experience that this is utterly impossible; in his despair, he is too apt to run clean away into all manner of moral abandonment, self-deceit and hypocrisy (cloaked, however, mostly under an aspect of the most respectable devotion); or else he openly runs, like a mad dog, into atheism. But if any man say, that such a doctrine as this I lay down is false, is impious; I would charitably refer that man to the history of Christendom for the last 1800 years; and ask him, whether, in spite of all the maxims of Christ, that history is not just as full of blood, violence, wrong, and iniquity of every kind, as any previous portion of the world's story? Therefore, it follows, that so far as practical results are concerned—regarded in a purely earthly light—the only great original moral doctrine of Christianity (i.e., the Chronometrical gratuitous return of good for evil, as distinguished from the horological forgiveness of injuries taught by some of the Pagan philosophers), has been found (horologically) a false one; because after 1800 years' inculcation from tens of thousands of pulpits, it has proved entirely impracticable.[9]

This doctrine is a reformulation of the Calvinistic distinction between saving faith and good works, but whether Melville intended this to be an ironical lecture on the tragic concepts of orthodoxy or his own tragic revision of the transcendentalist doctrine of correspondence is perhaps impossible to determine. It is really both. But for the interpretation of Melville's own character it would be important to know, if one could, whether Melville retained to the end a positive, "chronometrical" faith, or whether he became increasingly embittered and despondent. The concluding lines of *White Jacket*, in which he pictures mankind on board a "fast-sailing, never-sinking world-frigate, of which God was the shipwright," sailing under sealed orders, can be interpreted as a confession of either faith or despair:

Let us not give ear to the superstitious, gun deck gossip about whether we may be gliding, for, as yet, not a soul on board of us knows—not even the Commodore himself: assuredly not the Chaplain: even our Professor's scientific surmisings are vain. . . . And believe not the hypochondriac dwellers below hatches, who will tell you, with a sneer, that our world-

[9] Herman Melville, *Pierre; or, The Ambiguities* (New York, 1929), pp. 294–300.

frigate is bound to no final harbor whatever. . . . For how can this world-frigate prove our eventual abiding place, when, upon our first embarkation, as infants in arms, her violent rollings—in after life unperceived—makes every soul of us sea-sick? Does not this show, too, that the very air we here inhale is uncongenial, and only becomes endurable at last through gradual habituation, and that some blessed, placid haven, however remote at present, must be in store for us all? . . .

Oh, shipmates and world-mates, all round! We the people suffer many abuses. . . . In vain from Lieutenants do we appeal to the Captain; in vain—while on board our world-frigate—to the indefinite Navy Commissioners, so far out of sight aloft. Yet the worst of our evils we blindly inflict upon ourselves; our officers can not relieve them, even if they would. From the last ills no being can save another; therein each man must be his own saviour. For the rest . . . let us not mutiny . . . let us never forget that,

> Whoever afflict us, whatever surround,
> Life is a voyage that's homeward-bound! [10]

His long poem *Clarel* is similarly ambiguous. It is a commentary on the Holy Land and its pilgrims. Like Christ, Clarel weeps over Jerusalem, more in pity than in disgust, but also like Christ he takes a personal interest in the many types of pilgrims and their ideals. Three characters, especially, are treated with great sympathy, Clarel (a theological student), Vine (a recluse),[11] and Rolfe, a transcendentalist of the Thoreau type. These three Americans, representing the three dominant strains in Melville's own mind, confront many types of Latins, Greeks, Jews, and Arabs, and lastly they listen attentively to the skepticism of two European critics of civilization, especially of American civilization. An American (Ungar) adds to his exposition of fatalism the following bitter reflections on America.

> Ay, Democracy
>
>   . . .
>
> Arch-strumpet of an impious age,
> Upstart from ranker villanage,
> 'Tis well she must restriction taste,
> Nor lay the world's broad manor waste:

[10] Herman Melville, *White Jacket*, pp. 463–65.
[11] Vine is supposed by Henry Wells to portray Hawthorne.

Asia shall stop her at the least,
That old inertness of the East.

.   .   .

But in the New World things make haste;
Not only men, the *state* lives fast—
Fast breeds the pregnant eggs and shells,
The slumberous combustibles
Sure to explode. 'Twill come, 'twill come!
One demagogue can trouble much:
How of a hundred thousand such?
And universal suffrage lent
To back them with brute element
Overwhelming? What shall bind these seas
Of rival sharp communities
Unchristianised? Yea, but 'twill come!
"What come? Your Thirty Years (of) War."

.   .   .

Dead level of rank commonplace:
An Anglo-Saxon China, see,
May on your vast plains shame the race
In the Dark Ages of Democracy.

.   .   .

To feel the arrest of hope's advance,
And squandered last inheritance;
And cry—'To Terminus build fanes!
Columbus ended earth's romance:
No New World to mankind remains!' [12]

These pessimistic lines are exceptionally vigorous, at least for Melville, and seem to reflect his own opinions. Nevertheless, the poem does not end on this note. The three Americans, though they are unable to refute these charges, express a common faith in their destiny and a repudiation of the naturalistic evolutionism and "scientific" faith of their European critics.

If Luther's day expand to Darwin's year,
Shall that exclude the hope—foreclose the fear?

.   .   .

[12] Melville, *Clarel*, II, 240, 249–50.

> Yea, ape and angel, strife and old debate—
> The harps of heaven and dreary gongs of hell;
> Science the feud can only aggravate—
> No umpire she betwixt the Chimes and knell;
> The running battle of the star and clod
> Shall run for ever—if there be no God.[13]

The story of Billy Budd, Melville's final expression of the tragedy, is open to the same varieties of interpretation that haunt the reader of his earlier works.

It is right and true to call *Billy Budd* Melville's "testament of acceptance"; but we must be careful not to understand either too much or too little by the word acceptance. Melville's "acceptance" was not based on any denial of the tragic facts of life or any ignorance of the inexorable logic of these facts. The world which we are shown in his last book is figuratively—as he had called it long before in *White Jacket*—and literally, a man-of-war world, and the story of *Billy Budd* is as stark a tragedy as an American writer even to this day has ever penned.[14]

This comment by William Ellery Sedgwick really leaves the question of Melville's "acceptance" as baffling as ever.

— *29* —

SPIRITUAL SOCIALISM AND SPONTANEITY

HENRY JAMES the Elder was the most searching intellect among the rebels, but his rebellion took so paradoxical a form that he was compelled to resort on the one hand to futile gestures of "spontaneity" and on the other to a mystical faith in the divinity of mankind. He was one of the most conspicuous characters among those who cultivated individuality in extraordinary ways; he believed, however, that his characteristic spontaneity was not an individual trait, but a

---

[13] *Ibid.*, p. 297 (Epilogue).
[14] William Ellery Sedgwick, *Herman Melville; the Tragedy of Mind* (Cambridge, 1944), pp. 233-34.

spiritual grace in which all men share. His aim was to reconcile individualism and collectivism in terms of a secular conception of spirituality, but in practice he achieved little more than to be a mild gad-fly. For he covered his savage satire with a most genial piety and expressed it in a most endearing, easy style. He was a brilliant writer and certainly one of the most daring and original theologians in the history of antinomianism.

Antinomianism needs to be explained. It is religious rebellion against law and moral order; it conceives the life of the spirit as antithetical to self-reliant, self-centered morality. What makes Henry James's antinomianism especially significant is that he gave it secular form, conceiving political democracy as an expression of faith in human nature and in the progress toward a society in which law, government, "and all private differences are bound to disappear." He carries antinomianism into the economic field by contrasting the economic aspects of "the uncleanness of our present morality" with spiritual society in God in which property disappears with *proprium* (the Swedenborgian term for selfhood).[1]

Henry James was familiar with the distinction between free grace and moral effort even in his youth, having heard it expounded at home by his Calvinist father, later at Union College, by President Eliphalet Nott, and from 1835 to 1837 at Princeton Seminary by the redoubtable Archibald Alexander and Charles Hodge, as well as by the more humane Samuel Miller. At Princeton the battle was raging between the old lights and new lights of Presbyterianism. The new lights of Andover and Yale, the followers of Jonathan Edwards, were being charged by the so-called orthodox, whose headquarters were at Princeton, with having moralized grace. The new-light doctrine that the original sin of Adam was merely "representative" sin, that God's will is primarily an expression of "disinterested benevolence" and God's wrath a "vindictive" love of justice was regarded by the old school as subordinating God's sovereignty to his justice and justifying the Divine economy of redemption by appealing to man's sense of justice. Though James felt the force of the Calvinistic distinction between

---

[1] See Henry James, *Lectures and Miscellanies* (New York, 1852), pp. 15, 37, 48; Lecture I, "Democracy and Its Issues"; Lecture II, "Property as a Symbol."

morality and salvation, he became thoroughly disgusted with the orthodox portrait of God's character.

The scheme postulates God as a being of such essential malignity . . . as to require that His thirst of blood once aroused by the sin of His own abject and helpless creatures, should be slaked only in one of two ways either . . . by the substantive reduction of these creatures themselves to eternal misery; or else . . . by the substitution in their place of an exquisitely innocent victim. . . . Judged of by either alternative this scheme . . . reduces the Divine name indeed below the level of the lowest diabolism.[2]

Nevertheless, a rationalized version of Calvinism remained the foundation of his philosophy. He was disgusted by the attitude of the Unitarians and transcendentalists toward Calvinism and wrote to his friend Emerson, very pointedly:

You don't look upon Calvinism as a fact at all; wherein you are to my mind philosophically infirm—impaired in your universality. I can see in Carlyle the advantage his familiarity with it gives him over you with a general audience. What is highest in him is built upon that lowest. At least so I read; I believe Jonathan Edwards redivivus in true blue would, after an honest study of the philosophy that has grown up since his day, make the best possible reconciler and critic of this philosophy—far better than Schelling redivivus.[3]

He left Princeton abruptly and went to England, where he was introduced by his friend Joseph Henry to the great physicist Michael Faraday. Faraday was both intellectually and personally congenial to James and made him acquainted with a most extraordinary variety of Calvinism. For Faraday belonged to the Glasite Church, or the Sandemanians, a small Scottish sect of separatists which believed that God's Kingdom is merely spiritual and had succeeded in reducing justification by faith to very simple terms in order to counteract the current enthusiasm of the evangelicals. Robert Sandeman, following the teachings of his father-in-law, John Glas, had explained that faith is nothing more than ordinary belief in the truth of a proposition in view of the evidence, that such belief is either spontaneous or im-

[2] Cited in Ralph Barton Perry, *The Thought and Character of William James* (Boston, 1935), I, 13n; "Inheritance and Vocation."
[3] Cited in Austin Warren, *The Elder Henry James* (New York, 1934), pp. 49–50.

possible, and that the essence of religion lies, not in a will to believe, but in the rites of fellowship among those believers on whom grace has been bestowed by God out of his sovereign pleasure. His followers developed a simple form of congregational fellowship: frequent communion, sharing of goods, no salaried clergy, and no secular concerns. "Here no man's pride is flattered; no man can find any ground to presume that the Deity regards him more than others." [4] To this ultra-democratic, ultra-simple piety James became a wholehearted convert. From then on, with Sandeman, he regarded all ecclesiastical religion as "Phariseeism" and "self-righteous moralism." He published an American edition of Sandeman's *Letters* in 1838 and in 1840 wrote a brief treatise entitled *Remarks on the Apostolic Gospel*.[5] That Henry James took his new gospel very seriously is evident from the following description of his spiritual condition and of the crisis to which it led him.

From the day of my birth I had not only never known what it was to have an honest want, a want of my nature, ungratified, but I had also been able to squander, upon the will of my personal caprice, an amount of sustenance equal to the maintenance of a virtuous household. And yet thousands of persons directly about me, in all respects my equals, in many respects my superiors, had never in all their lives enjoyed an honest meal, an honest sleep, an honest suit of clothes, save at the expense of their own personal toil or of that of some parent or child, and had never once been able to give the reins to their personal caprice without an ignominious exposure to severe social penalties. It is, to be sure, perfectly just that I should be conveniently fed and lodged and clad, and that I should be educated out of my native ignorance; but it is a monstrous affront to the divine justice or righteousness that I should be guaranteed, by what calls itself society, a life-long career of luxury and self-indulgence, while so many other men and women, my superiors, go all their days miserably fed, miserably lodged, miserably clothed, and die at last in the same ignorance and imbecility, though not, alas! in the same innocence, that cradled their infancy.

Now, I had long felt this deep spiritual damnation in myself growing out of an outraged and insulted divine justice, had long been pent up in spirit to these earthquake mutterings and menaces of a violated conscience, with-

---

[4] Robert Sandeman, *Letters on Theron and Aspasio*, quoted in Warren, *The Elder Henry James*, p. 36.

[5] See Austin Warren, *op. cit.*, p. 236.

out seeing any clear door of escape open to me. That is to say, I perceived with endless perspicacity, that, if it were not for the hand of God's providence visiting with constant humiliation and blight every secret aspiration of my pride and vanity, I should be more than any other man reconciled to the existing most atrocious state of things. I knew no outward want; I had the amplest social recognition; I enjoyed the converse and friendship of distinguished men; I floated in fact on a sea of unrighteous plenty; and I was all the while so indifferent, if not inimical in heart, to the divine justice, that save for the spiritual terrors it ever and anon supplied to my lethargic sympathies, to my swinish ambition, I should have dragged out all my days in that complacent sty, nor have ever so much as dreamed that the outward want of my fellows—their want with respect to nature and society—was in truth but the visible sign and fruit of my own truer want, my own more inward destitution with respect to God. . . . Imagine, then, my glad surprise, my cordial relief, when in this state of robust religious nakedness, with no wretchedest fig-leaf of ecclesiastical finery to cover me from the divine inclemency, I caught my first glimpse of the spiritual contents of revelation, or discerned the profoundly philosophic scope of the Christian truth. This truth at once emboldened me to obey my own regenerate intellectual instincts without further parley, in throwing the Church overboard, or demitting all care of my religious character to the devils, of whom alone such care is an inspiration. . . . Spiritual Christianity means the complete secularization of the Divine name, or its identification henceforth only with man's common or natural want,—that want in which all men are absolutely one,—and its consequent utter estrangement from the sphere of his private or personal fulness, in which every man is consciously divided from his neighbor; so that I may never aspire to the Divine favor, and scarcely to the Divine tolerance, save in my social or redeemed natural aspect,—that is, as I stand morally identified with the vast community of men of whatever race or religion, cultivating no consciousness of antagonist interests to any other man, but on the contrary frankly disowning every personal hope towards God which does not flow exclusively from his redemption of human nature, or is not based, purely and simply, upon his indiscriminate love to the race.[6]

To this "glimpse of the spiritual contents of revelation" James was led by reading the works of Swedenborg in 1841. The Sandemanians had destroyed "self-hood" in him and had made him a thoroughgoing

[6] Henry James, *The Literary Remains of the late Henry James,* edited by William James (Boston, 1885), pp. 89–91, 92, 93.

antinomian; [7] Swedenborg's writings (especially Garth Wilkinson's liberal interpretation of them) gave him a positive conception of "divine-natural humanity." James now began to interpret ecclesiastical Christianity not only as Phariseeism but also as an extension of "Deism" or natural religion. In opposition to the whole tendency to interpret human nature biologically, in terms of individual organisms, he preached the doctrine that man's nature or substance is a collective spiritual being, the "Grand Man" of Swedenborg's theory, the "divine society" of the Fourierists. "Society," conceived as the fellowship of men who have ceased to believe in individual independence, is the "redeemed form of man," and God is thoroughly human, being simply "the great and holy and unconscious mass" of mankind.

The Divine being or substance is Love,—love without any the least set-off or limitation of self-love; infinite or creative love in short. And it communicates itself to the creature, accordingly, in no voluntary or finite, but in purely spontaneous or infinite, measure—in a way, so to speak, of overwhelming *passion;* so that we practically encounter no limit to our faculty of appropriating it, but on the contrary sensibly and exquisitely feel it to be our own indisputable being; feel it to be in fact our inmost, most vital, and inseparable *self* and unhesitatingly call it *me* and *mine, you* and *yours,* cleaving to it as inmost bone of our bone and veritable flesh of our flesh, and incontinently renouncing all things for it. [8]

For what is one's *nature* as a creature? It is abject want or destitution. To be created is to be void of all things in one's self and to possess them only in another; and if I am the creature accordingly of an infinite creator, my want of course must be infinite. The nature of a thing is what the thing is in itself, and apart from foreign interference. And evidently what the creature is in himself, and apart from the creator, is sheer nothingness; that is to say, sheer want or destitution. [9]

Thus creation is not a something outwardly achieved by God in space and time, but a something inwardly wrought by him within the compass exclusively of human nature or human consciousness. [10]

It is an easy enough thing to find a holiday God who is all too selfish to be touched with the infirmities of his own creatures . . . and who is willing,

---

[7] The Sandemanians repudiated antinomianism technically, but they nevertheless encouraged it by their antimoralism, and James went farther in this direction than did the leaders of the sect.

[8] *Ibid.,* p. 36*n.*   [9] *Ibid.,* pp. 27–28.   [10] *Ibid.,* p. 37.

accordingly, to accept our decorous Sunday homage in ample quittance of obligations so unconsciously incurred on our part, so lightly rendered and so penuriously sanctioned on his. Every sect, every nation, every family almost, offers some pet idol of this description to our worship. But I am free to confess that I have long outgrown this loutish conception of deity. I can no longer bring myself to adore a characteristic activity in the God of my worship, which falls below the secular average of human character. In fact, what I crave with all my heart and understanding,—what my very flesh and bones cry out for,—is no longer a Sunday but a week-day divinity, a working God, grimy with the dust and sweat of our most carnal appetites and passions, and bent not for an instant upon inflating our worthless pietistic righteousness, but upon the patient, toilsome, thorough cleansing of our physical and moral existence from the odious defilement it has contracted, until we each and all present at last in body and mind the deathless effigy of his own uncreated loveliness.[11]

I for my part will cherish the name of him alone whose insufficiency to himself is so abject that he is incapable *of realizing himself except in others.* In short, I neither can nor will spiritually confess any deity who is not essentially *human,* and existentially thence exclusively *natural;* that is to say, devoid of all distinctively personal or limitary pretensions.[12]

Religion in the old virile sense of the word has disappeared from sight and become replaced by a feeble Unitarian sentimentality. The old religion involved a conscience of the profoundest antagonism between God and the worshipper, which utterly refused to be placated by anything short of an unconditional pledge of the utmost divine mercy.[13]

Religion was once a spiritual life in the earth, though a very rude and terrible one; and her conquests were diligently authenticated by the divine spirit. Then she meant terror and amazement to all devout self-complacency in man; then she meant rebuke and denial to every form of distinctively *personal* hope and pretension towards God; then she meant discredit and death to every breath of a Pharisaic or Quaker temper in humanity, by which a man could be led to boast of a "private spirit" in his bosom, giving him a differential character and aspect in God's sight to that of other men, especially the great and holy and unconscious mass of his kind.[14]

Morality is the summer lustihood and luxuriance of self-love, clothing its mineral ribs with vegetable grace, permeating its rigid trunk with sap,

[11] *Ibid.,* pp. 39–40.

[12] *Ibid.,* p. 42.

[13] *Ibid.,* p. 48*n.*

[14] *Ibid.,* p. 49*n.*

decorating its gnarled limbs with foliage, glorifying every reluctant virgin bud and every modest wifely blossom into rich, ripe motherly fruit. Religion is the icy winter which blights this summer fertility, which arrests the ascent of its vivifying sap, and humbles its superb life to the ground, in the interests of a spring that shall be perennial, and of autumns bursting with imperishable fruit. In other words, religion has no substantive force. Her sole errand on earth has been to dog the footsteps of morality, to humble the pride of selfhood which man derives from nature, and so soften his interiors to the reception of divine truth, as that truth shall stand fulfilled in the organization of human equality or fellowship.[15]

Our government is emphatically a *popular* government, the only truly popular government under the sun; and that is the true excuse it offers for the apparently infirm practical working it exhibits in comparison with aristocratic governments. If it were instituted and administered in the interest of a class, every voter no doubt would be eager to do his duty. But it was instituted in the interest of the unclassed or oppressed, in defence of the victim of established civic and religious privilege wherever he might be found; to lift his children from the dunghill and seat them beside the princes of the earth. And as soon as these ends have been accomplished it will shrivel up and disappear.[16]

I, for my own part, renounce root and branch the conservative logic. That is to say, I both deny with heart and understanding that man is by creation moral, and cherish with heart and understanding the most revolutionary hopes and aspirations with respect to our existing moralistic regimen. I wish it to be distinctly noted, moreover, that the discrepancy between us is not merely scientific, having regard only to the surface of action, but strictly philosophic, as reaching to and renewing the very substance of the mind. The conservative idea, for example, is that our selfhood or felt freedom constitutes our true *life*, our inseparable *being*, the sole veritable life or being we derive from God; whereas I maintain on the contrary that it does no such thing: that it constitutes at most our finite or conscious *existence*,— that is, the mere *quasi* life, the mere *phenomenal* or apparitional being we derive from an altogether unconscious *natural* community or fellowship which we are under with respect to our kind.[17]

Unquestionably we do *as a people* constitutionally reject—in the symbols of priest and king—the only two hitherto sacred pillars upon which the ark of man's salvation has rested, or which have based his public and private right-

[15] *Ibid.*, pp. 54–55.   [16] *Ibid.*, p. 197.   [17] *Ibid.*, pp. 201–2.

eousness; and it is very clear that we could not have rejected the symbol unless the substance had first come empowering us so to do. That is to say, we as a people are without any proper political and religious life or consciousness which is not exclusively generated by the social spirit in humanity, or the truth of an approaching marriage between the public and private, the universal and the particular interests of the race; so that our future welfare, spiritual and material, stands frankly committed to the energies of that untried spirit. Happy they who in this twilight of ever-deepening spiritual unbelief within the compass of the old symbolic Church, and hence of ever-widening moral earthquake, confusion, and desolation within the compass of the old symbolic State, intelligently recognize the serene immaculate divinity of the social spirit, feel their souls stayed upon the sheer impregnable truth of human society, human fellowship, human equality, on earth and in heaven! For they cannot fail to discern in the gathering "clouds of heaven," or the thickening obscuration which to so many despairing eyes is befalling the once bright earth of human hope, the radiant chariot-wheels of the long-looked-for Son of Man, bringing freedom, peace, and unity to all the realm of God's dominion.[18]

The most eloquent and dramatic expression of James's philosophy of democracy is his Fourth of July Oration at Newport, Rhode Island, after the outbreak of the Civil War. In it he represents the United States as the inheritor of Europe's struggles against class society and as, therefore, a nation privileged to *begin* its course with the faith in individual liberty secure. He regards the nation's supreme task to be the achievement of a collective democracy in which all men are sacred as members of the spiritual union of mankind. Having formulated this democratic ideal, he asks,

Now, such being the undoubted spirit of our polity, what taint was there in its material constitution, in our literal maternal inheritance, to affront this righteous paternal spirit and balk its rich promise, by turning us its children from an erect sincere hopeful and loving brotherhood of men intent upon universal aims, into a herd of greedy luxurious swine, into a band of unscrupulous political adventurers and sharpers, the stink of whose corruption pervades the blue spaces of ocean, penetrates Europe, and sickens every struggling nascent human hope with despair? [19]

[18] *Ibid.*, pp. 176–77.
[19] Henry James, *The Social Significance of Our Institutions*; an oration delivered . . . at Newport, R.I., July 4th, 1861 (Boston, 1861), p. 31. The address is reprinted in full in Blau, ed., *American Philosophic Addresses, 1700–1900*, pp. 234–56.

His answer was, the twin evils of slavery and "Mammon," which have been at the root of American politics and "civilization," must be eliminated from the spiritual body of the people, otherwise America must become "the most contemptible people on earth; a people that bartered away the fairest spiritual birthright any people ever yet were born to, for the foulest mess of material pottage ever concocted of shameless lust and triumphant fraud." [20]

Following Fourier, Henry James used "civilization" as a term of contempt to symbolize moralized man, and he did not spare the most cultivated of his close friends among the transcendentalists. He referred pointedly to

that very large number of persons who live and thrive in contentment with the existing very infirm constitution of society: poets, literary essayists, scholars, artists, transcendental aspirants or idealists, men of science . . . all of whom blindly regard morality as the absolute law of human life. [21]

James was extremely critical of Emerson's ideas, although they were personally on good terms. The gospel of self-reliance was to him the extreme of pride and sin. The Unitarians he ridiculed because they "preserved the semblance of a church" and condemned because they were the most moralistic of all churches. He satirized as well what he called moralism outside the churches, "as Transcendentalism, as 'ethical culture,' as philanthropy," and in general "the New England conscience, with its fussy self-consciousness and self-culture." [22]

Much more evidence could be gathered from Henry James's writings to demonstrate the thoroughness of his rebellion against transcendentalist individualism. But it is important to call attention to the fact that his reassertion of Calvinism was a revival of Platonic idealism.

The idealism implicit in Henry James's thought is made explicit in a lucid, succinct passage.

There are three realms of life in man, one exterior or physical, one interior or psychical, one inmost or spiritual; or one realm of body, one of mind or soul, and one of spirit; and each of these realms claims its proper unity or organization, the first being *sensibly* organized, the second being *scientifically* organized, the third being *philosophically* organized. Now each

[20] *Ibid.*, p. 40.   [21] Warren, *The Elder Henry James*, p. 202.
[22] *Ibid.*, p. 203.

of these organizations or unities demands of course its own appropriate light. The sun is the light of sense. Reason is the light of science. Revelation is the light of philosophy. Each of these lights is absolute in its own sphere, and good for nothing out of it. The light of the sun is essential to my bodily health, the light of reason to my mental health, the light of Revelation to my spiritual health. But if I attempt to make one light do another's duty, I infallibly reduce my intelligence to fatuity on the one hand, or exalt it to madness on the other. For these various realms of life in man agree not directly, but by inversion; their accord is one not of continuity, but of correspondence; and if, accordingly, I use the light of one realm to illumine the objects of another one, I shall only be able to see things upside down, and hence hopelessly falsify my own understanding. Thus our senses make us acquainted with finite existence, and demand only the light of the sun, the moon, and the stars; science makes us acquainted with relative existence, and demands, therefore, a purer light than that of sense, the light of reason; but philosophy alone makes us acquainted with infinite and absolute existence, and it demands, consequently, not merely a subtler light than that of nature, but a more penetrating and less flickering one than that of reason, even the serene and steadfast ray of Revelation.

The spiritual world, the world of man's true immortality, the true realm of the Divine creation, is shut up, of course, to the experience of its subject, or confined to his interior consciousness, defying sensible scrutiny and scientific analysis alike; so that we should have been forever utterly incapable of discerning, or even imagining it, were it not for the commanding light of Revelation. Revelation, which is the truth of the Divine Incarnation, teaches us that there is no life of man so abject, no soul of man so infamous in a purely conventional estimation, or when measured by mere ecclesiastical and political necessities, in which the immaculate Divine Love does not maintain his intimate abode, and which he will not one day visibly irradiate with all his infinite sanctity and power. It declares that, in spite of all appearances to the contrary, our true life is an immortal one, not derived from our natural progenitors, standing in no natural gifts of any sort, whether of beauty or wit or intellect or temper, much less in any purely personal accomplishments, such as wealth or learning or manners or station, but flowing exclusively from the living acknowledgment of the Divine name, which means the hearty practical recognition of human fellowship. In short, Revelation ascribes to the whole human race the unity of a man before God, having but one body and one spirit, one Lord, one faith, and one baptism, one God and Father of all, who is above all and through all and in all: this man being evidently social, as implying such a unity of all the mem-

312 GUIDE TO THE LITERATURE FOR PART V

bers with each individual member and of each with all as will finally obliter-
ate the iniquities of caste upon earth, or do away with all that arbitrary and
enforced inequality among men which is the pregnant source of our existing
vice and crime.[23]

No more radical critique of liberalism has appeared in this country,
though there have been many more realistic. Perhaps the most immediate practical achievement of Henry James's philosophy was its
effect on the mind of William James. Of this we shall say more later,
but it will serve both to characterize the thought of Henry James and
to anticipate the contrasting point of view of William to quote from
William's Introduction to his father's *Literary Remains:*

Any absolute moralism is a pluralism; any absolute religion is a monism. It
shows the depth of Mr. James's religious insight that he first and last and
always made moralism the target of his hottest attack, and pitted religion and
it against each other as enemies, of whom one must die utterly, if the other is
to live in genuine form. The accord of moralism and religion is superficial;
their discord radical. Only the deepest thinkers on both sides see that one
must go.[24]

GUIDE TO THE LITERATURE OF PART V

Although there have been many studies of this theme, the literary emphasis has so predominated that such works need not long detain us here. The
standard early treatment is Octavius B. Frothingham, *Transcendentalism
in New England* (Boston, 1876), which contains information derived
from its author's personal acquaintance with the major figures of New
England transcendentalism. Of later works, H. C. Goddard, *Studies in
New England Transcendentalism* (New York, 1909), and Van Wyck
Brooks, *The Flowering of New England* (New York, 1936), contain
material of value for the study of the ideas of the transcendentalists. F. O.
Matthiessen, *American Renaissance; Art and Expression in the Age of
Emerson and Whitman* (London and New York, 1941), while limited in
extent, shows deep penetration into the intellectual characteristics of the
movement.

[23] James, *The Social Significance of Our Institutions,* pp. 43–45.
[24] James, *The Literary Remains of the Late Henry James,* pp. 118–19.

CHAPTER 23

On Theodore Parker, the biography by Henry Steele Commager, *Theodore Parker* (Boston, 1936), gives a good portrait and excellent bibliographical information. There is a good discussion of Parker in F. G. Bratton, *The Legacy of the Liberal Spirit; Men and Movements in the Making of Modern Thought* (New York, 1943). The question of the extent to which Parker embraced transcendental philosophy is discussed critically in a Columbia University dissertation by J. Edward Dirks, which has not yet been published. There is a good article by F. A. Christie on "Theodore Parker and Modern Theology," *Meadville Journal*, XXV (1930–31), 3–17.

The extent of Brownson's and Parker's familiarity with transcendental philosophy is examined critically by René Wellek, "The Minor Transcendentalists and German Philosophy," *New England Quarterly*, XV (1942), 652–80. In Van Wyck Brooks, *The Flowering of New England* (New York, 1936), pp. 193–95, there is a brief but suggestive discussion of the importance of Scottish thought, notably that of Carlyle, for American transcendentalism. Parker's lecture, "Transcendentalism," was reprinted in his *Works*, Vol. VI, pp. 1–37. His sermon "The Philosophical Idea of God," is reprinted in Blau, *American Philosophic Addresses, 1700–1900*, pp. 663–79.

CHAPTER 24

Ronald V. Wells, *Three Christian Transcendentalists* (New York, 1943), contains an account of James Marsh, Caleb Sprague Henry, and Frederic Henry Hedge, to which this chapter is much indebted. His bibliography is comprehensive; the following items are selected as of particular value for the history of philosophy.

Marjorie Nicolson, "James Marsh and the Vermont Transcendentalists," *Philosophical Review*, XXXIV (1925), 28–50, and John Dewey, "James Marsh and American Philosophy," *Journal of the History of Ideas*, II (1941), 131–50, contain supplementary information on Marsh. *The Remains of the Reverend James Marsh, D.D.*, edited with a memoir by Joseph Torrey (2d edition, New York, 1845), contains Marsh's papers; Marsh's edition of Samuel T. Coleridge's *Aids to Reflection* (Burlington, Vt., 1829), includes the "Preliminary Essay" in which Marsh avowed his reasons for introducing Coleridge to American readers. Marsh also edited Coleridge's *The Friend* (Burlington, Vt., 1831). An early unsigned review of these

American editions of Coleridge's works, with incidental discussion of "German metaphysics," showing some familiarity with the materials and much sympathy with the transcendental method, appeared in the *Christian Examiner*, XIV (1833), 108–29. Julian Ira Lindsay, "Coleridge and the University of Vermont," *Vermont Alumni Weekly*, Vol. XV (1936), Nos. 13–15, discusses the tradition established by Marsh's interest.

Besides the discussion in Wells's *Three Christian Transcendentalists*, there have been no studies of the work of Henry. Henry's works include the following writings of philosophical interest: *Principles and Prospects of the Friends of Peace* (Hartford, Conn., 1834), "Additional Discourses and Essays," in William Whewell and Caleb S. Henry, *On the Foundation of Morals* (Andover, 1839); *The Position and Duties of the Educated Men of the Country* (New York, 1840); *The Gospel: a Formal and Sacramental Religion* (Boston, 1846); *Dr. Oldham at Greystones and His Talk There* (New York, 1860); *Considerations on Some of the Elements and Conditions of Social Welfare and Human Progress* (New York, 1861); and *Satan as a Moral Philosopher; with Other Essays and Sketches* (New York, 1877). Henry's edition of Victor Cousin's *Elements of Psychology* (Hartford, 1834), has an interesting introduction; but there is even better introductory material in the fourth edition, New York, 1856.

O. W. Long has written a biographical study of *Frederic Henry Hedge; a Cosmopolitan Scholar* (Portland, Me., 1940). Of Hedge's works, the following give a clear view of his ideas: *Reason in Religion* (Boston, 1866); *The Primeval World of Hebrew Tradition* (Boston, 1870); *Ways of the Spirit and Other Essays* (Boston, 1877); and *Atheism in Philosophy* (Boston, 1884).

CHAPTER 25

The literature on transcendentalism in general and on Emerson in particular is enormous, and no attempt will be made to review it here. We shall call attention merely to several recent attempts to discover the philosophical tenets of the movement and their sources. René Wellek, in an article entitled "Emerson and German Philosophy," *New England Quarterly*, XVI (1943), 41–62, summarizes the evidence for direct German influence and notes the major misinterpretations of the German. He points out in the earlier article, mentioned above, that though Ticknor, Everett, and Bancroft were the first to become acquainted with German transcendentalism, they took little interest in its philosophy. He concludes as follows:

What attracted the American thinkers was rather the fact that the German philosophy shared with them a common enmity to the methods and results of eighteenth-century British empiricism and to the tradition of skepticism and materialism in general. Among the Transcendentalists, one can distinguish two groups: a metaphysical, comprising Emerson and Alcott; and a theological, which includes Ripley, Parker, and Brownson, and which advocates, in effect, an intuitive philosophy of religion. The latter are akin to the French eclectics, to the common sense philosophers (though they were less empirical in their methods), and to German thinkers who, like Herder, Jacobi, and Schleiermacher, were in constant warfare with the main representatives of German speculative philosophy. Brownson, who stands somewhat apart, most clearly realizes the dangers of German subjectivism, expounding an extreme objectivist intuitionism. Emerson and Alcott, though they share their friends' trust in intuition, are far more interested in a philosophy of nature in which nature appears as a symbol or emblem of the internal world of our mind and of the mind of God. In spite of the obvious distinctions between the two friends, they thus both continue the Neoplatonic tradition (p. 61).

Another work which brings out the contrast between the Platonism (derived from Channing and Coleridge) and the subjectivism (from the German romantics) is Henry David Gray, *Emerson; a Statement of New England Transcendentalism as Expressed in the Philosophy of Its Chief Exponent* (Palo Alto, Calif., 1917). Gray thinks that the evolutionary point of view gradually emerged in Emerson as a reconciliation of these two types of idealism, but he gives inadequate attention to the idea of development in nature, civilization, and individuals which is at the heart of German romanticism.

The question of the relation of transcendentalism to puritanism is reviewed by Perry Miller, "From Edwards to Emerson," *New England Quarterly*, XIII (1940), 589–617, and in Frederic I. Carpenter, "The Genteel Tradition; a Re-interpretation," *New England Quarterly*, XV (1942), 427–43. In this connection it is worth referring to George Santayana, "The Genteel Tradition in American Philosophy," in *Winds of Doctrine* (New York, 1912), pp. 186–215, and *The Last Puritan* (New York, 1936), which is really a statement of New England idealism.

It is well to remember that in addition to the Platonic and German strains of idealistic thought there came a significant importation of oriental mysticism. This aspect of transcendentalism has been explored by Frederic I. Carpenter, *Emerson and Asia* (Cambridge, Mass., 1930), and more thoroughly by Arthur Christy in his book *The Orient in American Transcendentalism* (New York, 1932), and in numerous articles.

In addition to the standard edition of Emerson's works, the following recent additions to the publication of Emerson's writings should be mentioned: Arthur Hale McGiffert, *Young Emerson Speaks* (Boston, 1938), which publishes some of the sermons of the days when Emerson was still in the Unitarian ministry, the complete *Letters* (New York, 1939), edited by Ralph L. Rusk, in six volumes, and the *Uncollected Lectures* (New York, 1932), edited by Clarence Gohdes.

The philosophical reader will be interested in comparing the interpretations of Emerson's mind by William James, "Address at the Emerson Centenary in Concord," in *Memories and Studies* (New York, 1911), pp. 19–34, George Santayana, "Emerson," in *Interpretations of Poetry and Religion* (New York, 1900), pp. 217–33, and John Dewey, "Emerson," in *Characters and Events* (New York, 1929), I, 67–77.

Kenneth W. Cameron, *Emerson the Essayist; an Outline of His Philosophical Development through 1836* (Raleigh, N.C., 1945), Volume I, discusses Emerson's major philosophical sources, including various types of Platonism, Berkeley, Coleridge, Swedenborg, Cousin, and Goethe; it also gives a critical examination of Emerson's *Nature;* Volume II is especially useful, because it brings together early essays by minor transcendentalists whose ideas and interests prove that the movement had greater philosophical depth and variety than is commonly supposed. Unfortunately, this work appeared too late for me to make the use of it which it deserves.

Various aspects of Emerson's thought and its sources are treated by Stewart G. Brown, "Emerson's Platonism," *New England Quarterly,* XVIII (1945), 325–45, Merrell R. Davis, "Emerson's 'Reason' and the Scottish Philosophers," *New England Quarterly,* XVII (1944), 209–28, and A. Robert Caponigri, "Brownson and Emerson: Nature and History," *New England Quarterly,* XVIII (1945), 368–90.

CHAPTER 26

The most adequate portrait of Bronson Alcott is Odell Shepard's *Pedlar's Progress; the Life of Bronson Alcott* (Boston, 1937). For a description of Alcott's Fruitlands the chief work is Clara Endicott Sears, *Bronson Alcott's Fruitlands* (Boston, 1915), which contains also Louisa Alcott's "Transcendental Wild Oats." From the point of view of philosophy there is additional information in F. B. Sanborn and William T. Harris, *A. Bronson Alcott; His Life and Philosophy* (Boston, 1893), Denton J. Snider, *A Writer of Books in His Genesis* (St. Louis, 1910), and Austin Warren, "The Concord School of Philosophy," *New England Quarterly,* II (1929), 199–233.

The extensive literature on Brook Farm and on Fourierist socialism in America has been supplemented admirably in recent years by the studies of Arthur E. Bestor, Jr., notably in his essay, *American Phalanxes; a Study of*

Fourierist Socialism in the United States (Yale University Library), and in several articles, especially "Fourierism in Northampton; a Critical Note," *New England Quarterly*, XIII (1940), 110–22.

CHAPTER 27

There are several biographies of Thoreau, none of which are very useful for the interpretation of his philosophy. The standard Walden edition of Thoreau's works has been supplemented by his *Collected Poems*, edited by Carl Bode (Chicago, 1943). A critical review of this volume by Henry W. Wells, "An Evaluation of Thoreau's Poetry," *American Literature*, XVI (1944), 99–109, throws light on Thoreau's intellectual as well as his literary sources. See, too, Arthur Christy's researches on Thoreau's *Journal*, which emphasize (possibly overemphasize) the oriental influence.

Of recent critical articles on Thoreau, we mention two: Charles A. Madison, "Henry David Thoreau: Transcendental Individualist," *Ethics*, LIV (1943–44), 110–23, and Joseph J. Kwiat, "Thoreau's Philosophical Apprenticeship," *New England Quarterly*, XVIII (1945), 51–69.

CHAPTER 28

The basic critical work on Melville was begun by Raymond Weaver, with the publication of *Herman Melville, Mariner and Mystic* (New York, 1921), and the editing of his works, and a separate edition of his *Shorter Novels*, including the important "Billy Budd, Foretopman." The interpretation of Melville's enigmatic poem, *Clarel*, is made still more difficult by Weaver's publication of his *Journal Up the Straits*, New York, 1935. This poem is the chief subject of Henry W. Wells's essay on Melville, entitled "A Religious Quest," in *The American Way of Poetry* (New York, 1943). The religious aspect of Melville was discussed by William Brasswell, *Melville's Religious Thought* (Durham, N.C., 1943). A brief selection from Melville's poems was made by F. O. Matthiessen, Norfolk, Conn., 1944.

The psychological analysis of Melville's thought and character is still being pursued; noteworthy contributions are William Ellery Sedgwick, *Herman Melville; the Tragedy of Mind* (Cambridge, Mass., 1944), Lewis Mumford, *Herman Melville* (New York, 1929), and F. O. Matthiessen, *American Renaissance* (London and New York, 1941).

Sedgwick gives the impression that Melville was writing high tragedy of the Hamlet-Lear type; but I doubt whether it is fair either to Melville or to classical tragedy to put his work in that context.

Other important critical works on Melville's thought include Charles

Robert Anderson, *Melville in the South Seas* (New York, 1939), William Brasswell, *Herman Melville and Christianity* (Chicago, 1936), and Karl Heinrich Sundermann, *Herman Melvilles Gedankengut, eine kritische Untersuchung seiner weltanschaulichen Grundideen* (Berlin, 1937), which is an academic analysis of Melville's chief ideas. Especially useful is Part II, "Religiöse Elemente in Melvilles Werk," which contains (pp. 37–57) an analysis of *Clarel*.

E. L. Grant Watson, "Melville's *Pierre*," *New England Quarterly*, III (1930), 195–234, psychoanalyzes Melville, while George C. Homans, "The Dark Angel, the Tragedy of Herman Melville," *New England Quarterly*, V (1932), 699–730, presents a philosophical analysis.

CHAPTER 29

There are sketches of the character and philosophy of Henry James the Elder in the writings of his sons, notably in William James's Introduction to *The Literary Remains of Henry James* (Boston, 1885), and in Henry James, *Notes of a Son and Brother* (New York, 1914). There is an excellent discussion of James's philosophical development in Part I of Ralph Barton Perry, *The Thought and Character of William James* (Boston, 1935), and in the Appendix to Vol. II there are several philosophical letters between William James and his father. Austin Warren, *The Elder Henry James* (New York, 1934), gives a good account of the life and philosophy of James; this work contains a bibliography of James's writings and of the chief works about him. James's Fourth of July address, "The Social Significance of Our Institutions," is reprinted in Blau, ed., *American Philosophic Addresses, 1700–1900*, pp. 234–56.

The only comprehensive account of the Glasite or Sandemanian church through which Henry James was led to his extraordinary form of Calvinism is an unpublished dissertation by John T. Hornsby, *John Glas; a Study in the Origins, Development and Influence of the Glasite Movement* (1936), typescript copies of which are available at the University of Edinburgh library and the library of the School of Religion, Butler University, Indianapolis.

For the background of the Swedenborgian liberalism which Henry James represents see the writings of J. J. Garth Wilkinson, Marguerite B. Block, *The New Church in the New World* (New York, 1932), Chapters XI–XII, and Herbert W. Schneider and George Lawton, *A Prophet and a Pilgrim* (New York, 1942), Chapters II–III.

—VI—

EVOLUTION AND HUMAN PROGRESS

COSMIC PHILOSOPHIES

IN 1859, while *The Origin of Species* was coming off the press in England, a boy at Middletown, Connecticut, was anxiously casting about for a faith to take the place of "the most repulsive form of Calvinism" in which he had been reared and which he now definitely rejected. John Fiske was only seventeen, but he had become absorbed in Greek literature and history, in comparative linguistics, and in "geological speculations," none of which fields of knowledge fits into the system of Christian theology. He had turned to the liberal Calvinists for light, but they were worse than useless to him. "The rhetorical work of Bushnell," he later confessed, "with its total ignorance of physical science, did more to shake my faith than anything else." In his groping he stumbled upon two works which at once afforded him a glowing faith and a life work: von Humboldt's *Kosmos* and Buckle's *History of Civilization*. The former was to him "the epic of the universe"; the latter explained to him the cause of progress. Together they would give a complete science of nature and of morals. But could they be put together? Could the sciences of human action be shown to depend on the sciences of nature? Is there a universal law governing both natural and human history? Such a law, if it could be found, would not only restore natural theology to the exalted place from which it had fallen but also embrace the growing young science of the rise of civilization, the philosophy of human progress. A social physics! He must find it. Within a few months he had discovered positivism, with its classification of the sciences and its law of historical stages, proving that the social sciences must be based on the physical. He discovered also that Herbert Spencer intended to improve upon Comte's system by his law of universal progress and his prospectus of an all-inclusive, synthetic philosophy. Fiske subscribed at once to the series of volumes of *Synthetic Philosophy*.

The demand for cosmic philosophy was insistent and general at that time in America, as well as in Europe, for here, too, the prestige of natural science was growing, and there spread a general fear among moralists and theologians that unless they could come to terms with natural law and natural history they must either take the high and unorthodox ground of the Kantian transcendentalists or renounce their pretensions to the use of inductive methods and appeal to facts. The independence of moral science was increasingly untenable and, moreover, undesirable. It was much better to be able to see in human history the patterns of a universe which is itself, as von Humboldt said, "ever growing and unfolding in new forms." Or, to quote John Fiske's exuberant words, "man and nature alike are traversing the bridge of Time" whose "beginning and end are immersed in the utter darkness of eternity." This cosmos of romantic naturalism was not the static, eternal order of nature believed in by deism, but a moving order, temporal, phenomenal, and progressive. The world itself now appeared as an organism, whose career in time can be observed even though its origin and substance must remain forever unknowable. Though such a world seemed less secure than one in the hand of an over-arching Providence, it seemed more intelligible, more exciting, and a more appropriate home for man than the damnable affair pictured in orthodoxy or the merely revolving and gravitating universe of the Newtonians. Thus, in the name of deanthropomorphization, these cosmic philosophers of the nineteenth century fashioned themselves a natural order congruous with their own particular social order.

The infinite and absolute Power, which Anthropomorphism has in countless ways sought to define and limit by metaphysical formulas, thereby rendering it finite and relative, is the Power which Cosmism refrains from defining and limiting by metaphysical formulas, thereby acknowledging —so far as the exigencies of human speaking and thinking will allow—that it is infinite and absolute. Thus in the progress from Anthropomorphism to Cosmism the religious attitude remains unchanged from the beginning to the end. And thus the apparent antagonism between Science and Religion, which is the abiding terror of timid or superficial minds, and which the Positive Philosophy did comparatively little to remove, is in the Cosmic Philosophy utterly and for ever swept away.[1]

Note how Fiske here emphasizes the advantages of naturalism over humanism for theism. For him and for many other deeply religious

[1] John Fiske, *Outlines of Cosmic Philosophy* (London, 1874), I, 184.

philosophers of the time the discovery of the relativity of natural knowledge came as a great liberation for faith, a new ground for asserting the existence of an infinite, transcendent power, and a more objective method than that of the idealists for arriving at their own goal of the Absolute. Fiske was learned, but not inventive; he did little more than to expound Spencer's philosophy from the point of view of this enthusiasm for cosmic theism, and he was both annoyed and perplexed when he discovered that Spencer himself did not understand the importance of bringing in the idea of the cosmos. To Spencer the synthesis of the positive sciences was a primary objective; to Fiske, on the other hand, the sciences were interesting because they led him to "the epic of nature," and nature was interesting because it led him to God.

The extent to which his cosmic theism led Fiske away from his youthful enthusiasm for Positivism came to light when he delivered two notable lectures before the Concord Summer School of Philosophy; his 1884 lecture he entitled *The Destiny of Man,* and his 1885 lecture, *The Idea of God.* In the Preface to this second lecture Fiske expressed his surprise at discovering that *The Destiny of Man* had been commonly interpreted as indicating a "conversion" on his part. He therefore explained that he was now merely adding another chapter to his "cosmic philosophy" in pointing out that the doctrine of evolution had worked a counter-Copernican revolution and had restored man to "his old position of headship in the universe, even as in the days of Dante and Aquinas." He did not undertake to say how far his interpretation agreed with Spencer's doctrine of the Unknowable. "On such an abstruse matter it is best that one should simply speak for one's self." [2] He then proceeded to describe God as follows.

The "infinite and eternal Energy from which all things proceed," and which is the same power that "in ourselves wells up under the form of consciousness," is certainly the power which is here recognized as God. The term "unknowable" I have carefully refrained from using; it does not occur in the text of this essay. It describes only one aspect of Deity, but it has been

[2] John Fiske, *The Idea of God as Affected by Modern Knowledge* (Cambridge, 1887), Preface, p. xxv. In describing a "solemn talk about God" with Huxley in 1879 he commented: "Huxley unburdened himself to me of some of his innermost thoughts—poor creatures both of us, striving to compass thoughts too great for the human mind" (Clark, *Life and Letters of John Fiske,* p. 412).

seized upon by shallow writers of every school, treated as if fully synonymous with Deity, and made the theme of the most dismal twaddle that the world has been deluged with since the days of mediaeval scholasticism. The latest instance is the wretched positivist rubbish which Mr. Frederic Harrison has mistaken for criticism, and to which it is almost a pity that Mr. Spencer should have felt called upon to waste his valuable time in replying. That which Mr. Spencer throughout all his works regards as the All-Being, the Power of which "our lives, alike physical and mental, in common with all the activities, organic and inorganic, amid which we live, are but the workings,"—this omnipresent Power it pleases Mr. Harrison to call the "All-Nothingness," to describe it as "a logical formula begotten in controversy, dwelling apart from man and the world" (whatever all that may mean), and to imagine its worshippers as thus addressing it in prayer, "O x^n, love us, help us, make us one with thee!" If Mr. Harrison's aim were to understand, rather than to misrepresent, the religious attitude which goes with such a conception of Deity as Mr. Spencer's, he could nowhere find it more happily expressed than in these wonderful lines of Goethe:—

> "Weltseele, komm, uns zu durchdringen!
> Dann mit dem Weltgeist selbst zu ringen
> Wird unsrer Kräfte Hochberuf.
> Theilnehmend führen gute Geister,
> Gelinde leitend, höchste Meister,
> Zu dem der alles schafft und schuf."

Mr. Harrison is enabled to perform his antics simply because he happens to have such a word as "Unknowable" to play with. Yet the word which has been put to such unseemly uses is, when properly understood, of the highest value in theistic philosophy. That Deity *per se* is not only unknown but unknowable is a truth which Mr. Spencer has illustrated with all the resources of that psychologic analysis of which he is incomparably the greatest master the world has ever seen; but it is not a truth which originated with him . . . Among all the Christian theologians that have lived, there are few higher names than Athanasius, who also regarded Deity *per se* as unknowable, being revealed to mankind only through incarnation in Christ. It is not as failing to recognize its value that I have refrained in this essay from using the term "Unknowable"; it is because so many false and stupid inferences have been drawn from Mr. Spencer's use of the word that it seemed worth while to show how a doctrine essentially similar to his might be expounded without introducing it. . . .

The universe as a whole is thrilling in every fibre with Life,—not, indeed, life in the usual restricted sense, but life in a general sense. The distinction, once deemed absolute, between the living and the not-living is converted into a relative distinction; and Life as manifested in the organism is seen to be only a specialized form of the Universal Life.

The conception of matter as dead or inert belongs, indeed, to an order of thought that modern knowledge has entirely outgrown. If the study of physics has taught us anything, it is that nowhere in Nature is inertness or quiescence to be found. All is quivering with energy. . . .

The infinite and eternal Power that is manifested in every pulsation of the universe is none other than the living God. . . . The everlasting source of phenomena is none other than the infinite Power that makes for righteousness. Thou canst not by searching find Him out; yet put thy trust in Him, and against thee the gates of hell shall not prevail; for there is neither wisdom nor understanding nor counsel against the Eternal.[3]

Well might Fiske's hearers think that he had returned to the faith of his fathers. For, though the letter of his cosmic philosophy had changed little, the spirit was Christian, and the intent was conciliatory. Even the transcendentalists gathered at Concord could not quarrel with him.

Fiske's lecture on *The Idea of God* at Concord was one of a symposium devoted to the question: "Is Pantheism the Legitimate Outcome of Modern Science?" A less evasive answer to this question came from another member of the symposium, Francis Ellingwood Abbot. His lecture was expanded and published under the title *Scientific Theism*. The argument which he here presented for what he called "scientific realism" had been the substance of his Ph.D. dissertation at Harvard in 1881. But when he took his doctor's degree Abbot was already an old man of 44, discouraged and beaten; a martyr who felt that he had sacrificed everything to his faith in "scientific philosophy." A few years later, 1887, he made a last attempt to secure recognition among academic philosophers: he took over Josiah Royce's classes at Harvard while Royce was on leave of absence and then published his lectures under the title *The Way Out of Agnosticism*. But Royce, on his return, having found his own "way out," attacked Abbot savagely and warned "the liberal minded public concerning Dr. Abbot's philosophical pretentions." The poor man at last gave up the fight in despair.

[3] Fiske, *The Idea of God as Affected by Modern Knowledge* (Cambridge, 1887), pp. xxv–xxviii, 149–50, 166, 167.

He had struggled long for liberal support. In 1868, contrary to the advice of his friend, Chauncey Wright, he had resigned his Unitarian pulpit, on the ground that he could no longer conscientiously preach a Christian gospel. He had been unsuccessful in his attempt to induce the whole Unitarian Church to renounce Christianity and, together with O. B. Frothingham and other independents, had founded *The Free Religious Association,* devoted to "the interests of pure religion" and "the scientific study of theology." For three decades this association was an influential agency for the promotion of "a rational religion without a priesthood; a moral code without a theology; a God without a dogmatic system; a religion of action." [4] Abbot personally, however, was more interested in theology than in "action," and he used the pages of *The Index,* of which he was editor from 1870 to 1880, to expound "a radical's theology." His best book, *Scientific Theism,* was of little use to the cause of free religion, but it was a major contribution to American philosophic realism. On the basis of a careful critique of Kant's exploitation of the distinction between phenomena and noumena, Abbot made an excellent exposition of objective relativism. He seems to have antedated Charles S. Peirce in repudiating modern nominalism and in defending a realism not based on Scottish intuitionalism, but on an independent analysis of the objectivity of relations. As early as 1864 he published articles in which he argued that since "relations cannot possibly be objects of sensuous perception" and nevertheless "we really know the objective relations of things, there must be some faculty of pure and immediate cognition of relations." This "faculty" he termed "the perceptive understanding," and he contended that such an understanding is continually exhibited in scientific, experimental observation and that it is distinct from "common sense," on the one hand, and, on the other, from both the "understanding" and the "reason" of the Coleridgeans. He was aware that his criticism of Kant was cognate to Hegel's, but he regarded his system as superior to Hegel's in that it was quite free of idealistic presuppositions.

RELATIONISM OR SCIENTIFIC REALISM (of which *universalia inter res* may be adopted as an apt formula) teaches that universals, or genera and species, are, *first,* objective relations of resemblance among objectively

---

[4] Sidney Warren, *American Freethought, 1860–1914* (New York, 1943), p. 101.

existing things; *secondly*, subjective concepts of these relations, determined in the mind by the relations themselves; and, *thirdly*, names representative both of the relations and the concepts, and applicable alike to both. This is the view logically implied in all scientific classifications of natural objects, regarded as objects of real scientific knowledge. But, although empirically employed with dazzling success in the investigation of Nature, it does not appear to have been ever theoretically generalized or stated.

This view rests for its justification upon a broader principle; namely, that of the *Objectivity of Relations*, as opposed to the principle of the *Subjectivity of Relations*, which is the essence of the Nominalistic doctrine of universals inculcated by modern philosophy. . . .

The theory of Scientific Philosophy (by which is meant simply the philosophy that founds itself theoretically upon the practical basis of the scientific method) teaches that knowledge is a dynamic correlation of object and subject, and has two ultimate origins, the cosmos and the mind; that these origins unite, inseparably yet distinguishably, in experience, *i.e.*, the perpetual action of the cosmos on the mind *plus* the perpetual reaction of the mind on the cosmos and on itself as affected by it; that experience, thus understood, is the one proximate origin of knowledge; that experience has both an objective and a subjective side, and that these two sides are mutually dependent and equally necessary; that the objective side of experience depends on the real existence of a known universe, and its subjective side on the real existence of a knowing mind; that experience includes all mutual interaction of these, whether sensitive or cognitive, and is utterly inexplicable even as subjective sensation, unless its sensitive and cognitive elements are equally recognized; that this extended conception of experience destroys the distinction of noumena and phenomena, as merely verbal and not real; that "things-in-themselves" are partly known and partly unknown; that, just so far as things are known in their relations, they are known both phenomenally and noumenally, and that the possibility of experimentally verifying at any time their discovered relations is the practical proof of a known noumenal cosmos, meeting every demand of scientific certitude and furnishing the true criterion and definition of objective knowledge. . . .

Experience, therefore, is the beginning and the end of the scientific method, mediated by reason and imagination; and experience itself is the actual meeting, the dynamic correlation, the incessant action and reaction, of the human mind and its cosmical environment. The scientific method, therefore, is a living organic process, the true and only organon for the discovery of truth; and the proof of its validity is the rapid progress of actual discovery in the experiential study of the universe. . . .

The Scotch school held, not only that the things which we perceive exist, but also that they exist as we perceive them; whereas the philosophy of science will hold that the crudities of sense-perception and the confused inferences of uninstructed "common sense" are to be corrected by scientific discovery, and will therefore present, as the veritable outward fact, the subtile and often recondite relations which her formulated laws express. . . . These, not to mention other important differences, are quite enough to signalize the vast divergence between the philosophies of science and of "common sense," and to show that scientific realism is of a type wholly distinct from that of the Scotch school. . . .

"But," it will be asked, "do you seriously mean to defend the exploded doctrine that the universe is known as a Thing-in-itself, a *Ding-an-sich*, a Noumenon?"

That is exactly what I mean. But I deny that the doctrine is exploded, and I also deny that it has ever yet been set forth in its true light. . . .

Now the root of modern idealism, whether in its transcendental or experiential form, is the theory of *Phenomenism*—the theory that nothing can be known except "phenomena," and that all phenomena depend for their existence on individual human consciousness alone. It is this theory of phenomenism, the life-principle of modern philosophy, which most formidably opposes the theory of *Noumenism* (scientific realism or scientific ontology), the life-principle of modern science. This profound and fundamental issue between PHENOMENISM AND NOUMENISM lies at the bottom of all other issues of modern thought . . .[5]

On the basis of this critical epistemology, Abbot then defended the theological conception of an "infinitely intelligible" universe, which is both an infinite organism or subject and an infinite "immanent relational constitution" or object.

Teleology, say what one will, cannot be escaped by any device in the comprehension of Nature; it is either openly confessed in, or else surreptitiously introduced into, all philosophical systems of evolution . . . Teleology conjoined with Monism yields the organic theory of evolution or Scientific Theism, which includes only so much of Pantheism as is really true and has appeared in every deeply religious philosophy since the very birth of human thought.[6]

[5] Francis Ellingwood Abbot, *Scientific Theism* (Boston, 1885), pp. xi–xii, 39–40, 60, 66–67, 70–72.

[6] *Ibid.*, pp. 212, 213–14.

Another type of speculative natural philosophy, which likewise provided a religious cosmology for laymen and scientists, came from men whom Swedenborg had inspired to work out, each for himself, a mystical metaphysics of creation. They used Swedenborg's basic ideas, but they used them as he had done, not to expound an ecclesiastical philosophy of history and judgment, not even the official system of the Church of the New Jerusalem, but to clothe natural history in the garments of spirituality. Science suggested to them a more meaningful pattern in natural events than the mere order of cause and effect.

As early as the winter of 1837–38 and as far west as Cincinnati the theme of man's divine nature was being expounded by Alexander Kinmont in a remarkable series of lectures on *The Natural History of Man*. Kinmont had been born in Scotland, raised a Calvinist, educated at the University of Edinburgh, and had come to this country as a school teacher in 1823. At Bedford, Pennsylvania, where he was principal of the academy, he became engrossed in the writings of Swedenborg and found in them a way of reconciling his classical studies, to which he was particularly devoted, with modern science and Christian theology. He now considered human nature, not as corrupt, but as still the divine image, and the progress of man from savagery to science appeared to him as the evolution of the mastery of man's "divine" nature over his material body and environment. What made his exposition of this theme particularly sensational was that he undertook by this theory of progress to counteract a popular tendency among Western educational reformers to abandon classical education in favor of a combination of Biblical and "American" education. He presented man's cultural heritage as the most essential feature in his *natural* equipment. Man, he explained, is molded by natural forces, and what chiefly distinguishes the environment of a civilized American from his savage neighbor is his possession of European culture. But Kinmont was no mere classicist; having defended the classical heritage as a natural power, he then turned with an eloquent enthusiasm to picture the glories of the new age that is dawning, especially in America. In this new age man is privileged to hear "the voice of truth and nature" directly through the revelations of natural science; he can discard "the idols of fancy" and is "less disposed to look at religion through its sects, at government through factions, at nature through theories, and at thought through words; but will have entered into closer communion with God, country, nature, and mind" [7] through an education that crowns the liberal arts with natural science.

Developing a similar theme, the Honorable Job Durfee, chief justice of Rhode Island, in 1843 discoursed on *The Influence of Scientific Discovery and Invention on Social and Political Progress*. To him the recent revolutionary development of steam power was not merely an instance of man making progress, it was a revelation of the divine "law of progress" and of a "high destiny" planned by God himself for a new age. Hear him expound the cosmic meaning of "this invention of Watt."

Sprung, armed for its mission, from the head of the progressive humanity, it cometh forth the genuine offspring of that one Eternal Reason which hath ruled through all ages past. It embraceth within itself, struggling for utterance, the history of millenniums to come. It standeth before the portals of the future, but as no veiled Isis, as no mute and motionless Harpocrates. It hath a language its own; and as it moveth to its task, it talketh freely of its mission. Thou unambiguous prophet! What a voice for the future speaketh from the expanding volume of thy force! What a tale to the future is foretokened in the movements of thy demon strength! Great fashioner of the destinies of nations! Thou hast hardly commenced thy career of victory; but when it is finished, all lands and all seas shall lie beneath thy feet, at once conquered and glorified by thy conquest! . . .

What becomes of those doctrines of social and political reform, with which our land is now so rife, and with which the public ear is so incessantly abused? What becomes of those ideas of a natural, absolute, unlimited and uncontrollable popular sovereignty, which is at once to bring humanity to perfection by establishing a *natural* liberty and a *natural* equality in *social* and *political* life? . . . They would cut clear from the past; they would establish a new theory of human nature, and base a human progress upon ideas and laws their own. Well! let them do it; but let them do it, as they must, with material their own. Let them create their world, and their man and woman, after their own image, and then, on their principles, run their course of events in rivalry with that of Divine Providence . . .

Change indeed must come, but then let it come by force of the necessary

[7] Alexander Kinmont, *Twelve Lectures on the Natural History of Man and the Rise and Progress of Philosophy* (Cincinnati, 1839), p. 353. The last lecture, from which this quotation is taken, was entitled "On the Elements of American Civilization."

law of progress. So shall the present still ever build and improve on a patrimony formed by the deeds of heroic virtue, and the labors of exalted intellect. So shall the great and glorious be added to the great and glorious, and the labors of the illustrious dead still be made fruitful by the labors of illustrious living, time without end.[8]

Durfee elaborated his "law of progress" into a system of idealistic pantheism, to the exposition of which he gave the grandiose title of *The Panidea; or, An Omnipresent Reason Considered as the Creative and Sustaining Logos*. According to this system the Absolute Reason or Divine Logos is gradually "assimilating" the world unto himself, drawing each "natural form" toward its "natural perfection" (material forms toward "immutability," and spiritual forms toward "progress" or toward union with "the divine image"). The "logic of progress" is therefore to be found in the successive approaches of man toward stable forms or types, each of which can be assimilated to "the *Homo Universalis* or Theanthropoid," which universal life of "multiform humanity" is identical with the creative Divine Mind.

An even more poetic exposition of "spiritual wisdom" is contained in two remarkable volumes by Henry James, Sr., *Christianity the Logic of Creation* (1857) and *Substance and Shadow* (1863). James interpreted evolution as a dual process: a process of *creation*, whereby God, through the growth of consciousness in man, removes man from both the shadows or unsubstantial forms of "nature" (the realm of mere cause and effect) and the spiritual or spontaneous unity with

[8] Job Durfee, *The Complete Works* (Providence, 1849), "Oration Delivered before the Phi Beta Kappa Society of Brown University, September 6, 1843," pp. 343-45. Reprinted in Blau, ed., *American Philosophic Addresses, 1700-1900*, pp. 383-414. Another passage from this same address (p. 342) is of considerable interest just now. Judge Durfee speculates on the consequences of the invention of the steam boat and the railroad for the problems of military defense: "Have we any choice but to radiate our country with communications for its defence, that the whole war force of the nation may be thrown with railroad speed on any point of danger? This system of defence may not be adopted till the shock of some foreign invasion, or some terrible internal convulsion, forces upon the government the necessity of adopting it; and then, if it be the will of God that we continue one people, it will, and must be adopted. When it is done, this union will be complete; its duration will depend on no written scroll of parchment; on no variable popular breath; its strength on no constitutional constructions changing to suit the temper of the times, but the constitution itself, resolved by the law of progress, shall take form, over the whole face of the land, in bands of iron."

Himself and thus creates isolated, self-conscious individuals, and a counter-process of *redemption*, whereby God gradually reunites man with Himself by revealing to him a "spiritual philosophy" to lift him above the delusions of natural science. The chief delusion of natural science is the belief that a man is an independent being; in discovering his dependence on "humanity" and on "spiritual substance" the individual is saved. This doctrine has the appearance of conventional Christian theology, but its meaning is completely transformed when we remember that James meant by God "humanity's redeemed form."

There is no God but the Lord, or our glorified *Natural* humanity, and whatsoever other deity we worship is but a baleful idol of our spiritual fantasy, whom we superstitiously project into nature to scourge us into *quasi* or provisional manhood, while as yet we are blind to the spiritual truth.[9]

These Swedenborgian interpretations of the cosmos and of evolution reflect an eighteenth-century background of Cartesian dualism and mysticism. More prevalent in the nineteenth century were the systems founded on German romanticism, especially Goethe and Schelling. There were three notable attempts to propagate in America this idealistic German *Naturphilosophie*, as a philosophy of science, in addition to the numerous versions of transcendentalism. The first of these was Johann Bernhard Stallo's *General Principles of the Philosophy of Nature* (1848), which was largely an exposition of the philosophies of nature of Schelling, Hegel, and Oken. Stallo came to this country from Germany at the age of sixteen and learned most of his German idealism while he was lecturing at St. John's College (Fordham), New York, 1844–47. In 1849 he returned to Cincinnati, where he practiced law, lectured on scientific theory, and participated in democratic politics. He later repudiated much of his German *Naturphilosophie* and in a series of articles in *The Popular Science Monthly* (1873–74) and in a volume entitled *The Concepts and Theories of Modern Physics* (1882) expounded a more naturalistic system. In these writings he undertook a critique of the atomic theory, as well as of absolutism, and expounded with remarkable foresight a thoroughgoing theory of physical relativism.

[9] Henry James, *Society the Redeemed Form of Man* (Boston, 1879), p. 264. See also Warren, *The Elder Henry James*, p. 213.

All the reality we know is not only spatially finite, but limited in all its aspects; its whole existence lies in relation and contrast.[10]

If we reverse the proposition, that a body acts where it is, and say that a body is where it acts, the inconceivability [of action at a distance] disappears at once. One of the wisest utterances ever made on this subject is the saying of Thomas Carlyle . . . "You say a body cannot act where it is not? With all my heart; but, pray, where is it?" Of course, a reconstitution of our concepts of material presence, in the sense here indicated, would be in utter conflict with the theory of the mechanical construction of matter. . . . Such a reconstitution is necessary.[11]

As there is no Unconditional in subjective thought, so there is no Absolute in objective reality. There is no absolute system of coordinates in space to which the positions of bodies and their changes can be referred; and there is neither an absolute measure of quantity, nor an absolute standard of quality. *There is no physical constant.*[12]

Another German who made an enduring contribution to the spread of natural philosophy in America was Dr. Paul Carus, whose liberalism compelled him to flee from Dresden to America. His first work, *Monism and Meliorism,* appeared in 1885. Two years later he became editor of *The Open Court* and later of *The Monist,* two periodicals which have been of great service in promoting philosophical thought in America. Though Dr. Carus himself was a vigorous apostle of "two-aspect monism" and preached his faith in cosmic order as the very heart of all religion, he at the same time cultivated a respect for other philosophies; his personal catholicity and his liberal editorial policies were an influential factor in awakening an ignorant American public to the basic problems and traditions, both Western and Eastern, of free and critical speculation on the import of natural knowledge.

Dr. Carus did not call himself a philosopher. He preferred to be considered a theologian; and although he was often accused of being an atheist, he insisted that he was an atheist who loved God. It was in the study of the Science of Religion and the Religion of Science that his deepest interests lay . . .[13]

---

[10] *Popular Science Monthly,* IV (1873–74), 102.
[11] *Ibid.,* p. 107.
[12] *Ibid.,* p. 231.
[13] Catherine Cook, ed., *The Point of View; an Anthology of Religion and Philosophy Selected from the Works of Paul Carus* (Chicago, 1927), Preface, p. viii.

He preached reverence for science.

Science is the embodiment of the immutable world-order of the Logos that was in the beginning, of God in His revelation.

Whenever God speaks to man, it is not in the earthquake of bigotry or dogma, nor in the fire of fanaticism but he comes in the still, small voice . . . of science, for science is an utter surrender of what we wish to believe to a recognition of the actual fact.

Science is sometimes erroneously supposed to be a human invention; it is represented as the truth of man, which is contrasted with the divine revelation of religious dogma as being the truth of God . . . but science is not of human make. . . . It is a revelation which cannot be invented but must be discovered. There is a holiness in mathematics and there is ethics in the multiplication table.[14]

The chief service to American cosmology performed by men like Fiske, Youmans, Draper, Stallo, and Carus was to make known in this country the more important European philosophies of science and to create here some public recognition of the ways in which the new conceptions of nature and natural order were effecting a revolution in European philosophy and theology.

Of a quite different character was the cosmological speculation of Charles Sanders Peirce, for though he made a careful study of the European systems, particularly the German, he made highly original and ingenious revisions in them, which are gaining steadily in historical importance in spite of the fact that in his own generation they were wrapped in various kinds of obscurity. Like Abbot, he revolted against the reigning nominalism and phenomenalism and laid a well-constructed foundation for realism. But, more than Abbot, he built on this foundation a theory of evolution which possessed scientific erudition as well as cosmological originality. Apparently he began to formulate his "synechistic agapastic tychism" under the influence of Schelling.

I was born and reared in the neighborhood of Concord—I mean in Cambridge—at the time when Emerson, Hedge, and their friends were disseminating the ideas they had caught from Schelling, and Schelling from Plotinus, from Boehm, or from God knows what minds stricken with the monstrous mysticism of the East. But the atmosphere of Cambridge held

[14] *Ibid.*, pp. 118–19.

many an antiseptic against Concord transcendentalism; and I am not conscious of having contracted any of that virus. Nevertheless, it is probable that some cultured bacilli, some benignant form of the disease was implanted in my soul, unawares, and that now, after long incubation, it comes to the surface, modified by mathematical conceptions and by training in physical investigations.[15]

I carefully recorded my opposition to all philosophies which deny the reality of the Absolute, and asserted that "the one intelligible theory of the universe is that of objective idealism, that matter is effete mind." This is as much as to say that I am a Schellingian, of some stripe; so that, on the whole, I do not think Dr. Carus has made a very happy hit in likening me to Hume, to whose whole method and style of philosophizing I have always been perhaps too intensely averse. . . .[16]

My views were probably influenced by Schelling,—by all stages of Schelling, but especially by the *Philosophie der Natur*. I consider Schelling as enormous. . . . If you were to call my philosophy Schellingism transformed in the light of modern physics, I should not take it hard.[17]

From absolute idealism Peirce took over an evolutionary idea, quite different from the popular concept of "development" or "unfolding": the universe, which was at first mere chaos, is gradually becoming an orderly, intelligible being by acquiring "habits of mind." Three principles govern this process: (1) spontaneity, freedom, variability, chance —the world has a tendency to "sport," to take chances, and none of nature's doings are perfectly precise. This element of chance or spontaneity, Peirce thought, is particularly evident and important in the structure and behavior of protoplasm; this living substance, "man's glassy essence," is conspicuously able to learn, to form habits, but there is no reason to suppose that *only* living tissue can form habits. (2) Uniformity, law, continuity is the second principle. The primeval spontaneity gives way to regularity. Individuals move together in reciprocal tension or "struggle," holding each other in place. Matter's law-abidingness is by no means evidence of a purely mechanical order; on the contrary, insofar as it is orderly it exhibits mental traits.

---

[15] Charles Sanders Peirce, *Collected Papers*, ed. by Hartshorne and Weiss (Cambridge, 1931–35), VI, 86–87.

[16] *Ibid.*, VI, 415.

[17] In a letter to William James, quoted in Ralph Barton Perry, *The Thought and Character of William James* (Boston, 1935), II, 415–16.

(3) Generality, habit, assimilation, kinds—this factor in evolution accounts for its direction. Regularity grows or "spreads." Peirce identified the spread or generality of orderly movement in nature with the growth of concepts or universals in mind. The natural attraction which orders things into classes or species is the basic principle of evolution: it is purpose, desire, or "evolutionary love," and like Platonic love it is the source of knowledge, since it aims at generality.

Evolution is nothing more nor less than the working out of a definite end. . . . No classes can be more fundamental nor broader than those which are defined by the purpose. A purpose is an operative desire. Now a desire is always general; that is, it is always some *kind* of thing or event which is desired; at least, until the element of will, which is always exercised upon an individual object upon an individual occasion, becomes so predominant as to overrule the generalizing character of desire. Thus, desires create classes, and extremely broad classes. But desires become, in the pursuit of them, more specific.[18]

An apple pie is desired. Now, observe that we seldom, probably never, desire a single individual thing. What we want is something which shall produce a certain pleasure of a certain kind. To speak of a single individual pleasure is to use words without meaning. We may have a single experience of pleasure; but the pleasure itself is a quality. . . . An apple pie, then, is desired—a good apple pie, made of fresh apples, with a crust moderately light and somewhat short, neither too sweet nor too sour, etc. But it is not any particular apple pie; for it is to be made for the occasion; and the only particularity about it is that it is to be made and eaten today. For that, apples are wanted . . . But desire has nothing to do with particulars; it relates to qualities. Desire is not a reaction with reference to a particular thing; it is an idea about an idea, namely, the idea of how delightful it would be for me, the cook's master, to eat an apple pie. However, what is desired is not a mere unattached quality; what is desired is that the dream of eating an apple pie should be realized in Me; and this Me is an object of experience.[19]

This simple illustration of the "realization of desire" is the pattern on which love works on a cosmic scale.

The starting-point of the universe, God the Creator, is the Absolute First; the terminus of the universe, God completely revealed, is the Absolute

---

[18] Peirce, *Collected Papers*, "Principles of Philosophy," 1.205–6.
[19] *Ibid.*, 1.341–42.

Second. . . . If you hold that there is a definite drift to the course of nature as a whole, but yet believe its absolute end is nothing but the Nirvana from which it set out, you make the two points of the absolute to be coincident, and are a pessimist. But if your creed is that the whole universe is approaching in the infinitely distant future a state having a general character different from that toward which we look back in the infinitely distant past, you make the absolute to consist in two distinct real points and are an evolutionist. The last view is essentially that of Christian theology, too. The theologians hold the physical universe to be finite, but considering that universe which they will admit to have existed from all time, it would appear to be in a different condition in the end from what it was in the beginning, the whole spiritual creation having been accomplished, and abiding.

If all things are continuous, the universe must be undergoing a continuous growth from non-existence to existence. There is no difficulty in conceiving existence as a matter of degree. The reality of things consists in their persistent forcing themselves upon our recognition. If a thing has no such persistence, it is a mere dream. Reality, then, is persistence, is regularity. In the original chaos, where there was no regularity, there was no existence. It was all a confused dream. This we may suppose was in the infinitely distant past. But as things are getting more regular, more persistent, they are getting less dreamy and more real.[20]

Peirce interpreted the Darwinian theory of natural selection in terms of "merely fortuitous variations," and made little attempt to reconcile it with his theory of evolutionary love. He did, however, attempt to fit the principles of natural selection into his three categories.

The principle of sporting is the principle of irregularity, indeterminacy, chance. . . . The principle of heredity is the principle of the determination of something by what went before, the principle of compulsion, corresponding to will and sense. The principle of the elimination of unfavorable characters is the principle of generalization by casting out of sporadic cases.[21]

To all such cosmological and evolutionary speculation there was at least one stanch opponent among American scientific philosophers— Chauncey Wright, of Northampton, Massachusetts, mathematician, computer for the *Nautical Almanac,* recording secretary of the American Academy of Arts and Sciences, sometime lecturer at Harvard, member of the famous "Metaphysical Club," devoted disciple of both Mill and Darwin. Wright and Peirce had many long discussions on the philosophical interpretation of natural science, Peirce contending

[20] Peirce, *Collected Papers,* 1.175, 1.362.   [21] *Ibid.,* 1.399.

for realism, teleology, and his general theory of evolution as the growth of order out of chaos, Wright trying to persuade him that there is no pattern in universal history, but mere "cosmical weather," and that Darwinism is not to be interpreted as a general method of evolution but a special application of utilitarianism to problems of biological survival. Wright defended critically and stubbornly an empiricist version of natural science and a utilitarian theory of morals and teleology. His general conception of the universe as well as of human life had been beautifully and succinctly expressed in one of his earliest articles:

Man finds himself everywhere mirrored in nature. Wayward, inconstant, always seeking rest, always impelled by new evils, the greatest of which he himself creates,—protecting and cherishing or blighting and destroying the fragmentary life of a fallen nature,—incapable himself of creating new capacities, but nourishing in prosperity and quickening in adversity those that are left,—he sees the workings of his own life in the strife of the elements. His powers and activities are related to his spiritual capacities, as inorganic movements are related to an organizing life. The resurrection of his higher nature is like a creation, secret, sudden, inconsequent. "The wind bloweth where it listeth, and thou hearest the sound thereof, but canst not tell whence it cometh, and whither it goeth." [22]

In a passage which was undoubtedly directed against Peirce's theory of evolution, though he referred it to Anaxagoras, Wright criticized the theory of a primeval chaos and asserted his belief in an "actual" chaos.

It is common to speak of Anaxagoras as having introduced into the philosophy of nature the *nous*, or the independent agency of intelligence. It is not so commonly seen that he introduced along with this, and in antithesis to it, a still more characteristic idea, that of a primeval chaos. The antichaotic *nous* of Anaxagoras is not that of the physicists and the pantheists. The only chaos contemplated by the ancient atomists is the one they saw around them always existing; one which had always existed in the indeterminate confused actual order, at any time, of the universe as a whole.[23]

Wright believed in cyclical processes, but not in a general evolutionary trend. These cyclical processes, he thought, were to be explained on

[22] Chauncey Wright, "The Winds and the Weather," *The Atlantic Monthly*, I (1858), 279.
[23] Chauncey Wright, *Philosophical Discussions* (New York, 1877), p. 382.

mechanical principles. The careers of solar systems, for example, he tried to explain on the basis of simple thermodynamics.

The living forces of all moving bodies, *minus* the potentials of their forces of gravitation, *plus* the mechanical values of their heat, *equal* to a constant quantity,—is the precise formula to which our cosmical speculations should conform.[24]

The distribution of the stars will be accounted for, not on the hypothesis of simple attractive or repulsive forces, but by the distributions of matter and heat through the interstellar spaces, and by their actions and reactions, not as centres of simple forces, but as the receptacles of concrete masses and motions, and as the sources of diffused motions and matters, none of which can ever be lost or destroyed; that their motions will be found to result principally from those of the medium of diffused materials, from which they are aggregated precipitates, and into which they are evaporated by heat.

This is at present only an hypothesis, but it is not teleological in any sense of the term. The most obvious objection to it is the theory that there is "a universal tendency in nature to the dissipation of mechanical energy," a theory well founded, nay, demonstrated, if we only follow this energy as far as the present limits of science extend. But to a true Aristotelian this theory, so far from suggesting a dramatic *dénouement*, such as the ultimate death of nature, only propounds new problems. What becomes of the sun's dynamic energy, and whence do the bodies come which support this wasting power? . . .

Scientific demonstration is slow and painful, the work of time and patience. All that can now be presented are problems, but these are scientific problems. They are concerned with the details of an elementary order, which science has a right to presume, and not with the abstract features of an external order, which science has no right to presume.[25]

Against the theory of evolution and against Spencer's theory, in particular, he wrote unequivocally:

We strongly suspect that the law of "evolution" will fail to appear in phenomena not connected, either directly or remotely, with the life of the individual organism, or the growth of which this law is an abstract description. And, heterodox though the opinion be, we are inclined to accept as the soundest and most catholic assumption, on grounds of scientific method, the too little regarded doctrine of Aristotle, which banishes cosmology from the realm of scientific inquiry, reducing natural phenomena in their cosmical

[24] *Ibid.*, p. 19.   [25] *Ibid.*, pp. 86–88.

relations to an infinite variety of manifestations (without a discoverable tendency on the whole) of causes and laws which are simple and constant in their ultimate elements.

The laws of archetypes of nature are properly the laws of invariable or unconditional sequence in natural operations. And it is only with the objective relations of these laws, as constituting the order of nature, that natural science is concerned. Their subjective relations, origin, and essential being belong to the province of transcendental metaphysics, and to a philosophy of faith. According to this division, there can never arise any conflict between science and faith; for what the one is competent to declare, the other is incompetent to dispute. Science should be free to determine what the order of nature is, and faith equally free to declare the essential nature of causation or creation.[26]

[The theologian] should refrain from attributing any special plan or purpose to the creation, if he would find in science a constant support to religious truth. But this abstinence does not involve a withdrawal of the mind from the proper religious interests of natural science, nor weaken a legitimate faith in final causes. Even the Newtonian mechanism of the heavens, simple, primordial, and necessary as it seems, still discloses to the devout mind evidence of a wisdom unfathomable, and of a design which transcends interpretation; and when, in the more complicated order of organic life, surprising and beautiful adaptations inspire in the naturalist the conviction that purpose and intelligence are manifested in them,—that they spring from a nature akin to the devising power of his own mind,—there is nothing in science or philosophy which can legitimately rebuke his enthusiasm,— nothing, unless it be the dogmatism which would presumptuously interpret as science what is only manifest to faith, or would require of faith that it shall justify itself by proofs.

The progress of science has indeed been a progress in religious truth, but in spite of false theology, and in a way which narrow theologians have constantly opposed. It has defined with greater and greater distinctness the boundary between what can be discovered and what cannot. It has purified religious truth by turning back the moral consciousness to discover clearly in itself what it had obscurely divined from its own interpretations of nature. It has impressed on the mind of the cautious inquirer the futility, as well as the irreverence, of attempting a philosophy which can at best be but a finer sort of superstition, a real limitation to our conceptions of final causes, while apparently an extension of them.[27]

[26] *Ibid.*, pp. 7, 7n–8n.
[27] *Ibid.*, p. 41.

Though Wright discounted the scientific value of philosophical speculation, he defended it in its own right as a significant human enterprise, along with religion, morals, and the arts. It should be estimated, he said,

rather by the dignity of its motives, and the value it directs us to, than by the value of its own attainments. To condemn this pursuit because it fails to accomplish what science does, would be to condemn that which has formed in human nature habits, ideas, and associations on which all that is best in us depends. . . . Theology was Philosophy developed in the interests of Religion or of religious feeling, and Metaphysics was cultivated in the interests of Theology. Both aimed at truth; both were determined by the same love of simplicity and unity in knowledge, which determines all search after truth; but neither cared for simple truth alone. When pursued for the truth of fact alone, they both degenerate into affectation and emptiness.[28]

Philosophy, morals, and religion, to say nothing of the arts, were for Wright not only practical in nature, but each of them ought to be understood as an independent concern, with its own motives and values. Religion is primarily concerned with moral problems, but unlike secular ethics it disregards considerations of utility and relativity, concentrating its attention on those duties which have an "absolute or unconditional character," irrespective of any "object or end." [29] In general, Wright attempted to conceive both religion and morals as independent of particular "creeds and codes," and he regarded this independence as of great value to him. For example, he tried to dissuade his friend F. E. Abbot, from renouncing his pulpit on the ground that

the test of a true faith is emotional and moral, not intellectual. . . . To stake any serious human concern on the truth of this or that philosophical theory seems to me in the highest degree arrogant and absurd. . . . Men conclude in matters affecting their own welfare so much better than they can justify rationally. . . . The explanations which men have hitherto given of their beliefs in practical rules of conduct afford the best possible evidence of the practical weakness of theory even in the most important matters. . . . Nothing so much justifies that shameful assumption by ecclesiastical bodies of control over speculative opinions as the inconsiderate

[28] *Ibid.*, p. 52.
[29] Chauncey Wright, *Letters* (Cambridge, 1878), p. 98.

preaching of such opinions, in place of the warnings, encouragements, sympathies, and persuasions of the true religious instructor. The lessons which he has to deliver are really very easy to understand, but hard to live up to.[30]

One of these lessons which are "easy to understand, but hard to live up to" was of particular importance to Wright, namely, the danger of transforming all recognized values into moral imperatives.

There are many actions which, though they may be recognized as obligatory by the conscience of the one who does them, ought not to be imposed as such on any one by any other human being. . . . For, by this reasoning, the more worthy an act is, the more obligatory the act would be, and saintliness would be imperatively demanded of us,—the Calvinist paradox. It is not by laws and legal sanctions, nor yet by opinion and moral sanctions, but only by worship,—the positive reverence due to the highest of even human virtues,—that such virtues have a foothold in the world.[31]

Chauncey Wright's own morals were, as he confessed, almost entirely those of a scientist, and he formulated clearly what he conceived a scientific ethics (i.e., morals of and for science) to be. The natural, "subjective" desire for knowledge must become an "objective" motive by ceasing

to be associated with our fears, our respects, our aspirations,—our emotional nature; when it ceases to prompt questions as to what relates to our personal destiny, our ambitions, our moral worth; when it ceases to have man, his personal and social nature, as its central and controlling objects. A curiosity which is determined chiefly or solely by the felt imperfections of knowledge as such, and without reference to the uses this knowledge may subserve, is prompted by what we call an objective motive.

A spirit of inquiry which is freed from the influence of our active powers, and the interests that gave birth to theological and metaphysical philosophies, —which yields passively and easily to the direction of objective motives, to the felt imperfections of knowledge as such,—is necessarily, at all times, a weak feeling; and before a body of systematic, well-digested, and well-ascertained scientific truth had been generated, could hardly have had any persistent influence on the direction of inquiry.

The motives to theological and metaphysical speculation exist from the beginning of civilized human life in the active emotional nature of man. . . .

The questions of philosophy proper are human desires and fears and

[30] *Ibid.*, pp. 61, 101, 135.   [31] *Ibid.*, p. 118.

aspirations—human emotions—taking an intellectual form. Science follows, but does not supersede, this philosophy. The three phases which the positivists assign to the development of the human mind—the Theological, the Metaphysical, and the Positive or Scientific—are not in reality successive, except in their beginnings. They co-exist in all the highest developments of civilization and mental activity.[32]

There are morals to be drawn from science as well as a science from morals. It is tame bathos, perhaps, instead of vague sublimity, to rest from scientific effort in the following reflection—but I make it nevertheless: How much better for truth is patient induction and the use of judgment, than obedient deduction, humility, and submission to judgment? . . . Such patient, busy dealing with truth is sometimes falsely called humility. It is properly a reasonable pride; though if a metaphysician were to come down to it, it might be regarded as an act of humility. It is not humility to walk and climb when one sees clearly that he cannot fly; it is simply good sense.[33]

— 31 —

SPECULATIVE BIOLOGY

AMERICAN interest in the origin of species goes back at least as far as an evening in 1787 when the Reverend Samuel Stanhope Smith, of the College of New Jersey, delivered an "ingenious and learned oration" before the American Philosophical Society at Philadelphia "On the Causes of the Variety of Complexion and Figure in the Human Species." When this address was published the author added to it *Strictures on Lord Kaims's Discourse on the Original Diversity of Mankind.* There was keen interest among the Edinburgh philosophers in the science of human progress and in the attempt to lay the foundations for a natural history of mankind. As a contribution to this subject Lord Kames had tried to prove that mankind must have been diversified from its beginning. For, he argued,

certain it is that all men, more than all animals, are not equally fitted for every climate. There were therefore created different kinds of men at first, according to the nature of the climate in which they were to live. And

[32] Wright, *Philosophical Discussions*, pp. 49–50.
[33] Wright, *Letters*, p. 256.

if we have any belief in providence, it ought to be so. Because men, in changing their climate usually become sickly and often degenerate.[1]

Many of Lord Kames's arguments were no better than this, and many of the supposed anthropological facts on which he rested his case turned out to be the tall tales of travelers. Dr. Smith had a relatively easy case in proving that the known varieties of men could be accounted for as the effects of either climate or "the state of society" or both, and he closed his oration with the triumphant reflection:

A just philosophy will always be found to be coincident with true theology. The writers who, through ignorance of nature, or through prejudice against religion, attempt to deny the unity of the human species do not advert to the confusion which such principles tend to introduce. The science of morals would be absurd; the law of nature and nations would be annihilated; no general principles of human conduct, of religion, or of policy could be framed; for, human nature, originally, infinitely various, and, by the changes of the world, infinitely mixed, could not be comprehended in any system. The rules which would result from the study of our own nature, would not apply to the natives of other countries who would be of different species; perhaps, not to two families in our own country, who might be sprung from a dissimilar composition of species. Such principles tend to confound all science, as well as piety; and leave us in the world uncertain whom to trust, or what opinions to frame of others. The doctrine of one race, removes this uncertainty, renders human nature susceptible of system, illustrates the powers of physical causes, and opens a rich and extensive field for moral science.[2]

Nevertheless, the problem became more acute during the following decades. In 1839 a Philadelphia ethnologist, Samuel George Morton, published *Crania Americana,* in which he came to the startling conclusion that the American Indians were a truly aboriginal race and had never been connected with the Caucasians. In subsequent researches he discovered evidence of other original races. During the forties his views were gaining support both here and abroad. Professor Louis Agassiz, of Harvard, shocked his orthodox friends by supporting Morton's views and by adding his own reasons for believing that mankind, though a single "species," is divided into a number of

[1] Samuel Stanhope Smith, *An Essay on the Causes of the Variety of Complexion and Figure in the Human Species . . . [and] Strictures on Lord Kaims's Discourse, on the Original Diversity of Mankind* (Philadelphia, 1787); "Strictures," p. 2.
[2] *Ibid.,* pp. 109–10.

"original varieties." To make matters worse, Agassiz tried to comfort his religious friends with the following philosophical argument.

We recognize the fact of the unity of mankind. It excites a feeling that raises men to a most elevated sense of their connection with each other. It is but the reflection of that divine nature which pervades the whole being. It is because men feel thus related to each other, that they acknowledge those obligations of kindness and moral responsibility which rest upon them in their mutual relations. Where the relationship of blood has ceased, do we cease to acknowledge that general bond which unites all men of every nation? By no means. This is the bond which every man feels more and more the farther he advances in his intellectual and moral culture, and which in this development is continually placed upon higher and higher ground, so much so, that the physical relation arising from a common descent, is finally lost sight of in the consciousness of higher moral obligations. It is this consciousness which constitutes the true unity of mankind.[3]

This would not do! A merely moral unity was not enough. The Reverend James W. Alexander pointed out that it was not a matter of indifference "whether the nature which fell in Eden, was that which we inherit, and whether the humanity which Jesus bore upon the cross and carried into heaven, was that of all mankind." [4] In 1850 a physician, Dr. J. Bachman, D.D., of Charleston, S.C., and a Presbyterian clergyman, Thomas Smyth, both attempted replies. But in 1854 Morton's position was again espoused by J. C. Nott and George R. Gliddon in their elaborate volume *Types of Mankind,* which concluded "there exists a *Genus Homo,* embracing many primordial Types or Species." [5] Gliddon here added to the ethnological arguments an ingenious work on "Hebrew Nomenclature," in which he revived the Biblical arguments for the existence of "pre-Adamite races." It was no small comfort, therefore, to hear John W. Draper, the eminent physiologist of New York University, take issue with Agassiz and say "I do not contemplate the human race as consisting of varieties, much less of distinct species."

Dr. Nott had contended that "blacks and whites do not amalgamate

[3] J. L. Cabell, *The Testimony of Modern Science to the Unity of Mankind* . . . with an introductory notice by James W. Alexander (New York, 1859), pp. 144–45; quoting L. Agassiz, "Geographical Distribution of Animals," *Christian Examiner,* XLVIII (1850), 181–204.

[4] *Ibid.,* pp. vi–vii.

[5] Nott and Gliddon, *Types of Mankind* (Philadelphia, 1854), p. 465.

perfectly, but obey the laws of hybridity." [6] To which Dr. Bachman replied, giving evidence from Charleston, S.C., that the mulattoes "are upright and virtuous, and are professors of religion . . . and are fully as prolific as either the whites or blacks." Hereupon Professor James Dwight Dana, of Yale, commented:

It strikes us naturally with wonder, that even in senseless plants, without the emotional repugnance of instinct, and with reproductive organs that are all outside, the free winds being often the means of transmission, there should be a rigid law sustained against intermixture. The supposed cases of perpetuated fertile hybridity are so exceedingly few as almost to condemn themselves, as no true examples of an abnormity so abhorrent to the system. They violate a principle so essential to the integrity of the plant-kingdom, and so opposed to Nature's whole plan, that we rightly demand long and careful study before admitting the exceptions. [7]

There was here more than a touch of "Civil War nerves," and the anti-slavery emotions were being dragged into the issue. The publication in 1856 of an American edition of Count A. de Gobineau's *The Moral and Intellectual Diversity of Races*, with its arguments for the "permanent inequality" of races, added fuel to both sides, since it took no definite stand on the question of origins. Similarly disquieting and complicating were the new but inconclusive evidences reported in Darwin's *Voyage of a Naturalist around the World* (1855). There were frequent references to the fact that Alexander von Humboldt, whose *Cosmos* had been translated and was just then appearing, had commented sentimentally on the sad view that mankind may not be a unity after all.

Into this heated controversy dropped Darwin's *On the Origin of Species by Means of Natural Selection; or, The Preservation of Favoured Races in the Struggle for Life*, and it was taken by all except the most farseeing and the professional biologists as primarily a contribution to this controversy. In fact, it seemed superficially that Darwin's additional evidences of the influences of the environment on species would strengthen the faith in the original unity of man. And when Agassiz came out in opposition to Darwin, and Asa Gray, a pious

[6] *Ibid.*

[7] Cited in Cabell, *op. cit.*, p. 133*n*, from J. D. Dana, "Thoughts on Species," *Bibliotheca Sacra*, XIV (1857), 854–74.

theist, came out in favor, there was rejoicing in the "unity" camp. Only gradually did it dawn on the readers that there was in Darwin's book more than a discussion of a technical biological issue and that not merely the unity of man but also his creation was at stake, and not merely creation but also teleology in general. The popular storm over Darwinism did not break until the publication of *The Descent of Man,* in 1871.

There was, however, at least one prompt, critical review of the *Origin of Species* in which some of the basic philosophical problems of Darwinism were raised. Professor Francis Bowen, of Harvard, published in *The North American Review,* which he edited, one of the first American reviews to appear, and certainly the first to look beyond the immediate biological controversies to the problem of explaining the origin of the human mind and to foreshadow the metaphysics of "emergence," which soon became popular. He wrote:

The theory, if accepted at all, must be accepted as a whole. . . . Mr. Darwin is bound to account for the origin of the human species just as much as for that of the lowest insect. He confesses as much, when he says that, after the general reception of his system, "psychology will be based on a new foundation, that of the necessary acquirement of each mental power and capacity by gradation"; and that "light will be thrown on the origin of man and his history." He is bound, therefore, to find the means of bridging over, by imperceptibly fine gradations, the immense gap which now separates man from the animals most nearly allied to him,—a gap not only between the two structural forms, which, however unlike, may still be affirmed to be of the same kind, but between reason and instinct, where nearly all psychologists are agreed that the difference is in kind, and not in degree. Here surely, as we remarked in the outset, it is the student of physical science who, instead of protesting against intrusion by others, is himself intruding upon psychological and metaphysical ground, and aiming to break up the previously well-established division of the sciences.

Now the tendency of Mr. Darwin's theory, or rather of the facts upon which it is founded, is to enlarge the domain of what is thus, in one sense, arbitrary and contingent, or dependent on free volition, in nature, and to limit the action of secondary causes to a comparatively subordinate part in the economy of the universe. Our author denies that the same physical antecedents are always followed by the same consequents; he affirms that irregular and unexpected variations are perpetually interrupting the chain of orderly succession, and compelling us to seek for a cause *ab extra*, or out of the phenomena themselves,—a free, or, as he would call it, a capricious cause, to account for the aberrant results. While seeking with so much zeal to disprove the necessity of any fresh exertion of creative power to explain the origin of a new species, he traces back that origin to countless "variations," departures from law, divergences from type, every one of which, on his own principles, is just as much an act of creation as the primary calling forth of light out of darkness.[8]

The problem, suggested by Bowen, of explaining in Darwinian terms the transition from "instinct to reason" worried Darwin himself, and he communicated his worries to his first enthusiastic American disciple, Chauncey Wright. Darwin was inclined to solve the problem in terms of variations of language, due to "unconscious selection" and in this connection he wrote to Wright: "As your mind is so clear, and as you consider so carefully the meaning of words, I wish you would take some incidental occasion to consider when a thing may properly be said to be effected by the mind of man."[9] Chauncey Wright set to work at once and produced his remarkable essay, *The Evolution of Self-Consciousness*, which, though it failed to answer Darwin's problem, gave a fresh impetus to empirical psychology in America. Wright's argument was an attempt to combine utilitarianism and natural selection. Without assuming the appearance of new "faculties" in man's animal ancestors, he thought he could account for the appearance of language and reason on the supposition that because of environmental changes the old faculties (especially memory and imagination) were put to new *uses*. Images or gestures might have served, without being intended for that purpose, as signs; and out of the habit of inventing signs there would then naturally emerge (especially in a social animal) the conscious use of signs and finally self-consciousness. For, though consciousness is naturally directed outward, it is "sufficiently vivid in itself to engage distinct attention" and hence to arouse a distinct type of action, namely, reflection.

Reflection would thus be, not what most metaphysicians appear to regard it, a fundamentally new faculty in man, as elementary and primordial as

[8] Francis Bowen, review of Darwin's *Origin of Species*, *North American Review*, XC (1860), 501–2, 506.

[9] See Philip P. Wiener, "Chauncey Wright, Darwin and Scientific Neutrality," *The Journal of the History of Ideas*, VI (1945), 34.

memory itself, or the power of abstractive attention, or the function of signs and representative images in generalization; but it would be determined in its contrasts with other mental faculties by the nature of its objects. On its subjective side it would be composed of the same mental faculties— namely, memory, attention, abstraction—as those which are employed in the primary use of the senses. It would be engaged upon what these senses have furnished to memory; but would act as independently of any orders of grouping and succession presented by them, as the several senses themselves do of one another.[10]

What is most remarkable in this essay is Wright's appreciation of the difference between consciousness and self-consciousness, and his serious effort to explain the latter, when most of his contemporaries were preoccupied with the former.

Wright, encouraged by Darwin, conceived a new type of science of the mind, a new teleology, which would evaluate consciousness, habits, manners, morals in terms of their utility for the survival of the race, or for "the greatest happiness of the greatest number." This science was to be a synthesis of utilitarianism and Darwinism. In reporting his conversation with Darwin he wrote to a friend:

I am sometime to write an essay on matters covering the ground of certain common interests and studies . . . for which the learned title is adopted of *Psychozoölogy,*—as a substitute for "animal psychology," "instinct," and the like titles,—in order to give the requisite subordination (from our point of view) of consciousness in men and animals, to their development and general relations to nature.[11]

We find ourselves acting the more reasonably and more for the real ends of nature, in proportion as these are not our immediate motives, but give place to more completely devoted, single-purposed, and therefore effective powers, or to instincts and habits; which we should, nevertheless, as reasonable beings, subject theoretically, or in our philosophy of life and duty, to the test of the good they subserve in the economy of life.

Utilitarianism needs to be supplemented, in order to meet misunderstandings, by a Philosophy of Habit, and to lay down among its practical principles that, since motives are effective, not in proportion to their usefulness or reasonableness, but rather to their singleness or instinctiveness, therefore it is reasonable to foster and to rely practically on the force of proper habits and just, natural inclinations. In the serene and unopposed play of these,—

[10] Wright, *Philosophical Discussions*, p. 217.
[11] *Letters of Chauncey Wright*, p. 248.

and especially in their concord or harmonious play,—there is a source of happiness to the agent, which the sentimental moralist mistakes for the real, or natural, end of virtue, but which belongs to it only as a habit, or as a body of mutually supporting or concordant habits; and is quite distinct from the happiness or well-being to which as virtuous or reasonable habits and inclinations they are or should be adapted. Dignity is a weight with the will, or an effective source of happiness, which these powers of habit and instinct gain from their mutual support or harmonious action, and from their persistent influence, and which would be the natural result of accordance with the harmonious real ends of life. It is to questioned and artificial rules of life, and to the morals of legislation rather than to the instincts of the individual conscience, that the utilitarian test is of greatest practical importance. Nature has not waited for human reason to discover or to test all the instincts and disciplines best adapted for keeping the surviving races of men in the most flourishing condition; just as she did not wait for physiological science to disclose the uses of color, but secured them in her economy by making them the delight and one, apparently, of the most important ends of vision, though really one, as we have seen, of its most important means.[12]

"Nature," says Cicero, "has inclined us to the love of mankind; and this is the foundation of laws" (*fundamentum juris*). This is both the rational and the disciplinary foundation, the ground and the efficacy of laws; since fear becomes a moral power only by its sanction; and even those laws which we may be said to observe instinctively, or as ends from the start and in themselves, are instinctively associated with the love of mankind, with the wish for the greatest good of the greatest number. On this wish hang all the law and the prophets.[13]

Utilitarianism sits in permanent judgment over all law-*making*, over all devices of expediency, whether these be deductions from laws, or exceptions to the existing and acknowledged rules of duty. Its reliance on the forces of habit and instinct is not for rational guidance, but for practical efficacy; yet these are so important to its aims, that they are not safely to be disregarded, or unnecessarily opposed, or weakened by substituting for them habitually the calculations of expediency.[14]

Innate predispositions to perceptions and actions, which, *if right* in their directive agency, are in accordance with reason,—that is, with the results of experience and observation,—are not thereby made a standard, or at any

[12] *Ibid.*, pp. 282–83.   [13] *Ibid.*, pp. 288–89.   [14] *Ibid.*, p. 291.

rate an independent standard, for self-culture. The way to follow Nature is to observe the means which, in accordance with the cosmic laws or conditions of Nature, and of human nature, are found to be conducive to self-sanctioned ends in the higher social or moral life of man, or in his reflective social nature; *naturam observare* is the way *naturam sequi*. This research observes the conditions of necessity, the laws of inevitable sequence in cosmic nature, and seeks to join to them the ideals of life in such manner as will realize or make actual these ideals as perfectly as possible in outward action. In this relation, Nature is not a teacher, but only a part of the lesson, and is a guide only in the sense in which a mountain-pass is a guide; namely, the limits within which our efforts are saved from total failure.[15]

The Nature still deserving our worship is the harmony of an elevated ideal standard, pragmatically opposed to the claims of traditional institutions and sanctions.[16]

In these few paragraphs Chauncey Wright sketched beautifully a *Psychozoölogy* which, if he had lived to develop it, would certainly have been one of the major works in the history of American thought and probably a classic expression of naturalistic utilitarianism as a normative science.

Another attempt to solve the problem of mental evolution came about the same time from John Fiske, and his use of the associationist psychology was not unlike Wright's. He, too, following Spencer, pointed out that a new environment would serve to give old "nerve-channels" new functions. Given the great growth of the cerebrum (to be explained by the general principles of natural selection), man enjoyed a new, "critical" opportunity to transform the processes of habit-forming into the processes of consciousness.

As long as the psychical life consists solely in the passage of nervous undulations along permanent pre-established channels, there is no consciousness. Consciousness, as already shown, implies continual discrimination, or the continual recognition of likenesses and differences; and this process implies a rapid succession of changes in the supreme ganglia. Now this rapid succession of changes occurs when a vast number of relations are brought together in a single ganglion, or group of ganglia, as in the cerebrum, in order to be compared with each other. . . .

Obviously, therefore, when the number of impressions sent in to the

---

[15] *Ibid.*, p. 329.　　　　[16] *Ibid.*, p. 330.

brain from moment to moment exceeds the number of thoroughly permeable channels which have been formed there, so that there is a brief period of tension during which occur the nutritive changes implied in the transmission of the disturbance through the appropriate channels, then there arise the phenomena of conscious intelligence. . . .

The view of cerebral action here adopted settles the long-vexed question between the Lockian and Kantian schools as to the sources of knowledge; and the verdict, while partly favourable to each of these schools, is not wholly favourable to either. . . .

The strength of Locke's position lay in the assertion that all knowledge is ultimately derived from experience,—that is, from the intercourse between the organism and the environment. The strength of Kant's position lay in the recognition of the fact that the brain has definite tendencies, even at birth. The Doctrine of Evolution harmonizes these two seemingly-opposite views, by showing us that in learning we are merely acquiring latent capacities of reproducing ideas.[17]

Fiske then proceeded to show how human dependence on the learning process created family life and a social environment and how in turn the social environment explains the subsequent evolution of intelligence and civilization.

It was the lengthening of infancy which ages ago gradually converted our forefathers from brute creatures into human creatures. It is babyhood that has made man what he is. The simple unaided operation of natural selection could never have resulted in the origination of the human race.

There is a period after birth when its character can be slightly modified by what happens to it after birth, that is, by its experience as an individual. It becomes educable. It is no longer necessary for each generation to be exactly like that which has preceded. A door is opened through which the capacity for progress can enter. . . .

At some remote epoch of the past—we cannot say just when or how—our half-human forefathers reached and passed this critical point, and forthwith their varied struggles began age after age to result in the preservation of bigger and better brains, while the rest of their bodies changed but little.

But this steady increase of intelligence, as our forefathers began to become human, carried with it a steady prolongation of infancy. As mental life became more complex and various, as the things to be learned kept ever multiplying, less and less could be done before birth, more and more must

[17] John Fiske, *Outlines of Cosmic Philosophy* (London, 1874), II, 154, 155, 160, 161.

be left to be done in the earlier years of life. So instead of being born with a few simple capacities thoroughly organized, man came at last to be born with the germs of many complex capacities which were reserved to be unfolded and enhanced or checked and stifled by the incidents of personal experience in each individual. In this simple yet wonderful way there has been provided for man a long period during which his mind is plastic and malleable, and the length of this period has increased with civilization until it now covers nearly one third of our lives. It is not that our inherited tendencies and aptitudes are not still the main thing. It is only that we have at last acquired great power to modify them by training, so that progress may go on with ever increasing sureness and rapidity.[18]

Among the American biologists there were several who took a speculative turn and expanded their researches into philosophies of evolution in general and into theories of the origin and development of the human mind in particular. Of these, Alexander Winchell was a pioneer; he had already worked out a general evolutionary philosophy on the basis of modern geology before Darwin's work appeared and was, therefore, prepared to extend it readily to biological evolution, whereas most of his colleagues were unprepared and adapted themselves reluctantly to the new ways of thinking. On the other hand, just because he was well-grounded in the old teleology, he failed to appreciate Darwin's departure from it. Winchell graduated from Wesleyan University in 1847 and became professor of geology and zoology at Syracuse University, where for several years he was also chancellor. He was thus in a position to preach evolutionary doctrine in the religious circles among whom it was least palatable, and hence he deserves to be regarded as doubly a pioneer. As a teacher he had an unusual gift of constructing out of geological evolution, paleontology, and human archaeology a romantic story which captivated the imaginations of his hearers. He also succeeded in telling the whole tale of evolution in terms of a Universal Intelligence and Will, so that the discovery of relentless law in nature came, not as a shock, but as evidence of God's intelligence in choosing an orderly method of creation from among "the infinite storehouse of possible plans under which the Supreme Power might have proceeded. . . . This great all-embracing,

---

[18] John Fiske, *Excursions of an Evolutionist* (Cambridge, 1902), Standard Library Edition, in *The Miscellaneous Writings of John Fiske*, VII, 280, 286, 287–88.

all-confronting, all-enduring fact inspires our souls with awe; it illuminates the dark realm of matter with the sunlight of a divine revelation; it moves our souls with a sentiment of humble and profound adoration." [19]

Winchell was aware of the fact that in conceiving evolution as he did, he was but continuing the teleology of Paley and the deists.[20] He thought he had sufficient scientific evidence to justify his belief that man is the culmination of the evolutionary process, on the ground that nature is evidently designed as a home for man [21] and that in human intelligence the mind of the infinite creator is finally revealed. As for man's body, it is the final biological creation, because

Man first and alone assumed a perpendicular attitude, and turned his countenance toward heaven, and talked with the Being who formed him. . . . It is evident no farther progress can be made in this direction. The elevation of the spinal axis has reached a mathematical limit; the consummation of organic exaltation is attained. These various considerations concur in justifying the assumption that the Author of Nature regards his work as completed.[22]

As for man's mind,

To seek knowledge is to aspire to reproduce the thoughts of the divine mind. So far as man thinks the divine thoughts, he possesses a faculty akin to the divine intelligence; so far he partakes of the divine nature; so far he comes into a sympathetic union with the Being whose existence is before all and beyond all. I believe, too, that all intelligences whether dwellers in an angelic realm or on other planets, whether inhabitants of our system or other systems, understand the truths of nature as we understand them. There is but one geometry; there is but one body of transcendental philoso-

---

[19] Alexander Winchell, *Walks and Talks in the Geological Field* (New York, 1886), p. 311.

[20] Alexander Winchell, *Sketches of Creation* (New York, 1870), p. vi.

[21] "How admirably the constitution of the Drift is suited to human wants! To us it looks as if it had been an intentional preparation for man. There are persons, however, who prefer to say it is not so; but man is here only because the situation is one which permits him to be here. But we are sure, at least, that a happy coördination exists between our necessities and our surroundings; and the constitution of things which brings enjoyment out of the coördination is a beneficent constitution."—Alexander Winchell, *Walks and Talks in the Geological Field*, p. 33.

[22] *Sketches of Creation*, pp. 378–79.

phy. In these we find the common thoughts and the common language of universal intelligence. In the unity of intelligence we find a bond of brotherhood and sympathy between the dwellers in distant worlds and between all and the Supreme Intelligence.

One common aspiration stirs every human soul—to accommodate itself to the Supreme Being whose existence it feels, or more explicitly understands, and whose authority it unhesitatingly recognizes. While this common religious nature expresses the unity of mankind, it has also a higher significance. The correlative of the religious consciousness is God. Man and his Creator, therefore, constitute one system—a complete system, the unity of which is expressed in a body of reciprocal relations between God and man.[23]

The Platonic foundation of Winchell's thought is evident even in his technical, scientific exposition of geological and biological evolution: he represented epochs and orders as "dominant ideas," [24] and he regarded "the history of life" as literally a "succession of ideas in the mind of God." He was most impressed by what he called "prophetic ideas" or those "facts which show the ideas of the far-off coming ages wandering in advance of their time among the creations of an existing world, like streaks of morning light."

It is as if the thoughts of the Creator were busied with the plans of the distant future, while his hands are occupied with the work of to-day. Thus were incorporated in the organisms of one age hints of the features which were to blossom and unfold in the dominant ideas of the following one. Thus grew into being those "prophetic types" which show that *One Intelligence* has ordered creation—an intelligence to which the past and the future are both present.[25]

It was the fact that "nature has always issued her bulletins" that made evolution an exciting inquiry for Winchell. He turned the familiar argument based on "vestiges" into an argument for prediction. He believed there could be no biological evolution beyond man (for reasons given above), but he looked ahead calmly to the "death of the

[23] *Walks and Talks in the Geological Field*, pp. 316–17.
[24] "Life has presented itself not so much in a series of sharply-restricted organic *forms*, rising or descending in regular order, as in a succession of *dominant ideas*, each in its own age expressing itself in more than one organic type. . . . The forms styled 'synthetic' or 'comprehensive' types may perhaps be generalized under the formula of *dominant ideas*."—*Sketches of Creation*, pp. 317–18.
[25] *Ibid.*, pp. 319–20.

solar system," of which there were many "prophetic ideas." After describing very graphically the termination of life, light, and heat, he exclaimed: "But there must be progress after the funeral of the sun." [26] Though no objective evidence of such progress can be found now, Winchell accepted as circumstantial evidence the widespread human belief in world-cycles. He cited some of the oriental faiths on this theme and then concluded that the Infinite Creator in all probability creates new cycles of evolution upon the "deaths" of the old. In this way he reconciled his evolutionary science with his "transcendental philosophy" and reconciled "the method of life" with "cycles of matter." Evolution itself is but a particular example of "the supreme law of free intelligence." [27]

Though Winchell regarded the order of nature and the freedom of intelligence as "one empire" and did not hesitate to speak of "the mind in matter," he took no interest in speculations regarding the evolution of mind in nature. Like many other theists of his time he was content to prove that matter is inert without mind or will, and having thus defended the faith in free agency, he felt free to accept the Darwinian (or any other reputable) theory of the evolution of man's "organism." He emphasized the "missing link" between man's ability to understand how he was created and the inability of other animals. Though he did not believe (like Mivart and other dualistic critics of Darwin) that the soul *must be* distinct and eternal, yet he failed to see the practical possibilities of an evolutionary psychology. In general, he was less interested in speculations concerning "specific creations" in evolution than in the principle of "the unity of organic history." He made a few careful, critical remarks in "the field of metaphysics," pointing out that evolution should not be regarded as a physical force, since it does not follow physical formulae, but as a pattern of "ideas," or creative energies. "The organism of the universe . . . is not eternal and demands a power superior to itself to originate and conserve it." [28] From this point of view he interpreted Darwinism, pointing out the improbability of many organisms *varying*

[26] *Ibid.*, p. 417.
[27] Alexander Winchell, *The Doctrine of Evolution* (New York, 1874), p. 9.
[28] *Ibid.*, p. 106. See his lectures *Theologico-Geology* (1857) and *Creation the Work of One Intelligence* (1858).

together in such a manner as to make Darwinian natural selection operative and arguing that natural selection itself must, therefore, have been designed. He also pointed out very clearly that natural selection is merely a "residual effect," not "an innate active impulse to deviation," [29] that it is a truism to assert that "the weakest go under," and that it is not the struggle itself but some other cause which makes animals fit to survive in the struggle.

Less picturesque than Winchell's philosophy, but no less influential in gaining a respectful hearing for the theory of evolution in Western pioneer society was the philosophy of creative evolution expounded by Joseph Le Conte. He was a graduate of the College of Physicians and Surgeons in New York City, a research student at Harvard under Agassiz and Gray, and then he made notable contributions to geology both in the field and in theoretical interpretation. He lived, taught, and explored in widely scattered regions of the North, the South, and the West, but his greatest influence was exerted at the University of California, where he taught from 1874 until his death, in 1901. Apart from his numerous discoveries in geology, he regarded his chief scientific contribution to have been his theory of the transmutation of forces, which he published in 1859 under the title "The Correlation of Physical, Chemical, and Vital Force." In philosophy he was an enthusiastic champion of the general theory of evolution. In his early days he defended Agassiz's theory of "development" against the new Darwinian theory of "evolution by derivation," but under the stimulus of his studies in continuity and transmutation he became an ardent preacher of the new evolution interpreted as a process of continuous creation by an immanent will in nature. Evolution, he exclaimed,

is, indeed, glad tidings of great joy which shall be to all peoples. Woe is me, if I preach not the Gospel. Literally, it can be shown that all the apparent irreligious and materialistic implications of science are reversed by this last child of science, or rather this daughter of the marriage of science and philosophy.[30]

He regarded evolution as not merely a plausible induction from the facts of geology and biology, but as an axiomatic principle of science,

---

[29] *The Doctrine of Evolution*, p. 49.
[30] Joseph Le Conte, *The Autobiography*; ed. by William Dallam Armes (New York, 1903), p. 336.

being the law of causation in time, as gravitation is the law of causation in space.

Evolution is *absolutely certain* . . . evolution as a law of derivation of forms from previous forms; evolution as a law of continuity, as a universal law of becoming. In this sense it is not only certain, it is axiomatic. . . . The nexus between *successive events in time* (causation) is far more certain than the nexus between *coexistent objects in space* (gravitation). The former *is a necessary truth*, the latter is usually classed as a contingent truth.[31]

Le Conte traced the "individuation" of energy from "gross matter" through life to "spirit" and self-consciousness. The individuation of life reaches its climax in man, and the individuation of spirit in "the Divine Person" of Christ. Seen in the light of this "universal design," all "separate design" arguments become needless, and all evil is seen to end in good.

In all departments of thought except science, forms of thought, whether embodied as a theory, a creed, or a political organization, are at first in some sense natural and enthusiastic embodiments, necessary for life and helpful to growth, then gradually become hardened into a shell which is at first protective and conservative, but finally obstructive and arrestive, and must therefore be broken and cast off, if necessary, with violence. Such forms in their early stage are embodiments of living, active, *effective* truth; in their second stage are protective, conservative, perhaps *useful* dogmas; in their third stage are dead and therefore *hurtful* dogmas—are dead bodies from which we must pray to be delivered. Those who regard these forms only in their early effectiveness—in their living time—are apt to conclude that they are necessary to human progress, and that all the evils of the present are due to throwing them off. Those, on the contrary, who look only on the dead shell, imagine them the cause of unmixed evil only, both now and at all times. Only the philosophic thinker perceives their essentially provisional character as the agents and conditions of growth, but not the final form of perfect reason.[32]

The complete individuation and separation of spirit from the general fund of divine energy pervading nature, is the essential characteristic of man . . . Separation from God. Alas! is this, then, it will be asked, the sum of our

[31] Joseph Le Conte, *Evolution; Its Nature, Its Evidences, and Its Relation to Religious Thought*, 2d ed., revised (New York, 1894), pp. 65–66.

[32] Joseph Le Conte, "Illustrations of a Law of Evolution of Thought," *Princeton Review*, LVIII (1881), 390.

philosophy? Yes, I answer: separation *physically*, but only in order to unite again with Him *morally*. Physical *bonds* are broken only that thereby higher moral, personal relations may be established. As by the nebular hypothesis the earth must break away from *cohesive* connection and become a separate planet before she can establish higher *gravitative* relations with the central sun and with other planets, and move with them in sweet accord, making spheral music; even so spirit must break away from cohesive physical connection with the divine energy and become a distinct self-conscious entity, before she can enter into higher moral relations with the central sun of righteousness or with other spirits, and move with them in the beauty of holiness, making far sweeter moral harmony. As in the physical cosmos the law of cohesion is replaced by the freer law of gravity, even so in the moral cosmos must the law of necessity be replaced by the free law of love. In both the former condition is a preparation for the latter.

But the upward tendency which runs through all nature does not stop with man. It is again taken up by man and carried forward in a higher sphere. As spirit in the womb of nature gradually grew to higher and higher conditions until it broke away and came to birth and freedom in man, so the spirit of man immediately enters into a new and higher embryonic condition, to reach by evolution a new spiritual birth and a higher moral freedom as *regenerated man*. As nature through all geological times struggled slowly upward to reach its final term, its goal, its *ideal*—in a word, to *finish its work* in man; so man immediately enters upon a new race to reach *his* goal and ideal—the *divine man*.[33]

Le Conte called this theory "evolutional idealism." Though his pupil, Josiah Royce, rejected many of its features and enthusiasms, it had a formative influence on Royce's own version of idealism.

Another biologist who overindulged in philosophy was the Pennsylvania Quaker, Edward Drinker Cope (1840–97). He was a paleontologist, professor at the University of Pennsylvania, an explorer in many Western scientific expeditions and a belated champion of Lamarckian theories in biology. As a scientist he repudiated a priori speculation and tried, as he said, to "separate truth from the metaphysics," but his speculations on "the origin of the fittest," which to him were genuinely scientific hypotheses, were to his fellow-biologists excursions into dubious inferences based on unverifiable assumptions.

[33] Joseph Le Conte, "Man's Place in Nature," *Princeton Review*, LIV (1878), 775–803.

He himself entitled his theory of "archaesthetism" (the hypothesis of a primeval mind or consciousness), as "metaphysical evolution," but he thought he had good evidence for it. To his mind it was the foundation of an evolutionary psychology as well as of a scientific theism. He thought it essential to the theory of evolution that the processes of organic development should be explained as the work of inner forces, rather than as merely the result of "natural selection" by the environment. He stated his case well.

It has seemed to the author so clear from the first as to require no demonstration, that natural selection includes no *actively* progressive principle whatsoever; that it must first wait for the development of variation, and then after securing the survival of the best, wait again for the best to project its own variations for selection. In the question as to whether the latter are any better or worse than the characters of the parent, natural selection in no wise concerns itself.[34]

Accordingly, Cope accounted for "the *origin* of the fittest" by assuming a unique type of energy, which he called "growth-force" or "bathmic" energy and which had the distinctive power of counteracting the normal dissipation of energy or entropy. This power, which is revealed by living cells when they divide and causes organisms to grow, he identified with consciousness, will, or mind. Mind thus appeared as primarily an adapting mechanism, enabling the organism through conscious effort to develop habits useful to its survival.

The lowest forms of life show evidences of the possession of sensation and memory, and thus have the possibility of the development of mind. The result of the possession of sensation and memory is the capacity for forming a simple judgment.[35]

Sensation, even in its lowest form, is something more than the operation of a merely mechanical energy. It is not analogous, as some have affirmed, to chemical reaction. The tendency of energy in the inorganic world is to dissipate. Sensation is profitable to its possessors in enabling them to resist this tendency. The dead products of conscious action are profitable.[36]

When we enter the realm of consciousness we are in a universe which is in some respects not subject to the scales and the measure of the materialist.

[34] Edward Drinker Cope, *The Origin of the Fittest* (New York, 1887), p. 175.
[35] Edward Drinker Cope, *The Descent of Man*, in *Evolution*; popular lectures and discussions before the Brooklyn Ethical Association (Boston, 1889), pp. 166–67.
[36] *Ibid.*, p. 167.

No doubt every act of consciousness requires for its performance the expenditure of energy, but there are some of the functions of mind which are not correlated with the amount of energy expended in producing them, so far as relates to their mental quality. Of all mental acts this is especially true of the formation of a judgment as the result of a consideration of inducements, or reasons, or the mutual pressure of motives. No matter whether the judgment be free or not, the consideration of, the estimation of, and surrender to, reasons, is a process outside the pale of the scales of the physicist or physiologist. This is the most important fact known to man. It shows that although his mind is bound to its material basis, it controls that basis, within limits, by purely mental processes, which are *per se* entirely free from the trammels of matter, although they may not be free from the laws of mental action.[37]

Moral will power then represents the highest attribute of mind, whether greater or lesser, and we must suppose that it has, like other mental functions, a correspondingly peculiar molecular basis. And it must be the creator of this basis under the general law of the limited control of mind over physical energy. It seems eminently reasonable that the development of will in man should eventuate in the production of a type of energy similar in kind to that which expresses will in Deity, and that it should be persistent in the one case as it is in the other.[38]

Cope developed this theory not only as a natural theology, but also as a theme for the interpretation of the history or "evolution" of morals.

The organized moral qualities can not normally transcend in power, as motives of human action, those which secure man's physical preservation. Lines of men in whom the sympathetic and generous qualities predominate over the self-preservative, must inevitably become extinct. Evolution can produce no higher development of the race (whatever may sometimes appear in individuals) than an equivalency in these two classes of forces. Beyond this the organization of the social faculties of the brain must always be repressed in the race, so that we can only expect to attain an equilibrium between them and the more purely selfish ones, as the very highest result of unassisted evolution. In this position the judgment is suspended between the opposing classes of motives; and it must ever remain doubtful in general as to whether resulting action will be just and right or the reverse. . . . So it

[37] *Ibid.*, p. 168.
[38] Edward Drinker Cope, reply to Montgomery's review of his *Theology of Evolution*, in *Open Court* (1887–88), I, 360.

would appear that no organized faculty of *self-sufficient altruistic justice* can be derived by the process of mental evolution. The result is rather a continued struggle between justice and injustice.[39]

The direction of action under stimulus is determined by intelligence, which is, as has been above maintained, the product of experience. Intelligence is organized or classified knowledge, and directs the activities set on foot by the likes and dislikes, that is, the affections. *When there is knowledge, there is no need for spontaneous action or free will*, since action is determined by the organization of the mind. Even if the mind is conscious of insufficient knowledge, an inducement to seek knowledge is supplied, and according to the result of investigation will be the direction of knowledge.

But we are here brought to face the case where knowledge can not be or is not obtained. This is the condition of the two questions of the practice of morals, and the nature of the future life. The evolution of mind consists of a continual advance from the known into the unknown, and a transfer of the unknown into the known. So long as there is any inducement to progress of this kind, and nature responds to inquiry, development will go on.[40]

Here is sketched in bold strokes a version of the genetic theory of intelligence which was to play so important a role in subsequent American philosophy. Cope was hard pressed to defend this theory of the adaptive power of consciousness against the prevailing belief in psycho-physical parallelism,[41] and in his defense he showed that he was fully aware of the importance for both moral philosophy and psychology of his views. Like William James, he saw in them a basis for faith in panpsychism and in freedom, but he was most concerned to exhibit them as a functional interpretation of consciousness. Unfortunately, he was caught in the Lamarck-Weissmann dispute over the inheritance of acquired characteristics, and thus gave the impression that his theory of consciousness was bound to stand or fall with Lamarckian biology. Unfortunately, too, he added to his functional theory of consciousness, a speculation (admittedly unverifiable) suggesting the existence of a "general mind" or unspecialized consciousness antecedent to the particular minds in organisms. This theistic doctrine was based on the Spencerian faith in evolution from the homogeneous to the hetero-

[39] Edward Drinker Cope, *The Origin of the Fittest*, pp. 237–38.
[40] *Ibid.*, p. 239.
[41] Versus Montgomery, below.

geneous and consequently found little favor either among the religious or among the scientific. He likewise adopted Spencer's suggestion that the instinct of hunger is basic to the development of intelligence, and the instinct of sex basic to social and moral relations. This thesis led him to write uncritically on woman suffrage, on the effect of psychological sex differences, on government, and on other highly speculative applications of pseudo-biology.

Though he was not intellectually an American, Edmund Montgomery (1835–1911) should be mentioned among the philosophical biologists whose works contributed to the debate on evolution, for he may well become more influential in the future than he has been to date. The story of his romantic life need not be told here, since it has been made public recently.[42] Suffice it to say that he was a physician, born in Scotland, educated in Germany, an enthusiastic 1848 Liberal, who emigrated (with his wife, the sculptress Elizabeth Ney) to Texas in 1870. In America he lived the life of a hermit-scientist, but published voluminously both philosophical essays and scientific experiments on protoplasm. His researches on man's "living substance" and his criticism of the theories of living cells were soon antiquated, but the philosophical conclusions which he drew were prophetic of growing tendencies in modern philosophy and deserve to be read both for their literary vigor and their ingenious contribution to epistemology and emergent evolutionism. His discussion with E. D. Cope in *The Monist* is particularly brilliant.

In Munich he wrote and later (1871) published *Die Kant'sche Erkenntnisslehre widerlegt vom Standpunkt der Empirie—Ein vorbereitender Beitrag zur Begründung einer physiologischen Naturauffassung.* Here he attacked the idealistic theory of perception thoroughly and, like Peirce and Abbot, constructed on the basis of this critique a realistic, vitalistic, empiricism which he called "naturalism" and confidently expected to grow with the biological sciences until it had displaced both idealism and materialism (mechanism). He thought that the peculiar properties of protoplasm (man's "sub-

---

[42] I. M. Stephens, "Edmund Montgomery, the Hermit Philosopher of Liendo Plantation," *Southwest Review*, XVI (1931), 200–35. An interesting article by Morris T. Keeton, "Montgomery—Pioneer of Organicism," is to appear shortly in the *Journal of the History of Ideas.*

stantiality") explained, how out of the unconscious, lifeless energies of matter, man became equipped with a body of conscious experience ("the perceptual organism"), which was a product of blind forces and yet had a light-like quality of illuminating or "revealing" the forces that gave it birth. The content of consciousness is to be interpreted, not as a self-contained, self-referring reality, but as an organic system of "all-revealing signs." As a naturalist he assumed that "only an evolutionally developed pre-established harmony can here render the definite percept arising within the percipient strictly and minutely representative of the corresponding perceptible entity subsisting outside the percipient's being." [43] His chief argument for believing in the organic unity of perception-and-perceived came, not from his biological evolutionism, but from his empirical critique of Kantian epistemology. Nevertheless, he interpreted the growth of consciousness as a culmination of the evolutionary process, transforming the universe from "the silence of the mutely toiling spheres" into a "sense-revealed universe," "becalmed," and radiant with "beauty and appraised worth." [44] Quality is added to quantity.

Nature, artificially unaided, has at every step of her developmental changes introduced new formations into the causative nexus, which have essentially modified pure mechanical necessity in qualitatively incalculable ways.[45]

The world as actually perceived by us is a phenomenon arising in each of us as individual awareness; with this most enlightening recognition, the question of mechanical necessity and qualitative development discloses itself as far more profoundly complicated than has as yet been indicated . . . The world we perceive and apprehend, with all its qualitative and quantitative appearances, becomes therewith ideally transfigured.[46]

The immediate objects of physical research, as actually present in consciousness, are as such perceptual signs of definite modes of activity inferred as occurring in and among extra-conscious existents. These conscious signs of extra-conscious activities, consisting of perceived or conceived modes of motion, are themselves forming part of definite percepts occupying visual space. It is with the visibly revealed characteristics of extra-conscious existents that physical science mainly occupies itself.[47]

[43] Edmund Montgomery, *Philosophical Problems in the Light of Vital Organization* (New York, 1907), p. 137.

[44] *Ibid.*, p. 445.　　[45] *Ibid.*, p. 302.　　[46] *Ibid.*, p. 303.　　[47] *Ibid.*, p. 304.

Physical science as at present constituted can, therefore, not be accepted as an adequate interpretation of the perceptible world. Nor does its alleged unbroken necessity and equivalence of occurrences, as figured out in an endless chain of mere mechanical causation, hold good at any stage of the developmental process in real creative, extra-conscious nature, to which all perceptible things, we ourselves included, owe their gradual elaboration and present existence.

Qualitative developmental elaboration of extra-conscious, interdependent, and interacting power-endowed existents is the essential fact to be recognized in perceptible nature, not interpretable as the mere necessary and causatively equivalent concatenation of mechanically moved inert masses.[48]

Montgomery was clearly one of the most erudite and enthusiastic members of a group of biologists, each apparently working independently, who laid the foundations of emergent, organic evolutionism and of empirical naturalism. Like Peirce, he called attention to the operation of spontaneity or unpredictable behavior in living cells, and, like Abbot, he recognized the difference between organic and mechanistic methods of interpreting living beings and natural processes. But quite apart from their contributions to evolutionary theory, Peirce, Abbot, and Montgomery jointly deserve study and recognition for their effective critiques of Kantian psychology and for thus making the beginnings of the distinctive realistic theory of knowledge which has come to flourish in America.

— 32 —

EVOLUTIONARY THEOLOGY

DURING the early part of the nineteenth century the theologians had been kept busy trying to interpret the religious significance of the discoveries of geology. These discoveries were at first attacked as speculative adventures by impious imaginations, but as the concrete verifications kept pouring in and when Sir Charles Lyell finally crowned the science with the philosophical principle of uniformitarianism, doubt vanished, and the only question that remained was one of

[48] *Ibid.*, pp. 307–8.

adapting the Biblical version to the truth as revealed by science. Two theologically gifted geologists led the way in adapting the Biblical story of creation to the evolutionary story of geological epochs. One of these, Alexander Winchell, has already been described as a speculative biologist. The other was Edward Hitchcock, pupil of Benjamin Silliman at Yale, who in 1825 became professor of natural history and chemistry at Amherst, and from 1845 to 1854 was president of that college. In *The Religion of Geology* (1851) he produced an influential pioneer work of theological reconstruction and paved the way for the general acceptance of his thesis that "the exclusive object of revelation is of a moral character." [1] His genial sophistication was remarkably effective in reconciling theists to the general idea of evolution. The best illustration of his rhetorical method as well as of his theological views is his address before the Porter Rhetorical Society of the Andover Theological Seminary (1852) on "The Relations and Mutual Duties between the Philosopher and the Theologian." He spoke as follows:

True science employs terms that are precise, definite, literal, with scarcely more than one meaning, and adapted only to cultivated minds. Religion, especially the Bible, makes use of language that is indefinite, loose, and multiform in signification, often highly figurative, and adapted, not only to the popular mind, but to men in an early and rude state of society. Science, for instance, could not, as the Bible can and does, represent the work of creation in one chapter as occupying six days, and in the next chapter as completed in one day. It could not, like the Bible, speak of the sun's rising and setting, and of the earth's immobility. Meteorology could not describe the concave above our heads as a solid expanse, having windows or openings for the rain to pass from the clouds beyond. Nor could physiology represent the bones to be the seat of pain, or psychology refer intellectual operations to the region of the kidneys. Neither could systematic theology in one place represent God as having repented that he had made man, and in another exhibit him as without variableness or shadow of turning. But all this can the Bible do in perfect consistency with its infallible inspiration, because it was the language of common life; and common sense can interpret it, so that every suspicion of self-contradiction shall vanish. Indeed, had its language been strictly scientific, it might have formed a good text book in philosophy, but it would have been a poor guide to salvation. . . .

We should not conclude that Job meant to reveal the Copernican

[1] Edward Hitchcock, *The Religion of Geology* (Boston, 1851), p. 3.

system because he speaks of the earth as hanging upon nothing; especially as in another place he refers to the pillars on which the earth rests. But both phrases are quite natural and proper for one of the most allegorical books of the Bible when regarded as vivid poetical images. The grand distinction between the Bible and all other professed revelations is, not that it has anticipated scientific discoveries, but that there is nothing in its statements which those discoveries contradict or invalidate. . . .

A scientific man, desirous of extending his discoveries into the domain of religion, ventures upon interpretations of Scripture, or statements of doctrine, that show him quite ignorant of both. The practised theologian points out the fallacy of his reasoning so clearly as to wound his pride. But, instead of generously confessing his error, he resorts to charges of bigotry, narrowmindedness, and ignorance of science, and dogmatically maintains that science is to be followed, whatever becomes of revelation. He shows towards it and its defenders the same bitter, bigoted spirit which he censures in his opponents. . . . The most illiberal of all bigots are those who fancy themselves the very pinks of liberality; and pride never assumes such lofty airs as when it curls the lip of the self-satisfied philosopher who is destitute of Christian humility. . . . Christianity stands on too firm and broad a base to be overturned by one or a hundred such blows as have hitherto been aimed against it. The true policy is to wait for a time, to see whether we fully understand the new views, and whether they conflict with the letter or the spirit of revelation. Suppose the theologian should take ground which he is compelled afterwards to abandon, and to fall in with the new discovery. With how bad a grace will he come over to the new ground after severely denouncing as infidels those who accepted it! How likely to lose the public respect, and to make sceptics of those who were before only indifferent! How mortifying must it have been to the theologians who, one hundred and fifty years ago, denounced astronomy, to see its discoveries at length introduced into the almanac, and testifying of their bigotry to all classes! . . .

Suppose it should appear that the laws of distribution in the species and varieties of the lower animals, which is the grand argument for proving a diversity of origin in the case of man, should be found greatly modified in respect to him, by his cosmopolite character and ability, through superior mental endowments, to adapt himself to different circumstances. Suppose we should find examples of varieties of men, who have passed from the highest to the lowest races, save in color, through the influence of deteriorating causes long acting. Suppose it should appear that ethnology and psychology are entitled to as much weight in their testimony on this subject as zoölogy, and that they should pronounce in favor of a unity of origin.

Suppose it should be found that many other elements of this most difficult subject are yet not well enough understood to reason from, and demand long and patient investigation. Or make the most unfavorable supposition, viz., that the preponderance of evidence favors the idea of a diversity of origin. Is it quite certain that we must give up the Bible, or its more important doctrines? Would the discrepancy appear so great as it did when the Copernican system was first announced? Shame on us, that we feel so fearful in respect to God's Word, and those eternal truths that form the groundwork of the scheme of salvation! Right is it that we should address ourselves manfully to every argument that bears upon revelation; but how unwise, when it is wholly unnecessary, to take ground which we may be compelled with a bad grace to relinquish! [2]

The worry over geology had scarcely subsided when, as the passage quoted from Hitchcock suggests, a new and worse conflict appeared over the question of human origins. The secular issues raised have already been described; it remains to give some account of the spontaneous variations among theologians in their desperate efforts to adapt themselves to the new scientific climate created by Darwin, Huxley, and Spencer and by their American disciples, John Fiske, Chauncey Wright, E. Youmans, John W. Draper, and Andrew D. White.

The courageous thing to do was to defy evolutionary theory on the ground that it was not genuine science, but merely the old design argument weakened by the omission of a designer. True science, they thought, could not possibly conflict with true theology, because it would not meddle with teleology. This was the strategy of several leading controversialists, Orestes Augustus Brownson, the radical and independent Catholic, Charles Hodge of Princeton University, author of *What Is Darwinism?* (1874), Professor Enoch F. Burr of Amherst College, author of *Pater Mundi* (1873), and Professor Andrew P. Peabody of Harvard University, author of *Christianity and Science* (1874). Peabody was especially explicit in pointing out that he felt free to question the truth of evolution precisely because evolution is a speculative theory and not science. This position became increasingly difficult to maintain as scientists increasingly embraced the evolutionary view. At least one theologian, the president of Columbia College,

[2] Edward Hitchcock, *Religious Truth, Illustrated from Science* (Boston, 1857), pp. 65–66, 66–67, 80, 90–91, 92–93.

who had tried stubbornly to maintain it, was forced to the ignominious and truculent attitude:

Much as I love truth in the abstract, I love my hope of immortality more. . . . If this, after all, is the best that science can give me, give me, then, I pray, no more science. Let me live on in my simple ignorance, as my fathers lived before me; and when I shall at length be summoned to my final repose, let me still be able to fold the drapery of my couch about me and lie down to pleasant, even though they be deceitful, dreams.[3]

What made this position doubly uncomfortable was that some of the scientists were ready to make peace on these easy terms, since they regarded theology as harmless because useless. John Fiske, for example, like Darwin himself, admitted freely:

The consistent theist will always occupy an impregnable position in maintaining that the entire series in each and every one of its incidents is an immediate manifestation of the creative action of God. . . . To say that complex organisms were directly created by the Deity is to make an assertion which, however true in a theistic sense, is utterly barren.[4]

The more intelligent theologians, unwilling to be "utterly barren," followed the pattern outlined by the geologists Winchell and Hitchcock, announcing frankly their belief in evolution and admitting that the Bible should not be regarded as a scientific text. The Reverend James Woodrow, for example, uncle of Woodrow Wilson, president and professor of natural science of the University of South Carolina, took this position. In 1884 he delivered a notable address [5] to the Alumni Association of the Presbyterian Theological Seminary, at Columbia, South Carolina, where he held the chair of "Perkins Professor of Natural Science in connexion with Revelation." He made an eloquent and clear exposition of his view that the Bible was "almost certainly" not intended to teach science and admitted his belief in evolution as "mediate creation." As a consequence of this address he was promptly dismissed from the faculty of the seminary.

There was, however, a more positive task for evolutionary theologians to perform in addition to the mere recognition of scientific

[3] F. A. P. Barnard, "The Law of Disease," *College Courant*, XIV, 27.
[4] John Fiske, *Darwinism and Other Essays* (Boston, 1885), pp. 7–8.
[5] See Blau, ed., *American Philosophic Addresses, 1700–1900*, pp. 488–513.

truth on its own authority: the evolutionary point of view had to be presented as a new version of a traditional faith, as itself the substance of the Christian gospel. There arose two chief types of evolutionary theology in America: one was inspired chiefly by Darwin and found its stronghold among the Presbyterians; the other was inspired chiefly by Spencer and found its stronghold among the Unitarians; the one gave a supernatural sanction to the struggle for existence, the other preached the optimistic faith in "the evanescence of evil."

One of the first theological expounders and adapters of Darwinism in America was James McCosh of Princeton. Before coming to America, as early as 1850, he had written *The Method of the Divine Government*, a work that enjoyed great popularity in Scotland as well as here, going through ten editions. In it he had argued that God has an infinite treasury of spontaneous variations which he introduces into the normal course of events, and which makes his government a combination of law and of "special providences," or "adaptations," as McCosh called them. He also pointed out how this government by apparently accidental and practically "invisible" variations adds a temporal dimension to Leibniz's version of the perfect chain of being. He criticized Leibniz, Comte, Spencer, and the natural theology of the Enlightenment in general for believing that there is only a general providence or law of progress in the world. He reasserted the Calvinist faith in special providences, in spontaneous or unpredictable acts of God whereby some are elected and others rejected, and restated the argument from design, which was the commonplace of natural theology, to include the gradual achievement of fitness or adaptation in nature by means of numerous "accidental" interferences with the normal course of events. In other words, he located God's design or "method," not in the immediate fitness of organs or mechanisms to perform their functions, but in the general plan by which fitness was achieved through what appears on the surface to be arbitrary selection. When Darwin's *Origin of Species* appeared, in 1859, he saw almost at once that his theory of "Divine government" could be identified with the doctrine of natural selection. Why not interpret the variations which Darwin called spontaneous, chance, or accidental differences, and for which he did not pretend to give an explanation, as supernatural choices of an intervening Designer? Natural selection and divine election amounted to the same thing in practice, or, to quote McCosh: "Supernatural design produces natural selection." [6]

McCosh used this Calvinistic version of Darwinism very effectively to criticize the uniformitarianism and mechanism of Spencer and the positivists. He also emphasized struggle as a basic factor in the divine economy, contrasting the tragic aspects of Calvinism and Darwinism with the superficial optimism of the Spencerians. Those who survive in the "moral struggle" of history are not the heroes of physical power or of intelligence, but those who have "moral power."

Of all acts of cowardice, the meanest is that which leads us to abandon a good cause because it is weak, and join a bad cause because it is strong. . . . I thank the great God that I have always been kept from the prevalent form of idolatry . . . which worshipped the rising sun. . . . We have to see to it that, in the struggle of life, we stand by right, and not by might, being sure that in the end the right shall have might. . . .

It may still be that the strongest, the fittest, are to prevail; but it is becoming evident that the strongest and the fittest are not physical, or even intellectual strength, but the moral forces supported by the righteous God. But all this is to be accomplished and manifested by a struggle. "The whole creation groaneth and travaileth in pain together until now." Our academic theists were refusing to look at our world under this aspect. Even some of our sentimental Christians were turning away from it. It is a curious circumstance that it is science that has recalled our attention to it.

Our Cosmos has been formed in ages past out of warring elements; and

[6] James McCosh, *The Religious Aspect of Evolution* (New York, 1888), p. 7. In this connection he quoted with approval from Isaac Taylor's *Natural History of Enthusiasm*: "Those unforeseen accidents which so often control the lot of men, constitute a superstratum in the system of human affairs, wherein peculiarly the Divine providence holds empire for the accomplishment of its special purposes. It is from this hidden and inexhaustible mine of chances, as we must call them, that the Governor of the world draws, with unfathomable skill, the materials of his dispensations towards each individual of mankind." James McCosh, *The Method of the Divine Government Physical and Moral* (London, 1874), p. 164. McCosh continues with the following comment: "If, in contemplating the general order that pervades the world, we seemed to fall in with beautiful figures rectilinear and circular, we feel now, in dealing with these fortuities, that we are ascending to curves of a higher order, and figures of greater complexity; or rather as if we had got an infinitesimal calculus, in which every one thing is infinitely small, but in which the infinite units produce magnitudes and forces infinitely great. The curves . . . form, an instrument unequalled at once for its potency and its pliability, its wide extended range, and the certainty with which it hits the point at which it aims." *Ibid.*

we seem to see at this present time broken-up worlds, the debris of dread catastrophes. There is evidence that suffering and death have been in our earth since sentient life appeared, and reigning over those "who had not sinned after the similitude of Adam's transgression." The struggle in the pre-Adamite ages is an anticipation, perhaps a prefiguration, of the more terrible struggle in the post-Adamite period. In the time now present, history and travel disclose ignorance and misery spread over the earth, with destructive wars breaking forth ever and anon even in the most enlightened nations. And if you ask science what it can do to remove the evils, it tells you that, . . . while it may so far restrain, it cannot subdue the disease which lies deep down in the depths of the human heart. . . . We see the battle raging all around us in this city and in every city, in every dwelling and in every heart. Christianity thus appears in our world in analogy and in accordance with all that has gone before—a new power to contend with evil, and overcome it. The history of our world is thus a unity from the commencement to the present time.[7]

While McCosh was making Darwinian theology at Princeton, Asa Gray was doing a similar work at Harvard. Though he was a botanist by profession, not a theologian, he professed to be an orthodox Christian. He represented himself as "philosophically a convinced theist, and religiously an acceptor of the 'creed commonly called the Nicene,' as the exponent of the Christian faith."[8] I quote a few passages from his Yale Divinity School Lectures of 1880, entitled *Natural Science and Religion.*

Views like these of Darwin's when formulated by religious instead of scientific thought, make more of Divine providence and fore-ordination than of Divine intervention; but perhaps they are not the less theistical on that account. Nor are they incompatible with "special creative act," unless natural process generally is incompatible with it,—which no theist can allow. No Christian theist can eliminate the idea of Divine intervention any more than he can that of Divine ordination; neither, on the other hand, can he agree that what science removes from the supernatural to the natural is lost to theism. But, the business of science is with the course of Nature, not

[7] James McCosh, *Christianity and Positivism; a Series of Lectures to the Times on Natural Theology and Apologetics* (New York, 1871), pp. 62, 70, 72, 339–41. There is a considerable literature among theologians on "The Pre-Adamites." See Alexander Winchell, *Preadamites* (Chicago, 1880), for suggestive references.

[8] George Frederick Wright, "The Debt of the Church to Asa Gray," *Bibliotheca Sacra*, XLV (1888), 523, quoting Gray's *Darwiniana* (1876), p. vi.

with interruptions of it, which must rest on their own special evidence. Still more, it is the business of science to question searchingly all seeming interruptions of it, and its privilege, to refer events and phenomena not at the first but in the last resort to Divine will.

View these high matters as you will, the outcome, as concerns us, of the vast and partly comprehensible system, which under one aspect we call Nature, and under another Providence, and in part under another, Creation, is seen in the emergence of a free and self-determining personality.

I accept Christianity on its own evidence, which I am not here to specify or to justify; and I am yet to learn how physical or any other science conflicts with it any more than it conflicts with simple theism. I take it that religion is based on the idea of a Divine Mind revealing himself to intelligent creatures for moral ends. We shall perhaps agree that the revelation on which our religion is based is an example of evolution; that it has been developed by degrees and in stages, much of it in connection with second causes and human actions; and that the current of revelation has been mingled with the course of events.[9]

No theory of evolution can be entertained which implies impassable limitations on God's spontaneity in manifesting himself to our most deeply implanted wants.[10]

The chief difference between McCosh's and Gray's versions of Darwinism is that Gray emphasized a general providence and McCosh the special providences. Gray was more critical of the design argument and defended the doctrine of providence on the ground that "teleology is equally difficult" in theology and in evolution, but that "without the implication of a superintending wisdom, nothing is made out and nothing credible." [11] Gray is careful to explain that he does not believe in "creation *from* all time," which leads to deism and fatalism, or in "creation *through* all time," which leads to the idealist belief in an immanent Deity, but in a creator who "now and then, and only now and then . . . puts his hand directly to the work," and thus creates *in* time.[12]

Dr. George Frederick Wright, Professor of the Harmony of Science and Revelation at Oberlin College, was the most outspoken defender

[9] Asa Gray, *Natural Science and Religion* (New York, 1880), pp. 77, 102–3, 106–7.
[10] Wright, *op. cit.*, p. 528.
[11] *Ibid.*, p. 525, quoting Gray's *Darwiniana*.
[12] *Ibid.*, p. 527, quoting Gray's *Darwiniana*, p. 158.

of the thesis that Darwinism is "the Calvinistic interpretation of nature." [13] If Calvinism is a foe to sentimentalism in theology, so is Darwinism in natural history. Wright regarded both as realistic, distrusting the reign of law and speculative reason, and as critical of the argument from fitness to design. "Fitness" and "design" must be sought in the system as a whole, not in "immediate uses." Darwin, he maintained, restored a true doctrine of design and "rescued natural history from the depressing influence of empiricism and positivism." [14] Darwin proved that particular waste in nature is not wasteful in general. More specifically, Wright regarded Darwin's account of the origin of man's body as analogous to the "traducian theory" among the Calvinists, which accounted for the origin of an individual soul by tracing it back to Adam's soul, from which it inherits original sin. In opposition to Spencer, he argued against an individualistic outcome of evolution. "Through the action of natural selection in the human race, the social and political organism is likely to be developed at the expense of the individual. The individual, as a social force, is already becoming a mere rudiment. He is in danger of becoming an organ rather than a being." [15] He gives us a grim picture of the struggle for existence and concludes his account with the observation: "Race has warred on race, and individual has been brought into sharp competition with his fellow. The mystery is that the higher forms of life have been preserved at all. The hand of Providence certainly is not dispensed with, but rather called for, by this theory." [16]

These illustrations must suffice for the present to substantiate my generalization that Darwinism was used by the Calvinists to support the ideas of supernatural selection and design, revelation, transcendent deity, moral struggle, and social conflict.

[13] George Frederick Wright, "Some Analogies between Calvinism and Darwinism," *Bibliotheca Sacra*, XXXVII (1880), 76. A similar work was being carried on at Princeton by Charles Woodruff Shields, Professor of the Harmony of Science and Revealed Religion, and author of *The Final Philosophy* (New York, 1877). But Shields made no use of the concept of evolution in general, confining his critique to the special technical controversies in current science.

[14] George Frederick Wright, *Scientific Aspects of Christian Evidences* (New York, 1898), p. 110.

[15] George Frederick Wright, in *Bibliotheca Sacra*, XXXVII (1880), 56–57.

[16] Wright, *Scientific Aspects of Christian Evidences*, p. 103.

A very different version of theological evolutionism arose among the Unitarians, an optimistic doctrine stressing progressive salvation through immanent design, evolutionary love, a faith in the natural growth of intelligence, virtue, and peace. The Darwinian theologies were theocentric; these liberalistic versions were humanistic.

Even in these liberal circles Spencer's philosophy was, of course, criticized and condemned as too materialistic and agnostic. But it was nevertheless taken seriously, and in the modified form preached by Fiske, the Spencerian conception of evolution was readily detached from his materialism, hedonism, and agnosticism and was adapted to liberal theology and to the transcendentalist heritage.

One of the first wholehearted preachers of this type of evolution was Minot J. Savage (1841–1918), Unitarian minister in Boston and New York, who in 1876 published *The Religion of Evolution*. Savage did not interpret natural selection as *laissez faire,* and he pointed out that "human selection" is also natural; however, he did present the natural progress of evolution as an alternative to "proposed 'short-cuts' " "that lead to nowhere in particular." [17] Among the short-cuts criticized by him from this evolutionary point of view are communism, the single tax, Tolstoy's ideal country, industrial co-operation, state socialism, or nationalism, and any schemes that attempt to build perfect cities of "imperfect bricks."

James Thompson Bixby (1843–1921),[18] another example of this type of evolutionary theologian, devoted the first part of his lectures entitled *The Crisis in Morals* to a critique of Spencer's ethics. In criticizing Spencer Bixby expresses his admiration for him as the chief exponent of evolution and regards him as "in the forefront of our intellectual leaders." The second part of his work is a "positive reconstruction" in which he tries to prove that

[17] Minot J. Savage, "The Effects of Evolution on the Coming Civilization," in *Evolution;* popular lectures and discussions before the Brooklyn Ethical Association (Boston, 1889), p. 376.

[18] James T. Bixby, with an A.B. and a B.D. from Harvard, was professor of religious philosophy at Meadville Theological School and for twelve years chairman of the Liberal Ministers' Association. In addition to numerous articles in the *Unitarian Review* and the *Andover Review,* he published in 1891 a book entitled *The Crisis in Morals,* a second edition of which appeared in 1900 under the title *The Ethics of Evolution.*

a consistent scheme of evolution, as it traces back the line of conscious life, does not bring thought face to face with abrupt gaps, nor needs to resort to magical transformations, but it finds the development which it traces, proceeding from appropriate germs and principles in a moral universe, and aiming at a higher and more definite goal than that of mundane happiness. The doctrine of evolution, therefore, does not weaken, but fortifies, the natural and rational sanctions of ethics.[19]

Charles Fletcher Dole (1845–1927), a graduate of Harvard and of Andover Seminary, was theologically very close to Bixby, but politically more radical.

The most scholarly writer of this group was Francis Howe Johnson, for years a Congregational minister at Andover, Massachusetts, and a prominent contributor to the *Andover Review*. His book, *What Is Reality? An Inquiry as to the Reasonableness of Natural Religion and the Naturalness of Revealed Religion* (Boston, 1891), is one of the most philosophical expressions of liberal theological evolutionism in New England. His work was enriched by its author's familiarity with the philosophies of Hermann Lotze, J. B. Stallo, and Andrew Seth, in addition to the usual evolutionist literature, and with the psychology of William James.

Johnson, though a theist, is quite ready to identify his God with a "stream of tendency," to regard Him as immanent in nature and as "limited by both his ends and his means." It is demonstrated by evolutionary science, so Johnson argues, that though the Creative Intelligence of the world may intervene occasionally in the manner called by the Darwinians "natural selection," a method which Johnson thinks would better be labeled "unintelligent repression," He operates increasingly through conscious intelligence as it is found in man. Johnson criticizes and minimizes the idea of unconscious intelligence, as a contradiction in terms, and emphasizes Cope's doctrine that even the instinctive and automatic mechanisms in animals, by which they are adapted to their environments, are the vestiges of an original intelligent or conscious adaptation. Similarly he assumes, following the arguments of some of the German romanticists, that the adaptive qualities of protoplasm are not purely physical but are accompanied by "atomic consciousness." And as for the struggle for existence among

[19] James T. Bixby, *The Ethics of Evolution* (Boston, 1900), pp. 3–4.

animals, he gives evidence to prove that, though it undoubtedly oper- ates as Darwin claims, it is only one of God's means, and that many animals, notably the ants, manage to survive by mutual aid rather than through struggle. In man, the greater utility of co-operation and of conscious intelligence is, he thinks, indisputable and gives adequate support for an optimistic evolution and theology.

It has seemed to some that if, notwithstanding these antagonisms, we persist in assuming an intelligent Creator, we are forced to think of him as one who amuses himself, one who delights in the spectacle of an infinitely varied conflict,—a conflict which tests and develops all the skill and energies of his curiously fashioned gladiators. Does not the care that protects and continues all these conflicting orders resemble the care that such a being would take to insure the vigor of the instruments of his pleasure? And, further, does not the progressive aspect of creation suggest just that craving for variety and novelty in entertainment which would characterize such a mind? Does not the history of mankind, ever fighting and destroying one another for ideals that are never realized, frenzied by enthusiasms that are anon seen to be the outcome of illusions, harmonize altogether with such a conception?

The imaginations of our Teutonic and Scandinavian ancestors were so impressed by these facts that they constructed for themselves a religion of which warfare was the central idea. Odin, the creator and sustainer of every kind of life, the being who pervades the universe, working in and through all animate and inanimate things, is above all else the god of battle. . . .

Odin is not the god whom we worship. We have not, indeed, ceased to admire bravery or, when our attention is turned to it, to recognize the dis- ciplinary advantages of conflict. But a new vision of good has supplanted the old one. Our God is "the God of peace and love." His heroes are those who forgive their enemies, who do good unto all men as they have op- portunity, who live lives of gentleness and self-effacement. His kingdom is a kingdom of peace. The ideal society toward which he is leading his creatures is one from which violence and all forms of oppression have been forever banished by love and mutual helpfulness.

Now the question for our natural theology to answer is this,—Does the Scandinavian or the Christian ideal find the strongest endorsement in na- ture?

The Lord our God is not only a great God, He is beyond all peradventure a *good* God. As judged by his works, He desires and labors for that which men call goodness. The ideals that man is striving to realize are *his* ideals; and the efforts that we make in the direction of goodness are not altogether ours, they are God working in us, for the bringing about of the great end toward which the process of creation has been moving from the beginning even until now.

The first clear revelation of the knowledge of good and evil comes to every individual soul through transgression. The light and moral humiliation of Christianity do their work at a later stage. Nor does this exhaust the analogy. The whole process is repeated again and again. We never outgrow the tree of the knowledge of good and evil. The frequent appropriation of its stimulating fruit is the condition of spiritual growth. The Christian fall is experienced, not indeed every time we are guilty of transgression, but every time our eyes are opened to hitherto disregarded imperfections and to the existence of a higher moral standard; and our Christian life is made fuller and deeper every time we are impelled by our sense of insufficiency to draw more largely on the strength of the Saviour of our spirits. This is the divine method from beginning to end.[20]

This type of liberalism and optimism was difficult to maintain for long; its inherent weaknesses and superficial adaptations, its too ready and too clever coupling of incompatibles, soon were exposed. In the *Andover Review*, for example, at the same time Johnson and Bixby were expounding this humanistic and humanitarian faith as though it were based on natural science, a young critic, John Dewey, was pointing out that

man may be one form through which the course of evolution passes; but that is all that he can be. What, then, in bold Anglo-Saxon, is the sense of talking about the goal of the process of evolution being a goal for man, except that it be something in which he is absorbed, swallowed up, forever lost?

The process is one of conflict; its very condition is opposition, competition, selection, survival. The ideal is harmony, unity of purpose and life, community for well-being—a good which does not admit of being competed for, but in which all must share.[21]

This type of criticism had already become familiar through Huxley's critique of evolutionary ethics, but Dewey was more disconcerting to these theologians than was Huxley, because he also attacked their re-

[20] Francis Howe Johnson, *What Is Reality?* (Boston, 1891), pp. 347–49, 362, 474.
[21] John Dewey, "Ethics and Physical Science," *Andover Review*, VII (1887), 586, 580.

liance on consciousness as an independent force in nature, the very being of God. He pointed out, in terms borrowed from Hegel, that precisely because existence is organic through and through, psychical processes are not autonomous, and must be understood in their organic functions as part of a living, growing personality. He said pointedly, too, that just as intelligence is not an "independent autonomous faculty" of the organism, so spiritual life is not independent of the social, organic environment. And he used this organic conception of the Spirit, not only to refute Spencer but also to give the organic theory of nature an idealistic, rather than a theistic, direction.

By the turn of the century the liberal theologians had cut loose from Spencer entirely and also from biology and were expounding a Christian version of moral evolution. Henry Ward Beecher's *Evolution and Religion* was obviously an exploitation of evolutionary concepts for evangelical purposes; there was scarcely even a pretext of science in him. His successor at Plymouth Church, Brooklyn, Lyman Abbott, was a more genuine evolutionist, since he believed in the evolution of revelation, the evolution of immortality, the evolution of anything; but he paid little or no attention to biological evolution, except to dismiss it politely in the Preface to his *The Theology of an Evolutionist* (1897).

It would be difficult to find anywhere a more noble statement of the profound mystery of life than is to be found in the writings of Darwin, Huxley, and Herbert Spencer. The very word "agnostic," which has been applied by these gentlemen to themselves, and which was, indeed, first employed by Huxley, is an indication of their frank recognition that the universe cannot be comprehended by finite man. The creed of the evolutionist is all embodied in the statement that life is a growth. But growth is itself a mystery; and the statement that the universe is full of mysteries is not inconsistent with the statement that the history of the universe is a history of growth.[22]

There was a flood of such evangelical appropriation of evolutionary language and enthusiasm. The popularity in America of Henry Drummond's *Natural Law in the Spiritual World* (1890) and *The Ascent of Man* (1894) was symptomatic of this trend; at Andover, Drummond found an American disciple in George Harris, whose *Moral Evolution* (1899), though less inspiring than the writings of his Eng-

[22] Lyman Abbot, *The Theology of an Evolutionist*, p. vii.

lish contemporary, was used widely as an academic text and as a source of texts for sermons.

The culmination of such adaptation of evolutionary thought to theology came with the idea, promulgated before Darwin by Cardinal Newman, but now reasserted in a bolder form, that revelation itself evolves. The Reverend Theodore T. Munger, for example, in his formulation of "the New Theology," wrote without evasion:

The Bible, like the order of history, is a continually unfolding revelation of God; it is a book of eternal laws and facts that are evolving their truth and reality in the process of history. Its full meaning is not yet disclosed; it is an ever-opening book. It is always leading man in the right direction, but it does not show him at once, in clear light, the whole domain of truth. It is, therefore, a book to be constantly and freshly interpreted; it may mean to-morrow more than it means today.[23]

Evolution in general was interpreted by Munger as "the creative process," which is identical with the increasing revelation of God's goodness and which issues in "man as a moral being." To him, as to Fiske, science itself must regard man as "the final form in creation," for even though the universe is not anthropocentric, further biological development is possible only in man's moral evolution.[24]

— 33 —

GENETIC SOCIAL PHILOSOPHY

It cannot be too soon understood that science is one, and that whether we investigate language, philosophy, theology, history, or physics, we are dealing with the same problem, culminating in the knowledge of ourselves. Speech is known only in connection with the organs of man, thought in connection with his brain, religion as the expression of his aspirations, history as the record of his deeds, and physical sciences as the laws under which he lives. Philosophers and theologians have yet to learn that a physical fact is as sacred as a moral principle. Our own nature demands from us this double allegiance.[1]

[23] Theodore T. Munger, *The Freedom of Faith*, pp. 19 ff.; cited in Frank Hugh Foster, *The Modern Movement in American Theology* (New York, 1939), p. 64.
[24] See his sermon, "Man the Final Form in Creation," reprinted in Blau, ed., *American Philosophic Addresses 1700–1900*, pp. 712–27.
[1] Louis Agassiz, "Evolution and the Permanence of Type," *The Atlantic Monthly*, XXXIII (1874), 95.

WITH these words Professor Agassiz greeted Darwin's *The Expression of the Emotions in Man and Animals,* and he added: "I can only rejoice that the discussion has taken this turn, much as I dissent from the treatment of the subject." It was the old botanist's intellectual testament to an evolutionary generation and set before it the aims of philosophical reconstruction. For, if science is one, natural knowledge must lead to self knowledge. To this task the new biology brought excellent instruments of analysis: "adaptation to the environment," "spontaneous variation," "struggle for existence," "survival value," these were concepts, at once physical and teleological, which could readily be applied to all phases of culture and to the criticism of all institutions. The genetic method thus offered a program for moralists and social scientists which transferred the center of evolutionary interest from the problems of human origins and divine plans to the problems of daily life and contemporary society.

There developed rapidly the new science of social psychology, the genetic account of logic, language, custom, and law as instances of organic adaptation to the demands of a social environment and as relative to changing conditions. What made the enterprise of genetic social psychology particularly significant was the failure on the part of the earlier generation of evolutionary naturalists to take social evolution seriously. All animals were regarded as essentially struggling, each for its own existence, even within a single species. Each organism was part of the "external," physical environment of every other. The struggle was conceived individualistically even by those who were chiefly interested in the theory of the survival of species or "favored races." This was particularly true of the Spencerians, for Spencer's *Sociology,* which appeared in the early seventies, formulated the principles of political and economic individualism in terms of "the survival of the fittest." Thus, what Bagehot had more properly called "social physics" came to be known unfortunately as "social Darwinism," and, despite Huxley's best efforts, Darwin's biology was popularly condemned for making inevitable Spencer's sociology.

In the United States the situation was even more ironic than in England, for Spencer's best-known American disciple, John Fiske, repudiated the harsher forms of the ethics of the survival of the fittest and had given his own social, altruistic and religious turn to evolutionary theory. It remained, therefore, for another Yankee to champion

Spencer's sociology. This champion was found in the professor of political and social science in Yale College, William Graham Sumner. According to his colleague William Lyon Phelps, he argued with his students as follows:

"Professor, don't you believe in any government aid to industries?"
"No! it's root, hog, or die."
"Yes, but hasn't the hog got a right to root?"
"There are no rights. The world owes nobody a living."
"You believe then, Professor, in only one system, the contract-competitive system?"
"That's the only sound economic system. All others are fallacies."
"Well, suppose some professor of political economy came along and took your job away from you. Wouldn't you be sore?"
"Any other professor is welcome to try. If he gets my job, it is my fault. My business is to teach the subject so well that no one can take the job away from me." [2]

And in 1879, in the face of the general depression, he was lecturing publicly as follows:

If we do not like the survival of the fittest, we have only one possible alternative, and that is the survival of the unfittest. The former is the law of civilization; the latter is the law of anti-civilization. We have our choice between the two, or we can go on, as in the past, vacillating between the two, but a third plan—the socialist desideratum—a plan for nourishing the unfittest and yet advancing in civilization, no man will ever find. [3]

Sumner was, of course, giving expression not only to Spencer's sociology but also to the traditional Yankee morals of self-reliance, thrift, and prudence. "Let every man be sober, industrious, prudent, and wise, and bring up his children to be so likewise, and poverty will be abolished in a few generations." [4] When old-fashioned Scottish economy thus dressed itself in the wolf's clothing of social Darwinism, it was highly important for the good naturalist shepherds to come to the rescue with a more social Darwinism.

[2] William Lyon Phelps, "When Yale Was Given to Sumnerology," *The Literary Digest International Book Review* (1925), III, 661; cited in Richard Hofstadter, *Social Darwinism in American Thought 1860–1915* (Philadelphia, 1944), p. 39.

[3] William Graham Sumner, *Essays*, ed. by A. G. Keller and M. R. Davie (New Haven, 1934), II, 56; cited in Hofstadter, *op. cit.*, p. 43.

[4] *Ibid.*, I, 109; cited in Hofstadter, *op. cit.*, p. 47.

What made the problem all the more acute was the growth of the new psychology of "animal intelligence," which tended to transfer the whole philosophy of mind to the theory of "selective thinking." Consciousness was no longer interpreted as the faculty of receiving passively external impressions or of intuiting reality, it was explained "functionally" as allied with the feeling-groping mechanism of the organism to select the proper means for the satisfaction of organic needs and was hence naturally subservient to the emotions, the emotions themselves being, either practically or "vestigially," mechanisms of adaptation and weapons of survival. When James's *Psychology* appeared, in 1890, this conception of mind as an active, selective type of behavior, became at once popular and gave to psychology the ambition of being, as James said, "a natural science." Such a conception of the nature of mind played into the hands of the individualistic sociology. For, in place of the old assumption that the mind aimed at reason and reason at truth, it now became necessary to justify the very categories of reason and scientific methods themselves as serviceable "variations" in the biological process of natural selection. James used Darwinism effectively to undermine Spencer's whole theory that the mind is molded by "external" forces and that it reproduces the order of experience. The mind of man is, according to James, the product of a series of *spontaneous* variations, no one of which is explicable in terms of natural law. The variations come, we know not how, but once produced they are evaluated by the environment, the useful ones enduring. James even represented man's varied attempts to invent useful systems of interpreting the world as a conflict between man's mental trial-and-error and the "outer order," and in this struggle the "scientific" ways of thinking proved "congruous" and hence survived.

The peculiarity of those relations among the objects of our thought which are dubbed "scientific" is this, that although they no more are inward *reproductions* of the outer order than the ethical and aesthetic relations are, yet they do not conflict with that order, but, once having sprung up by the play of the inward forces, are found—some of them at least, namely the only ones which have survived long enough to be matters of record—to be *congruent* with the time- and space-relations which our impressions affect.

In other words, though nature's materials lend themselves slowly and discouragingly to our translation of them into ethical forms, but more readily into aesthetic forms; to translation into scientific forms they lend themselves with relative ease and completeness. The translation, it is true, will probably never be ended. The perceptive order does not give way, nor the right conceptive substitute for it arise, at our bare word of command. It is often a deadly fight; and many a man of science can say, like Johannes Müller, after an investigation, *"Es klebt Blut an der Arbeit."* But victory after victory makes us sure that the essential doom of our enemy is defeat.

The aspiration to be "scientific" is such an idol of the tribe to the present generation, is so sucked in with his mother's milk by every one of us, that we find it hard to conceive of a creature who should not feel it, and harder still to treat it freely as the altogether peculiar and one-sided subjective interest which it is. But as a matter of fact, few even of the cultivated members of the race have shared it; it was invented but a generation or two ago.[5]

Mental evolution, therefore, is not to be formulated in terms of natural laws, according to James, but in terms of "random images, fancies, accidental out-births of spontaneous variation in the functional activity of the excessively instable human brain." [6] Hence there are no laws of history.

Originally all these things and all other institutions were flashes of genius in an individual head, of which the outer environment showed no sign. Adopted by the race and become its heritage, they then supply instigations to new geniuses whom they environ to make new inventions and discoveries; and so the ball of progress rolls. But take out the geniuses, or alter their idiosyncrasies, and what increasing uniformities will the environment show? We defy Mr. Spencer or any one else to reply.

The plain truth is that the 'philosophy' of evolution (as distinguished from our special information about particular cases of change) is a metaphysical creed, and nothing else. . . .

The spencerian 'philosophy' of social and intellectual progress is an obsolete anachronism, reverting to a pre-darwinian type of thought. . . . I for my part cannot but consider the talk of the contemporary sociological school about averages and general laws and predetermined tendencies, with its obligatory undervaluing of the importance of individual differences, as the most pernicious and immoral of fatalisms. Suppose there is a social equilibrium fated to be, whose is it to be,—that of your preference, or mine? There lies the question of questions, and it is one which no study of averages can decide. . . .

[5] William James, *The Principles of Psychology* (New York, 1890), II, 639–40.
[6] William James, *The Will to Believe; and Other Essays in Popular Philosophy* (New York, 1897), p. 247.

The moving present in which we live with its problems and passions, its individual rivalries, victories, and defeats, will soon pass over to the majority and leave its small deposit on this static mass, to make room for fresh actors and a newer play. And though it may be true, as Mr. Spencer predicts, that each later zone shall fatally be narrower than its forerunners; and that when the ultimate lady-like tea-table elysium of the Data of Ethics shall prevail . . . still even in this shrunken and enfeebled generation . . . battles and defeats will occur, the victors will be glorified and the vanquished dishonored just as in the brave days of yore, the human heart still withdrawing itself from the much it has in safe possession, and concentrating all its passion upon those evanescent possibilities of fact which still quiver in fate's scale.[7]

With this romantic conception of human history and mental powers, James added his own variety of individualism to the Darwinian social philosophies. It was the antithesis of Sumner's, being anti-Spencer, anti-natural law, and anti-laissez-faire. Nevertheless, it presented an additional obstacle to those moralists who had an evolutionary faith in the progress of civilization.

The first substantial contribution toward a genetic social psychology came, as we have seen, from John Fiske's theory that evolution had taken a "psychic" turn. This theme was greatly elaborated by Lester F. Ward. In 1893 he published *The Psychic Factors of Civilization*, in which, as he explained, he attempted to perfect his *Dynamic Sociology* (1883) by "building the superstructure higher and laying the foundation deeper." The deeper foundations were derived from Schopenhauer; the higher superstructure was an attempt to apply the theory of social forces to the solution of practical social problems and thus to lay the foundations for a new science, which he called "meliorism, the science of the improvement or amelioration of the human or social state." Schopenhauer had helped Ward to understand the true relation between will and intellect. He now interpreted social action as a positive art motivated by the power of will or desire. Intellect or objective mind does not precede feeling, or subjectivity, as he had formerly held following the associationist psychology; it follows upon the subjective powers of desire. For subjectivity, or will, is reality and life. This Schopenhauerian psychology, which was in general similar to James's, gave Ward the idea that with the advent of social will or social activity evolution had taken a new turn.

[7] *Ibid.*, pp. 253, 254, 259–60, 261–62.

Animated, the same as the lower animals only more intensely, by desires, seeking those higher and more generalized pleasures which collectively go by the name of happiness, man has, almost as unconsciously as the lower animals, put forth varied, multiplied, and incessant efforts, attended by universal, continual, and restless activity, and resulting in wide-spread, radical, and colossal changes in all his surroundings. Not always useful, any more than were those of the humbler creatures, these changes in his environment have nevertheless been upon the whole progressive, and constitute, taken together, what is known as civilization. Not themselves the object of either Nature or Man, their true beneficiary, in so far as they have resulted in benefit, has been society, which is with respect to them as impersonal and unconscious as Evolution must be conceived to be of the results of animal activity. . . .

The dynamics of society is, in the main, the antithesis of the dynamics of animal life. The psychic element referred to, supplants "nature" by *art*. If we call biologic processes natural, we must call social processes artificial. The fundamental principle of biology is natural selection, that of sociology is artificial selection. The survival of the fittest is simply the survival of the strong, which implies and would better be called the destruction of the weak. If nature progresses through the destruction of the weak, man progresses through the protection of the weak. And so it is throughout. The terms are all reversed.[8]

Ward saw that intelligence or, as he now termed it for polemic purposes, "intuition," is not a reflective faculty, but is "intensely practical" in a social environment.

With man in the social state, however primitive, foresight was exercised, which is itself a form of the intuitive faculty, and the habit of making *provision* for the future arose. This had the immediate effect to render his wants unlimited by his immediate appetite. The consequence was that his desire for the means of subsistence, instead of being periodical, became continuous and the pursuit of this end was incessant. . . . Both the passion and the means of satisfying it were conditions to the development of society itself, and rightly viewed they have also been leading factors in civilization. But here, as man must cope with man, a struggle went on similar, only on a higher intellectual plane, to that which goes on in the animal world, a veritable struggle for existence.

In this great struggle brute force played a diminishing part, and mind an

8 Lester F. Ward, *The Psychic Factors of Civilization* (Boston, 1893), pp. 129–30, 135.

increasing one. Low cunning and animal sagacity, though very prominent, were more and more supplanted by more refined and subtle manifestations of the same psychic principle. This advance was greatly accelerated by the growth of institutions and the establishment of codes of conduct requisite to life in collectivity. The rude animal methods were intolerable, and by natural selection, if not otherwise, society discarded them.[9]

In this way Ward explained the working of a "social will," and it gave him a new basis for believing in Comte's ideal of "sociocracy" or collective social action. His dynamic sociology, therefore, not only became an effective counter to Sumner's and Giddings's but also inspired the younger generation of American sociologists to abandon the evolutionary prejudices which Spencer had displayed. It also supported the efforts being made by the liberal theologians to transform the evolutionary faith into a positive social gospel.

The most ardent spokesman for genetic social psychology was James Mark Baldwin, of Princeton and Johns Hopkins universities. He had been educated in idealist social philosophy, but following the new animal psychology and evolutionary science he became an enthusiastic genetic scientist, who, without abandoning his philosophical idealism, managed to give it a Darwinian dress. He saw that as a philosophical formula the ideas of the "general will," of "identity-in-difference," and of the dialectical theories of life are "the purest tautology." [10]

Baldwin, like Ward, regarded social science as essentially psychological on the theory that man, living in a social environment, develops through "social heredity" an inner life and social self, which are inexplicable in terms of merely biological natural selection. To this process of selection in society he gave the name "organic selection" and regarded this type of evolution as the emergence of a distinct stage in the evolutionary process; evolution thus became truly progressive. In the learning process, which Baldwin thought to be governed largely by trial-and-error, play, and imitation, the individual is "accommodated" to the group; he becomes a "socius," a social self. In his individual development he roughly recapitulates the whole evolution of the race.

[9] *Ibid.*, pp. 156–57.
[10] James Mark Baldwin, "Notes on Social Psychology and Other Things," *The Psychological Review*, IX (1902), 57–58.

"Personal coöperation" and "group selection," then, become the cornerstones of the more critical and adequate social philosophy which utilizes the Darwinian principle of selection. The use of these conceptions has largely, and should completely, supersede the application directly to society of vague and superficial biological and physical analogies.

The cruder forms of struggle for existence in the biological sense, the forms that depend upon physical offense and defense, are largely done away with when we come to the stage of active social coöperation. In rude societies, it survives in the indulgence of the coarser emotions and passions which are not yet reduced to the form in which they serve social use rather than private gratifications. Private revenge, for example, and lynch law remain in some communities. Some forms of direct struggle survive too on account of the countenance they continue to have in actual social sanction, during the slow processes of the evolution of the agencies of social control and law. But coöperation within the group is really the final enemy to these sorts of individualism; and we find that it is outside the group, in the realm of inter-group selection, that the struggle remains one of direct life-and-death competition. War we still have with us, and also the protective tariff, the exclusion of aliens from our food and labor markets, etc., all devices for providing for our own people regardless of what effect this may have upon other people who are in fact just as human and just as hungry as we are.

It is fair to say, therefore, that there is a progressive suppression within the group of the grosser, more biological forms of struggle for existence, progressing with the advance in social coöperation and organization; but that they still find illustration in the struggle which a social group as a unit wages with other similar units or groups. Even here, however, the struggle tends to be waged with other than physical weapons. The growth of mind, making the group organization ever more effective, shows itself efficient also in the foreign relations of the group. War and all other sorts of racial rivalry become as much struggle of wits as struggle with hands and guns. In war the sting of defeat is not measured by numerical loss of men, but by the humiliation of national pride and the losses of racial prestige. The costliness of victory contributes to the pride and glory of its achievement.

These considerations may introduce us to the form of struggle for existence which is distinctly psychological in character, and which does not allow of any sort of biological explanation.[11]

Baldwin's chief interest, however, was not the psychology of inter-group relations, but the study of ways in which groups fashion their

[11] James Mark Baldwin, *Darwin and the Humanities* (Baltimore, 1909), pp. 45–46, 56–57, Library of Genetic Science and Philosophy, II.

members. He made a particularly elaborate analysis of how social adaptation explains both the growth of an individual's mind and the evolution of mind in general. A mind is a social product; Baldwin's "genetic logic" was an attempt to show systematically how this is true, by tracing the genesis of each "faculty." He distinguished three chief stages in mental evolution: (1) the pre-logical, animistic, and mystic type of thought, in which the dualisms of mind and object have not yet appeared; (2) logical or scientific thought in which this dualism is "mediated"; and (3) hyperlogical thought, or aesthetic immediacy, in which the appreciation of beauty overcomes the need for mediation. Unfortunately for this type of "genetic logic" its psychology has proved to be less scientific than it was supposed to be and has afforded philosophers an instructive lesson in the exploitation of natural science by ingenious speculation.

A more enduring contribution to social analysis was made by a group at Chicago, Albion Small, John Dewey, James H. Tufts, George H. Mead, W. I. Thomas, and Thorstein Veblen. Like Baldwin and the earlier geneticists, they emphasized the qualitative difference between social acts or habits and merely physiological adaptation to the physical environment. They showed by a behavioral analysis that social relations are categorically different from other relations. Their psychology of "social acts" provided a new and more radical approach to the genetic theory of mind. Dewey, for example, criticized Baldwin for not giving a consistently social theory of mental development.

Mr. Baldwin . . . appears to reconcile the genetic and the intuitive views by taking them both by turns. . . .
The chief value of the genetic method is that it enables us to *substitute* a scientific statement of the nature of personality and society, and their relations to each other, for a metaphysical one.[12]

His chief contribution toward social psychology was to show the importance of occupational and moral interests in the evolution of human experience. In 1894 Dewey pointed out that Lester Ward and other evolutionists had not taken genetic analysis seriously enough, but had carried over uncritically too much pre-Darwinian psychology, and in 1902 he ridiculed Spencer's use of anthropological material.

[12] John Dewey, "Social Interpretations," *Philosophical Review*, VII (1898), 408*n*, 629.

We do not escape from an inorganic conglomerate conception of mind by just abusing the 'faculty' psychology. Our standpoint must be more positive. . . .

The biological point of view commits us to the conviction that mind, whatever else it may be, is at least an organ of service for the control of environment in relation to the ends of the life process.

If we search in any social group for the special functions to which mind is thus relative, occupations at once suggest themselves. Occupations determine the fundamental modes of activity, and hence control the formation and use of habits. These habits, in turn, are something more than practical and overt. "Apperceptive masses" and associational tracts of necessity conform to the dominant activities. The occupations determine the chief modes of satisfaction, the standards of success and failure. Hence they furnish the working classifications and definitions of value; they control the desire processes. Moreover, they decide the sets of objects and relations that are important, and thereby provide the content or material of attention, and the qualities that are interestingly significant. The directions given to mental life thereby extend to emotional and intellectual characteristics. So fundamental and pervasive is the group of occupational activities that it affords the scheme or pattern of the structural organization of mental traits. Occupations integrate special elements into a functioning whole. . . .

The further problem of genetic psychology is then to show how the purely immediate personal adjustment of habit to direct satisfaction, in the savage, became transformed through the introduction of impersonal, generalized objective instrumentalities and ends; how it ceased to be immediate and became loaded and surcharged with a content which forced personal want, initiative, effort and satisfaction further and further apart, putting all kinds of social divisions of labor, intermediate agencies and objective contents between them. This is the problem of the formation of mental patterns appropriate to agricultural, military, professional and technological and trade pursuits, and the reconstruction and overlaying of the original hunting schema.

But by these various agencies we have not so much destroyed or left behind the hunting structural arrangement of mind, as we have set free its constitutive psycho-physic factors so as to make them available and interesting in all kinds of objective and idealized pursuits—the hunt for truth, beauty, virtue, wealth, social well-being, and even of heaven and of God.[13]

[13] John Dewey, "Interpretation of Savage Mind," *The Psychological Review*, IX (1902), 219–20, 229–30.

Thomas described the evolution of the varied interests of civilized man out of the primitive preoccupation with "food and sex," trying to "trace the 'red thread' of consciousness through the different variables of society: ideas, institutions, beliefs, sentiments, language, arts, literature"; he thus laid the foundations for a more biological and behavioristic folk psychology than had been provided by Wundt.

This idea of the transformation of the hunting complex through occupational changes and the evolution of new types of culture gave to the Chicago school a new type of social psychology, to say nothing of its implications for genetic logic, and this social psychology was at once applied by Dewey and his colleagues to the problems of education and morals. Albion Small's "dynamic" sociology, for example, conceived the science of society as an integral part of social "growth" or reform. Tufts showed how such an evolutionary method in ethics could be used to give new meaning to the idealistic doctrine of self-realization. Mead made the most detailed and systematic contribution to this theory of the social formation of the self by his analysis of language and symbolical processes. He took his departure from Wundt's theory of gesture and developed it into a radically social theory of thought.

Since organism and environment determine each other and are mutually dependent for their existence, it follows that the life-process, to be adequately understood, must be considered in terms of their interrelations.

The social environment is endowed with meanings in terms of the process of social activity; it is an organization of objective relations which arises in relation to a group of organisms engaged in such activity, in processes of social experience and behavior. . . . The relation of the social process of behavior—or the relation of the social organism—to the social environment is analogous to the relation of the processes of individual biological activity —or the relation of the individual organism—to the physical-biological environment.

A social organism—that is, a social group of individual organisms—constitutes or creates its own special environment of objects just as, and in the same sense as, an individual organism constitutes or creates its own special environment of objects.[14]

[14] George H. Mead, *Mind, Self & Society; from the Standpoint of a Social Behaviorist* (Chicago, 1934), p. 130.

The human animal as an individual could never have attained control over the environment. It is a control which has arisen through social organization. The very speech he uses, the very mechanism of thought which is given, are social products. His own self is attained only through his taking the attitude of the social group to which he belongs. He must become socialized to become himself. So when you speak of this evolution, of its having reached a certain climax in human form, you must realize that it reaches that point only in so far as the human form is recognized as an organic part of the social whole. Now, there is nothing so social as science, nothing so universal. Nothing so rigorously oversteps the points that separate man from man and groups from groups as does science. There cannot be any narrow provincialism or patriotism in science. Scientific method makes that impossible. Science is inevitably a universal discipline which takes in all who think. It speaks with the voice of all rational beings. It must be true everywhere; otherwise it is not scientific. But science is evolutionary. Here, too, there is a continuous process which is taking on successively different forms.[15]

Mead's social theory of the mind and the self thus culminated in his idealization of the evolution of reason or of science as the most universal of human societies.

Mead and his colleagues in social psychology thus recognized in the institutionalization of intelligence a stage in human evolution. Reciprocal adaptation of men to their institutions and of institutions to men meant that the environment, too, could be changed, and that social reform could be regarded as a continuation and culmination of biological evolution.

If we admit that the evolutionary process consists in a mutual determination of the individual and his environment—not the determination of the individual by his environment, moral necessity in conduct is found in the very evolutionary situation. The possibility of intelligent action waits upon the determination of the conditions under which that action is to take place. . . . It is because the man must recognize the public good in the exercise of his powers, and state the public good in terms of his own outgoing activities that his ends are moral. But it is not the public good which comes in from outside himself and lays a moral necessity upon him, nor is it a selfish propensity that drives him on to conduct. . . .

It is this healthful, aggressive, moral attitude, which it seems to me is

[15] George H. Mead, *Movements of Thought in the Nineteenth Century* (Chicago, 1936), p. 168.

encouraged by the recognition that moral consciousness is the most concrete, the most inclusive of all. Here we must abstract from nothing, and here we cannot appeal from ourselves to a power without ourselves that makes for righteousness. In the fulness of immediate experience, with the consciousness that out of the struggle to act must arise all power to mediate action, lies salvation.

Nowhere is this point of view more needed than in the struggles which fill our industrial and commercial life. The individual is treated as if he were quite separable from his environment; and still more is the environment conceived as if it were quite independent of the individual. Both laborer and the society which employs him are exhorted to recognize their obligations to each other, while each continues to operate within its own narrow radius; and because the employer regards the labor union as a fixed external environment of his activity, and would have all the relations between laborer and employer determined by the method in which he bargains and does business, he becomes a narrow individualist; and because the laborer would determine these same relations by the methods which he has used in building up this union, he becomes a socialist. What will take that and other allied problems out of the vicious circles in which they are at present found, is the recognition that it is the incompleteness with which the different social interests are present that is responsible for the inadequacy of the moral judgments. If the community educated and housed its members properly, and protected machinery, food, market, and thoroughfares adequately, the problems at present vexing the industrial world would largely disappear. We resent the introduction of the standard of life into the question of the wages; and yet if the social activities involved in the conception of the standard of life were given full expression, the wage question would be nearly answered. Every such problem is the inevitable indication of what has been left undone, of impulses checked, or interest overlooked. We turn back to history and talk about the evolution of man as if his environment were not the projection of himself in the conditions of conduct, as if the fulfillment of the Law and the Prophets were not the realization of all that is in us. The sources of power lie in that which has been overlooked.[16]

This passage, which might have been written by any one of the "Chicago school," formulates admirably the way in which genetic psychology became a philosophical orientation for social action and reform. Albion Small, writing as a disciple of Lester Ward, conceived the dis-

[16] George H. Mead, "The Philosophical Basis of Ethics," *International Journal of Ethics*, XVIII (1908), 316, 317–19.

covery of the laws of social development as an instrument of "scientific" or evolutionary socialism.

Society never reaches a state of stable equilibrium. Changes in thought and feeling produce modifications of functions, which, in turn, influence structure. On the other hand, structures tend to resist change and to give activities a permanent character. The term "social growth" or "evolution" may be appropriately applied to this unceasing change in ideals and arrangements, which is more popularly described as progress. To study this growth of society, to discover laws of development, and to bring psychical forces to bear so that they may direct and hasten the movement toward a higher plane of collective and individual life, is the task of the scientific social reformer.[17]

All the members of this philosophical group were active participants in educational and industrial reforms and regarded their activities as educators, arbitrators, and politicians as continuous with their theoretical reconstructions of the theory of thought.[18]

The exception was Thorstein Veblen, who looked upon his evolutionary theories of economic institutions and upon science in general as the fruit of "idle curiosity." He was personally the most "inactive" and unsocial member of this highly active group; his theories, on the other hand, were intensely polemical and practical in their bearings. He himself, it seems, enjoyed their irony and display of learning as if they were his own little contribution to that "conspicuous waste" and "higher learning" which he in his books analyzed so mercilessly. As a student he had come under the influence of the biologized or Darwinized version of neo-Kantian philosophy prevalent at Johns Hopkins, and he continued his philosophical studies at Yale under Noah Porter and Ladd. Arrived at Chicago in 1892, he began at once to apply evolutionary theory to economics, particularly to the growth of socialism. He revolted against both the classical British economics (which he later called "marginal utility economics") and the German historical school of Schmoller. To him true science was "causal" science, causation was "impersonal" and "cumulative," and a truly genetic social science would "trace the cumulative "working out of the eco-

[17] Albion W. Small, and George E. Vincent, *An Introduction to the Study of Society* (New York, 1894), pp. 238–39.
[18] See the discussions of instrumentalism and pragmatism, below, chs. 39, 41.

nomic interest in the cultural sequence." [19] He entered wholeheartedly into the spirit of the new "active" psychology and interpreted economic processes, not in terms of natural law, but in terms of interests or teleological actions; and he interpreted these interests in their "causal" relations, that is, in terms of their social efficacies and efficiencies. Their cumulative effects or evolution could be traced disinterestedly and strictly impersonally. For the theory of progress, as distinct from the science of causation, he had only scorn, regarding all such habits of inquiry as vestiges of "animism" and of faith in providence.

The first significant application which he made of his genetic economics was *The Theory of the Leisure Class: an Economic Study in the Evolution of Institutions* (1899). In this volume he explained the habits and standards of the present leisure class, its "conspicuous waste," inefficiency, sporting interest, and predatory character, as a vestige of a once useful, fighting class which possessed genuine "prowess" and lived on robbery or slavery. The story of the gradual degradation of this class from its ancient wielding of economic power to its present display of "pecuniary strength" afforded Veblen an extraordinary opportunity to apply what he regarded as Darwinian methods to social history and, at the same time, to write a brilliant critique of the contemporary "invidious," "non-causal" class relations. The causal processes were those of "the industrial republic," that is, of the productive efficiencies of modern technology. The "price system" and the pecuniary interests in investment he regarded as uneconomical, unproductive vestiges of past cultures.

Thus, Veblen's economics is a particularly good illustration of the general tendency in this Chicago group to shift their interest gradually from genetic methods to functional criticism and from social evolution to social reconstruction.

[19] Thorstein Veblen, "Why Is Economics Not an Evolutionary Science?" *Quarterly Journal of Economics*, XII (1898), 394.

DESPERATE NATURALISM

The great stream of time and earthly things will sweep on just the same in spite of us. It bears with it now all the errors and follies of the past, the wreckage of all the philosophies, the fragments of all the civilizations, the wisdom of all the abandoned ethical systems, the debris of all the institutions, and the penalties of all the mistakes. It is only in imagination that we stand by and look at and criticize it and plan to change it. Everyone of us is a child of his age and cannot get out of it. He is in the stream and is swept along with it. All his sciences and philosophy come to him out of it. Therefore the tide will not be changed by us. It will swallow up both us and our experiments. It will absorb the efforts at change and take them into itself as new but trivial components, and the great movement of tradition and work will go on unchanged by our fads and schemes. The things which will change it are the great discoveries and inventions, the new reactions inside the social organism, and the changes in the earth itself on account of changes in the cosmical forces. These causes will make of it just what, in fidelity to them, it ought to be. The men will be carried along with it and be made by it. The utmost they can do by their cleverness will be to note and record their course as they are carried along, which is what we do now, and is that which leads us to the vain fancy that we can make or guide the movement. That is why it is the greatest folly of which a man can be capable, to sit down with a slate and pencil to plan out a new social world.[1]

TO most men this submission to existence comes naturally as an adaptation to environment, but in every generation there are sensitive spirits to whom the discovery that man shares an animal existence and an animal faith with other species comes as the revelation of poetic truth. In their unreflective thinking they go along with their fellows, "conquering" nature and managing their affairs, but in the privacy of philosophical reflection they awake from their pragmatic nightmares to observe calmly how even they are caught in the grip of natural forces. This knowledge of their bondage then appears to them as a precious liberty, not granted to other animals, of living in disillusionment; they "bear their fetters with an air." They now

[1] William Graham Sumner, *War and Other Essays* (New Haven, 1911), pp. 209-10.

play the role of seers and join the great company of heavenly reporters, alternately urging their fellows to emancipation and then fleeing alone for refreshment to their private world of imagination. They continue to live naturally, making their way among struggling powers, but they make a sharp distinction between their groping intelligence and their speculative freedom; as knowing ones, their proper business is to bear witness to truth, to describe as from an elevation the innocent, dark, dreaming play of natural forces, from which they have only half escaped. In America the era of evolutionary enthusiasm produced at least four such spirits who will continue to live in history.

William Graham Sumner was a conformist in principle, whom circumstances forced to become a reformer. As a priest of the Episcopal Church (his father was English and Anglican), and as professor of political and social science in Yale College (1872–1909) he lived what to him was a "simple and monotonous" life, singularly devoted to truth. To his friends, who marveled that a Christian minister could also be so fervently in communion with nature, he explained that he once put his religious beliefs in a drawer and that when he later opened it the drawer was empty. All his beliefs, in fact, had this power of vanishing into convictions as they were filed away into their proper places in his cabinet full of "the science of society." He was a believer, not in the fashion of sentimental piety or in possession of a reasoned faith, but in the spontaneous resignation of his mind to the normal conditions of life which are always a combination of orderliness and chance, of the element of law and of "the aleatory element." The former, institutionalized, gives us science; the latter, religion. These two institutions, therefore, supplement each other. Experience is a mixture of convention and wonder, half prudence, half gambling. What we call "brute facts," for which Sumner had an extraordinary respect, are partly to be understood as normal events, partly as "acts of God." Sumner understood both the secular and the sacred idioms for trust in the natural order, and he was, therefore, not torn by a double allegiance, but could devote himself wholeheartedly and religiously to his science. Like Herbert Spencer, whom he resembled even more than he followed, he respected the "constitution of nature" to such a degree that in his efforts to be cosmically law-abiding and to fall into no "artificial" ways he became a great iconoclast.

His ultimate and favorite way of looking at the order of nature was in terms of "the mores." Our folkways govern all of us, so he taught, and their hold on us is not an external coercion but the "internal life energy" of forces that are at once natural and social. "Nature her custom holds"; this text from Shakespeare was to him a veritable gospel. Our practical standards and habitual conduct arise "no one knows whence or how," since our historical knowledge is fragmentary, but they may be presumed to have been originally useful variations. They have a natural career, for "in time they lose power, decline, and die, or are transformed"; when they change they change naturally, because changed circumstances impel them. They must keep an inner consistency, too, and especially they must remain consonant with the economic system, the basic "mores of maintenance," as well as with the general "state of the arts." The mores are automatic, "factual" bonds; they have the might to make right and should be regarded, not as principles of what ought to be or as vestiges of what has been, but as governors of what is. To be civilized means to live by the mores; to defy them or to seek "artificially" to change them is both folly and wickedness.

In our democratic culture, for example, it is both natural and moral for us to "love one another" while each minds his own business. To mind each other's business, however, and to care for those whom we do not really love is artificial and ineffective. To struggle "for himself and those he cares for" is spontaneously recognized by a modern man as at once his business and his duty, or, in other words, our mores are such that "moral energy" is the energy of individuals. "Social machinery," such as the state, is not an independent source of moral power, but merely a channel for exerting individual powers. Institutions merely "give back the energy they cost"; in themselves they produce nothing. Co-operation, therefore, like prayer, is evidence of human need, not a magic source of power. The state cannot give us "free grace," nor can government give us capital. Capital is the natural fruit of frugality, and each producer naturally feels most secure when he is the protector of his own earnings and the promoter of his own interests. Social classes, or different types of individuals, naturally respect each other and abide by their contracts, but when they are asked to look after each others' interests they merely waste their own powers.

They undertake to govern each other in the hope of "being paternalized," only to find in the end that they are all "being policed." To seek protection for one's own family, property, or capital is normal and effective; to protect the drunkard, who should remain in the gutter where nature puts him, is not only a waste of resources which should be put to productive use but also an artificial, fruitless attempt to interfere with the natural weeding out of the unfit. "Huxley lost his grip in that *Evolution and Ethics* thing of his." A morality that attempts to go counter to nature is futile. The industrious, frugal, honest man, though he be forgotten by politicians, is the favorite of nature; he is still the norm of our culture, and his ways should continue to be the folkways until a changed material environment shall produce, by the methods of natural adaptation, a new body of mores.

With this simple conformist philosophy Sumner faced not only the classroom but also the larger world of affairs. In the classroom he could hold his own, for his system was extremely neat; but in the world he met one difficulty after another. Even in his early days as the rector of a church he found himself out of step with the mores of his group. He had to be a partisan of the broad-church wing against current high-church tendencies, and he became an editor of *The Living Church*, in which position he was supposed to champion reforms. Leaving the ministry for a field of wider liberty, he settled down to the teaching of social science at Yale only to find his liberty questioned by President Porter. He was asked not to use Spencer's *Principles of Sociology* as a textbook. Had he been using the *First Principles* or the *Psychology*, no questions would have been asked, for Porter himself used these works in his classes; but Spencer's *Sociology*, said Porter, was "pamphleteering," and, besides, it treated theism with "freedom and unfairness" and with "cool and yet sarcastic effrontery." Sumner, of course, would not yield, and a serious controversy ensued, involving the trustees of the college. Then he was forced into a long fight to liberalize the Yale curriculum, including in it more science and more electives. He entered local politics as a Republican, but was outwitted by the professional politicians on local issues and repudiated by them nationally because he opposed protectionism. "I found out that I was likely to do more harm in politics than almost any other kind of man, because I did not know the rules of the game and did not want to learn them." He would not defend paper currency and free silver, and therefore the Democratic Party was closed to him. When he saw the country turning toward imperialism, he opposed the trend as vigorously as he could. He became increasingly desperate in politics: "We shall all have to vote for Teddy in 1908 in order to ward off Bryan and Hades. If I do it, I shall be disgraced forever." [2] Meanwhile, the trends in sociology and economics were going against him, and he found himself usually out of step with the times. Were the mores really changing? He comforted himself with his pure science of society and his industry as a scholar. He might, like his industrious, frugal father, be an independent, though forgotten, man. Even this comfort was denied him; he was forced into the championship of one lost cause after another. Most ironical was his famous attempt to save "the forgotten man." According to Sumner's theory:

The Forgotten Man is delving away in patient industry, supporting his family, paying his taxes, casting his vote, supporting the church and the school, reading his newspaper, and cheering for the politician of his admiration, but he is the only one for whom there is no provision in the great scramble and the big divide. [3]

"He works, he votes, generally he prays," but, alas, "he always pays —yes, above all, he pays." He must, therefore, be protected against imposition and injustice. Thus, Sumner was compelled to admit that the mores of individualism were in danger and he made both himself and "the forgotten man" unforgettable as symbols of a departing faith and a moribund morality.

Henry Adams's despair was the antithesis of Sumner's, the despair of a man who had taken Emerson's advice to "hitch his wagon to the star of reform," who, therefore, was in principle a lover of motion and change, [4] but who learned to understand his own futile career and that of mankind in general as in the grip of forces beyond human control and as a dissipation of energy which resembles chaos more than progress. As a youth at the outbreak of the Civil War he plunged gaily into

[2] A. G. Keller, *Reminiscences of William Graham Sumner* (New Haven, 1933), p. 84.

[3] William Graham Sumner, *The Forgotten Man and Other Essays* (New Haven, 1919), p. 491.

[4] *Ibid.*, p. 231.

politics, assuming that he was destined to live in the White House; he embarked confidently on his diplomatic career in high English society, on his career as a literary journalist, and on his residence in Washington, in the expectation that he was a statesman in the making. His bewilderment was bottomless when he found President Grant and his like entrenched in power, the Democratic Party hopeless as a refuge, and all the Adamses advising him to accept an assistant professorship in medieval history at Harvard. He was politically disillusioned not merely on his own account but on account of democracy in general, for he had hoped to be, like his grandfather, a leader in shaping a new national democracy on sober, scientific principles. But now—to quote one of the characters in his novel of 1880,

What was it all worth, this wilderness of men and women as monotonous as the brown stone houses they lived in? In her despair she had resorted to desperate measures. She had read philosophy in the original German, and the more she read, the more she was disheartened that so much culture should lead to nothing—nothing.[5]

To a senator, who had been orating against evolutionary doctrines, this same character replies:

You are very hard on the monkeys. . . . The monkeys never did you any harm; they are not in public life; they are not even voters; if they were, you would be enthusiastic about their intelligence and virtue. After all, we ought to be grateful to them, for what would men do in this melancholy world if they had not inherited gaiety from the monkeys—as well as oratory.[6]

[5] Henry Adams, *Democracy; an American Novel* (New York, 1880), p. 2.
[6] *Ibid.*, pp. 102–3. Another character, Nathan Gore, a literary man from Massachusetts who aspires to a governmental post abroad, speaks very seriously in answer to the question "Do you yourself think democracy the best government and universal suffrage a success?" The views he expresses may well have been those held by Adams at this time:
"These are matters about which I rarely talk in society; they are like the doctrine of a personal God; of a future life; of revealed religion; subjects which one naturally reserves for private reflection. But since you ask for my political creed you shall have it. I only condition that it shall be for you alone, never to be repeated or quoted as mine. I believe in democracy. I accept it. I will faithfully serve and defend it. I believe in it because it appears to me the inevitable consequence of what has gone before it. Democracy asserts the fact that the masses are now raised to a higher intelligence than formerly. All our civilization aims at this mark. We want to do what we can to

With such fits of cynicism Henry Adams tried to console himself, but they afforded him no insight into the causes of the general collapse.

It was not until the crash of 1893 that he understood, as he later put it, that he and his generation had been "mortgaged to the railroads," and that both Boston and Washington were in the power of the "goldbugs" of New York and the robber barons of Wall Street. His younger brother, Brooks Adams, was able to adapt himself intellectually to this situation by working out a philosophy of history which explained it. All history, he discovered, is a seesaw struggle between concentration and dissipation of energy, between fear and greed.

The theory proposed is based upon the accepted scientific principle that the law of force and energy is of universal application in nature, and that animal life is one of the outlets through which solar energy is dissipated.

Starting from this fundamental proposition, the first deduction is, that, as human societies are forms of animal life, these societies must differ among themselves in energy, in proportion as nature has endowed them, more or less abundantly, with energetic material.

Thought is one of the manifestations of human energy, and among the earlier and simpler phases of thought, two stand conspicuous—Fear and Greed. Fear, which, by stimulating the imagination, creates a belief in an invisible world, and ultimately develops a priesthood; and Greed, which dissipates energy in war and trade.

Probably the velocity of the social movement of any community is proportionate to its energy and mass, and its centralization is proportionate to its velocity; therefore, as human movement is accelerated, societies centralize. In the earlier stages of concentration, fear appears to be the channel through which energy finds the readiest outlet; accordingly, in primitive and scattered communities, the imagination is vivid, and the mental types produced are religious, military, artistic. As consolidation advances, fear

---

help it. I myself want to see the result. I grant it is an experiment, but it is the only direction society can take that is worth its taking; the only conception of its duty large enough to satisfy its instincts; the only result that is worth an effort or a risk. Every other possible step is backward, and I do not care to repeat the past. I am glad to see society grapple with issues in which no one can afford to be neutral.

". . . I have faith; not perhaps in the old dogmas, but in the new ones; faith in human nature; faith in science; faith in the survival of the fittest. Let us be true to our time, Mrs. Lee! If our age is to be beaten, let us die in the ranks. If it is to be victorious, let us be first to lead the column. Anyway, let us not be skulkers or grumblers."—(*Ibid.*, pp. 76–78).

yields to greed, and the economic organism tends to supersede the emotional and martial.[7]

But Henry Adams found little comfort in so ready an explanation; he was himself habitually seized alternately by fear and greed, spending half his time hoarding his financial patrimony like a "goldbug" and the other half in gloomy prediction of the final collapse of the whole system. Such rhythms of concentration and dissipation of energy were the stuff of experience, but they were not a "scientific law" of history. Brooks's theory, he thought, might be interpreted as a piece of Darwinism, since it proved "the survival of the cheapest," but what he himself sought was a genuine, physical science of history, that is, a formula which would measure human experience and history in terms of the known laws of physical science. Entropy was merely the second law of thermodynamics; a true science of history would integrate the theory of the dissipation of energy into a still more general theory of force, less human, more mathematical. So he brooded for years, "growling like an Englishman" at his contemporaries, waiting powerlessly and feverishly like a "conservative Christian anarchist" for the day of doom and for some inspiration that would make it intelligible.

While he was thus heaping scorn on the social order and like Job vindicating his own principles, he was also like Job silenced into humility by being overwhelmed with God's natural power. In 1870 he was called to the bedside of his sister, who was dying in agony from tetanus. Suddenly he had a "serious consciousness" of nature's "attitude towards life" as "a nightmare, an insanity of force."

For the first time, the stage-scenery of the senses collapsed; the human mind felt itself stripped naked, vibrating in a void of shapeless energies, with resistless mass, colliding, crushing, wasting, and destroying what these same energies had created and labored from eternity to perfect. Society became fantastic, a vision of pantomime with a mechanical motion; and its so-called thought merged in the mere sense of life, and pleasure in the sense. The usual anodynes of social medicine became evident artifice. Stoicism was perhaps the best; religion was the most human; but the idea that any personal deity could find pleasure or profit in torturing a poor woman, by accident,

[7] Brooks Adams, *The Law of Civilization and Decay; an Essay on History* (New York, 1943), pp. 59–60.

with a fiendish cruelty known to man only in perverted and insane tempera-
ments, could not be held for a moment. For pure blasphemy, it made pure
atheism a comfort. God might be, as the Church said, a Substance, but He
could not be a Person.[8]

Then, in 1884, when his wife died, he fled his social and political
interests, insisted that he was dead to the world, and accompanied his
artist friend John La Farge to the Orient. There he found nirvana, or
"the peace of God," as he preferred to call it, a dumbfounded resignation to the inevitable, beyond grief and tragedy—the attitude so eloquently expressed by St. Gaudens' marble figure, presiding over the
Adams tomb in Rock Creek Cemetery, Washington, D.C. But in the
Orient there awakened in him at the same time that he entered nirvana
a spontaneous enjoyment of colors, forms, and pantomime, an aesthetic
life rich in sense and imagery, but not moving or moral in its consequences. In this attitude of double detachment he returned to Europe
and suddenly found that medieval history, which at Harvard had
bored him, had come to life in him. He composed his *Mont Saint
Michel and Chartres* and became conscious of the power of the Virgin.
He became absorbed in the theme of "The Dynamo and the Virgin,"
two forces between which he felt caught. He felt caught in the sense
that he was carried away by powers which he failed to formulate. The
theology of miraculous power did not help him to understand the
"real presence" of the Virgin, but Gothic art did.

Without the conviction of her personal presence, men would not have been
inspired; but, to us, it is rather the inspiration of the art which proves the
Virgin's presence, and we can better see the conviction of it in the work than
in the words. Every day, as the work went on, the Virgin was present, directing the architects.[9]

The measure of this devotion, which proves to any religious American
mind, beyond possible cavil, its serious and practical reality, is the money it
cost. . . . Five thousand million francs is a thousand million dollars, and
this covered only the great churches of a single century. . . . The share of
this capital which was—if one may use a commercial figure—invested in
the Virgin . . . expressed an intensity of conviction never again reached
by any passion, whether of religion, of loyalty, of patriotism, or of wealth;

[8] Henry Adams, *The Education of Henry Adams* (Boston, 1918), pp. 288–89.
[9] Henry Adams, *Mont Saint Michel and Chartres* (Boston, 1904), p. 105.

perhaps never even paralleled by any single economic effort, except in war. . . . Expenditure like this rests invariably on an economic idea. . . . The investment was based on the power of Mary as Queen of Heaven.[10]

Gradually Henry Adams worked out a most ingenious and fantastic philosophy of force. There might be, he now thought, a progress in the "phases" of force which could be called an evolution of emergent forms of energy, but which had nothing to do with the conventional theories of human progress. It reduced history to physics. He worked out a theory of historical gravitation (attraction or pressure) and cultural acceleration according to which the "phases" of substance (solid, liquid, gaseous, radiant, ethereal, and spatial) correspond to successive epochs. The forces appeared in order of intensity. There was first the "solid" era of instinct or of control by the automatic drives of animal nature, chief among them the energy of reproduction; then the religious period under the power of faith; then the mechanical period; then the electrical period, which began with the invention and general application of the dynamo; there would follow a brief "ethereal phase," when thought would reach "the limit of its possibilities." This would end history, but there would still remain an indefinite period of "space" or pure mathematics, whose empirical content is difficult to predict; it might mean that energy would subside as into nirvana, "into an ocean of potential thought." However,

if, in the prodigiously rapid vibration of its last phases, Thought should continue to act as the universal solvent which it is, and should reduce the forces of the molecule, the atom, and the electron to that costless servitude to which it has reduced the old elements of earth and air, fire and water; if man should continue to set free the infinite forces of nature, and attain the control of cosmic forces on a cosmic scale, the consequences may be as surprising as the change of water to vapor, of the worm to the butterfly, of radium to electrons.[11]

If the law of acceleration holds in history, as it must, it may be possible to calculate roughly the dates of the great transformations of energy on the basis of the law of inverse squares. The length of the first period is incalculable; the religious period (about 90,000 years) ended with .

[10] *Ibid.*, p. 95.
[11] "The Rule of Phase Applied to History," in Henry Adams, *The Degradation of the Democratic Dogma* (New York, 1920), p. 309.

Galileo in 1600; the mechanical period, in 1870; [12] the electrical period, in 1917; the ethereal period, after four hectic years, in 1921. When Henry Adams died in 1918 he thought his predictions might be literally verified.

As a "science of history" this fantastic scheme is ridiculous, and Henry Adams would no doubt be amused to see historians studying it seriously. Even as a philosophy of emergent evolutionism it is little more than an old man's toy. What was important about it and gave it meaning to Henry Adams himself was that it provided a picturesque mythology for his conviction that the transition from the nineteenth century to the twentieth was a crisis in the history of power. He thought of himself as at home in the eighteenth century and educated by the nineteenth century, but for the age of electricity or radiant energy he felt wholly unprepared.

It is a new century, and what we used to call electricity is its God. I can already see that the scientific theories and laws of our generation will, to the next, appear as antiquated as the Ptolemaic system, and that the fellow who gets to 1930 will wish he hadn't. The curious mustiness of decay is already over our youth, and all the period from 1840 to 1870. The period from 1870 to 1900 is closed. I see that much in the machine-gallery of the Champ de Mars. The period from 1900 to 1930 is in full swing, and, gee-whacky! how it is going! It will break its damned neck long before it gets through, if it tries to keep up the speed. [13]

He feared the twentieth century as an age when man would be wrecked even more than he had been by the energies that nature dissipates through him.

Bombs educate vigorously [he wrote] and even wireless telegraphy or airships might require the reconstruction of society . . . the new American—the child of incalculable . . . electric power and radiating energy . . . must be a sort of God compared with any former creation of nature. [14]

[12] The span of approximately 300 years of this period is the basis for the whole calculation.

[13] Henry Adams, *Letters* (*1892–1918*) ed. by Worthington Chauncey Ford (Cambridge, 1938), II, 301.

[14] *The Education of Henry Adams*, p. 496.

We are no beggars! What care we
  For hopes or terrors, love or hate?
What for the universe? We see
Only our certain destiny
  And the last word of Fate.

Seize, then, the Atom! rack his joints!
  Tear out of him his secret spring!
Grind him to nothing!—though he points
To us, and his life-blood anoints
  Me—the dead Atom-King! [15]

These verses from his "Prayer to the Dynamo" should be supplemented by several stanzas of his "Prayer to the Virgin."

Help me to bear! not my own baby load,
  But yours; who bore the failure of the light,
The strength, the knowledge and the thought of God,—
  The futile folly of the Infinite!

     . . .

For centuries I brought you all my cares,
  And vexed you with the murmurs of a child;
You heard the tedious burden of my prayers;
  You could not grant them, but at least you smiled.

If then I left you, it was not my crime,
  Or if a crime, it was not mine alone.
All children wander with the truant Time.
  Pardon me too! You pardoned once your Son!

For He said to you:—"Wist ye not that I
  Must be about my Father's business?" So,
Seeking his Father he pursued his way
  Straight to the Cross towards which we all must go.

So I too wandered off among the host
  That racked the earth to find the father's clue.
I did not find the Father, but I lost
  What now I value more, the Mother,—You! [16]

[15] Mabel La Farge, *Letters to a Niece and Prayer to the Virgin of Chartres* (Cambridge, 1920), p. 130, "Prayer to the Dynamo."
[16] *Ibid.*, pp. 134, 126, "Prayer to the Virgin of Chartres."

Edwin Arlington Robinson composed poetry of a quite different vein, though to the superficial reader he, too, seems to chant endlessly the futility of the infinite. On the contrary, the infinite pursuit of absolute truth seemed to Robinson the only possible form of freedom and meaning for beings whose careers are fated. "A few, by fate's economy shall seem to move the world the way it goes," [17] but this is illusion. Man's only power is the power of self-knowledge, and the exercise of even this power costs him struggle and despair. For the light of knowledge discloses only darkness. To live in the knowledge of darkness, however, is vastly different from simply being in the dark; by courage man can be an idealist though his existence is material. This is the idea and the ideal underlying practically all Robinson's poetry.

Robinson spoke of himself as a "New England conscience," and this self-characterization is typically enigmatic. His fatalism may represent a secularized version of Puritan determinism, fortified by materialistic mechanism. His conscientious, relentless pursuit of self-knowledge may be the Puritan sense and confession of sin transformed into psychoanalysis. His poetry may be a series of exercises in the Last Judgment. Certainly he strove to know objectively, without sentimentality and with perfect sincerity; he could bear unflinchingly the doom of damnation. Thus he was closer to the old New England than to Emerson and Thoreau; he despised both self-reliance and escape.

But the peculiar and bitter quality of Robinson's idealism was not characteristic of New England. When a youth at Harvard College in the early nineties he came under the spell of Hardy and Schopenhauer, and, as was then fashionable, he reveled in a sentimental pessimism. It is highly probable that Royce's *Spirit of Modern Philosophy*, with its sympathetic exposition of Schopenhauer and its portrayal of the life of moral judgment as a life of courage or endurance, made a lasting impression on him. In any case, Robinson rapidly outgrew the sentimental pathos in Hardy's conception of tragedy and became obsessed with the tragedy of knowledge, with the agony of penetrating layer after layer of illusion in order to get the real truth, the truth of human bondage. He followed Royce, too, in believing that this abso-

---

[17] Edwin Arlington Robinson, "The Man against the Sky," in *Collected Poems* (New York, 1937), p. 67.

lute understanding is achieved, not through scientific description, but through sympathetic appreciation.

Robinson's poems can be grouped as successive applications of this theory to different aspects of human existence. The earliest group, culminating in *The Man against the Sky*, put man in his cosmic setting and struggle for "light" on the dark "shadows" of material existence.

> Let us, the Children of the Night,
> Put off the cloak that hides the scar!—
> Let us be Children of the Light,
> And tell the ages what we are! [18]

In these poems both his philosophy and his verse are relatively conventional. Then followed a series of poems centering on man's efforts to escape his "castles"—the castles symbolizing a combination of romantic love and chivalric duty. He used the Arthurian legend to illustrate the conflict of love and duty and the romantic mechanisms of escape; *Merlin* is the outstanding poem of this series. He next considered man's "houses," the problems of marriage, and portrayed their various "doors" as all opening out into "the night." Lastly, he wrote about "dragons and chimneys," the blind will of "the people" and the economic struggle for power. His great poem on this theme, truly a classic tragedy, is *King Jasper*.

The idea for "King Jasper" had come to Robinson, walking down State Street in Boston during the bank holiday, following the inauguration of Franklin Roosevelt, and the name of his protagonist was that of the mine down which the last of his patrimony had vanished thirty-five years before. He was distrustful of a contemporaneous theme but could not resist the temptation to write what he called his "treatise on economics." He gave the poem a triple significance—first, as a story of six unhappy beings, caught in a cataclysm of all that is life to them; then, as a symbolic drama of the disintegration of the capitalistic system; and, last, as an allegory of ignorance and knowledge and aspiration.[19]

[18] Estelle Kaplan, *Philosophy in the Poetry of Edwin Arlington Robinson* (New York, 1940), p. 12; quoted from *The Children of the Night* in Hermann Hagedorn, *Edwin Arlington Robinson* (New York, 1938), p. 101.

[19] *Ibid.*, pp. 128–29; quoted from Hagedorn, *op. cit.*, p. 369.

The only character in this tragedy which survives the social cataclysm is Zoë, the incarnation of vitality and intelligence, freed from all habits of introversion and from the moralism of "the New England conscience." The poem is a masterpiece of irony and a demonstration that Robinson was capable of analyzing the social environment as well as the inner play of motives with deep feeling, yet with complete aloofness, like a chained Prometheus surveying the restless, blind motions of all other beings.

Among the sad young metaphysical poets at Harvard in the nineties, each inspired by the same truth, but living apart in unsocial unison, was George Santayana. As an undergraduate he, too, had been charmed by Royce's Schopenhauer, and during his postgraduate year or two in Berlin he had heard Deussen give his lectures on Schopenhauer and nirvana. When he returned, in 1888, to take his doctor's degree under Royce, he begged to write on Schopenhauer, but was compelled to write, what proved to be a perfunctory chore, an essay on Lotze. Meanwhile, he nourished a double enthusiasm, not unlike Schopenhauer's, an enthusiasm kindled apparently by Paulsen's lectures in Berlin on Greek ethics, during the first semester, and on Spinoza's *Ethics* during the second. He understood the antithesis and synthesis of Hebraism and Hellenism: "naturalism as to the origin and history of mankind, and fidelity, in moral sentiment, to the inspiration of reason, by which the human mind conceives truth and eternity, and participates in them ideally." [20]

During his youthful romanticism Santayana conceived of natural piety as a union of Greek, Spinozist, and pessimist ethics. Apparently, if we may trust his sonnets, he turned to natural religion as a substitute for a Christian faith that was no longer tolerable. "I came down from Golgotha to thee, Eternal Mother." It was not a comfortable religion, but beautiful, and above all, intellectually courageous; he was not seeking comfort and felt strong enough to wake from "that summer's trance" of youth "to find despair before us, vanity behind." He gave poetic expression to his more than Promethean defiance in his "extravagant drama" *Lucifer*. Here is an attempt to bring the Greek and Christian gods together, but neither convinces the other, and in the

[20] George Santayana, *The Middle Span* (New York, 1945), pp. 6–7.

end both prove powerless. With Lucifer, arch-rebel, he finally takes
his firm but desolate stand.

> Great God, when thy frail son of Galilee
> Forsaken on the cross was nigh to death,
> Into thy hands he yielded up his breath.
> Death's vain forgetting hath no balm for me.
> Hereafter I shall look upon the sun
> In sorrow, for my circle is not run,
> The circle of mine endless misery.
> My pang is greater than a man's could be
> Whose father was in heaven and who, forsooth,
> Thought to be happy. And I needs must find
> A greater, dearer comforter than he.
> O truth, O truth, eternal bitter truth,
> Be thou my refuge when all else is blind!
> Thou art the essence of my lofty mind;
> At thy pure wells I will renew my youth.
> Thy joyless bosom never was unkind
> To him who loved thee; let us now be one.
> I have no other friend, I have resigned
> All love but thine. My foolish life is done.
> But O ye hills that I have known of old,
> Unravished of the sun, ye snowy flock
> For ever sleeping, take me to your fold
> And in your flanks of adamantine rock
> Entomb my fiery heart. Over me spread
> Your frozen shroud and wreathe me in ice-flowers,
> To watch with you through everlasting hours
> And not remember. Lo! I lift my head
> Into the void, in scorn of all that live
> Through hope and anguish and insensate wars.
> For, knowing grief, I have forgot to grieve,
> And, having suffered, without tears receive
> The visitation of my kindred stars.[21]

In 1898 the poet became a professor, and there ensued a period
of more than a dozen years which Santayana in retrospect regards

[21] George Santayana, *Lucifer; a Theological Tragedy* (Chicago, 1899), pp.
186–87.

as "the middle years" of "somnambulism," but which, judged by the record, were exceedingly fruitful and on the whole pleasant years of academic fellowship and production. If we may apply to Santayana's life his own scheme for describing the phases of human progress, we should call these years his "rational" period, leading him from his prerational poetry to his post-rational soliloquy. This sober period began with Royce's lectures on Hegel's *Phenomenologie des Geistes,* with William James's lectures on psychology, and with Santayana's own lectures on the philosophy of history. As he became more intimately acquainted with the history of philosophy, art, and religion, there dawned on him the theme of *The Life of Reason.* This charming exposition of human progress, of both the subjective and objective growth of reason in man and society, is a combination of Aristotelian ethics and Hegelian phenomenology and deserves to hold an enduring place among the classic formulations of the genteel tradition. Of it may truly be said what Santayana says of his later "system," that "it aspires to be only a contribution to the humanities, the expression of a reflective, selective, and free mind." [22] It is not original, but it is catholic and says systematically, elegantly, what every professor of philosophy tries to say. In the first and theoretically basic volume, *Reason in Common Sense,* he expounded James's psychology as an analysis of experience. He explained how the "flux" (James's "stream of consciousness") is organized into intelligible "concretions" (objects) by the selective or discriminating activity of "intent," interest or will (James's "intelligence" or "sagacity"). Concretions based on association by contiguity yield knowledge of physical objects; those based on association by similarity yield ideas or terms of discourse. Hence knowledge has two poles: physics, the disclosure of concretions in existence, and dialectics, the clarification of ideas, values and objects of "intent." The "concretions in discourse" he occasionally calls "stable essences," and they are clearly distinguished from the flux of experience, on the one hand, and from physical existence, on the other.

In its objective embodiment the life of reason takes the form of institutions: society, religion, art, and science. In their careers these institutions exhibit the same pattern of life which individual experience exhibits. Three levels or phases of progress can be distinguished: the

[22] Santayana, *The Middle Span,* p. 156.

prerational, life being controlled by the natural impulsions of instinct, desire, and custom; the rational, life being controlled by the conscious expression, clarification, and objectification of these impulsions; the postrational, life being subordinated to the free play of consciousness and imagination. The successive volumes of *The Life of Reason* describe these three levels of society, religion, art, and science.

Philosophies, too, as he explained in later essays, share the same career; they arise naturally as "maps of action" or creatures of "animal faith," but they gradually generate a life of their own, in which the normal life of man is transformed into the patterns of "pictorial space," "sentimental time," and "literary psychology." These patterns of reflection when considered in relation to their origins and ends, may serve man's happiness and enlightenment, but they may become ends in themselves and carry the mind off into realms of free speculation and mystic joys to the complete disregard of their natural reference and uses.

As soon as Santayana could renounce his academic duties, he devoted himself to this post-rational art of being a free spirit. It chanced that soon after he broke loose from America the world broke into war, and the energies of most men have been consumed in conflict ever since. Santayana, however, persisted in the great renunciation; he did not flee nature or seek escape in supernatural mysticism, but he looked down on society, humanism, and morals from his solitary, skeptical eminence, where in cultivated innocence and Olympian charity he could clearly see that man's practical concerns are "only natural."

Impartial reflection upon ultimate things tends to purify, without condemning, all the natural passions, because being natural, they are inevitable and inherently innocent, while being *only* natural, they are all relative and, in a sense, vain. . . .

Spirituality is only a sort of return to innocence, birdlike and childlike. Experience of the world may have complicated the picture without clouding the vision. . . . Although intellect arises quite naturally, in the animal act of dominating events in the interests of survival, yet essentially intellect disengages itself from that servile office (which is that of its organ only) and from the beginning is speculative and impartial in its own outlook, and thinks it not robbery to take the point of view of God, of the truth, and of eternity. . . .

. . . when ultimately the spirit comes face to face with the truth, convention and absurdity are out of place; so is humanism and so is the genteel tradition; so is morality itself. . . .

A strained holiness, never without its seamy side, ousts honourable virtue, and the fear of so many enemies becomes the greatest enemy of the soul. No true appreciation of anything is possible without a sense of its *naturalness*, of the innocent necessity by which it has assumed its special and perhaps extraordinary form.[23]

He imagined himself in the position of a Luther or a Spinoza, ready to stand alone, "unpledged and naked, under the open sky," confessing a natural piety and courage; but unlike them he renounced even a faith in Providence and a love of natural order.

Does it not begin to appear that the solitude of a naked spirit may be rather well peopled? In proportion as we renounce our animal claims and commitments, do we not breathe a fresher and more salubrious air? May not the renunciation of everything disinfect everything and return everything to us in its impartial reality, at the same time disinfecting our wills also, and rendering us capable of charity? [24]

Undistracted and in solitude, he now surveyed the realms of being and constructed a systematic ontology to serve as a natural home for a free spirit. He abandoned his Jamesian "common sense," his belief in the empirical mixture of "intent" and "flux," of will and stream of consciousness, and reverted to a Humean psychology. The intuition of discrete essences, he claimed, could be completely divorced from "animal faith" in objects. Nothing given need exist, for knowledge is not derived through intuition of the given, but by interaction of organisms with other material objects. The play of imagination or intuition is emancipated by the discovery that science has a pragmatic, animal foundation. Thus Santayana brought his youthful enthusiasm for Schopenhauer up to date, deepened by a more skeptical phenomenology and a more behavioristic epistemology. The four volumes of *The Realms of Being*, exploring in succession essence, matter, truth, and spirit, expound this union of skepticism and animal faith as a systematic

[23] George Santayana, *The Genteel Tradition at Bay* (New York, 1931), pp. 46, 64, 65, 71–72, 73.

[24] George Santayana, *Obiter Scripta; lectures, essays and reviews* (New York, 1936), p. 287.

ontology. The work is, however, more than an ontology, for into it Santayana has woven what worldly wisdom he possesses as well as his sense of beauty. It is undoubtedly one of the masterpieces of philosophic construction, and will undoubtedly survive our times, since it is addressed to a reflective reader of any age or culture and seeks to express in a fresh idiom an enduring truth. It would be idle to quarrel with its author by insisting that it should be interpreted in the perspective of recent American thought as an attempt to give calm and direction to the several winds of doctrine that stormed about him at Harvard and that have continued to blow at cross purposes in American philosophy, for it can stand as a monumental achievement wherever philosophy may flourish. It is, nevertheless, just to point out that there is so much of "the ultimate Puritan" in its austerity and so much of naturalistic metaphysics in its doctrine that it necessarily betrays its natural origin in America, whatever may be its eventual fortunes under clearer skies and among peoples of more delicate taste.

GUIDE TO THE LITERATURE FOR PART VI

For this subject in general see Richard Hofstadter, *Social Darwinism in American Thought, 1860–1915* (Philadelphia, 1944), Ch. I, "The Coming of Darwinism," and Ch. II, "The Vogue of Spencer"; Morris R. Cohen, "A Brief Sketch of the Later Philosophy," *The Cambridge History of American Literature*, III, 226–65; Sidney Ratner, "Evolution and the Rise of the Scientific Spirit in America," *Philosophy of Science*, III (1936), 104–22; Bert James Loewenberg, "Darwinism Comes to America, 1859–1900," *Mississippi Valley Historical Review*, XXVIII (1941), 339–68, and "The Reaction of American Scientists to Darwin," *American Historical Review*, XXXVIII (1932–33), 657–70; and Arthur O. Lovejoy, "The Argument for Organic Evolution before 'The Origin of Species,'" *Popular Science Monthly*, LXXV (1909), 499–514, 537–49. Merle Curti, *The Growth of American Thought* (New York, 1943), Chapter XXII, "Evolutionary Thought in a Utilitarian Society," deals chiefly with the later phases of evolutionary thought and their relations to instrumentalism and pragmatism. In Chapter XXI, "The Delimitation of Supernaturalism," however, pp. 543–54, there is a survey of the rise of evolutionary philosophy in America.

CHAPTER 30

John Spencer Clark, *The Life and Letters of John Fiske,* 2 vols. (Boston and New York, 1917), is an entertaining account not merely of the thought and career of Fiske but also of the chief currents of cosmic philosophy of the time. *The Letters of John Fiske,* edited by his daughter, Ethel F. Fisk (New York, 1940), are unfortunately not indexed. The volume contains many interesting letters not included in Clark's *Life.* Of special interest are Fiske's earliest letters as a college student and his letters to Spencer and Darwin, particularly those of 1871. In his letter to Darwin, April 21, 1880, he wrote, "Huxley told me last year that he thought I could do more for the doctrine of evolution in history than in any other line." This comment and Fiske's varying reactions to it recur frequently and throw considerable light on Fiske's reputation as a philosopher. The reactions of Spencer and Darwin to the emphasis on the "cosmic" are found in the letters for 1874–75. Fiske's chief philosophical works were: *Outlines of Cosmic Philosophy Based on the Doctrine of Evolution* (Boston, 1874); *The Destiny of Man Viewed in the Light of His Origin* (Boston, 1884); *The Idea of God as Affected by Modern Knowledge* (Boston, 1885); and *Through Nature to God* (Boston, 1899). In addition to these, attention is called especially to the essays in Vols. VII, "Excursions of an Evolutionist," and VIII, "Darwinism and Other Essays," of his *Miscellaneous Writings* (Boston and New York, 1902).

Edward L. Youmans founded and edited the *Popular Science Monthly* and made its pages a vehicle for carrying evolutionary ideas to the American public. He also edited the volume *Herbert Spencer on the Americans and the Americans on Herbert Spencer* (New York, 1883). John W. Draper, in addition to writing for *Popular Science Monthly,* wrote an account of *The Conflict of Religion and Science* (New York, 1874). Draper's *Evolution; Its Origin, Progress, and Consequences* (New York, 1877), provides a convenient summary of his views; it was originally delivered as an address before an institute of Unitarian ministers at Springfield, Mass., October 11, 1877. Andrew D. White, president of Cornell University, delivered his blow for the evolutionary theory by the publication of his *History of the Warfare between Science and Theology* (New York, 1896).

The Works of Job Durfee, edited with a Memoir by his son, were published at Providence, R.I., 1849. His address "On the Influence of Scientific Discovery and Invention upon Social and Political Progress" is reprinted in Blau, *American Philosophic Addresses, 1700–1900,* pp. 383–414. Alexander Kinmont's *Twelve Lectures on the Natural History of Man and the*

Rise and Progress of Philosophy were posthumously published at Cincinnati, 1839, with a biographical sketch. The works of Henry James the Elder have already been given on p. 318.

J. B. Stallo, after he had cast off "the spell of Hegel's ontological reveries," published a series of articles defining his newer understanding of "The Primary Concepts of Modern Physical Science," in the *Popular Science Monthly:* "The Theory of the Atomic Constitution of Matter," III (1873), 705–17; "The Atomic Constitution of Matter as a Postulate of Thought," IV (1873–74), 92–109; "The Assumption of the Essential Solidity of Matter," IV (1873–74), 219–31; and "Inertia and Force," IV (1873–74), 349–61. The substance of these articles was expanded into his book, *The Concepts and Theories of Modern Physics* (New York, 1882). Paul Carus provided a guide to his own thought in the volume *Philosophy as a Science; a Synopsis of the Writings of Paul Carus* (Chicago, 1909), which contains, in addition to Carus's Introduction, summaries of all his books and a list of his articles and editorials in *The Monist* and *Open Court.*

The addresses at the Concord Summer School in 1885, as a symposium on the question, "Is pantheism the legitimate outcome of modern science?" were published as follows: John Fiske, *The Idea of God as Affected by Modern Knowledge* (Boston, 1885), and Francis Ellingwood Abbot, *Scientific Theism* (Boston, 1885), were published independently, Abbot's book in expanded form; the contributions of the other participants were published as read in the *Journal of Speculative Philosophy*, XIX (1885): Andrew P. Peabody, pp. 337–52; Edmund Montgomery, pp. 352–63; George H. Howison, pp. 363–84; William Torrey Harris, pp. 407–28. Montgomery's paper also appeared in the *Index*, n.s., Vol. VI (August 27, 1885), and Howison's in the *Overland Monthly*, ser. 2, VI (December, 1885), 646–58. A brief account of the symposium is to be found in the beginning of Abbot's *Scientific Theism*, p. vii.

On Francis Ellingwood Abbot, the only published work of any proportion is F. A. Christie's article in the *Dictionary of American Biography.* Abbot's lectures as substitute for Royce at Harvard were published under the title *The Way Out of Agnosticism.* Royce's review, "Dr. Abbot's 'Way Out of Agnosticism,'" *International Journal of Ethics*, I (1890–91), 98–113, touched off a hot dispute. Abbot replied to Royce in a pamphlet entitled *Professor Royce's Libel; a public appeal for redress to the corporation and overseers of Harvard University* (Boston, 1891). The remaining published contributions to the controversy were included in the *Nation*, Vol. LIII (July–Dec., 1891): Charles S. Peirce, p. 372, favoring Abbot's position; William James, p. 389, maintaining a judicious balance; Royce's counsel, Joseph B. Warner, p. 408, giving the "facts"; Abbot, p. 426, replying to Warner, after which the editor of the *Nation* declined to print more letters on the question. There is an extended discussion of Abbot's *Scientific Theism* in L. Carrau, *La Philosophie religieuse en Angleterre depuis Locke jusqu'a nos jours* (Paris, 1888), pp. 251–69, and a brief account in Sidney Warren, *American Freethought, 1860–1914* (New York, 1943), pp. 100–101 and *passim*. Edmund Montgomery reviewed *Scientific Theism* in the *Index*, n.s., VI (1885–86), 438–41; 450–53.

Abbot's major works were: *Scientific Theism; or, Organic Scientific Philosophy* (Boston, 1885); *The Way Out of Agnosticism; or, The Philosophy of Free Religion* (Boston, 1890); and *The Syllogistic Philosophy; or, Prolegomena to Science*, 2 vols. (Boston, 1906). In addition he wrote an important article, "The Philosophy of Space and Time," *North American Review*, XCIX (1864), 64–116, and a critical account of Herbert Spencer's work, "Philosophical Biology," *North American Review*, CVII (1868), 377–422. Among his contributions to the thought of "free religion," his "A Radical's Theology," *The Radical*, II (1867), 585–87, and "The Genius of Christianity and Free Religion," in Blau, *American Philosophic Addresses, 1700–1900*, pp. 683–708, are of particular interest. Chauncey Wright's criticism of "A Radical's Theology" and other letters to and about Abbot are included in *Letters of Chauncey Wright* (Cambridge, 1878).

By "syllogistic philosophy" Abbot meant that human knowledge is based on the "Threefold Reality of Universals as its Constituent Molecules; 1. Objective Reality in the Real Genus, or Universal of the First Power; 2. Subjective Reality in the Ideal Concept, or Universal of the Second Power; and 3. Objective-Subjective Reality in the Real-Ideal World, or Universal of the Third Power" (*Syllogistic Philosophy*, II, 311).

On Peirce's philosophy of evolution see Morris R. Cohen's introduction to Charles S. Peirce, *Chance, Love, and Logic* (New York, 1923); H. G. Townsend, *Philosophical Ideas in the United States* (New York, 1934), chap. xi, "Logical Realism: Chance"; and Charles Hartshorne, "Charles Sanders Peirce's Metaphysics of Evolution," *New England Quarterly*, XIV (1941), 49–63. Two articles by Philip P. Wiener on Peirce's evolutionism and Metaphysical Club and their relation to pragmatism are in Vol. VII, (1946) of the *Journal of the History of Ideas*. See also Ralph Barton Perry, *The Thought and Character of William James* (Boston, 1935), Vol. I, chap. xxxii, "Charles Peirce." There are attempts to describe Peirce's rebellion against New England culture by James Feibleman, "The Relation of Peirce to New England Culture," *American Journal of Economics and*

Sociology, IV (1945), 99–107, and Frederic I. Carpenter, "Charles Sanders Peirce, Pragmatic Transcendentalist," *New England Quarterly*, XIV (1941), 34–48. Of Peirce's writings, the essays which are related to his theory of evolution are his review of A. C. Fraser's edition of *The Works of George Berkeley*, in the *North American Review*, CXIII (1871), 449–72, Peirce's earliest defense of antinominalism, and the essays collected in *Chance, Love, and Logic* (New York, 1923). Many of these important essays are in Justus Buchler, *The Philosophy of Peirce: Selected Writings* (New York, 1940). There are scattered bits of Peirce's cosmology in all six volumes thus far published of *The Collected Papers of Charles S. Peirce*, ed. by C. Hartshorne and P. Weiss (Cambridge, 1931–35), but the best material is to be found in Vols. I and VI.

On Chauncey Wright see John Fiske, "Chauncey Wright," in *Darwinism and Other Essays* (Boston, 1902), pp. 74–104, originally published as a review of Wright's *Philosophical Discussions*; William James, "Chauncey Wright," in *Collected Essays and Reviews* (New York, 1920), pp. 20–25; Ralph Barton Perry, *The Thought and Character of William James* (Boston, 1935), chap. xxxi, "Chauncey Wright"; Gail Kennedy, "The Pragmatic Naturalism of Chauncey Wright," in *Studies in the History of Ideas*, ed. by the Department of Philosophy, Columbia University, III (New York, 1935), 477–503; and Philip P. Wiener, "Chauncey Wright's Defense of Darwin and the Neutrality of Science," *Journal of the History of Ideas*, VI (1945), 19–45. There are scattered references to Wright in the papers of Charles S. Peirce, in F. W. Maitland, *The Life and Letters of Leslie Stephen* (New York, 1906), and in Simon Newcomb, *The Reminiscences of an Astronomer* (Boston, 1903). Wright's *Philosophical Discussions* were edited with a biographical sketch by Charles Eliot Norton (New York, 1877), and some of the *Letters of Chauncey Wright* were collected and edited by James B. Thayer, with interspersed memoirs by Thayer and other friends of Wright (Cambridge, 1878). Of Wright's essays and reviews, the following are of particular interest: "The Wind and the Weather," *Atlantic Monthly*, I (1857), 272–79; "A Physical Theory of the Universe," *North American Review*, XCIX (1864), 1–33, reprinted in *Philosophical Discussions*; "Natural Theology as a Positive Science," *North American Review*, C (1865), 177–85, reprinted in *Philosophical Discussions*; "The Philosophy of Herbert Spencer," *North American Review*, C (1865), 423–76, reprinted in *Philosophical Discussions*; "Mill on Hamilton, *Nation*, I (1865), 278–81; "The Limits of Natural Selection," *North American Review*, CXI (1870), 282–310, reprinted in *Philosophical Discussions*; "The Genesis of Species," *North American Re-*

view, CXIII (1871), 63–82, reprinted in *Philosophical Discussions;* "Evolution by Natural Selection," *North American Review,* CXV (1872), 1–30, reprinted in *Philosophical Discussions;* "The Evolution of Self-Consciousness," *North American Review,* CXVI (1873), 245–310, reprinted in *Philosophical Discussions;* "McCosh on Tyndall," *Nation,* XX (1875), 277–79, reprinted in *Philosophical Discussions;* and "German Darwinism," *Nation,* Vol. XXI (1875), reprinted in *Philosophical Discussions.*

CHAPTER 31

The chief contributions to the controversy over the unity of mankind were: Samuel Stanhope Smith, *An Essay on the Causes of the Variety of Complexion and Figure in the Human Species* (Philadelphia, 1787); Samuel G. Morton, "Hybridity in Animals Considered in Reference to the Question of the Unity of the Human Species," *American Journal of Science and Arts,* 2d ser., III (1847), 38–50, 203–12; C. Pickering, *Races of Men and Their Geographical Distribution,* published in 1848 as Vol. IX of the *Reports* of the United States Exploring Expedition of 1838–42; Thomas Smyth, *The Unity of the Human Races Proved to Be the Doctrine of Scripture, Reason, and Science: with a Review of the Present Position and Theory of Professor Agassiz* (New York, 1850; rev. and enl. ed., Edinburgh, 1851); L. Agassiz, "Geographical Distribution of Animals," *Christian Examiner,* XLVIII (1850), 181–204; J. Bachman, *The Doctrine of the Unity of the Human Race Examined on the Principles of Science* (Charleston, 1850); Josiah C. Nott and George R. Gliddon, *Types of Mankind* (Philadelphia, 1854), which contains an important article by Louis Agassiz entitled "Of the Natural Provinces of the Animal World and Their Relations to the Different Types of Man," in which the distinguished scientist supports the hypothesis of original varieties; John W. Draper, *Human Physiology, Statistical and Dynamical* (New York, 1856); J. D. Dana, "Thoughts on Species," *Bibliotheca Sacra,* XIV (1857), 854–74; and J. L. Cabell, *The Testimony of Modern Science to the Unity of Mankind* (New York, 1859). J. P. Lesley, *Man's Origin and Destiny Sketched from the Platform of the Physical Sciences* (Boston, 1868), especially Lecture V, "On the Unity of Mankind," argued for the original diversity of man and concluded his survey of the evidence with the pious suggestion, "Let us praise God for our place in this procession of mysteries. If natural history should hereafter teach the truth of our descent from these inferior beings, Christianity will always teach humility. Let us comfort our pride by remembering that everything has been good and perfect in its day and generation" (2d ed., Boston, 1881, p. 121).

The general position out of which the pre-Adamite theory arose was stated thus by Alexander Winchell: "Our written history does not extend back to the origin of man. The Mosaic records, which are undoubtedly the oldest of our authentic documents, represent the western portion of Asia as swarming with a population tolerably advanced in the arts at a period two or three thousand years antecedent to our era. There was, consequently, a long interval of human history still anterior to this date" (*Sketches of Creation*, New York, 1870, p. 350). The pre-Adamite theory was an attempt to fill this long interval in such a way that neither the evolutionary theory nor the authenticity of the Scriptures need be questioned. A discussion of the earlier pre-Adamite literature can be found in Alexander Winchell, *Preadamites; or, A Demonstration of the Existence of Men before Adam; together with a Study of Their Condition, Antiquity, Racial Affinities, and Progressive Dispersion over the Earth* (Chicago, 1880), chap. xxix, "Pre-adamitism in Literature."

For the scientific reaction to Darwin see Bert J. Loewenberg, "The Reaction of American Scientists to Darwin," *American Historical Review*, XXXVIII (1932–33), 657–70. Philosophically, the more important reviews of Darwin's *Origin of Species* were: Francis Bowen, "The Latest Form of the Development Theory," *North American Review*, XC (1860), 474–506; Asa Gray, "Darwin and His Reviewers," *Atlantic Monthly*, VI (1860), 406–25; Louis Agassiz, "Prof. Agassiz on the Origin of Species," *American Journal of Science and Arts*, XXX (1860), 142–54; Chauncey Wright, "The Limits of Natural Selection" and "The Genesis of Species," both originally published in the *North American Review* and reprinted in Wright, *Philosophical Discussions* (New York, 1877); Francis Ellingwood Abbot, "Philosophical Biology," *North American Review*, CVII (1868), 377–422; Louis Agassiz, "Evolution and the Permanence of Type," *Atlantic Monthly*, XXXIII (1874), 92–101.

Alexander Winchell held various academic positions, was one of the founders and an early president of the Geological Society of America, and wrote voluminously both on scientific topics and speculative themes arising out of his scientific thinking. His bibliography extends to more than 250 published items; his manuscripts, including letters, are preserved in the collections of the Minnesota Historical Society. For his evolutionary speculations the following are his most important works: *Sketches of Creation* (New York, 1870); *The Doctrine of Evolution; Its Data, Its Principles,*

Its Speculations, and Its Theistic Bearings (New York, 1874), which includes a survey of the various theories of evolution and a sharp criticism of the Darwinian theory; *Reconciliation of Science and Religion* (New York, 1877); *Preadamites* (Chicago, 1880); *Geological Excursions* (Chicago, 1884); *Walks and Talks in the Geological Field* (New York, 1886); and *Speculative Consequences of Evolution* (Ann Arbor, 1888).

Joseph LeConte's *Autobiography* (New York, 1913) contains information about his surrender to theistic evolution. In addition, the following works clarify his position: *Religion and Science* (New York, 1874); "Man's Place in Nature," *Princeton Review*, LIV (1878), 775–803; "Evolution in Relation to Materialism," *Princeton Review*, LVII (1881), 149–74; *Evolution; Its Nature, Its Evidence, and Its Relationship to Religious Thought* (New York, 1888); *The Conception of God; a Philosophical Discussion concerning the Nature of the Divine Idea as a Demonstrable Reality* (New York, 1897), a discussion in which the other participants were Josiah Royce, George Holmes Howison, and Sidney E. Mezes.

Henry Fairfield Osborn, *Cope, Master Naturalist* (Princeton, 1931), is a lively portrait showing the massiveness of Cope's scientific labors and giving a general history of his philosophical speculations, especially pp. 527–74. Osborn cites much interesting correspondence and gives a complete bibliography of Cope. The treatment emphasizes Osborn's polemic with Cope over Lamarckianism. C. T. Stockwell, *New Modes of Thought, Based upon the New Materialism and the New Pantheism; Including a Tribute to Edward Drinker Cope* (Boston, 1901), is a record of intellectual discipleship, asserting that Cope "gives us the *scientific* affirmation of God and Immortality." Stockwell also wrote *The Evolution of Immortality* (Chicago, 1888), which is an extension and specific application of Cope's notion of the "great Mind." Cope's *Origin of the Fittest* (New York, 1886), is a collection of various papers written between 1868 and 1884. The introduction summarizes the development of Cope's theory and its relation to the theories of others. Of special interest are the following papers: "The Origin of Genera" (1868), "The Hypothesis of Evolution, Physical and Metaphysical" (1870), "Consciousness in Evolution" (1875), and "Archaesthetism" (1882). Edmund Montgomery's review of Cope's *Theology of Evolution*, in the *Open Court*, I (1887), 160–64; 217–20; 274–77; 300–303 introduced a controversial discussion between the two, *Open Court*, I (1887), 285–88, 358–61, which is valuable for its succinct summaries of Cope's views and for distinguishing his system from both mechanism and idealism. In this discussion Cope revealed what theism meant to him. In general he is here shown at his critical best. Cope's *Primary Factors of Organic Evolution* (Chicago, 1896) is the latest and most complete exposition of his views; for his philosophy of evolution, chaps. ix, "The Energy of Evolution," and x, "The Function of Consciousness," are especially important.

Morris T. Keeton has written an excellent brief account of Edmund Montgomery's biological and philosophical speculations, "Montgomery—Pioneer of Organicism," which is to appear in a forthcoming issue of the *Journal of the History of Ideas*, accompanied by a list of Montgomery's published writings. I. M. Stephens, "Edmund Montgomery, the Hermit Philosopher of Liendo Plantation," *Southwest Review*, XVI (1931), 200–235, sketches the biography of Montgomery with particular stress on his ideas. Of his writings, those which are most important for his philosophy of evolution are: *Die Kant'sche Erkenntnisslehre widerlegt vom Standpunkt der Empirie* (Munich, 1871); "The Dependence of Quality on Specific Energies," *Mind*, V (1880), 1–29; "The Unity of the Organic Individual," *Mind*, V (1880), 318–36, 465–89; "Causation and Its Organic Conditions," *Mind*, VII (1882), 209–30, 381–97, 514–32; "Is Pantheism the Legitimate Outcome of Modern Science?" *Journal of Speculative Philosophy*, XIX (1885), 352–63; "Space and Touch," *Mind*, X (1885), 227–44, 377–98, 512–31; "Transcendentalism and Evolution," *The Index*, n.s., V (1885), 463–66, 474–77; "Scientific Theism," *The Index*, n.s., VI (1885–86), 438–41, 450–53, a review of Francis Ellingwood Abbot's book of that name; "Cope's *Theology of Evolution*," *Open Court*, I (1887), 160–64, 217–20, 274–77, 300–303; "Concluding Remarks in the Discussion 'Is Monism Untenable?'" *Open Court*, IV (1890), 2511–12; "Automatism and Spontaneity," *Monist*, IV (1893), 44–64; "The Integration of Mind," *Mind*, n.s., IV (1895), 307–19; "Are We Conscious Automata?" *Proceedings of the Texas Academy of Science*, I, No. 5 (1896), 65–80; "Actual Experience," *Monist*, IX (1899), 359–81; *Philosophical Problems in the Light of Vital Organization* (New York, 1907).

CHAPTER 32

The chief American literature concerning the religious implications of evolutionary geology is described by Conrad Wright, "The Religion of Geology," *New England Quarterly*, XIV (1941), 335–58. Wright gives particular attention to Benjamin Silliman, Edward Hitchcock, and James Dwight Dana. To the literature which he surveys should be added the writings of Alexander Winchell, for which see above, *The Education of Henry Adams*, chap. xv, "Darwinism," for which see below, and the writings of Tayler Lewis, especially his *Six Days of Creation* (Schenectady, 1878).

There are several accounts of the religious reactions to biological evolution as reflected in the periodical literature of the time. Unfortunately these articles do not distinguish between the more critical and philosophical theologians and the popular attacks in popular church journals. The most comprehensive treatment of the subject is by Windsor Hall Roberts, *The Reaction of American Protestant Churches to the Darwinian Philosophy, 1860–1900*. Abstract of a dissertation submitted to the Department of History of Chicago University in 1936 (Chicago, 1938). Dr. Roberts analyzes the general theological reaction as follows: an earlier wave of "alarmism," a "mild group of hesitating compromisers" in the seventies, followed "in the early eighties by a group of enthusiastic evolutionists, lay and clerical, who had been captivated by the Spencerian optimism." He attempts an interesting, though probably premature, statement of "theology's final adjustment," which includes an analysis of the literature of the early twentieth century. In addition, see Sidney Ratner, "Evolution and the Rise of the Scientific Spirit in America," *Philosophy of Science*, III (1936), 104–22; Arthur M. Schlesinger, "A Critical Period in American Religion, 1875–1900," *Proceedings*, Massachusetts Historical Society, LXIV (1932), 525–27; and Bert James Loewenberg, "Darwinism Comes to America, 1859–1900," *Mississippi Valley Historical Review*, XXVIII (1941), 339–68, and "The Controversy over Evolution in New England," *New England Quarterly*, VIII (1935), 232–57, which is devoted less to New England than to the general run of religious periodicals. The philosophical theologians are discussed in Frank Hugh Foster, *The Modern Movement in American Theology* (New York, 1939), chap. iii, "The Reception of Evolution by Theologians," and in Daniel Day Williams, *The Andover Liberals; a Study in American Theology* (New York, 1941), chaps. ii, "Evolutionary Philosophies," iii, "Ethics and Evolution," and v, "Evolution and Historical Criticism."

Noteworthy Publications in Evolutionary Theology

1860   Louis Agassiz, "On the Origin of Species," *American Journal of Science and Arts*, XXX (1860), 142–54.

Francis Bowen, "Darwin on the Origin of Species," *North American Review*, XC (1860), 474–506.

D. R. Goodwin, "Darwin on the Origin of Species," *American Theological Review*, II (1860), 326–44.

Asa Gray, "Darwin and His Reviewers," *Atlantic Monthly*, VI (1860), 406–25.

John A. Lowell, "Darwin on the Origin of Species," *Christian Examiner*, LXVIII (1860), 449–64.

1861 J. P. Thompson, "Does Science Tend to Materialism?" *New Englander*, XIX (1861), 84–101.

W. C. Wilson, "Darwin on the Origin of Species," *Methodist Quarterly Review*, XLIII (1861), 605–25.

1863 Edward Hitchcock, "The Law of Nature's Constancy Subordinate to the Law of Change," *Bibliotheca Sacra*, XX (1863), 489–561.

1867 W. N. Rice, "The Darwinian Theory of the Origin of Species," *New Englander*, XXVI (1867), 603–35.

1871 John Bascom, "Darwin's Theory of the Origin of Species," *American Presbyterian Review*, 3d ser., Vol. III (1871), 349–79.

—— Science, Philosophy, and Religion (New York, 1871).

James McCosh, Christianity and Positivism (New York, 1871).

J. B. Tyler, "Evolution in Natural History as Related to Christianity," *New Englander*, XXX (1871), 464–70.

1872 John Bascom, "Evolution as Advocated by Herbert Spencer," *Princeton Review*, XLIV (1872), 496–515.

Orestes A. Brownson, "Darwin's Descent of Man," in his Works, (Detroit, 1882–87), Vol. IX.

Frederick Gardiner, "Darwinism," *Bibliotheca Sacra*, XXIX (1872), 240–89.

J. S. Stahr, "Theories of Evolution and Theology," *Mercersburg Review*, XIX (1872), 439–50.

1873 Enoch F. Burr, Pater Mundi (Boston, 1873).

S. R. Calthorp, "Religion and Evolution," *Religious Magazine and Monthly Review*, L (1873), 193–213.

Daniel S. Martin, The Relation of Christian Education to Modern Phases of Science (Albany, N.Y., 1873).

1874 Charles Hodge, What Is Darwinism? (New York, 1874). Contains a good bibliography of types of evolutionary theory.

Andrew P. Peabody, Christianity and Science (New York, 1874).

1875 Charles W. Shields, Religion and Science in Their Relation to Philosophy (New York, 1875).

1876 James T. Bixby, Similarities of Physical and Religious Knowledge (New York, 1876).

Asa Gray, Darwiniana (New York, 1876).

James McCosh, The Development Hypothesis; Is it Sufficient? (New York, 1876).

Minot J. Savage, The Religion of Evolution (Boston, 1876).

George F. Wright, "Recent Works Bearing on the Relation of Science to Religion," *Bibliotheca Sacra*, XXXIII (1876), 448–93, 656–94.

1877   Charles W. Shields, The Final Philosophy (New York, 1877).

1878   John T. Duffield, "Evolution Respecting Man, and the Bible," *Princeton Review*, LIV (1878), 150–77.

Frederick Gardiner, "The Bearing of Recent Scientific Thought upon Theology," *Bibliotheca Sacra*, XXXV (1878), 46–75.

Tayler Lewis, The Six Days of Creation (Schenectady, 1878).

Andrew P. Peabody, "Science and Revelation," *Princeton Review*, LIV (1878), 760–83.

1880   Asa Gray, Natural Science and Religion (New York, 1880).

Andrew P. Peabody, "The Religious Aspects of the Logic of Chance and Probability," *Princeton Review*, LVI (1880), 303–20.

George F. Wright, "Some Analogies between Calvinism and Darwinism," *Bibliotheca Sacra*, XXXVI (1880), 48–76.

1881   Joseph LeConte, "Evolution in Relation to Materialism," *Princeton Review*, LVII (1881), 149–74.

Moses S. Phelps, "Anthropomorphism," *Princeton Review*, LVII (1881), 120–44.

1883   J. M. Whiton, "Darwin and Darwinism," *New Englander*, XLII (1883), 51–64.

1884   Francis H. Johnson, "Theistic Evolution," *Andover Review*, I (1884), 363–81.

1885   Francis H. Johnson, "Co-operative Evolution," *Andover Review*, III (1885), 326–46, 436–55.

1886   Henry Ward Beecher, Evolution and Religion (New York, 1885).

Theodore T. Munger, "Evolution and the Faith," *Century*, XXXII (1886), 108–18.

1887   John Dewey, "Ethics and Physical Science," *Andover Review*, VI (1887), 573–91.

1888   James McCosh, The Religious Aspects of Evolution (New York, 1888).

George F. Wright, "The Debt of the Church to Asa Gray," *Bibliotheca Sacra*, XLV (1888), 523–30.

1889   Minot J. Savage, Evolution (New York, 1889).

1891   James T. Bixby, The Crisis in Morals (Boston, 1891).
        Francis H. Johnson, What Is Reality? (Boston and New York, 1891).
        Theodore T. Munger, The Appeal to Life (Boston, 1891).
        Newman Smyth, Old Faiths in New Light (New York, 1891).
1892   Lyman Abbott, The Evolution of Christianity (Boston and New York, 1892).
        Minot J. Savage, The Irrepressible Conflict Between Two World Theories (Boston, 1892).
1896   George Harris, Moral Evolution (Boston and New York, 1896).
1897   Lyman Abbott, The Theology of an Evolutionist (Boston and New York, 1897).
1898   George F. Wright, Scientific Aspects of Christian Evidences (New York, 1898).
1900   James T. Bixby, The Ethics of Evolution (Boston, 1900).
        Charles W. Shields, Scientific Evidences of Revealed Religion (New York, 1900).
1904   Newman Smyth, Through Science to Faith (New York, 1902).
1909   Charles F. Dole, The Ethics of Progress (New York, 1909).
1910   Charles F. Dole, The Coming Religion (Boston, 1910).
1927   Charles F. Dole, Victorious Goodness; an Epic of Spiritual Evolution (New York, 1927).

CHAPTER 33

The best and most recent introduction to the general subject matter of this chapter is Richard Hofstadter, *Social Darwinism* (Philadelphia, 1944). The antithesis between William Graham Sumner and Lester Ward is portrayed admirably. Though the treatment is confined largely to the political and economic ideas, there is at least some indication of the general philosophical orientation, especially in the case of the pragmatists. It is misleading to call Sumner a Darwinist, for his ideas were specifically those of Spencer. The bibliography is extensive and includes many recent works. Fay Berger Karpf, *American Social Psychology* (New York, 1932), Part II, gives a more extensive analysis of the philosophical and psychological theories, especially those of Ward, James, Baldwin, Cooley, Ross, Mead, and Dewey. See also Charles A. Ellwood, *A History of Social Philosophy* (New York, 1938), for expositions of Sumner and Ward. For references to William James see below, pp. 578–79, 583.

On Lester Ward, there are two major works, Emily Palmer Cape, *Lester F. Ward; a Personal Sketch* (New York, 1922), and Samuel

Chugerman, *Lester Ward, the American Aristotle* (Durham, N.C., 1939), which, as their subtitles suggest, go to opposite extremes. A critical work on Ward as a philosopher is to be desired. Ward himself collected practically all his minor writings into six volumes entitled *Glimpses of the Cosmos* (New York, 1913–18). For the particular subject under discussion here, his *Psychic Factors of Civilization* (Boston, 1893) is most important. John Dewey reviewed this work in the *Psychological Review*, I (1894), 400–411. Of Ward's essays, the following have the greatest philosophical interest (the numbers given are those attached to the essays in *Glimpses of the Cosmos*): "Cosmic and Organic Evolution," 1877, No. 89; "Feeling and Function as Factors in Human Development," 1880, No. 106; "Kant's Antinomies in the Light of Modern Science," 1882, No. 120; "Scientific Basis of Positive Political Economy," 1882, No. 121; "Commentary on *Dynamic Sociology*," 1883, No. 145; "Professor Sumner's Social Classes," 1884, No. 169; "Mind as a Social Factor," 1884, No. 179; "Moral and Material Progress Contrasted," 1885, No. 201; "The Use and Abuse of Wealth," 1887, No. 218; "Asa Gray and Darwinism," 1888, No. 240; "Some Social and Economic Paradoxes," 1889, No. 250; "The Course of Biologic Evolution," 1890, No. 265; "The Transmission of Culture," 1891, No. 290; "Neo-Darwinism and Neo-Lamarckism," 1891, No. 291; "The Psychologic Basis of Social Economics," 1893, No. 331; "Commentary on *The Psychic Factors of Civilization*," 1893, No. 349; "The Political Ethics of Herbert Spencer," 1894, No. 355; "Status of the Mind-Problem," 1894, No. 357; "Static and Dynamic Sociology," 1895, No. 381; "Ethical Aspects of Social Science," 1896, No. 411; "The Gospel of Action," 1899, No. 461.

I. Woodbridge Riley, *American Thought from Puritanism to Pragmatism* (New York, 1915), pp. 216–28, is a good statement of Baldwin's evolutionary theory. Vahan D. Sewny, *The Social Philosophy of James Mark Baldwin* (New York, 1945), is the most recent critical summary of his ideas. H. G. Townsend, *Philosophical Ideas in the United States* (New York, 1934), pp. 230–33, summarizes Baldwin's "pancalism" as expounded in his *Genetic Theory of Reality*. James Edwin Creighton, "Darwin and Logic," *Psychological Review*, XVI (1909), 170–87, reprinted as Chap. X of J. E. Creighton, *Studies in Speculative Philosophy* (New York, 1925), criticizes Baldwin's genetic logic from an idealist point of view. Baldwin's works include: *A Handbook of Psychology* (New York, 1889–91); *Elements of Psychology* (New York, 1893); *Mental Development in the Child and the Race* (New York, 1895); *Social and Ethical Interpretations in Mental Development; a Study in Social Psy-*

chology (New York, 1897), of which there were noteworthy critical reviews by James H. Tufts, in the *Psychological Review*, 1898, and John Dewey, in the *Philosophical Review*, 1898, Baldwin's rejoinders to both of which are published in appendices to the 3d ed., New York, 1902; *Development and Evolution* (New York, 1902); *Fragments in Philosophy and Science: Collected Essays and Addresses* (New York, 1902); *Thought and Things; a Study of the Development and Meaning of Thought or Genetic Logic*, 3 vols. (New York, 1906–11); *Darwin and the Humanities* (Baltimore, 1909); *The Individual and Society; or, Psychology and Sociology* (Boston, 1911), which is the best statement of Baldwin's social philosophy; and *Genetic Theory of Reality; Being the Outcome of Genetic Logic as Issuing in the Aesthetic Theory of Pancalism* (New York, 1915), which was projected as the fourth volume of *Thoughts and Things*, but became a summary and restatement of Baldwin's whole philosophy as a system; it is particularly interesting for its close relation to Royce's theory of interpretation and appreciation.

An excellent critical account of various ways in which evolutionary methods have been applied to ethics is found in C. M. Williams, *A Review of the Systems of Ethics Founded on the Theory of Evolution* (New York, 1893). The author was a student of Professor Moses Stuart Phelps at Yale and made no attempt himself to contribute to evolutionary theory except by his extremely judicious critique. His own philosophy, which comes out best in the last chapter, "The Ideal and the Way of Its Attainment," reveals his sympathy for social idealism.

A more extensive guide to the writings of the Chicago school will be found below, pp. 580–82. The most important works are included in the bibliography of Hofstadter's *Social Darwinism*. For a general characterization of this school see Charles H. Judd, *Psychology* (New York, 1907). George Sidney Brett, *A History of Psychology* (London, 1921), III, 259–68, discusses the historical significance of Dewey's and James's psychologies. Fay Berger Karpf, *American Social Psychology; Its Origins, Development, and European Background* (New York, 1932), is of particular value for this group. For the general orientation of the Chicago school, the University of Chicago *Decennial Publications* (Chicago, 1903) are valuable.

Of special interest in the context of genetic social psychology are the following articles by John Dewey: "The Reflex Arc Concept in Psychology," *Psychological Review*, III (1896), 357–70; "Evolution and Ethics," *Monist*, VIII (1898), 321–41; and "The Need for Social Psychology," *Psychological Review*, XXIV (1917), 266–77.

W. I. Thomas's chief publications in the field of social psychology were: "The Scope and Method of Folk Psychology," *American Journal of Sociology*, I (1896), 434–45; "The Province of Social Psychology," in Congress of Arts and Sciences, Universal Exposition, St. Louis, 1904, *Proceedings*, Howard J. Rogers, ed. (Boston and New York, 1906), V, 861–68; *Source Book for Social Origins* (Boston, 1909), in the introduction to which, Thomas interprets the instrumentalist theory of mind, with its emphasis on control of the environment, as an extension of genetic method; and "The Behavior Pattern and the Situation," *Publications of the American Sociological Society*, XXII (1928), 1–13.

E. A. Ross, *Social Psychology* (New York, 1908), was influenced largely by Tarde and the French school and contributed little to the theory of evolution; Ross, however, emphasized the social nature of mind.

On G. H. Mead see T. V. Smith, "The Social Philosophy of George Herbert Mead," *American Journal of Sociology*, XXXVII (1931–32), 368–85, and Grace Chin Lee, *George Herbert Mead, Philosopher of the Social Individual* (New York, 1945), which presents Mead's ideas as a coherently integrated system and discusses the somewhat obscure relationship between *The Philosophy of the Present* and Mead's social psychology. This book also includes a good bibliography. Of Mead's articles, the following are important in the context of genetic social psychology: "The Working Hypothesis in Social Reform," *American Journal of Sociology*, V (1899), 367–71; "The Definition of the Psychical," University of Chicago, *Decennial Publications*, III (1903), 77–112; "Concerning Animal Perception," *Psychological Review*, XIV (1907), 383–90; "The Philosophical Basis of Ethics," *International Journal of Ethics*, XVIII (1908), 311–23; "Social Psychology as Counterpart to Physiological Psychology," *Psychological Bulletin*, VI (1909), 401–8; "What Social Objects Must Psychology Presuppose?" *Journal of Philosophy*, VII (1910), 174–80; "Social Consciousness and the Consciousness of Meaning," *Psychological Bulletin*, VII (1910), 397–405; "The Mechanism of Social Consciousness," *Journal of Philosophy*, IX (1912), 401–6; "The Social Self," *Journal of Philosophy*, X (1913), 374–80; "A Behavioristic Account of the Significant Symbol," *Journal of Philosophy*, XIX (1922), 157–63; "Scientific Method and the Moral Sciences," *International Journal of Ethics*, XXXIII (1923), 229–47; "The Genesis of the Self and Social Control," *International Journal of Ethics*, XXXV (1924–25), 251–77.

Joseph Dorfman, *Thorstein Veblen and His America* (New York, 1935), is not only the best critical work on Veblen, but also provides in chaps. vi–viii a description of the personnel and significance of the Chicago

School. R. L. Duffus, *The Innocents at Cedro; a Memoir of Thorstein Veblen and Some Others* (New York, 1944) is largely anecdotal, but contains biographical side lights of value. The following works by Veblen relate to the theme of this chapter: "Kant's Critique of Judgement," *Journal of Speculative Philosophy*, XVIII (1884), 260–74, reprinted in *Essays in Our Changing Order* (New York, 1934); Veblen's dissertation at Yale, "Ethical Grounds of a Doctrine of Retribution," which was based on a thorough examination of Spencer and Kant, prepared him for this work; "The Army of the Commonweal," *Journal of Political Economy*, II (1893–94), 456–61, reprinted in *Essays in Our Changing Order;* "Why Is Economics Not an Evolutionary Science?" *Quarterly Journal of Economics*, XII (1897–98), 373–97, reprinted in *The Place of Science in Modern Civilization* (New York, 1919); "The Preconceptions of Economic Science," *Quarterly Journal of Economics*, XIII (1898–99), 121–50, 396–426, XIV (1899–1900), 240–69, reprinted in *The Place of Science in Modern Civilization; The Theory of the Leisure Class; an Economic Study of the Evolution of Institutions* (New York, 1899), a review of which, by Lester F. Ward, was published in the *American Journal of Sociology*, V (1900), 829–37; *The Theory of Business Enterprise* (New York, 1904); "The Place of Science in Modern Civilization," *American Journal of Sociology*, XI (1906), 585–609, reprinted in *The Place of Science in Modern Civilization;* "The Evolution of the Scientific Point of View," *University of California Chronicle*, X (1908), 396–416, reprinted in *The Place of Science in Modern Civilization;* and "Christian Morals and the Competitive System," *International Journal of Ethics*, XX (1909–10), 168–95, reprinted in *Essays in Our Changing Order.*

CHAPTER 34

On Sumner, Harris E. Starr, *William Graham Sumner* (New York, 1925), is the standard biography, and should be supplemented by the personal material in Albert G. Keller, *Reminiscences (Mainly Personal) of William Graham Sumner* (New Haven, 1933). Sumner's contributions to sociology and sociological method are discussed in Maurice R. Davie, ed., *Sumner Today* (New Haven, 1940); R. E. Park, "The Sociological Methods of William Graham Sumner," in Social Science Research Council Committee on Scientific Method in the Social Sciences, *Methods in Social Science*, S. A. Rice, ed. (Chicago, 1931), pp. 154–62; C. H. Cooley, *Sociological Theory and Social Research* (New York, 1930), chap. xi; and H. E. Barnes, "William Graham Sumner (1840–1910)," *Sociological Review*, XIV (1922), 209–12. The miscellaneous papers of Sumner were edited by Albert G. Keller, in a series of four volumes: *War and Other Essays* (New Haven, 1911); *Earth Hunger and Other Essays* (New Haven, 1913); *The Challenge of Facts and Other Essays* (New Haven, 1914); and *The Forgotten Man and Other Essays* (New Haven, 1918). Albert G. Keller and Maurice R. Davie, eds., *Selected Essays of William Graham Sumner* (New Haven, 1924), makes a convenient introduction to Sumner's ideas, though many of the essays are republished only in part, without indications of omissions. The autobiographical sketch included here and also published elsewhere, though brief, contains some interesting comments. The four volumes of William G. Sumner and Albert G. Keller, *The Science of Society* (New Haven, 1927–28), are an attempt on the part of Sumner's younger colleague to complete his most ambitious enterprise, but for philosophical purposes, the heart of this enterprise is found in Sumner's *Folkways* (Boston, 1907). The preface and first five chapters contain most of the theoretical material. The remainder of the volume is a collection of more or less related bits of morality and hardly justifies its reputation. A chronological listing of the most important of Sumner's other works follows.

1873 "Introductory Lecture to Courses in Political and Social Science," printed for the first time in The Challenge of Facts and Other Essays, pp. 391–403.

1877 "Democracy and Responsible Government; address at Providence, R.I., June 20, 1877, before the Phi Beta Kappa Society of Brown University," printed in the *Providence Evening Press*, June 21, 1877; reprinted in The Challenge of Facts and Other Essays, pp. 243–86.

1881 "Sociology," *Princeton Review*, LVIII (1881), 303–23; reprinted in War and Other Essays, pp. 167–92.

1882 Andrew Jackson as a Public Man; What He Was, What Chances He Had, and What He Did with Them (Boston and New York, 1882), "American Statesmen Series."

Political Economy and Political Science, comp. by W. G. Sumner, D. A. Wells, W. E. Foster, R. L. Dugdale, and G. H. Putnam, New York Society for Political Education, 1882. "Economic Tracts No. 2."

"The Science of Sociology; a Speech at the Farewell Banquet to Herbert Spencer, November 9, 1882," printed in E. L. Youmans, ed., Herbert Spencer on the Americans and the Americans on Herbert Spencer (New York, 1883), pp. 35–40; reprinted in The Forgotten Man and Other Essays, pp. 401–5.

1883   "The Forgotten Man," printed for the first time in The Forgotten Man and Other Essays, pp. 465–95.

What Social Classes Owe to Each Other (New York, 1883).

"The Philosophy of Strikes," *Harper's Weekly*, XXVII, No. 1396 (September 15, 1883), 586; reprinted in The Forgotten Man and Other Essays, pp. 239–46.

1885   Protectionism; The —Ism which Teaches That Waste Makes Wealth (New York, 1885); reprinted in The Forgotten Man and Other Essays, pp. 9–111.

Collected Essays in Political and Social Science (New York, 1885). The first significant collection of Sumner's essays contains: "Bimetalism" (1879), "Wages" (1882), "The Argument against Protective Taxes" (1881), "Sociology" (1881), "Theory and Practice of Elections" (1880), "Presidential Elections and Civil Service Reform" (1881), "Our Colleges before the Country" (1884).

1886   "Who Win by Progress?" *The Independent* (November 25, 1886); reprinted in The Challenge of Facts and Other Essays, pp. 169–74.

"The New Social Issue," *The Independent* (December 23, 1886); reprinted in The Challenge of Facts and Other Essays, pp. 207–12.

1887   "What Makes the Rich Richer and the Poor Poorer?" *Popular Science Monthly*, XXX (1887), 289–96; reprinted in The Challenge of Facts and Other Essays, pp. 65–77.

"The Abolition of Poverty," *The Independent* (August 25, 1887); reprinted in Earth Hunger and Other Essays, pp. 228–32.

"The State As an 'Ethical Person,' " *The Independent* (October 6, 1887); reprinted in The Challenge of Facts and Other Essays, pp. 201–4.

1888   "Democracy and Plutocracy," *The Independent* (November 15, 1888); reprinted in Earth Hunger and Other Essays, pp. 283–89.

"Definitions of Democracy and Plutocracy," *The Independent* (December 20, 1888); reprinted in Earth Hunger and Other Essays, pp. 290–95.

1889   "The Conflict of Plutocracy and Democracy," *The Independent*

(January 10, 1889); reprinted in Earth Hunger and Other Essays, pp. 296–300.

"What Is Civil Liberty?" *Popular Science Monthly*, XXXV (1889), 289–303; reprinted in Earth Hunger and Other Essays, pp. 109–30.

"The Challenge of Facts" (written some time in the 1880's under the title "Socialism." Present title given by A. G. Keller, Sumner's editor); printed for the first time in The Challenge of Facts and Other Essays, pp. 17–52.

1890   Alexander Hamilton (New York, 1890); "Makers of America."

1894   "The Absurd Effort to Make the World Over," *Forum*, XVII (1894), 92–102; reprinted in War and Other Essays, pp. 195–210. This article is a general critique of "Bellamy and his comrades in opinion" who are opposed to industrial capitalism.

1896   "The Fallacy of Territorial Extension," *Forum*, XXI (1896), 416–19; reprinted in War and Other Essays, pp. 285–93.

"Earth Hunger or the Philosophy of Land Grabbing"; printed for the first time in Earth Hunger and Other Essays, pp. 31–64.

1899   "The Conquest of the United States by Spain; a lecture before the Phi Beta Kappa Society of Yale University, January 16, 1899," *Yale Law Journal*, VIII (1899), 168–93; printed as a separate pamphlet (Boston, 1899); reprinted in War and Other Essays, pp. 297–334.

"The Power and Beneficence of Capital," The Saving Banks Association of the State of New York, Proceedings of the Sixth Annual Convention (New York, 1899), pp. 77–95; reprinted in Earth Hunger and Other Essays, pp. 337–53.

1904   "Reply to a Socialist (The Fallacies of Socialism)," *Collier's Weekly* (October 29, 1904), pp. 12–13; reprinted in The Challenge of Facts and Other Essays, pp. 55–62.

1906   "Protectionism Twenty Years After" (title given by A. G. Keller); address at a dinner of the Committee on Tariff Reform. Published by the Reform Club Committee on Tariff Reform. Series 1906, No. 4, August 15, 1906; reprinted in The Forgotten Man and Other Essays, pp. 131–38.

1909   "The Mores of the Present and the Future," *Yale Review*, XVIII (1909), 233–45; reprinted in War and Other Essays, pp. 149–64.

1910   "Religion and the Mores," *American Journal of Sociology*, XV

(1910), 577–91; reprinted in War and Other Essays, pp.
129–46.

1911   "War," *Yale Review*, n.s., I (1911), 1–27; reprinted in War and
Other Essays, pp. 3–40.

The Education of Henry Adams (Boston, 1918) is an autobiography in
form, but the reader should remember that the author is developing a philosophical theme and taking liberties with his own life in order to enhance the
plot. This is particularly true of the section on Darwinism. The published
letters in *The Letters of Henry Adams, 1858–1891*, ed. by Worthington
Chauncey Ford (Boston, 1930), and in *A Cycle of Adams Letters, 1861–
1865*, ed. Worthington Chauncey Ford, 2 vols. (Boston, 1920), make it
quite clear that his concern over evolutionary theory was a relatively late
development. His review of Lyell's *Principles of Geology*, in the *North
American Review*, CVII (1868), 465–501, confirms the impression given
by the letters that his interest in uniformitarianism was at that time superficial
and that he did not think of himself as a Darwinian. For his medieval interpretations, the chief sources are *Mont Saint-Michel and Chartres* (Boston,
1904), the famous chapter on "The Dynamo and the Virgin," in *The
Education of Henry Adams*, and Mabel La Farge, *Letters to a Niece and
Prayer to the Virgin of Chartres, by Henry Adams, with a Niece's Memories*
(Boston, 1920). His philosophy of history is expounded in "The Tendency
of History" (1894), a letter to the American Historical Association, and
"The Rule of Phase Applied to History," both published in *The Degrada-
tion of the Democratic Dogma* (New York, 1919). It should be noted that
the title "The Degradation of the Democratic Dogma" represents Brooks
Adams rather than Henry. The best exposition of Henry Adams's views of
democracy is contained in his anonymously published *Democracy; a Novel
Commenting on American Government* (New York, 1880). Succinct
expositions and criticism of the philosophy of history will be found in James
Truslow Adams, "Henry Adams and the New Physics," *Yale Review*,
XIX (1929–30), 283–302; Roy F. Nichols, "The Dynamic Interpreta-
tion of History," *New England Quarterly*, VIII (1935), 163–78; James
Stone, "Henry Adams's Philosophy of History," *New England Quarterly*,
XIV (1941), 538–48. For the relation between the theories of Brooks
Adams and Henry see Charles A. Beard's "Introduction" to his edition of
Brooks Adams, *The Law of Civilization and Decay; an Essay on History*
(New York, 1943). More light on Henry Adams's life and on his relation
to his brothers is cast by the last chapter, "The Fourth Generation," of

James Truslow Adams, *The Adams Family* (Boston, 1930); on pp. 348–49 there is a letter of Henry Adams, not elsewhere published, which is of special philosophic interest, since in it Adams defines his "stoic" faith. In the first volume of Henry Adams, *History of the United States during the Administration of Jefferson and Madison* (New York, 1890), there is a survey of American culture at the end of the eighteenth century.

Brooks Adams's economic interpretations of American history are found in the following works: *America's Economic Supremacy* (New York, 1900); *The New Empire* (New York, 1902); and *The Theory of Social Revolutions* (New York, 1913).

Edwin Arlington Robinson's *Collected Poems* (New York, 1937) includes his latest poems. Analysis of the chief philosophical poems will be found in Estelle Kaplan, *Philosophy in the Poetry of Edwin Arlington Robinson* (New York, 1940). This volume also gives an account of Robinson's philosophical interests and development and a good bibliography of the secondary literature. Herman Hagedorn, *Edwin Arlington Robinson; a Biography* (New York, 1938), is a good biography, and Henry W. Wells, "The New England Conscience," in *The American Way of Poetry* (New York, 1943), pp. 89–105, is an excellent recent interpretation. Students of American history will be particularly interested in a poem entitled "On the Way," *Collected Poems*, pp. 474–84, in the form of a dialogue between Alexander Hamilton and Aaron Burr, which describes with great acuteness the "parting of the ways" not only of these two characters but also of the two conflicting social ideals that are basic to American life.

It is unnecessary to list the writings by George Santayana or about him, since adequate bibliographies are available, especially in *The Philosophy of George Santayana*, ed. by Paul A. Schilpp (Evanston and Chicago, 1940), "Library of Living Philosophers," Vol. II, and in George Santayana, *Obiter Scripta; Lectures, Essays and Reviews* (New York, 1936), ed. by Justus Buchler and Benjamin Schwartz.

Most informative for his intellectual career is his "Brief History of My Opinions," first published in G. P. Adams and W. P. Montague, *Contemporary American Philosophy* (London, 1930), II, 239–57. Two volumes of his autobiography have appeared, the first entitled *Persons and Places* (New York, 1944), and the second, *The Middle Years* (New York, 1945). Among his writings the following are particularly important for the understanding of the conflict between naturalism and idealism in his thought: "Aversion from Platonism," "Cloud Castles," "Cross-Lights," "Society and Solitude," "Literature and Culture," "Reversion to Platonism," and "On My Friendly Critics," in *Soliloquies in England and Later*

Soliloquies (New York, 1922); his Herbert Spencer Lecture entitled "The Unknowable" and his Spinoza lecture entitled "Ultimate Religion," both included in *Obiter Scripta* (New York, 1936); "The Appeal to the Super-natural," in *The Genteel Tradition at Bay* (New York, 1931); "Three Proofs of Realism," in *Essays in Critical Realism* (New York, 1920), where his biological theory of knowledge is expressed even more clearly than in the latter part of *Skepticism and Animal Faith* (New York, 1923); "Normal Madness" and "The Secret of Aristotle," in *Dialogues in Limbo* (New York, 1925); "Distraction" and "General Review of *Realms of Being*," in *The Realm of Spirit* (New York, 1940). The two characters Oliver and Mario, in *The Last Puritan* (New York, 1935), dramatize the conflict between the moralistic and aesthetic, the Puritan and the Latin, elements of his thinking.

— VII —

IDEALISMS

ACADEMIC AWAKENING

THE passage from orthodoxy to idealism was an almost invisible transition, but its total effect was startling; it produced a revolution in American higher education and a renaissance of the pursuit of philosophy as a reflective, systematic enterprise. "Philosophy," during the last quarter of the nineteenth century, became the name of an independent department in the faculties of our standard colleges and universities. Whether this was a gain or a loss for the art of philosophizing is still a moot point, but it was clearly a significant change in the curriculum, and this change in philosophy's academic status was not without its more general cultural implications. Philosophical thinking and writing became professionalized, and as a result American *systems* of philosophy began to be produced. That full-grown, native systems of philosophy should appear so late among American institutions was due largely to the fact, to which we alluded in discussing the rise of academic orthodoxy, that philosophical thinking had been an integral element in the chief theological, political, and economic systems of thought, and that there was little demand for philosophy as an independent discipline until "mental philosophy" appeared. We have now to describe the breaking up of "mental philosophy" as an academic discipline into "mental science" or psychology on the one hand and, on the other, a residue of speculative thought now conceived as intellectually ultimate, as "philosophy proper" or *philosophia prima*, an amalgam of cosmology, metaphysics, and epistemology. Professionalized philosophy and psychology, independent of theology, rhetoric, and politics, independent in essence or ideal even of pedagogy, though its professors usually make a living as teachers, was itself a German importation; it is, therefore, intelligible that German schools of idealism were the first to gain systematic expression in American life.

The beginnings of this emancipation came from the leaders of orthodoxy themselves. In their attempts to keep up with the latest literature on the subject, they were driven to pay increasing attention to the German literature. Even before the Civil War it had become fashionable for American professors with scholarly ambitions to spend at least a year in German universities, and after the war this fashion spread rapidly. Thus, one after another of the theologically trained addicts to "common sense" orthodoxy, who were in the habit of treating philosophy as an adjunct to divinity, became personally acquainted with the critical and secular tendencies in German idealism. They had turned to German idealism in the hope of finding comfort against English positivism and empiricism, but the comfort had to be purchased at a high price, and it proved in the end worthless. G. Stanley Hall, who was one of these American "mental philosophers," awakened from his orthodox slumbers in Germany, described the academic situation in 1879 as follows:

there are less than half a dozen colleges or universities in the United States where metaphysical thought is entirely freed from reference to theological formulae. Many teachers of philosophy have no training in their department save such as has been obtained in theological seminaries, and their pupils are made far more familiar with the points of difference in the theology of Parks, Fairchilds, Hodges and the like, than with Plato, Leibnitz or Kant. Many of these colleges were established by funds contributed during periods of religious awakening, and are now sustained with difficulty as denominational outposts by appeals from the pulpit and sectarian press. The nature of the philosophical instruction is determined by the convictions of constituencies and trustees, while professors are to a great extent without independence or initiative in matters of speculative thought. . . .

Some of the professorlings of philosophy are disciples of disciples of Hopkins, Hickok, Wayland, Upham, Haven. Most have extended their philosophical horizon as far as Reid, Stewart, Hamilton.[1]

The last impressive champions of orthodoxy were James McCosh and his colleague, Charles Woodruff Shields, who naturally kept the Scottish faith at Princeton, where American Presbyterians continued to look up to the hills of Scotland for authoritative help.[2] But McCosh

[1] G. Stanley Hall, "Philosophy in the United States," *Mind; a Quarterly Review of Psychology and Philosophy,* IV (1879), 90.

[2] Shields, who was professor of the harmony of science and religion, was not to be shaken from his faith that he had "the final philosophy"; *Philosophia Ultima; or "Christian Science"* he called his voluminous reconciliation of philosophical and theological orthodoxies.

finally had to take some account of Schelling and Hegel. He looked upon idealism as an irresponsible "raising of our associated sentiments to the rank of cognitions" [3] and, in particular, suspected the German speculative systems of being pantheistic skepticism "disguised as idealism." He hoped to be able to dismiss them as passing fashions.

The man of genius, like Schelling, will create an ingenious theory, beautiful as the golden locks of the setting sun; the man of vigorous intellect, like Hegel, will erect a fabric which looks as coherent as a palace of ice: but until they can be shown to be founded on the inherent principles of the mind, or to be built up of materials thence derived, I wrap myself up in philosophic doubt, as not being sure whether they may not disappear while I am gazing on them. [4]

The other leaders of orthodoxy, however, Francis Bowen of Harvard and Noah Porter of Yale, incorporated much of German idealism into the framework of their "common sense." Bowen, in his long career, witnessed the rise and decline of New England literary transcendentalism and attempted to appreciate its wide appeal; he dealt with it quite sympathetically in his historical sketches. The influence of Bowen's philosophical idealism is most conspicuous in his theology, for, though he tried to remain theologically orthodox, he speculated quite freely; witness the following excerpt from his article with the sensational title "Christian Metempsychosis."

It is far more reasonable to believe that the future life which we are taught to expect will be similar to the present one, and will be spent in this world, tho we shall carry forward to it the burden or the blessing entailed upon us by our past career. Besides the spiritual meaning of the doctrine of regeneration, besides the new birth which is "of water and of the Spirit," there may be a literal meaning in the solemn words of the Saviour, "Except a man be born again, he cannot see the kingdom of God." [5]

Bowen was, however, too sober and conservative to indulge in extravagant speculation, and in the end he relied chiefly on Sir William Hamilton's logic, of which he was the most expert exponent.

But even in this field he was obliged to study the German rivals,

[3] *First and Fundamental Truths*, p. 306. Cf. in this connection James McCosh, *A Criticism of the Critical Philosophy* (New York, 1884).

[4] James McCosh, *The Intuitions of the Mind Inductively Investigated* (New York, 1867), p. 75.

[5] Francis Bowen, "Christian Metempsychosis," *Princeton Review*, LVI (1881), 329.

for his colleague Charles Carroll Everett published in 1869 the fruits of industrious note taking of lectures attended in Berlin under the elaborate title *The Science of Thought; a System of Logic after the Principles of the Hegelian School, as Expounded by Gabler, of Berlin.* Everett explained that he was "charmed by the beauty and simplicity" of Hegel's system and that it contained the "maximum of form and the minimum of formalism." Everett also makes the significant remark that next to Hegel he was most indebted to Schopenhauer.

The most brilliant of metaphysicians, the clearest and most satisfactory, for the most part, in his details; the most unsatisfactory in his grand results; whose system, with its sad centre of pessimism, is like a rich and tempting fruit, fair without, but rotten at its heart.[6]

Noah Porter, too, had attended lectures in Berlin and was willing to accept much of the critical philosophy as he heard it expounded there. It seemed to him to "settle once for all the question that science, philosophy, experience, common sense, and faith rest on certain fundamental principles which must in some way or other be justified to man's critical examination, if he would justify his confidence in any kind of knowledge."[7] He welcomed such critical idealism especially as an antidote to "Coleridge's American disciples," whom he ridiculed as "artful dodgers," who "if pressed to any logical conclusion, find their refuge in some Coleridgian term, and hide themselves from their pursuers in a convenient mist."[8] He likewise welcomed a Kantian ethics to counteract the attempts by evolutionary naturalists and mechanists to capture moral science.[9] Porter, however, adopted more than the critical method, he saw the advantage of the German idealist theory of the Absolute over the Hamiltonian philosophy of the unconditioned, and his famous text *Elements of Intellectual Science* (1871, dedicated to Trendelenburg), culminates in the doctrine: "The universe is a *thought* as well as a *thing.* . . . We assume that this Abso-

[6] Charles Carroll Everett, *The Science of Thought* (Boston, 1869), Preface, p. xiii.

[7] Noah Porter, "The Kant Centennial," *Princeton Review*, LVII (1881), pp. 394–424.

[8] Noah Porter, "Coleridge and His American Disciples," in *Bibliotheca Sacra*, IV (1847), p. 170.

[9] See his "The Sciences of Nature versus the Science of Man, a Plea for the Science of Man," a lecture delivered before the ΦBK Society of Harvard University in 1871; reprinted in Blau, ed., *American Philosophical Addresses, 1700–1900*, pp. 457–85.

lute exists, in order that thought and science may be possible. . . . We do not demonstrate that God exists, but that every man must assume that He is." [10]

The first American theologian and professor to become a systematic expositor of German idealism was Laurens Perseus Hickok (1798–1888), of Union College. He was, like Caleb Sprague Henry, inspired during his college days by that remarkable teacher Eliphalet Nott and was determined as a professor of theology (at Western Reserve and at Auburn Seminary) to work out a thoroughly critical, rational theology. It is worth noting that his earliest published work is an expression of critical, practical idealism; in 1833, while he was minister at Litchfield, Conn., he delivered before the Connecticut Peace Society a beautifully reasoned and eloquent address on *The Sources of Military Delusion and the Practicability of Their Removal.* After Hickok's retirement from the presidency of Union College, in 1868, he lived at Amherst, Mass., where he could be with his nephew and former student Julius H. Seelye, professor of philosophy and later president of Amherst College, who revised his most popular texts and thus continued his influence for several academic generations. Unfortunately, these texts, the *Moral Science* (1880; a revision of his *Moral Science*, 1853) and the *Mental Science* (1882; a revision of his *Empirical Psychology*, 1854), reduce the idealist philosophy to a minimum and give the impression that Hickok, like Seelye, was little more than a typical, orthodox educator. It is, therefore, to the earlier volumes that we must turn to get an adequate idea of Hickok's critical system.

In his *Moral Science*, though this text as a whole was conventional, he showed his independence of current opinion by his outspoken treatment of the theory of the state, which was conceived in a Hegelian manner. He distinguished three "modes" of sovereignty, or "positive authority": "civil government," or objective legislation through rewards and penalties; "divine government," or objective legislation through love and loyalty; "family government," a synthesis of the other two modes. The state, the divine administration, and the family are objective moral powers, existing in their own right and creating "public freedom." True liberty is the freedom of the community; individual freedom he described as "the most hopeless bondage."

[10] Noah Porter, *Elements of Intellectual Science* (New York, 1871), p. 555.

All other conceptions of popular liberty but such as rests upon the choice of the state, which is the whole society in its unity, and this choice, directed to the legitimate end of its highest civilization in its own right, are but conceptions of that which in its very definition will be licentiousness.[11]

The authority of the state is thus given extensive power, including "the right to control all property." In the revision of 1880 the political theory is modified considerably; though the power of the state over all property is reasserted, the concept of "public freedom" disappears, and the emphasis is shifted to the "organic unity of mankind."

Hickok's expositions of empirical psychology and ethics were not significantly different from the other current texts, except for incidental innovations, such as his introductory section on "Anthropology," in which he stresses the influence of physical factors on the mind, not merely in the medical manner of Benjamin Rush but also in emphasizing racial and cultural diversities. There is also in his "Introduction" a clear statement of his realistic epistemology, in which he describes introspection as "the inverted method of the mind's operation."

The old habit of throwing attention outwards is now to be broken up, and an entire inversion of the mental action is to be practiced. The mind is to make its own phenomena its study, and turn the attention inward upon its own action. . . . The organs of sense must be shut up, and the material world shut out, and the mind for the time shut in upon itself, and made to become familiar with its own action. . . . When this habit of introspection has been gained, the investigation of mental facts becomes not only possible, but facile and delightful.[12]

Such habitual, introspective "experience in consciousness is *knowledge;* and when this is confirmed by an appeal to universal consciousness we have that knowledge which rests upon *common sense.*"[13] But *philosophical* or *rational* knowledge rests on "those a priori conditions which give the necessary and universal laws to experience, and by which intelligence itself is alone made intelligible."[14] Hickok, there-

---

[11] Laurens Perseus Hickok, *Moral Science* (Schenectady, N.Y., 1853), pp. 156–57.
[12] Laurens Perseus Hickok, *Empirical Psychology*, 1st ed. (New York, 1854), pp. 16, 17.
[13] Laurens Perseus Hickok, *Rational Psychology; or, The Subjective Idea and the Objective Law of All Intelligence* (Schenectady, 1854), p. 97.
[14] *Ibid.*, p. 21.

fore, in 1848 while he was teaching theology at Auburn Seminary, worked out his *Rational Psychology* for a double purpose: to provide a "rational" ontology for theism and to provide a "rational" form of transcendentalism in the face of the literary variety which was turning in a "pantheistic," "mystic," and "profane" direction.

The importance of such an investigation thoroughly made can not well be over estimated, and especially in view of what is so emphatically and with probable truth affirmed by a learned friend in his Introduction to "Plato against the Atheists," that "the next battle ground of Infidelity will not be the Scriptures. What faith there may remain will be summoned to defend the very being of a God, the great truth, involving every other moral and religious truth—the primal truth—*that* He is, *and that he is the rewarder of all who diligently seek him.*"

A true, complete, and sound transcendental philosophy was, perhaps, never more to be desired, though the name was never so sadly perverted and vilified. Like the Hebrew champion, it has been blinded and bound and made to grind in the prison-house of the uncircumcised; but in its recovered strength it may terribly avenge itself, when placed between the pillars of that profane temple in which it has been exposed to mockery.[15]

Hickok reconstructed Kant's doctrine of the categories into a system of three "a priori intellectual operations" corresponding to the three faculties of sense, understanding, and reason. After an exceptionally critical account of sense experience, culminating in an extraordinary section on "the valid being of the phenomenal," he developed the "constructive" functions of the understanding and engaged in "exposing false systems of nature," among which systems he included Cudworth's Platonism and the Edwardean theologians of New England. The culmination of his critique was the analysis of a priori "comprehension" in reason. The a priori intellectual operation of reason, he claimed, referred "wholly to the supernatural" and covered "the ground that Kant has excluded from all speculative philosophy and put within the peculiar region of what, with him, is the practical reason." [16] Reason, according to Hickok, can comprehend pure spontaneity or activity.

This reason-conception of simple pure activity is thus wholly unconditioned to space, time, and a nature of things; and is apriori conditional for

---

[15] *Ibid.*, pp. 105–6.   [16] *Ibid.*, p. 159.

all transcending of nature. It were wholly impossible to find any passage out from nature to the supernatural, except in this reason-conception of a pure agency which can come within none of the conditions that belong to nature, and has none of the necessitated connections of a discursive judgment. But such pure activity is the conception of *pure spontaneity;* and this must stand as our first element of Personality. . . .

The complete Idea of the Reason, as faculty for an operation of Comprehension, is thus given in the compass of the Absolute in personality. *Nature may be comprehended in a pure Spontaneity, Autonomy, and Liberty: or, which is the same thing—Reason may comprehend Nature in the compass of an Absolute Person.*[17]

The *Rational Cosmology* (1858) begins where the *Rational Psychology* left off.

There must somewhere be a position from whence it may clearly be seen, that the universe has laws which are necessarily determined by immutable and eternal principles. Nothing in nature, and equally so not nature itself, can be made intelligible except as it has been subjected to rational principle, and such principle must both have been, and been made controlling, in the very origination of nature, or nature must forever be without meaning or end. That principle, then, to an all-perfect insight, must disclose within itself what the facts must be, and no induction of facts can at all be needed by the absolute reason.[18]

The knowledge of absolute reason, or God, can never be an "object for the judgments of the connecting understanding," but only an "object for the insight of the reason." "Enough that in creation we find unequivocal certainty of facts that originated out of nature." [19] The only evidence we have that God is rational is that his creation culminates in reason. Hickok drew an eloquent portrait of creation as a restless "self-finding and self-losing" until in man it finally comes to rest in rational communion with the Creator.

All creation is as yet means to ends, and the attainment is not yet made of an end that can be self-satisfactory and thus ultimate. The antagonist and diremptive forces work on and never finish; the life-force builds up the

---

[17] *Ibid.,* pp. 569, 620.
[18] Laurens Perseus Hickok, *Rational Cosmology; or, The Eternal Principles and the Necessary Laws of the Universe* (New York, 1858), p. 3.
[19] *Ibid.,* p. 257.

plant, and pushes out perpetual buds in self-reduplication, and throws off its seed after its kind in the perpetuation of its species, but at no point does the plant turn back upon itself and come to any self-finding; and then the animal inwardly digests and respires, has locomotion and sensation, and a perpetual circulation of life and feeling about a centre, but in all this going out from and coming back to a centre, there is no capability to remain and retain itself at the centre. So soon as there is a self-finding there is also a self-losing, and thus only a successive self-feeling with no self-possession. The most intense animal sensation is perpetually transitional, and never comes to any abiding self-consciousness. All is thus nature; conditioned succession; determined but interminable births and deaths; and as yet nowhere the capability to rest in any consummation.

With this reason cannot be satisfied. The Absolute Spirit cannot rejoice in his own work except as it is made at last complete in itself, and possessing that which has an intrinsic excellency that may properly use and exhaust for itself all this universe of created means, and be an end in which they are swallowed up. Without such a crown on nature, her last birth and growth is wholly meaningless, and there has been nothing to work *from*, and nothing to work *for*, and therefore nothing worthy of the Great Architect to work *out*.

Superinduced upon this animal life, there must be the force of reason, which can read principles and law in itself and control all animal feeling by them, and hold all of nature that is in him freely and joyfully subject to them. Such a union of the animal and the rational will be *the human;* not thing, but person; in nature, and yet supernatural. While he can use all nature's means for his ends, he can also know and commune with the God who reveals himself in nature, as partaking himself of his likeness. God may not only express himself in him as in all his works, but may reveal himself to him in ways which none of his created works can express, and bring him thus intelligently and eternally in adoring communion.[20]

In his next great work, *Humanity Immortal; or, Man Tried, Fallen, and Redeemed* (1872), Hickok rounded out his theory of man as the final form of creation by trying to "comprehend in full Idea" the history of man as a process of the resurrection of his natural life into eternal life. Man is pictured as in an "intermediate state" awaiting the final judgment when the limitations of man's finite spirit, his inability to "comprehend the equity of many transactions" of the creator will be removed, and God's design will be "cleared up."

[20] *Ibid.*, pp. 252–54.

The latent skepticism in this theory of human history was felt by no one more keenly than by Hickok himself. He had been attacked repeatedly by orthodox ministers as a pantheist, but such charges worried him less than did his own realization that reliance on a priori principles and laws, though it might prove the existence of absolute reason, left the course of human experience intelligible only in terms of the mythology of redemption. A thoroughly rational understanding of human experience seemed impossible in terms of either revealed theology or merely natural law. Hickok, therefore, became preoccupied with a logic of history. After a careful study of both the Aristotelian and the Hegelian logics as rationalizations of experience he concluded that "the Aristotelian cannot move and the Hegelian cannot rest." He, therefore, made a last and bold attempt to construct "a logic of concrete universality," which he called *The Logic of Reason, Universal and Eternal* (1875). In this reworking of idealistic logic he attempted to overcome the dualism between the rational and the empirical methods which underlay all his other works and to trace the outlines of absolute experience in human experience; that is, he tried to show that even here and now there are elements in human experience which are characterized by being "self-essential, self-intelligent, self-sufficient, self-possessed, and self-approved." He expressed his hope that mathematical logic might be freed from its limitations as a purely abstract science and might become the foundation of a "universal" science in terms of which "concrete universals" would be adequately formulated.

Although few, comparatively, now see that such better logic is the only way to escape an all-pervading scepticism, yet the full belief that the period is not far distant when this must become a general conviction, and a new and better logic be a wide-felt want, lays an additional claim upon us to do what we may, not only to hasten on this certain issue, but also to do what we can to meet this coming want.[21]

The academic awakening at Amherst, for which Hickok laid such excellent foundations, was conducted to a remarkable renaissance by the work of one of his disciples, Charles Edward Garman. He had misspent much of his time in college memorizing "the light," as Presi-

---

[21] Laurens Perseus Hickok, *The Logic of Reason, Universal and Eternal* (Boston, 1875), p. 4.

dent Seelye called Hickok's texts; but, in the years that followed, he achieved, through independent study and reflection, a personal realization of the significance of idealistic doctrine. Kant's philosophy in particular blossomed into new life in his own experience. Garman devoted his whole life to the art of making students feel academic problems as vital personal concerns. He thought that just as his own generation had been preoccupied with the religious crisis precipitated by naturalism, so the next generation must be preoccupied with the social crisis that was being precipitated by the growth of "greed and graft." Idealism meant to him, therefore, the doctrine of a double citizenship—citizenship in nature and citizenship in the state. He used Hickok's social philosophy with great effectiveness to teach "spiritual principles" or objective norms as critical substitutes in both knowledge and conduct for "anthropomorphic" prejudices. Instead of using Hickok's texts, however, he distributed a series of his own "pamphlets" to his classes in order to exhibit the practical significance of philosophical *problems* (one at a time) and thus to prepare his students for serious discussion in class and intelligent reading of the texts. His method of teaching was an excellent statement of his idealism. To G. Stanley Hall he expounded it as follows:

Years ago when I taught geometry I found that the students would oftentimes make it a mere intellectual puzzle or mental gymnastics, but that by applying some of the problems to questions in surveying, in astronomy, and in physics, I could bring the men to realize that in studying geometry they were gaining citizenship in the universe, and they were at once led to interpret their lives as far as possible in terms of these propositions. In taking up philosophy I have attempted to do something of that same kind of work; I present the fundamental positions from the point of view of the history of the discussions in psychology, in philosophy, and ethics, and to some extent of those in political obligations. It makes the matter as serious and personal as possible, and as a result it has often cost the students a very great effort to satisfy themselves instead of simply meeting the requirements of the recitation room. . . .

The earlier life of the students has been one of imitation and obedience to authority; it corresponds to traditionalism in tribal or national existence. The great requisite for a young person is to form habits. . . . But there comes a time when the young man must assume responsibility for what he does; there must be self-possession and self-direction instead of dependence on authority, and this is a new experience to him, an experience which many shrink from even in very little things. . . .

There is no hope for a young man at this time if he does not meet the obligations of life with the spirit of self-reliance, but to do this he must have some confidence in his own judgment and the standards by which he judges. . . . The average student needs help, at least to this extent, to show him that he cannot make any hypothesis which will be a reasonable basis for his knowledge of the physical world and of natural science that does not involve as its basis something more than the physical world. I believe the place to take this up is with Kant's "Practical Reason". . . .

The great need of our students from a practical point of view is an ideal; the great danger is that they will become visionary.[22]

In this way Garman transformed the lifeless text of Seelye, who was known as "the deepest-down-divingest, the longest-under-stayingest, and the greatest up-mud-bringingest of all the writers in philosophy,"[23] into a personal discipline which created a score of distinguished American thinkers. His enthusiasm was contagious, for he sincerely believed that the philosophical awakening in academic New England would be the beginning of a great reform in American life:

Why should not the colleges and universities be the true American castles— castles that shall never fall to ruins, castles that shall serve our civilization so faithfully that it shall never cease to grow?

Has not our own Connecticut valley—or rather I should include a little larger part of New England, beginning with Yale on the south, extending to Dartmouth on the north, holding Harvard in her right hand, Williams in her left, while she cherishes Amherst, Smith, and Mount Holyoke so near to her geographical heart (to borrow a phrase from Professor W. S. Tyler),—has not this part of New England exercised as large an influence on the educational, religious, and political life of our times as the fortunes of the Rhine valley on the warfare of bygone centuries? Is this anything more than the beginning? Is not our future all before us? Are we not face to face with a new movement destined to give new power and influence to the college graduate? [24]

Garman's faith in a Kantian idealism as a power to reform American morals and religion was shared by a notable group of teachers, each

[22] Charles Edward Garman, *Letters, Lectures and Addresses*, ed. by Eliza Miner Garman (Cambridge, 1909), pp. 58–60, 69, 70.
[23] *Ibid.*, p. 443.   [24] *Ibid.*, p. 483.

with his own variant system, but each succeeding in kindling in his students a sense of the importance of philosophy and thus creating a source of "spiritual energy" independent of the churches. These idealists, without intending to set up rival pulpits to those in the churches, nevertheless emancipated academic faith and morals from clerical domination, as the literary transcendentalists had done outside academies. Almost all of them were theists, but they approached God through criticism rather than through prayer and developed the secular spirituality of which Marsh and Henry had been prophets. There was George Herbert Palmer at Harvard, teaching a social ethics that was intended to mediate between Puritanism and Hegelianism. There was George Holmes Howison at the Massachusetts Institute of Technology and later at the University of California, teaching a pluralistic, personalistic idealism. There was Borden Parker Bowne, at Boston University, teaching and preaching a more monistic personalism. There was Moses Stuart Phelps of Yale, Middlebury, and Smith, who would have been one of the foremost in the group had he not been killed accidentally at the early age of thirty-four. There were John Bascom and John E. Russell of Williams College, A. C. Armstrong of Wesleyan University, George Trumbull Ladd of Yale, George Fullerton of the University of Pennsylvania, George Sylvester Morris of Johns Hopkins and Michigan, John Grier Hibben and Alexander T. Ormond of Princeton, Jacob Gould Schurmann of Cornell, and, of course, Nicholas Murray Butler of Columbia.[25] These great teachers, animated by a common inspiration, not only laid the foundations of the professional pursuit of philosophy in the United

[25] The situation at Columbia was typical. Professor Charles M. Nairne, imported from Scotland, was an old war horse of orthodoxy. As early as April 13, 1863, the trustees, according to the unpublished diary of G. T. Strong, resolved "to sweep away Professor Nairne's 'Empirical Aesthetics,' Ontology, 'Circular Notation,' cobwebs, Scotch metaphysics, Hickok and humbug, and to substitute for these shadows of moonshine tangible concrete instruction in the History of Literature and the History of Philosophy, such as McVickar used to give us." Finally in the seventies they looked around for a professor of physiological psychology and had the misfortune of appointing Archibald Alexander of Princeton, who in addition to knowing nothing of physiological psychology proved to be a worse teacher than Nairne. Gradually Nicholas Murray Butler, returned from studies in Germany, organized critical instruction in philosophy and psychology. The first seminar was offered in 1885–86. Butler became professor of philosophy in 1889, and in 1890 he established a graduate "School of Philosophy."

States, but gave to systematic philosophy a serious, critical function in American life which soon showed its power far beyond academic walls.

— 36 —

SCHOOLS OF IDEALISM

OUT of this academic renaissance, the great generation of near-great professors of philosophy, each working out independently an American version of German idealism, there grew several schools of philosophy which have endured for more than a generation and which perpetuate each a distinctive type of idealism. Before describing these durable and traditional schools in their American dress we ought at least to mention several picturesque, though ephemeral, groups having a semi-academic form and engaging in animated discussions, which were not the less philosophical for appearing to the more professional professors of idealism as amateur, devotional, and idiosyncratic, unworthy of the Ph.D.

There was, first of all, the St. Louis school, whose origins we have already described.[1] The Philosophical Society of St. Louis was exceedingly diversified in its interests and achievements. It edited *The Journal of Speculative Philosophy* (1867–93) and *The Western*, a "Review of Education, Science, Literature and Art." Harris, Brokmeyer, and Snider devoted themselves chiefly to translating and expounding the German classics of transcendentalism, notably Goethe and Hegel. Their aim was, not to found a school, but to raise the cultural level of St. Louis society in the hope that, with St. Louis as a center, American life in general might cultivate more spiritual forms of speculation and finer arts.

It was because Harris and his companions thought they saw in the Hegelian philosophy a sword wherewith to smite the three-headed monster of anarchy in politics, traditionalism in religion and naturalism in science, that they found courage to undertake and the perseverance to carry through the task of naturalizing it in America.[2]

[1] See above, pp. 179–84.
[2] J. H. Muirhead, "How Hegel Came to America," *The Philosophical Review*, XXXVII (1928), 239.

The meetings and lectures of this group were successful in reaching men of affairs, school teachers, journalists, lawyers, and thus in stimulating the community at large more than the conventional, aloof Washington University in St. Louis even tried to do. G. Stanley Hall described the character of the St. Louis group with amused sympathy:

There is such a pleasing sense of liberty in the perpetual recurrence of dialectic alternatives, and yet of security, inspired by the regularity with which the beats and clicks of the triadic engine are heard, and above all there is such a largeness and scope in the formula of Hegel, as if the Universe itself might be "done" once for all by reading a few thousand pages, that it is no wonder his sun should rise upon the new as it sets in the old world. Where every thing is an open question it is pleasing to feel that "all progress is advancement in the consciousness of freedom." But this is not all. No one can spend a week among the philosophical coteries of St. Louis without feeling—still more perhaps than by reading the *Journal*—that these causes, aided by the influences of reaction from a severely practical and business life, have awakened the faculty of philosophy to a most hopeful and inquiring receptivity.[3]

Snider was an enthusiast for pagan Greek culture, Brokmeyer was a boisterous iconoclast, and Harris, the most academically respectable of the group, though he was a Christian of a sort and fanatically fond of his particular theory of the Trinity, was generally recognized and repeatedly attacked as a "pantheist." When the society broke up, Brokmeyer becoming lieutenant governor of the state, Harris going to Concord, Mass., and then into educational administration on a national scale, Snider was left in solitary splendor to print and "publish" by the labor of his own hands his fifty queer books. He tried to organize a "Communal University" but was finally content with "The Denton J. Snider Association for Universal Culture," as he called the small group who attended his weekly lectures.

Meanwhile, there grew up in neighboring cities, directly or indirectly related to the activities of the St. Louis group, several Platonic academies. The most flourishing of these was at Jacksonville, Ill.,

[3] G. Stanley Hall, "Philosophy in the United States," *Mind; a Quarterly Review of Psychology and Philosophy*, IV (1879), 100. Hall's own interests are amusingly revealed in a comment which follows this passage: "Should Mr. Harris decide to open his *Journal* to psychological as well as to metaphysical discussions, and in preference to the aesthetical selections which have been so often weary and unprofitable, it would soon become not only self-supporting but remunerative."

under the leadership of a physician, Hiram K. Jones. Early in the 1860's he and several friends organized a "Plato Club."

Three friends met in an upper chamber, to decide how they might best inaugurate a plan which should serve once a week to draw them away from the absorbing cares of every-day life, and elevate them to some purer realm from whose heights life in all its interests might appear in its true relations, and where mind and heart might be so strengthened and sweetened that the toil and stress of life's battle might be more easily and courageously borne.[4]

The club was so successful that in 1883 its scope was enlarged; "The American Akademe" was organized, and the *Journal of the American Akademe* began publication. The organization's aim was

to promote the knowledge of Philosophic Truth, and to co-operate in the dissemination of such knowledge, with a view to the elevation of the mind from the sphere of the sensuous life into that of virtue and justice, and into communion with the diviner ideas and nature.[5]

Better known than the American Akademe was its contemporary, the Concord Summer School of Philosophy and Literature (1879–88), which met in the famous structure built especially for it, adjacent to Alcott's residence. Its leaders were A. Bronson Alcott, F. B. Sanborn, and W. T. Harris; it ended when Harris became United States Commissioner of Education.

This was an idea which had been brewing in the mind of Bronson Alcott ever since the early 1840's when he had visited James P. Greaves's school near London. It had been given much encouragement through the contacts which Alcott established in his various journeys through the Midwest and he had talked the idea over with Jones in Jacksonville on occasion, realizing that interest in such a school was as strong as, if not stronger, in the Midwest than it was in the East. In a very important sense, it can be said that if Jones and the Plato Club had not been successful in their own way and enthusiastic about such schemes, the Concord School might never have come into being. It was Jones's visit to Concord in 1878 that brought the movement to fruition, for on that occasion, Alcott, Jones, Sanborn and Emerson agreed that the auspicious moment had arrived for such a venture.

[4] Paul Russell Anderson, "Hiram K. Jones and Philosophy in Jacksonville," *Journal of the Illinois State Historical Society*, XXXIII (1940), 492.

[5] *Ibid.*, pp. 504–5.

When the school opened in 1879 its two chief attractions were Jones and William Torrey Harris, both midwesterners; S. H. Emery, Jr., of Quincy, leader of the Plato Club there, became its permanent director. A good many of those who attended the lectures were from the Midwest. In a sense, it can fairly be said that the founding of this school was an occasion for the Midwest to implant philosophy once again in the soil of the East. Newspapers commonly spoke of this as a midwestern triumph of culture.[6]

Whether or not the summer school was as "midwestern" as this account leads us to believe, it is certainly true that its chief purpose was to give an opportunity to the western Hegelians and the New England transcendentalists to hear each other and to attempt some sort of synthesis. Its chief significance, however, lay, not in the realization of this purpose, but in the recognition and publicity which it gave to philosophy as an independent and important aspect of "culture."

Conceived as a sequel to the Concord Summer School was Davidson's Summer School of the Culture Sciences at Glenmore, in the Adirondacks. Among other teachers of Latin and Greek in the St. Louis high schools during Harris's administration of them was a Scotsman named Thomas Davidson. He became an active member of the St. Louis Philosophical Society and a contributor to the *Journal of Speculative Philosophy*. Through Harris he became familiar with Rosenkranz's interpretation of Hegel, and he tried for a time to share Harris's conviction that Hegel and Aristotle were trying to say the same thing. Harris made elaborate analyses of the psychological significance (especially for the theory of perception and recognition) of the various figures of the syllogism, and had concluded that the Aristotelian logic is important, not because it teaches us how to reason, but because it teaches us "the rationale of our otherwise unconscious processes of perceiving and knowing, and gives us self-knowledge." The study of Greek philosophy seemed to Harris the prerequisite for understanding Hegel, and to understand Hegel seemed to Harris the prerequisite for understanding psychology.

Up to date almost no commentator in Europe or America has been able to explain Hegel's philosophy as a continuation of any philosophy previously offered to the world. It is all out of whole cloth. . . . It is more nearly akin to Aristotle's Metaphysics—the eleventh book—than anything else

[6] *Ibid.*, pp. 499–500.

that we know. And we are safe in saying this because Hegel himself communicates this as his opinion that his philosophy is a philosophy of pure thought in the very sense that Aristotle conceives *nous*. . . . In 1863 I commenced to work in Hegel's History of Philosophy and from that time on Plato and Aristotle began to have a wonderful light which grew slowly from decade to decade. . . . The most wonderful passage in Aristotle . . . is selected by Hegel as the closing sentence of his Encyclopedia of Philosophy. . . . Aristotle shows that the Absolute must be an activity, a self-moved. And his great thought is that the activity and its object are one. "Thinking and being are one" is not a Hegelianism, but as old as Aristotle at least. The activity of speculative insight produces what is perceived.[7]

Such looking at Aristotle through Hegelian spectacles became disgusting to Davidson. He dismissed Hegel abruptly and, being an excellent linguist, went directly to Plato and Aristotle. His primary philosophical interest in their study, however, was identical with Harris's, to understand how "thinking and being are one." His interest in this problem was religious, too. He had outgrown Scottish orthodoxy, but he sought earnestly, pathetically, for a substitute for the fellowship of the church. It was not Christian theology that interested him, but Christian society. Toward Harris's habit of everlastingly deriving the Christian Trinity from Aristotle's syllogisms he showed the greatest contempt, but he, nevertheless, sought some working synthesis of Hellenic and Christian idealisms. It occurred to him that possibly the Greek Orthodox Church might possess such a synthesis, so to Athens he went, spending the greater part of three years with Greek monks and metropolitans. Disappointed in his quest, he turned to Italy; possibly the Catholic Church might be catholic in spirit and in truth. He was again disappointed, but he stumbled by good fortune on the Rosminian Community at Domodossola. Here he found an "ontologism" that satisfied him philosophically and a simple society that satisfied him emotionally. Here was an idealistic individualism that, nevertheless, believed in "the commonwealth of humanity." Here were "men whose lives were full of God, who were never out of the attitude of prayer, whose acts formed one long catalogue of self-sacrificing kindnesses." Full of this Rosminian enthusiasm, Davidson went to England and organized The Fellowship of the New Life,

[7] Letter to D. H. Harris, April 15, 1909.

one branch of which later became the Fabian Society. Foreseeing the English drift toward socialism, which he hated, he returned to the United States in 1884 and founded an American branch of the fellowship. The "declaration of principles" for this fellowship states:

The religion of the Fellowship consists of a determined endeavor to know well, to love well, and to do well.

In endeavoring to know well, the members of the Fellowship, far from depending solely on individual reason or experience, seek light and aid from every quarter; from every age and people; from religion, science, and philosophy; from nature and art; from reason and faith. Knowing that their own mental and moral status, the very conceptions by which they interpret experience, and the thought by which they unite them into a known world, as well as the language by which they express all this, are not their own products, but are the outcome of a process of mental unfolding dating back far beyond the dawn of recorded history, and are to be understood only through a knowledge of this process, they can look only with pity upon those persons who, having no comprehensive acquaintance with the history of human conceptions, rashly undertake, with their crude notions, to pronounce upon the great problems of life and mind. They are, therefore, neither dogmatists, skeptics, nor agnostics, but reverent students of the world of nature and of mind, seeking to supplement their own experience and conclusions with the experience and conclusions of the serious men and women of all time. . . .

Mere indiscriminate loving, vague philanthropic sentiment, and enthusiasm for abstractions, such as humanity, law, etc., it rejects as unprofitable and wasteful. True love is that which seeks the highest good of its object, and rejoices in that good. It is merely another name for a desire to realize and abide with perfection.

. . . It is only when a man has his head and heart well trained that he can act well. Without a comprehension of the end of all action, and of the various tendencies of different actions, he will act blindly from prejudice, passion, or impulse; without well-regulated sympathies, all his actions will have a wrong emphasis and hence be abortive. Such wrong emphasis we see in all those philanthropic movements whose chief aim is men's physical comfort and the indiscriminate removal of that powerful natural corrective, suffering. With such movements the Fellowship, realizing how beneficial suffering may be, has no sympathy. Better to suffer and be strong, than to be comfortable and weak. While the Fellowship seeks to foster coöperation for good works, it hopes for its best results from individual character and

effort. It seeks to avoid all publicity and to do its work quietly and unob-
trusively in the hearts of men. It calls upon each of its members to be a living
power for good, not only in one way or in one connection, but in all ways
and in all connections, in the smallest things as well as in the greatest. Its
ultimate aim is the good man and the good woman, the intelligent, loving,
vigorous character, that seeks good and good alone.

Such is the Religion of The Fellowship of the New Life, such attitude its
only bond of union.[8]

One of the activities of this fellowship was to carry on a summer school
of philosophy similar to that of Concord. Davidson organized his first
summer school at Farmington, Conn., in 1888, but moved in 1890 to
the Adirondacks, where his "Summer School of the Cultural Sciences"
was conducted annually even for several years after his death in 1900.
A typical prospectus for one of these summer schools will suggest to
the reader the importance of these occasions for the history of idealism
in America.

MORNING COURSES

I. THE PHILOSOPHY OF T. H. GREEN

June 17. Green's Theory of Cognition and its place in the History of
   Thought. By Thomas Davidson. . . .
June 18. Green's Treatment of the Relation of Feeling to Reality. By
   H. N. Gardiner. . . .
June 19. Green's Ethical System. By Stephen F. Weston. . . .
June 20. Green's Ethical System viewed in its Relation to Utilitarianism.
   By W. Douw Lighthall. . . .
June 23. Green's Political Theory. By Percival Chubb. . . .
June 24. Green's Religious Philosophy. By John Dewey. . . .

II. THE RELATIONS OF CHURCH AND STATE

June 25. The Politico-Philosophical View. By Professor John Dewey. . . .
June 26. The Free-Religious View. By Reverend W. J. Potter. . . .
June 27. The Historical-Philosophical View. By W. T. Harris. . . .
June 30. The Humanitarian View. By H. D. Lloyd. . . .
July 1. The Scholastic or Roman Catholic View. By Brother Agarias.
July 2. The Unitarian View. By the Reverend A. N. Alcott. . . .

[8] William Knight, *Memorials of Thomas Davidson* (Boston, 1907), pp. 49–51.

I. THE GREEK MORALISTS

(By Thomas Davidson)

June 17. Aeschylus. The Ethical Interpretation of Mythology.
June 18. Aeschylus. Ethical Theory. Man's Relations to Family, Society,
State, and God.
June 19. Socrates. The Relation of Intelligence to Moral Freedom.
June 20. Plato. The State as the Embodiment of Reason and Justice.
June 23. Aristotle. The Good. The Golden Mean. The Ideal Life.
June 24. Aristotle. The State as a School for Life.

II. PRIMARY CONCEPTS OF ECONOMIC SCIENCE

June 25. Wealth. By Percival Chubb.
June 26. Value. By W. M. Salter. . . .
June 27. Property. By Percival Chubb.
June 30. Land. By Stephen F. Weston.
July   1. Labor. By Stephen F. Weston.
July   2. Capital. By W. M. Salter.[9]

While such courses were being conducted during the summers, Davidson was busy during the winters with his "Breadwinner's College," in New York City, a school for workers, conducted evenings, Saturdays, and Sundays, which, under the direction of Morris R. Cohen, survived the founder for several years as "The Davidson Society" and the Davidson Schools. This educational institution was regarded by Davidson as his crowning work, for it united all the aspects of the spiritual life which were most dear to him.

Our own little society already does something to combine the advantages of the College and the Church with those of the home. We form a School in so far as we help each other to master the world's wisdom and learning—a Church in so far as we encourage each other to form and to live up to the highest ideals—a Home in so far as we try to cultivate among ourselves those deep, cordial relations which unfortunately are seldom found outside of the home.

[9] *Ibid.*, pp. 56–57.

There is nothing that the world of to-day needs so much as a new order of social relations, a new feeling between man and man. We may talk and teach as long as we like, but until we have a new society with ideal relations and aims we have accomplished very little. All great world movements begin with a little knot of people, who, in their individual lives, and in their relations to each other, realize the ideal that is to be. To live truth is better than to utter it.[10]

Somewhat similar in aim to Davidson's practical idealism and more enduring in its institutional achievements was the Ethical Culture Movement, which is still an international organization. It originated with the Society for Ethical Culture, in New York, founded in 1876 by Felix Adler, and it spread rapidly to other American cities, where similar societies were organized. These societies are religious fellowships, "where men seek the highest" and unite "to assert the supreme importance of the ethical factor in all the relations of life—personal, social, national, and international, apart from any theological or metaphysical considerations." Dr. Adler, the son of a distinguished Reform rabbi and reared in the doctrines of German Reform Judaism, felt deeply the appeal of a free and universal religion of right and duty, as it was conceived by Kant and preached by idealists, notably by transcendentalists like Emerson. At the same time, he became interested in "organized democracy" and wished to participate in collective reform movements to a degree that was then unpopular among religious institutions. To socialize the all-too-individualistic moral idealism of the Kantians was his primary aim, and for this purpose he found philosophical support in the works of German academic socialists, especially Hermann Cohen and Albert Lange. Through Trendelenburg, too, he was directed toward the metaphysics of Aristotle, much of which seemed congenial to his rational ethics. Gradually Adler wove these various strands into a coherent philosophy, which, quite apart from the intellectual impetus it gave to the ethical movement, represents one of the major types of idealism that have flourished in America. It was the first systematic attempt in America to develop a functional theory of the various vocations of man and to use this theory as a critique of contemporary institutions. It was particularly effective in formulating the ideas of "free religion" and in leading the scattered

[10] *Ibid.*, p. 84.

forces of "free thought" or popular atheism into a more idealistic philosophy with more practical aims. As a leader in the Free Religious Association, as a neighbor and friend of Davidson's School in the Adirondacks, as a promoter of civic and educational reforms, Dr. Adler was particularly concerned to preach a philosophy which possesses both reason and energy.

Ethics has lain in the lap of theology, which was itself corrupted by the attempt to apply to ethical problems the inadequate principle of causality in the form of creation theories, while again in recent times, by way of reaction against theology, the solution of ethical questions is sought for in the empirical disciplines where a measure at least of objective certainty has rewarded the investigators. Even Kant, who asserted the independence of ethics, actually made it dependent on Newtonian science. The great task now is, strictly to carry out the idea of the independence of ethics, not indeed as if its principles were unrelated to those of science and art, but in the sense of independently investigating the problems *peculiar* to ethical consciousness. . . .

Thus the things of earth are to be used as instrumentalities by which we are to become aware of the spiritual reality. Only that the disparateness of the physical world and the ethical universe should ever be kept in the foreground. Every effort to solve the riddle by somehow identifying the two has failed. To account for the existence of a finite world of indefinite extensibility side by side with a universe *ex hypothesi* infinite is impossible. Instead of seeking to explain let effort go toward utilizing. Let the *world* be used instrumentally for the purpose of verifying the existence of *universe*.

For the average man, and indeed for all men, the test of the truth of a theory is in the practice to which it leads. Abstract metaphysical arguments appeal only to a few, and even for them the formula in its abstract guise is unconvincing. Look at the mathematical figure, and see whether the axioms hold good. Look at the sequent phenomena and see whether the so-called law of nature is exemplified. And so with respect to conduct: look at the ways of human behavior traced out in accordance with the plan of the ethical manifold, and see whether such behavior wins the approval of the spiritual nature implicit within you. This is not a transcendental derivation of ethics. The ideal of the infinite society is a fulguration *out of* ethical experience, to be ever renewed *in it*. We build not only our world, but our universe. . . .

The ethical principle is not a working hypothesis, like those provisionally used in science. It is the outgrowth of the functional finalities. It is a postulate. The specific moral laws, or expressions of the ethical principle indeed, are changeable, being the product of the principle with the varying empirical conditions of human society. The fundamental principle is unchangeable. . . .

The instrumental view is precisely that in which modern society has most at stake, on the working out of which the solution of our most pressing problems,—such as the labor problem, the problem of the family, the problem of patriotism and international relations—is entirely dependent. If Kant has failed at this point, as I believe he has, his usefulness as a guide in the reconstruction of modern life is seriously diminished. What he had set out to demonstrate, the inalienable worth of man, remains; but foundations other than his must be found. For the formula "not merely as a means but also as an end" I would substitute: Treat every man as a spiritual means to thine own spiritual end and conversely . . . treat the extent and the manner in which we are to use one another as means being determined by the criterion that our exchange of services shall conduce to the attainment of each other's ends as ethical beings conjointly.[11]

Quite independent of the Ethical Culture Movement, but likewise inspired by a critique of Kantian individualism, was the personal idealism of George H. Howison, which eventuates in an ethical pluralism not unlike Adler's idea of "the spiritual manifold." Howison, like Davidson, was a member of the St. Louis Philosophical Society during its early years. He was at that time (1865–70) a teacher of mathematics at Washington University, but his dominant interests were centered in the Kant Club, which met in the home of W. T. Harris and studied Brokmeyer's attempt to translate Hegel's *Phenomenology.* Hoping for a more congenial teaching appointment, he left St. Louis for Boston, where he became professor of logic and the philosophy of science at the Massachusetts Institute of Technology (1872–78). G. Stanley Hall said Howison lectured "on the logic of grammar in the spirit of Aristotle and Trendelenburg," [12] but when Howison returned from his two years in Germany (1878–80), where he came under the spell of Michelet, his lectures took a different turn, and like Michelet he expounded "the 'Absolute Idea' as a Reason eternally

---

[11] Felix Adler, *An Ethical Philosophy of Life* (New York, 1918), pp. 132–33, 134, 135, 138–39.

[12] G. Stanley Hall, *op. cit.,* p. 100. On the same page Hall writes: Howison's "course of lectures on the history of philosophy is extended and thorough, though attended largely by ladies."

personal, and the ground and source of the personality in man, instead of a mere bond of Logical Energy, coming first to consciousness in human nature." [13] After expounding his version of personal idealism in occasional lectures at Harvard and at the Concord Summer School, Howison finally (1884) settled down in his permanent academic home at the University of California, where both as teacher and as founder and inspirer of the Philosophical Union he exerted a lasting influence. From his own summary statement of his personalistic pluralism and of his picturesque theory of the "eternal republic of God" we quote a few paragraphs here, and we shall have occasion to refer to it later, when we discuss its relation to Royce's idealism.

I. All existence is either (1) the existence of *minds*, or (2) the existence of *the items and order of their experience;* all the existences known as "material" consisting in certain of these experiences, with an order organized by the self-active forms of consciousness that in their unity constitute the substantial being of a mind, in distinction from its phenomenal life.

II. Accordingly, Time and Space, and all that both "contain," owe their entire existence to the essential correlation and coexistence of minds. This coexistence is not to be thought of as either their simultaneity or their contiguity. It is not at all spatial, nor temporal, but must be regarded as simply *their logical implication of each other in the self-defining consciousness of each.* And this recognition of each other as all alike self-determining, renders *their coexistence a moral order.*

III. These many minds, being in this mutual recognition of their moral reality the determining ground of all events and all mere "things," form the eternal (i.e., unconditionally real) world; and by a fitting metaphor, consecrated in the usage of ages, they may be said to constitute the "City of God." In this, all the members have the equality belonging to their common aim of fulfilling their one Rational Ideal; and God, the fulfilled Type of every mind, the living Bond of their union, reigns in it, not by the exercise of power, but solely by light; not by authority, but by reason; not by efficient, but by final causation—that is, simply by being the impersonated Ideal of every mind.

IV. The members of this Eternal Republic have no origin but their purely logical one of reference to each other, including thus their primary reference to God. That is, in the literal sense of the word, they have no origin at all—no source in *time* whatever. There is nothing at all, prior to

[13] John Wright Buckham and George Malcolm Stratton, *George Holmes Howison, Philosopher and Teacher* (Berkeley, 1934), p. 69.

them, out of which their being arises; they are not "things" in the chain of efficient causation. They simply *are*, and together constitute the eternal order. . . .

VII. This Pluralism held in union by reason, this World of Spirits, is thus the genuine *Unmoved One that moves all Things*. Not the solitary God, but the whole World of Spirits including God, and united through recognition of him, is the real "Prime Mover" of which since the culmination of Greek philosophy we have heard so much. Its oneness is not that of a single inflexible Unit, leaving no room for freedom in the many, for a many that is really many, but is the oneness of uniting harmony, of spontaneous coöperation, in which every member, from inner initiative, from native contemplation of the same Ideal, joins in moving all things changeable toward the common goal.

VIII. This movement of things changeable toward the goal of a common Ideal is what we have in these days learned to call the process of Evolution.[14]

Here Howison is consciously enlarging Kant's doctrine of "the native spontaneity of the human mind" to construct a continuous a priori science of both the moral and the sensible domains, and thus he is reconstructing the metaphysics of "free spirits," which in Berkeley's system centers in the unifying function of the divine mind, but which in Howison's system gives expression to a more democratic, pluralistic type of unity achieved by the community of human minds.

Coming now to the American "schools" of idealism in the stricter sense of academic traditions, we can distinguish four main types of idealism, each having an influential academic headquarters, a founding father, and a generation of more or less faithful disciples; these may be conveniently identified as follows:

1. Personalism: Boston University, Borden Parker Bowne

2. Speculative or Objective Idealism: Cornell University, James Edwin Creighton

3. Dynamic Idealism: Michigan University, George Sylvester Morris.

4. Absolute Idealism: Harvard University, Josiah Royce

Of these, personalism has remained closest to the fold of theism and of academic orthodoxy, has served most explicitly as a philosophy of a religion, and has maintained most conspicuously the external

[14] *Ibid.*, pp. 128–30.

marks of a coherent school. It has been useful in breaking down the
sectarian intellectual barriers of the Methodist Church, which had
inherited the evangelical fear and scorn of unrevealed doctrines, but
which in giving ear to its personalist theologians has become accustomed to philosophical forms of speech and even, if we regard its most
courageous leaders, to philosophical habits of mind. Professor Bowne,
of Boston University, was one of the most gifted teachers and independent minds of his generation, and his books, though antiquated in
doctrine, are still interesting reading for their clarity and vigor of
thought and expression. Bowne addressed himself boldly to two major
problems in the academic philosophy of his time: he exposed the weaknesses of the faculty psychology and expounded the empirical reality
of the self as a substitute for the antiquated faith in a substantial soul.
His first philosophical inspiration came to him when he was a student
at New York University, where he wrote a vigorous critique of Spencer. Then, during his postgraduate studies in Germany he came under
the influence of Lotze and realized at once the important bearings of
his theory of the empirical self for the criticism of academic orthodoxy
on the one hand and of British empiricism on the other. The self, or
person, in Lotze's theory, is an ultimate, empirical reality, whose unity
is given as basic to both experience and nature. Bowne developed the
theistic implications of this "transcendental empiricism" and reconstructed the Kantian doctrine of the categories. Arguing on the basis
of the principle of sufficient reason, he concluded that persons can be
caused only by persons and that the ultimate cause or creator must be
"at least personal." Bowne was well aware that speculative hypotheses
or postulates are not useful for "the advance of knowledge," but he
defended them, nevertheless, as inevitable and natural forms of man's
will.

Hypotheses are of two kinds. Some are simply offered as explanations of
the facts, and give us no new control over the facts. They are necessary to
satisfy the demand for a sufficient reason; and when no competing hypothesis satisfies the mind as well, we hold it for the mental peace it brings,
although we cannot use it to advance knowledge. Such are the atomic
theory, most of the doctrines of geology, many of the theories of physics,
the theistic view of the world, etc. None of these are fruitful in practical
research; they are simply theories which are necessary to explain the actual

order of facts. Their proof or verification consists in showing that the facts shut us up to such a view.

The other order of hypotheses admits of deduction, and puts us in control of phenomena. The proof of these consists not merely in their adequacy to the observed facts, but in the agreement of their implications with other facts not originally contemplated or observed. The law of gravitation, the ether theory of light, are examples. These can be used to advance knowledge, and are generally mathematical. Once in a while a speculator of positivist leanings decides that only the latter class of hypotheses is to be allowed. The former he rejects as unverifiable figments of fancy. Unfortunately, he does not always have the clearest notion as to what verification means; and, besides, he has the human mind against him.[15]

Bowne's *Studies in Theism* (1879), *Philosophy of Theism* (1887), and *Principles of Ethics* (1893) were popular textbooks, especially in Methodist seminaries and colleges. His *Personalism* (1908) gave systematic formulation to a distinct school of idealistic philosophy and theology. The more recent champions of this school, notably G. A. Coe, E. S. Brightman, A. C. Knudson, and R. T. Flewelling, have defended personalism less on the basis of conventional cosmology, as did Bowne, and more as a philosophy of values or ideals. Personality, they say, being the locus of all value, perspective, and meaning, is also the ultimate empirical reality, and God is the person of persons. Though this philosophy is evidently a defense of theism and, in that sense, a kind of Christian apologetics, it is not a mere revival of the "mentalistic" or Berkeleyan argument for idealism. Its approach is psychological, but its psychology is critical of empiricism. Brightman, especially, has subordinated his theism and his defense of belief in a "finite God" to a generalized axiology or metaphysics of value, which brings his version of personalism somewhat closer to Howison's, Calkins's, and Leighton's, as well as to other current forms of idealist thought. The "finite self" or empirical datum is conceived by these idealists as conscious activity, and such activity is most clearly present in acts of valuation or selection. Objective mind, if it exists, is to be discovered in the norms by which selves govern themselves and each other. By this method personalists have succeeded in developing

[15] Borden P. Bowne, *Theory of Thought and Knowledge* (New York, 1897), pp. 208-9.

further Bowne's monadology, teleology, and ethics, without committing themselves to the cosmological arguments for theism on which his earliest works were based. They are, for the most part, content to rest their case on the doctrine that "the only world-view in which values and meanings can have a permanently real status is one for which minds, personalities, and their values are supreme." [16]

Antithetical to personalism is the objective idealism of the Cornell University type. Here a philosophy of spirit has flourished which is indifferent to psychology and which conceives the only complete empiricism to be an understanding of human experience in its historical course and institutional forms. This study of "objective mind," as it has been carried on at the Sage School of Philosophy of Cornell, was the American wing of the movement within idealism which in both Germany and England combined a critical analysis of the categories (the Kantian heritage) with an historical conception of the human spirit (the Hegelian heritage). A critical logic and a philosophy of history were thus united to form a theory of experience as an organic whole, both in the individual and in society.

The first head of the Sage School, later president of the university, was Jacob Gould Schurman. He had received his enthusiasm for Kant in Scotland and had carried it with him to Canada, where for years he taught philosophy at Dalhousie College. When he was called to Cornell in 1886, he developed the idea that critical idealism was especially significant for America because it was essentially the great mediator, and it was America's destiny to be the great mediator among nations. Schurman's interpretation of Kant emphasized the way in which he succeeded in reconciling the empiricism of Hume with the rationalism of Leibniz, and he elaborated the doctrine of the categories into a science of the necessary forms of empirical reason. He conceived the a priori and the a posteriori elements in knowledge as supplementary to each other and as equally essential for any science. Similarly, he conceived philosophy's chief function to be that of mediating between the sciences and the arts. When he launched the *Philosophical Review* in 1892 he explained the function of this periodical in terms of cultural mediation, and he added the idea that American philosophy would be

[16] J. A. Leighton, "The Principle of Individuality and Value," in *Contemporary Idealism in America,* ed. by Clifford Barrett (New York, 1932), p. 160.

doubly mediatorial, because American culture in general must be the great reconciler of the East and the West.

As the mixing-place of the Same and the Other (to apply the striking terminology of Plato), there is every reason to believe that America will be the scene on which that master-demiurgus, the human spirit, will manifest its next world-phase of philosophical discovery, interpretation, and construction. . . . Greek culture was characterized by freedom,—freedom of government for the city-states, freedom of action for the individual, and freedom of thought in religion (which possessed no uniform system of doctrine and no regularly organized priesthood endowed with external power). On the other hand, Greek culture was characterized by respect for custom and law and by subordination of the individual to the whole. These opposite features attained to a full harmony of development about the time of the origin of Greek Philosophy. To them it owes, on the one hand, its originality and independence; on the other, its orderliness, its system, its constructive tendencies. If these favoring aspects of Greek civilization are not to-day reproduced in the American love of independence and the American respect for law, in the American union of half a hundred "sovereign" commonwealths with all their county and town governments under one federal head, in the American churches with their democratic organization and their multifarious and plastic creeds, in American freedom of thought and speech which has always tended to build and not merely to destroy; then one can scarcely imagine where they are to be found, even in approximation, among the peoples of the earth.

That a combination of endowments, culture, and circumstances, so favorable to the development of Philosophy, should exist in a nation numbering between sixty and seventy millions, is a most hopeful augury for the future of human civilization. We are not required, however, to nourish our spirits on expectation merely. The signs and omens already move towards their fulfilment. What is prefigured in the conditions is even now becoming the hatch and brood of time. Never before in our history has there been so deep and so widely diffused an interest in philosophical subjects. The light, unreflective, optimistic mood of earlier days may not have deserted us, but we cannot conceal the fact that the nation enters upon the second century of its career with a new feeling of unrest and a temper of greater seriousness and reflection. . . . If it were safe to prophesy from the "seeds and weak beginnings" of things "as yet not come to life," one might venture to forecast from this vigorous philosophical activity, taken in conjunction with the parity of conditions, a harvest of thought like that gathered in Greece in the fourth century before Christ, or that which came to maturity in Germany scarce three generations ago. But in one respect there will be an important difference. The new birth of Philosophy amongst ourselves will be the final outcome of devotion to special philosophical interests and of cultivation of special philosophical domains. Our classic systems, if ever we form them, will rest on a much wider induction of facts than any preceding philosophical systems. It is fortunate, indeed, that the spirit of specialization has taken possession of Philosophy, and we may congratulate ourselves on the special investigations and special publications conducted by Americans. But division of labor is profitless without co-operation.[17]

When Schurman became president of Cornell University, in 1892, his place at the head of the Sage School was taken by one of his former students at Dalhousie, James Edwin Creighton, who until his death, in 1924, was the chief representative of the Cornell school of idealism. Associated with him was an exceptionally competent staff: Frank Thilly (disciple of Paulsen and translator of some of his works and other German texts), William A. Hammond, Ernest Albee, to mention only the first generation of a distinguished line of teachers and scholars. At Cornell were trained the greater part of a generation of professors of philosophy in the United States, and through them the Cornell theories and methods came to exert a dominant role in philosophical instruction and research. Through the initiative of the Cornell school, too, the American Philosophical Association was formed in 1902, with Creighton as its first president. That Cornell should play this leading part in professional and co-operative philosophical studies was no accident; it was but the practical application of its objective conception of mind and of its belief in the social nature of thought. In his presidential address Creighton made this clear.

In every department of investigation the conviction seems to be growing that intellectual companionship and coöperation are essential to real progress. The underlying assumption is that it is necessary in scientific work to combine forces and to work, not as a number of isolated individuals, but as a social group of coöperating minds. We have learned that to isolate oneself intellectually is to render one's work unfruitful; that there is in every generation a main drift of problems within which we must work, if we wish to contribute anything to the common cause.[18]

[17] Jacob Gould Schurman, ed., "Prefatory Note," *The Philosophical Review*, I (1892), 3–4, 5.
[18] James Edwin Creighton, *Studies in Speculative Philosophy* (New York, 1925), p. 7.

And in one of his finest essays he developed the same idea.

The mind is a whole, and if its social nature is demonstrated in certain forms of experience, we should hardly expect to find it, in any one of its aspects, remaining isolated and self-centered. Nevertheless, both in popular thinking and in psychological analysis there is a tendency to regard the thinking mind as a particular form of existence, somehow enclosed within a body, and expressing the functioning of a brain. Just as one body keeps another body out of the same space, so the thinking mind of the individual is regarded as isolated, repellent, exclusive. The thinker is taken to be a solitary being, wrestling with his own problems alone and unassisted. By the power of his mind he is supposed to create truth through his own analysis and meditations. . . . As opposed to this contention, I wish to suggest that the process of verification always involves, either directly or indirectly, the coöperation and interplay of a plurality of minds. It is with the support and in the light of the thoughts of other men that the individual is able to free himself from subjective fancies and hasty generalizations, and so to attain to universal truth. The result is not original in the sense that it has sprung wholly from his brain, but it is the product of many minds working together. . . . Thinking is the outcome of the functioning of a society of minds, not of an abstract individual mind, just as morality, and political institutions, and religion spring from and belong to such an organic unity of individuals. "Without society no individual," is a statement that applies to man as a thinker no less than to man as a moral or political being.[19]

For the same reason that thought must be social, it must be historical; the continuity and unity of experience must become a conscious possession.

Philosophical science is not "natural" science, and cannot "accept its facts" from the latter. To do so would be to put "psychologism" and "naturalism" in place of philosophy. But philosophy, to be philosophy at all, has to *humanize* its facts, that is, to look at them from the standpoint of complete and self-conscious human experience, for it is only from this standpoint that a meaning for them can be found. The philosopher is thus essentially a humanist rather than a naturalist, and his closest affiliations are with the sciences that deal with the products of man's thought and purposive activity. In his relation to natural science, he is concerned less with the facts regarded objectively than with the thinking operations by which these facts were obtained. He does not adopt the standpoint of natural science, but

[19] *Ibid.*, pp. 50–51.

transforms it utterly, and gives to natural facts a new interpretation in terms of conscious experience. Similarly, the abstract view of nature as a whole which the physical naturalist furnishes, has to be humanized by philosophical interpretation, *which construes the facts differently,* finding in nature the congeniality with the mind of man through which alone it is intelligible. And, on the other hand, the philosophical standpoint necessitates a different account of the facts of mind from that given by the psychological "naturalist." The merely subjective standpoint of the latter cannot be taken as starting-point any more than the merely objective standpoint of the physicist. Just as philosophy humanizes the physical facts by viewing them in relation to mind, so it also objectifies subjective facts by viewing them as functions through which the individual realizes his unity with nature and with his fellow-men.[20]

The reader will recognize in these passages the spirit of *Geisteswissenschaft.* Such idealism was humanistic in method as well as in interest. Nature was to be interpreted as man's environment, the habitat of his experience, neither external nor central. Similarly, the individual, nature's polar opposite, is neither central nor incidental to mind. Nature, society, and individual together form a community of thought and culture. Creighton, in his own thinking, as well as in his teaching and editing, insisted that there could no longer be "pioneering," there could only be contributory labor in the great cultivated field of the arts and sciences. To think is to work with other minds at common tasks. This doctrine was obviously no mere epistemology or even a mere program for academic scholarship; it was in America, as in Germany and England, an attempt to give new vitality to philosophy (*Lebensphilosophie*) by integrating it with the widest possible areas of human action and memory. As in the case of most philosophical ideas, and certainly of most ideals, the doctrine of what is real is the index to what is important; so the assertion that all experience is an absolute, coherent, organic whole was part of an energetic attempt to make it so.

Even more consciously concerned with the logic of life than was Cornell was the school of dynamic idealism which flourished for a few years at Johns Hopkins University and for a longer period at the University of Michigan. This school emphasized the biological as well

[20] *Ibid.,* p. 23.

as the cultural nature of human experience. George Sylvester Morris, a graduate of Dartmouth College and a student at Union Theological Seminary, was one of the many young liberals in divinity who chose to continue his studies in Germany instead of ascending to the pulpit and, as a result of this choice, permanently forsook the profession of the Christian ministry to devote himself to the teaching of philosophy. He came under the influence of Ulrici of Halle and of Trendelenburg at Berlin; they taught him to seek the truth, not in the pseudo-Christian Hegelian theology, but in a genuine "science of being," a transcendentalism enlightened by Aristotle's metaphysics. After his return to the United States in 1868 he endured several years of intellectual and academic groping. He went to Michigan in 1870 to teach modern languages and literature, but it was not until 1878, when he undertook to teach at both Johns Hopkins and at Michigan, that his career as the founder of a distinctive school of idealism in America was assured.

He carried back with him from Germany an enthusiasm for the activistic interpretation of the Kantian categories and for an assimilation of idealism to Aristotelian conceptions of movement, development, growth, and actualization. Acts of thought, Morris explained, following Trendelenburg and other neo-Kantian voluntarists, are literally motions, and the categories of thought are categories of movement. Hence the science of mind can be assimilated to the science of the other natural forms of energy. The creative (formative) powers of mind can be understood as natural energies, free because spontaneous or elemental. This analysis of the life of reason was intended as a critique of the Hegelian overemphasis on logic and dialectic. The "movement" of thought in the course of history was, according to Morris, less a *logical* sequence of "theses" than it was a growth of living activities. Morris used this interpretation of the creative activity of mind as a point of view from which to criticize the "identity-systems" of Spinoza, Leibniz, and Hegel and to contrast in general the philosophical methods of analysis with those of mathematics and dialectic. He thought of philosophy as an independent and distinctive science, "experimental" in a sense, but radically different in method and aim from the mechanical sciences on the one hand and the mathematical or logical on the other. To him it was the science of the life or soul (in the Aristotelian sense) of the body, the science of experience as it is lived or "in act." Criticizing the British empiricists like Mill and Spencer, he wrote:

The search for a fundamental, spiritual, living, and absolute reality, like that of Self, by psychological inquiries pursued under the limitations, and determined by the presuppositions, of the method of purely physical science, must necessarily be fruitless. The very fact that the search, thus prosecuted, is hopelessly unavailing, while yet the "belief in self" persists in the mind of the inquirer as one which "no hypothesis enables us to escape," should, apparently, be of itself sufficient to convince him and the whole cohort of his followers that the method in which he and they put all their trust, and which they style "experimental," is—not, indeed, in its proper sphere, inexperimental, but—abstract, partial, incomplete, and not commensurate with the whole nature and content of experience; requiring, therefore, to be supplemented by a larger and more liberal, but not less strictly scientific, method, which is not unknown to philosophy and which, not being arbitrarily conceived and forcibly imposed on experience, but simply founded in and dictated by the recognition of experience in its whole nature, is alone entitled to be termed fully and without qualification "experimental." . . .

The theoretical sensationalist (as Locke, Hume, *et al.*,) and the critical idealist (Kant), who start with the express or implicit assumption of the mechanical relation as the fundamental one between subject and object, come quickly to the conclusion that the true object is an unknown and unknowable substrate or thing-in-itself, which the subject-forms of intelligence never reach. This conclusion is a *reductio ad absurdum* of the premise on which it rests. The science of knowledge has nothing to do with unknowable objects. It has no ground on which to posit their existence. It has positive ground for absolutely denying their existence, for *knowing* that they do not exist . . . The phenomenal object is not a vail or screen effectually to shut out from us the sight of the noumenal object. Nor is the former separated from the latter by an impassable interval. On the contrary, to thought it instrumentally reveals the true object. . . .

In other words, that *is* which is *known*. Knowledge and being are correlative terms. When we know therefore what is the true *object* of *knowledge*, we know what is the final and absolute significance of the terms *being* and *reality*.[21]

With this combination of epistemological realism and romantic voluntarism, Morris tried to put philosophy on a strictly scientific

[21] George S. Morris, *Philosophy and Christianity* (New York, 1883), pp. 287, 44–45, 70.

basis without subordinating it to other sciences. Such an enterprise was particularly significant at Johns Hopkins, where the natural experimental sciences were being championed for the first time as the center of academic research. And, in this attempt to defend an idealism as a science among sciences, Morris was unable to convince either President Gilman or G. Stanley Hall, who regarded his system as essentially moral philosophy, not natural science. He was obliged to give up the attempt at Johns Hopkins and to return to Michigan with the reputation of being a moralist.

Meanwhile, his colleague at Johns Hopkins, C. S. Peirce, was working on his own revision of the Kantian categories, relating them to his particular conception of the biology of mind and expounding his own version of the theory of continuity. Though Peirce and Morris shared these basic interests and problems, they differed radically in their attitude toward mathematics. Morris had a technical appreciation for mathematical logic, but he failed to see its significance for philosophy.

When G. Stanley Hall was added to the Johns Hopkins faculty, after he had been trained in the laboratories of Wundt and other German psychologists, he introduced experimental, physiological psychology to America and looked upon the metaphysics of Morris and Peirce as too speculative to be biological. John Dewey, who came from Vermont in 1883 and studied primarily under Morris, felt the force of these divergent forms of philosophical biology and, making critical use of all of them, began to prepare his own system of "psychology," which appeared as a text in 1887. Dewey began this work under Morris with his Ph.D. research on "Kant's psychology." His thesis, like Thorstein Veblen's contemporary article in the *Journal of Speculative Philosophy* (likewise inspired by Morris), centered on Kant's theory of judgment as a mediating function in human experience. He tried to prove that Kant's theory made "reason or spirit the center and organic unity of the entire sphere of man's experience," that in virtue of his assigning this central position and function to intelligence (Morris's word for Kant's "reason"), Kant was the founder of true philosophic method, and that "so far as he was false to it he fell into his own defects and contradictions."

In 1884 Dewey joined Morris at Michigan, and Morris spent the 1885 summer abroad, chiefly in Scotland and England, where he met the British idealists, especially Edward Caird, F. H. Bradley, and William Wallace. From that time on until Morris's death in 1889 both Morris and Dewey became increasingly reconciled to Hegel, regarding him as basically an objective empiricist, whose aim was to exhibit the "mediation" or integration of human experience through intelligence. This Hegelian version of their idealism was expounded more systematically by Dewey than by Morris. What Morris had called "the special science of philosophy" appeared in Dewey's version as "the objective method in psychology." (It will be recalled that Snider and some of the other St. Louis Hegelians were using the term "psychology" in this broad sense.) In explaining why psychology is "a central science," Dewey writes:

All the other sciences deal only with facts or events which are known, but the fact of *knowledge* thus involved in all of them no one of them has said anything about. It has treated the facts simply as *existent* facts, while they are also *known* facts. But knowledge implies reference to the self or mind. Knowing is an intellectual process, involving psychical laws. It is an activity which the self experiences. A certain *individual* activity has been accordingly presupposed in all the *universal* facts of physical science. These facts are all facts known by some mind, and hence fall, in some way, within the sphere of psychology. This science is accordingly something more than one science by the side of others; it is a central science, for its *subject-matter*, knowledge, is involved in them all. . . .

We find the unity of the psychical processes . . . and therefore their ultimate explanation, in the fact that man is a self; that the essence of self is the self-determining activity of will; that this will is an objectifying activity, and that, in objectifying itself, it renders itself universal. The result of this activity is *knowledge*. The objectified will is science; the objectifying activity is the intellect. This will or activity also renders an account *to itself* of its own doings. It is internal to itself. The objective universal result is at one and the same time existent in the medium of the individual's consciousness. This subjective aspect of the activity is feeling. As expressing the furtherance or hinderance of the activity, it is pleasure or pain; as an accompaniment of an actual realization, it possesses content and is qualitative.

The activity which is both subjective and objective, which unites the individual and the universe, which finds its motive in feeling and its result in knowledge, and at the same time changes this known object into the felt subject is the will, the unity of psychical life. . . .

Mind has not remained a passive spectator of the universe, but has produced and is producing certain results. These results are objective, can be studied as all objective historical facts may be, and are permanent. They are the most fixed, certain, and universal signs to us of the way in which mind works. Such objective manifestations of mind are, in the realm of intelligence, phenomena like language and science; in that of will, social and political institutions; in that of feeling, art; in that of the whole self, religion. Philology, the logic of science, history, sociology, etc., study these various departments as objective, and endeavor to trace the relations which connect their phenomena. But none of these sciences takes into account the fact that science, religion, art, etc., are all of them products of the mind or self, working itself out according to its own laws, and that, therefore, in studying them we are only studying the fundamental nature of the conscious self. It is in these wide departments of human knowledge, activity, and creation that we learn most about the self, and it is through their investigation that we find most clearly revealed the laws of its activities.[22]

Dewey developed the objective psychology of the will still further in his *Outlines of Ethics* (1891). It was while Dewey was engaged in revising this system of ethics that he discovered instrumentalism in James's *Psychology*, and he consequently abandoned the elaborate idealistic framework of his biological approach to logic and ethics for a more naturalistic, less esoteric terminology.

It is, therefore, to another associate of Morris's that we must turn for a more concrete working out of dynamic idealism. Alfred H. Lloyd, who came to the University of Michigan in 1891, was for many years (until 1927) an influential teacher and dean (after 1915) at that university, but he was less well known elsewhere than his colleagues. His four books were, with the exception of *Dynamic Idealism* (1898), particular applications of his philosophy, rather than expositions of it, and were extremely abstruse, ironical, and subtle. Even the general exposition of his dynamic idealism was made unpalatable to the majority of his prospective readers by professing to be "the metaphysics of psychology" and "to give a distinct, explicit doctrine of the soul." In other words, Lloyd's language gave the impression that he was a rank reactionary, but the substance of his doctrine was so unconventional that it gave religious comfort to no one. Lloyd was an unusually independent thinker. Even as a youth his independence asserted itself. Like

[22] John Dewey, *Psychology* (New York, 1887), pp. 4, 423, 11–12.

his colleagues Morris and Dewey, he received much of his early training in Vermont. When he graduated from St. Johnsbury Academy he was headed for the ministry, and friends were prepared to support him while at Dartmouth College and while in seminary. He preferred, however, to work his way through Harvard, where he was graduated in 1886, believing halfheartedly in Unitarianism, but apparently more inspired by Royce's methodical skepticism and Abbot's organicist theism. In Germany he became still further preoccupied with philosophical criticism. Throughout his career and in all his thinking he glorified doubting as the surest sign and source of idealism. To live critically, said this modern Socrates, is the essence of mental activity. The world of acts, he said repeatedly, is the living, present union of matter and form, of things and ideas.

Matter as organic is intelligent, and mind as dynamic is material or substantial. . . . Soul . . . is the fulfilling organic activity, or the substance, in which an organic matter and a dynamic mind are one. . . .

Relationship among things is the criterion neither of a life nor of a mind that exists apart from the substance of the universe. It is, however, the criterion of substance itself, and as the central truth about things it bears this witness: *The universe itself lives; the universe itself thinks.*[23]

Lloyd emphasized the creative function of doubt, not merely as a methodological device, but because, as he put it characteristically, "we must believe in the things we doubt." The struggle of opposites, the life of dialectic, was to him the most concrete and empirical pattern of life; hence, his development of the Hegelian philosophy of history, with its meeting of antitheses, was to him, not the mere celebration of paradox, which to the hasty reader it appears to be, but his appreciation of the seriousness of living issues or conflicts. To think, meant, in Lloyd's system, to see a problem as a problem; the mind "mediates," even when it fails to solve a problem, by feeling the opposing pulls of vital forces. It is impossible here to give the reader a just idea of the brilliance and irony of Lloyd's expositions and of the futility of his conclusions. Perhaps one specimen, taken from his *Philosophy of History*, will give the reader a taste at least of his original applications of

[23] Alfred H. Lloyd, *Dynamic Idealism* (Chicago, 1898), pp. 159 and the page facing the title page.

the Hegelian dialectic. He is expounding the three stages of social growth: society at one with itself, society alienated from itself, and society restored to itself. And, in the course of his analysis of the process of alienation (the theory of revolution), he writes:

Psychologically or sociologically, the time can not but come when labor and thought will return to each other. Thus, whenever science is afield, it is well to look for a revolution. But this is anticipating.

A society's thought is long in developing and we need to follow the process of the development in its several moments before we can adequately comprehend how it must culminate in a revolution. That alienation is a forerunner of revolution is quite evident, but the successive details of the process are important, although their differences may prove to be only in degree. Accordingly, with reference particularly to the three social classes, already named, the thinkers, the officials, and the laborers, I have found it convenient to recognize five moments in the alienating process, these moments, namely: (1) the moment of consciously asserted patriotism; (2) the moment of aesthetic self-appreciation; (3) the moment of the cosmopolitan spirit; (4) the moment of assumed and cultivated naturalism, and (5) the moment of spiritual surrender and resignation. Thus, here they are in a table, with the contemporary class changes:

FIVE MOMENTS IN A SOCIETY'S ALIENATION FROM ITSELF

Order of Moments.	Thinkers.	Officials.	Laborers.	Historical Illustration.
1	Law-makers.	Public guardians or patriots.	Slaves.	Greece before Pericles' time.
2	Artists.	Conscious and critical citizens.	Paid servants.	The age of Pericles.
3	Scientists.	Politicians.	Artisans.	The period just before Socrates.
4	Philosophers.	Fatalists or time-servers.	Revolutionists.	The Socratic Period.
5	Religious leader or monarch.	Followers or disciples.	Hirelings.	Greece a Christian-Roman province.

A mere glance at this table shows a progressive increase in the degree of the alienation of the society as a whole from itself, from its institutions and traditions, or—otherwise put—a progressive increase in the degree of the independence or individual freedom of the members of society.[24]

The written words of Morris, Lloyd, and of Dewey during his early years, though they state clearly enough what dynamic idealism meant to the members of this school, fail to portray the liveliness of their teaching. Their idealism was dynamic in a double sense, for not only did it teach that thinking is the most active form of life, but each of these thinkers in his own way exhibited personally this union of energy and thought.

Lastly, we turn to the type of idealism which we have labeled "absolute idealism," though this label does not distinguish it properly. It denotes Josiah Royce's several versions of the doctrine of the absolute and his successive attempts to appropriate the special features of the other schools in order to paint a comprehensive, not an eclectic, portrait of God. Royce, at Harvard, succeeded in being a school all by himself, and, though he did not create a clique of idealists, he made his own exposition sufficiently vivid and impressive to affect deeply many types of philosophers in many lands. Let us give him a separate chapter.

— 37 —

JOSIAH ROYCE

TWO years after the University of California opened its doors at Berkeley (1873), a red-haired, freckled lad, named Josiah Royce, had already obtained from it an A.B. and was on his way to study in Germany. His graduation thesis on "The Theology of Aeschylus's Prometheus" had made such a strong impression on several prosperous pioneers that they offered him enough California gold to spend two years in Germany reading Schelling, Schopenhauer, and Pfleiderer, and hearing the lectures of Lotze at Göttingen. He returned to America just in time to get one of the first fellowships at

---

[24] Alfred H. Lloyd, *Philosophy of History; an Introduction to the Philosophical Study of Politics* (Ann Arbor, Mich., 1899), pp. 154–55.

Johns Hopkins. There he wrote his thesis on "The Possibility of Error" and was examined by Morris in the history of philosophy. After receiving his doctors degree (1878) he returned to California to teach logic and rhetoric; within a few years he was on his way east again, to teach literature and philosophy at Harvard. Everyone was impressed by him at once, and within three years he was invited by President Eliot to give the Lowell Lectures, for one thousand dollars. Mr. Lowell, the patron of the lectureship, explained to the young man that since the lectures were to be about religion he would be obliged to sign a simple creed before the deal could be closed. Whereupon the youth announced that he would sign no creed for money, and instead of delivering the Lowell Lectures he went to work on an essay entitled *California; a Study of American Character*. The close of this essay is worth quoting:

It is the State, the Social Order, that is divine. We are all but dust, save as this social order gives us life. When we think it our instrument, our plaything, and make our private fortunes the one object, then this social order rapidly becomes vile to us; we call it sordid, degraded, corrupt, unspiritual and ask how we may escape from it forever. But if we turn again and serve the social order and not merely ourselves, we soon find that what we are serving is simply our own highest spiritual destiny in bodily form. *It* is never truly sordid or corrupt or unspiritual; it is only *we* that are so when we neglect our duty.[1]

What a perfect beginning for a romantic idealist! In this mood, his big head and high brow full of Prometheus, Schopenhauer, Schelling, and California, he wrote his first flamboyant, philosophical homily, entitled, *The Religious Aspect of Philosophy*.

This volume is a clever dialectical exploitation of pessimism and skepticism. The argument falls into two parts: the *moral* problem of pessimism; and the *logical* problem of judgment. How is ethical doubt possible? And how is error possible? He begins with Schopenhauer's pessimism, which, in the last analysis, turns out to be a moral despair over the fact that it is impossible to prove that any particular ideal *ought* to be accepted by every rational soul. But he has no sooner drunk the bitter dregs of this doubt than he discovers that "the truth of the

[1] Josiah Royce, *California; a Study of American Character* (Boston, 1886), p. 501.

matter is concealed in the doubt." The very fact that the failure to discover some particular absolute *"ought"* makes the inquirer pessimistic,
implies that he has in him the moral will or demand that all particular
ideals *ought to be harmonized.* To one whom moral conflict makes
pessimistic, the good of moral peace must be self-evident. Therefore
empirical pessimism is possible only because an absolute ideal is asserted in the very act of pessimism. This absolute ideal he formulates:
So live as though thine and thy neighbor's life were one to thee.

This is a restatement of the Kantian ethics of the Good Will. He
reformulated it later as the philosophy of loyalty, the categorical im-
perative of which is: Be loyal to loyalty. He tries to give concrete content to this formula in the following maxims: (1) Don't try to be
happy as an individual—nothing particular can be final. (2) Organize
all life. Find work for the life of the coming moral humanity, which
shall be so comprehensive and definite that each moment of every
man's life in that perfect state, however rich and manifold men's lives
may then be, can be and will be spent in the accomplishment of that
one highest impersonal work.[2] Organization is achieved perfectly in
science and in the state. He talks about the state with the fervor of a
Prussian or a Californian. Art is only an imperfect agency of organization, since artists cultivate individuality.

Having achieved this moral insight, Royce now turns to theological
skepticism. Is there a God? This may have two meanings: it may mean,
Is there a creator and governor of the universe, i.e., Is there an absolute
power? Or it may mean: Is there an absolute postulate, an absolute
truth? For God as a power, he finds no proof. The whole world of external powers need not be postulated at all, it can be absolutely doubted.
Furthermore, a single absolute cause would be identical with its effect.
The external world of causes is therefore *essentially* pluralistic, the
realm of strife, doubt, dissolution and evolution, good and evil, constant opposition.

In the realm of postulates, however, we are faced with the same
situation as in the realm of moral ideals. To admit finite error implies
absolute truth; this was the burden of his Johns Hopkins thesis. For
how is error possible?

[2] Josiah Royce, *The Religious Aspect of Philosophy* (Boston, 1885), p. 211.

Let us take the now so familiar suggestion of our great humorist about the six people that take part in every conversation between two persons. If John and Thomas are talking together, then the real John and Thomas, their respective ideas of themselves, and their ideas of each other, are all parties to the conversation. Let us consider four of these persons, namely, the real John, the real Thomas, John as Thomas conceives him, and Thomas as John conceives him. When John judges, of whom does he think? Plainly of that which can be an object to his thoughts, namely, of *his* Thomas. About whom then can he err? About his Thomas? No, for he knows him too well. . . . About the real Thomas? No, for . . . he has nothing to do with the real Thomas in his thought, since that Thomas never becomes any part of his thought at all. "But," says one, "there must be some fallacy here, since we are sure that John can err about the real Thomas!" Indeed he can, say we; but ours is not this fallacy. Common sense has made it. Common sense has said: Thomas never is in John's thought, and yet John can blunder about Thomas. How shall we unravel the knot?

A present thought and a past thought are in fact separate, even as were John and Thomas. Each one means the object that it thinks. How can they have a common object? Are they not once for all different thoughts, each with its own intent? But in order to render intelligible the existence of error about matters of fact, we must make the unintelligible assumption, so it would seem, that these two different thoughts have the same intent, and are but one.

Either there is no such thing as error, which statement is a flat contradiction, or else there is an infinite unity of conscious thought to which is present all possible truth.[3]

In other words, an idea cannot be true or false to itself but only to another idea, and this to a third, ad infinitum. Therefore, if any thought is an error, it is so only because there is an infinite judge. Other idealists had worried about the possibility of truth. It took a romantic genius to see that error is just as difficult to achieve as truth, on idealistic principles.

May not error be *possible* without being *actual?* Or obversely, does not this dialectic prove merely that the *possibility* of absolute truth is infinitely remote? No, says Royce. For *bare* possibility is no possibility at all; the conditions which make error possible must be actual, and

---

[3] *Ibid.,* pp. 408, 419–20, 424.

since the infinite judge is a necessary condition of the possibility of error, He must be actual, if *error* is actual. Therefore, Royce concludes, in almost ecstatic fervor and with the full diapason of his California rhetoric: "Infinite error and evil are actual and are eternally so judged by an inclusive infinite thought. In this religious insight the mind can rest." Royce is fully aware that this Absolute is not the God of the churches, but it is the "religious aspect of philosophy," it is the reconciliation of romantic pessimism and absolute unity. It is the formal harmony that makes conflict possible.

The perfection of this argument became less conspicuous as Royce worked over it in succeeding expositions, for as he grew older he became more concerned with its concrete application to ethics and science, so that he continually changed the terms of the argument while keeping its form intact.

The first empirical difficulty which was impressed on Royce was the difficulty of unifying separate minds or individuals. It is easy to say: "Live as if thine and thy neighbor's life were one to thee." But how is it possible to do so? The two lives are not one and no amount of living *as if* will make them really one. As for the Absolute, for Him the two are so essentially united that it is impossible that they should be two. How can God experience individuality? And how can man act as an individual, though he is merely an act of God? Here Schopenhauer came to Royce's rescue. From the point of view of the world of idea, or as Royce called it, "the world of description," this is impossible. Two consciousnesses cannot coalesce into one; two ideas are two ideas and cannot be compounded. But from the point of view of will, or as Royce called it, "the world of appreciation," unity is possible. Two wills can operate in concert. By *love* or mutual appreciation men can transcend their individual selves and live in genuine unity. Likewise, God, though his ideas are not our ideas, can by an act of love, or attention, select an individual as an object of his appreciation. It is as though we lived in windowless cells, open to the sky. We can communicate with each other only indirectly, by language, by science, by symbols, though we are all aware of the same sky above us and share in the "reflective publicity" of a common light or will. God, on the contrary, looks down and sees us all together, at once; but he can ap-

preciate us only one at a time, as individuals. Therefore, the fact that
we exist as individuals is proof that God is more than a mere judge or
thought; He is a will, an attentive self.

In Royce's address before the Philosophical Union of California,
1895 (published as *The Conception of God*, 1897), the proof of the
reality of the Absolute is again taken up from a different angle, namely,
in terms of experience. He is here trying to meet the objections of
Howison and the personalists. The thesis is developed that human experience implies absolute experience.

> Every intelligent interpretation of an experience involves, however, the
> appeal from this experienced fragment to some more organized whole of
> experience, in whose unity this fragment is conceived as finding its organic
> place. To talk of any reality which this experience indicates, is to conceive
> this reality as the content of the more organized experience. To assert that
> there is any absolutely real fact indicated by our experience, is to regard this
> reality as presented to an absolutely organized experience in which every
> fragment finds its place. . . .
> Our result then is this: There is an Absolute Experience, for which the
> conception of an absolute reality is fulfilled by the very contents that get
> presented to this Experience. This Absolute Experience is related to our
> experience as an organic whole to its own fragments.[4]

Royce's idealism is here practically identical with the Cornell-
Bosanquet type, and it need not surprise us that Howison and the personalists were not convinced. How is individual freedom possible in
such a scheme of "absolute experience" of which individual selves are
mere "fragments"? Royce was apparently less worried about individual
freedom than he was about the dilemma of either theism or organicism
into which the personalists were trying to force him.

Royce had proceeded thus far, when he hit upon a happy term that
revealed to him how the two dimensions of reality (will and idea, appreciation and description) are related—the term, "meaning." Meaning has a double role. I can mean to do something, that is, I can
intend something; and I can mean an external object in the sense of
referring to it. The former, the act of intention or purpose, he called

[4] Josiah Royce and others, *The Conception of God; a Philosophical Discussion concerning the Nature of the Divine Idea as a Demonstrable Reality* (New York, 1897),
pp. 42–44.

an internal meaning, and the latter, the act of reference, he called an external meaning. Internal and external meanings are but two phases of a single purpose. Our internal meanings, our wills or purposes, demand objectification or external realization; and our external meanings, or ideas, demand to be appropriated as fulfillments or satisfactions of our internal meanings. What we call the external world, therefore, exists as the ideal or objective toward which our purposes draw us. Reality is the objective fulfillment of individualized aims.

All this is little more than a restatement of German idealism with the emphasis on the absolute will and with William James's doctrine of selective attention transformed into a theology. In England, F. H. Bradley was struggling with the same dialectic that troubled Royce, and Royce was considerably disturbed over Bradley's contention that the Infinite is purely ideal or abstract, not to be found in existence. Bradley, in other words, like most philosophers, felt baffled when he stumbled upon a situation involving an infinite regress; whereas Royce had been glorying in the Infinite, seeing in it, not a predicament, but the ground for certainty. Royce was now hard put to it to show that an infinite could actually exist.

But at this point Charles Peirce took pity on Royce and gave him a piece of advice that transformed his philosophy radically. Peirce said in effect: Royce, why don't you study mathematical logic? It would clarify your problem and tighten your philosophic system. Royce took the advice and discovered just what he needed: the mathematical idea of an infinite series and the idea of the community of interpretation. On the basis of these ideas he reworked his entire system. His supplementary essay to Volume I of *The World and the Individual* was devoted to this task. Here he tried to prove, on the basis of Peirce's suggestions, that the infinite is not a sign of "irrationality" in existence, as it was for Bradley, but a sign of "perfect order," i.e., of a "well-ordered series."

The order of integers, for example—let this infinite series of discrete numbers represent the series of individual selves in the Absolute. Between any two integers it is possible to insert a series of fractions which is also infinite, so that the structure of the series of fractions by which any two integers are connected serves to interpret or reproduce the structure of the series of integers. Such a series is self-imaging or "self-interpreting." It is infinite, not because it is endless, but by its very structure, i.e., its members interpret each other in terms of the structure of the whole. Such self-interpreting situations or series can exist and are not mere mathematical constructions. For example, said Royce, a map which includes itself among the things mapped, implies an infinite series of maps. So also the thought of thought, the ideal of the ideal, the oughtness of oughts, the knowledge of knowledge. Such situations are simply existential examples of mathematically well-ordered series. To return to our series of integers, imagine two of them trying to communicate by means of middle terms (fractions); this infinite series of communication, though it prevents the integers from coalescing into unity, nevertheless serves to describe truly how the integers are related to each other. So individuals are linked triadically into a community of interpretation. A interprets B to C. This triadic linkage is infinite and is the basic pattern of reality.

In this way Royce transferred his argument from the traditional problem of knowledge, with its dualistic problem of the relation between idea and object, purpose and goal, etc., to an entirely different ground—the ground of language, the social use of symbols. By shifting the problem of knowledge from the dyadic relations of epistemology to the triadic relations of interpretation, Royce achieved a fresh and important reconstruction of idealistic philosophy. He was helped to this conception not only by Charles Peirce but also by Howison's theory of the City of God.

He now saw clearly that knowledge is social and that if reality is to exhibit the same structure it too must be social. He took over bodily Peirce's doctrine of the infinite community of scientists engaged in the co-operative pursuit of ultimate truth and transformed it into a metaphysics. The world is a self-interpreting community of individuals.

A process of interpretation involves, of necessity, an infinite sequence of acts of interpretation. It also admits of an endless variety within all the selves which are thus mutually interpreted. These selves, in all their variety, constitute the life of a single Community of Interpretation, whose central member is that spirit of the community whose essential function we know. In the concrete, then, the universe is a community of interpretation whose life comprises and unifies all the social varieties and all the social communities which, for any reason, we know to be real in the empirical world which our social and our historical sciences study. The history of the universe, the whole order of time, is the history and the order and the expression of this Universal Community.[5]

This doctrine he called an absolutistic pragmatism. He embraced the pragmatic theory of knowledge and extended it to a theory of reality.

Within the empirical limits of human communication he had no difficulty in expounding the meaning of his system, but he had to resort to somewhat fantastic hypotheses about communication between natural objects in general. Here he fell back on his doctrine of the acts of the divine attention. God sees the whole series as a unity, simultaneously in an eternal now, but he attends to individuals successively. This gives the appearance of temporal patterns, of evolution. God interprets the whole as we do a piece of music. The form of the whole composition is essential to the understanding of each phrase. We finite phrases in the cosmic music can only guess at the plan of the composition and can make out only occasional repetitions and cadences. The mountains and stars with their longer rhythms or "time-spans" might interpret God to us on a larger scale, could they communicate with us. But we can communicate only with beings that share our time span, our rate of vibration, so to speak. The particular forms of space and time by which we are limited in communication (or science) must not be attributed to the structure of the community as a whole. The so-called "laws of nature" are really forms of communication. Thus, physical science has its relative function and serves to make physical objects more or less intelligible to each other within the limits of physical communication.

The type of community which Royce means is exhibited even better in the church than in science. The true church, and here Royce's idealism reverts to Calvinism, is a community of memory and hope, a unity of faith and redeeming grace. In himself the individual is a lost soul, and any acts of disloyalty on his part must be atoned for by greater loyalty on the part of others. Ordinary political society does not conform to this type of community, for it breeds individualism, and individualism is "the sin against the Holy Ghost." To be a real individual, one must be a loyal member, for only through God's grace in the community is salvation, self-hood, possible. For God is simply the

[5] Josiah Royce, *The Problem of Christianity* (New York, 1913), II, 272–73.

"spirit-of-the-community," the essence of loyalty. The love of God, that is, loyalty to loyalty, implies complete submission to his will.

Where does Royce locate this true church? The Christian churches have wandered far from this Pauline primitive model. The modern state, as above indicated, is not a true community. A true community would not generate members who wish to be free. Science is a genuine community of interpretation insofar as it remains true to its co-operative quest of truth. The "Great Community" is real, however, not because it happens to be physically embodied, but because it is the eternal moral basis of order. It is what I ought to be loyal to and what I ought to believe. Its reality consists fundamentally in its relation to the will—it is a task which every rational being is obligated to undertake.

In one of his last books Royce indicated that "the Hope of the Great Community" in economic society rests chiefly on the extension of insurance. For insurance is an association on the triadic principle of interpretation: the insured, the insurer, and the beneficiary. In insurance associations the barrier to association becomes itself the basis of an association and disloyalty an opportunity for loyalty. Royce recommended insurance against war; and I suppose, were he living today, he would recommend insurance against unemployment, class conflicts, graft, and other forms of disloyalty. Insurance against insurance would make dialectically the most perfect community, though its time span would no doubt be brief. This co-ordination of church and insurance company will no doubt be regarded by the old-worldly reader as a typical Yankee trick. It is instructive, nonetheless, showing the ability of a fearless and conscientious idealist to adapt his thought to changing realities.

— 38 —

DOWN TO THE PRESENT

THE schools of idealism are no longer clear and distinct. There are important recent works which in the main carry on the traditions of one or the other of these schools, and at least a mention of them will be found in the accompanying guide to the literature. But the leaders among recent idealists have broken loose from their traditional moorings and are reconstructing idealism to such an extent that even the term "idealism" is obscured and there are numerous expressions among idealists of the wish to transcend idealism. Since the days of Royce there has been a general unbending of systems and a refusal to take any "ism" too seriously. There are now about as many types of idealism as there are idealists, and the historian must turn prophet who seeks to discover trends and emergent uniformities amid so much diversity. Under these circumstances the reader who wishes to know the recent history of American idealism may do well to turn at once to the record of production as it appears in the guide to the literature and there face the bewildering array of "facts," instead of attending to the following attempt to discern general tendencies. For the present chaos is more intelligible to him who can see into the future than to him who has followed its past. However, a few generalizations may be hazarded as tentative truth, "so help me future experience"— as Royce said of James's pragmatism.

Recent idealist literature seems less concerned to make idealism itself an issue.[1] This attitude stems partly from the desire to free idealism from the dubious and incidental epistemology with which it has been contaminated since Locke and which Boodin, for example, dismisses as "the philosophical disease, psychologitis." The schools of speculative and dynamic idealism were both scornful of the so-called problem of the external world, and their disciples seem to be increasingly annoyed by those critics [2] who think idealism is committed to a British phenomenalism or even to German phenomenology. Idealism means to many of them something at least as old and catholic as Platonism, and to some of them (notably Urban and recently the Californian neo-orientalist Aldous Huxley) an Anglo-Catholic synthesis of Platonism and Aristotelianism, called *philosophia perennis*. Regardless of the particular controversy over the historical reality of a *philosophia perennis*, there is a widespread attempt to conceive ideal-

[1] See especially the references to Boodin, Cunningham, De Laguna, Parker, Sheldon, and Urban.

[2] See, for example, the writings of mentalists like Miss Calkins and some of the personalists, and the epistemological critiques of idealism by realists like Perry, Pratt, Montague, and others.

492 DOWN TO THE PRESENT

ism as more than a school of modern philosophy and to regard it as a variant form of the age-old search for objective mind.

The theory of objective mind, which has certainly been one of the major themes of idealists, has been cultivated brilliantly by logicians and metaphysicians of various schools and has consequently become a relatively cumulative, fruitful, and independent philosophic inquiry and doctrine. It has given to rationalism new life and critical foundations and has compelled not only idealists but also realists, pragmatists, and positivists to re-examine the ancient problem of the relation of ontology to logic. In other words, the American critiques of the Kantian doctrine of the categories have born fruit in a revival of metaphysics relatively free from persistent epistemological polemics.

The philosophical "adventures" of such critical spirits as Cohen, Lewis, McGilvary, Perry, Savery, Schmidt, Whitehead, and Woodbridge, whose early thought was steeped in the study of Kant and whose systems are revisions of the critical approach to natural knowledge, reveal that the idealist heritage is still identifiable if one looks closely into the obscure corners of their moral ideas, but that in their major work they have departed from romantic transcendentalism toward naturalistic interpretations of objective order and scientific principles of evidence.[3]

The emphasis on mind as objective logical structure has grown at the expense of the Absolute. Though the conception of the Absolute has not disappeared, it has certainly been weakened and robbed of its "religious availability," to use a current phrase. What there remains of Royce's glorified Absolute, who might make some pretension to being a surrogate for a really religious divinity, is too abstract and impersonal to serve well the cause of theism. There remain among most idealists the belief in an objective and intelligible structure, the faith in "the spirit of the community" of truth seekers as an ultimate body of truth, and the devotion to a perfect Platonic God, the principle of ultimate values and the creator of all that is good. But the good God is not omnipotent, and the rational order is impersonal. Hence, idealism has ceased to be a Christian apologetic in its doctrine of God, and

[3] The "objective relativists," like Mead and McGilvary, should also be mentioned here, though they will be discussed later, pp. 550–52.

is either religiously negligible [4] or theologically radical.[5] This shift
in interest from problems of religious theism to problems of secular
reason and value is, of course, a situation which has overtaken philosophy in general, and idealists have but moved with the times, popular
prejudice to the contrary notwithstanding. But precisely because idealism has shifted its ground and its values conspicuously, it is as yet
difficult to estimate the meaning of this shift historically. Most conspicuous and widespread has been the shift toward a temporal theory
of reality. Not only reason, truth, value, and being but also the Absolute itself have been given a temporal context.[6] This is due in part to
the influence of James, Dewey, Bergson, and Whitehead, in part to
the development of physical relativity theories, and in part to the prevalence of evolutionary concepts. In adapting itself to the temporal
and natural sciences and to "process philosophies" idealism has under-
gone a major transformation. For according to the newer theories
absolute experience is no longer divorced from human, temporal experience as an object of religious or logical faith, but is conceived as a
factor in actual experience, a human possession in time and at times.

One is tempted to conclude, perhaps prematurely, that there are
emerging two types of idealism, reminiscent of the dualism of the
Enlightenment and indicative of the continued vitality of the Kantian *Critiques*—a moral and a natural idealism. The idealist theories
of value and morals, so-called axiologies, have developed their own
categories and systematic implications without becoming too inex-
tricably involved in cosmologies, theories of evolution, and other attempts to identify the natural order with the moral order. Some
metaphysics, of course, and some attempts to deal with the relations between moral and natural science are inevitable, at least for idealists, but
there has been a considerable cultivation of idealistic moral philosophy
with a minimum of cosmology.[7]

On the other hand, there has developed a natural idealism, which

[4] Cf. the conceptions of the Absolute in Blanshard and Cunningham.

[5] Cf. the theologies of Adams, Boodin, Brightman, Hocking, Parker, Schmidt,
Singer, and Urban.

[6] Cf. especially the writings of Adams, Boodin, Cunningham, De Laguna, Hocking,
Parker, and Sheldon.

[7] See, for example, the writings of Adler, Everett, Fite, Hendel, and Tufts.

may be tending to an outright naturalistic idealism—if I may use such a term without giving too much offense or seeming too confused. These traditionally opposite approaches to truth are, as Sheldon has forcefully argued, more compatible in life than they appear to be in theory and may even be regarded as complementary to each other. Be that as it may, idealistic speculation recently has become not merely reconciled to natural science, but positively concerned with problems of natural knowledge. Creighton's and Santayana's insistence that philosophy is humanistic, concerned with the affairs of the spirit, merely tolerant of nature, hence poetic rather than scientific, seems to be a position shared by comparatively few idealists today. Singer has been one of the most radical and eloquent exponents of an experimentalist idealism, and the following excerpts from his critique of Schelling's romanticism state with wonderful precision not only his own position but also the basic issues as they now present themselves to many philosophers, idealist and otherwise.

Whether we take idealism to imply a doctrine of a priori forms, or a doctrine recognizing some or all *reals* to be *ideals,* your modern experimental scientist is an idealist on both counts. But it is no longer an accident, as one may think it to have been with Kant, that he is an idealist on *both* counts. If we had time to look into the matter more closely, we should find that the scientist's eternal task of finding new forms to which observation can be adjusted is imposed upon him as a condition to the progressive reduction of his probable error, i.e., a condition to the indefinite approach of the observed appearances is the *real* of which each observation is an *appearance.* . . . We have taken the modern analogue of Kant's theoretical philosophy to lie in a present-day theory of the conditions that make scientific progress possible. This progress we define to be a transition from a remoter to a closer approximation to a limiting conception. That limiting conception we call, in traditional terms, the ideal reality, Nature. Should we not, then, look for the analogue of Kant's practical philosophy in some later theory of the conditions that make possible another kind of progress—a progress to be defined as a transition from a lower to a higher order of approximation to another limiting conception, this other limiting concept being some such ideal as tradition would call the really Good, or the true God? Does the idealistic realism in which the experimentalist development culminates include theories of this kind, theories which might be called the system's practical philosophy? None, I should say, of sufficient following and influence to deserve analysis here; yet some of us who have given the matter patient thought have come to feel that such a theory can and ought to be developed within the limits of experimental method. . . . But for this ideal to be real, i.e., really to guide the conduct of our brief, struggling lives, it must fulfil several conditions that Kant's *Gottesidee* did not meet. It must be much more sharply defined in terms that would make it clear to every man willing to think out his own deepest desires, why it is that to make the struggle toward this ideal the regulative principle of his whole life is a necessary condition to the only contentment a finite life can know. If these requirements are met in the only way in which some of us conceive that they could be met, the interdependence of progress toward the ideal reality which is Nature, and progress toward the ideal reality which is God would be clear enough: to religious progress, scientific progress would prove itself a necessary condition; to scientific progress, religious progress would prove to be the one adequate incentive. . . .

Seeking a name to stand for the relation of God to his world, we could find it in no such categories as causation or production, terms which stand for general concepts. We now find it in the name, *creation,* a word which stands for nothing conceivable, but for something intimately realizable. This realization begins with the immediate intuition of that freedom which each senses in his own spontaneous gestures; it ends in the divination of a like freedom in the Maker whose work is Nature. But who says Maker says in English what the Greek would call a Poet.

. . . It is by pure intuition that each is aware of his own moments of freedom; it is still by pure intuition that he divines a like freedom in others, be they plain men, his neighbors, or demigods creating works of art, or God the All-Creator.

Why have the scientific and the romantic reorientations of thought toward idealism and realism been throughout mutually unhelpful? Why do the two types of idealistic realism in which they culminate remain mutually unintelligible? It is because what constitutes evidence for the one school stands in at least one and sometimes two respects, in direct contradiction to what the other school demands of evidence. Deeper cleavage than this, separating one thinker from another, there cannot be; it goes to the very root of things. . . . Must scientist and romanticist always remain strangers to each other, uncollaborative, unsympathetic, even where they are trying to think out an answer to the same ultimate question? For example, I used to wonder whether it were possible to reconcile those religious views that may be arrived at by non-experimental methods (rationalist, intuitionist, or both) with such views as an experimentalist may develop without departing from the rules of evidence that govern him in all his science. I wonder no longer; the thing is impossible. Where understandings of evidence are antithetical, no synthesis of conclusions is even a meaningful hypothesis. What then? Is the disciple of each school to confine his reading to the literature of his own school's past and present; is he to leave unread and unpondered the literature of every other doctrine? Those who in ready answer quote from the "ancient wisdom of childhood" that fable of the two sides to a shield may be right in their lesson, but inexperienced in the cost of applying it. That end has to be very important to attain which one is willing to pay what it costs, say, an experimentalist to read a romantic, or a romantic an experimentalist. Yet at no less price can these two minds, which between them influence the greater part of the thinking world, come to a mutual understanding of the most fundamental things in which they differ.[8]

GUIDE TO THE LITERATURE FOR PART VII

CHAPTER 35

The best surveys of the beginnings of academic idealism in America are J. H. Muirhead, "How Hegel Came to America," *Philosophical Review*, XXXVII (1928), 226–40, G. Stanley Hall, "Philosophy in the United States," *Mind*, IV (1879), 89–105, A. C. Armstrong, Jr., "Philosophy in the United States," *Educational Review*, X (1895), 1–11, and "Philosophy in American Colleges," *Educational Review*, XIII (1897), 10–22, and Benjamin Rand, "Philosophical Instruction in Harvard University from 1636 to 1906," Part III, *Harvard Graduates' Magazine*, XXXVII (1928–29), 291–311.

The inclinations toward idealism among essentially Scottish philosophers, notably Francis Bowen and Noah Porter, have already been noted; see pp. 241, 245. There is a long and favorable critique of Hickok's *Rational Psychology* by Tayler Lewis in *Bibliotheca Sacra*, VIII (1851), 181–217, 346–77. An unsigned article "Dr. Hickok's Philosophy," *Bibliotheca Sacra*, XVI (1859), 253–78, is laudatory in tone. The writer, presumably one of the editors (Edwards A. Park and Samuel H. Taylor), began his survey of Hickok's views with the statement "Unless we incorrectly estimate their intrinsic worth, they represent the highest attainments in speculative thought

---

[8] Edgar A. Singer, Jr., "Thoughts on a Translation of Schelling's *Weltalter*; a Review Article," *The Review of Religion*, VIII (1943), 44–45, 48–49, 52, 53.

which the American mind has yet reached; and if we are not mistaken, respecting the increasing force of their influence, they promise to found a school of philosophy with a prominent and permanent place in the history of the world's speculation" and concluded with the prediction (unfounded in historical retrospect) that "if American philosophy is to have a history, the course of its stream and the bulk of its waters can appear in no other channel than the one he has indicated." An unfavorable review from the point of view of Scottish common sense by Professor Edwin Hall of Auburn Theological Seminary of Hickok's revised edition of the *Rational Psychology* was published in the *Princeton Review* for October, 1861. This called forth a reply and a defense of Hickok's rational idealism, as a more adequate approach to theism than common sense could provide, by Tayler Lewis, "The Two Schools of Philosophy," *American Theological Review*, IV (1862), 102–34, an anonymous defense in a later issue of the *Princeton Review*, and two articles by Hickok himself, "Modern Philosophy Pantheistic," *American Theological Review*, IV (1862), 199–227, and "Psychology and Skepticism," *American Theological Review*, IV (1862), 391–414. To all of these Professor Hall replied in "The Rational Psychology and Its Vindications," *American Theological Review*, IV (1862), 611–42, reaffirming the point of view of "natural realism." Garman's review of the Seelye revision of Hickok's *Empirical Psychology* appeared in the *New Englander*, XLI (1882), 770–77. Towards the end of the review Garman said of the book, "It carefully avoids all dogmatism, and strives to be only a guide, like the manuals we use in chemistry. It is the Manual of Mental Analysis; forcing the student to make investigations for himself. It simply teaches him how to listen to, and to voice the testimony of his own consciousness."

Hickok's most important works were: *The Sources of Military Delusion, and the Practicability of Their Removal* (Hartford, 1833), *Rational Psychology; or, The Subjective Idea and the Objective Law of All Intelligence* (Auburn, N.Y., 1849), *A System of Moral Science* (Schenectady, N.Y., 1853), *Empirical Psychology; or, The Human Mind as Given in Consciousness* (Schenectady, 1854), *Rational Cosmology; or, The Eternal Principles and Necessary Laws of the Universe* (New York, 1858), *Creator and Creation; or, The Knowledge in the Reason of God and His Work* (New York, 1872), *Humanity Immortal or, Man Tried, Fallen and Redeemed* (Boston and New York, 1872), *The Logic of Reason, Universal and Eternal* (Boston and New York, 1874), "Evolution from Mechanical Force," *Princeton Review*, LIV (1878), 567–605. The revisions of Hickok's works by Julius H. Seelye appeared as follows: *A*

System of Moral Science (Boston, 1880), *Empirical Psychology; or, The Science of Mind from Experience* (Boston, 1882).

The best introduction to the career and thought of Charles Edward Garman is *Letters, Lectures, and Addresses of Charles Edward Garman*, a memorial volume, edited by Eliza Miner Garman (Boston, 1909). The first three sections are biographical; the remainder of the volume is a compilation of Garman's chief essays and classroom pamphlets. Included, on pp. 478–86, is his "response on the occasion of the presentation of the commemorative volume." The editors of this commemorative volume, *Studies in Philosophy and Psychology*, by former students of Charles Edward Garman (Boston, 1906), included as a preface Garman's letter of 1898 to G. Stanley Hall explaining his method of teaching philosophy. Among the contributors to the *Studies* were J. H. Tufts, F. C. Sharp, F. J. E. Woodbridge, E. W. Lyman, E. B. Delabarre, and R. S. Woodworth.

The chief works of the most notable of the first generation of idealist teachers with the exception of those founders of schools who will be discussed below, are the following: John Bascom of Williams College, for a brief time also first president of the University of Wisconsin, and his successor at Williams, John E. Russell, and Moses Stuart Phelps and his successor, H. Norman Gardiner, at Smith College were both geographically and intellectually close to Garman. Of these, Bascom was by far the most prolific and influential because of his writings in fields bordering on philosophy, especially in social theory. His philosophic works were: *Political Economy* (Andover, Mass., 1859), *Aesthetics; or, The Science of Beauty* (Boston, 1862), *The Philosophy of Rhetoric* (Boston, 1866), "Consciousness: What Is It?" *American Presbyterian Review*, 3d series, I (1869), 478–91, *Principles of Psychology* (New York, 1869), *Science, Philosophy and Religion* (New York, 1871), "Darwin's Theory of the Origin of Species," *American Presbyterian Review*, 3d series, III (1871), 349–79, "Evolution as Advocated by Herbert Spencer," *The Presbyterian Review*, n.s., I (1872), 496–515, *Philosophy of Religion; or, The Rational Grounds of Religious Belief* (New York, 1876), *Ethics; or, The Science of Duty* (New York, 1879), *Natural Theology* (New York, 1880), "Philosophical Results of a Denial of Miracles," *Princeton Review*, LVII (1881), 85–94, *Problems in Philosophy* (New York, 1885), *An Historical Interpretation of Philosophy* (New York, 1893), *Social Theory: A Grouping of Social Facts and Principles* (New York, 1895), *Evolution and Religion: or, Faith as a Part of a Complete Cosmic System* (New York, 1897). Russell wrote *A First Course in Philosophy* (New York, 1913). Gardiner and Phelps wrote only contributions to periodicals, of which Phelps's article on "Anthropomorphism," *Princeton Review,* LVII (1881), 120–44, is an exceptionally good theistic critique of Spencer, in which the opening chapters of Spencer's *First Principles* are described as "a metaphysical circus, in which the captive concepts rise as high as the paper hoops, and then, falling back, are one after the other led out of the ring."

At Yale, in addition to Noah Porter, George Trumbull Ladd was important for his critical studies of German idealism, especially Kant, Hegel, and Lotze. His own works, though voluminous, were less important for philosophy than for physiological psychology: *Philosophy of Mind; an Essay in the Metaphysics of Psychology* (New York, 1895), *Philosophy of Knowledge; an Inquiry into the Nature, Limits, and Validity of the Human Cognitive Faculty* (New York, 1897), *A Theory of Reality; an Essay in Metaphysical System upon the Basis of Human Cognitive Experience* (New York, 1899), *Philosophy of Conduct; a Treatise of the Facts, Principles, and Ideals of Conduct* (New York, 1902), *The Philosophy of Religion; a Critical and Speculative Treatise of Man's Religious Experience and Development in the Light of Modern Science and Reflective Thinking* (2 vols., New York, 1905), *Knowledge, Life and Reality; an Essay in Systematic Philosophy* (New York, 1909).

Nicholas Murray Butler, among his many educational achievements, was the first teacher and organizer of critical graduate philosophical instruction at Columbia University and was especially active in keeping in contact with later German idealism. With him at Columbia were J. H. Hyslop, who, after his early studies in idealist ethics, turned increasingly toward psychical research, and George S. Fullerton, who went from Columbia to the University of Pennsylvania and there gathered an influential group of philosophers. Fullerton developed his idealism in the direction of realism. His most important work was *A System of Metaphysics* (New York, 1904). Edgar A. Singer, Jr., *Fool's Advice* (New York, 1925), pp. 175–94, contains Singer's tribute to George Stuart Fullerton, originally published in the *Journal of Philosophy,* XXII (1925), 589–96.

At Princeton, President J. Grier Hibben and Alexander T. Ormond introduced idealism into McCosh's stronghold of Scottish realism. McCosh's resistance can be gauged by his articles "Contemporary Philosophy: Historical," *Princeton Review* LIV (1878), 192–206, "Contemporary Philosophy: Mind and Brain," *Princeton Review,* LIV (1878), 606–32, and "A Criticism of the Critical Philosophy," *Princeton Review,* LIV (1878), 889–915. Hibben was especially important as editor and translator. Ormond wrote *Foundations of Knowledge* (New York, 1900) and *The Concepts of Philosophy* (New York, 1906).

At Harvard, George Herbert Palmer was an enthusiastic teacher of the new idealism. His *Autobiography of a Philosopher* (Boston, 1930), and his autobiographical introduction to Vol. I of *Contemporary American Philosophy*, ed. by G. P. Adams and W. P. Montague (New York, 1930), are an excellent introduction to the academic awakening of this period. He also wrote *The Field of Ethics* (Boston, 1901), *The Nature of Goodness* (Boston, 1903), *The Problem of Freedom* (Boston, 1911), and *Altruism; Its Nature and Varieties* (New York, 1920). Charles Carroll Everett, though more conservative, was important for his idealistic philosophy of religion. His Hegelian logic, *The Science of Thought; a System of Logic after the Principles of the Hegelian School* (Boston, 1869), culminates in a theory of "dynamic induction," and in a section on "problems of life," or "the logic of events." Everett's use of dynamic categories is extraordinarily complacent. He represents Hegel and Spencer as "in polar antagonism . . . tunnelling a mountain from different sides. . . . They meet midway. . . . It shows that the forms of thought and those of the objective world are one." Morally, too, he reflects the same optimism, arguing that the individual must follow the logic of events by falling in with "the grand movement of life and of history." Of Everett's other works, *Theism and the Christian Faith* (New York, 1900), a series of lectures delivered in the Harvard Divinity School, is worthy of mention as an expression of his thought.

CHAPTER 36

The literature of the St. Louis school and the Concord Summer School has already been listed; see pp. 220, and 316. The scattered idealist clubs and "academies" have been described by Paul Russell Anderson in the *Journal* of the Illinois State Historical Society, XXXIII (1940), 478–520, and XXXIV (1941), 50–83.

On Thomas Davidson see the excellent sketch by C. M. Bakewell in the *Dictionary of American Biography* and his description of Glenmore in the Adirondacks, which is going to be published soon. Professor Bakewell has also edited the documents in connection with Davidson's Breadwinners' College in New York City, under the title *The Education of the Wage Earners* (New York, 1904). Bakewell's introduction supplements his other biographical sketches. Davidson's "The Task of the Twentieth Century" is reprinted from the *International Journal of Ethics*, XII (1901–2), 23–43, as Chapter II. Chapter III, Davidson's 1898 address on "The Educational Problem Set by the Nineteenth Century to the Twentieth" was the immediate occasion for the organization of the school. Chapter V contains a number of Davidson's letters to members of his classes, and the final chapter, VI, contributed by Morris R. Cohen, tells the history of the school after the founder's death. Cohen also wrote the article on Thomas Davidson in Monroe's *Cyclopedia of Education* and several articles in Vols. I (1901) and II (1902) of the *Alliance Review*. *Memorials of Thomas Davidson, the Wandering Scholar*, collected and edited by William Knight (Boston, 1907), includes some of Davidson's lectures and letters, and reminiscences of some of his associates, including Percival Chubb, Felix Adler, William James, and Havelock Ellis. An appendix lists Davidson's writings, both published and unpublished. William James's memorial article, "Thomas Davidson: a Knight-Errant of the Intellectual Life," originally published in *McClure's Magazine* for May, 1905, is reprinted in William James, *Memories and Studies* (New York, 1917), pp. 75–103. There is a sketch of Davidson from W. T. Harris's point of view in Kurt F. Leidecker's biography of William T. Harris (New York, 1946).

The literature on the Ethical Culture Movement is too extensive to list here, and among Felix Adler's writings only two are mentioned: *An Ethical Philosophy of Life* (New York, 1918) and *The Reconstruction of the Spiritual Ideal* (New York, 1924). The reader will find in these books not only the essence of Adler's philosophy but also an introduction to the work of the Ethical Culture Society. A definitive biography by Horace L. Friess is forthcoming.

G. Holmes Howison, Philosopher and Teacher; a Selection from His Writings with a Biographical Sketch, ed. by John Wright Buckham and George Malcolm Stratton (Berkeley, Cal., 1934), includes a complete bibliography of Howison's publications and gives an excellent presentation of Howison's career and philosophy.

The personalist school of idealism is represented first by the works of Borden Parker Bowne: *Studies in Theism* (New York, 1879), *Metaphysics* (New York, 1882), *Introduction to Psychological Theory* (New York, 1886), *Philosophy of Theism* (New York, 1887), *Principles of Ethics* (New York, 1892), *The Theory of Thought and Knowledge* (New York, 1897), *The Christian Revelation* (New York, 1898), *Theism* (New York, 1902), *The Immanence of God* (Boston, 1905), *Personalism* (Boston, 1908), *Studies in Christianity* (Boston, 1909), and his posthumously published sermons, *The Essence of Religion* (Boston, 1910), and lectures, *Kant and Spencer; a Critical Exposition* (Boston, 1912). Francis J. McConnell, *Borden Parker Bowne* (New York, 1929), is an excellent exposition. There are many articles about Bowne, of which we select as representative: *Methodist Review*, Bowne Memorial issue, May-

June, 1922, A. C. Knudson, "Bowne as Teacher and Author," *The Personalist*, I, No. 2 (July, 1920), 5–14, G. H. Jones, *Lotze und Bowne; eine Vergleichung Ihrer philosophischen Arbeit* (Jena, 1909), C. B. Pyle, *The Philosophy of Borden P. Bowne* (Columbus, O., 1910), and José Antonio Fránquiz Ventura, *Borden Parker Bowne's Treatment of the Problem of Change and Identity* (Rio Piedras, Puerto Rico, 1942). Edgar Sheffield Brightman, "Personalism and the Influence of Bowne," *Proceedings* (1926) of the Sixth International Congress of Philosophy (New York, 1927), pp. 161–67, in addition to its discussion of Bowne also lists the chief members of his school. Among their works the following are outstanding.

Brightman, Edgar Sheffield, A Philosophy of Ideals (New York, 1928).
—— The Problem of God (New York, 1930).
—— "The Dialectical Unity of Consciousness and the Metaphysics of Religion," Proceedings of the Seventh International Congress of Philosophy (London, 1931), pp. 70–77.
—— "The Finite Self," in Contemporary Idealism in America, ed. by Clifford Barrett (New York, 1932), pp. 171–95.
—— "The Given and Its Critics," Religion in Life, I (1932), 134–45.
—— "A Temporalist View of God," Journal of Religion, XII (1932), 545–55.
—— Moral Laws (New York, 1933).
—— "The Definition of Idealism," Journal of Philosophy, XXX (1933), 429–35.
—— Personality and Religion (New York, 1934).
—— "An Empirical Approach to God," Philosophical Review, XLVI (1937), 147–69.
—— A Philosophy of Religion (New York, 1940).
—— The Spiritual Life (New York, 1942).
Coe, George Albert, The Psychology of Religion (Chicago, 1916).
Flewelling, Ralph Tyler, Personalism and the Problems of Philosophy (New York, 1915).
—— The Reason in Faith (New York, 1924).
—— Creative Personality (New York, 1926).
Knudson, Albert Cornelius, The Philosophy of Personalism (New York, 1927).
—— The Doctrine of God (New York, 1930).
—— The Validity of Religious Experience (New York, 1937).

Of philosophical works less intimately associated with Bowne's type of personalism, but representing a generally personalist approach to philosophy, the following may be mentioned.

Calkins, Mary Whiton, The Persistent Problems of Philosophy (New York, 1907).
—— "The Idealist to the Realist," *Journal of Philosophy*, VIII (1911), 449–58.
—— "The Foundation in Royce's Philosophy for Christian Theism," *Philosophical Review*, XXV (1916), 282–98.
—— "The Personalistic Conception of Nature," *Philosophical Review*, XXVIII (1919), 115–46.
—— "The New Rationalism and Objective Idealism," *Philosophical Review*, XXVIII (1919), 598–605.
—— "The Philosophical Credo of an Absolutistic Personalist," in Contemporary American Philosophy, ed. by G. P. Adams and W. P. Montague (New York, 1930), I, 199–218.
Leighton, Joseph Alexander, Typical Modern Conceptions of God; the Absolute of German Romantic Idealism and of English Evolutionary Agnosticism (New York, 1902).
—— Man and the Cosmos; an Introduction to Metaphysics (New York, 1922).
—— Religion and the Mind of Today (New York, 1924).
—— The Individual and the Social Order; an Introduction to Ethics and Social Philosophy (New York, 1926).
—— Individuality and Education; a Democratic Philosophy of Education (New York, 1928).
—— "My Development and Present Creed," in Contemporary American Philosophy, ed. by G. P. Adams and W. P. Montague (New York, 1930), I, 425–41.
—— "The Principle of Individuality and Value," in Contemporary Idealism in America, ed. by Clifford Barrett (New York, 1932), pp. 133–67.

The Cornell school of speculative or objective idealism received its first impetus from the founder of the Sage School of Philosophy, Jacob Gould Schurman, whose writings were devoted chiefly to the interpretation of Kant. He took an active part in the polemic over evolutionary ethics as the titles of his chief works show: *Kantian Ethics and the Ethics of Evolution* (London, 1881), *The Ethical Import of Darwinism* (New York, 1887), and *Agnosticism and Religion* (New York, 1896).

The chief exponent and most influential member of the school was James Edwin Creighton, who was widely known among college students for his popular text in logic, but whose philosophical influence is much wider than his writings indicate. Some account of his influence is contained in the following memorial articles: G. Watts Cunningham, "In Memoriam: James Edwin Creighton," *International Journal of Ethics*, XXXV (1925), 214–16; Katherine Gilbert, "James E. Creighton as Writer and Editor," *Journal of Philosophy*, XXII (1925), 256–64; William A. Hammond, "James Edwin Creighton," *Journal of Philosophy*, XXII (1925), 253–56; George H. Sabine, "The Philosophy of James Edwin Creighton," *Philosophical Review*, XXXIV (1925), 230–45; Frank Thilly, "The Philosophy of James Edwin Creighton," *Philosophical Review*, XXXIV (1925), 211–20. Additional information and a good discussion of Creighton's philosophy is to be found in H. G. Townsend, *Philosophical Ideas in the United States* (New York, 1934), pp. 187–95. Creighton's chief articles were collected and published as *Studies in Speculative Philosophy* (New York, 1925).

As American correspondent of *Kantstudien*, Creighton wrote three articles on Kantian thought in America: "The Philosophy of Kant in America," *Kantstudien*, II (1897–98), 237–52, "American Current Literature on Kant," *Kantstudien*, III (1898–99), 148–59, "Kantian Literature in America since 1898," *Kantstudien*, VII (1902), 409–19. In these articles he gives a brief survey of the history of New England transcendentalism, *The Journal of Speculative Philosophy*, and the Concord School of Philosophy, and in reviewing current idealistic literature in America takes the occasion to give his critical opinions of G. T. Ladd, Josiah Royce, A. T. Ormond, and J. G. Schurman.

As an index to the extensive academic influence of Cornell, we mention some of the contributors to *Philosophical Essays in Honor of James Edwin Creighton*, by former students in the Sage School of Philosophy of Cornell University, ed. by George Holland Sabine (New York, 1917), and their academic institutions at that time: K. E. Gilbert, North Carolina; G. H. Sabine, Missouri; R. A. Tsanoff, Rice Institute; E. L. Hinman, Nebraska; J. W. Wright, Lake Forest; E. B. Talbot, Mount Holyoke; E. L. Schaub, Northwestern; E. Jordan, Butler College; H. G. Townsend, Smith College; E. H. Holland, Kansas; G. W. Cunningham, Texas; J. A. Leighton, Ohio State; G. A. de Laguna, Bryn Mawr; W. P. Pillsbury, Michigan; E. C. Wilm, Boston; A. H. Jones, Brown; T. de Laguna, Bryn Mawr.

In the *Philosophical Review*, XXVI (1917), 315–38, there is a discussion of the theme of A. O. Lovejoy's presidential address "Progress in

Philosophical Inquiry," largely by members of the Cornell school. This address raised the issue forcibly to what extent philosophy is a co-operative inquiry, and the discussion of the address reveals the concern of the objective idealists to promote the community of knowledge.

For an interesting discussion of the nature of the ethical community see Frank Thilly's discussion of Felix Adler's *An Ethical Philosophy of Life,* entitled "The Kantian Ethics and Its Critics," *Philosophical Review,* XXVII (1918), 647–50, and his review which follows, pp. 651–56.

The writings of Thilly, Hammond, Albee, and other members of the school are scattered in various periodicals. Some of their most important articles in the *Philosophical Review* are listed here to indicate their thought: E. Albee, "The Significance of Methodological Principles," XV (1906), 267–76, "The Present Meaning of Idealism," XVIII (1909), 299–308, W. A. Hammond, "Hylozoism," IV (1895), 394–406, "The Significance of the Creative Reason in Aristotle's Philosophy," XI (1902), 238–48, G. H. Sabine, "The Concreteness of Thought," XVI (1907), 154–69, "The Material of Thought," XVI (1907), 285–97, "Liberty and the Social System," XXV (1916), 662–75, "The Concept of the State as Power," XXIX (1920), 301–18, "Logic and Social Studies," XLVIII (1939), 155–76, F. Thilly, "The Self," XIX (1910), 22–33, "The Relation of Consciousness and Object in Sense-Perception," XXI (1912), 415–32, "Romanticism and Rationalism," XXII (1913), 107–32, "Sociological Jurisprudence," XXXII (1923), 373–84. Thilly's textbooks in ethics and in the history of philosophy and his translations of Paulsen and other German authors were widely used. Albee wrote *A History of English Utilitarianism* (London, 1902). Hammond made contributions primarily in the field of aesthetics.

George S. Morris's career and writings are described in R. M. Wenley, *The Life and Works of G. S. Morris* (New York, 1917), which includes a complete bibliography of Morris's writings. Morris's and Lloyd's relation to the early thought of John Dewey and Dewey's idealism are discussed by Morton G. White, *The Origin of Dewey's Instrumentalism* (New York, 1943). Dewey's own comments on Morris in Wenley's volume are particularly interesting. A critical treatment of Morris's philosophy and a selection from his essays is being prepared by Marc E. Jones. Of Morris's writings, those that are historically most important are his articles on Trendelenburg, notably the article inserted in his translation of Ueberweg's *History of Philosophy,* Vol. II. His other important works were: "Philosophy at Johns Hopkins University," *Journal of Speculative Philosophy,* XIII (1879), 398–99, *British Thought and Thinkers; Introductory Studies,*

Critical, Biographical, and Philosophical (Chicago, 1880), "Kant's Transcendental Deduction of the Categories," *Journal of Speculative Philosophy,* XV (1881), 253–74, "Philosophy and Its Specific Problems," *Princeton Review,* n.s., IX (1882), 208–52, *Philosophy and Christianity* (New York, 1883), which was the published version of Morris's lectures on the Ely Foundation at Union Theological Seminary, and *Hegel's Philosophy of the State and of History; an Exposition* (Chicago, 1887).

Of John Dewey's works, those which best represent his ideas during the period of his association with Morris are: "The Psychological Standpoint," *Mind,* XI (1886), 1–19, "Psychology as Philosophic Method," *Mind,* XI (1886), 153–73, *Psychology* (New York, 1887, 3d revised edition, 1891), "Knowledge as Idealisation," *Mind,* XII (1887), 382–96, *Outlines of a Critical Theory of Ethics* (Ann Arbor, Mich., 1891).

There are brief biographical sketches of Alfred Henry Lloyd by Ernest S. Bates in the *Dictionary of American Biography* and by his colleagues A. K. Cross, D. H. Parker, and R. M. Wenley in the *Journal of Philosophy,* XXV (1928), 124–30. Lloyd's books were: *Citizenship and Salvation; or, Greek and Jew, a Study in the Philosophy of History* (Boston, 1897), *Dynamic Idealism* (Chicago, 1898), *The Philosophy of History* (Ann Arbor, Mich., 1899), and *The Will to Doubt* (New York, 1902). His article "The Relation of Righteousness to Brute Facts," *International Journal of Ethics,* XVIII (1907–8), 418–33, is also of interest.

CHAPTER 37

There are many sketches of Royce by his colleagues, his contemporaries, and his students. Of these sketches we select the following: G. H. Palmer, "In Dedication: Josiah Royce," in *Contemporary Idealism in America,* ed. by Clifford Barrett (New York, 1932), pp. 3–9; George Santayana, *Character and Opinion in the United States* (New York, 1920), chap. iv; Ralph Barton Perry, *In the Spirit of William James* (New Haven, 1938), chap. i; and H. G. Townsend, *Philosophical Ideas in the United States* (New York, 1934), chap. x. James Edwin Creighton edited a volume of *Papers in Honor of Josiah Royce on His Sixtieth Birthday* (New York, 1916), which includes George Holmes Howison's "Josiah Royce; the Significance of His Work in Philosophy," pp. 3–16, and Richard C. Cabot's "Josiah Royce as a Teacher," pp. 238–44. Other contributors to this volume were John Dewey, Charles M. Bakewell, Lawrence J. Henderson, Mary Whiton Calkins, George P. Adams, William A. Brown, B. W. Bacon, W. H. Sheldon, E. G. Spaulding, Morris R. Cohen, Alfred H. Lloyd, Clarence I. Lewis, J. Loewenberg, E. E. Southard, E. A. Singer, H. H.

Horne, W. E. Hocking; the volume is concluded by "A Bibliography of the Writings of Josiah Royce," pp. 287–94, compiled by Benjamin Rand.

The correspondence between Royce and William James, published in *The Letters of William James,* ed. by Henry James (Boston, 1920), *passim,* and in Ralph Barton Perry, *The Thought and Character of William James* (Boston, 1935), *passim,* is informative; in Appendices V and VI Perry reproduces the famous discussion between James and Royce on the Absolute.

There is no need to list Royce's chief works here, but attention may be called to a few of his works that are often neglected: *California from the Conquest in 1846 to the Second Vigilance Committee in San Francisco (1856); a Study of American Character* (Boston, 1886), *Race Questions, Provincialisms, and Other American Problems* (New York and London, 1908), *The Problem of Christianity* (2 vols., New York, 1913), *War and Insurance* (New York, 1914), and "The Hope of the Great Community," *Yale Review,* V (1916), 269–91.

CHAPTER 38

It is impossible here to make a commentary on recent contributions to American idealism. An idea of the complexity of the problem may be gained from the discussion which appeared in the pages of the *Journal of Philosophy,* XXX (1933), including the following contributions: J. B. Pratt, "Is Idealism Realism?" pp. 169–78, Clifford Barrett, "Is Idealism Realism? a Reply in Terms of Objective Idealism," pp. 421–29, E. S. Brightman, "The Definition of Idealism," pp. 429–35, F. C. S. Schiller, "Is Idealism Incurably Ambiguous?" pp. 659–64, and J. B. Pratt, "What Is Speculative Idealism?" pp. 673–83. Some contemporary idealists have been listed in other contexts, and their works will not be repeated here; with this exception, the following alphabetical list of authors and their chief works should be consulted in connection with the attempt made in the text to indicate emerging types and currents of idealist thought.

Adams, George Plimpton, Idealism and the Modern Age (New York, 1918).
—— "Naturalism or Idealism," in Contemporary American Philosophy, ed. by G. P. Adams and W. P. Montague (New York, 1930), I, 65–86.
Bakewell, Charles Montague, "Continuity of the Idealist Tradition," in Contemporary Idealism in America, ed. by Clifford Barrett (New York, 1932), pp. 25–42.
Blanshard, Brand, The Nature of Thought (2 vols., London, 1939).

Blanshard, Brand, "Current Strictures on Reason," *Philosophical Review*, LIV (1945), 345–68.

Boodin, John Elof, "Nature and Reason," in Contemporary American Philosophy, I, 136–66.

—— "God and Cosmic Structure," in Contemporary Idealism in America, pp. 199–216.

—— God and Creation (New York, 1934), Vol. I, Three Interpretations of the Universe, Vol. II, God.

—— The Social Mind (New York, 1939).

—— Religion of Tomorrow (New York, 1943).

Cunningham, G. Watts, Five Lectures on the Problem of Mind (Austin, Tex., 1925).

—— "A Search for a System," in Contemporary American Philosophy, I, 251–74.

—— "On the Meaning Situation," in Contemporary Idealism in America, pp. 69–100.

—— The Idealistic Argument in Recent British and American Philosophy (New York, 1933).

—— "Perspective and Context in the Meaning Situation," *University of California Publications in Philosophy*, XVI, No. 2 (1935), 29–52.

Everett, Walter G., Moral Values (New York, 1918).

—— "In Vestigiis Veritatis," in Contemporary American Philosophy, I, 329–53.

Fite, Warner, "The Theory of Democracy," *International Journal of Ethics*, XVIII (1907–08), 1–18. A good exposition of an individualistic interpretation of democracy.

—— Moral Philosophy; the Critical View of Life (New York, 1925).

—— The Living Mind; Essays on the Significance of Consciousness (New York, 1930).

—— "The Impersonal Point of View and the Personal," in Contemporary American Philosophy, I, 357–81.

Hendel, Charles William, "The Meaning of Obligation," in Contemporary Idealism in America, pp. 239–95.

—— "The Status of Mind in Philosophy," *Journal of Philosophy*, XXXI (1934), 225–35.

—— "Reflections on the Spirit of Man," *Philosophical Review*, LII (1941), 162–87.

Hocking, William E., The Meaning of God in Human Experience (New Haven, 1912).

—— Human Nature and Its Remaking (New Haven, 1918).

—— Man and the State (New Haven, 1926).

—— Present Status of the Philosophy of Law and Rights (New Haven, 1926).

—— The Self; Its Body and Freedom (New Haven, 1928).

—— Types of Philosophy (New York, 1929).

—— "Some Second Principles," in Contemporary American Philosophy, I, 385–400.

—— "The Ontological Argument in Royce and Others," Contemporary Idealism in America, pp. 45–66.

—— Lasting Elements of Individualism (New Haven, 1937).

—— Thoughts on Death and Life (New York, 1937).

—— Science and the Idea of God (Chapel Hill, 1944).

Laguna, Theodore de, "The Way of Opinion," in Contemporary American Philosophy, I, 403–22.

Lewis, Clarence Irving, Mind and the World-Order (New York, 1929).

—— "Logic and Pragmatism," in Contemporary American Philosophy, II, 33–51.

Parker, DeWitt H., The Self and Nature (Cambridge, Mass., 1917).

—— The Principles of Aesthetics (Boston, 1920).

—— "Empirical Idealism," in Contemporary American Philosophy, II, 163–83.

—— Human Values (New York, 1931).

—— Substance and Experience (Ann Arbor, 1941).

Schmidt, Karl, The Creative I and the Divine (New York, 1937).

—— "An Approach to God," *Open Court*, XLV (1931), 344–56.

—— From Science to God; Prolegomena to a Future Theology (New York, 1944).

Sheldon, Wilmon Henry, The Strife of Systems and Productive Duality (Cambridge, Mass., 1919).

—— "The Task of Present-Day Metaphysics," in American Philosophy Today and Tomorrow (New York, 1935), pp. 449–61.

—— America's Progressive Philosophy (New Haven, 1942).

—— Process and Polarity (New York, 1944).

—— "Critique of Naturalism," *Journal of Philosophy*, XLII (1945), 253–70.

—— "Are Naturalists Materialists?" *Journal of Philosophy*, XLIII (1946), 197–209.

Singer, Edgar A., Jr., Modern Thinkers and Present Problems (New York, 1923).

—— Mind as Behaviour (Columbus, O., 1924).

Singer, Edgar A., Jr., Fool's Advice (New York, 1925).

—— "On Spontaneity," *Journal of Philosophy*, XXII (1925), 421–36.

—— "On the Conscious Mind: I, Definition of the Conscious; II, History of the Conscious," *Journal of Philosophy*, XXVI (1929), 561–75.

—— "Confessio Philosophi," in Contemporary American Philosophy, II, 289–310.

—— "On a Possible Science of Religion," *Philosophical Review*, XL (1931), 105–23.

—— The Contented Life (New York, 1936).

—— "Review of Frederick Bolman's translation of Schelling's The Ages of the World," *Review of Religion*, VIII (1943–44), 39–54.

Tsanoff, Radoslav A., "The Theory of Moral Value," in Contemporary Idealism in America, pp. 219–36.

—— Religion at the Crossroads (New York, 1942).

—— The Moral Ideals of Our Civilization (New York, 1942).

Urban, Wilbur M., Valuation; Its Nature and Laws (New York, 1909).

—— The Intelligible World; Metaphysics and Value (New York, 1929).

—— Language and Reality; the Philosophy of Language and the Principles of Symbolism (New York, 1939).

—— "Metaphysics and Value," in Contemporary American Philosophy, II, 356–81.

—— "The Philosophy of Spirit; Idealism and the Philosophy of Value," in Contemporary Idealism in America, pp. 103–129.

Wenley, Robert Mark, "An Unborn Idealism," in Contemporary American Philosophy, II, 385–411.

Woodbridge, Frederick J. E., The Purpose of History (New York, 1916).

—— The Realm of Mind (New York, 1926).

—— The Son of Apollo: the Themes of Plato (Boston, 1929).

—— "Confessions," in Contemporary American Philosophy, II, 415–38.

—— Nature and Mind (New York, 1937).

—— An Essay on Nature (New York, 1940).

Though not essays in idealism, Woodbridge's works are closely related to recent objective idealism.

— VIII —

RADICAL EMPIRICISM

PRAGMATIC INTELLIGENCE

WHEN William James proposed to make psychology a natural science, there was a rude awakening among American philosophers who, in their "critical" dogmatic slumbers, had become accustomed to the contrast between natural and moral science, as if it were the unshakable foundation of faith, as well as the customary foundation of all textbooks. In Europe the sensationalism of the British and the dynamic psychology of the French and the Germans had prepared the way for the idea that intelligence might be conceived as a natural process. But even Darwin, who in his work on conscience and the emotions was beginning to explore the field of psycho-biology, was extremely cautious. James, too, though he returned from Europe in 1868 inspired by Darwin, Helmholtz, Charcot, and other naturalists, was Kantian enough to retain the belief that morals rest on a priori foundations. But intelligence, the life of the soul, mental activity, this field which because of its teleological nature had been subordinated to moral science, *Geisteswissenschaft,* was now to be assimilated to biology. Henceforth reason was to be explained as a natural outgrowth of animal intelligence. Even the "dynamic" idealists protested against this idea. A rational ideal or moral end "which interprets, which gives meaning to, which unifies all processes" must have its basis, according to them, "in the rational and spiritual constitution of reality." Only if we "read physical causes in terms of rational purpose" can we incorporate "ethical ends in the very structure of reality." Physical science, in seeking to make man mechanical and to rob nature of its divinity, merely makes science inhuman.[1] And J. H. Hyslop, of Columbia University, expressed forcefully the general conviction when he wrote: "Evolution is explanatory, ethics is legislative. . . . Can we legislate for mankind upon the mere basis of power? . . . No doubt naturalistic theory well describes the actual influence of might in determining

---

[1] The passages quoted and the ideas here stated are taken from John Dewey, "Ethics and Physical Science," in *Andover Review,* VII (1887), 573–91.

things as they are." [2] But "rummaging in the brains of babies and savages . . . and then pronouncing for a theory of man's 'nature,' which left all the 'nature' out of it" is subversive of every high belief. "With this view of the subject we do not care what the practices of savages really are. We may still inquire whether they ought to be what they are." [3] "Science, indeed, can tell us nothing of the validity of virtue, duty, or good . . . their warrant being, in the last analysis, an inexpugnable consciousness of their right to us and authority over us." [4] What is true of our moral nature is true of our rational nature, so went the idealist's argument, and therefore psychology in general must rest on our "inexpugnable consciousness" of validity.

To these familiar and eminently sound objections the new school of biological and genetic empiricists turned deaf ears. Their natural science of the mind was not concerned with what we ought to think, but with how we think and why we believe what we do, whether our beliefs be reasonable or foolish, valid or invalid. This new psychology would no longer be normative, would not expound the rules of mental health; it would be clinical, explaining to men how their minds work even when they are working badly. Of these psychologists, William James became peculiarly important for philosophy. In 1878 his course at Harvard, previously entitled "Physiological Psychology—Herbert Spencer's Principles of Psychology," became "Philosophy 4. Psychology—Taine on Intelligence." He began modestly enough. In defending his new course to President Eliot he wrote:

A real science of man is now being built up out of the theory of evolution and the facts of archaeology, the nervous system and the senses. It has already a vast material extent, the papers and magazines are full of essays and articles having more or less to do with it. The question is shall the students be left—to the magazines, on the one hand, and to what languid attention professors educated in the exclusively literary way can pay to the subject? Or shall the College employ a man whose scientific training fits him fully to realize the force of all the natural history arguments, whilst his concomitant familiarity with writers of a more introspective kind preserves him

[2] J. H. Hyslop, "Evolution and Ethical Problems," in *Andover Review*, IX (1888), 348–66.

[3] These two passages are from J. H. Hyslop's review of Schurman's *Ethical Import of Darwinism*, in *Andover Review*, IX (1888), 203–6.

[4] J. G. Schurman, *The Ethical Import of Darwinism* (New York, 1887), p. 264.

from certain crudities of reasoning which are extremely common in men of the laboratory pure and simple?

Apart from all reference to myself, it is my firm belief that the College cannot possibly have psychology taught as a living science by anyone who has not a first-hand acquaintance with the facts of nervous physiology. On the other hand, no mere physiologist can adequately realize the subtlety and difficulty of the psychologic portions of his own subject until he has tried to teach, or at least to study, psychology in its entirety. A union of the two "disciplines" in one man, seems then the most natural thing in the world.[5]

Soon he turned his experimental empiricism, that is, his combination of evolution, physiology and introspection, upon philosophical beliefs themselves; he took "the sentiment of rationality" into his psychological laboratory for clinical investigation. He had a disconcerting and impudent habit of asking why there are so many articles of faith, tenaciously held, for which there can be little evidence or objective validity. And this impudence became the philosophy of pragmatism when he began to psychologize truth itself and to ask how we come to believe in validity or when we are satisfied that a proposition is verified. He raised these questions, not in the spirit of materialism, but in the spirit of "common sense," in the hope of gaining experimental evidence for his conviction that "the human mind always has and always will be able to interpret facts in accordance with its moral interests." [6] It was small comfort to the orthodox to hear this reassertion of the subordination of reason to morals when morals themselves were dethroned from the transcendent seat of reason and set adrift among human "interests."

There had been anticipations of such pragmatism. As far back as 1864 [7] F. E. Abbot had attacked the nominalism of phenomenalism, had argued that man has a direct experience of the objectivity of relations, and that, in general, the principles of validity were not mere a priori forms of the understanding, but fruits of experience. He was not merely repeating the Scottish common sense faith in intuition; he was suggesting a radical, realistic epistemology, according to which

[5] Ralph Barton Perry, *The Thought and Character of William James* (Boston, 1935), II, 11.

[6] In a public lecture of 1877; see Perry, *op. cit.*, p. 27.

[7] F. E. Abbot, "The Philosophy of Space and Time," *North American Review*, XCIX (1864), 64–116.

the mind is neither a passive "activity of representation" nor a creative act of ordering phenomena, but is engaged in "action and reaction" with objects-in-relation; the resultant "percepts," he explained, were "mental vision or the perception of relations." Hence universals or objective relations are perceived by a process of experimentally ana- lyzing things-in-relation, not by a process of synthesizing discrete phenomena. Abbot thus had the basic ideas of an organic, biological psychology, but he had neither the psychological interest nor the scientific equipment to develop them adequately; for him this realistic theory of knowledge was but a prolegomenon to "scientific theism" and organismic cosmology. It was, therefore, left to naturalists like Edmund Montgomery to add to such criticism of Kant a more positive, biological theory of consciousness and mind. Meanwhile, Abbot's friend Chauncey Wright, whom Abbot's arguments had failed to shake from his reliance on Hamilton's metaphysics, was shaken by J. S. Mill's critique of Hamilton and by Darwin's *Origin of Species*. In 1873 he was discussing "psychozoology" with Darwin when Darwin put to him the haunting question, When may things be said to be in mind? Wright's notable essay *The Evolution of Self-Consciousness* [8] was a radical, though speculative, attempt to give a biological framework to mental processes and faculties.

As Abbot failed to convert Wright to realism, so Wright failed, in "almost daily" discussions, to convert C. S. Peirce to biological utilitar- ianism. Nevertheless, Peirce saw the problem and was working out his own pragmatic theory of universals. The first indication from Peirce's pen of the direction his thoughts were taking is to be found in his re- view of the Fraser edition of Berkeley.[9] The relevant passages are worth quoting as the earliest formulation of his pragmatic realism and of his theory of truth as the goal or final outcome of co-operative, experimental research.

It is anticipated that the Berkeleyan treatment of the question of the validity of human knowledge and of the inductive process of science, which is now so much studied, is such as to command the attention of scientific men to the idealistic system. To us these hopes seem vain. The truth is that

[8] See above, p. 348.
[9] C. S. Peirce, "The Works of George Berkeley," *The North American Review*, CXIII (1871), 449-72.

the minds from whom the spirit of the age emanates have now no interest in the only problems that metaphysics ever pretended to solve. The abstract acknowledgment of God, Freedom, and Immortality, apart from those other religious beliefs (which cannot possibly rest on metaphysical grounds) which alone may animate this, is now seen to have no practical consequence whatever. . . . Whatever interest it has had has been due to a hope that the solution of it would afford the basis for sure and useful maxims concerning the logic of induction,—a hope which would be destroyed so soon as it were shown that the question was a purely metaphysical one. This is the prevalent feeling, among advanced minds. It may not be just; but it exists. And its existence is an effectual bar (if there were no other) to the general acceptance of Berkeley's system. . . .

Human opinion universally tends in the long run to a definite form, which is the truth. Let any human being have enough information and exert enough thought upon any question, and the result will be that he will arrive at a certain definite conclusion, which is the same that any other mind will reach under sufficiently favorable circumstances. Suppose two men, one deaf, the other blind. One hears a man declare he means to kill another, hears the report of the pistol, and hears the victim cry; the other sees the murder done. Their sensations are affected in the highest degree with their individual peculiarities. The first information that their sensations will give them, their first inferences, will be more nearly alike, but still different; the one having, for example, the idea of a man shouting, the other of a man with a threatening aspect; but their final conclusions, the thought the remotest from sense, will be identical and free from the one-sidedness of their idiosyncrasies. There is, then, to every question a true answer, a final conclusion, to which the opinion of every man is constantly gravitating. He may for a time recede from it, but give him more experience and time for consideration, and he will finally approach it. The individual may not live to reach the truth; there is a residuum of error in every individual's opinions. No matter; it remains that there is a definite opinion to which the mind of man is, on the whole and in the long run, tending. On many questions the final agreement is already reached, on all it will be reached if time enough is given. The arbitrary will or other individual peculiarities of a sufficiently large number of minds may postpone the general agreement in that opinion indefinitely; but it cannot affect what the character of that opinion shall be when it is reached. This final opinion, then, is independent, not indeed of thought in general, but of all that is arbitrary and individual in thought; is quite independent of how you, or I, or any number of men think. Everything, therefore, which will be thought to exist in the final opinion is real, and nothing else. . . . Any truth more perfect than this destined conclusion, any reality more absolute than what is thought in it, is a fiction of metaphysics. . . .

It is plain that this view of reality is inevitably realistic; because general conceptions enter into all judgments, and therefore into true opinions. Consequently a thing in the general is as real as in the concrete. It is perfectly true that all white things have whiteness in them, for that is only saying, in another form of words, that all white things are white; but since it is true that real things possess whiteness, whiteness is real. It is a real which only exists by virtue of an act of thought knowing it, but that thought is not an arbitrary or accidental one dependent on any idiosyncrasies, but one which will hold in the final opinion.

This theory involves a phenomenalism. But it is the phenomenalism of Kant, and not that of Hume. Indeed, what Kant called his Copernican step was precisely the passage from the nominalistic to the realistic view of reality. It was the essence of his philosophy to regard the real object as determined by the mind. That was nothing else than to consider every conception and intuition which enters necessarily into the experience of an object, and which is not transitory and accidental, as having objective validity. In short, it was to regard the reality as the normal product of mental action, and not as the incognizable cause of it.

This realistic theory is thus a highly practical and common-sense position . . . and science as it exists is certainly much less nominalistic than the nominalists think it should be. Whewell represents it quite as well as Mill. Yet a man who enters into the scientific thought of the day and has not materialistic tendencies, is getting to be an impossibility. So long as there is a dispute between nominalism and realism, so long as the position we hold on the question is not determined by any proof *indisputable*, but is more or less a matter of inclination, a man as he gradually comes to feel the profound hostility of the two tendencies will, if he is not less than man, become engaged with one or other and can no more obey both than he can serve God and Mammon. If the two impulses are neutralized within him, the result simply is that he is left without any great intellectual motive. There is, indeed, no reason to suppose the logical question is in its own nature unsusceptible of solution. But that path out of the difficulty lies through the thorniest mazes of a science as dry as mathematics. Now there is a demand for mathematics; it helps to build bridges and drive engines, and therefore it becomes somebody's business to study it severely. But to have a philosophy is a matter of luxury; the only use of that is to make us feel comfortable and easy. It is a study for leisure hours; and we want it supplied in an elegant, an agreeable, an interesting form. The law of natural selection, which is the precise analogue in another realm of the law of supply and demand, has the most immediate effect in fostering the other faculties of the understanding, for the men of mental power succeed in the struggle for life; but the faculty of philosophizing, except in the literary way, is not called for; and therefore a difficult question cannot be expected to reach solution until it takes some practical form. If anybody should have the good luck to find out the solution, nobody else would take the trouble to understand it. But though the question of realism and nominalism has its roots in the technicalities of logic, its branches reach about our life. The question whether the *genus homo* has any existence except as individuals, is the question whether there is anything of any more dignity, worth, and importance than individual happiness, individual aspirations, and individual life. Whether men really have anything in common, so that the *community* is to be considered as an end in itself, and if so, what the relative value of the two factors is, is the most fundamental practical question in regard to every public institution the constitution of which we have it in our power to influence.[10]

Peirce here asserted propositions which were destined to become bones of contention for several generations and are fundamental in the history of pragmatism: (1) The question of the validity of knowledge may be approached and settled inductively as a scientific problem; (2) Experimental verification is based on faith in an eventual agreement among observers, and the universals eventually held by the community of knowers constitute reality and truth; (3) Kant's doctrine that the real object is determined by the mind is to be interpreted as meaning that the objectively valid universals in our experience of objects are normal products of a community of "mental action," not incognizable causes; (4) Science is to be freed from contamination with nominalism, individualism, and materialism by reviving realism through mathematical logic; (5) Philosophy and mathematics must discard their leisurely elegance and take on a practical form by addressing themselves to proving the reality of community.

During the seventies these propositions were subjected to protracted discussion by Wright, Peirce, James, Abbot, and a few other members of the so-called Metaphysical Club. In describing the meetings of this club Peirce wrote:

[10] *Ibid.*, pp. 450, 455–56, 457, 472.

It may be that some of our old-time confederates would today not care to have such wild-oats-sowings made public, though there was nothing but boiled oats, milk, and sugar in the mess. Mr. Justice Holmes, however, will not, I believe, take it ill that we are proud to remember his membership; nor will Joseph Warner, Esq. Nicholas St. John Green was one of the most interested fellows, a skillful lawyer and a learned one, a disciple of Jeremy Bentham. His extraordinary power of disrobing warm and breathing truth of the draperies of long worn formulas, was what attracted attention to him everywhere. In particular, he often urged the importance of applying Bain's definition of belief, as "that upon which a man is prepared to act." From this definition, pragmatism is scarce more than a corollary; so that I am disposed to think of him as the grandfather of pragmatism. . . . Wright, James, and I were men of science, rather scrutinizing the doctrines of the metaphysicians on their scientific side than regarding them as very momentous spiritually. The type of our thought was decidedly British. I, alone of our number, had come upon the threshing-floor of philosophy through the doorway of Kant, and even my ideas were acquiring the English accent.

. . . Our metaphysical proceedings had all been in winged words (and swift ones, at that, for the most part), until at length, lest the club should be dissolved, without leaving any material *souvenir* behind, I drew up a little paper expressing some of the opinions that I had been urging all along under the name of pragmatism. This paper was received with such unlooked-for kindness, that I was encouraged, some half dozen years later, on the invitation of the great publisher, Mr. W. H. Appleton, to insert it, somewhat expanded, in the *Popular Science Monthly* for November, 1877 and January, 1878.[11]

Of these three "men of science" Wright departed least from the path of positivism and was for that reason dubbed by Peirce an "acute but shallow fellow." [12] He clung to his motto: "Nothing justifies the development of abstract principles in science, but their utility in enlarging our concrete knowledge of nature." [13] But he admitted that,

[11] Peirce, *Collected Papers*, ed. by Charles Hartshorne and Paul Weiss (Cambridge, 1934), V, 7–8.

[12] Perry, *The Thought and Character of William James*, II, 439.

[13] "The Philosophy of Herbert Spencer" (1865), reprinted in Wright, *Philosophical Discussions* (New York, 1877), p. 56. He added: "The ideas on which mathematical Mechanics and the Calculus are founded, the morphological ideas of Natural History, and the theories of Chemistry are such working ideas,—finders, not merely summaries of truth." *Studies in the History of Ideas* (New York, 1935), III, 498.

whereas the utility of theological and metaphysical speculations is entirely moral or practical, the utility of scientific abstractions may be cognitive insofar as they afford "consequences capable of sensuous verification, or by yielding such consequences in conjunction with ideas which by themselves are verifiable." [14] This doctrine was but the reassertion of the basic principle of empiricism, with the emphasis shifted from the problem of the origin of ideas to the problem of the verification of ideas. Wright made a more substantial advance over traditional empiricism, however, when on the basis of this principle he raised the question of the concrete utility of the distinction between subject and object and said that it is not "the intuitive distinction it is supposed to be by most metaphysicians," but "a classification through observation and analysis" for the social purposes of "communication between members of a community." [15] Here was a new, radical empiricism, clearly formulated; unfortunately, Wright died soon after he had formulated it, and no one can tell whether if he had lived longer he would have developed it in the direction of Peirce or of James.

Peirce started with the same positivist maxim on which Wright had insisted: "Our idea of anything *is* our idea of its sensible effects, and if we fancy that we have any other we deceive ourselves and mistake a mere sensation accompanying the thought for a part of the thought itself. It is absurd to say that thought has any meaning unrelated to its only function." Our conception of an object, therefore, can be made clear by considering "what effects, that might conceivably have practical bearings" our object has. Had Peirce gone no farther in his now famous article on "How to make Our Ideas Clear" (1878), he would not have differed significantly from the positivism of Wright. His chief aim, however, was to show that even in these positivistic terms the reality and utility of "abstractions" or universals could be accounted for.

Reality, like every other quality, consists in the peculiar sensible effects which things partaking of it produce. The only effect which real things have is to cause belief, for all the sensations which they excite emerge into conscious-

---

[14] Wright, *Philosophical Discussions*, p. 47.
[15] "Evolution of Self-Consciousness," in Wright, *Philosophical Discussions*, pp. 217–19.

ness in the form of beliefs. The question therefore is, how is true belief (or belief in the real) distinguished from false belief (or belief in fiction). Now . . . the ideas of truth and falsehood, in their full development, appertain exclusively to the experiential method of settling opinion. . . .

Since belief is a rule for action, the application of which involves further doubt and further thought, at the same time that it is a stopping-place, it is also a new starting-place for thought. That is why I have permitted myself to call it thought at rest, although thought is essentially an action. The *final* upshot of thinking is the exercise of volition, and of this thought no longer forms a part; but belief is only a stadium of mental action, an effect upon our nature due to thought, which will influence future thinking.

The essence of belief is the establishment of a habit; and different beliefs are distinguished by the different modes of action to which they give rise. If beliefs do not differ in this respect, if they appease the same doubt by producing the same rule of action, then no mere differences in the manner of consciousness of them can make them different beliefs, any more than playing a tune in different keys is playing different tunes.[16]

In other words, Peirce thought that he had proved that a concept, a universal, or idea, as distinguished from a particular state of consciousness or feeling, could be defined pragmatically in terms of habits of belief and that these habits in turn are pragmatically habits of action. A habit is the biological embodiment of a general idea. This explanation of the reality of universals seemed to Peirce the central thesis of pragmatism; it was a very peculiar type of "action" with which he was concerned—the act of generalization.

I have seen more thoroughly than I used to do that it is not mere action as brute exercise of strength that is the purpose of all, but, say, generalization,—such action as tends toward regularization, and the actualization of the thought which without action remains unthought. . . . Much has led me to rate higher than ever the individual deed as the only real meaning there is in the concept; and yet at the same time to see more sharply than ever that it is not the mere arbitrary force in the deed, but the life it gives to the idea, that is valuable.[17]

Peirce insisted that the only conscientious and thorough pragmatism was one which "remembered" that

---

[16] Peirce, *The Philosophy of Peirce; Selected Writings;* ed. by Justus Buchler (New York, 1940), pp. 36–37, 28–29.

[17] Perry, *The Thought and Character of William James,* II, 222.

the only ultimate good which the practical facts to which it directs attention can subserve is to further the development of concrete reasonableness; so that the meaning of the concept does not lie in any individual reactions at all, but in the manner in which those reactions contribute to that development.[18]

But James was above all an individualist, and he was not inclined to agree with Peirce that "the meaning of the concept does not lie in any individual reactions at all." He worked out his own version of pragmatism. The first published suggestion of it came in 1878 in an article entitled "Brute and Human Intellect," published in the *Journal of Speculative Philosophy*; the scientific argument in this article was then cast into more philosophical and polemic form in his article "Are We Automata?" published in *Mind* and composed as a contribution to the British debate over parallelism. James is, in these articles, clearly influenced by Chauncey Wright, though he does not mention him by name and represents his position as Darwinian, as a justification for the view that feeling or consciousness has utility.

I have tried to show that all Reasoning depends on the ability of the mind to break up the totality of the phenomenon reasoned about into partial factors or elements, and to pick out from among these the particular one which, in our given theoretical or practical emergency, may lead to the proper conclusion. Another predicament will need another conclusion, and require another element to be picked out. The man of genius is he who will always stick-in his bill, as it were, at the right point, and bring it out with the right element—"reason" if the emergency be theoretical, "means" if it be practical—transfixed upon it. Association by similarity I have shown to be an important help to this breaking-up of represented things into their elements. But this association is only the minimum of that same selection of which picking out the right reason is a maximum. . . . Reasoning is but another form of that selective activity which appears to be the true sphere of mental spontaneity. . . .

The spontaneity of the mind does not consist in conjuring up any new non-sensational quality of objectivity. It consists solely in deciding what the particular sensation shall be whose native objectivity shall be held more valid than that of all the rest. . . .

[18] Peirce, *Collected Papers*, ed. by Hartshorne and Weiss, V, 2; from Peirce's article "Pragmatic and Pragmatism," in the *Dictionary of Philosophy and Psychology*, ed. by J. M. Baldwin (New York, 1902), II, 321-22.

These mental functions are already at work in the first beginnings of sensation and the simplest changes of sensation moreover involve consciousness of all the categories—time, space, number, objectivity, causality. There is not first a passive act of sensation proper, followed by an active production or projection ("inference") of the attributes of objectivity by the mind. These all come to us together with the sensible qualities, and their progress from vagueness to distinctness is the only process psychologists have to explain. . . .

The desire on the part of men educated in laboratories not to have their physical reasonings mixed up with such incommensurable factors as feelings is certainly very strong. Nothing is commoner than to hear them speak of conscious events as something so essentially vague and shadowy as even doubtfully to exist at all. I have heard a most intelligent biologist say: "It is high time for scientific men to protest against the recognition of any such thing as consciousness in a scientific investigation." In a word, feeling constitutes the "unscientific" half of existence, and any one who enjoys calling himself a "scientist" will be too happy to purchase an untrammeled homogeneity of terms in the studies of his predilection, at the slight cost of admitting a dualism which, in the same breath that it allows to mind an independent status of being, banishes it to a limbo of causal inertness from whence no intrusion or interruption on its part need ever be feared.

But Common Sense also may have its aesthetic demands, and among them may be a craving for unity. The spectacle of an ultimate and inexplicable dualism in the nature of things may be as unsatisfying as the obligation to calculate with heterogeneous terms. . . .

And now, who shall decide between such rival aesthetic needs? . . . Both alike are conceptions of the possible, and for any one dogmatically to affirm the truth of either is, in the present state of our knowledge, an extremely unscientific procedure.[19]

Here we have the essence of James's psychology as well as of his "will-to-believe" and pragmatism. The cerebrum, he argued, is flexible or made to be guided, and consciousness is evidently made for guiding, discriminating. The conclusion is irresistible—the cerebrum and consciousness *must* work together. Though he was morally certain of interaction, he refused, in his *Psychology,* to regard it as a scientific question and referred it to the metaphysical department of his thought —a convenient device which he employed often in his *Psychology.*

[19] William James, "Are We Automata?" *Mind; a Quarterly Review of Psychology and Philosophy,* IV (1879), 12, 11, 11n, 2–3, 3.

While he was writing these articles he was delivering a series of lectures at Johns Hopkins on the subject of interactionism, and closed them with the remark:

I, for one, as a scientific man and a practical man alike, deny utterly that science compels me to believe that my conscience is an *ignis fatuus* or outcast, and I trust that you too, after the evidence of this evening, will go away strengthened in the natural faith that your delights and sorrows, your loves and hates, your aspirations and efforts are real combatants in life's arena, and not impotent, paralytic spectators of the game.[20]

He had no sooner reached this conclusion than he applied it to the most speculative forms of thought and wrote his "Reflex Action and Theism." Here his own pragmatism was put in its characteristic form:

The willing department of our nature . . . dominates both the conceiving department and the feeling department; or, in plainer English, perception and thinking are only there for behavior's sake. I am sure I am not wrong in stating this result as one of the fundamental conclusions to which the entire drift of modern physiological investigation sweeps us. If asked what great contribution physiology has made to psychology of late years, I am sure every competent authority will reply that her influence has in no way been so weighty as in the copious illustration, verification, and consolidation of this broad, general point of view.[21]

[20] Perry, *The Thought and Character of William James*, II, 31. James had been "sleepless and restless" during his lecture engagement, worrying whether the girl to whom he had proposed marriage would make up her mind and say yes. When the awaited reply finally came, he and his non-automatic sweetheart were married and together they sent off the "Are We Automata?" article to *Mind*. The issue of automatism and materialism was raised again in connection with pragmatism in 1898, when James confessed that he had not taken into account the pragmatic value of "sentiment per se," and corrected his account (in the California lecture) of the pragmatic difference between materialistic and theistic cosmology by reference to the unsatisfactory performance of an "automatic sweetheart." C. C. Everett used a different illustration in calling his attention to this problem: "Suppose we think of a human-hearted chicken. It seems to me it would make considerable difference to one approximating this type, whether it had a mother-hen brooding over it or was kept warm in an incubator—even though it got everything out of the incubator that it could out of the hen. Is not at least one difficulty with materialism that it changes the world into an incubator?" (Letter to James, October 29, 1898. Published in Perry, *op. cit.*, II, 464). See also E. A. Singer's treatment of this issue in *Mind as Behavior* (Columbus, O., 1924), and William James, *The Meaning of Truth* (New York, 1909), p. 189n.

[21] William James, *The Will to Believe and other Essays in Popular Philosophy* (New York, 1897), p. 114.

Though the address at the Summer School of Ethics for 1895, entitled "The Will to Believe," came fourteen years later, it did little more than restate the voluntarism and "anti-gnosticism" of this early article. But its effect, when it was published in 1897 together with the earlier article and several others, was sensational. Even his friends were repulsed by it and interpreted it as a defense of action-for-action's-sake and a plea for believing what one wants to believe. Peirce, to whom the volume was dedicated, thought it "a very exaggerated utterance, such as injures a serious man very much," and wrote James as kindly as he could the remarks, quoted above, against "mere action," concluding:

As to "belief" and "making up one's mind," if they mean anything more than this, that we have a plan of procedure, and that according to that plan we will try a given description of behavior, I am inclined to think they do more harm than good.[22]

His friend John Jay Chapman wrote:

The state of mind of a man who justifies faith by the considerations you mention—is well enough. He makes himself content. His shanty will last his day. He's got some kind of tar or hopes that'll keep faith in him and prevent it from evaporating. But he'll never convey it—arouse it, evoke it —in another. . . . This is a somewhat roundabout way of saying that such a man hasn't got faith at all. The faith you begin to talk about has been so justified and bolstered, and drugged up and down, and ironed and wired— damme if I call that faith! Damned if I call that faith! . . .

Why all this pother—what *difference* does it make whether a man believes or not? Why is this question important enough to be discussed? . . . I had supposed that the idea of . . . the supposed connection between belief and conduct . . . was one of the busted ideas of the world, like astrology, or the divining rod—a thing containing some elements of truth worthy perhaps of investigation, but rather (at present) discredited on account of its manifest error. My own studies have led me to believe that there may be men who in some matters are sometimes influenced by the form of their religious tenets, and act and feel as they wouldn't have acted and felt but for some dogma; but this is so rare and so complex, and is of course rapidly disappearing.[23]

[22] Perry, *The Thought and Character of William James*, II, 222.
[23] *Ibid.*, p. 236.

To which James replied:

Faith indeed! Damme if I call that faith, either. It is only calculated for the sickly hotbed atmosphere of the philosophic-positivistically enlightened scientific classroom. To the victims of spinal paralysis which these studies superinduce, the homeopathic treatment, although you might not believe it, really does good.[24]

The clinical interest of the psychologist is here clearly expressed. But the relation between the pathology of belief and "fideism" [25] as a metaphysics became increasingly confused as the animated discussion over "the will to believe" continued. James finally admitted that he should have entitled his essay "A Critique of Pure Faith."

The issue came to the fore again in 1897, when James delivered before the Philosophical Union of the University of California his now famous address on "Philosophical Conceptions and Practical Results," in which he first referred to his point of view as pragmatism and attached it to Peirce's formulation of 1878. Peirce now, more than ever, repudiated James's individualistic version of his logical method, and thereafter he referred to his own doctrine as "pragmaticism." The immediate complications in the history of pragmatism are best told in Peirce's own words,

"Pragmatism" has gained general recognition in a generalized sense that seems to argue power of growth and vitality. The famed psychologist, James, first took it up, seeing that his "radical empiricism" substantially answered to the writer's definition of pragmatism, albeit with a certain difference in the point of view. Next, the admirably clear and brilliant thinker, Mr. Ferdinand C. S. Schiller, casting about for a more attractive name for the "anthropomorphism" of his *Riddle of the Sphinx*, lit, in that most remarkable paper of his on *Axioms as Postulates*, upon the same designation "pragmatism," which in its original sense was in generic agreement with his own doctrine, for which he has since found the more appropriate specification "humanism," while he still retains "pragmatism" in a somewhat wider sense. So far all went happily. But at present, the word begins to

---

[24] *Ibid.*, II, 237.

[25] Perry uses "fideism" in a technical sense to distinguish James's earlier and more general voluntarism from the more specific doctrines of his pragmatism and distinguishes both from his metaphysics. These distinctions are well sustained by Perry in his fuller analysis, but I have felt obliged to use these terms more loosely in this brief sketch.

be met with occasionally in the literary journals, where it gets abused in the merciless way that words have to expect when they fall into literary clutches. Sometimes the manners of the British have effloresced in scolding at the word as ill-chosen—ill-chosen, that is, to express some meaning that it was rather designed to exclude. So then, the writer, finding his bantling "pragmatism" so promoted, feels that it is time to kiss his child good-by and relinquish it to its higher destiny; while to serve the precise purpose of expressing the original definition, he begs to announce the birth of the word "pragmaticism," which is ugly enough to be safe from kidnappers.[26]

The reference here to F. C. S. Schiller indicates precisely what his distinctive contribution to pragmatism was. In the face of Peirce's repudiation of James's logic of sentiment or of willfulness, Schiller gave timely support to it by representing it as the logic of practical idealism. His general philosophical orientation was that of romantic, personal idealism, and he wished to emphasize the subjective factor in logic and science; but he had the misfortune of preaching it out of place. At Cornell, where he was instructor from 1893 to 1897, such a subjective idealism was unwelcome, and he returned to Oxford, where, though it was no less unwelcome, it was more picturesque and scandalous. In his last years, which he spent at the University of Southern California, he had become too much of a humanist to please the personalist theists entrenched there. His first important essay on "Axioms as Postulates" (1902) gave an experimentalist turn to empiricist logic. Instead of criticizing the Kantian categories and the supposedly necessary a priori truth, "historically and psychogenetically," and instead of regarding them as verified by past experience and evolutionary struggle, he regarded them as "problems for the philosophic mind," or as hypotheses for experimental testing. They are a priori in the sense that they are not the fruit of particular experiences; they are "demands" postulates made by the organism functioning as a self or whole upon the world as a whole.

When we speak of "the *a priori* principles implied in the existence of all knowledge," do we mean implied *logically* or *psychologically*? Are they, that is, the products of a *logical analysis* or *psychical facts*? Is the "priority" asserted priority *in time* (psychical fact) or priority *in idea* (logical order)?

---

[26] *The Monist*, XV (1905), 161–81; cited in Peirce, *Collected Papers*, ed. by Hartshorne and Weiss, V, 276–77.

Or *horribile dictu,* can it be that the *a priori,* as it is used, is a little of both, or each in turn, and that the whole apriorist account of our axioms rests on this fundamental confusion? . . .

Neither the apriorist nor the empiricist account is tenable. Both have proved unsatisfactory; the former because it represented the axioms as mere brute facts of our mental organisation (either entirely disconnected or connected only among themselves), the latter as the fictitious imprints of a psychologically impossible experience on a purely passive mind.

At bottom the failure of both accounts springs from the same source. Both are infected with an intellectualism which is a libel on our nature, and leads them to take too narrow a view of its endowment. Because of this common intellectualism they fail to realise the central fact which we always encounter so soon as we abandon the abstract standpoints of the lower sciences and try to conceive our relation to our experience as a whole, the fact that the living organism *acts as a whole.* Or to bring out separately the aspects of this central fact which empiricism and apriorism severally misinterpret, we may say that *the organism is active and the organism is one.* . . .

Thought must be conceived as an outgrowth of action, knowledge of life, intelligence of will, while the brain which has become an instrument of intellectual contemplation must be regarded as the subtlest, latest, and most potent organ for effecting adaptations to the needs of life. . . .

When we try to grasp experience as a whole, we must set ourselves above the encumbering abstractions of a psychological classification that has transgressed the limits of its validity. By conceiving the axioms as essentially postulates, made with an ultimately practical end, we bridge the gap that has been artificially constructed between the functions of our nature, and overcome the errors of intellectualism. We conceive the axioms as arising out of man's needs as an agent, as prompted by his desires, as affirmed by his will, in a word, as nourished and sustained by his emotional and volitional nature.[27]

Such logical theory was obviously close to James's pragmatism, and Schiller was well aware of the fact. He wrote:

Practical postulation is the real meaning of his much misconstrued doctrine of the "Will to believe." It is not so much exhortation concerning what we *ought to do* in the future as analysis of what we *have done* in the past. And the critics of the doctrine have mostly ignored the essential addition to the

[27] *Personal Idealism: Philosophical Essays by Eight Members of the University of Oxford,* ed. by Henry Sturt (London, 1902), pp. 72, 84, 85, 86.

"will to believe," viz. *"at your risk,"* which leaves ample scope for the testing of the assumed belief by experience of its practical results.[28]

Schiller's type of pragmatic logic was, however, of dubious value to James, who was being accused of subjectivism by Bradley, Royce, and other objective idealists, as well as being attacked by Peirce and natural scientists. James, therefore, had to guard against defining the "practical" too practically.

Why our predicaments and perplexities might not be theoretical here as well as narrowly practical, I wish that our critics would explain. They simply assume that no pragmatist *can* admit a genuinely theoretic interest. Having used the phrase "cash-value" of an idea, I am implored by one correspondent to alter it, "for every one thinks you mean only pecuniary profit and loss." Having said that the true is "the expedient in our thinking," I am rebuked in this wise by another learned correspondent: "The word expedient has no other meaning than that of self-interest. The pursuit of this has ended by landing a number of officers of national banks in penitentiaries. A philosophy that leads to such results must be unsound."

But the word "practical" is so habitually loosely used that more indulgence might have been expected. When one says that a sick man has now practically recovered, or that an enterprise has practically failed, one usually means just the opposite of practically in the literal sense. One means that, altho untrue in strict practice, what one says is true in theory, true virtually, *certain to be* true. Again, by the practical one often means the distinctively concrete, the individual, particular, and effective, as opposed to the abstract, general, and inert. To speak for myself, whenever I have emphasized the practical nature of truth, this is mainly what has been in my mind. "Pragmata" are things in their plurality; and in that early California address, when I described pragmatism as holding that "the meaning of any proposition can always be brought down to some particular consequence in our future practical experience, whether passive or active," I expressly added these qualifying words: "the point lying rather in the fact that the experience must be particular than in the fact that it must be active." [29]

But, by thus stressing the "particular" over the "active" he ran into the objections of Peirce and the Chicago school. He seemed unable to "satisfy" anyone.

---

[28] *Ibid.*, p. 91n.
[29] William James, *The Meaning of Truth; a Sequel to "Pragmatism"* (New York, 1909), pp. 208–10.

Bradley and Royce were hospitable to James's emphasis on empirical verification, provided he, in turn, would admit that an absolute had to be postulated pragmatically in order to prevent the process of verification from becoming an endless and futile quest. Royce made his criticism very pointed.

Let us suppose that a witness appears, upon some witness-stand, and objects to taking the ordinary oath, because he has conscientious scruples, due to the fact that he is a recent pragmatist, who has a fine new definition of truth, in terms of which alone he can be sworn. Let us suppose him, hereupon, to be granted entire liberty to express his oath in his own way. Let him accordingly say, using, with technical scrupulosity, my colleague's definition of truth: "I promise to tell whatever is expedient and nothing but what is expedient, so help me future experience." I ask you: Do you think that this witness has expressed, with adequacy, that view of the nature of truth that you really wish a witness to have in mind? Of course, if he were a typical pragmatist, you would indeed be delighted to hear his testimony on the witness-stand or anywhere else. But would you accept his formula? . . .

To reduce truth to expediency, is to go about crying *cash, cash,* in a realm where there is no cash of the sort that loyalty demands, that every scientific inquiry presupposes, and that only the unity of the experiences of many in one furnishes.

If we must, then, conceive recent pragmatism under the figure of a business enterprise,—a metaphor which my colleague's phraseology so insistently invites,—I am constrained therefore to sum up its position thus: First, with a winning clearness, and with a most honorable frankness it confesses bankruptcy, so far as the actually needed cash payments of significant truth are concerned. Secondly, it nevertheless declines to go into the hands of any real receiver, for it is not fond of anything that appears too absolute. And thirdly, it proposes simply and openly to go on doing business under the old style and title of the truth. "After all," it says, "are we not, every one of us, fond of credit values?" [30]

James, in reply, was inclined, on considerations of intellectual comfort or "moral holidays," to allow the pragmatic value of an absolute standard for those who needed occasional or ultimate rest, but he refused to admit that an absolute is *logically* necessary.

Explaining why I do not believe in the absolute myself . . . yet finding that it may secure "moral holidays" to those who need them, and is true in

[30] Josiah Royce, *The Philosophy of Loyalty* (New York, 1908), pp. 331–32, 346–47.

so far forth (if to gain moral holidays be a good), I offered this as a conciliatory olive-branch to my enemies. But they, as is only too common with such offerings, trampled the gift under foot and turned and rent the giver. . . . Using the pragmatic test of the meaning of concepts, I had shown the concept of the absolute to *mean* nothing but the holiday giver, the banisher of cosmic fear. One's objective deliverance, when one says "the absolute exists," amounted, on my showing, just to this, that "some justification of a feeling of security in presence of the universe," exists, and that systematically to refuse to cultivate a feeling of security would be to do violence to a tendency in one's emotional life which might well be respected as prophetic.

Apparently my absolutist critics fail to see the workings of their own minds in any such picture, so all that I can do is to apologize, and take my offering back. The absolute is true in *no* way then, and least of all, by the verdict of the critics, in the way which I assigned! [31]

He was on the point of surrendering on the issue of the "abstract" nature of truth to Peirce and the idealists, by distinguishing between "truth" and "truthfulness" and professing to be concerned exclusively with the latter, when he received the following stiff warning from Dewey.

For a pragmatist to say that the question is "almost purely academic" gives the unbeliever too much chance to blaspheme, doesn't it? Or, on the other hand, if this is an almost purely academic question, how can it be admitted that "truthfulness" is so much the more important idea, as the last paragraph indicates? I should not venture to write you about this if I did not know positively that these two paragraphs have been both a stumbling-block to those who had not made up their minds, and a cause of congratulation to the anti-pragmatists. . . .

While my main purpose in writing is merely to raise this question of advisability, it seems to me that Strong's article . . . brings out very clearly the confusion of your critics which you are endeavoring to meet by your distinction between "truth" and "truthfulness." "Is it true that Napoleon landed in Provence on the last day of March, 1814?" If this means anything, it means either (*a*) Is the *statement, idea or belief* that Napoleon landed etc., true? or, (*b*) Is the landing (the bare existential fact) of Napoleon a truth? Now the thoroughgoing rationalist (*e.g.*, Royce) holds, as I understand him, that the bare existential fact *qua* fact *is* itself of the *nature* of truth, *i.e.*, is already, externally at least, an absorbed element in a

[31] James, *The Meaning of Truth*, pp. viii–x.

truth (and therefore intellectual) system. Now Strong (and many of your other critics) do *not* hold this any more than you do. Strong's "true that Napoleon landed" can only be an elliptic statement for, "the idea or belief is true." Now it seems to me that we need only hold the critics (of the non-absolute-idealism type) up to the distinction between brute existences or occurrences (which certainly are not "truths") and the intellectual . . . statements *about* those existences (to which alone the character of truth-falsity does appertain), to make them see that the confusion lies with them, and that truth (and not merely truthfulness) may well be a relation between the *effects* of the existence in question and the *effects* of the intellectual position or assertion in question. . . .

You will pardon this suggestion, I hope, but it seems to me that to concede, for the sake of better understanding, to the critic that a happening is the same as a truth, is to admit the very point in which his own confusion resides, and, by encouraging him in that confusion to prevent exactly the better understanding which you have aimed at? [32]

This was excellent polemic advice from a skilled dialectician, but it was too much for James. He was beginning to weary of the whole "truth" controversy and was pointing out that for him pragmatism was merely a methodological preliminary for the fruitful discussion of his real philosophy—radical empiricism. Let Schiller and Dewey make a philosophy, if they chose to do so, out of what to him was merely a "method of conducting discussions."

What do we mean by "truth"? What is it known-as? Those are questions which if once opened up for discussion, will make each side respect the other a little more. I am amused at the way *my* name has been dragged in as that of the father of all this way of thinking. I recognize it as a continuation of partial thoughts which I have expressed; but "pragmatism" never meant for me more than a method of conducting discussions (a sovereign method, it is true), and the tremendous scope which you and Dewey have given to the conception has exceeded my more timid philosophizing. I welcome it, and admire it, but I can't yet think out certain parts of it; although something inside of me feels sure that they can be successfully thought out, and that it will then be a great day for Philosophic Man. . . .

I must be very damp powder, slow to burn, and I must be terribly respectful of other people, for I confess that it is only after reading these things (in spite of all you have written to the same effect, and in spite of your tone of

[32] Perry, *The Thought and Character of William James*, II, 530, 531.

announcing judgment to a sinful world), that I seem to have grasped the full import for life and regeneration, the *great* perspective of the program, and the renovating character for *all things,* of Humanism; and the outwornness as of a scarecrow's garments, simulating life by flapping in the wind of nightfall, of all intellectualism, and the blindness and deadness of all who worship intellectualist idols. . . . It is queer to be assisting at the *éclosion* of a great new mental epoch, life, religion, and philosophy in one. . . .

It is important to show the public that the function of concepts is practical, but it disconcerts the beginner to be told that the very concepts you use in doing so are themselves deliquescent; and after all, our experience ought to have by this time established *some* of them in pragmatic solidity. . . . I thus pedagogically insert the thin end of the wedge with which you [Schiller] and Dewey are engaged in splitting up the whole thickness of the cake of epistemology. There is room for both of our methods; but the result of your notes and criticisms will be to make me confess more explicitly to the provisionality of my forms of statement.[33]

"To show the public that the function of concepts is practical" was indeed important for John Dewey and his "Chicago school." Dewey had been from the beginning preoccupied with the logic of practice and had discovered in James's *Psychology* the instrumentalist logic that revolutionized his own ethical theory. An early letter from Dewey to James, following the publication in 1891 of his *Outlines of a Critical Theory of Ethics,* reveals how James helped him to free himself from "preceptual ethics."

The present preceptual structure is so great, and such a weighty thing, both in theory and in practice, that I don't anticipate any success for the book, but when one man like yourself expresses what you wrote me, the book has already succeeded.

But unless a man is already living in the gospel and not under the law, as you express it, words thrown at him are idle wind. He doesn't understand what you mean, and he wouldn't believe you meant it, if he did understand. The hope seems to be with the rising generation. . . . Many of my students, I find, are fairly hungering. They almost jump at any opportunity to get out from under the load and to believe in their own lives. . . .

I don't know that I told you that I have had a class of four graduates going through your psychology this year, and how much we have all enjoyed

[33] *Ibid.,* pp. 502, 505, 512.

it. I'm sure you would be greatly gratified if you could see what a stimulus to mental freedom, as well as what a purveyor of methods and materials, your book has been to us.[34]

While James was thus helping Dewey to formulate a "psychological ethics" based, not on precepts, but on actual, active, desires, another friend, a journalist named Franklin Ford, was showing him how from a social perspective, too, intelligence and morals could be treated as a subject for experimental investigation. In the Preface to his 1891 *Ethics* Dewey had called attention particularly " . . . to the idea of desire as the ideal activity in contrast with actual possession; to the analysis of individuality into function including capacity and environment; to the treatment of the social bearings of science and art (a point concerning which I am indebted to my friend, Mr. Franklin Ford)." [35] He now abandoned the whole system, which he had laboriously and abstrusely constructed on the basis of dynamic idealism, and developed a new system (and course) of ethics, in two parts, psychological ethics and social ethics. It was in the double frame of reference of this ethical system that Dewey and his colleagues conceived the famous *Studies in Logical Theory* (1903), which marked the rise of the "Chicago school" of instrumentalism.

We have already noted the biological and evolutionary reconstruction of idealism which had been going on in and around Dewey at Michigan and Chicago.[36] He was accustomed to thinking of thought as activity and of the laws of thought as laws of movement or development. He had also worked out, in dialectical terms, the mediating function of judgment. When James's *Psychology* appeared, with its doctrine of the teleological nature of essences, and Peirce's articles on "evolutionary love," with their doctrine of universals as embodied in habits, he realized that the interpretation of the categories as "regulative ideas" for action could be generalized and applied to all ideas. All ideas are teleological or instrumental; the analysis of this thesis could now be shifted from the ground of genetic speculation to the ground of empirical psychology. Dewey was thus prepared to describe the "mediation" of experience in terms of the "reflex-arc concept" and to abandon the idealistic metaphysics of activity for a physiological

[34] *Ibid.*, p. 517.
[35] Cited in *ibid.*, p. 518*n*.
[36] See above, pp. 389, 477.

analysis of an act of judgment. The first systematic expositions of this theory were made simultaneously by Dewey, in his article, "Logical Conditions of a Scientific Treatment of Morality," by Mead, in his article, "The Definition of the Psychical," and by A. W. Moore, in his article, "Some Logical Aspects of Purpose." Of these, Moore's approach was the most direct and simple; he pointed out that both Royce and James take ideas to be purposive, but that they fail to explain precisely what happens when an experience of "restlessness and dissatisfaction," of "capricious, baffling, brute reality," is transformed into an experience of "fulfilled meaning." In detail he criticizes Royce for appealing vaguely to absolute experience instead of working out his problem carefully.

This absolutely "fragmentary" character of human experience is an abstraction of the relatively disintegrated condition into which experience temporarily falls, which abstraction is then reinstated, as a fixed quality, overlooking the fact that experience becomes fragmentary only that it may again become whole. The absolute system, the final fulfilment, is in the same case. It too is but the hypostatized abstraction of the function of becoming whole, of wholing and fulfilling, which manifests itself in the "pauses of satisfaction." . . .

Restlessness is not generated in a vacuum. But why should this activity get into a condition to be described as "indefinite restlessness" and dissatisfaction?

Repugnant as it will be to many to have psycho-physical, to say nothing of biological, doctrines introduced into a logical discussion, I confess that, at this point facing the issue squarely, I see no other way. And it appears to me that just at this point it is the fear of phenomenalistic giants that has kept logic wandering so many years into the wilderness. . . .

Precisely because, then, the idea "as a plan" is projected and constructed in response to this restlessness must its fulfilment be relevant to it. It is when the idea as a purpose, a plan, born out of this matrix of restlessness, begins to aspire to the absolute system, and attempts to ignore or repudiate its lowly antecedents, that the difficulties concerning fulfilment begin. They are the difficulties that beset every ambition which aspires to things foreign to its inherited powers and equipment. . . .

Surely not in "a certain absolute system of ideas," which is "the object of love and hope, of desire and will, of faith and work, but never of present finding," shall we seek [reality]. Rather precisely in the loving and hoping, desiring and willing, believing and working, shall we find that reality in which and for which both the "World as fact" and the "World as idea" have their being.[37]

Dewey's article "The Logical Conditions of a Scientific Treatment of Morality" was less polemical against absolute idealism and more concerned to break down the Kantian dualism between judgments of fact and judgments of value. He developed the doctrine that ideas or universals can be located in experience as plans or habits of decision and that this functional approach to the nature of ideas in experience emphasizes not only continuity between action and judgment, but also between scientific and ethical judgment. He refers specifically to Peirce's theory as coming "along diverse lines" to the same results.

The generic propositions or universals of science can take effect . . . only through the medium of the habits and impulsive tendencies of the one who judges. They have no *modus operandi* of their own. . . .

So far as I know, Mr. Charles S. Peirce was the first to call attention to this principle, and to insist upon its fundamental logical import (see *Monist*, Vol. II, pp. 534–36, 549–56). Mr. Peirce states it as the principle of continuity: A past idea can operate only so far as it is psychically continuous with that upon which it operates. A general idea is simply a living and expanding feeling, and habit is a statement of the specific mode of operation of a given psychical continuum. I have reached the above conclusion along such diverse lines that, without in any way minimizing the priority of Mr. Peirce's statement, or its more generalized logical character, I feel that my own statement has something of the value of an independent confirmation. . . .

All generic scientific propositions, all statements of laws, all equations and formulae, are strictly normative in character, having as their sole excuse for being, and their sole test of worth, their capacity to regulate descriptions of individual cases. And the view that they are shorthand registers, or abstract descriptions, confirms instead of refuting this view. Why make a shorthand and unreal statement if it does not operate instrumentally in firsthand dealings with reality? . . .

So far as the scientific judgment is identified as an act, all *a priori* reason disappears for drawing a line between the logic of the material of the recognized sciences and that of conduct. . . .

The point of view which is here presented is, of course, distinctly pragmatic. I am not quite sure, however, of the implications of certain forms of

[37] John Dewey, *Studies in Logical Theory* (Chicago, 1903), pp. 369, 374, 375, 382.

pragmatism. They sometimes seem to imply that a rational or logical statement is all right up to a certain point, but has fixed external limits, so that
at critical points recourse must be had to considerations which are distinctly
of an irrational or extralogical order, and this recourse is identified with
choice and "activity." The practical and the logical are thus opposed to each
other. It is just the opposite which I am endeavoring to sustain, viz., that
the logical is an inherent or organic expression of the practical, and hence
is fulfilling its own logical basis and aim when it functions practically. I have
no desire to show that what we term "science" is arbitrarily limited by *outside* ethical considerations; and that consequently science cannot intrude itself into the ethical sphere; but precisely the contrary, viz., that just because
science is a mode of controlling our active relations with the world of experienced things, ethical experience is supremely in need of such regulation.
And by "practical" I mean only regulated change in experienced values.[38]

In his *Studies in Logical Theory* Dewey then proceeded to apply
this instrumentalist theory of ideas to the theory of logical objects.
He put his argument in the form of a critique of Lotze's *Logic,* in
order that he might make clear how he could agree with the objective
idealists' criticisms of Lotze's radical separation of thought from its
subject matter, without falling into their own conclusion that thought
must be "constitutive" of reality. By showing that ideas, abstractions,
or "logical objects" have a specific role in experience, namely, to
clarify confused activities, he could avoid Lotze's dualism of thought
versus reality without asserting the idealist doctrine that reality is
thought. This meant to Dewey and his colleagues not merely the
emancipation of the theory of knowledge from idealism but also from
metaphysics of any kind. They had a science of intelligence.

Had William James lived to see the publication in 1938 of Dewey's
Logic; the Theory of Inquiry, in which the experimentalist theory of
knowledge is given its completest expression, he might have seen in
this volume an approximation, at least, to that "immortal work" which
he did not live to write; Dewey's *Logic* embodies many of James's
specifications. He wrote.

I want to write and publish, if I can do it, another immortal work, less
popular but more original than *Pragmatism,* which latter no one seems
rightly to understand,—representing it as a philosophy got up for the use of

[38] John Dewey, *Logical Conditions of a Scientific Treatment of Morality* (Chicago,
1903), pp. 14, 14*n*, 13*n*, 13, 10*n*.

engineers, electricians and doctors, whereas it really grew up from a more subtle and delicate theoretic analysis of the function of knowing than previous philosophers had been willing to make.[39]

— 40 —

EXPERIENCE AND NATURE

WHILE William James was working away at his "natural science" of psychology, he was consciously dismissing metaphysical problems—dismissing them, not from his own mind, where they were firmly lodged, but from his science of mind. He intended first of all to be empirical in the methodological sense, and he informed the reader of his *Principles of Psychology*, from time to time, that he was postponing certain problems which could not be settled by empirical evidence to "the end of the work," but when he came to the end and wrote his final metaphysical chapter, "Necessary Truths and the Effects of Experience," he could not possibly treat all the postponed problems; the most he could do was to state the form into which the problems arising in experience must be cast in order to make them problems about natural fact. He formulated this "philosophical" problem as follows:

We distinguish . . . between the empirical order of things, and their rational order of comparison; and, so far as possible, we seek to translate the former into the latter, as being the more congenial of the two to our intellect. . . .

Any assimilation of things to terms between which such classificatory relations, with their remote and mediate transactions, obtain, is a way of bringing the things into a more rational scheme. . . .

There is thus a large body of *a priori* or intuitively necessary truths. As a rule, these are truths of *comparison* only, and in the first instance they express relations between merely mental terms. Nature, however, acts as if some of her realities were identical with these mental terms. So far as she does this, we can make *a priori* propositions concerning natural fact. The aim of both science and philosophy is to make the identifiable terms more

[39] Perry, *The Thought and Character of William James*, II, 468.

numerous. So far it has proved easier to identify nature's things with mental terms of the mechanical than with mental terms of the sentimental order.

The widest postulate of rationality is that the world *is* rationally intelligible throughout, after the pattern of *some* ideal system. The whole war of the philosophies is over that point of faith.[1]

James was thus prepared to enter "the war of the philosophies" with the attempt to construct an "ideal system" more inclusive than the mechanical system and less rigid than the system of absolute theism. This system he would call "radical empiricism"; it would not be a methodology, but an interpretation of nature as "identifiable with mental terms."

To clear the decks of nonempirical, "metaphysical" problems, he devised pragmatism; it was intended to facilitate and clarify "philosophical discussion." Unfortunately, it did the opposite; it became one more bone of contention and one more scheme for "justifying" unverifiable faiths. Amid the confusions and distractions of the methodological strife, James made what progress he could on his philosophical system.

A more serious obstacle than pragmatism was the problem of the nature of consciousness, which had haunted James, as it haunted his contemporaries, and which he never solved to his own satisfaction. The *function* of consciousness he had analyzed adequately; consciousness is a "fighter for ends," or at least "it seemed to be so." But the *being* of consciousness—what could it be? His own account of his struggle with this problem is an amusing revelation of how difficult it is to be radically empirical. He had succeeded in describing consciousness as a "stream," as something continuous, whose parts were organically related and which might, therefore, be expected to function as an "organ." But when he attempted to fit this unified mental activity into a physical world, whose elements were atomic and whose relations were "external," he saw the hopelessness of his task.

On the principles of the corpuscular or mechanical philosophy, the only realities are the separate molecules, or at most the cells. Their aggregation into a "brain" is a fiction of popular speech. Such a fiction cannot serve as the objectively real counterpart to any psychic state whatever. Only a

---

[1] William James, *The Principles of Psychology* (New York, 1890), II, 676, 677.

genuinely physical fact can so serve. But the molecular fact is the only genuine physical fact—whereupon we seem, if we are to have an elementary psycho-physic law at all, thrust right back upon something like the mind-stuff theory, for the molecular fact, being an element of the "brain," would seem naturally to correspond, not to the total thoughts, but to elements in the thought.

What shall we do? Many would find relief at this point in celebrating the mystery of the Unknowable and the "awe" which we should feel at having such a principle to take final charge of our perplexities. Others would rejoice that the finite and separatist view of things with which we started had at last developed its contradictions, and was about to lead us dialectically upwards to some "higher synthesis" in which inconsistencies cease from troubling and logic is at rest. It may be a constitutional infirmity, but I can take no comfort in such devices for making a luxury of intellectual defeat. They are but spiritual chloroform. Better live on the ragged edge, better gnaw the file forever! . . .

Many readers have certainly been saying to themselves for the last few pages: "Why on earth doesn't the poor man say *the Soul* and have done with it?" . . .

The Soul invoked, far from making the phenomena more intelligible, can only be made intelligible itself by borrowing their form,—it must be represented, if at all, as a transcendent stream of consciousness duplicating the one we know.

Altogether, the Soul is an outbirth of that sort of philosophizing whose great maxim, according to Dr. Hodgson, is: "Whatever you are *totally* ignorant of, assert to be the explanation of everything else." . . .

. . . it is logically impossible that the same thing should be *known as the same* by two successive copies of the same thought. As a matter of fact, the thoughts by which we know that we mean the same thing are apt to be very different indeed from each other. We think the thing now in one context, now in another; now in a definite image, now in a symbol. . . . but nevertheless we always *do* know which of all possible subjects we have in mind. Introspective psychology must here throw up the sponge; the fluctuations of subjective life are too exquisite to be arrested by its coarse means. It must confine itself to bearing witness to the fact that all sorts of different subjective states do form the vehicle by which the same is known . . .

In the successive judgments, all sorts of new operations are performed on the things, and all sorts of new results brought out, without the sense of the main topic ever getting lost. At the outset, we merely *have* the topic; then we *operate* on it; and finally we have it again in a richer and truer way. A compound conception has been substituted for the simple one, but with full consciousness that both are of the Same. . . .

The result of the thoughts' operating on the data given to sense is to transform the order in which experience *comes* into an entirely different order, that of the *conceived* world.[2]

These fields of experience that replace each other so punctually, each knowing the same matter, but in ever-widening contexts, from simplest feeling up to absolute knowledge, *can* they have no *being* in common when their cognitive function is so manifestly common? The regular succession of them is on such terms an unintelligible miracle. If you reply that their common *object* is of itself enough to make the many witnesses continuous, the same implacable logic follows you—how *can* one and the same object appear so variously? . . .

Sincerely, and patiently as I could, I struggled with the problem for years, covering hundreds of sheets of paper with notes and memoranda and discussions with myself over the difficulty. How can many consciousnesses be at the same time one consciousness? How can one and the same identical fact experience itself so diversely? The struggle was vain; I found myself in an *impasse*. I saw that I must either forswear that "psychology without a soul" to which my whole psychological and kantian education had committed me,—I must, in short, bring back distinct spiritual agents to know the mental states, now singly and now in combination, in a word bring back scholasticism and common sense—or else I must squarely confess the solution of the problem impossible, and then either give up my intellectualistic logic, the logic of identity, and adopt some higher (or lower) form of rationality, or, finally, face the fact that life is logically irrational. . . .

For my own part, I have finally found myself compelled to *give up the logic*, fairly, squarely, and irrevocably. It has an imperishable use in human life, but that use is not to make us theoretically acquainted with the essential nature of reality. . . .

I should not now be emancipated, not now subordinate logic with so very light a heart, or throw it out of the deeper regions of philosophy to take its rightful and respectable place in the world of simple human practice, if I had not been influenced by a comparatively young and very original french writer, Professor Henri Bergson. Reading his works is what has made me bold. . . .

The particular intellectualistic difficulty that had held my own thought so long in a vise was . . . the impossibility of understanding how "your" experience and "mine," which "as such" are defined as not conscious of

[2] *Ibid.*, I, 178–79, 180, 347, 480, 481, 482.

each other, can nevertheless at the same time be members of a world-experience defined expressly as having all its parts co-conscious, or known together.[3]

What made James's dilemma so hopeless was that in the twenty years intervening between his *Psychology* and his *Pluralistic Universe* he had given up the assumption, which was at the time of the *Psychology* "the fundamental assumption of *every* philosophic school," that consciousness is a distinct order of existence and had adopted a relational theory of consciousness. There are indications that even in the *Psychology* he had his doubts about this orthodox assumption and that he saw the possibility of escaping from the dilemma of parallelism by the unconventional "back door" of denying that the two types of existence are external to each other, but he could not decide which of the two is primary. Throughout the *Psychology* he alternates between the functional, biological approach and the introspective, "stream of thought" approach. Both were empirical, but they were compatible only so long as James ruled out "philosophical" issues and pretended to be concerned with a positivistic, natural science. Every reader knew, and James even better than his readers, that he would be obliged sooner or later to take a stand on the metaphysical question.

The decision came in 1904, with the publication of his article "Does 'Consciousness' Exist?" which constitutes the opening chapter of his *Essays in Radical Empiricism*. Here, too, James tells his own history.

I have got to working altogether outside of psychological lines, as some articles which I have recently sent you will show. I am interested in a metaphysical system ("Radical Empiricism") which has been forming itself within me, more interested, in fact, than I have ever been in anything else . . .[4]

For twenty years past I have mistrusted "consciousness" as an entity; for seven or eight years past I have suggested its non-existence to my students, and tried to give them its pragmatic equivalent in realities of experience. It seems to me that the hour is ripe for it to be openly and universally discarded.

To deny plumply that "consciousness" exists seems so absurd on the face

[3] William James, *A Pluralistic Universe* (New York, 1908), 206, 207–8, 212, 214, 221.

[4] Ralph Barton Perry, *The Thought and Character of William James* (Boston, 1935), II, 387.

of it—for undeniably "thoughts" do exist—that I fear some readers will follow me no farther. Let me then immediately explain that I mean only to deny that the word stands for an entity, but to insist most emphatically that it does stand for a function. . . .

To be radical, an empiricism must neither admit into his constructions any element that is not directly experienced, nor exclude from them any element that is directly experienced. For such a philosophy, *the relations that connect experiences must themselves be experienced relations, and any kind of relation experienced must be accounted as "real" as anything else in the system.* . . .

Now, ordinary empiricism, in spite of the fact that conjunctive and disjunctive relations present themselves as being fully co-ordinate parts of experience, has always shown a tendency to do away with the connections of things, and to insist most on the disjunctions. . . .

Continuity here is a definite sort of experience; just as definite as is the *discontinuity-experience* which I find it impossible to avoid when I seek to make the transition from an experience of my own to one of yours. In this latter case I have to get on and off again, to pass from a thing lived to another thing only conceived, and the break is positively experienced.[5]

What James did, in effect, was to expand his psychological doctrine of continuity in consciousness into a metaphysical doctrine of continuity in being between "things and thoughts." He conceived of the common world in which we exist as both things and thinkers as "a world of pure experience," a world of experience which is, at the same time, no one's experience exclusively. He was helped in defending such a postulate of "neutral" experience by the use of pragmatic argument.

Your objects are over and over again the same as mine. If I ask you *where* some object of yours is, our old Memorial Hall, for example, you point to *my* Memorial Hall with *your* hand which I see. If you alter an object in your world, put out a candle, for example, when I am present, *my* candle *ipso facto* goes out. It is only as altering my objects that I guess you to exist. If your objects do not coalesce with my objects, if they be not identically where mine are, they must be proved to be positively somewhere else. But no other location can be assigned for them, so their place must be what it seems to be, the same.

---

[5] James, *Essays in Radical Empiricism*, 3, 42, 42–43, 49.

Practically, then, our minds meet in a world of objects which they share in common.[6]

If radical empiricism were merely the common-sense, realistic view that "our minds meet in a world of objects," there would be less novelty in it as a metaphysics than there is in the pragmatic method by which it is defended. But for James a mind could not be "directly experienced" unless it were felt; the world of feeling was ultimate for his empiricism, and even after he had abandoned belief in the existence of consciousness, he put emphasis on *feelings* of activity, of effort, of relation. He emphasized the domain of emotional experience because it was traditionally excluded by naturalists from the objective world and because he agreed with Royce that experience can be unified in "the world of appreciation" more immediately than in "the world of description."

The world is surely the *total* world, including our mental reaction. The world *minus* that is an abstraction, useful for certain purposes, but always envelopable. Pure naturalism is surely envelopable in wider teleological or appreciative determinations. Most men try so to surround it. You talk as if from the point of view of truth such trials were condemned in advance. But we pragmatists not only justify them, but say that the constitution of the world of naturalistic truth itself can only be understood by bringing it into line with the appreciative truth.[7]

He now saw the psychological possibility of the "meeting of minds" in the sense of "the compounding" of consciousness or the merging of personal experience in a "mother sea" of consciousness. He had always taken panpsychism seriously, and he now feared that he might be forced into the position of a psychic monism in which individuality is lost as utterly as in the "absolute experience" of the idealists or the ocean of nirvana. How could he defend his "pluralistic universe" and individualism, if he admitted the "compounding" of minds? Was his metaphysics of continuity endangering the indeterminism of his moral philosophy?

The absolute is not the impossible being I once thought it. Mental facts

[6] *Ibid.*, p. 79.
[7] Perry, *The Thought and Character of William James*, II, 476.

do function both singly and together, at once, and we finite minds may simultaneously be co-conscious with one another in a superhuman intelligence. It is only the extravagant claims of coercive necessity on the absolute's part that have to be denied by *a priori* logic. As an hypothesis trying to make itself probable on analogical and inductive grounds, the absolute is entitled to a patient hearing. . . .

In spite of rationalism's disdain for the particular, the personal, and the unwholesome, the drift of all the evidence we have seems to me to sweep us very strongly towards the belief in some form of superhuman life with which we may, unknown to ourselves, be co-conscious. We may be in the universe as dogs and cats are in our libraries, seeing the books and hearing the conversation, but having no inkling of the meaning of it all.[8]

William James speculated in this fashion to the end; his empiricism was tempered by his marvelous imagination and extreme tolerance. Anything *logically* possible seemed to appeal to him as a suggestion worth taking seriously; it was his mind rather than his experience that kept his universe open.

Peirce's empirical metaphysics of continuity took a decidedly different direction from that of James. His philosophical system was not a metapsychological account of experience, but rather a map of experience made as a preliminary to scientific inquiry. It was his substitute for the transcendental deduction of the categories. He called it phenomenology, or phaneroscopy. A phenomenon, or phaneron, is, in Peirce's usage, any object of the mind regardless of its reality. The observation of the most general traits of experience is a discipline imposed on us by experience itself, for we are compelled by facts to reconstruct our world of fancy in order to anticipate and govern future disturbances.

We live in two worlds, a world of fact and a world of fancy. Each of us is accustomed to think that he is the creator of his world of fancy; that he has but to pronounce his fiat, and the thing exists, with no resistance and no effort; and although this is so far from the truth that I doubt not that much the greater part of the reader's labor is expended on the world of fancy, yet it is near enough the truth for a first approximation. For this reason we call the world of fancy the internal world, the world of fact the external world. In this latter we are masters, each of us, of his own voluntary muscles, and

[8] James, *Essays in Radical Empiricism; a Pluralistic Universe*, II, 292–93, 309.

of nothing more. But man is sly, and contrives to make this little more than he needs. Beyond that, he defends himself from the angles of hard fact by clothing himself with a garment of contentment and of habituation. Were it not for this garment, he would every now and then find his internal world rudely disturbed and his fiats set at naught by brutal inroads of ideas from without. I call such forcible modification of our ways of thinking the influence of the world of fact or *experience*. But he patches up his garment by guessing what those inroads are likely to be and carefully excluding from his internal world every idea which is likely to be so disturbed. Instead of waiting for experience to come at untoward times, he provokes it when it can do no harm and changes the government of his internal world accordingly.[9]

Phenomenology is the first of three parts of philosophy and is related to the sciences according to the following scheme.

I. *Theoretical Science*
   1. *Inquiry* (sciences of observation)
      a. Mathematics (observation of imaginary objects)
      b. Philosophy (coenoscopic observation, i.e., ordinary observation, requiring no special instruments, or techniques)
         (1) Necessary (observation of universal experience)
            (*a*) Phenomenology
            (*b*) Normative sciences (logic, ethics, esthetics)
            (*c*) Metaphysics (called by the ancients "physics," coenoscopic natural science)
         (2) "Vitally important truths and sentimental conservatism" "All sensible talk about vitally important topics must be commonplace, all reasoning about them unsound, and all study of them narrow and sordid." [10]
   2. *Review*
II. *Practical Science*
      "Pedagogics, gold-beating, etiquette, pigeon-fancying, vulgar arithmetic, horology, surveying, navigation, etc. . . . I must confess to being utterly bewildered by its motley crowd." [11]

By "coenscopic observation" of the most universal aspects of universal experience we discover three categories: quality, fact, and thought,

[9] Peirce, *Collected Papers*, (Cambridge, 1931–35), I, 321.   [10] *Ibid.*, I, 677.
[11] *Ibid.*, I, 243.

which for convenience's sake Peirce labels firstness, secondness, and thirdness.

Though Peirce's theory of categories can be traced back to 1860, when he distinguished in mathematics between icons, indices, and symbols, and to 1867, when he classified "characters" into qualities, relations, and representations,[12] he began his systematic phenomenology about 1890, when he drafted a work entitled "A Guess at the Riddle." He remarked at the beginning of his draft, "And this book, if ever written, as it soon will be if I am in a situation to do it, will be one of the births of time." [13] This first draft might well be described, continuing his own metaphor, as labor pains; in it he indulges in many ingenious speculations, applying his three categories to all kinds of particular subject matter, from the syllogism to protoplasm. But during the nineties he developed the doctrine more systematically in connection with the logic of mathematics; in 1902 phenomenology became a prominent part of his "Minute Logic," and in 1903 it was embodied into the "Lectures on Pragmatism."

Peirce's phaneroscopy should not be identified with what is now generally known as phenomenology. It is not the phenomenology of any particular subject matter, least of all is it the phenomenology of phenomena. It is not "the statement of what appears," but "the study of what seems"; it is an analysis, not an assertion of fact or a mere description of the given. It resembles other phenomenologies in that it does not involve a theory of reality. As Peirce elaborated the doctrine, he distinguished between the purely formal analysis of phenomena and their material analysis. The basic formal structures are monads, dyads, and polyads, but all polyads can be analyzed into compound triads. Monads are individuals; dyads are polar relatives; triads are comprehensions. For example, if I may venture a mathematical illustration not employed by Peirce, given three points, A, B,

[12] *Ibid.*, I, 560–67. Peirce relates how, as a youth, he was led by his father, the mathematician, to study Kant's doctrine of the categories, how he came to the conclusion that Kant was right in asserting that the categories of thought have a sort of dependence on formal logic, and how he then proceeded through a study of Aristotle and Duns Scotus to a logical and metaphysical realism. His paper "On a New List of Categories" was published in the *Proceedings* of the American Academy of Arts and Sciences for 1867. In 1893 he intended to make it Chapter I of his "Grand Logic."

[13] *Ibid.*, I, 181*n.* See also above, pp. 335–36.

and C, the points are each monads; the end points of the lines AB, BC, and AC, taken as pairs, are dyads, and the area of the triangle ABC is a triad. When these structural distinctions, which are applicable universally to any phenomenon, are interpreted as material "elements" of any phenomenon, they yield the basic "metaphysical" distinctions of quality, fact, and law. Feelings, for example, in their qualitative uniqueness are individuals, not events or facts, and they are as such timeless, repeatable, "mere may-bes not necessarily realized," not logically general, not even pleasures or pains; they are "suchness" without any occurrence. "Mere may-being gets along without any realization at all." [14] Facts, events, existences, however, are by nature dyadic, polar, involving struggle, tension, will. Ideas or meanings are triads, involving representation, generality, habit. Thus, we may distinguish metaphysically three basic types of being: possibility, existence, generality.

Occasionally Peirce suggested that the categories evolved out of each other, and he thus attempted to link his phenomenology with his theory of evolution.

When I say nullity consists of the possibility of the monad; that the unit consists of the possibility of the dyad, and the like, such statements have a Hegelian sound. Undoubtedly they are intrinsically of that nature. I follow an order of evolution in such phrases, the possibility evolves the actuality. So does Hegel. He reaches each category from the last preceding by virtually calling "next!" What his process [is] of making the next come and of recognizing it when it emerges is, however important it may be, yet, comparatively speaking a detail, wherein I sometimes agree with the great idealist and sometimes diverge from his footsteps—for my own method has resulted from a more deliberate examination of the exact theory of logic (in which Hegel's age, and especially his own country, and more especially he himself were decidedly weak), and consequently has a broader form, capable of diversification to adapt itself to the special form of the germinal conception. It is not yet time to formulate it. I apply it; the reader follows it with approval if he can. [15]

This passage is probably to be interpreted as a half-serious attempt to outdo Hegel's *Phenomenology*. Peirce, with his exquisite sense of humor, played with his categories to the end of his life; they proved

[14] *Ibid.*, I, 304.   [15] *Ibid.*, I, 453.

an excellent toy. It is probably more just to him to follow the phenomenology speculatively into its possible applications, rather than to attempt to make of his many excursions into the metaphysical wilderness a straight, smooth highway of doctrine. Peirce was fond of "leading principles," but he seemed singularly indifferent to the directions in which they led him.

Another "seminal mind" among the metaphysicians of radical empiricism was George H. Mead. Mead was first of all a social psychologist; [16] he had learned to conceive mind, not in terms of individual consciousness, but in terms of social acts. He might easily have been tempted to follow idealists like Royce (his teacher) in what he called "the grandiose undertaking to bring the whole of reality within experience" and to construct a theory of reality based on the structure of an absolute community. But he did the opposite. He interpreted the emergence of communities and minds as one instance of a more general process of natural emergence. Experience and reality must, according to him, both be understood as existents, and "to exist" means to be in a temporal present, to have a past and a future. A temporal present is the ultimate form and locus of existence, and "the world is a world of events." The endless emerging of novelties, the participation in natural occurrences and passing perspectives, the precarious being of becoming—this is what it means to be. Such passing and plural presents do not take place in any eternal order of nature. Nature as a whole is unintelligible and an eternal present is a contradiction in terms. The objectivity of existence and knowledge must, therefore, be found here and now, in the interrelations or relativity of perspectives. Since experience is neither absolute nor subjective, it can be objective, in the sense that objectivity is understood in the theory of relativity. It is both relational and fluid, organic and temporal.

According to Mead, reality is an aggregate of temporal perspectives or "situations," each situation being as ultimate as any, and each being defined in terms of some novelty or "repugnant fact" which demands a reconstruction of inherited perspectives before it can be assimilated to an objective order. Each situation or present has its own past, which though it is irrevocable as an existent is being continually

[16] See the account of his psychology above, pp. 391–93.

reinterpreted and recovered. Each present also has its own future, which the present tries to anticipate, but which as it comes into existence brings new events, new perspectives, and hence creates new situations. Life is thus just one situation after another, and, what is worse, one situation in another. Any event is complicated by being relative to several perspectives. Whenever events are re-presented, participating in the activities of several presents, the possibility of community and experience emerges. Communities of experience have two primary dimensions: the temporal dimension is mental, being the review of the past in view of the future, and the spatial or "distance" dimension is the "area of manipulation." By the reconstruction of the past and by the reception of distant things into the acts of an organism, the mechanism of multiple perspectives is created, which makes it possible for one present to see itself as others see it and thus to attain self-knowledge. With such an increase in the "radius of manipulation" natural processes are significantly transformed. Motions become symbolical reactions, masses become social environments, and individuals become selves. Thus, the emergence of intelligent experience among natural processes is itself an event which changes a natural "situation" enormously, but never completely destroys its temporal and contingent character.

The cogredient world answers to the organization of response with reference to any possible action. A moving object within that field, if it is an object of attention, introduces an attitude of adjustment. With every change of position of the object, there is a suggested congruous reconstruction of the landscape. The degree of reconstruction depends upon the scope of suggested responses which the moving object entails. . . .

We live in a universe whose past changes with every considerable change in our scientific account of it, and yet we are prone to look for the meaning of our biological and social life in fixed forms of historical institutions and the order of past events. We prefer to understand the family, the state, the church, and the school by forms which history has given to their social structures rather than by finding the meaning of the history of the institutions in the functions and services which our social science exhibits.

The whole development of social institutions has, however, moved away from the theological interpretation and has found the meaning of life in the present rather than in the past and in the future. A metaphysics of the type of pragmatism was a natural American outgrowth. It is entirely in harmony with the will to power through the understanding of nature.[17]

The emphasis on social acts and moral conduct characterizes most of Mead's metaphysics, but with the growth of relativism in modern natural science and the construction of systems of naturalistic realism such as those of Whitehead, Russell, and McGilvary, he was stimulated to apply his "philosophy of the act" to physical science. In his Carus Lectures *The Philosophy of the Present,* published in 1932, shortly after his death, he sketched what amounts to a pragmatic rendering of Whitehead's *Process and Reality,* and he gave a more detailed analysis of his radical relativism in a series of remarkable essays, chief of them being "The Experimental Basis of Natural Science" and "The Process of Mind in Nature." These essays are extremely difficult to read, for they reflect, in addition to the clumsy "functional" language of the early days of the Chicago school, his groping for new concepts of scientific method which would overcome both the Newtonian "bifurcation of nature" and the realists' abstractions from experience. But with all their difficulties and exploratory excursions these essays represent the most thoroughgoing attempt made by a radical empiricist to construct a metaphysics for physics.

What Mead tried to do for natural science Dewey, in his Carus Lectures, *Experience and Nature* (1925), tried to do for man's less technical transactions with nature. The most "practical" and common concerns of human existence, which Peirce dismissed as too "bewildering" and which Mead refined beyond recognition, are here treated with extraordinary directness, informality, and urbanity. Dewey's lectures can scarcely be regarded as a system of metaphysics, but they do more justice to more phases of human life than any other American contribution to radical empiricism has as yet done.[18] There is no attempt made to describe nature as such, and hence there will probably always be those who will interpret his philosophy of human existence

[17] George Herbert Mead, *The Philosophy of the Act* (Chicago, 1938), pp. 228, 626.

[18] "Although Dewey's book is incredibly ill written, it seemed to me after several rereadings to have a feeling of intimacy with the inside of the cosmos that I found unequaled. So me-thought God would have spoken had He been inarticulate but keenly desirous to tell you how it was." Oliver Wendell Holmes, *Holmes-Pollock Letters* (Cambridge, 1941), II, 287.

as a theory of nature tainted with subjectivism. But Dewey, like George S. Morris and the other Michigan idealists, had always taken the existence of the so-called "external" world for granted and had never regarded the *existence* of nature as open to serious question. As early as 1909 Dewey wrote to James that his "instrumental theory of knowledge is clearly self-contradictory unless there are independent existences of which ideas take account and for the transformation of which they function." And he added, "I have repeated *ad nauseam* that there are existences prior to and subsequent to cognitive states and purposes, and that *the whole meaning of the latter* is the way they intervene in the control and revaluation of the independent existences." [19] Nevertheless, there was in Dewey's thinking a gradual drift toward naturalism, not in the sense that he developed a theory of nature, but in the sense that he became increasingly aware of the ontological implications of his theory of human existence. In 1907 he wrote to James:

My own views are much more naturalistic, and a reaction against not merely intellectualistic and monistic idealism but against all idealisms, except, of course, in the sense of ethical ideals. Now, I seem to myself to be nearer you than I am to Schiller on this point, yet I am not sure. On the other hand, Schiller in his later writings seems to emphasize that the good consequence which is the test of an idea, is *good* not so much in its own nature as in meeting the claims of the idea, whatever the idea is. And here I seem to be nearer to him than to you.[20]

What Dewey and Mead called "the active process" seemed to them so comprehensive, embracing both nature and human experience, that no theory of it as a whole was either needed or possible.

I cannot help feeling that an adequate analysis of activity would exhibit the world of fact and the world of ideas as two correspondent objective statements of the active process itself,—correspondent because each has a work to do, in the doing of which it needs to be helped out by the other. The active process itself transcends any possible objective statement (whether in terms of fact or of ideas) simply for the reason that these objective statements are ultimately incidental to its own ongoing—are for the sake of it. It is this transcendence of any objectified form, whether perceptual or con-

[19] Perry, *The Thought and Character of William James*, II, 532.
[20] *Ibid.*, pp. 528–29.

ceptual, that seems to me to give the clue to freedom, spontaneity, etc.; and to make it unnecessary to have recourse to such a hypostatizing of chance as Peirce seems to me to indulge in. I always feel as if he were engaging (as respects his "chance") in just the same sort of conceptual construction he is protesting against. I must say, however, that I can see how far I have moved along when I find how much I get out of Peirce this year, and how easily I understand him, when a few years ago he was mostly a sealed book to me.[21]

Even more than Peirce, it was Woodbridge who encouraged Dewey to think naturalistically, to take metaphysics empirically, and to write *Experience and Nature*.

For Dewey, as for Mead, nature is a name for temporal changes or events that are more or less co-ordinated. This dynamic, or "active," world has its determined past and its future possibilities. For the *present*, it is a process of *determination* or *mediation*—possibilities are being utilized continually, in building up a cumulative, determinate, growing *past*, the experienced world. The course of events is not fixed, and though we may call it evolution, there is no fixed order of evolution, for existence is precarious at any time.

The visible is set in the invisible; and in the end what is unseen decides what happens in the seen; the tangible rests precariously upon the untouched and ungrasped. The contrast and the potential maladjustment of the immediate, the conspicuous and focal phase of things, with those indirect and hidden factors which determine the origin and career of what is present, are indestructible features of any and every experience. We may term the way in which our ancestors dealt with the contrast superstitious, but the contrast is no superstition. It is a primary datum in any experience.

We have substituted sophistication for superstition, at least measurably so. But the sophistication is often as irrational and as much at the mercy of words as the superstition it replaces. Our magical safeguard against the uncertain character of the world is to deny the existence of chance, to mumble universal and necessary law, the ubiquity of cause and effect, the uniformity of nature, universal progress, and the inherent rationality of the universe. These magic formulae borrow their potency from conditions that are not magical. Through science we have secured a degree of power of prediction and of control; through tools, machinery and an accompanying technique we have made the world more conformable to

[21] *Ibid.*, pp. 522–23.

our needs, a more secure abode. We have heaped up riches and means of comfort between ourselves and the risks of the world. We have professionalized amusement as an agency of escape and forgetfulness. But when all is said and done, the fundamentally hazardous character of the world is not seriously modified, much less eliminated. . . .

What has been said sounds pessimistic. But the concern is not with morals but with metaphysics, with, that is to say, the nature of the existential world in which we live. It would have been as easy and more comfortable to emphasize good luck, grace, unexpected and unwon joys, those unsought for happenings which we so significantly call happiness. We might have appealed to good fortune as evidence of this important trait of hazard in nature. Comedy is as genuine as tragedy. But it is traditional that comedy strikes a more superficial note than tragedy. And there is an even better reason for appealing to misfortunes and mistakes as evidence of the precarious nature of the world. . . . When we pull out a plum we treat it as evidence of the *real* order of cause and effect in the world. For this reason it is difficult for the goods of existence to furnish as convincing evidence of the uncertain character of nature as do evils. It is the latter we term accidents, not the former, even when their adventitious character is as certain.[22]

In such a course of events it is natural that beings should be born who feel the problem of evil and who worry about it more than they do about the problem of good. It is morals, not metaphysics, that leads us to be conscious of and responsible for mistakes, while we take the more regular and satisfactory course of events for granted as an objective order. Strictly speaking, however, all acts are of both the organism and its environment. Any distinction between agent and object, stimulus and response, is a secondary distinction made for the sake of controlling activity. Agency is attributed now here, now there; but primarily nature is composed neither of free agents nor of inert masses, but of movements, of bodies interacting, transacting.

It is meaningless to call such a world as a whole, organic or alive, intelligent or purposive. It is all these in turn and in spots. But in itself it is what it is from time to time and no meaning can be given it as a whole. Meanings, purposes, ideas, minds are being generated continually along with other specific products of natural activities. Hence, mind must be understood as a particular kind of activity in its natural relations or functions with other activities. Mind ultimately must be

[22] John Dewey, *Experience and Nature* (Chicago, 1925), pp. 43-44, 45.

understood by what it does relatively, that is, in its environment. What, then, is the distinctive function of mind? According to Dewey it is to redirect activities by an anticipation of their consequences. Mind is simply nature feeling her way, groping in her own darkness by her own light, trying herself out, finding out for herself what she can and cannot do. In short, the career of the human mind has a significance for nature as well as for man. Reason is neither the stuff nor the primary structure of nature; reason is a natural growth, a form of life. But life itself remains a precarious existence among other existences.

Fidelity to the nature to which we belong, as parts however weak, demands that we cherish our desires and ideals till we have converted them into intelligence, revised them in terms of the ways and means which nature makes possible. When we have used our thought to its utmost and have thrown into the moving unbalanced balance of things our puny strength, we know that though the universe slay us still we may trust, for our lot is one with whatever is good in existence. We know that such thought and effort is one condition of the coming into existence of the better. As far as we are concerned it is the only condition, for it alone is in our power. To ask more than this is childish; but to ask less is a recreance no less egotistic, involving no less a cutting of ourselves from the universe than does the expectation that it meet and satisfy our every wish. To ask in good faith as much as this from ourselves is to stir into motion every capacity of imagination, and to exact from action every skill and bravery.[23]

— 41 —

EMPIRICAL RADICALISM

IT seems appropriate to give at least some account of the practical applications of pragmatism and experimentalism in American culture, for without a knowledge of these applications the pragmatic meaning of the movement in philosophy must be lost. Such an account should begin with the applications of the theory of knowledge to the sciences, since it was to the union of logic and scientific method that this philosophical movement was most immediately devoted. In their social interests and political beliefs these empiricists were so variously

[23] *Ibid.*, pp. 420–21.

radical that it would be preposterous to regard them all as ideologists for any particular social program. The only concern which they really shared and which gave pragmatic unity to their polemics was the union of philosophy and science; philosophy was to submit its problems to experimental formulation and verification, and science was to become methodologically self-conscious or philosophical. But to examine the various ways in which mathematics, biology, psychology, and physics have appropriated pragmatic methodology, or, using the more technical language, to sketch the history of "behaviorism" and "operationalism" in these sciences, would result in too difficult and specialized a story to inflict on the readers of this book. Suffice it to note the general tendency among the sciences mentioned to purify themselves of concepts and hypotheses that are useless in the laboratory and to define the abstractions that are useful in the terms recommended by Peirce. Thus, there was laid a foundation in American science for the more recent movement of logical positivism, imported from abroad, which has given technical elaboration to some aspects of the pragmatic movement and has corrupted others. It has attempted to promote a greater "unity of science" than the pragmatists ever dreamed of and has shifted the emphasis of scientific logic from factual experimentation to verbal or semantic manipulation. The positivism of pragmatism has become more extreme, and the empiricism too logical to be "radical."

The history of pragmatism's application to religion can be more readily told here than the recent scientific history, because it had the opposite effect: its influence was anti-technical, popular, and sentimental. James shocked both theologians and philosophers by the loose, cavalier way in which he dismissed their "deepest" problems. They were intent on making faith more reasonable and theology more philosophical; he took for granted that there is something essentially "extravagant" and super-rational, if not supernatural, in religion as it is lived spontaneously, which must defy all attempts to make it appear rational. He no doubt acquired this conviction early from his father, and though he repudiated the monism and "socialism" of his father, he retained his anticlericalism, antirationalism, and antimoralism.

As early as 1874 he had read Benjamin Paul Blood's *Anaesthetic Revelation*, one of the "stepping-stones" of all his thinking thereafter. The last work to be written and published during his own lifetime was in praise of this writer, and bore the title "A Pluralistic Mystic." In 1888 he had been attracted by Edmund Gurney's "hypothetical supernaturalism"—with its idea of an "invisible order continuous with the present order of nature"; and from this there is a natural transition to the "piecemeal" or "crass" supernaturalism of 1902.[1]

His general defiance of theological knowledge was already explicit in his early article "Reflex Action and Theism," but by 1902, when he composed his famous Gifford Lectures, *The Varieties of Religious Experience,* he had become more dogmatic in his convictions.

The contention of philosophy . . . is . . . that religion can be transformed into a universally convincing science. . . . The fact [is] that no religious philosophy has actually convinced the mass of thinkers. . . .

In all sad sincerity I think we must conclude that the attempt to demonstrate by purely intellectual processes the truth of the deliverances of direct religious experience is absolutely hopeless. . . .

We must therefore, I think, bid a definitive good-by to dogmatic theology. In all sincerity our faith must do without that warrant. Modern idealism, I repeat, has said good-by to this theology forever. Can modern idealism give faith a better warrant, or must she still rely on her poor self for witness? . . .

When all is said and done, has Principal Caird—and I only use him as an example of that whole mode of thinking—transcended the sphere of feeling and of the direct experience of the individual, and laid the foundations of religion in impartial reason? Has he made religion universal by coercive reasoning, transformed it from a private faith into a public certainty? Has he rescued its affirmations from obscurity and mystery?

I believe that he has done nothing of the kind, but that he has simply reaffirmed the individual's experiences in a more generalized vocabulary. And again, I can be excused from proving technically that the transcendentalist reasonings fail to make religion universal, for I can point to the plain fact that a majority of scholars, even religiously disposed ones, stubbornly refuse to treat them as convincing. . . .

Philosophy lives in words, but truth and fact well up into our lives in ways that exceed verbal formulation. There is in the living act of perception always something that glimmers and twinkles and will not be caught, and for which reflection comes too late. No one knows this as well as the phi-

[1] Ralph Barton Perry, *The Thought and Character of William James* (Boston, 1935), II, 334.

losopher. He must fire his volley of new vocables out of his conceptual shot-gun, for his profession condemns him to this industry, but he secretly knows its hollowness and irrelevancy. . . .

A critical Science of Religions might . . . eventually command as general a public adhesion as is commanded by a physical science. Even the personally non-religious might accept its conclusions on trust, much as blind persons now accept the facts of optics—it might appear as foolish to refuse them. Yet as the science of optics has to be fed in the first instance, and continually verified later, by facts experienced by seeing persons; so the science of religions would depend for its original material on facts of personal experience, and would have to square itself with personal experience through all its critical reconstructions. It could never get away from concrete life.[2]

Here theology and philosophy are conceived as not even instrumental or "mediating," but as directly opposed to the essential variety, privacy, and irrationality of religious experience.

What keeps religion going is something else than abstract definitions and systems of logically concatenated adjectives, and something different from faculties of theology and their professors. All these things are after-effects, secondary accretions upon a mass of concrete religious experiences, connecting themselves with feeling and conduct that renew themselves in *saecula saeculorum* in the lives of humble private men. If you ask what these experiences are, they are conversations with the unseen, voices and visions, responses to prayer, changes of heart, deliverances from fear, inflowings of help.[3]

The effect of James's appeal to "religious experience" was, therefore, to discount the intellectual aspects of religious belief and the conventional aspects of institutionalized religion. It was not merely the variety of religious experiences, but the abnormality or "subliminal" quality of religious consciousness that seemed to James the essential fact of religion. And he presented his clinical cases of "sick souls," not in order to raise problems of mental health, but rather in order to show that "healthy mindedness" is an abnormality for religion. For this reason, he assumed that some form of "crass supernaturalism," some

[2] William James, *The Varieties of Religious Experience; a Study in Human Nature* (New York, 1903), pp. 454n, 455, 448, 453–54, 456–57, 456.

[3] From James's California lecture on "Philosophical Conceptions and Practical Results" (1898), in *Collected Essays and Reviews* (New York, 1920), pp. 427–28.

type of theistic metaphysics or cosmology, must cling to any religion that is genuine and that therefore the belief in a God whose attributes are essentially "moral" or related to human experience can be defended as a necessary element of religious experience, though it cannot serve as a basis for a rational theology.

Dewey's empiricism in matters of religion is less "extravagant." Like James he believes that there is a religious quality in experience which is relatively independent of conventional beliefs and practices of institutional religions. But he wants "religious values" kept free from all kinds of cosmology and supernaturalism; he is a humanist. "The opposition between religious values as I conceive them and religions are not to be bridged. Just because the release of these values is so important, their identification with the creeds and cults of religions must be dissolved." [4] He seeks the religious element of human experience, not in the abnormalities of private consciousness, but in "shared experience." He regards religious faith as something that men can and should have in common, uniting them in their basic enterprise of relating what together they experience as real with what together they hold to be ideal. God as the symbol for this union of believers and as the name for the partial union of actuality and ideality, is an object of loyalty rather than of affirmation. Dewey is, therefore, content with a minimum of theology and cosmology and a maximum of naturalistic liberalism.

It would be possible to mention several other significant variations of religious empirical radicalism, but these two illustrations, James and Dewey, may serve to indicate the ways in which pragmatism has reinstated a theory of faith and at the same time sought to discredit all conventional institutions, authorities, theologies, and creeds. But even more important than the pragmatic theory of faith has been the notion of religious experience as something emotional, immediate, mystical, which is to be understood in terms of psychology or pos-

---

[4] John Dewey, *A Common Faith* (New Haven, 1934), p. 28. Note also the following biographical statement written by his daughter. Referring to Mrs. Dewey, she says: "She had a deeply religious nature but had never accepted any church dogma. Her husband acquired from her the belief that a religious attitude was indigenous in natural experience, and that theology and ecclesiastic institutions had benumbed rather than promoted it."—Jane M. Dewey, "Biography of John Dewey," in *The Philosophy of John Dewey*, ed. by P. A. Schilpp (Evanston, 1939), p. 21.

sibly anthropology and throws light on human nature and human "adjustments" rather than on the universe as a whole.

James's persistent interest in religion and theism, which was certainly a major factor in pragmatism's popularity, alienated many of his more "tough-minded" friends, who labored to take sentiment out of moral philosophy and to give pragmatism the hard aspect of political and economic realism. Of these, none was more outspoken than Justice Oliver Wendell Holmes, who had participated in many of the early metaphysical discussions at Harvard, had welcomed James's *Psychology*, and had become the recognized leader of legal pragmatism, but who, when James's *Pragmatism* appeared, wrote to his friend Sir Frederick Pollock,

I think pragmatism an amusing humbug—like most of William James's speculations, as distinguished from his admirable and well written Irish perceptions of life. They all of them seem to me of the type of his answer to prayer in the subliminal consciousness—the spiritualist's promise of a miracle if you will turn down the gas. As I have said so often, all I mean by truth is what I can't help thinking. . . . William James's argument for free will, to give another example written many years ago, seemed to me just like the one I have mentioned, and fitted to please free thinking Unitarian parsons and the ladies. I always think of a remark of Brooks Adams that the philosophers were hired by the comfortable class to prove that everything is all right. I think it *is* all right, but on very different grounds. . . . The aim and end of the whole business is religious. . . . But for that conclusion I don't believe we ever should have heard from him on the subject, taking that as the significance of the whole business I make it my bow.[5]

Justice Holmes, however, had his own type of sentimentality—the glory of the struggle of life, the value of decisive action, the futility of the search for ultimate meanings.

Life is action, the use of one's powers. As to use them to their height is our joy and duty, so it is the one end that justifies itself.[6]

Realize life as an end in itself. Functioning is all there is—only our keenest pleasure is in what we call the higher sort. I wonder if cosmically an idea is any more important than the bowels.[7]

[5] *Holmes-Pollock Letters* (Cambridge, 1941), I, 138–40.
[6] Oliver Wendell Holmes, *Speeches* (New York, 1913), p. 85.
[7] *Holmes-Pollock Letters*, II, 22.

Such "celebration of mere vital excitement" was to James as repulsive as James's religious speculations were to Holmes.

It is curiously childish to me, and Wendell always forgets that on his own terms the dutiful people also fulfil his law. Even they live hard, and enjoy the struggle with their opposing devils! So let them alone! . . . Mere excitement is an immature ideal, unworthy of the Supreme Court's official endorsement.[8]

The sentimental, rugged individualism which Holmes preached was not a new philosophy among Yankees and had no direct relation to pragmatism; but when he applied it critically to legal judgment he produced a sensational theory of jurisprudence which began the highly important movement known as legal pragmatism or realism. Holmes applied James's "anti-gnosticism" to the common law.

The life of the law . . . has not been logic: it has been experience. . . . The felt necessities of the time, the prevalent moral and political theories, intuitions of public policy, avowed or unconscious, even the prejudices which judges share with their fellow men, have had a good deal more to do than the syllogism in determining the rules by which men should be governed.[9]

With such empiricism as a point of departure, he formulated in 1897 his famous pragmatic definition of law as "the prediction of the incidence of the public force through the instrumentality of the courts." And in the same notable address, *The Path of the Law*, he continued:

I often doubt whether it would not be a gain if every word of moral significance could be banished from the law altogether, and other words adopted which should convey legal ideas uncolored by anything outside the law. We should lose the fossil records of a good deal of history and the majority got from ethical associations, but by ridding ourselves of an unnecessary confusion we should gain very much in the clearness of our thought. . . . The language of judicial decision is mainly the language of logic. And the logical method and form flatter that longing for certainty and for repose which is in every human mind. But . . . behind the logical form lies a judgment as to the relative worth and importance of competing legislative grounds. . . . There is a concealed, half conscious battle on the question of legislative policy, and if any one thinks that it can be settled

[8] Perry, *The Thought and Character of William James*, II, 251.
[9] Oliver Wendell Holmes, *The Common Law* (Boston, 1881), p. 1.

deductively, or once for all, I only can say that I think he is theoretically wrong. . . .

The law can ask no better justification than the deepest instincts of man. . . .

Philosophy does not furnish motives, but it shows men that they are not fools for doing what they already want to do.[10]

This radical voluntarism in legal philosophy was more than an attack on the antiquated deductive theory of law which had already been disposed of by the historical and evolutionary school of jurisprudence; it was an effective application of Peirce's maxim for conceptual definition to judicial procedure. The judge could, on the basis of Holmes's philosophy, turn to the empirical consequences of legislation in order to determine the meaning of an enactment. This opened the door wide to what came to be called sociological jurisprudence and the courts became frankly agents of governmental policy. Holmes himself treated the collectivist tendencies in legislation with "cynical acid," but he was tolerant enough to enforce those tendencies when they clearly expressed the will of the legislature, though as a citizen he condemned them as tyrannical. He would not pit his "reason" against the "deepest instincts" of the people or conceive it his moral duty to obstruct the popular "passions," as the old theory of checks and balances taught. He was personally a foe of moralism and considered that he was doing the law a real service by robbing it of its black dignity, its clerical robes, and its privileged position among pulpits, in order to set it firmly with a utilitarian footing on the level ground of the market place.[11]

---

[10] Oliver Wendell Holmes, *Collected Legal Papers* (New York, 1920), pp. 179–83, 200, 316. The last quotation is from his essay on "Natural Law."

[11] Personally, however, he continued to cultivate the genteel life of a gentleman and felt a disdain for the hard labors to which his own theories were condemning future judges. The following passage from a letter to Sir Frederick Pollock reveals this contrast between his personal dignity and his democratic jurisprudence: "Brandeis the other day drove a harpoon into my midriff with reference to my summer occupations. He said you talk about improving your mind, you only exercise it on the subjects with which you are familiar. Why don't you try something new, study some domain of fact? Take up the textile industries in Massachusetts and after reading the reports sufficiently you can go to Lawrence and get a notion of how it really is. I hate facts. I always say the chief end of man is to form general propositions—adding that no general proposition is worth a damn. Of course a general proposition is simply a string

It remained for Roscoe Pound, in theory, and Judges Brandeis and Cardozo, in practice, to develop a sociological jurisprudence in terms of which moral principles and social policy could support each other.

The judge makes the actual law by a process of trying the principles and rules and standards in concrete cases, observing their practical operation and gradually discovering by experience of many causes how to apply them so as to administer justice by means of them. . . .

The infusion of morals into the law through the development of equity was not an achievement of legislation, it was the work of courts. The absorption of the usages of merchants into the law was not brought about by statutes but by judicial decisions. When once the current of juristic thought and judicial decision is turned into the new course our Anglo-American method of judicial empiricism has always proved adequate. Given new premises, our common law has the means of developing them to meet the exigencies of justice and of molding the results into a scientific system. Moreover it has the power of acquiring new premises, as it did in the development of equity and the absorption of the law merchant. Indeed fundamental changes have been taking place in our legal system almost unnoticed, and a shifting was in progress in our case law from the individualist justice of the nineteenth century, which has passed so significantly by the name of legal justice, to the social justice of today even before the change in our legislative policy became so marked.[12]

Here the point of view is shifted slightly from the voluntarism of James and Holmes to the social ethics of Dewey and Tufts, Brandeis and Cardozo; the law exists, not to serve the various wills for power in "the struggle which is life," but to satisfy wants by the art which is government.

Jurists began to think in terms of human wants or desires rather than of human wills. They began to think that what they had to do was not simply to equalize or harmonize wills, but, if not to equalize, at least to harmonize the satisfaction of wants. They began to weigh or balance and reconcile claims or wants or desires, as formerly they had balanced or reconciled wills.

---

for the facts and I have little doubt that it would be good for my immortal soul to plunge into them, good also for the performance of my duties, but I shrink from the bore—or rather I hate to give up the chance to read this and that, that a gentleman should have read before he dies. I don't remember that I ever read Machiavelli's *Prince* —and I think of the Day of Judgment."—*Holmes-Pollock Letters*, II, 13–14.

[12] Roscoe Pound, *The Spirit of the Common Law* (Boston, 1921), pp. 176, 184–85.

They began to think of the end of law not as a maximum of self-assertion, but as a maximum satisfaction of wants. Hence for a time they thought of the problem of ethics, of jurisprudence, and of politics as chiefly one of valuing; as a problem of finding criteria of the relative value of interests. In jurisprudence and politics they saw that we must add practical problems of the possibility of making interests effective through governmental action, judicial or administrative. But the first question was one of the wants to be recognized—of the interests to be recognized and secured. Having inventoried the wants or claims or interests which are asserting and for which legal security is sought, we were to value them, select those to be recognized, determine the limits within which they were to be given effect in view of other recognized interests, and ascertain how far we might give them effect by law in view of the inherent limitations upon effective legal action.[13]

We Americans are committed not only to social justice in the sense of avoiding things which bring suffering and harm, like unjust distribution of wealth; but we are committed primarily to democracy. The social justice for which we are striving is an incident of our democracy, not the main end. It is rather the result of democracy—perhaps its finest expression—but it rests upon democracy, which implies the rule by the people. And therefore the end for which we must strive is the attainment of rule by the people, and that involves industrial democracy as well as political democracy. . . .

Can any man be really free who is constantly in danger of becoming dependent for mere subsistence upon somebody and something else than his own exertion and conduct? Financial dependence is consistent with freedom only where claim to support rests upon right, and not upon favor. . . .

The freedom of the individual is as much an essential condition of successful democracy as his education. If the Government permits conditions to exist which make large classes of citizens financially dependent, the great evil of dependence should at least be minimized by the State's assuming, or causing to be assumed by others, in some form, the burden incident to its own shortcomings.

The cost of attaining freedom is usually high.[14]

On the left wing of this empiricist movement in American law is a group of so-called realists who aspire to an objective science of law, free of moral principles, "jural postulates," and other forms of "transcendental nonsense." They fear that under cover of utilitarian theories

[13] Roscoe Pound, *An Introduction to the Philosophy of Law* (New Haven, 1922), pp. 89–90.

[14] Louis Dembitz Brandeis, *The Social and Economic Views of Mr. Justice Brandeis;* collected by Alfred Lief (New York, 1930), pp. 382, 369.

of the general happiness the champions of sociological jurisprudence are inclined to smuggle in certain general social ends, democratic dogmas, principles of legal order, and other moral criteria which are not really empirical. They seek a "normative science" built up on the actual aims and interests of men, not on general ends or values. Their emphasis is on civil, rather than criminal law, and they think of the problems of law as a lawyer would—as problems of predicting judicial decisions. They want to be assured that any legal rules and moral values which are introduced into jurisprudence are strictly instrumental to the practical process of settling rival claims, that they can be empirically verified, and that they are not mere *obiter dicta*, lending *ex post facto* glamor to a decision, but doing no intellectual work.

A diversity similar to that which is exhibited in the pragmatic approaches to the law confronts us when we examine the pragmatic approaches to politics. William James was temperamentally as well as philosophically an individualist; he had a horror of "bigness" as such, a distaste for all but the most local politics, a passionate hatred of imperialism, and even a loathing for "the bitch-goddess, success." He believed in heroism and the strenuous life, but he conceived these virtues quite personally and on a small scale; to the many little private strugglers he was sympathetic and helpful, but toward large-scale political issues and conflicts, with the exception of the fight against imperialism, he showed little philosophical concern. Dewey, on the contrary, had developed his ethics largely in terms of the major political and economic issues of his time and has been so much preoccupied with "the public and its problems" that there have been complaints from time to time that he does not believe in private individuals at all. Dewey's social philosophy, however, is built upon his ethics of self-realization, and what he calls "the new individualism" is the belief that collective action and public experience are necessary to give to any individual an "effective freedom" and a practical understanding of the implications of his particular interests and needs. He has become the chief American exponent and patron saint of democratic socialism.

More important, however, for our history than the political opinions of pragmatic philosophers are the pragmatic habits of political thinking that have grown up more or less spontaneously among practical politicians, until there has come into being a conscious ideology of recent

American social experience, which, though it is not yet integrated into a well-constructed system, can be recognized as a peculiarly American social theory. Unfortunately for our purposes, this theory is recognizable more clearly as a social force than as a body of doctrine, but we may sketch its chief features roughly and tentatively, remembering that they are likely to change, not without much notice, but with no more than a faint warning from "the situation." First of all, this ideology has been conspicuous negatively by its failure to work out a philosophy of history, and this failure is eloquent testimony to its pragmatic temper. Even the economic interpretation of American history, which under the inspiration of the Marxians made a little headway among historians and promised to give to American politics a more realistic perspective than the conventional histories afforded, is apparently being abandoned (too hastily) by Beard and its other friends. And even this interpretation of history has remained a technical tool of historians rather than a philosophical framework for history in general. Neither the Marxian nor any other philosophy of history since the decline of the Hegelian enthusiasm has made a serious impression on American social philosophy. American utopians and Americanized Christian philosophers now and then capture the popular imagination, but on the whole they are less effective in giving historical perspective than they are in contributing to the dominant concern for "human nature" on the one hand and for the faith in progress on the other. Recent American faith in progress has been grounded, not on history, but on confidence in our human and natural resources. This takes us to a second trait of political pragmatism: it is primarily a theory of power, or rather of powers, pluralistic and opportunistic. What Dewey said about philosophy in general seems peculiarly to reflect the spirit of recent American political philosophy.

Philosophy in America will be lost between chewing a historic cud long since reduced to woody fiber, or an apologetics for lost causes (lost to natural science), or a scholastic, schematic, formalism, unless it can somehow bring to consciousness America's own needs and its own implicit principle of successful action.[15]

The headquarters of this philosophy were in Chicago. Of the social

[15] John Dewey and others, *Creative Intelligence* (New York, 1917), p. 67.

psychology developed there by Dewey, Tufts, Mead, and Veblen we have given an account above.[16] They formulated a theory of democracy not merely as a form of government but also as a mode of associated living, based on the ideas that individuality and freedom are themselves social products and that a democratic society is one which subordinates its institutions to the basic aim of permitting its members to grow intellectually and emotionally by widening their "areas of shared concern," by promoting means of communication and public expression, and by giving all a responsible participation in the processes of social and physical control. This ideal was applied by Dewey to the reform of education, by Jane Addams to the reform of urban society and international relations, by Veblen and Ayres to the reform of industrial management and vested interests. The philosophy was given a more technical and systematic elaboration as a theory of government by Arthur F. Bentley and by the Chicago trinity, Charles E. Merriam, H. D. Lasswell and T. V. Smith. Smith, particularly, has shown how the pragmatic philosophy can be applied to the theory of equality, the art of compromise, and the ethics of "democratic discipline." Bentley, Beard, and Merriam have been leaders in formulating politics in terms of the interaction of "pressure-groups" and in thus providing a practical, pluralistic substitute for the Marxian concepts of class-conflict in a society where classes are vague, but conflicts continual. In the form of "experimental economics" this philosophy was then carried by Tugwell and other New Dealers to Washington, where it passed through the ordeal by fire.

Radical empiricism faced a much more delicate task when it turned from these rough and tumble social arts to the fine arts; John Dewey and Albert C. Barnes made the culminating application of empirical and pragmatic analysis in their attempt to analyze artistic activity and to show how the fine arts and the most imaginative enjoyments of "consummatory experience" are continuous with the concerns of everyday living. Barnes showed how both the artist, for whom art is a skill or technique of creation, and the appreciator, who enjoys the works of the art of others, require analytic intelligence, discipline, and communicativeness; aesthetic experience, therefore, is at least no less intellectual and social than scientific and technological experience. Dewey

[16] See pp. 389-95.

made the most of this theme, for it gave him an excellent opportunity to show how the enjoyment of ends and the pursuit of aims are related.

When artistic objects are separated from both conditions of origin and operation in experience, a wall is built around them that renders almost opaque their general significance, with which esthetic theory deals. Art is remitted to a separate realm, where it is cut off from that association with the materials and aims of every other form of human effort, undergoing, and achievement. A primary task is thus imposed upon one who undertakes to write upon the philosophy of the fine arts. This task is to restore continuity between the refined and intensified forms of experience that are works of art and the everyday events, doings, and sufferings that are universally recognized to constitute experience.[17]

We reach a conclusion regarding the relations of instrumental and fine art which is precisely the opposite of that intended by seclusive estheticians; namely, that fine art consciously undertaken as such is peculiarly instrumental in quality. It is a device in experimentation carried on for the sake of education. It exists for the sake of a specialized use, use being a new training of modes of perception. The creators of such works of art are entitled, when successful, to the gratitude that we give to inventors of microscopes and microphones; in the end, they open new objects to be observed and enjoyed. This is a genuine service; but only an age of combined confusion and conceit will arrogate to works that perform this special utility the exclusive name of fine art.[18]

From this last quotation, and indeed from most of Dewey's writings, one gets the impression that all things "are carried on for the sake of education." "Philosophy," he said, "is the general theory of education," and the arts, we may conclude, are its general practice. To speak in this way of the life of the mind as a process of education is, of course, to use the term "education" in a very broad sense. But it is no accident, from the point of view of radical empiricism, that education should be so broadly conceived. The discipline of the schoolroom is, as Dewey pointed out in one of his earliest and most influential books, *School and Society*, merely an early phase of the basic discipline of human life. There is nothing academic about learning, and no limits can be assigned to the process.

[17] John Dewey, *Art as Experience* (New York, 1934), p. 3.
[18] John Dewey, *Experience and Nature* (Chicago, 1925), p. 392.

Our present education . . . is highly specialized, one-sided and narrow. It is an education dominated almost entirely by the mediaeval conception of learning. It is something which appeals for the most part simply to the intellectual aspect of our natures, our desire to learn, to accumulate information, and to get control of the symbols of learning; not to our impulses and tendencies to make, to do, to create, to produce, whether in the form of utility or of art. The very fact that manual training, art and science are objected to as technical, as tending toward mere specialism, is of itself as good testimony as could be offered to the specialized aim which controls current education. Unless education had been virtually identified with the exclusively intellectual pursuits, with learning as such, all these materials and methods would be welcome, would be greeted with the utmost hospitality.

While training for the profession of learning is regarded as the type of culture, as a liberal education, that of a mechanic, a musician, a lawyer, a doctor, a farmer, a merchant, or a railroad manager is regarded as purely technical and professional. The result is that which we see about us everywhere—the division into "cultured" people and "workers," the separation of theory and practice. . . . While our educational leaders are talking of culture, the development of personality, etc., as the end and aim of education, the great majority of those who pass under the tuition of the school regard it only as a narrowly practical tool with which to get bread and butter enough to eke out a restricted life. If we were to conceive our educational end and aim in a less exclusive way, if we were to introduce into educational processes the activities which appeal to those whose dominant interest is to do and to make, we should find the hold of the school upon its members to be more vital, more prolonged, containing more of culture. . . .

The introduction of active occupations, of nature study, of elementary science, of art, of history; the relegation of the merely symbolic and formal to a secondary position; the change in the moral school atmosphere, in the relation of pupils and teachers—of discipline; the introduction of more active, expressive, and self-directing factors—all these are not mere accidents, they are necessities of the larger social evolution. . . .

If we once believe in life . . . then will all the occupations and uses . . . then will all history and science, become instruments of appeal and materials of culture to . . . imagination, and through that to the richness and the orderliness of . . . life. Where we now see only the outward doing and the outward product, there, behind all visible results, is the readjustment of mental attitude, the enlarged and sympathetic vision, the sense of growing power, and the willing ability to identify both insight and capacity with the interests of the world and man. Unless culture be a superficial polish, a veneering of mahogany over common wood, it surely is this—the growth of the imagination in flexibility, in scope, and in sympathy, till the life which the individual lives is informed with the life of nature and of society.[19]

In Dewey's thought the terms "democracy" and "education" are practically synonyms, and both are intended to designate what it means to live by the principles of radical empiricism.

Democracy is belief in the ability of human experience to generate the aims and methods by which further experience will grow in ordered richness. Every other form of moral and social faith rests upon the idea that experience must be subjected at some point or other to some form of external control; to some "authority" alleged to exist outside the processes of experience. Democracy is the faith that the process of experience is more important than any special result attained, so that special results achieved are of ultimate value only as they are used to enrich and order the ongoing process. Since the process of experience is capable of being educative, faith in democracy is all one with faith in experience and education. All ends and values that are cut off from the ongoing process become arrests, fixations. They strive to fixate what has been gained instead of using it to open the road and point the way to new and better experiences.

If one asks what is meant by experience in this connection, my reply is that it is that free interaction of individual human beings with surrounding conditions, especially the human surroundings, which develops and satisfies need and desire by increasing knowledge of things as they are. Knowledge of conditions as they are is the only solid ground for communication and sharing; all other communication means the subjection of some persons to the personal opinion of other persons. Need and desire—out of which grow purpose and direction of energy—go beyond what exists, and hence beyond knowledge, beyond science. They continually open the way into the unexplored and unattained future.[20]

[19] John Dewey, *The School and Society* (Chicago, 1900), pp. 41–44, 72–73.
[20] John Dewey, "Creative Democracy—the Task before Us," in *The Philosopher of the Common Man* (New York, 1940), p. 227.

GUIDE TO THE LITERATURE FOR PART VIII

The controversy over pragmatism in the philosophical journals centered about the publication of William James's California lecture, "Philosophical Conceptions and Practical Results," *University of California Chronicle* (1898) pp. 24, which was reprinted, with slight changes, under the title, "The Pragmatic Method," *Journal of Philosophy*, I (1904), 673–87, F. C. S. Schiller's *Humanism* (London, 1903), and John Dewey's *Studies in Logical Theory* (Chicago, 1903). Of the extensive literature, more or less polemic, which ensued, discussing radical empiricism, pragmatism, instrumentalism, and experimentalism as a movement in philosophical thinking and in American culture, we select the following:

Irving King, "Pragmatism as a Philosophic Method," *Philosophical Review*, XII (1903), 510–24.

H. H. Bawden, "The Necessity from the Standpoint of Scientific Method of a Reconstruction of the Ideas of the Psychical and the Physical," *Journal of Philosophy*, I (1904), 62–68.

Josiah Royce, "The Eternal and the Practical," *Philosophical Review*, XIII (1904), 113–42.

J. A. Leighton, "Pragmatism," *Journal of Philosophy*, I (1904), 148–56.

J. M. Baldwin, "The Limits of Pragmatism," *Psychological Review*, XI (1904), 30–60.

H. H. Bawden, "What Is Pragmatism?" *Journal of Philosophy*, I (1904), 421–27.

William James, "Does 'Consciousness' Exist?" *Journal of Philosophy*, I (1904), 477–91.

—— "A World of Pure Experience," *Journal of Philosophy*, I (1904), 533–43, 561–70.

R. B. Perry, "Conceptions and Misconceptions of Consciousness," *Psychological Review*, XI (1904), 282–96.

William James, "Humanism and Truth," *Mind*, n.s., Vol. XIII (1904), 457–75.

—— "The Thing and Its Relations," *Journal of Philosophy*, II (1905), 29–41.

—— "The Essence of Humanism," *Journal of Philosophy*, II (1905), 113–18.

F. J. E. Woodbridge, "The Nature of Consciousness," *Journal of Philosophy*, II (1905), 119–25.

B. H. Bode, " 'Pure Experience' and the External World," *Journal of Philosophy*, II (1905), 128–33.

C. H. Judd, "Radical Empiricism and Wundt's Philosophy," *Journal of Philosophy*, II (1905), 169–76.

William James, "How Two Minds Can Know One Thing," *Journal of Philosophy*, II (1905), 176–81.

—— "Is Radical Empiricism Solipsistic?" *Journal of Philosophy*, II (1905), 235–38.

—— "The Place of Affectional Facts in a World of Pure Experience," *Journal of Philosophy*, II (1905), 281–87.

W. P. Montague, "The Relational Theory of Consciousness and Its Realistic Implications," *Journal of Philosophy*, II (1905), 309–16.

John Dewey, "The Realism of Pragmatism," *Journal of Philosophy*, II (1905), 324–27.

A. H. Lloyd, "The Personal and the Factional in the Life of Society," *Journal of Philosophy*, II (1905), 337–45, especially the concluding paragraphs.

John Dewey, "The Postulate of Immediate Empiricism," *Journal of Philosophy*, II (1905), 393–99.

C. V. Tower, "A Neglected 'Context' in 'Radical Empiricism,' " *Journal of Philosophy*, II (1905), 400–408.

C. M. Bakewell, "An Open Letter to Professor Dewey concerning Immediate Empiricism," *Journal of Philosophy*, II (1905), 520–22.

W. T. Bush, "An Empirical Definition of Consciousness," *Journal of Philosophy*, II (1905), 561–68.

F. J. E. Woodbridge, "Of What Sort Is Cognitive Experience?" *Journal of Philosophy*, II (1905), 573–76.

John Dewey, "Immediate Empiricism," *Journal of Philosophy*, II (1905), 597–99.

P. Hughes, "Dr. Bush's Definition of Consciousness," *Journal of Philosophy*, II (1905), 629–30.

John Dewey, "The Knowledge Experience and Its Relationships," *Journal of Philosophy*, II (1905), 652–57.

B. H. Bode, "Cognitive Experience and Its Object," *Journal of Philosophy*, II (1905), 658–63.

W. T. Bush, "Reply to Dr. Hughes," *Journal of Philosophy*, II (1905), 663–64.

John Dewey, "The Knowledge Experience Again," *Journal of Philosophy*, II (1905), 707–11.

—— "The Terms 'Conscious' and 'Consciousness,' " *Journal of Philosophy*, III (1906), 39–41.

P. Hughes, "Rejoinder [to W. T. Bush]," *Journal of Philosophy*, III (1906), 42.

W. T. Bush, "The Privacy of Consciousness," *Journal of Philosophy*, III (1906), 42–45.

H. Nichols, "Professor James's 'Hule,' " *Journal of Philosophy*, III (1906), 64–70.

J. A. Leighton, "Cognitive Thought and 'Immediate' Experience," *Journal of Philosophy*, III (1906), 174–80.

W. H. Sheldon, "The Quarrel about Transcendency," *Journal of Philosophy*, III (1906), 180–85.

F. C. S. Schiller, "Thought and Immediacy," *Journal of Philosophy*, III (1906), 234–37.

John Dewey, "Reality as Experience," *Journal of Philosophy*, III (1906), 253–57.

B. H. Bode, "Realism and Pragmatism," *Journal of Philosophy*, III (1906), 393–401.

W. B. Pitkin, "The Relation between the Act and the Object of Belief," *Journal of Philosophy*, III (1906), 505–11.

J. E. Russell, "The Pragmatist's Meaning of Truth," *Journal of Philosophy*, III (1906), 599–601.

W. B. Pitkin, "A Problem of Evidence in Radical Empiricism," *Journal of Philosophy*, III (1906), 645–50.

William James, "Mr. Pitkin's Refutation of 'Radical Empiricism,' " *Journal of Philosophy*, III (1906), 712.

R. W. Sellars, "The Nature of Experience," *Journal of Philosophy*, IV (1907), 14–18.

F. C. S. Schiller, "A Pragmatic Babe in the Wood," *Journal of Philosophy*, IV (1907), 42–44.

W. B. Pitkin, "In Reply to Prof. James," *Journal of Philosophy*, IV (1907), 44–45.

J. E. Russell, "Pragmatism as the Salvation from Philosophic Doubt," *Journal of Philosophy*, IV (1907), 57–64.

H. Nichols, "Pragmatism vs. Science," *Journal of Philosophy*, IV (1907), 122–31.

William James, "Pragmatic Conception of Truth," *Journal of Philosophy*, IV (1907), 141–55.

John Dewey, "The Control of Ideas by Facts," *Journal of Philosophy*, IV (1907), 197–203, 253–59, 309–19.

E. B. McGilvary, "The Stream of Consciousness," *Journal of Philosophy*, IV (1907), 225–35.

F. C. S. Schiller, "The Pragmatic Cure of Doubt, "*Journal of Philosophy*, IV (1907), 235–38.

J. E. Russell, "A Reply to Dr. Schiller," *Journal of Philosophy*, IV (1907), 238–43.

William James and J. E. Russell, "Controversy about Truth," *Journal of Philosophy*, IV (1907), 289–96.

J. B. Pratt, "Truth and Its Verification," *Journal of Philosophy*, IV (1907), 320–24.

R. B. Perry, "A Review of Pragmatism as a Theory of Knowledge," *Journal of Philosophy*, IV (1907), 365–74.

William James, "A Word More about Truth," *Journal of Philosophy*, IV (1907), 396–406.

R. B. Perry, "A Review of Pragmatism as a Philosophical Generalization," *Journal of Philosophy*, IV (1907), 421–28.

W. T. Bush, "The Continuity of Consciousness," *Journal of Philosophy*, IV, (1907), 428–32.

R. W. Sellars, "Prof. Dewey's View of Agreement," *Journal of Philosophy*, IV (1907), 432–35.

W. A. Brown, "The Pragmatic Value of the Absolute," *Journal of Philosophy*, IV (1907), 459–64.

William James, "Prof. Pratt on Truth," *Journal of Philosophy*, IV (1907), 464–67.

F. C. S. Schiller, "Pragmatism vs. Skepticism," *Journal of Philosophy*, IV (1907), 482–87.

J. E. Russell, "A Last Word to Dr. Schiller," *Journal of Philosophy*, IV (1907), 487–90.

F. C. S. Schiller, "Ultima Ratio?" *Journal of Philosophy*, IV (1907), 490–94.

William James, "The Absolute and the Strenuous Life," *Journal of Philosophy*, IV (1907), 546–48.

A. W. Moore, "Professor Perry on Pragmatism," *Journal of Philosophy*, IV (1907), 567–77.

E. B. McGilvary, "Realism and the Physical World," *Journal of Philosophy*, IV (1907), 683–92.

A. O. Lovejoy, "The Thirteen Pragmatisms," *Journal of Philosophy*, V (1908), 1–12, 29–39.

John Dewey, "What Does Pragmatism Mean by Practical?" *Journal of Philosophy*, V (1908), 85–99.

A. R. Gifford, "The Pragmatic Hulē of Mr. Schiller," *Journal of Philosophy*, V (1908), 99–104.

J. B. Pratt, "Truth and Ideas," *Journal of Philosophy*, V (1908), 122–31.

William James, " 'Truth' versus 'Truthfulness,' " *Journal of Philosophy*, V (1908), 179–81.

H. M. Kallen, "The Pragmatic Notion of Hulē," *Journal of Philosophy*, V (1908), 293–97.

M. Meyer, "The Exact Number of Pragmatisms," *Journal of Philosophy*, V (1908), 321–26.

John Dewey, "The Logical Character of Ideas," *Journal of Philosophy*, V (1908), 375–81.

A. W. Moore, "Truth Value," *Journal of Philosophy*, V (1908), 429–36.

E. B. McGilvary, "The Chicago 'Idea' and Idealism," *Journal of Philosophy*, V (1908), 589–97.

A. Schinz, "Professor Dewey's Pragmatism," *Journal of Philosophy*, V (1908), 617–28.

John Dewey, "Objects, Data, and Existences: a reply to Professor McGilvary," *Journal of Philosophy*, VI (1909), 13–21.

E. B. McGilvary, "Experience and Its Inner Duplicity," *Journal of Philosophy*, VI (1909), 225–32.

W. P. Montague, "The True, the Good and the Beautiful from a Pragmatic Standpoint," *Journal of Philosophy*, VI (1909), 233–38.

A. W. Moore, "Anti-Pragmatisme," *Journal of Philosophy*, VI (1909), 291–95.

—— "Pragmatism and Solipsism," *Journal of Philosophy*, VI (1909), 378–83.

John Dewey, "The Dilemma of the Intellectualist Theory of Truth," *Journal of Philosophy*, VI (1909), 433–34.

A. Schinz, "A Few Words in Reply to Professor Moore's Criticism of 'Anti-Pragmatisme,' " *Journal of Philosophy*, VI (1909), 434–38.

W. P. Montague, "May a Realist Be a Pragmatist?" *Journal of Philosophy*, VI (1909), 460–63, 488–90, 543–48, 561–71.

H. Wodehouse, "Professor James on Conception," *Journal of Philosophy*, VI (1909), 490–95.

H. M. Kallen, "Dr. Montague and the Pragmatic Notion of Value," *Journal of Philosophy*, VI (1909), 549–52.

A. O. Lovejoy, "Pragmatism and Realism," *Journal of Philosophy*, VI (1909), 575–80.

J. E. Boodin, "What Pragmatism Is and Is Not," *Journal of Philosophy*, VI (1909), 627-35.

H. M. Kallen, "The Affiliations of Pragmatism," *Journal of Philosophy*, VI (1909), 655-61.

In addition to this group of articles, through which the development of pragmatism as a movement is clearly portrayed, there are a few books which represent attempts at the systematization of pragmatism and some critical articles which deserve special comment. A. O. Lovejoy, "The Thirteen Pragmatisms," *Journal of Philosophy*, V (1908), 1-12, 29-39, is one of the most searching critiques of the pragmatic theory of knowledge; it does not, as its title suggests, identify diverse movements in pragmatism, but it formulates clearly thirteen propositions prominent in pragmatic literature and points out to what extent they are incompatible with each other. A. C. Armstrong, "The Evolution of Pragmatism," *Journal of Philosophy*, V (1908), 645-50, attempts a genetic account of the history of pragmatism. I. Woodbridge Riley, "Transcendentalism and Pragmatism: a comparative study," *Journal of Philosophy*, VI (1909), 263-66, is another early historical account. J. B. Pratt, *What Is Pragmatism?* (New York, 1909), Addison W. Moore, *Pragmatism and Its Critics* (Chicago, 1910), and H. Heath Bawden, *The Principles of Pragmatism: a Philosophical Interpretation of Experience* (Boston and New York, 1910) are early attempts by individuals to define and criticize the pragmatic movement; the most important justification was, however, the co-operative volume, *Creative Intelligence*, ed. by John Dewey (New York, 1917), which included contributions by Dewey, Moore, H. C. Brown, G. H. Mead, B. H. Bode, H. W. Stuart, J. H. Tufts and H. M. Kallen. Dewey wrote a historical account, "The Development of American Pragmatism," in *Studies in the History of Ideas*, Vol. II, ed. by the Department of Philosophy of Columbia University (New York, 1925), pp. 351-77. The account of pragmatism in the *Encyclopedia of the Social Sciences* is by H. M. Kallen. A full-length historical study is Eduard Baumgarten, *Der Pragmatismus: R. W. Emerson, W. James, J. Dewey* (Frankfurt a.M., 1938). Later critical studies include F. J. E. Woodbridge, "The Promise of Pragmatism," *Journal of Philosophy*, XXVI (1929), 541-52, G. H. Mead, "The Philosophies of Royce, James, and Dewey in Their American Setting," *International Journal of Ethics*, XL (1930), 211-31, and William Savery, "The Significance of Dewey's Philosophy," in *The Philosophy of John Dewey*, ed. by Paul Arthur Schilpp (Evanston and Chicago, 1939), pp. 479-513, which is more general than its title, attempting to place pragmatism in its setting among philosophical movements and in American culture; it also discusses in more detail than Lovejoy's earlier article doctrines which are more or less loosely connected with pragmatism, such as the logic of relations, neutralism, perspective realism, tychism, and naturalism.

There is a bibliography of Peirce's works appended to *Chance, Love, and Logic*, ed. by M. R. Cohen (New York, 1923). Six volumes of Peirce's *Collected Papers*, ed. by Hartshorne and Weiss, have thus far been published. Pragmatic elements appear in Peirce's thought in his early review of Fraser's edition of Berkeley, *North American Review*, CXIII (1871), 449-72. Of Peirce's later papers, those which apply most directly to the theme of this part were published in the *Monist*, in 1891-93 and 1905-6. The first five papers are reprinted in *Chance, Love and Logic:* "The Architecture of Theories," pp. 157-78, "The Doctrine of Necessity Examined," pp. 179-201, "The Law of Mind," pp. 202-37, "Man's Glassy Essence," pp. 238-66, "Evolutionary Love," pp. 267-300. In the 1905-6 group were: "What Pragmatism Is?" *Monist*, XV (1905), 161-81, "The Issue of Pragmaticism," *Monist*, XV (1905) 481-99, and "Prolegomena to an Apology for Pragmaticism," *Monist*, XVI (1906), 492-546. Justus Buchler, *Charles Peirce's Empiricism* (New York, 1939), is a thorough critical study which should be supplemented by articles on special aspects of Peirce's thought, of which the following are of particular interest: Ernest Nagel, "Charles S. Peirce; Pioneer of Modern Empiricism," *Philosophy of Science*, VII (1940), 69-80; James K. Feibleman, "Peirce's Phaneroscopy," *Philosophy and Phenomenological Research*, I (1940), 208-16; A. W. Burks, "Peirce's Conception of Logic as a Normative Science," *Philosophical Review*, LII (1943), 187-93, and Philip Wiener's forthcoming articles in the *Journal of the History of Ideas*. The *Journal of Philosophy* Vol. XIII, No. 26 (December 21, 1916) was a memorial issue which contained the following papers: Josiah Royce and Fergus Keenan, "Charles Sanders Peirce," pp. 701-9; John Dewey, "The Pragmatism of Peirce," pp. 709-15 (reprinted as a supplementary essay in *Chance, Love, and Logic*, pp. 301-8); Christine Ladd Franklin, "Charles S. Peirce at the Johns Hopkins," pp. 715-22; Joseph Jastrow, "Charles S. Peirce as a Teacher," pp. 723-26; and Morris R. Cohen, "Charles S. Peirce, and a Tentative Bibliography of his published Writings," pp. 726-37.

Ralph Barton Perry compiled an *Annotated Bibliography of the Writings of William James* (New York, 1920). Perry's *Thought and Character of William James* (Boston, 1935) is an indispensable companion to any serious reader of James. Appendix X to Volume II of this work includes James's attempts to reply to the "Bode-Miller" criticism of his theory of consciousness.

Essays Philosophical and Psychological in Honor of William James (New York, 1908) included as philosophic contributors G. S. Fullerton, W. T. Bush, John Dewey, W. P. Montague, F. J. E. Woodbridge, C. A. Strong, W. B. Pitkin, D. S. Miller, A. O. Lovejoy, F. Adler, H. G. Lord, G. A. Tawney, H. C. Brown, and K. Gordon. Contributing psychologists were R. S. Woodworth, F. L. Wells, N. Norsworthy, J. M. Cattell, and E. L. Thorndike. More recent volumes in honor of James are *In Commemoration of William James, 1842-1942* (New York, 1942) to which Henry James, J. M. Kallen, D. S. Miller, E. B. Holt, John Dewey, J. S. Bixler, R. B. Perry, G. S. Brett, D. C. Williams, H. W. Schneider, J. R. Kantor, V. Lowe, C. Morris, E. W. Lyman, A. Metzger, and W. H. Hill contributed addresses at various celebrations of the hundredth anniversary of James's birth, and *William James the Man and the Thinker* (Madison, Wis., 1942), a publication of the addresses delivered at the similar celebration at the University of Wisconsin, including those by G. C. Sellery, M. C. Otto, D. S. Miller, N. Cameron, C. A. Dykstra, John Dewey, B. H. Bode, and J. S. Bixler. Studies of James's philosophy include Théodore Blau, *William James; sa théorie de la connaissance et la vérité* (Paris, 1933), Umbero Cugine, *L'Empirismo radicale di W. James* (Genova, 1925), and Ethel E. Sabin, *William James and Pragmatism* (Lancaster, Pa., 1916). F. C. S. Schiller wrote on "William James and Empiricism," *Journal of Philosophy*, XXV (1928), 155-62; Wendell T. Bush, "William James and Panpsychism," appeared in *Studies in the History of Ideas*, II (New York, 1925), pp. 313-26. John Dewey is the author of an important recent critical essay, "The Vanishing Subject in the Psychology of James," *Journal of Philosophy*, XXXVII (1940), 589-99.

F. C. S. Schiller's works include the following: "Axioms as Postulates," in *Personal Idealism*, ed. by H. C. Sturt (London, 1902), pp. 47-133, *Formal Logic, a Scientific and Social Problem* (London, 1912), and *Logic for Use; an Introduction to the Voluntarist Theory of Knowledge* (New York, 1930) in definition of his logical position; and, in presentation of his more general "humanistic" position, *Humanism, Philosophical Essays* (London, 1903), *Studies in Humanism* (New York, 1907), and *Our Human Truths* (New York, 1939). Stephen S. White has written *A Comparison of the Philosophies of F. C. S. Schiller and John Dewey* (Chicago, 1940). William James's comments on the similarities and dissimilarities between his own pragmatism and Schiller's humanism are to be found in his review of Schiller's *Humanism*, *Nation*, LXXVIII (1904), 175-76, in "Humanism and Truth," *Mind*, n.s., Vol. XIII (1904), 457-75, in "Humanism and Truth Once More," *Mind*, n.s., Vol. XIV (1905), 190-98, and in his review of Marcel Hébert's *Le Pragmatisme et ses diverse formes anglo-américaines,* in *Journal of Philosophy,* V (1908), 689–94.

Milton H. Thomas and H. W. Schneider, *A Bibliography of John Dewey, 1882–1939* (New York, 1939), is the most complete listing of Dewey's work. The introductory essay, "Dewey's Eighth Decade," is by H. W. Schneider. In the earlier edition of the Thomas and Schneider *Bibliography of John Dewey* (New York, 1929) Schneider's introductory essay considers "John Dewey's Empiricism." *John Dewey, the Man and His Philosophy* (Cambridge, Mass., 1930) contains addresses delivered in New York in honor of Dewey's seventieth birthday. The speakers were J. R. Linville, W. H. Kilpatrick, E. C. Moore, J. H. Newlon, I. L. Kandel, G. H. Mead, H. W. Schneider, J. R. Angell, Jane Addams, J. H. Robinson. *The Philosopher of the Common Man* (New York, 1940) contains essays in honor of John Dewey to celebrate his eightieth birthday. The contributors include H. M. Kallen, A. E. Murphy, E. Nagel, A. C. Barnes, J. H. Randall, Jr., W. Hamilton, E. W. Patterson, and Hu Shih, and the volume also contains an important statement by Dewey, "Creative Democracy—the Task before Us," pp. 220–28. *The Philosophy of John Dewey,* ed. by Paul A. Schilpp (Evanston and Chicago, 1939), which was the first volume of the "Library of Living Philosophers," includes a biography of John Dewey, ed. by Jane M. Dewey, pp. 3–45, critical articles by J. Ratner, J. H. Randall, Jr., D. A. Piatt, B. Russell, H. Reichenbach, A. E. Murphy, D. Parodi, G. Santayana, G. W. Allport, H. W. Stuart, G. R. Geiger, S. C. Pepper, E. L. Schaub, J. L. Childs, H. H. Kilpatrick, A. N. Whitehead, and W. Savery, and Dewey's reply to the criticisms expressed in these articles under the title "Experience, Knowledge, and Value: a Rejoinder," pp. 515–608. Sidney Hook, *John Dewey; an Intellectual Portrait* (New York, 1939), W. T. Feldman, *The Philosophy of John Dewey; a Critical Analysis* (Baltimore, Md., 1934), and F. Leander, *The Philosophy of John Dewey; a Critical Study* (Göteborg, 1939) are attempts at critical evaluation of Dewey's thought.

The writings of George H. Mead in the field of genetic social psychology have already been discussed, pp. 391, 430. There is a bibliography of his works appended to George H. Mead, *Mind, Self, and Society from the Standpoint of a Social Behaviorist,* ed. by Charles W. Morris (Chicago, 1934), pp. 390–92. Morris's introduction to this volume should be consulted with A. E. Murphy's critique of *The Philosophy of the Act* in *Journal of Philosophy,* XXXVI (1939), 85–103. Among Mead's works on pragmatic empiricism are: "Scientific Method and Individual Thinker," in *Crea-*

tive Intelligence, ed. by John Dewey (New York, 1917), pp. 176–227; "The Objective Reality of Perspectives," in *Proceedings of the Sixth International Congress of Philosophy* (New York, 1926), pp. 75–85; "The Nature of Aesthetic Experience," *International Journal of Ethics,* XXXVI (1926), 382–92; "A Pragmatic Theory of Truth," in *Studies in the Nature of Truth, University of California Publications in Philosophy,* XI (1929), 65–88; "The Nature of the Past," in *Essays in Honor of John Dewey* (New York, 1929), pp. 235–42; *The Philosophy of the Present* (Chicago, 1932), Mead's lectures on the Paul Carus Foundation; *Mind, Self, and Society* (Chicago, 1934), *Movements of Thought in the Nineteenth Century* (Chicago, 1936), and *The Philosophy of the Act* (Chicago, 1938). Dewey's remarks at Mead's funeral were published in the *Journal of Philosophy,* XXVIII (1931), 309–14; his review of Mead's *Mind, Self, and Society* and *Movements of Thought in the Nineteenth Century* appeared in the *New Republic,* LXXXVII (July 22, 1936), 329–30. T. V. Smith has written on "The Social Philosophy of George Herbert Mead," *American Journal of Sociology,* XXXVII (1931), 368–85; "George Herbert Mead and the Philosophy of Philanthropy," *Social Service Review,* VI (1932), 37–54; and "The Religious Bearings of a Secular Mind: George Herbert Mead," *Journal of Religion,* XII (1932), 200–213. Grace Chin Lee, *George Herbert Mead, Philosopher of the Social Individual* (New York, 1945), is a recent attempt to present Mead's ideas in systematic form.

Addison W. Moore, though not a prolific writer, made several important contributions to the literature of pragmatism: *The Functional versus the Representational Theories of Knowledge in Locke's Essay* (Chicago, 1902), *Existence, Meaning and Reality in Locke's Essay and in Present Epistemology* (Chicago, 1903), "Some Logical Aspects of Purpose," in *Studies in Logical Theory,* ed. by John Dewey (Chicago, 1903), pp. 341–82, *Pragmatism and Its Critics* (Chicago, 1910), and "Reformation of Logic," in *Creative Intelligence,* ed. by John Dewey (New York, 1917), pp. 70–117.

James Hayden Tufts has written much in the field of ethics from a pragmatic viewpoint. In addition to his co-authorship with John Dewey of *Ethics* (New York, 1908), revised edition, New York, 1932, Tufts wrote *Our Democracy, Its Origins and Its Tasks* (New York, 1917), "The Moral Life and the Construction of Values and Standards," in *Creative Intelligence,* ed. by John Dewey (New York, 1917), pp. 354–408, *The Ethics of Co-operation* (Boston and New York, 1918), "Individualism and American Life," in *Essays in Honor of John Dewey* (New York, 1929), pp. 389–401, *Recent Ethics in Its Broader Relations* (Berkeley, Cal., 1930), and

America's Social Morality; Dilemmas of the Changing Mores (New York, 1933). Tuft's credo, "What I Believe," appeared in *Contemporary American Philosophy,* ed. by G. P. Adams and W. P. Montague (New York, 1930), II, 333–53.

Other writings that contributed to the development of the pragmatic movement were Henry Waldgrave Stuart, "Valuation as a Logical Process," in *Studies in Logical Theory,* ed. by John Dewey (Chicago, 1903), 227–340, and *The Logic of Self-Realization* (Berkeley, Cal., 1904); Horace M. Kallen, "Value and Existence in Philosophy, Art, and Religion," in *Creative Intelligence,* ed. by John Dewey (New York, 1917), pp. 409–67, *Culture and Democracy in the United States* (New York, 1924), and *Individualism, an American Way of Life* (New York, 1933), as well as earlier articles which have already been listed; Sidney Hook *The Metaphysics of Pragmatism* (Chicago, 1927) and "A Pragmatic Critique of the Historico-Genetic Method," in *Essays in Honor of John Dewey* (New York, 1929), pp. 156–74; Max C. Otto, *Things and Ideals, Essays in Functional Philosophy* (New York, 1924), *Natural Laws and Human Hopes* (New York, 1926), and *The Human Enterprise* (New York, 1940); Herbert W. Schneider, "The Theory of Values," *Journal of Philosophy,* XIV (1917), 141–54, "Instrumental Instrumentalism," *Journal of Philosophy,* XVIII (1921), 113–17, and "Moral Obligation," *Ethics,* L (1939), 45–56; John Herman Randall, Jr., "Dualism in Metaphysical and Practical Philosophy," in *Essays in Honor of John Dewey* (New York, 1929), pp. 306–23; Sterling P. Lamprecht, "Empiricism and Natural Knowledge," *University of California Publications in Philosophy,* XVI (1940), 71–94; and Arthur F. Bentley, *Behavior, Knowledge, Fact* (Bloomington, Ind., 1935) and a series of articles with Dewey in *Journal of Philosophy,* 1945–46.

CHAPTER 41

The applications of radical empiricism to various fields are far too numerous for detailed presentation.

Radical empiricism in the scientific field has produced two movements, behaviorism and operationism. Behaviorism is represented best in the writings of Edward Lee Thorndike, John B. Watson, and Charles Judson Herrick. Thorndike's writings include *Educational Psychology* (New York, 1903), *The Original Nature of Man* (New York, 1913), *Fundamentals of Learning* (New York, 1932), *Human Nature and the Social Order* (New York, 1940), and *Man and His Works* (Cambridge, Mass., 1943). The high priest of behaviorism was John B. Watson, whose works on this theme are *Behavior; an Introduction to Comparative Psychology* (New York, 1914), *Psychology from the Standpoint of a Behaviorist* (Philadelphia, 1919), *Behaviorism* (New York, 1925), *The Ways of Behaviorism* (New York, 1928), and, with William McDougall, *The Battle of Behaviorism* (London, 1928). Herrick has written *Fatalism or Freedom; a Biologist's Answer* (New York, 1926), *The Thinking Machine* (Chicago, 1929), and a stimulating essay, "The Natural History of Experience," *Philosophy of Science*, XII (1945), 57–71. Outstanding works of operationists are Percy W. Bridgman's *The Logic of Modern Physics* (New York, 1927), *The Nature of Physical Theory* (Princeton, N.J., 1936), and several monographs and articles by Ernest Nagel.

. Radical empiricism in religious thought took its start from William James's Gifford Lectures, *The Varieties of Religious Experience; a Study in Human Nature* (New York and London, 1902), although James himself had anticipated some of his later positions in "Reflex Action and Theism," *Unitarian Review*, XVI (1881), 389–416. This, with other "essays in popular philosophy," was reprinted in *The Will to Believe* (New York, and London, 1897), and was the subject of Ettie Stettheimer's critical study, *The Will to Believe as a Basis for the Defense of Religious Faith* (New York, 1907). Julius Seelye Bixler wrote *Religion in the Philosophy of William James* (Boston, 1926) and has followed along the empirical path in *Immortality and the Present Mood* (Cambridge, Mass., 1931), "Can Religion Become Empirical?" in *The Nature of Religious Experience; Essays in Honor of Douglas Clyde Macintosh* (New York, 1937), pp. 68–92, and *Religion for Free Minds* (New York, 1939). Frederick J. E. Woodbridge presented "The Moral Aspects of Pragmatism," *Church Congress Journal* (1913), 200–205, and the relations between "Faith and Pragmatism," *Chronicle*, XIV (1914), 319–23. Edward Scribner Ames and James Bissett Pratt started from a Jamesian concern for the psychology of religious experience, which in both men has broadened into a fully empirical account of religion; Ames wrote *The Psychology of Religious Experience* (Boston and New York, 1910), *The New Orthodoxy* (Chicago, 1925), "Religious Values and Philosophical Criticism," in *Essays in Honor of John Dewey* (New York, 1929), pp. 23–35, and *Religion* (New York, 1929); Pratt, although he was unable to follow James in other fields, became under the influence of James an empiricist in religious study, having written *The Psychology of Religious Belief* (New York, 1907), *The Religious Consciousness* (New York, 1920), *Why Religions Die* (Berkeley, Cal., 1940), and *Can We Keep the Faith?* (New Haven, Conn., 1941). Herbert W. Schneider wrote "Faith," *Journal of Philosophy*, XXI (1924), 36–40, and "Radical Empiricism and Religion," in *Essays in Honor of John Dewey,* (New York, 1929), pp. 336–53. John Herman Randall, Jr., wrote "The Religion of Shared Experience," in *Philosopher of the Common Man* (New York, 1940), pp. 106–45. The publication of John Dewey's Terry Lectures, *A Common Faith* (New Haven, Conn., 1934), led to much controversy, especially in the pages of the *Christian Century,* where Henry Nelson Wieman questioned Dewey's theism, and in the *New Republic* and *New Masses,* where Dewey was accused of "capitulation" to God. A recent critical study of radical empiricism and religion is James A. Martin, Jr., *Empirical Philosophies of Religion* (New York, 1945).

There have been several stages of development in the application of radical empiricism to legal thought. These vary from the empiricism of Mr. Justice Holmes to the most extreme legal realism, and are discussed in much detail in Edwin N. Garlan, *Legal Realism and Justice* (New York, 1941), in which the introductory chapter and the selective bibliography are particularly worthy of attention. Oliver Wendell Holmes, Jr., *Collected Legal Papers* (New York, 1921) and *The Common Law* (Boston, 1938), should be supplemented by *Holmes-Pollock Letters,* ed. by M. DeWolfe Howe (Cambridge, Mass., 1941), *The Mind and Faith of Justice Holmes,* ed. by Max Lerner (Boston, 1944), Morris R. Cohen, "Justice Holmes and the Nature of Law," *Columbia Law Review,* XXXI (1931), 352–67, Francis Biddle, *Mr. Justice Holmes* (New York, 1942), and by Daniel J. Boorstin, "The Elusiveness of Mr. Justice Holmes," *New England Quarterly,* XIV (1941), 478–87. The relations between Holmes and William James are treated by Ralph Barton Perry, *The Thought and Character of William James* (Boston, 1935). The sociological emphasis in jurisprudence appears notably in the work of Roscoe Pound and Mr. Justice Brandeis. Pound's writings include "Do We Need a Philosophy of Law?" *Columbia Law Review,* V (1905), 339–53, "The Need for Sociological Jurisprudence," *Green Bag,* XIX (1907), 607–15, "The Scope and Purpose of Sociological Jurisprudence," *Harvard Law Review,* XXIV (1911), 591–619, XXV (1912), 140–68, 489–516, "The End of Law as Developed in Juristic Thought," *Harvard Law Review,* XXVII (1914), 195–234, 605–28, XXX (1917), 201–25, *The Spirit of the Common Law* (Boston, 1921), *An Introduction to the Philosophy of Law* (New Haven, 1922), *Interpretations of Legal History* (New York, 1923), "The Call for a Realistic Jurisprudence," *Harvard Law Review,* XLIV (1931), 697–711, and "Fifty Years of Jurisprudence," *Harvard Law Review,* L (1937), 557–82, LI (1938), 444–72, 777–812. W. L. Grossman wrote of "The Legal Philosophy of Roscoe Pound," *Yale Law Journal,* XLIV (1935), 605–18.

K. N. Llewellyn replied to Pound's criticisms of legal realism in "Some Realism about Realism—Responding to Dean Pound," *Harvard Law Review*, XLIV (1931), 1222–64, and included a selective bibliography of actual work done on law by realists. For Brandeis see *The Social and Economic Views of Mr. Justice Brandeis*, ed. by Alfred Lief, with a foreword by Charles A. Beard (New York, 1930), Louis D. Brandeis, "Living Law," *Illinois Law Review*, X (1916), 461–71, *Other People's Money* (revised ed., Washington, D.C., 1932), and Alpheus T. Mason, *Brandeis and the Modern State* (Washington, D.C., 1933). Benjamin N. Cardozo wrote *The Nature of the Judicial Process* (New Haven, 1922) and *The Growth of Law* (New Haven, 1924), and a noteworthy evaluation of legal realism in his "Address," *New York State Bar Association Reports*, LV (1932), 263–307. For criticism of Cardozo's legal thinking see E. W. Patterson, "Cardozo's Philosophy of Law," *University of Pennsylvania Law Review*, LXXXVIII (1939), 71–91, 156–76, and Beryl H. Levy, *Cardozo and the Frontiers of Legal Thinking* (New York, 1938). On the general theme of sociological jurisprudence see F. Parsons, *Legal Doctrine and Social Progress* (New York, 1911). Early statements of a realistic jurisprudence can be found in J. W. Bingham, "Legal Philosophy and the Law," *University of Illinois Law Review*, IX (1914), 98–119, and A. L. Corbin, "The Law and the Judges," *Yale Review*, n.s., Vol. III (1914), 234–50. More recent expositions are those of K. N. Llewellyn, "A Realistic Jurisprudence—the Next Step," *Columbia Law Review*, XXX (1930), 431–65, and *The Bramble Bush* (New York, 1930); M. Radin, "The Theory of Judicial Decision," *American Bar Association Journal*, XI (1925), 357–62, "Legal Realism," *Columbia Law Review*, XXXI (1931), 824–28, and *Law as Logic and Experience* (New Haven, 1940); E. S. Robinson, *Law and the Lawyers* (New York, 1935); F. V. Harper, "Some Implications of Juristic Pragmatism," *International Journal of Ethics*, XXXIX (1929), 269–90, and "The Pragmatic Process in Law," *International Journal of Ethics*, XLI (1931), 305–28; Jerome Frank, "Realism in Jurisprudence," *American Law School Review*, VII (1934), 1057–76, and *Law and Politics* (New York, 1939); W. Nelles, "Toward Legal Understanding," *Columbia Law Review*, XXXIV (1934), 862–89, 1041–75; E. W. Patterson, "Pragmatism as a Philosophy of Law," in *The Philosopher of the Common Man* (New York, 1940), pp. 172–204; W. H. Hamilton, "The Path of Due Process of Law," in *The Constitution Reconsidered*, ed. by Conyers Read (New York, 1938), pp. 167–91; and F. S. Cohen, "Scientific Method and Law," *American Bar Association Journal*, XIII (1927), 303–9, and "Transcendental Nonsense and the Functional Approach," *Columbia Law Review*, XXXV (1935), 809–41. Critics of realistic jurisprudence include W. B. Kennedy, "Pragmatism as a Philosophy of Law," *Marquette Law Review*, IX (1924), 63–77, and L. L. Fuller, "American Legal Realism," *University of Pennsylvania Law Review*, LXXXII (1934), 429–62. More detailed references on the controversy are made available in E. N. Garlan, *Legal Realism and Justice* (New York, 1941), in the bibliographical footnotes on pp. 4–17.

G. H. Sabine, "The Pragmatic Approach to Politics," *American Political Science Review*, XXIV (1930), 865–85, describes a general approach which is best exemplified in the political thought of the Chicago School, and recently illustrated in C. E. Merriam, *Public and Private Government* (New Haven, 1944), and *Systematic Politics* (Chicago, 1945). Notable for his excursions into political life as well as for his theoretical statements is T. V. Smith, whose relevant works are *Beyond Conscience* (New York, 1934), *The Promise of American Politics* (Chicago, 1938), *The Democratic Way of Life* (revised ed., Chicago, 1939), and *Discipline for Democracy* (Chapel Hill, N.C., 1942). Arthur F. Bentley, *The Process of Government* (Bloomington, Ind., 1908), was one of the first expressions of the pressure-group theory of politics. John Dewey, "Force, Violence, and Law," *New Republic*, V (Jan. 22, 1916), 295–97, was instrumental in freeing the positive concept of power of control from the implications of the theory of coercion or force.

Thorstein Veblen, "The Place of Science in Modern Civilization," *American Journal of Sociology*, XI (1906), 585–609, has been taken by Stuart, and with reservations by Dorfman as an attack on pragmatism. In it Veblen represents pragmatism as encouraging the perversion of the "instinct of workmanship" into a competitive sportsmanship, and he defends the ideals of pure science as opposed to the emphasis on applied science, but this criticism must not be interpreted as indicating a general repudiation of the empirical movement in social philosophy, to which Veblen himself contributed. His attitude is like that of Peirce, and for that matter of all the leaders, in emphasizing the importance of experimental verification for "pure" science and philosophy. Veblen's works illustrating this attitude are *The Vested Interests and the State of the Industrial Arts* (New York, 1919), *The Place of Science in Modern Civilization and Other Essays* (New York, 1919), *The Engineers and the Price System* (New York, 1921), *Absentee Ownership and Business Enterprise in Recent Times* (New York, 1923), and *Essays in Our Changing Order* (New York, 1934). On the general theme of radical empiricism in economics see also S. N. Patten, "Pragmatism and Social Science," in *Essays in Economic Theory*, ed. by R. G. Tugwell (New

York, 1924), Rexford G. Tugwell, "Experimental Economics," Chapter XV of Tugwell and others, *The Trend of Economics* (New York, 1924), and Herbert W. Schneider, "Pragmatism and Property," *Journal of Legal and Political Sociology*, Vol. I, Nos. 3 and 4 (April, 1943), pp. 5–9.

The pragmatic approach to art is most fully illustrated in John Dewey, *Art as Experience* (New York, 1934). Other exponents of this attitude are Harold C. Brown, "Art, Action, and Affective States," in *Essays in Honor of John Dewey* (New York, 1929), pp. 49–65, Irwin Edman, "A Philosophy of Experience as a Philosophy of Art," in *Essays in Honor of John Dewey* (New York, 1929), pp. 122–32, Horace M. Kallen, *Indecency and the Seven Arts and Other Adventures of a Pragmatist in Aesthetics* (New York, 1930), and *Art and Freedom* (New York, 1942), Kate Gordon, "Pragmatism in Aesthetics," in *Essays Philosophical and Psychological in Honor of William James* (New York, 1908), pp. 459–82, and Albert C. Barnes, "Method in Aesthetics," in *Philosopher of the Common Man* (New York, 1940), pp. 87–105.

The literature of pragmatism in educational thinking is far too extensive to be summarized here. John Dewey's *Experience and Education* (New York, 1938) sums up the faith and the wisdom of a life devoted to education. Frederick J. E. Woodbridge wrote of "Pragmatism and Education," *Education Review*, XXXIV (1907), 227–40. William H. Kilpatrick's "Certain Conflicting Tendencies within the Present-day Study of Education," in *Essays in Honor of John Dewey* (New York, 1929), pp. 175–90, and his books *Education for a Changing Civilization* (New York, 1926), *Education and the Social Crisis* (New York, 1932), and *Group Education for a Democracy* (New York, 1940), illustrate Kilpatrick's educational philosophy. The application of G. H. Mead's thought to educational problems has been set forth in Alfred S. Clayton, *Emergent Mind and Education; a Study of George H. Mead's Bio-social Behaviorism from an Educational Point of View* (New York, 1943). Boyd H. Bode has been a consistent advocate of the pragmatic approach to education; see his *Modern Educational Theories* (New York, 1927), *Fundamentals of Education* (New York, 1928), and *Progressive Education at the Crossroads* (New York and Chicago, 1938). Paul Crissman, "The Temper of American Pragmatism," *Educational Forum*, V (1941), 261–67, is a general statement of the relation of educational pragmatism to its philosophic ancestry.

INDEX

INDEX

Bowen, Francis, 241; views on political economy, 114 f.; theory of origin of human mind: metaphysics of emergence foreshadowed, 347 f.; philosophical idealism, 443 f.

—— *American Political Economy*, 114; "Christian Metempsychosis," 443; "Darwin on the Origin of Species," 424; "The Latest Form of the Development Theory," 421; *Treatise of Logic*, 256; *On the Application of Metaphysical and Ethical Science to the Evidences of Religion*, 255; *Principles of Political Economy*, rev. under title *American Political Economy*, 211

Bowers, Claude G., *Jefferson and Hamilton: Jefferson in Power: The Young Jefferson*, 81

Bowne, Borden Parker, 250, 453; personalist school of idealism, 467-69, 501; chief members of his school and their works, 502

—— *The Christian Revelation: The Essence of Religion: The Immanence of God*, 501; *Introduction to Psychological Theory*, 256, 501; *Kant and Spencer . . . : Metaphysics*, 501; *Personalism: Philosophy of Theism*, 468, 501; *Principles of Ethics*, 256, 468, 501; *Studies in Christianity*, 501; *Studies in Theism*, 468, 501; *Theism: The Theory of Thought and Knowledge*, 501

Boyd, James R., *Eclectic Moral Philosophy*, 255

Bradley, F. H., 477, 487, 530, 531

Bradsher, E. L., *Mathew Carey*, 211

Brandeis, Louis D., 563n, 564; quoted, 565

—— "Living Law": *Other People's Money: The Social and Economic Views of Mr. Justice Brandeis*, ed. by Alfred Lief, 585

Brasch, F. E., "The Newtonian Epoch in The American Colonies": "The Royal Society of London . . . ," 85

Brasswell, William, *Herman Melville and Christianity*, 318; *Melville's Religious Thought*, 317

Bratton, F. G., *The Legacy of the Liberal Spirit . . .* , 313

Breadwinner's College, 461, 500

Brett, George Sidney, *A History of Psychology*, 253, 429

Bridgman, Percy W., *The Intelligent Individual and Society*, 583; *The Logic of Modern Physics*, 583; *The Nature of Physical Theory*, 583; *The Nature of Thermodynamics*, 583

Brightman, Edgar Sheffield, 468, "The Definition of Idealism," 502, 507; "The Dialectical Unity of Consciousness . . ." : "An Empirical Approach to God": "The Finite Self . . .": "The Given and Its Critics": *Moral Laws*: "Personalism and the Influence of Bowne": *Personality and Religion: A Philosophy of Ideals: A Philosophy of Religion: The Problem of God: The Spiritual Life*: "A Temporalist View of God," 502

Brisbane, Albert, 287

Brokmeyer, Henry, 454, 455, 464; Hegelianism, 180; pattern for understanding the national life, 181; political activities and office, 184

Brodie, Fawn M., *No Man Knows My History . . .* , 216

Brook Farm, 156, 287; Hawthorne's view of, 138

Brooklyn Daily Eagle, 127; excerpt, 135

Brooks, Van Wyck, *The Flowering of New England*, 312, 313; *The World of Washington Irving*, 212

Brown, Harold C., "Art, Action, and Affective States," 587

Brown, Stewart G., "Emerson's Platonism," 316

Brown, Thomas, 229, 246, 247

Brown, W. A., "The Pragmatic Value of the Absolute," 575

Brownson, Henry F., biography of his father, 218

Brownson, Orestes A., 83, 130, 185, 213, 228, 286, 368; democratic ideas and

82; *The Revolutionary Generation* . . . , 77

Gronlund, Laurence, Fabian type of socialist doctrine, 201-3; socialist organizations in colleges, 203

—— *The Co-operative Commonwealth*, 201, 222; *Our Destiny* . . . , 202, 222

Grossman, W. L., "The Legal Philosophy of Roscoe Pound," 584

Grotius, Hugo, 238

Groups and members, 387 ff.

Guizot, F. P. G., 125; *History of Civilization*, 274

Gurney, Edmund, 558

Habit, defined, 522

Hacker, Louis M., and B. B. Kendrick, *The United States since 1865*, 221

Hagedorn, Herman, *Edwin Arlington Robinson* . . . , 436

Hall, Edwin, "The Rational Psychology . . . ," 497

Hall, G. Stanley, quoted, 442, 455, 464; at Johns Hopkins: introduced experimental physiological psychology, 476

—— . . . *American College Text-books and Teaching in Logic* . . . , 254; "Philosophy in the United States," 251, 496

Hall, Lawrence Sargent, quoted, 136

—— *Hawthorne, Critic of Society*, 213

Hamilton, Alexander, 50, 105; quoted, 52; bibliography, 81, 209; social philosophy, 90-100; early influences, 90 f.; public finance: view of money power, 92 f., 110, 111; excerpts from writings of, exposing boldness and modernity of his philosophy, 94-98; bitterness of last years, 99

—— *Industrial and Commercial Correspondence of* . . . : *Papers on Public Credit, Commerce and Finance* . . . , 209; *Report on Manufactures*, 93, 94; *Reports on Public Credit*, 94; *Works* . . . , 209

—— John Jay, and James Madison, *The Federalist*, 81

Hamilton, Edward J., *The Human Mind* . . . , 256

Hamilton, W. H., "The Path of Due Process of Law," 585

Hamilton, Sir William, 241, 256, 443, 444, 516

Hammond, William A., 471; "Hylozoism," 505; "James Edwin Creighton," 504; "The Significance of the Creative Reason in Aristotle's Philosophy," 505

Hanna, Mark, 203

Hardy, Thomas, 408

Harley, L. R., *Francis Lieber* . . . , 218

Harmon, Frances B., *The Social Philosophy of the St. Louis Hegelians*, 220

Harmony, Ind., Rappite community, 147, 156

Haroutunian, Joseph, *Piety versus Moralism* . . . , 252

Harper, F. V., "The Pragmatic Process in Law," 585; "Some Implications of Juristic Pragmatism," 585

Harrington, Sir James, 49, 52, 115*n*

Harris, George, *Moral Evolution*, 379, 427

Harris, Thomas Lake, views and works: community founded, 152 f.

Harris, William Torrey, 417, 454, 455, 464; study of Hegel: *Journal* . . . published by, 180; quoted, 182; contribution to national education, 184; association with Alcott and the Concord School, 184, 289, 456; Greek philosophy the prerequisite for understanding Hegel, 457

—— F. B. Sanborn, and *A. Bronson Alcott* . . . , 316

Harrison, Frederic, 324

Hartley, David, 229

Hartshorne, Charles, 419; ". . . Peirce's Metaphysics of Evolution," 418

Harvard College, 60, 63, 277

Harvard University, Royce's teachings at, 482 ff.

Hatcher, William B., *Edward Livingston* . . . , 212

Mudge, Eugene T., *The Social Philosophy of John Taylor* . . . , 82

Muelder, W. G., and M. Sears, *The Development of American Philosophy*, 30, 31

Muhlenberg, Henry, 73

Muirhead, J. H., "How Hegel Came to America," 496

Mulford, Elisha, gave fresh impetus to Hegelian idealism through religious expression of the ideals of democracy, 185-91; Munger's articles on, 220
—— *The Nation*, 185-89, 220, 221; *The Republic of God*, 185, 189, 190, 220, 221

Mumford, Lewis, *Herman Melville*, 317

Munger, Theodore T., 380; *The Appeal to Life*, 427; "Evolution and the Faith," 426; "Personal Impressions of Dr. E. Mulford": "The Works of Elisha Mulford," 220

Murdock, Kenneth B., *Increase Mather; the Foremost American Puritan*, 27

Nagel, Ernest, "Charles S. Peirce . . . ," 578

Nairne, Charles M., 453n

Napoleon III (Louis Napoleon), 174

Napoleonic struggle, reactions following, 261

Nathanson, Jerome, *Forerunners of Freedom* . . . , 217

Nation, The (Mulford), 220, 221; excerpts, 185-89, *passim*

National Bank Bill, 120

Nationalism, two schools of Federalist philosophy, the constitutionalist and the bill of rights schools, 89; Whig nationalism, 89-115; economic, of Alexander Hamilton, 90-100, 209; romantic, following disillusionment with Europe, 100 ff.; J. Q. Adams the best theoretical expositor of new, 102 ff.; intellectual development through outstanding political economists, 105-15, 210-12; Whiggism found best embodiment in economic nationalism, 105; transition

from classical republicanism to Jacksonian democracy (*q.v.*): the common man, 115-32; concept of Young America's progress and destiny, 133-44; transition from Whig to Democratic nationalism, 133; frontier type of social philosophy: communities established, and their religious and economic faiths, 144-59; problem of relating liberty and union, 159-77; compromises with democracy followed by evasion, 159; political scientists who led in development of theory, 169, 177; idealistic democracy: influence of Hegel and the Hegelians, 177-93; equality and solidarity, 193-207; movement created by Bellamy's work: philosophical orientation of his nationalism, 197 ff.; guide to the literature, 207-22; *see also* Democracy; *also entries under subjects treated*

Nationalism and Internationalism (Lieber), 169

Nationalist, The, 202

Nationalist Bellamy clubs, 197, 200

Nationalists, 206

National Republicans, *see* Whig Party

Natural history, first important American work in, 73

Natural History of Enthusiasm (Taylor), 371n

. . . *Natural History of Man, The* (Kinmont), 329

Natural idealism one of two types of idealism emerging, 493

Naturalism, desperate, during era of evolutionary enthusiasm, 396-415, 431-37; four famous philosophers, 397; Sumner's conformist philosophy and contribution to sociology, 397-400; Henry Adams's pessimism and later Nirvana, 400-407; Robinson's philosophical interests and poems, 408-10; conflicts in the philosophy of Santayana, 410-15; Dewey's drift toward, 553

Natural Law in the Spiritual World (Drummond), 379

Natural liberties, 9 f.

Phalanx communities, 156
Phaneroscopy, 546 ff.; defined, 548
Phelan, M., *Handbook of All Denominations*, 215
Phelps, Moses Stuart, 429, 453; "Anthropomorphism," 426, 498 f.
Phelps, William Lyon, 382
Phenomenologie . . . (Hegel), 412, 549
Phenomenology, 546 ff.
Philosopher of the Common Man, The, 580
Philosophia Brittanica (Martin), 238
Philosophia perennis, 491
Philosophical and Practical Treatise on the Will, A (Upham), 240
"Philosophical Conceptions and Practical Results" (W. James), 527, 572
Philosophical Essays in Honor of James Edwin Creighton, 504
Philosophical Review, 469
Philosophical Society of St. Louis, 454 f., 457, 464
Philosophical thinking joined to social action, 35
Philosophical Union, 465
Philosophie der Natur (Schelling), 335
Philosophy, during Puritanism and the Enlightenment did not exist as special field of inquiry or body of doctrine, 225; became a technical discipline in academic curricula, 225 f., 250; faculty psychology, 232 ff., 253 f.; division into natural and moral, 238; exploitation of the moral faculties, 242-46, 254-56; change in academic status: thinking and writing professionalized: why systems of philosophy appeared late, 441; union with science, 557; *see also* Mental philosophy; Orthodoxy
Philosophy of History (Lloyd), 479, 506
Philosophy of Human Nature (Buchanan), 228, 252
Philosophy of John Dewey, The, ed. Schilpp, 580
Philosophy of Natural History (Smellie), 238
Philosophy of Right (Hegel), 181
Philosophy of Theism (Bowne), 468, 501

Philosophy of the Present, The (Mead), 430, 552, 581
Pickering, C., *Races of Men . . .*, 420
Pickering, Timothy, 102
Pierce, Franklin, 136, 137, 139, 140
Pierre (Melville), excerpts, 295-98
Pietist theory of love, 11-18, 65; Edwards's reworking of Puritan theory under stimulus of, 13 ff.; empiricist argument for holy love, 16; pietism of Channing, 61, 65 f.
Piety, and secular morality distinguished, 231; love of God defined as, 264 f.
Pilgrim congregations, 146
Pioneers! Oh Pioneers! (Whitman), 158 f.
Pitkin, W. B., "In Reply to Prof. James": "A Problem of Evidence in Radical Empiricism": "The Relation between the Act and the Object of Belief," 574
Planning, Hildreth's up-to-date theory of social and scientific, 127
Plato Club, 456
Platonic academies, 455
Platonism, Scottish Enlightenment grounded on, 246
Platonism, Cambridge, 5, 10, 18 f., 31
Platonism and empiricism in colonial America, Platonic heritage of the Puritans, 3-11; pietist theory of love, 11-18; reconstructed by Edwards, 17; immaterialism, 18-26; guide to the literature, 26-32
Pluralism, personalistic, 465
"Pluralistic Mystic, A" (W. James), 558
Pluralistic Universe (W. James), 543
Plymouth Pilgrims, 146
Political economists, intellectual development of nationalism by outstanding, 105-15, 210-12
Political economy, Hamilton's theory based on, 90, 94, 98; first systematic treatise by an American, 107
Political Economy (Mill), 196
Political Economy (Raymond), 112
Political Economy (Wayland), 243
Political power, money basis, 91 ff.